Contents

State and Society

State and Society

A Social and Political History of Britain since 1870

Fifth Edition

Martin Pugh

Bloomsbury Academic
An imprint of Bloomsbury Publishing Plc

BLOOMSBURY
LONDON · OXFORD · NEW YORK · NEW DELHI · SYDNEY

Bloomsbury Academic

An imprint of Bloomsbury Publishing Plc

50 Bedford Square	1385 Broadway
London	New York
WC1B 3DP	NY 10018
UK	USA

www.bloomsbury.com

BLOOMSBURY and the Diana logo are trademarks of Bloomsbury Publishing Plc

This fifth edition first published 2017
Reprinted 2017

First edition published 1994
Second edition published 1999
Third edition published by Hodder Education in 2008
Fourth edition published by Bloomsbury Academic in 2012

© Martin Pugh, 2017

British Library Cataloguing-in-Publication Data
A catalogue record for this book is available from the British Library.

ISBN:	HB:	978-1-4742-4345-2
	PB:	978-1-4742-4346-9
	ePDF:	978-1-4742-4348-3
	ePub:	978-1-4742-4347-6

Library of Congress Cataloging-in-Publication Data
A catalog record for this book is available from the Library of Congress.

Cover design: Clare Turner
Cover images: (top) Protestors from the Occupy London Stock Exchange demonstration (Photo by Dan Kitwood/Getty Images); (bottom) People celebrate VE Day in London, 19 May 1945 (Photo by Picture Post/Hulton Archive/Getty Images).

Typeset by RefineCatch Limited, Bungay, Suffolk
Printed and bound in Great Britain

Part III The Period of Confusion: Collectivism versus Capitalism, 1918–40

18 The Loss of Great Power Status 398

Part V The Era of Reaction and Decline, 1970–2015

19 The Breakdown of the Post-war Consensus, 1970–9 419

20 The Era of Thatcherism 438

21 New Labour and the Blair Era 463

List of Illustrations

List of Tables and Figures

Tables

Figures

Preface to the Fifth Edition

In this new edition students will be able to follow through many of the key themes in modern British history including the evolution of a full democracy, the process whereby the labour movement became absorbed into the political system without overthrowing it, the advance of women to the central economic and political role they occupy today, the development of a society obsessed with consumerism, the rise of the empire to its territorial height after 1918 followed by its collapse in the thirty years after 1945 without significant controversy, and the gradual decline of Britain as a dominant industrial power to the shocking position today where manufacturing comprises a mere ten per cent of gross domestic product.

But above all I have thought it necessary to give full attention to explaining the profound change that has taken place since the late-Victorian period when British people were so confident about their national identity that they largely took it for granted. By 2015 virtually all the values and institutions that once sustained British national identity – empire, monarchy, industrialization, civil liberties, the Church, the Union with Scotland and Wales, the BBC – have either disappeared or lost much of their relevance. This has somehow crept up on the British people in the last 30–40 years and is generally neglected in the textbooks. For the historian it is especially concerning that today most English people do not even understand why Scotland has become so disillusioned with the Union. Accordingly the book explains the relationship between England, Scotland, Wales and Ireland in the late-Victorian period and how and when the Union unravelled. Some readers will be surprised that I locate the start of this process from around 1918 when the economic effects of the First World War undermined the economic rationale for the Union in Scotland even though the main political challenge dates from the 1960s onwards. I have also given attention to the major attempt to fashion a new post-colonial role and identity for Britain through participation in Europe, to explaining why, from the outset, much of the public was never really convinced about this alternative, and to considering the political mismanagement that has taken her to the edge of withdrawal from Europe today. If another edition of the book is published it may require some more radical reconsideration.

Martin Pugh, Slaley, Northumberland, October 2015

Part I

The Loss of Confidence, 1870–1902

1

The Retreat of the Industrial Revolution

During the mid-Victorian era Britain's superiority as a manufacturing, commercial and imperial force made her not just one of the Great Powers but, arguably, the greatest. Yet there was an element of illusion in this mid-Victorian triumphalism. In geographical terms Britain was the smallest of the Great Powers. With an army that was quite inadequate for the defence of her imperial possessions, she was lucky that the major powers were too preoccupied elsewhere to challenge her during the Victorian era. Britain's population, though growing rapidly, reached only 37.4 million by 1890, behind that of France, Germany, the United States, Russia, Austria-Hungary and Japan. Italy alone, whose claim to the status of a Great Power was dubious, had fewer people.

The beginnings of decline?

What, however, made the crucial difference to Britain's strength was her capacity to mobilize her human and physical resources for sophisticated and profitable economic activities more effectively than her rivals. After embarking on industrialization in the second half of the eighteenth century, she had ridden each wave of innovation – cotton textiles, iron and steel, railways – comfortably ahead of the other European states. Thus, by the middle of the nineteenth century her population had become uniquely industrialized; by 1871 only 11 per cent of her labour force worked in agriculture, and the proportion continued to fall. Her people had also become unusually urbanized – 65 per cent of them in 1870 and 78 per cent by 1901. This was two-and-a-half times the proportion in France and Germany. As a result of her early lead, Britain reached her peak as an industrial power in the 1860s. By that time she produced half the world's coal, over half the iron and steel, and nearly half the cotton goods, and possessed over a third of the world's merchant shipping. Russia, with over three times as many people and a huge land area, was an underdeveloped country by comparison.

Empire on the cheap

Britain made the most of her limited resources in other ways. Unlike all the great imperial states, apart from the United States, she largely avoided the diversion of her wealth into the armed forces, which received only 2–3 per cent of gross national produce in the mid-Victorian period. Such expenditure was widely considered 'unproductive'. Parsimony also reflected the traditional fear of a large standing army as a domestic political threat. Yet for all this, in times of crisis Britain proved quite capable of expanding her military effort by means of extra taxation and extensive borrowing. This was a purely temporary expedient. In peacetime her island position enabled her to concentrate on the Royal Navy, an economical form of defence, while maintaining an army of 240,000 men which, in view of Britain's huge interests, was extremely small. Victorian free-traders liked to argue that, as more and more nations were drawn into Britain's beneficent trading network, the causes of war would steadily diminish and military aggrandizement become a thing of the past.

Of course, the British Empire represented a major complication in this vision of international peace. Both formal possessions and informal commercial interests had to be defended and even extended. Even the supposedly non-imperial mid-Victorian period saw the addition of the Punjab, Sind, Burma and Hong Kong to British territory. Indeed, although the Victorians thought of themselves as presiding over an era of peace, the fact is that the Queen's men were actually fighting somewhere in the world in most years of her reign. But only the Crimean War in the 1850s involved a *European* opponent. On the whole, wars were short and economical engagements by a handful of men with native peoples in Asia and Africa. It is striking how little impression even a great threat like the Indian Mutiny of 1857 made on British policy. After that revolt British troops in India were increased, but from only 40,000 to 65,000, a tiny force for a huge Empire. British soldiers continued to be outnumbered more than two to one by the Indian sepoys on whom the British Raj relied. Indian troops were often used in campaigns in other parts of the Empire to supplement British forces. Moreover, they were paid for out of *Indian* revenues, not by the British taxpayer. The nineteenth-century Empire was run on a shoestring.

The 'Great Depression'?

It was during the 1870s that contemporaries seriously began to consider whether Britain had already passed her peak. After several buoyant years at the start of the decade, the economy suffered the sudden collapse of a speculative boom. By 1874 quantities of cheap wheat had begun to arrive from North America, severely undercutting the prices of British farmers. The slump of the 1870s was followed by another in the mid-1880s and by a third in the first half of the 1890s. Such cyclical fluctuations had, of course, characterized the mid-Victorian era too, but now they were regarded as symptoms of a long-term phenomenon – the 'Great Depression' from 1874 to 1896. This view gained credibility from a series of royal commissions, which gathered evidence from those farmers and manufacturers who were doing badly.

However, one must disentangle the various threads in the pattern of economic change. In one perspective British producers were experiencing pressures felt all over the world in a period of deflation. From the 1870s to the late 1890s, prices fell by about 40 per cent. This squeezed profits, put some out of business and seemed to mark a basic change from the buoyant mid-Victorian era, when business had been stimulated by mild inflation. But had Britain suffered disproportionately from the vicissitudes of the late nineteenth century? Had her long-term decline as an economic power really begun?

In many ways this seems improbable. Measurements of British gross domestic product show a continuous expansion of a fairly rapid order; by 1890 it was over 50 per cent greater than in 1870, for example. On the other hand, the average annual *rate* of growth was somewhat slower than in the pre-1870 period. Moreover, productivity, i.e. output per head of population, diminished significantly, especially in the period 1900–13. This suggests that contemporary complaints from the 1870s give a misleading impression about the *timing* of decline, but not, perhaps, about the underlying trend.

Foreign competition and relative decline

There is also plentiful evidence to suggest that Britain's economic performance deteriorated in relation to that of other advanced countries. However, this is true with respect to Germany and the United States rather than the other Great Powers. Between 1870 and 1913 the annual per capita rate of growth in manufacturing ranged from 0.6 per cent to 0.9 per cent in Britain; but in Germany the range was 1.7–3.9 per cent, and in America 2.1–3.2 per cent. The disparity was greatest after 1900 in spite of the Edwardian boom. A good indication of Britain's status is provided by the figures for manufacturing capacity. By 1880 she was still the world's leader, having increased her share in the 1860s and 1870s partly as a result of deteriorating performances of China and India. By 1900 Britain, Germany and the United States stood out as the top three producers; but America had comfortably overtaken Britain, and Germany was rapidly catching up. Of course, their faster rate of growth largely reflected the fact that they had started from a lower level of production than Britain. The exploitation of their greater resources and the application of British techniques and capital inevitably generated very rapid growth.

Which sectors declined?

Of course the figures for national output provide us with sweeping generalizations about a complex pattern of change. Britain's performance varied considerably from one sector to another. In some industries any talk of depression and decline seems premature. For example, British shipbuilders continued to enjoy great success up to 1914, both in exporting and in supplying the British merchant fleet and Royal Navy. The cotton textile industry also continued to make profits and to export over half its total output. But as one moves across the spectrum the picture begins to look less rosy. Railways are an example of a major industry whose profitability was declining, albeit only slightly, after 1870. The companies have been criticized for investing too much in dubious branch lines and duplicate facilities, and for having insufficient regard for the rate of return on capital. However, it is fair to say that much of their expenditure could not be avoided, especially on essential improvements in safety and the provision of extra capacity; they were also subject to legal controls on charges to their customers, and to pressure to improve wages. Similarly, the coal industry continued to expand output up to 1914, but its productivity declined steadily. This was partly a consequence of the deteriorating physical conditions in some of the older coalfields, but it also reflected a general failure by the many small companies to invest in mechanical methods and thereby improve efficiency. The coal industry's success was precariously founded on the urgent demand on the part of other rapidly expanding countries, but sooner or later its inefficiency would lead to a loss of markets. Even more than the railways, coal suffered from the fragmented pattern of private ownership which by the turn of the century had become inappropriate for such strategic industries.

Market loss was already taking place in agriculture, at least among the wheat-producers of southern and eastern England, whose prices

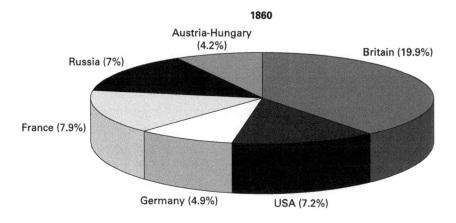

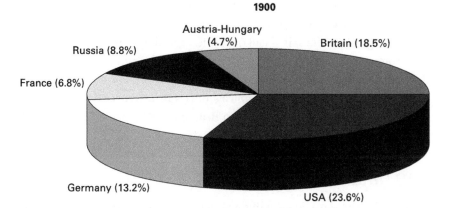

Figure 1.1 Relative output in manufacturers amongst the Great Powers*

*share of world output shown as a percentage

were drastically undercut by large-scale foreign farmers now able to take advantage of cheaper transport by rail and by sea. Here, too, improved technology in the form of combine harvesters was available but little used. However, while many farmers saw profits dwindle and went bankrupt, those who concentrated on dairying, livestock, fruit and market gardening profited from growing domestic demand and better prices. The worst example of decline was in the iron and steel industry. Manufacturers found that their prices were being severely undercut by German and American producers, largely because they had been too slow to adopt the more efficient technology available to them. As a result, exports diminished greatly.

The growth industries

Nonetheless, taken as a group, the traditional industries on which Britain's industrial revolution had been built – textiles, shipbuilding, railways, iron and steel – did not perform too badly. They continued to make profits even if their hold on world markets weakened. However, the world demand for the goods that Britain traditionally supplied was not very buoyant in the late nineteenth century. Thus in this period there was an urgent need to shift resources into the faster-growing sectors that formed the cutting edge of the new industrial revolution: electricity, chemicals, machine tools and motor cars. However, in none of these did Britain dominate as she had once done in the old staple industries. In particular, British firms failed to repeat what had been crucial to success in the first industrial revolution, namely, the mass production of a limited range of items. Both motor cars and machine tools were characterized by a large number of small companies, each manufacturing a wide range of products in small quantities, and thus at higher prices, than their competitors. British power stations were smaller and less efficient than those abroad, and as a result the British economy did not benefit from cheap electricity as early as others. In chemicals, once a British success story, only 11 per cent of world output originated in Britain by 1914, while Germany and the USA together accounted for nearly 60 per cent.

The balance of payments

By the 1890s the consequences of this loss of competitiveness began to make themselves apparent. Whereas formerly Britain had supplied nearly all her manufactured goods herself, she increasingly imported them; by 1914 25 per cent of all imports were manufactured items. Conversely, manufactured goods diminished as a proportion of British exports from three-quarters to

Table 1.1 Britain's balance of payments in 1900 (in £ millions)

Imports	Domestic exports	Re-exports	Net overseas earnings	Net invisible trade
523	291	63	103	109
Overall balance				
43				

a little over half between 1870 and 1914. In this way, the process that had made Britain such a wealthy country began to falter, for the greatest profit was to be made on sophisticated manufactured items, not on primary products like coal which loomed larger in British trade. Neither of the obvious solutions – improvements in the efficiency of the old industries and heavy investment in the growth sectors – was adopted. Contemporaries usually failed to diagnose the real problem, preferring to fix upon simpler explanations and remedies. Agricultural problems were attributed to unusually bad weather and to outbreaks of disease. Lost markets could be blamed upon rival countries who cheated by imposing tariffs or by dumping their own goods at artificially low prices in Britain. To some extent, however, the underlying deterioration in Britain's status as an exporter of manufactures was obscured. For as she was pushed out of the competitive markets of Europe and North America, she compensated to some extent by selling more in the easier markets of the less developed economies such as Latin and South America or China, as well as in the British Empire, where she enjoyed special advantages. Moreover, Britain's declining competitiveness did not, in this period, lead to any serious balance-of-payments problems because her deficits on visible trade were comfortably offset by the indirect exports earned through shipping, insurance, and the interest and dividends from investments made in foreign countries, all of which increased substantially between the 1870s and 1914.

Britain and free trade

The accepted diagnosis for Britain's modest relative decline in the late-Victorian era is that she failed to invest her resources in the growth sectors, thereby missing the greatest opportunities for profits and employment. But why? It is tempting to explain the situation in terms of Britain's pioneering role as the first industrialized society. Latecomers, it may be conjectured, have the advantage of being able to invest in the most recent and efficient technology. Yet this view has not commanded much support. As the most developed economy, Britain should have been in an excellent position to supply capital and re-equip herself at regular intervals so as to keep ahead of rivals. In the real world, however, economic decisions rarely grow out of purely rational economic considerations. Social and political factors have a very real bearing on British performance. As the first industrial nation, the British began to reap the benefits in the form of higher living standards earlier than other peoples. This may have been all the more true because of the system of responsible parliamentary government she enjoyed. The late-Victorian era witnessed huge increases in imported food, in luxury goods, and in expenditure on entertainment, travel and holidays. The influence of the consumer should not be regarded merely as an indulgence or as a cost borne by the economy; British consumers had made the initial phase of the industrial revolution possible. Moreover, concessions to consumers to maintain living standards were to serve governments well in times of crisis such as the First World War. British society was to prove itself steadier under strain, and better able to maintain industrial output, than those of Russia, Germany, Italy or France.

New support for protectionism

It was during the 1880s that some British businessmen and politicians began to question the policy of free trade on the grounds that it no longer served Britain's best interests. Certainly the imposition of new tariffs by Germany in the 1870s and by France and the USA in the 1890s contributed to the difficulties faced by some British exporters. The feeling that foreigners played unfairly by dumping goods at specially subsidized prices in Britain was directed at the Germans in particular, and culminated in a famous book by E.E. Williams, *Made in Germany*, published in 1896. On the whole, however, protectionism was of fairly marginal importance in Britain's economic decline, for the industries suffering from foreign competition had been undermined primarily by their own inefficient methods.

Nonetheless, by the 1880s the call for 'fair trade', which meant that Britain should force foreigners back to genuine free trade by threatening retaliatory tariffs, was on the face of it plausible and patriotic. Yet Britain remained loyal to free trade up to the First World War and beyond. There were a number of reasons for this. Manufacturing industry was never united on the subject of tariffs, and many major interests like cotton textiles, which were dependent on world markets both for cheap raw materials and for sales, strongly opposed protectionism. In addition, all manufacturers had to weigh the likely effects of tariffs in raising food prices at home and thereby subjecting them to severe pressure for higher wages. From the political perspective, the argument that Britain's huge urban population depended on the maintenance of supplies of cheap food from abroad seemed compelling, to say the least. It grew more so during the 1880s, as standards of living for working-class families rose as a result of the falling price and greater range of food available in the shops. Any check to this trend was likely to prove fatal for the government responsible.

Beyond this, it was argued that Britain's unique dependence on the state of the world economy for her prosperity made the maintenance of free trade a national interest. By freely importing food and raw materials, especially from the less developed countries, Britain helped to maintain their capacity to purchase her own manufactured items. The trade with India alone financed over 40 per cent of Britain's deficits. Thus Britain's interest lay in maximizing the level of world economic activity, both by her direct trade and by financial investments. As we have seen, overseas investments, which rose by around six times between 1870 and 1914, made a vital and growing contribution to national solvency, as did earnings from shipping and insurance. The conclusion is inescapable: contemporary opinion was correct in its belief that free trade was economically and politically justified for late-Victorian Britain. The most conspicuous cost of free trade was the shrinkage in agriculture; but the shift of resources out of areas of low productivity, and the concentration on the forms of agriculture that were most viable in British conditions, were entirely rational, though the readjustments were inevitably painful for some.

The banks and the question of investment

The debate over tariffs raises the wider question of the significance of the state in British economic development. The first industrial revolution had begun almost by accident without any deliberate support from the British state. But this experience was distinctly odd. Other European and American countries took it for granted that the state must play an active role in promoting industry, and historians have gradually come to recognize that hostility towards the state in Britain proved to be a source of long-term weakness.

Of course, there were strong empirical reasons why state intervention remained minimal during the mid-Victorian era. Contemporaries, impressed by the extraordinary rate of growth of British wealth and industry since the late eighteenth century, argued that governments had helped to promote this by abstaining from interference and keeping the burdens on productive industry as light as possible. Many Victorians regarded state action in the light of eighteenth-century and earlier practice: it implied the granting of special concessions and privileges to groups or individuals which tended to promote inefficiency and work to the detriment of the public interest. Thus a body like the East India Company had come under repeated attack; and its monopoly rights had been whittled away when the Company's charter came up for renewal by Parliament. Similarly, one of the arguments used against tariffs was that they almost inevitably led to corrupt deals between government and vested interests, with the result that a few profited at the expense of the country as a whole.

Anti-state ideology

However, it cannot be over-emphasized how peculiarly British this anti-state ideology was. German, French and American governments routinely dealt in special concessions, protective tariffs and subsidies for major works of construction from which the British largely abstained. But there were many other ramifications to the British hostility to the involvement of the state, some of which had damaging economic consequences. For example, Britain was slow to develop a national system of elementary or secondary education, not to mention the higher scientific and technological training of her population, by comparison with Germany and France. By the late nineteenth century the effects of this began to emerge in the form of an inadequate supply of skilled personnel in sectors like chemicals and engineering. It was also conspicuous that, whereas other governments used their diplomatic representatives abroad to promote the interests of their exporters, the British gave little or no help of that kind. Non-interference in business was one thing, but British attitudes often amounted to sheer neglect.

Indeed, at the heart of government there was no minister for industry who might have co-ordinated a positive strategy. The most relevant department, the Board of Trade, was dominated by a belief in free trade and a certain suspicion of manufacturing. Industry was poorly represented in parliament by comparison with land and finance. Indeed, businessmen had some reason for regarding such legislation as was enacted as unhelpful. A notorious example was the 1865 Locomotive Act, better known as the Red Flag Act, which required that someone carrying a red flag must precede any motor car by sixty yards and prohibited vehicles from going faster than four miles per hour in rural areas and two miles in towns. Not repealed until 1896, the Act was considered to have delayed the development of the motoring industry by thirty years. The Electric Lighting Act (1882) inhibited investment in and development of electricity which was largely run by inefficient local authority boards; as late as 1908 London's electricity was supplied by no fewer than seventy-two small companies for example. Of course, governments had to respect social concerns. Railway legislation in 1888 and 1894 was designed to improve safety and to limit charges paid by workmen. But the railways, run by too many small, privately-owned competing companies, were steadily losing efficiency and demanded rationalization under state control.

While Liberal and most Labour politicians were especially devoted to free trade, and to that extent were opposed to state intervention, the Conservatives were gradually converted to interventionism in the limited form of tariffs, or protectionism, during the 1890s. In his post-1903 campaign Joseph Chamberlain proposed a 10 per cent tariff on imports which was expected to protect the domestic market from foreign goods and, by implication, safeguard jobs. However, this was generally rejected by financiers, the civil service and by voters. Nonetheless, an energetic minister could promote the interests of British business. When Lloyd George became President of the Board of Trade in 1905, he swiftly took up several questions affecting the interests of businessmen and surprised them by his willingness to consult. For example, he reformed the law on patents so as to deter foreign companies from taking out patents merely with a view to checking British competition. But Lloyd George was clearly exceptional. Apart from free trade, the most important economic policy affecting British business was the maintenance of the gold standard. Yet here we have a most striking case of the detached stance adopted by government.

The dominance of the Bank of England

British monetary policy was determined not by the government but by the Bank of England. However, the Bank remained a private body run by a governor and a board of self-appointed representatives very few of whom represented manufacturing industry. Reflecting the interests of financiers and merchants, the Bank of England took a rather cosmopolitan, or, to its critics, unpatriotic, view of economic policy. Officially it endeavoured to protect the country's reserves of gold, thereby to maintain the international value of the pound sterling; keeping the pound on the gold standard was regarded as the prime object of policy. Unfortunately, Britain's gold reserves were invariably far too low for the job, and as a result the periodic loss of gold was regularly met by an increase in the bank rate which was designed to attract overseas funds back into Britain. This worked well for the financiers whom the Bank represented, but not for British manufacturers. They naturally suffered from the frequent fluctuations in bank rate; between 1851 and 1885 bank rate changed 285 times or every six weeks on average, and between 1880 and 1913 195 times or every eight weeks. Inevitably the effect was to inhibit investment and to exacerbate periods of depression by pushing down the level of production and employment. In countries such as Germany, by contrast, the central bank saw its role as promoting stability by *minimizing* sharp fluctuations in the trade cycle. Naturally this damaged the interests of British manufacturers but they were never a priority for the Bank; its narrow and complacent attitude represented a major handicap for the economy.

Lack of investment

Unhappily the attitude of the Bank reflected wider failings in the supply of capital to British industry. In the rest of the sector the merchant banks, the private banks and the joint-stock banks all enjoyed few contacts with industry and showed comparatively little interest in lending to industrialists. This failure in investment in the most efficient technology was reflected in poor and declining productivity in some sectors of the economy. In this respect British experience does seem to have been distinctive in that the banks in general were reluctant to lend to provincial industry. Both the joint-stock banks and the country banks provided only short-term loans rather than the long-term finance required by industry. All this stood in contrast to the more supportive practice of financial institutions in Germany, for example. During the early stages of industrialization this weakness had not been of great significance because it had proved possible to launch textile businesses without much capital, and what was required could be obtained by personal connections rather than through institutional sources. But the hand-to-mouth methods of the early entrepreneurs were scarcely adequate later in the nineteenth century, as industry became more sophisticated and the technology required grew more costly. One consequence was that a relatively high proportion of British firms remained small scale by comparison with Germany and failed to reap the advantages of mass production.

Investment goes abroad

Paradoxically, while much of domestic industry suffered from insufficient investment in the late-Victorian era, Britain did make huge and growing investments. But most of this went abroad. There is thus a prima facie case that this approach both diverted resources from home industries and accelerated the pace of technological innovation in foreign countries. Some of the evidence appears to bear this out. Between 1871 and 1913 Britain invested only 5–7 per cent of her gross national product at home, whereas the USA and Germany invested 12 per cent. Meanwhile Britain's net foreign investment rose from around £1,200 million in the 1870s to £4,000 million by 1914. Of this, approximately 40 per cent went to the Empire and 60 per cent to foreign countries. By 1914, 44 per cent of foreign capital in the world was British-owned.

But was this necessarily damaging to Britain? One must remember that by 1870 a high proportion of the new foreign investment was simply a matter of recycling the dividends now flowing in as a result of earlier investments abroad. Also, much depends on whether capital obtained a higher rate of return abroad than it would have done at home. If it did, then capital exports would have enlarged the national income and improved the growth rate of the economy. In a well-developed economy such as Britain's there were, after all, some sectors, such as transport, where further investment no longer yielded significant gains; in these cases diversion of resources to, say, Argentine railways could be perfectly rational. However, there is no consistent pattern of higher earnings on foreign as opposed to domestic investments; rather, a good deal of variation from year to year. It can certainly be argued that a really major diversion of capital into certain domestic industries would have yielded significant results in the long

Image 1 Workers in the Armstrong Vickers rowing club, Newcastle-upon-Tyne, c. 1900.

term. But it is generally the case that capital was not in short supply. Rather, there was a failure to make the most of the opportunities that existed both on the part of the financial institutions and on the part of businessmen.

The problem of entrepreneurship

Because of the intractability of the narrowly economic explanations for British economic problems, increasing attention has been given to *social* factors as an alternative or complementary line of explanation. This rests upon the assumption that there is a strong connection between a society's economic performance on the one hand and its social attitudes and cultural values on the other. In the case of Britain this has generated a number of ideas centred around the hypothesis that, in spite of the early industrial revolution, the spirit of entrepreneurship was never particularly strong in Britain, and that by the last third of the nineteenth century the economy suffered from a deterioration in entrepreneurial talent. From the very beginning the industrial process attracted criticism on account of the ugly and dirty urban development it entailed. By the 1870s this had resulted in a back-to-the-land movement which took the form of attempts to preserve footpaths, attractive countryside and open spaces in towns, to revitalize agricultural employment and to impart a rural quality to urban developments.

Did British enterprise decline?

Much interest focuses upon the middle classes and whether they ever really challenged the values of the traditional aristocratic elite effectively. Was their real objective to be assimilated into its ranks? Such a process could not be achieved overnight. First, the middle-class man must make his fortune. Then, so the argument runs, by the second and third generation business families often grew complacent and conservative about their economic interests and lost their entrepreneurial drive. It was tempting to enjoy wealth and leisure, or to use it to enhance one's status or diversify into other occupations – hence the migration by manufacturers out of city centres into salubrious rural enclaves, the purchase of land and country houses. Some sought recognition in the form of knighthoods and peerages, while others entered politics or helped their sons to do so. These forms of behaviour, so the argument runs, were all symptoms of the low status attached to industry in British society; consequently, those who had succeeded as manufacturers merely used their wealth and influence as a vehicle for further advance, but never saw business as the goal. The effect was compounded by a generational shift. The mid-Victorian era saw a major expansion of public schools. Thus middle-class men increasingly sent their sons to be educated alongside young aristocrats, thereby to acquire their values and aspirations. This gentrification of the bourgeoisie could subsequently be consolidated by means of marriages with the daughters of impecunious titled families.

The counter argument

Yet although there is a good deal of empirical support for the idea of entrepreneurial deterioration in several cases the implications drawn from the evidence must be questioned. For example, it seems doubtful whether the appeal of the rural idyll actually explains anything; similar ideals may be discerned in other advanced societies such as that of the USA, but do not appear to have inhibited successful entrepreneurship. Similarly it is undeniable that middle-class men entered Parliament in growing numbers during the late-Victorian and Edwardian era. They also began to win a substantial share of national honours; whereas before the 1880s few middle-class men received peerages, by the end of the century they accounted for over 40 per cent of all new creations. However, it is by no means obvious that such political success was necessarily associated with the decline or neglect of business enterprise. Political influence and connections could be used to promote economic interests.

The significance of education is also difficult to ascertain. No doubt the prevailing characteristics of public-school education – the dominance of the classics and the neglect of science – was its narrowness. Moreover, the schools reflected the aspirations of the *professional* middle classes in the sense that their object was to prepare boys for prestigious careers in the Indian civil service, the army, politics, the law, the Church and the home civil service – but not manufacturing. On the other hand, it is difficult to pin down the effects. There is an obvious problem over timing. If entrepreneurial decline is thought to be evident by 1870, this seems too early for public-school expansion to have made a major impact, though it might be relevant to post-1900 weaknesses. It is by no means clear that boys were either handicapped by their education or actually alienated from business. It has often been pointed out that the British aristocracy played a substantial part in the early industrial revolution, and its influence need not necessarily have been unhelpful. From the perspective of the middle-class businessman, the wider range of contacts resulting from public-school education could be seen as strengthening the family business, not as undermining it.

There is, however, a more basic problem with the entrepreneurial explanation. Is it possible to measure business skills so as to sustain generalizations about decline? At any point in time one can produce examples of family firms going downhill; but this would be true in any occupation. The significant thing is whether the evidence of a perfectly natural deterioration in some businesses is matched by evidence of new businesses growing from small beginnings, under the leadership of fresh recruits to the ranks of entrepreneurs.

New entrepreneurs

In fact late-Victorian Britain boasted an impressive range of new ventures which is difficult to square with the pessimistic view of British businessmen. Several of the sources of entrepreneurship are easily overlooked. For example, many men moved into the south and east of the country, taking advantage of falling land prices, to set up as dairy farmers and market gardeners supplying the huge London market with fresh produce. Another neglected area of enterprise is that of women. Among the middle classes this typically took the form of careers as novelists; but innumerable working-class women who took lodgers to help make ends meet moved on to become proprietors of guest houses and small shopkeepers. Perhaps the most notable evidence of the latter was the rapid spread of the fish-and-chip shop during the late-Victorian period. One must also remember the influx of entrepreneurial talent amongst the foreign immigrants of this period. This included Jews such as Sir Ernest Cassel and Montague Burton, John Brunner (of Swiss origin), Alfred Mond (a German), and several Americans, such as William Waldorf Astor and Gordon Selfridge.

Among the large-scale successes of the late nineteenth century one would have to include the chemical works established in Cheshire by Brunner and Mond which eventually gave rise to ICI. The 1890s particularly saw a major expansion of bicycle production by firms like Raleigh, using the traditional metalwork skills of the towns of the Midlands. William Lever advanced in the classical manner from the small beginnings of his father's shop to become the leading manufacturer of soap and the architect of Port Sunlight. In addition, a number of men made their fortunes through the development of chains of grocery stores, such as Hudson Kearley (the International Stores) and Thomas Lipton, who bought his own tea plantations so as to cut out the middlemen and reduce the price of tea to the consumer. Finally, the world of popular newspapers generated a number of successful businessmen, of whom Alfred

Harmsworth (later Lord Northcliffe) of the *Daily Mail* is the best known. It should be noted that Lipton received a knighthood and Kearley, Harmsworth and Lever peerages; moreover, Mond, Brunner, Lever and Kearley were all involved in politics (as Liberals) and several became MPs. It is not clear that this distracted them unduly from their role as businessmen.

But how much positive significance may be placed upon a catalogue of new businesses? At the least it undermines assumptions about the late nineteenth century as a period of unrelieved entrepreneurial failure. The successful men were repeating the practice of the early industrial entrepreneurs by marketing a cheap, mass-produced item. However, the examples of success also tell us something about the wider problems of the economy. First, nearly all these new enterprises were supplying *consumer* goods to the domestic market relatively free from external competition. Second, many of them managed to start out and to expand with only modest amounts of capital. In this sense they were not unlike the early cotton textile manufacturers. But their success could not easily be repeated in industry generally, which increasingly required major initial investment, sophisticated technology and skilled manpower.

Industrialization in perspective

The varied symptoms of incipient economic decline, albeit in the context of absolute economic strength, seem to justify some reassessment of the traditional emphasis placed on Britain's industrial revolution. Both because of Britain's role as the first industrial nation and because of assumptions about the *revolutionary* character of industrial change, it has always been natural to see the process as pervading all aspects of nineteenth-century British society. However, from the perspective of the early twenty-first century, when over a hundred years of decline has left Britain no longer a Great Power, it is much easier to see how exaggerated the traditional view was. In many ways it was possible for Britain to become an industrialized country without experiencing a thorough disruption of her existing ideas, institutions and practices.

To take the most obvious aspect, it is clear that the impact of industrialization on the organization of the economy was less dramatic than conventional accounts suggest. It comes as a surprise to find that even in manufacturing industry the average British workshop employed only twenty-nine men as late as 1898. And so much attention has been attracted to industries like textiles and coal that one can easily overlook the largest occupation in the country – domestic service – which grew in size during the nineteenth century. In many ways, therefore, pre-industrial forms of economic activity survived strongly right up to 1900. This point is complemented by recent studies of the wealth generated by British industrialists in the nineteenth century. Obviously many fortunes were made, but they were on a more modest scale than is often appreciated. By the end of the century the predominant sources of wealth amongst the millionaires or half-millionaires in Britain were land, banking and commerce, not manufacturing industry. Of course, the pattern was in a process of change; during the twentieth century the traditionally wealthy families often lost their pre-eminence. But in 1900, after a century of industrialization, the basic structure of the British social pyramid had not been significantly changed.

Finance and empire

As far as the character and quality of the British business elite is concerned, it is not necessary to assume a decline to recognize that in some respects their significance was always overestimated. The success of the original cotton entrepreneurs reflected a concatenation of favourable circumstances. They, and their successors, enjoyed the advantage of being not so much the most efficient as the *only* mass producers at least for many years. In this perspective, British economic supremacy was a rather special and brief phase, enjoyed rather fortuitously by a small country that depended heavily on transporting vital raw materials cheaply over long distances. Moreover, even in her Victorian heyday Britain's strength in the world economy reflected her role in finance and commerce rather than simply manufacturing. On the direct exchange of goods she enjoyed only a modest surplus; it was the indirect earnings that made her overall trade balance look strong.

The fact is that even at her peak Britain often showed herself slow to exploit the economic potential that beckoned. Perhaps we are too accustomed to the critical view of the ruthless Victorian capitalist as a keen-eyed hawk quartering the skies, perpetually ready to swoop on an opportunity. In reality he was often a cautious and slow-moving individual. This is abundantly clear if one looks at the broad record in what might be expected to have been a thoroughly exploited area – British India. The chief source of wealth derived from India in the nineteenth century was the land revenue laboriously gathered in by the civil service. But neither the East India Company before 1858 nor the British government thereafter showed a great concern for economic development. Private individuals worked fitfully at unlocking the country's great resources. Britain's tea continued to be obtained overwhelmingly from China until the 1890s. The jute industry was similarly left undeveloped for many years. It was not until the 1860s, when the Civil War in America interrupted Lancashire's cotton supplies, that India's output of cotton began to be extensively increased. Most striking was the fact that it took the Mutiny to make the development of a railway system a priority. Even so, private entrepreneurs were so reluctant that they had to be led by the Indian government, which guaranteed a 4.5 per cent rate of return on capital for the construction of a railway network. Taking overseas investment as a whole, about three-quarters of it went into loans to governments, public utilities and railways, and very little into manufacturing in the period 1870–1914. If Britain had a talent, it was very much for investment and commerce rather than for industry itself.

Continuity not revolution

This reminds us that British pursuit of economic success was always less single-minded than it must have appeared to outsiders. One traditional reading of nineteenth-century history had Britain falling to a series of challenges from the industrial middle class, as demonstrated by the extension of the vote in 1832 and the repeal of the Corn Laws in 1846. Yet there was never a complete clash of values and ideas between the old ruling groups and the rising classes, partly because the aristocracy itself had long been involved in capitalistic enterprise and continued to shore up its position by this means. In any case, it is now widely recognized that, in spite of isolated victories achieved by the reformers, British government was not taken over by middle-class interests. Parliament and the Cabinet continued to be dominated by the traditional landed and aristocratic families throughout the mid-Victorian era and even later still. Moreover, such increase as occurred in middle-class political representation was as much due to professionals like lawyers as to industrialists. Consequently, it is difficult to show that government policy was moulded by the interests of industrialists. This may seem a surprising claim. After all, by 1866 no fewer than 215 MPs had connections with railway companies, often as directors. But there is not much evidence that they significantly influenced the legislation dealing with railway interests, especially after 1870. Governments tended to take a wider view and to listen to criticism of the companies. Indeed, some scholars have argued that some industries like railways and electricity were seriously disadvantaged by government intervention. Similarly, when in the 1880s pressure developed among some manufacturers for protection against foreign competition, the party-political interests gave very little support, and the question of 'fair trade' had to wait another twenty years before it rose to the top of the political agenda. Britain was very far from giving priority to her manufacturing interests.

Further reading

The following give a good, comprehensive analysis of the performance of the economy:

Roderick Floud and Paul Johnson eds, *The Cambridge Economic History of Modern Britain, vol. II Economic Maturity, 1860–1939* (2004) is less quantitative and more reader friendly than earlier volumes.

Martin Daunton, *Wealth and Welfare: an economic and social history of Britain, 1851–1951* (2007)

S. Pollard, *Britain's Prime and Britain's Decline: the British Economy, 1870–1914* (1989)

J. Tomlinson, *Problems of British Economic Policy, 1870–1945* (1981)

S.B. Saul, *The Myth of the Great Depression, 1873–1896* (1969)

D.H. Aldcroft and H.W. Richardson, *The British Economy 1870–1939* (1969)

The debate about British entrepreneurship was most strikingly developed by an American scholar:

Martin Weiner, *English Culture and the Decline of the Industrial Spirit, 1850–1980* (1981)

It is also discussed in:

W.D. Rubinstein, *Capitalism, Culture and Decline in Britain, 1750–1990* (1993)

F.M.L. Thompson, *Gentrification and the Enterprise Culture in Britain, 1780–1980* (2001)

J. Raven, 'British History and the Enterprise Culture', *Past and Present*, 123, 1989

Martin Daunton, 'Gentlemanly Capitalism and British Industry, 1820–1914', *Past and Present*, 122, 1989

P.L. Payne, *British Entrepreneurship in the Nineteenth Century* (1974)

D.C. Coleman, 'Gentlemen and Players', *Economic History Review*, 26, 1973

A.J. Taylor, *Laissez-faire and State Intervention in Nineteenth-Century Britain* (1972)

2

Not Quite a Democracy

Victorian Britain enjoyed an unusual, possibly unique, form of government. On the one hand it operated a liberal, parliamentary system based on public debate and freely conducted elections; governments could be criticized and regularly overthrown without recourse to violence. Britons took pride in the independence of their judicial system and in civilian control over the armed forces. On the other hand, British politics bore the heavy imprint of traditional, autocratic elements. A good deal of power continued to be exercised by the hereditary House of Lords and the monarchy and participation was, in practice, limited by wealth and class. Parliament, the cabinet and local government were still dominated by men endowed with landed wealth and aristocratic titles. The 1880 House of Commons included 170 sons of peers and baronets, and of 101 Cabinet ministers between 1886 and 1916 47 were landowners and only 12 from financial and industrial backgrounds. The majority of people were unable to vote, women being entirely excluded from the franchise. Things had actually deteriorated in that while 5.5 per cent had enjoyed a vote in the eighteenth century, by 1832 it was only 2.6 per cent. Elections were frequently uncontested because of deals between rival parties or interests, and were invariably marred by the extensive corruption and intimidation of voters.

The system of government

This ill-assorted system was to some extent the result of the fact that, unlike other Western states, Britain lacked a written constitution. From time to time it was judged that the mixture of institutions and conventions through which government actually worked was unsatisfactory; innovations were made which grafted elements of liberalization upon the traditional structure but never thoroughly overhauled it. Hence the road to full democracy involved instalments of reform in 1832, 1867, 1885, 1918 and 1928. This gradual progress was complacently hailed as a 'Whig' strategy for promoting change without revolution in contrast to the upheavals typical of other European countries. However, the gaps between reforms were rather long and each generation was inclined to believe it had finally settled the question until pushed by popular pressure for reform.

A balanced constitution

Victorians believed they enjoyed a balanced or mixed form of government that deliberately prevented undue concentrations of power by dividing it between three institutions: the House of Commons, the House of Lords and the monarch, though not in equal proportions. The essential basis of a government's position consisted in its ability to command a majority in the Commons won at a general election. Provided this majority held together, a government might enjoy up to seven years in office, though in practice elections took place more frequently when the government's majority disintegrated. Usually, however, Victorian governments brushed off defeat on a bill and continued in office; their legislation occupied much less time than it does today, leaving more room for private backbenchers' bills. Governments' capacity to push their programmes through was handicapped because the party whips exercised only limited control over backbenchers, many of whom were elected for their local influence and personal standing and were not professional politicians anxious for promotion. Another limitation on government was the requirement that an MP who accepted certain ministerial posts must resign and fight a by-election; between 1868 and 1913 some 278 ministerial by-elections occurred of which only 56 were contested and 8 lost to the government.

Governments were also obstructed by the House of Lords which contained a high proportion of leading politicians. Among the prime ministers, for example, Salisbury and Rosebery sat in the upper house, and Disraeli first in one then in the other, while Gladstone was unusual in remaining in the Commons throughout. By convention the peers checked ordinary but not financial legislation. From the 1880s onwards their role increased as propertied interests reacted against Irish Home Rule and rallied increasingly behind the Conservatives. As a result they obtained an overwhelming hold in the upper house and major Liberal legislation was rejected, thereby threatening a constitutional crisis. However, before 1885 this obstructionism complicated but did not actually kill the Liberal programme. For although the peers invented a new rationale that they had a right to restrain a government whose policy lacked a popular mandate, they appreciated the dangers of such a strategy. If provoked too far, the Liberals might seek to arouse popular support not simply over the immediate issue but against the House of Lords and its privileges.

A constitutional monarchy?

The monarch still exercised considerable influence in the choice of prime ministers, though subject to the qualification that it was unwise to select one who did not command the loyalty of the party majority in the Commons; among Conservatives she chose Salisbury over Northcote in 1885 and among Liberals Rosebery over Harcourt in 1894. However, increasing party discipline inevitably curtailed the monarch's room for manoeuvre and 1837 was the last time that Parliament was dissolved on the accession of a monarch. Contrary to traditional belief, Queen Victoria found it hard to adjust to her dwindling role. This was the result of her excitable temperament, her partisanship and her limited understanding. Age and experience only made her increasingly truculent towards her prime ministers especially towards the Liberals, and Gladstone in particular. Following their victory at the 1880 election, she tried to offer the premiership to Lord Granville and Lord Hartington, but had to back down because Gladstone had effectively recaptured the party leadership. However, Queen Victoria continued to be guided by partisanship. She delayed the promotion to cabinet of such men as Sir Charles Dilke and Joseph Chamberlain, both of whom were suspect for their radicalism and republican sympathies. Worse, she undermined Gladstone as Prime Minister by showing his letters and her replies to the leader of the opposition; and she several times consulted Salisbury in order to ascertain whether a dissolution of Parliament would suit Conservative Party interests. Luckily for the Queen the politicians to whom she was so disloyal never revealed her behaviour to the public. It was, thus, the accession of King Edward VII that really marked the emergence of the modern constitutional monarchy. Edward acted much more as a figurehead above the controversies of party politics; as long as his elected government retained its majority he would not obstruct or undermine its work.

Gladstone and Victorian Liberalism

From the 1870s onwards, Victorian politics revolved increasingly around two coherent political parties. The traditional bipartisan character of politics

Table 2.1 Late-Victorian governments, 1859–1900

1859–65	Liberal	(Lord Palmerston)
1865–66	Liberal	(Earl Russell)
1866–68	Conservative	(Earl of Derby)
1868–74	Liberal	(W.E. Gladstone)
1874–80	Conservative	(Benjamin Disraeli)
1880–85	Liberal	(W.E. Gladstone)
1885–86	Conservative	(Lord Salisbury)
1886	Liberal	(W.E. Gladstone)
1886–92	Conservative	(Lord Salisbury)
1892–94	Liberal	(W.E. Gladstone)
1894–95	Liberal	(Lord Rosebery)
1895–1900	Conservative	(Lord Salisbury)

became anachronistic, both because of the polarization between Gladstone and Disraeli and because of the steady evolution of two elaborate party machines equipped with the professional organization, local branches, large membership, annual conferences and the official party policies that characterize modern parties. However, this must be qualified for Liberals and Conservatives still had a good deal in common. In Parliament both were dominated by gentlemen of independent means who did not depend on politics for their livelihood. Both retained their character as parties that originated in Parliament and, as yet, devoted little of their time to cultivating support in the country. They had also pursued somewhat similar policies during the mid-Victorian era, and the major divisions often occurred within rather than between the parties. Many politicians found themselves attached to a party more through family tradition than ideology.

The Liberals as the national party

There were, however, significant differences between them. The Liberals enjoyed a much better claim to be the *national* party, at least at the beginning of our period. Since 1846 they had been almost continuously in office, and were not defeated until the election of 1874. Under the leadership of Lord Palmerston the party became associated with a bold, patriotic foreign policy, free trade and cheap government – and thus with national prosperity and success. Moreover, the Liberals boasted a more broadly based support in the country, including the commercial middle classes, Whig landowners, small shopkeepers, skilled artisans and trade unionists. They spanned the divide between Anglicanism and Nonconformity; and their parliamentary majorities were drawn from Wales, Scotland and Ireland, not merely England. They were a more inclusive party than their rivals.

In spite of its frequent immersion in internal controversies, the Liberal Party also held a coherent overall view of politics. Perhaps the central element in this was free trade. The importance of free trade is often overlooked because after 1846 it largely ceased to be a matter of controversy. In fact, it was far from being an exhausted issue, for it still remained to whittle away the remaining duties on food, and the Conservatives, though they generally acquiesced in free-trade policy, remained susceptible to revivals of protectionism such as occurred during the 1880s and after 1903. Moreover, for Liberals free trade was much more than an economic expedient; it was regarded as a great *moral* cause because it helped to promote international peace through the maximization of commercial relations between the countries of the world. The pursuit of peace also complemented the policies of financial retrenchment and low taxation which mid-Victorian Liberals generally espoused.

In addition, most Liberals sympathized with policies designed to extend individual freedoms and remove artificial privileges. In foreign affairs this involved support for those, like the Greeks and Italians, struggling to achieve self-determination and representative government against authoritarian and clerical regimes. At home, a traditional tolerance towards religious variety led Liberals to advocate granting political and legal rights to Catholics, Jews and Nonconformists. Most of all, the extension of individual freedoms through parliamentary reform occupied a central place in popular Liberalism. Whereas many Conservatives regarded government as a necessary evil, Liberals emphasized its power for improvement. Theirs was fundamentally an optimistic creed. Their chief reservation about government was that unchecked power inevitably led to abuse and corruption – hence the need for scrutiny by Parliament and a free press.

The role of Gladstone

Despite this the Liberals, who had emerged during the 1850s via three coalitions of Whigs, Radicals and Peelites (that is free-trade Tories), were not completely united as the split over parliamentary reform in 1866 demonstrated. In this situation the key figure for Liberalism was W.E. Gladstone, who was both unifying and divisive. To the twenty-first-century mind he seems a remote figure; his combination of high-mindedness, intellect and religiosity is almost wholly absent from modern politics. Yet his strength lay in his capacity to reflect the typical concerns and values of Victorian society. Though he sprang from commercial wealth, Gladstone played the role of the traditional aristocrat-statesman with aplomb. He possessed roots in provincial England, an estate in Wales, a constituency in Scotland, and an abiding, if somewhat abstract, sympathy with the Irish. As a young man – the 'rising hope of the stern, unbending Tories' – he had opposed the 1832 Reform Bill. But his apprenticeship under Sir Robert Peel set Gladstone on the road to Liberalism via support for the repeal of the Corn Laws. As a staunch free-trader and sympathizer with liberal-nationalist movements in Europe, he gravitated naturally towards the Liberals in the 1850s. As Chancellor of the Exchequer he occupied a key role in government, and came to be seen as the inevitable leader of the party after the death of the elderly Palmerston and Lord John Russell. His obvious intellect and his massive industry made him the outstanding figure among the ranks of the conventional parliamentarians.

At a time when most leading politicians were remote from ordinary people Gladstone's growing reputation as a reformer, his oratorical powers and readiness to speak in the provinces exercised an appeal over the Radical Liberals in the country. This was the result of his work as Chancellor in assisting the popular press by abolishing the duties on paper, and also his public support for an extension of the parliamentary vote to workingmen. Gladstone had been genuinely impressed by changes in the Labour Movement since the decline of Chartism in the 1840s. The development of a responsible trade union organization and the readiness of workingmen to save money in Post Office savings accounts helped to convince him that there was nothing to fear from a judicious increase in the number of voters. This conviction was strengthened by his dismay at the behaviour of the 'upper ten thousand', whose political influence tended, in his view, towards profligate and self-serving policies. Thus Gladstone found himself in tune with the popular Liberal cry of 'Peace, Retrenchment and Reform'. By the 1860s he had grasped the fact that many working-class, radical leaders shared his own belief in checking government extravagance and keeping taxation low; he calculated that to enfranchise the top level of the working class would not only benefit the Liberal Party as against the Conservatives but also strengthen his hand against the vested interests that dominated Parliament up to the 1860s. In this sense there was a natural alliance between Gladstone and the working-class politicians in the 1860s and 1870s.

Gladstone and the Nonconformist conscience

Religion constituted another very important pillar in Gladstone's rise. By comparison with our own century, the Victorian era was much absorbed by religious concerns; and this certainly coloured politics throughout the nineteenth century. There were broadly three reasons for this. First, the Churches became alarmed at the extent to which, as the British population migrated to the towns, it escaped the influence of Christianity. The Church of England in particular began to invest a good deal of money in building new churches, organizing Sunday schools and establishing elementary schools in order to recover the lost congregations. But when the state began to intervene in educational provision, the voluntary schools inevitably became a matter of political controversy. Many Liberals believed that state schools should promulgate non-sectarian teaching.

Second, there had been a sustained rise in support for the Nonconformist Churches which, as measured by church attendance, threatened to overtake the Church of England. This in itself raised the question whether it was still appropriate for Anglicanism to enjoy the status and other benefits of being the established Church. Nonconformists also resented the legal discrimination which, for example, excluded them from the ancient universities and denied them burial by their own rites in consecrated ground. They increasingly resorted to political action to obtain redress, which took the form of promoting pressure groups that worked under the aegis of Liberalism.

Finally, the late nineteenth century witnessed fresh controversy over the reassertion of the Catholic Church in Europe generally and in Britain; this took the form of the spread of 'ritualism' within the Church of England, new recruits to Catholicism and the influx of Catholics from Ireland. The result was that politicians devoted a large proportion of their time to containing the effects of intractable religious controversies.

Gladstone was a High Anglican who took his religion much more seriously than most politicians. He was just as happy to write a religious tract as to draw up a parliamentary bill. Faced with divorce law reform in 1857, for example, it was natural to consider what the Bible had to say on the matter of marriage. There can be no doubt that he had a capacity to articulate late-Victorian moral and religious issues and to give a lead that neither his Tory opponents nor Liberal rivals like Joseph Chamberlain possessed. As a result, several of Gladstone's great crusades, such as Irish Disestablishment in 1868–9 and the Bulgarian Atrocities in 1876–80, had strong moral-religious overtones. This proved to be a considerable political strength, and it made him, in effect, the chief spokesman for what was dubbed the 'Nonconformist Conscience' in this period. His opponents, of course, resented what they saw as his sanctimoniousness; it was not, as one complained, that Gladstone always had the ace up his sleeve that irritated, but his assumption that God Almighty had put it there!

The impact of parliamentary reform

Since the Great Reform Act of 1832 there had been no major changes in the electoral system in Britain. Even that measure had left a total electorate of only 1.3 million by the 1860s – about one in five adult men. Radical Liberals felt that, until the electorate was expanded, Parliament would continue to be unrepresentative and uninterested in their grievances. For this reason the death in 1865 of Palmerston, who had been seen as an obstacle to reform, aroused great expectations. However, the case against reform remained compelling among contemporaries. The British system represented interests and communities not individuals; consequently it was widely thought that an employer could vote on behalf of his workers, a landowner for his tenants, a husband for his wife and a father for his daughter. Up to 1914 there were still seven ways of qualifying for a vote but most reflected property ownership; thus, if a man held property in several constituencies he could enjoy a vote in each one, a practice known as plural voting.

Consequently Russell and Gladstone tried to be cautious when meeting expectations in 1866. They introduced a modest franchise bill that would have lowered the existing requirement that a householder could vote if he paid an annual rent of £10 to one of £7. This would have enfranchised a few hundred thousand voters, most of whom were expected to be Liberals. It was thus in the interests of the Conservatives to combine with anti-reform Liberals to defeat the bill; the latter correctly feared that a wider electorate would help shift the balance of the Liberal Party towards the Radicals. Usually governments swallowed their pride after such a defeat and carried on. What made 1866 significant was that Gladstone and Russell resigned, thereby signalling their determination to return to the question of reform. As a minority government the Conservatives would not last long and Gladstone and Russell clearly anticipated returning to office after another general election in which they would be able to win a mandate for their bill.

For their part Lord Derby and Benjamin Disraeli knew from experience that taking minority office while the Liberals re-composed themselves did them little good. However they eventually decided to try to keep the Liberals divided by proposing a reform bill of their own. The surprising outcome was a much more sweeping reform than that envisaged in 1866. This was the result of Disraeli's dependence upon Radical Liberal MPs, who realized they could squeeze more from Disraeli than from Gladstone, to keep his bill afloat. This led him to accept amendments which extended the vote to all male owners and occupiers in borough constituencies, but not in counties, with twelve months continuous residence, thereby enfranchising many more

Table 2.2 Parliamentary voters in the United Kingdom, 1866–1911

Year	Number of voters in millions	Ratio of adult male population voting
1866	1.3	1 in 5
1869	2.4	1 in 3
1883	3.1	
1885	5.7	6 in 10
1911	7.9	6 in 10

working-class householders. The effect was to increase the number of electors from 1.3 million to 2.4 million by 1868 and to 3.1 million by 1883.

The significance of the Second Reform Act

Once the bill was passed the Derby-Disraeli ministry was overthrown, resulting in a general election at which the Liberals, as Gladstone had anticipated, were victorious. Consequently, although the bill had been a tactical triumph for Disraeli, his colleagues did not see it this way at the time; rather they felt it had been a mistake to try to outbid the Liberals. However, the 1867 Reform Act proved a major catalyst for further political change throughout the late-Victorian era. Some of the changes were direct effects in the shape of consequential legislation; others were indirect and long-term developments arising out of the reactions and responses of the parties to the wider franchise. Since many of the new voters were workingmen, they became vulnerable to influence by employers because voting continued to be a public act. The introduction of the secret ballot in 1872 was intended as a remedy, though its immediate effects were slight except in Ireland and in parts of Wales, where landlord influence had often been intimidatory. Yet it had indirect effects in making elections less rowdy and more suitable for participation by women.

Contemporaries also took alarm at the increase in expenditure in the form of bribery of the new electors, not to mention excessive drinking and violence that often followed. In the wake of the 1880 general election, Gladstone therefore enacted a Corrupt and Illegal Practices (Prevention) Act which introduced strict limits on expenditure and imposed severe penalties on politicians found guilty of malpractices. This proved to be a fairly effective measure, although two qualifications have to be made. Fighting parliamentary elections and cultivating a constituency, even by legitimate means, continued to be an expensive business; and this handicapped working-class organizations during the 1880s and 1890s. Also, the parties circumvented the legal restrictions on local expenditure by raising huge central funds, often by means of donations from wealthy businessmen in return for knighthoods and peerages; this money could be spent in the name of the party rather than the individual candidate without breaching the law.

The Third Reform Act

Tackling corrupt practices was clearly seen as a precondition for further extensions of the franchise to workingmen. Radical Liberals regarded the 1867 Reform Act as an illogical measure in that a worker who qualified for a vote as a householder if he resided in a borough lost it if he moved to a county constituency. They believed that extension of the new franchises to counties would enable them to tap extra support, and by 1884 Gladstone agreed to meet this demand in order to check the growing disillusionment among radicals with his government. Conversely, the Conservatives, fearful of losing seats in the counties, used their majority in the Lords to delay the bill. However, fearing the campaign launched by the Liberals to reduce the powers of the peers they gladly accepted a compromise: in return for passing the franchise bill they were given a scheme to redistribute the constituencies in 1885. This turned out to be another very radical change.

The post-1885 system involved a step towards equal-sized constituencies, in that new seats were to be created for units of population of 50,000. Moreover, the traditional two-member constituencies were largely abandoned. Now both counties and boroughs were carved up into single-member seats. The effect was to create constituencies dominated by a single economic interest or social class – coal mining, seaside resorts or suburbs of office workers; in the long term this promoted the growth of a class-based pattern of politics.

The Liberal Party becomes more radical

Less obvious but equally important were the stimulating effects of franchise reform in 1867 and 1884 on the strength and organization of radical Liberalism. When Gladstone won the 1868 election he at once came under pressure to tackle the grievances of a host of radical groups. However, Gladstone, who was in any case far from sympathetic to all the causes, determined to impose his own priorities. He followed up his deliberate campaign on Ireland during the election by introducing bills to disestablish and disendow the Church in Ireland in 1869–70. After this triumph, however, the government became embroiled in a series of reforms which were often dear to rank-and-file Liberals, but offended many wealthy supporters and vested interests. Several of these initiatives promoted individual opportunities by stripping away established privilege. For example, the University Tests Act opened up teaching fellowships at Oxford and Cambridge to non-Anglicans, the practice which allowed officers to buy their commissions in the infantry was abolished, and trade unions were granted the legal status enjoyed by other organizations.

A greater challenge to traditional vested interests was W.E. Forster's 1870 Education Act, which introduced a state system of elementary education though without abolishing the existing voluntary provision of schools by the Churches. Now elected school boards would be able to levy a special rate to build and run elementary schools where the existing provision was judged to be inadequate. Although such a reform was long overdue, the Church resented the competition from the state which would inevitably raise the standards required in schools. On the other hand, many Nonconformists resented the continuing role of the Anglican Church in schools because its religious teaching would enjoy a subsidy from public funds. This controversy rumbled on for many years. In the short term it led to a revolt against Forster's Bill by back-bench Liberals, and to the setting up of a new Nonconformist pressure group, the National Education League.

Internal party friction was also generated by the government's attempts to tackle another radical cause – temperance reform. H.A. Bruce's Licensing Bill provided for the introduction of licensed hours, police inspection of public houses, and penalties against the adulteration of beer. None of this was popular with brewers and publicans; and, as consumption of alcohol reached its peak in the early 1870s, it was unwelcome in the country at large. Yet this attempt at regulation fell far short of the aims of the temperance reformers, who wanted to eliminate drinking by the suppression of public-house licenses; by purging drink of its worst excesses, Gladstone's legislation seemed likely to make this ultimate objective less attainable. Again, this controversy ran on vigorously up to 1914.

Middle-class feminists formed another pressure group whose expectations had been raised by the political reforms of the 1860s. For women, too, the parliamentary vote appeared to be the key to achieving wider objectives; and feminists had some grounds for believing that, as Liberals justified the vote for men on the basis that they paid rates and taxes, so they would be prepared to enfranchise similarly qualified women. However, the women's suffrage amendments to the major reform bills by John Stuart Mill in 1867 and William Woodall in 1884 were rejected. Gladstone disliked women's suffrage on principle, but also feared that the inclusion of a women's clause in a franchise bill would give the House of Lords a good excuse to delay it. But despite becoming frustrated with Gladstone the feminists enjoyed a good deal of success. By the turn of the century the majority of Liberal MPs were suffragists. Under Liberal governments, women won the local government vote in 1869, the Married Women's Property Acts in 1870 and 1882, the raising of the age of consent in 1885, and the abolition of the Contagious Diseases Acts in 1886. Like the Nonconformists, the women grew steadily closer to the Liberal Party organization, though they were less well integrated, through the formation of the Women's Liberal Federation in 1887. But as with the other causes, the failure to achieve women's suffrage generated friction amongst Liberal activists for many years.

After three years of innovation and change, Gladstone's government began to suffer the fate of most reforming administrations; it lost momentum through sheer exhaustion, disappointment among its supporters and the controversy stirred up among the vested interests affected by reform. Many Whigs and middle-class Liberals were alarmed at what seemed to some an attack upon property by the legislation for Irish land reform and Irish Church disendowment. The suspicions of the wealthy were reflected in growing opposition in the House of Lords, and in a withdrawal of support for the Liberals by some Whig magnates at the 1874 election. On the other hand, many radicals were determined to push Gladstone further towards reforms such as the disestablishment of the Church in Wales and England. His government's defeat in the Commons in 1873 presaged the loss of the Liberals' majority in the subsequent general election in 1874.

Joseph Chamberlain and the National Liberal Federation

Despite these controversies and setbacks, the provincial radicals who ran local government and political pressure groups felt optimistic about their long-term prospects because they calculated that the extension of the electorate was exerting a stimulating effect on Liberal organization. Both traditional parties were, in fact, changing from small parliamentary elites into extraparliamentary movements. By the 1870s the Liberals were building up a substantial paid membership and an organization in every constituency. Popularly referred to as 'caucuses', these associations claimed to represent rank-and-file opinion and thus to have the right to select candidates who were committed to supporting radical causes in Parliament. The greater the dismay over Gladstone's reforms during 1868–73 the stronger the incentive to develop this organization. In effect the new National Liberal Federation (NLF), created in 1877, incorporated a range of radical pressure groups, such as the National Education League, the Reform League, the United Kingdom Alliance, and the Church Liberation Society, into a centralized, national party structure.

The chief inspiration behind the NLF was Joseph Chamberlain, a Liberal Lord Mayor of Birmingham and typical of the provincial radicals who were working their way up through the Liberal hierarchy in this period. He anticipated that, by compiling a programme of reforms and priorities for future Liberal governments, the NLF would effectively accelerate the radicalization of the party. Its work in the constituencies and at elections would help to change the composition of the parliamentary party and thereby realize the objectives of those who had agitated for the franchise in the 1860s.

The Midlothian campaign, 1879–80

From Chamberlain's perspective, Gladstone's leadership represented an asset to the radical cause – but only up to a point; for Gladstone not only dissented from many parts of the radical programme, he also disliked the emergence of an assertive party organization outside Parliament. However, he exercised such a powerful hold over popular emotions that for some years he managed to fend off the threat posed by Chamberlain. In 1874 Gladstone had retired but returned to active politics in 1877. He appeared to endorse the NLF, though in effect he intended to make use of it by appealing to the activists to back his new crusade against the persecution of Christians by the Turkish rulers of Bulgaria. In a famous election in Midlothian he extended the 'Bulgarian Atrocities' campaign to include attacks on Disraeli's imperial wars in South Africa and Afghanistan during 1878–9. The upshot was his triumphant re-election as MP for Midlothian in 1880 at the head of a Liberal majority in the country as a whole. Although neither Chamberlain nor the Whigs approved of Gladstone's campaign over the Bulgarian Atrocities, they were powerless to stop him. The Liberal victory at the 1880 election was attributed, rightly or wrongly, to Gladstone, and he returned to the premiership once again in an apparently strong position. However, this triumph led only to a frustrating period in which Gladstone became embroiled in Irish and imperial questions while domestic reform was neglected. Radical dissatisfaction steadily mounted, to such an extent that by 1885 Chamberlain was ready to join with Liberals from the Whig side of the party to drive him from the leadership. To this end Chamberlain launched a radical 'Unauthorised Campaign' in the country, pitched at the privileged classes 'who toil not, neither do they spin'; in this he advocated Church disestablishment, graduated income tax, taxation of landed wealth, and elected local government. He clearly hoped to capitalize upon the votes of the newly enfranchised labourers in the counties at the 1885 general election to undermine Gladstone's hold on the party.

The Home Rule split and Liberal decline

To a considerable extent the party was indeed moving in Chamberlain's direction. During the 1880s Whigs had already begun to leave the party, and a majority of the MPs supported at least part of the NLF programme by 1885. Whereas in 1868 only 64 MPs had been Nonconformists, there were 96 by 1886 and 177 by 1892. It was partly in order to arrest the drift towards Chamberlain and NLF policy that Gladstone launched a bold initiative early in 1886 by revealing that he had become converted to a policy of Home Rule for Ireland. However, this decision precipitated a split which drove many Whigs and a few radicals, led by Chamberlain, out of the Liberal Party as Liberal Unionists; but Gladstone nonetheless retained his position as Liberal leader until his final retirement in 1894. But why was Home Rule bitterly opposed in England? Some saw it as a strategic danger and some as offering encouragement to enemies of the empire. Others felt it would expose the Protestants of Ulster to Catholic domination. But the Irish movement was also seen as portending a great social revolution; the threat to landed property there could easily be extended to the mainland, and indeed the idea behind Gladstone's legislation for tribunals to control rents reappeared in legislation for Scottish crofters.

It has usually been thought that the effects of the Home Rule policy were largely negative for the Liberals in that it left the party electorally weaker, lacking funds, and out of office for most of the rest of the century. However, much depends on how long a time-frame one adopts. Irish Home Rule was symptomatic of a wider social and political reform and in the long run it compounded the evolution of Liberalism as a radical movement; it demonstrated to workingmen the party's progressive credentials. Although heavily defeated in 1886 Gladstone returned to office at the 1892 election and immediately tried to enact a second Home Rule Bill without success. But thereafter it was not clear what he wanted to do and much of its legislation was frustrated by the peers. In 1894 Sir William Harcourt pointed to the future with a radical budget that levied graduated death duties at 1 per cent on property worth £500 and up to 8 per cent on property worth £1 million.

This represented an important principle that wealth could be redistributed from the rich to the poor. As yet the peers did not dare to reject a budget. However, this was the post-Gladstonian agenda and in 1894 Gladstone resigned for the last time. His successor, Lord Rosebery, was temperamentally unable to handle a government, resigned in 1895 and suffered a massive electoral defeat. By the mid-1990s the Liberals had clearly lost their momentum. The advocates of the 'New Liberalism' were devising a fresh social agenda but as yet were not in influential positions in the party. Although in effect a Chamberlainite party they now lacked the bold, constructive leadership he would have provided. None of Gladstone's successors, Rosebery, Harcourt and Campbell-Bannerman, offered an equivalent source of inspiration. Rosebery himself divided the party by proposing to abandon Home Rule. The NLF was too focused on causes such as Home Rule, disestablishment and temperance that failed to arouse enough popular enthusiasm and the neglect of payment for MPs and votes for women suggested they were unwilling to live up to their democratic principles. Meanwhile some working-class Radicals were diverted into Socialist organizations because of the difficulties in being adopted as Liberal candidates. Things reached their nadir in 1899 when Liberals split several ways over the Boer War.

The Conservative revival under Disraeli and Salisbury

The split in the Tory Party over repeal of the Corn Laws in 1846 had left Conservatives with an unenviable reputation as a party of extreme protectionists and landowners lacking the competence for government; after 1841 the party did not win a general election until 1874 and governed only for brief intervals when the Liberals and Whigs had fallen out. It was more of a sectional than a national party based on the English rural counties. The loyalty to protectionism among the backwoodsmen gave Conservatives a reputation as out of touch with industrial Britain and lacking the confidence of the electorate.

Twentieth-century writing has traditionally credited Benjamin Disraeli with modernizing or liberalizing the party and emphasizes its progressive personalities in the party at the expense of the traditionalists. This is somewhat exaggerated. While Victorian Conservatives did adapt to change out of sheer necessity, this went against the grain, and their usual role was to resist change and to defend privilege, sometimes by introducing reforms before their rivals did so; for example, in 1889 they legislated for elective county councils in anticipation that Gladstone would pass a more democratic measure. The Reform Act of 1867, though it appeared to mark a comeback, was a case in point. The tactical triumph of Derby and Disraeli in passing the Reform Bill gave rise to a pervasive myth, popular among those Conservatives who wanted their party to become more progressive, that Disraeli had always *intended* to make a bid for a popular constituency for Conservatism and to democratize his party. In the words of *The Times* obituary, he 'found the Tory workingman as the sculptor finds the angel imprisoned in a block of marble'.

Disraeli and reform

On the contrary, Disraeli had no such ambitions, the party had no agreed view about reform and most Conservatives felt highly reluctant to indulge in reform. The euphoria over their parliamentary triumph rapidly evaporated in 1868 when the party slid to defeat by a margin of 116 seats. Lord Salisbury, one of the ministers who had resigned in protest over the reform bill, bitterly attacked Disraeli for having betrayed Conservative principles in a foolish attempt to outbid the Liberals. Nor was Disraeli himself quite the bold reformer later claimed by advocates of 'Tory democracy'. Far from having a broad vision about creating a new source of Conservatism, he had simply hoped to make some gains for his party in 1867 by redrawing the constituency boundaries to its advantage and by preventing Gladstone from reintroducing another damaging bill. He certainly shared the apprehensions of the traditionalist leaders about the emergence of an extraparliamentary organization. In 1867 the National Union of Conservative Associations had been established to promote the work of the existing Conservative workingmen's clubs; but it was confined to propaganda and local organization and had no role in policymaking. Just to make sure, in 1870 Disraeli created the Conservative Central Office, whose officials and funds were effectively controlled by the party leader, to run the organization.

On the other hand, Disraeli undoubtedly had a shrewd eye for a political opening, and he saw his opportunity in the shift of the Gladstonian Liberal Party towards a more radical position after 1867. The more the Liberals turned their backs on middle-of-the-road Palmerstonianism, the more credibly could the Conservatives appeal to the respectable, middle-class electorate. Harbingers of the new strategy appeared in Disraeli's speech at the Free Trade Hall, Manchester, in April 1872, in which he attacked the government for allowing radicalism to get out of control and for threatening the Church, the Crown and national security. Later that year, at the Crystal Palace, he made some celebrated if very brief references to social reform; but the real significance of the speech lay in his criticism of the external policies of the Liberals, notably the attempt to withdraw troops from New Zealand. This was blown up into an absurd claim that Gladstone intended to dismember the British Empire.

Conservative social reform

Yet Disraeli remained very cautious about his prospects of power. After the defeat of Gladstone in Parliament in 1873 he declined to take office, as he wanted to have a better chance of winning an election. When that election came, in 1874, it did produce a Conservative majority, the first since 1841, though the party still polled a minority of the votes – only 1.09 million compared to 1.28 million for the Liberals. The mid-Victorian mould of politics was not broken yet, though it was clearly cracking.

From 1874 to 1880 Disraeli enjoyed real power for the first time in his long career. Much attention has focused upon the remarkable concentration of social reforms enacted in these years, including the Artisans Dwellings Act, the Health Act, the Sale of Food and Drugs Act, and the Workmen and Employers Act. However, the Conservatives had been elected more through a middle-class revolt than through new working-class support. There is, in fact, little reason for thinking that the reforms reflected working-class pressure or attracted working-class recruits to Conservatism. With the exception of the legalization of peaceful picketing, the measures made no tangible impact on working-class life. This is hardly surprising. Most of the reforms grew out of civil servants' proposals to tighten up or to codify legislation passed by previous governments; they did not represent any considered or distinctive political strategy on Disraeli's part.

If the social reforms held any general significance for the Conservatives, it consisted, as with the 1867 Reform Act, less in the intrinsic importance of the measures than in the fact that they had been passed at all. The record restored to the party a reputation for competence in government which it had not enjoyed since the days of Peel. This impression was compounded by a careful approach to finance and economics. Unluckily for Disraeli, his premiership coincided with the influx of cheap imported grain. But he firmly resisted the farmers' pressure for tariff protection – a step that would have been calculated to revive fears about the Party. Moreover, the government adhered to sound Liberal finance. The duty on sugar was lifted; liability for income tax was raised from £100 income to £150; extra grants were given to local authorities to help keep the rates down; and the social reforms were very cheap for central government. All this was shrewdly calculated to reassure both traditional supporters and middle-class recruits alienated by the Liberals' radicalism.

The Disraelian legacy?

As a result Disraeli now seems in many ways an ephemeral influence upon Conservatism, but he did leave a lasting mark in his approach to foreign and imperial affairs. Seizing upon Gladstone's departure from existing policy, he adopted the flamboyant style of Palmerston and attempted to build for the Conservatives a reputation as the patriotic party. The opportunity to do this arose out of the conflict between Turkey and Russia in the Balkans in 1876. Disraeli took the view that Britain's national interest dictated that she should oppose Russia and support the Turks, because British communications with India would be jeopardized by any extension of Russian influence in the Mediterranean. By 1877, when Turkey was losing her war with Russia, this led Disraeli to dramatic gestures such as summoning troops from India, and brought the country dangerously close to a major war. Luckily for the Prime Minister, several other powers were keen to resolve the issue by means of a conference. This met at Berlin in 1878 and forced Russia to disgorge some of her gains, thus giving the British a diplomatic triumph at little cost as she could not have risked a war.

A succession of other initiatives and controversies kept foreign affairs very much to the fore in the 1870s. Disraeli purchased nearly half the shares in the Suez Canal Company for the British government; he raised Queen Victoria to new heights as Empress of India; and his representatives abroad engaged in two reckless wars of imperial expansion in South Africa and Afghanistan. Although Disraeli had not himself taken the initiative in these latter cases, it looked as though he had. Since every one of his imperial policies attracted criticism from Gladstone, it soon began to appear that the two parties had become polarized over imperialism. From this time onwards the Conservatives made it a deliberate strategy to associate themselves with the cause of the Empire, which they had previously disparaged, the monarchy, the armed forces and hostility to foreigners in general; they took to portraying their opponents as unpatriotic, even traitorous.

Yet in spite of both his new Palmerstonianism and his social reforms, Disraeli went down to a heavy defeat at the general election of 1880, and he died the following year. Although Gladstone's 1880 government was a very troubled one, the Liberals still went on to win the election of 1885, helped by the new county electorate. This casts some doubt on the claim that Tory fortunes had really been restored by Disraeli. The real turning-point in late-Victorian politics came in 1886. It was the three Conservative victories of 1886, 1895 and 1900 that decisively broke the long-standing Liberal hold on power.

1886 as the turning-point

How are we to account for this? To a large extent the Conservatives were simply lucky in being able to pick up the windfalls from the divisions on the Liberal side. Above all, Gladstone's dramatic conversion to Home Rule in 1886 precipitated a split that had been long in the making. It resulted in a breakaway party, comprising 78 Liberal Unionist MPs, at the 1886 election. In the country many Whigs and middle-class voters now shifted to the Conservatives, which made the party much stronger in areas like Scotland, the West Midlands and London. For purposes of propaganda the Conservatives made extensive use of the violence of the supporters of Home Rule in order to discredit the Liberals by association with terrorism; and the Gladstonian threat to the Union with Ireland served to corroborate the wider claim that only the Conservatives could be relied upon to defend Britain's strategic and imperial interests.

It proved easy to keep this message in the public eye during the 1880s and 1890s because these decades witnessed the emergence of new imperial powers and a succession of colonial conflicts. Famous episodes such as the death of General Gordon at Khartoum in 1885, when a relief force sent by Gladstone arrived too late, were perennially cited as proof of Liberal weakness. In fact, the acquisition of new territory in Africa proceeded as freely under Liberal governments as under Conservative, but the latter clearly exploited the trend more successfully. The Liberals, by comparison, were much more divided over the merits of imperial expansion. Not only the Whigs and Chamberlainites who had left the party, but also some of those like Lord Rosebery who stayed, supported 'forward' policies in Africa, in opposition to the so-called 'Little Englanders' who saw this as costly and unnecessary. These disagreements culminated in the Boer War of 1899–1902. Conservatives capitalized on the crisis brought about by that war by holding a general election two years early, in 1900, when the Liberals were divided and Salisbury could reap the advantage of patriotic loyalty towards the government.

The role of Lord Salisbury

In so far as the Conservatives were the authors of their revival Lord Salisbury's leadership assumes greater significance than Disraeli's. This

Table 2.3 General election results (seats won), 1865–1900

	1865	1868	1874	1880	1885	1886	1892	1895	1900
Conservative	294	274	356	238	250	316	268	341	334
Liberal Unionist						78	47	70	68
Liberal	364	384	245	353	334	191	273	177	184
Irish Nationalist	51	61	86	85	81	82	82	82	82
Labour							3		2

seems contrary to the traditional view in that he was a rather reactionary and out-of-touch peer who disapproved of most forms of political change. However, he was a skilful politician and over time showed an unexpected capacity for adaptation. Under Salisbury the Conservative electoral revival clearly owed a good deal to the drift of middle-class support to the party. No doubt issues like Home Rule, Disestablishment and infringements of property rights contributed to this. There is also some evidence that, in time, some of the Nonconformist enthusiasm for Liberalism weakened partly because many grievances had been resolved and because Methodists in particular were less concerned about Disestablishment. Wealthy Nonconformists increasingly saw themselves as part of the political and social status quo represented by the Conservatives, rather than as outsiders. The inclusion of a typical middle-class Nonconformist businessman like W.H. Smith in Tory governments epitomized the trend.

Moreover, the cautious financial policies adopted by Conservative governments helped to consolidate the new alliance with the middle classes. Until they were blown off course by the Boer War, Salisbury's Chancellors contrived to restrain expenditure and taxation more successfully than the Liberals. This suited Salisbury's doctrinal dislike of government intervention; he was one of those Conservatives who believed that government had little scope to do good and much for harm. The major innovation was a deliberate policy of reducing local taxation by giving local authorities grants-in-aid for specific purposes, financed from the Exchequer. The relief for rates on agricultural land and voluntary schools were blatant attempts to reward Tory supporters on Salisbury's part. In this sense the party clearly forfeited any Disraelian claim to represent the two nations; it chose instead to consolidate its position as the party around which wealth and property could rally.

Organizing Conservatism

By itself this might have been a dangerously narrow strategy. Indeed, the modest Liberal revival which gave Gladstone a victory in 1892 underlined the need to do more than rely upon the errors of their opponents. Conservatives had to make the most of their resources. In this they were considerably helped by the redrawing of the constituency boundaries in 1885 – a good example of Salisbury's tactical skill. By creating a pattern of single-member constituencies Conservatives were able to preserve their support and the influence of landowners where it was otherwise threatened by the spread of urban Liberalism into the counties. In due course the redistribution created dozens of new Conservative strongholds in suburbs and seaside resorts that were largely middle-class in character. In effect, then, gains for the Liberals arising from an extended electorate in 1885 could be balanced by Conservative gains from the redistribution.

Even so, the large new electorate obliged the Conservatives to work much harder at cultivating and mobilizing their support, especially now that much of the traditional expenditure was illegal. The party trained a body of professional agents both to register Conservative voters and to organize campaigns. It also developed constituency associations affiliated to the National Union throughout the country. This official party structure was significantly augmented by a mass membership enrolled under the auspices of the Primrose League, founded in 1883 by Lord Randolph Churchill. By the 1890s the Primrose League had recruited approximately a million members, of whom half were women, and its local 'habitations' or branches covered nearly all parts of the country and each social class. They gave the Conservatives a welcome supply of volunteer activists, thereby cancelling out the organizational advantage the Liberals had traditionally enjoyed in the constituencies. Also Conservatives capitalized effectively on the *social* activities of the Primrose League as a means of extending the reach of the party and holding supporters together in the periods between elections.

Nonetheless, the party had ultimately to sink or swim on the basis of its political message. On the whole, the leaders shrank from any 'Disraelian' appeal in the sense of offering social reforms. Salisbury's rooted aversion to improving legislation militated against this; instead, the party's message was cast more in negative terms. Conservatives could, for example, attack Liberal interventionism and improvement on such issues as temperance by championing the rights of the drinking classes. Essentially, Conservatives played the role of a conservative force by defending the status quo and exploiting traditional causes now threatened by radicals. This involved maintaining the Church Establishment and religious education, defending property and the British Empire, rallying to the Queen, and attacking foreigners in general and the Irish in particular, on the grounds that immigration threatened British jobs and reduced the supply of cheap housing. This was not an infallible recipe; Conservatives won late-Victorian elections more because the Liberal turnout was low than because their own vote was very high. But it clearly held together a wide range of support in all social classes sufficiently to keep the party in power for the best part of twenty years. In view of Salisbury's dire prognostications about the trend towards democracy in the 1860s, it was a surprisingly successful experiment in adaptation to political change.

The Liberal Unionist–Conservative coalition, 1895–1905

By far the most significant tactic employed by Salisbury was to form an alliance with the 93 Liberal Unionists led by Lord Hartington (later Duke of Devonshire) and Joseph Chamberlain, who had rebelled against Gladstone in 1886. Collaboration began in 1886 with electoral co-operation to ensure that Conservative and Liberal Unionists candidates did not stand against one another. Although Salisbury did not actually need a coalition after the 1895 election he formed one because he saw amalgamation as a logical step – and not just because they agreed over Home Rule. He felt that as Liberal reforms had run their course it was essential for the defenders of property to unite against threats to property posed by the Irish, trade unionism and Socialism. What seems surprising is that Salisbury was able to work with Chamberlain, the most radical and interventionist of Liberals. The explanation is that Chamberlain did manage to extract some social reforms, such as free elementary education, from the Conservatives and continued to advocate old-age pensions. Moreover, in time his interest in domestic reform was displaced by imperial expansion and for a wider strategy involving imperial federation and tariff reform. As a result the coalition won an election again in 1900 and lasted until 1905, A. J. Balfour succeeding Salisbury in 1902. Although the coalition became split this occurred among Conservatives themselves. Indeed by 1911 the Liberal Unionists had officially merged with the Conservative Party.

The Boer War and the crisis of Conservatism

However, as Colonial Secretary Chamberlain became partly responsible for the outbreak of the South African War in 1899 which Salisbury casually approved without realizing how disastrous it would be. Heavy British defeats exposed the inadequacy of the government's preparations while the conflict proved enormously costly in terms of lives, taxation and the National Debt. The war caused inflation, lowered real wages and raised new concerns about the physical deterioration of the British population all of which left Conservatism looking out of touch and too closely associated with wealth and privilege. In this situation Tory traditionalists wanted to stick to a negative view of the state, low taxation and minimal intervention, but Chamberlain characteristically advocated breaking out of the post-war deadlock with a bold programme of tariff reform that would boost the resources of the state. As a result the party became divided and uncertain about its policy and purpose especially under the leadership of Balfour. Salisbury's period of dominance had left the party ill-equipped to face the new century.

Socialism and the rise of the Labour Movement

From the late 1880s onwards both the existing parties felt obliged to take account of the intellectual and moral challenge posed by the new Socialist organizations and the emergence of an admittedly modest electoral rival as the Labour Movement became better organized. Since the campaigns for parliamentary reform in 1832 and repeal of the Corn Laws many working-class Radicals had collaborated with middle-class reformers including Richard Cobden, John Bright and latterly Gladstone. Although Chartism had dwindled as a movement since 1848, many of its ideas including manhood suffrage, secret ballot and payment of MPs continued to be advocated by Radicals. During the 1860s the demonstrations organized by Ernest Jones and Edmund Beales through the Reform League in support of franchise reform effectively

Table 2.4 Membership of trade unions in 1888

Metals, engineering and shipbuilding	190,000
Mining and quarrying	150,000
Textiles	120,000
Building	90,000
Transport	60,000
Clothing	40,000
Printing and paper	30,000
Other	70,000
Total	750,000

continued the moral-force tradition of Chartism. The backing of Bright and Gladstone, albeit heavily qualified, gave them a vital bridge into Parliament and the Liberal Party which their predecessors had not enjoyed. As the enfranchisement of manual workers in 1867 was largely attributed to Gladstone, rather than to Disraeli, politically aware workingmen looked to him for further instalments of reform. This was quite explicit in the case of the Agricultural Labourers' Union led by Joseph Arch in the 1870s. After its initial success the union quickly lost members, but instead it devoted its efforts to securing the enfranchisement of county labourers as the best way forward.

Trade unions and politics

It is easy to assume that working-class Liberalism was a mere anachronism with no roots and destined to disappear. However, this is to read backwards from later developments. In spite of Britain's early industrialization, the development of a mass trade union movement proved to be a very slow and difficult process. Many workers continued to be employed in quite small workshops where they had close relations with employers or in occupations like domestic service, where union organization was non-existent. Many workers were hampered in attempts to bargain by the availability of surplus supplies of labour which enabled employers to break strikes or ignore unions altogether. Throughout the nineteenth century trade union membership repeatedly collapsed in the wake of unsuccessful strikes. Unions were also handicapped by periods of economic depression, but conversely boom periods such as the early 1870s or the late 1880s often led to an upsurge in union fortunes, as the men enjoyed a temporary advantage when bargaining for better pay and conditions. For most groups of workers, suffering low pay or irregular employment, union membership was hardly a feasible proposition. But by the 1860s a fairly stable movement had emerged, based largely on skilled men in iron and steel, engineering, shipbuilding and similar trades. The craft unions levied high subscriptions, registered as Friendly Societies, and offered a range of welfare benefits that made membership a real attraction.

But how far could this organized body of men exercise political influence? Clearly the reforms of 1867 and 1884 had enfranchised not only skilled workers but some who were in fact too poorly paid to join unions. Also some of the new single-member constituencies were dominated by working-class electors, especially mining seats in South Wales, Yorkshire and north-east England. Yet it was not easy to translate this potential into direct political influence. The first stage in the assertion of working-class political ambitions was under way in the 1860s when the Trades Union Congress was established. Its immediate concern from 1869 onwards was to improve the legal status of trade unions, which was then the subject of an investigation by a royal commission set up in 1867. The evidence the commission received about the responsible conduct, sound finances and benefit schemes of the craft unions helped to convince sceptical politicians of the advisability of granting the unions the legal status they sought; this was achieved by Gladstone's 1871 legislation. Subsequently, the right to engage in peaceful picketing in support of a strike was conceded by Disraeli in 1875. In this way the unions began to function as a pressure group. The next step was to gain a direct footing in Parliament; but many union leaders felt this to be over-ambitious at this stage. One must remember that in a total labour force of some 12 million, union membership in the 1880s was still only 0.75 million, and 1.5 million by the early 1890s.

The 'Lib-Lab' members

Although the union leaders by no means lacked political awareness and ambitions they recognized that their members already felt an allegiance to the existing political parties. Cotton textile workers, for example, were notoriously divided between Conservative and Liberal loyalties. In Lancashire, Birmingham and London's East End, the Conservatives appeared to have won large numbers of working-class votes in the 1890s, but the leaders of the organized working class were for the most part enthusiastic Gladstonian Liberals. Free trade, financial retrenchment, parliamentary reform and avoidance of costly foreign adventures won their emphatic endorsement. Recognizing that most taxation was indirect and thus paid by workingmen and that much of the state's expenditure went to wealthier people, they endorsed Gladstone's preference for low taxation and financial retrenchment. The fact that many of these politically aware workingmen were also teetotallers, staunch Nonconformists and advocates of self-help made them natural adherents of Victorian Liberalism. They took their place along with the other radical groups that gathered beneath the umbrella of the Liberal Party. But if they were not socialists, nor were they Chamberlainites either as they demonstrated by their loyalty to Gladstone over Home Rule. Consequently, from Gladstone's perspective there could be no objection to direct parliamentary representation for such workingmen.

The breakthrough came in 1874, when two trades unionist officials were elected as 'Lib-Labs', that is, as candidates who were unopposed by the local Liberals and took the Liberal whip in Parliament. By the 1880s a dozen Lib-Labs had been elected, of whom the best known were Thomas Burt, the Northumberland miner, William Abraham, a Welsh miner, Henry Broadhurst, a stonemason, and Joseph Arch, the leader of the agricultural labourers. However, it proved difficult to extend working-class representation beyond the Lib-Lab bridgeheads most of which were in mining constituencies. The explanation for this lay partly in Liberal fortunes after the 1886 split with the Liberal Unionists, which left the party much worse off financially. As a result, local associations were often reluctant to adopt workingmen as candidates because they had little to contribute to their electoral expenses or to the annual revision of the electoral register. As yet, only a few trade unions felt able to bear these costs, and, since MPs received no salary until 1911, workingmen struggled to find alternative means of support.

Independent labour representation

The result was a frustrating period as ambitious workingmen maintained their pressure on the Liberals. Keir Hardie stood for election in Lanarkshire as an independent, but reminded the voters of his credentials as a Gladstonian. It is now clear that the Liberals missed an important opportunity in this period. Like Hardie many of the future leaders of the Labour Party largely enjoyed a close relationship with Liberalism; they agreed with its basic ideas and often served as agents or secretaries to Liberal politicians. Some such as Thomas Burt and John Burns did in fact become lifelong Liberal MPs; but Hardie, Ramsay MacDonald, Arthur Henderson and George Lansbury, each of whom nearly became Liberal MPs, were kept waiting too long and opted for an independent party instead.

However, there was also an ideological dimension to the movement towards independent labour representation. Although the early Labour leaders included men like Philip Snowden, who was dedicated to free trade and *laissez-faire* liberalism, others such as George Lansbury came increasingly under the influence of Socialist thinking. There was friction over the reluctance of the Liberals to implement an eight-hour working day and a growing realization of the failings of the capitalist system. The prevalence of poverty and underemployment in the 1880s and 1890s undermined confidence in Gladstonian economics and inevitably loosened the party's hold. 'I came to the conclusion', wrote Lansbury, 'that Liberalism would progress just so far as the great capitalist moneybags would allow it to progress, and so I took the plunge and joined the S[ocial] D[emocratic]

F[ederation].' By the late 1890s, when trade union membership had grown to almost two million, the prospects of establishing a new political party on the resources of the unions had improved greatly. The expansion of the movement also involved some modification in its composition as it now included more semi-skilled, less well-paid workers as well as a number of leaders, such as Will Thorne of the gasworkers and Ben Tillett of the dockers, whose views were more Socialist than Liberal. Being less effective as trade unions they were readier to adopt political methods to help their members. They stepped up the pressure on the TUC to adopt more radical policies such as the eight-hour day and to break with Liberalism.

The Socialist revival

On the face of it the cause of independent labour representation needed the distinctive ideology offered by Socialism to make the break with the conventional parties. It is often forgotten that late-Victorian Socialists argued not simply that unfettered capitalism was inhumane but that it was *inefficient*. They suggested that a free market was wasteful of resources and chaotic, producing excessive competition in some areas and inadequate investment in others. Perhaps the most effective exponent of Socialism was Robert Blatchford, author of *Merrie England* (1894) and editor of a newspaper, *The Clarion*. Blatchford put Socialism in the context of an older tradition of beneficial collective action and a more compassionate society that had been swept away by the industrial revolution; for him it was *British* not an alien import. He also expressed what to many seemed an abstract idea in familiar and concrete terms, pointing to the Victorian Post Office as a practical example of Socialism: 'It is standing proof that a vast and intricate business may be managed by the state without any spur of opposition or profit.'

Despite this the realization of a Socialist party for workingmen continued to be elusive. The Fabian Society, founded in 1884, attracted Sidney Webb and G.B. Shaw among others. But it was largely a middle-class organization that had no aspirations to become a mass party; it was sceptical about trade unionists and its members believed it could guide the existing parties towards Socialism by stages.

The Social Democratic Federation (SDF) was founded in 1881 but adopted Marxist Socialism in 1884. Its best-known members, H.M. Hyndman and William Morris, were articulate but quarrelsome and spent too much time on internal debates. Moreover the trade unions suspected that such organizations were designed to tap their funds for

Image 2 Labour MPs elected in 1906. Front row, Ramsay MacDonald (third from left), Arthur Henderson (fourth), Keir Hardie (fifth).

Socialism. Hence they had little to do with the SDF. As a result the SDF made more impact through its role in the great demonstrations by unemployed workers in Trafalgar Square in 1886 and 1887, events that attracted a good deal of sympathy both because of the plight of the workers and because of the repressive tactics used by the police to disperse the gatherings. But in parliamentary elections the SDF continued to poll very few votes and it never showed signs of developing into a mass movement. Most trade unionists preferred to participate in politics by forming trade councils in the major towns; this was a modest but economical way of bringing pressure to bear on local authorities and sponsoring the election of workingmen to municipal councils. The multiplication of elective local authorities after 1870 provided an excellent apprenticeship in politics for many workingmen.

The Independent Labour Party

Much greater success was enjoyed by the Independent Labour Party, formed in 1893. It was intended to pioneer the return to Parliament of workingmen free from any pacts or deals with other parties. It attracted most of the outstanding orators of the Labour Movement, including Keir Hardie, Ramsay MacDonald and Philip Snowden who had a foot in both Liberal and Socialist camps. Their Socialism involved relatively little emphasis on economics or state intervention; rather, they stood for ideas that were compatible with Liberalism including free trade, land reform and graduated taxation. For them Socialism was a matter more of morality, a vision of a society based on co-operation and brotherhood. This owed a good deal to the influence of the Christian moral code and to the arts of the lay preacher. Even the left-wing George Lansbury argued that Christ had been a social revolutionary.

The Independent Labour Party (ILP) was also a more democratic party than the SDF. It attracted the more independent-minded Socialists, and its emphasis on political reform made for continuity with the radical Liberal tradition. Indeed, the ILP claimed to be extending the work that was now being neglected by leading Liberals; Lansbury was one of those who reacted against the failure of the parliamentarians to respond positively to women's demand for the vote. And despite its base in the industrial north of England the ILP was also rather less working class in composition than its rhetoric suggested. A large proportion of the activists in this period were lower-middle-class men, often drawn from the families of manual workers who had acquired the education necessary to become clerks, schoolteachers, journalists, commercial travellers or insurance collectors. For a time the ILP appeared to be the coming force in politics. At the 1892 general election, three independent workingmen had won election to Parliament: Keir Hardie in West Ham, John Burns in Battersea and J. Havelock Wilson in Middlesbrough. But in 1895 all 28 ILP candidates were defeated. The party remained extremely short of funds, and even in local government it enjoyed only pockets of strength in places like Bradford.

The Labour Representation Committee, 1900

However, its leaders were realistic enough to recognize that they had not yet found the formula for a major breakthrough. In particular they had failed to tap the strength of the unions. But as the 1890s wore on and the Conservatives established their grip on politics, the various left-wing groups, the ILP, SDF and the Fabians, showed an increasing willingness to co-ordinate their efforts to create an effective party. The urgency appeared to increase now that growing numbers of skilled workers were facing unusually high unemployment as a result of the depression; this created dissatisfaction amongst the old-established unions over the political status quo. The effect was compounded by the Lyons v. Wilkins legal case which resulted in the conviction of a striking worker for picketing, thereby undermining the legislation of 1875. Everything seemed to point to the need for a new initiative to increase the influence of the unions in Parliament. Such a move also appeared feasible now that the unions' membership had reached 2 million and their reserve funds had risen from £1.4 million in 1893 to £3.7 million by 1900. This was the situation at the 1899 TUC session when the railway workers proposed the setting up of a new political organization; it was only narrowly approved by 546,000 votes to 434,000. But as a result in February 1900 129 delegates from trade unions and socialist societies met to establish the Labour Representation Committee whose object was to sponsor 'a distinct Labour group in Parliament who shall have their own whips, and agree upon their policy'. This was the organization that became the Labour Party in 1906.

At first the Labour Representation Committee (LRC) felt obliged to tread cautiously. Some of the major elements – miners, cotton textile and building workers – had not even joined the LRC. Even among its supporters the new body was as yet regarded as an improved pressure group rather than as a potential party of government. The founders avoided making any formal commitment to a Socialist ideology for fear of alienating the unions. But in order to keep the door open for sceptical middle-class Fabians, the LRC rejected the suggestion that its candidates should be restricted to workingmen. For the purpose of recruiting these disparate groups, the LRC's federal structure proved to be distinctly advantageous. It enabled each of the trade unions and Socialist societies to choose its own representatives to the executive, and to affiliate on behalf of its members at the low rate of ten shillings per thousand. Since only 350,000 members were affiliated during the first year, the LRC's income remained low. There was time to endorse only fifteen candidates for the general election of 1900, of whom two were elected, Keir Hardie at Merthyr Tydfil and Richard Bell at Derby. The LRC gained fresh momentum, however, from the Taff Vale case in 1901, when a trade union was made to pay compensation for the costs of a strike. This new blow from the courts stimulated a rapid rise in affiliations and an increase in the level of fees charged. In any case, by 1902 the political tide had turned against the Conservatives, and the LRC benefited from this at three by-elections. The success of Will Crooks at Woolwich, David Shackleton at Clitheroe and Arthur Henderson at Barnard Castle rapidly raised the profile of the fledgling party.

Further reading

On the transformation of British politics through the two-party system and parliamentary reform see:

G.R. Searle, *A New England? Peace and War 1886–1918* (2004)

G.I.T. Machine, *The Rise of Democracy in Britain 1830–1918* (2001)

J. Garrard, *Democratisation in Britain: Elites, Civil Society and Reform since 1800* (2002)

Martin Pugh, *The Making of Modern British Politics 1867–1945* (2002)

Brian Harrison, *The Transformation of British Politics 1860–1995* (1996)

Ben Griffin, *The Politics of Gender in Victorian Britain: Masculinity, Political Culture and the Struggle for Women's Rights* (2012)

E.A. Smith, *The House of Lords in British Politics and Society 1815–1911* (1992)

F.B. Smith, *The Making of the Second Reform Act* (1967)

Andrew Jones, *The Politics of Reform 1884–85* (1972)

The evolution of the Liberal Party is analysed in:

T.A. Jenkins, *The Liberal Ascendancy 1830–1886* (1994)

G.R. Searle, *The Liberal Party: Triumph and Disunity 1886–1929* (1992)

J.R. Vincent, *The Formation of the British Liberal Party 1857–68* (1966) – classic analysis of how the party came together from the chaotic conditions of mid-Victorian politics.

E. Biagini, *Gladstone* (2000)

E.J. Feuchtwanger, *Gladstone* (1975)

D.W. Bebbington, *The Nonconformist Conscience* (1982)

J.P. Parry, *Democracy and Religion: Gladstone and Liberalism 1867–75* (1986)

R. Jay, *Joseph Chamberlain* (1981)

Ian Cawood, *The Liberal Unionist Party: A History* (2012)

E. Biagini, *British Democracy and Irish Nationalism 1876–1906* (2007) – challenges the traditional negative view of Home Rule for the Liberals and argues for its positive significance in the long-term radicalisation of the party.

On the revival of Conservatism see:

E. Feuchtwanger, *Disraeli* (2000)

R. Blake, *Disraeli* (1966)

R. Shannon, *The Age of Disraeli 1868–1881* (1992)

R. Shannon, *The Age of Salisbury 1881–1902* (1996) – these two volumes are very dense accounts of the party from 1868 to 1902 best dipped into.

R. Blake, *The Conservative Party from Peel to Churchill* (1970)

B. Coleman, *Conservatism and the Conservative Party in Nineteenth-Century Britain* (1988)

D. Steele, *Lord Salisbury: a Political Biography* (1999) – a revisionist biography.

P. Marsh, *The Discipline of Popular Government: Lord Salisbury's Domestic Statecraft 1881–1902* (1978) – explains Salisbury as a skilled and adaptable manager.

G.R. Searle, *Country before Party: Coalition and the Idea of National Government in Modern Britain 1885–1987* (1995) – puts the coalition with the Liberal Unionists into wider context.

Martin Pugh, *The Tories and the People 1880–1935* (1985) – explains the role of the Primrose League as a popular Conservative organisation.

E.H.H. Green, *The Crisis of Conservatism* (1995) – analyses the intellectual problems faced by Conservatives towards the end of the century.

G.R. Searle, *The Quest for National Efficiency* (1971) – also examines the failings of conventional thinking in the 1890s.

The role of Socialist and Labour ideas is discussed in:

Paul Ward, *Red Flag and Union Jack: Englishness, Patriotism and the British Left 1881–1924* (1998) – an original book that reminds us that much of the working class was patriotic and right-wing.

John Callaghan, *Socialism in Britain since 1884* (1990)

Noel Thompson, *Political Economy and the Labour Party* (1996)

R.I. McKibbin, 'Why was there no Marxism in Great Britain?', *English Historical Review*, 99, 1984

For the organizational development of the Labour Movement see:

David Howell, *British Workers and the Independent Labour Party 1888–1906* (1983)

Martin Pugh, *Speak for Britain! A New History of the Labour Party* (2010)

R. Moore, *The Emergence of the Labour Party 1880–1924* (1978)

James Hinton, *Labour and Socialism* (1983)

Gordon Phillips, *The Rise of the Labour Party 1893–1931* (1992)

On three key pioneers of labour politics:

K.O. Morgan, *Keir Hardie: Radical and Socialist* (1975)

Chris Wrigley, *Arthur Henderson* (1990)

David Marquand, *Ramsay MacDonald* (1977)

3

The Victorian State
and its People

In the daily struggle for subsistence the majority of Victorians viewed their Westminster government as a remote and uncertain element; local authorities seemed much more relevant and immediate. But the most effective means of avoiding poverty and the workhouse was to rely upon the network of family, neighbours, trade unions and friendly societies.

The rising standard of living

Although generalization is risky, we can say that in the late-Victorian period a workingman would count himself reasonably fortunate if he enjoyed a regular weekly income of around 25s. During 1909–13, when a group of Fabian women in London investigated the living standards of typical families (Maud Pember Reeves, *Round About a Pound a Week* (1913)), they studied those who received between 18s. and 26s.; life in this range was a struggle, but more than bare subsistence could be achieved. However, many men earned less than this because of the casual and irregular nature of the work offered to them. There were also marked regional variations in wages; amongst agricultural labourers, one of the lowest-paid occupations, by 1900 a man received as little as 14s. in Dorset and Wiltshire because little alternative work was available, while in Northumberland, Durham and Lancashire, the effect of wider employment opportunities, the migration of workers into towns and emigration to America or the colonies was to reduce the surplus of labour and thus drive the basic agricultural wage up to 22s. As a result, many families simply found it impossible to support themselves: the official returns for paupers showed over twice as many in the south-west as in the northern counties. However, many families were saved from destitution because of the vital additional income of wives and children. Thus Lancashire, where the textile industry made the two-income family common, saw a relatively high standard of living in spite of the low level of wages.

However, the variation in manual workers' wages continued to be very wide at least until 1914. The most highly skilled workers in iron and steel smelting, boilermaking, shipbuilding and engineering could earn twice or even three times the wage of a casual unskilled labourer. At 30s. a comfortable life was possible, and a fortunate few might reach £2 a week. They could rent houses with more than four rooms and set aside a front parlour for 'best', equipped with such items of luxury as a piano. At the higher levels the so-called 'labour aristocrats' actually overtook the income of many of those in white-collar, lower-middle-class occupations. Clerks, for example, were typically in the £60–£100 a year range, though the most senior might earn £150. Male elementary schoolteachers received on average only £127 even by 1914. A salary of £3 a week was, in terms of social status, a critical one, for it meant that one paid income tax and could employ a servant – an indication of middle-class status.

Why did living standards rise?

These figures for money wages cannot, in themselves, convey a true idea of living standards. Even without changes in wage rates, many workingmen

Image 3 The first train to cross Canada arrives at Vancouver, 1886, reducing the price of bread in Britain.

raised their standards by simply moving out of the lowest-paid jobs into more skilled or more regular work. Whereas there had been 1.4 million agricultural labourers in 1850, there were only 0.97 million by 1911. Of course, increases in money wages did occur, as in the early 1870s, when the economy was expanding; however, it was usually the skilled minority that benefited most from this.

However, from the mid-1870s to the late 1890s a rather different pattern of improvement intervened. The difficulties faced by many employers resulted in a stagnation or even a reduction in money wages. Yet the effects were more than cancelled by a major and sustained drop in the price of most basic items of food. The catalyst in this process was the influx of cheap North American wheat, which virtually halved the price of bread in the shops by the 1890s. For most working-class families bread remained the staple item of consumption, though potatoes formed a growing element, especially in the north and Scotland. But many families responded to cheaper bread by diverting some of the surplus expenditure into other items of consumption, either more nutritious or more novel.

Improvements in diet

In the same period other sorts of food became cheaper, partly because of the long-term increase in supplies from far-flung parts of the world, or because of further cuts in the duties imposed by the government on tea, coffee, cocoa and sugar. Tea, as the 'cup that cheers but does not inebriate', was a favourite of Chancellors of the Exchequer. The price of sugar fell by 58 per cent between 1874 and 1900, and annual consumption rose to 80 lb. per head. Supplies of meat also improved significantly, partly through extra imports of live cattle from Europe, partly by the canning of beef from the United States and South America, and partly by the freezing of carcasses of lamb from Australia and New Zealand as well as American beef. Consequently the price of fresh meat had nearly halved by 1900, and it became a regular item of diet for most families for the first time. Improvements in transport and refrigeration also facilitated the rapid spread of fish-and-chip shops in this period. The combination of cheap flour and sugar promoted the mass production of biscuits by firms like Huntley and Palmer at Reading and Carr's of Carlisle, while the availability of domestic fruit supplies and imported sugar brought the jams of Chivers and Rowntree within reach of many families. Margarine was developed as a cheap substitute for butter, and tins of condensed, skimmed milk became an alternative to the fresh product, which was both expensive and frequently adulterated.

Table 3.1 Average price of wheat per imperial quarter, 1870–1900

Year	Price
1870	46s. and 11d.
1875	45s. and 2d.
1880	44s. and 4d.
1885	32s. and 10d.
1890	31s. and 11d.
1895	23s. and 1d.
1900	26s. and 11d.

Overall, the effect of these changes was to increase real wages by about one-third between 1875 and 1900; and since the key to the process was the fall in prices, which affected even the poorest families, one is justified in making a generalization about the late-Victorian period as one of substantially rising living standards. It was not until the end of the 1890s that prices rose again, and the inflationary effects of the Boer War led to some falling back in real wages at the beginning of the Edwardian period. This, however, could not reverse the steady advance towards a more varied and nutritious diet for the majority of families. Of course, the working-class appetite for novel and relatively expensive forms of food attracted a good deal of misguided criticism from middle-class Victorians at the time. In fact, many of the economical recipes they recommended were not only unappealing but impractical, either involving lengthy cooking or requiring equipment which poor housewives lacked. Instant meals such as fish and chips at one penny a head were, in fact, good value and very nutritious; potatoes supplied a high proportion of the required vitamins and minerals, while fish cooked in batter retained its food value.

Commercial innovation and state intervention

A number of other trends and innovations further promoted improved living standards in this period. Housewives were only too keen to use some of their spare cash to purchase materials to keep the home and the family clean. Hence the huge success of William Lever in selling one-penny bars of Lifebuoy soap to the working classes. There was, by contrast, a slight reduction in the consumption of alcohol after the peak in the early 1870s. As a proportion of consumer spending, drink fell from 15 to 12 per cent between the 1870s and the 1890s. The pressure to curtail alcohol consumption

Table 3.2 A late-Victorian family's weekly budget (family of three; income varied from 18s. and 9d. to the £1 3s. and 9d. shown here)

Item	Expenditure
rent	5s. and 6d.
coal	2s. and 2d.
coke	3½d.
insurance	7d.
meat	1s. and 6½d.
flour (14 lbs)	1s. and 5d.
bread meal (3½ lbs)	4½d.
butter (1 lb)	1s. and 2d.
milk (1 tin)	3½d.
lard (½ lb)	2½d.
bacon (1 lb)	9d.
sugar (4 lbs)	8d.
tobacco (3 ozs)	9d.
potatoes (7 lbs)	3d.
candles and matches	1½d.
lamp oil	2d.
cat's meat	1d.
starch (1 box)	2d.
boots (1 pair)	5s. and 11d.
soap (1 lb)	3d.
eggs	2d.
Gold Dust* (1 packet)	1d.
milk (fresh)	1d.
tea (½ lb)	9d.

* Household cleaning powder.

Source: Lady Bell, *At the Works* (1907)

at the family level was the greater because the price of this item did not fall in line with others. Another helpful, if marginal, trend was the spread of allotments, which gave some families access to cheap, fresh supplies of vegetables and eggs. More important was the intervention of the government in checking the adulteration of food and drink which was rampant during the mid-Victorian years. Not only was food diluted – sugar with sand and tea with hedgerow leaves, for example – but poisonous substances were commonly added to items like bread and beer in order to create a more attractive colour. Under the impact of successive legislation in 1860, 1872 and 1875, local authorities appointed inspectors to test food and to prosecute offenders. Finally, commercial developments also made a contribution to higher standards. For example, the practice of selling tea in sealed packets with a guarantee of purity, which had been pioneered by Horniman, was copied by Lipton, Brooke Bond and Lyons. Above all it was the Co-operative stores that made cheap but high-quality food available to ordinary families. In the late-Victorian period they were followed by new chain stores including Lipton, the International Stores and Home and Colonial.

Counter arguments

On the other hand, a number of qualifications must be made about the improvements in standards of living. Not everyone could take advantage of the pure and economical food at the Co-op. Poor families were obliged to buy from their corner shop because they needed credit and consequently paid a higher price for their food. There was clearly an increase in unemployment, although in the absence of reliable and comprehensive statistics it is impossible to say how great an impact it made. Income was not always wisely spent, nor was the food distributed fairly within the family. In particular wives notoriously deprived themselves of expensive items like meat in order to feed the male head of household. Also, the cost of other essentials like housing did not fall. The typical working-class rent bill was between 4 and 8 shillings a week. There was, however, some improvement in the quality of housing in the form of more gas lighting and water closets. In some areas overcrowding was reduced, but in the absence of new building slum property spread. Rural housing remained very poor and probably deteriorated because of a lack of new investment. In the towns, too, many of the landlords owned only a few properties, had little spare income, and failed to repair and improve unhealthy buildings. The effects of all this were evident in the poor health of many of the men who volunteered for service in the Boer War, and in the high infant mortality rates. During the 1880s, on average 142 out of every 1,000 babies died in the first year; and in the 1890s the average actually rose to 154 – a reminder that not everyone benefited fully from dietary improvements, and that the changes in food consumption took a generation or more to show results.

The persistence of mass poverty

The Victorians employed three strategies for dealing with the poverty in their society: self-help, charity and the Poor Law. What is significant about the last twenty years of the nineteenth century is that all three were increasingly recognized as unsatisfactory and inadequate. Consequently the problems of the poor moved a little higher up the political agenda; and although policies had not changed radically by 1900, the politicians had gained a clearer idea of the options available to them. The Victorian debate thus prepared the ground for action in the Edwardian and subsequent years; for example, William Beveridge, a university undergraduate much influenced by the 'discovery of poverty' around the turn of the century, was to leave his mark upon national welfare policies in the post-1945 era. Concern over poverty was stimulated and sustained by a series of revelations and investigations beginning with Andrew Mearns's pamphlet *The Bitter Cry of Outcast London* (1883), Charles Booth's monumental *Life and Labour of the People of London* (1887–1903), and B.S. Rowntree's *Poverty: A Study of Town Life* (1901). They influenced the debate in several ways.

Failings of the Poor Law

First, and simply, the studies suggested that poverty was much more widespread and persistent than had hitherto been thought. Around 28–30 per cent of the population were now described as being in a state of poverty. This stood in stark contrast to the official figures for paupers, which indicated 2–3 per cent; and it undermined complacent contemporaries who pointed to the diminution in the numbers of people receiving poor relief since mid-century. Since the reform of 1834, the poor-law system had run on the principle that those who enjoyed assistance from the rates should be required to enter the workhouse rather than receive a dole, and should there experience worse conditions than those faced outside. This, it was assumed, was a necessary means of maintaining the incentive to lead a self-supporting life. In practice the system had never been operated as uniformly as intended. Some guardians gave outdoor relief to the deserving poor, either out of humanity or because this was cheaper per head than indoor relief. However, orthodox critics charged that outdoor relief simply created more poverty, by encouraging people to apply to the guardians rather than help themselves. Yet if Booth and Rowntree were even approximately right, the bulk of the problem was not being touched by the poor-law authorities because people feared and resented the humiliating treatment in the workhouse: the separation from one's relations, the uniform, the disfranchisement and the prospect of a pauper's burial. Consequently the poor-law system found itself under attack from both the orthodox and the liberal reformers.

What caused poverty?

The second contribution of Booth and Rowntree was to focus attention on specific causes of poverty in terms of irregular or cyclical employment, low-paid occupations and old age. Since these were factors clearly outside the individual's control, much of the poverty could not reasonably be blamed upon moral failings. It was a sign of shifting perceptions that during the 1880s the word 'unemployment' came into vogue to describe an involuntary condition.

Finally, the investigations began to point the way towards more rational ways of tackling poverty. After all, the findings themselves were by no means entirely novel. In the 1850s Henry Mayhew had published similar revelations about the extent of destitution in London. In the 1860s the sudden rise in poverty in Lancashire owing to the interruption of raw cotton supplies by the American Civil War had underlined that men could be the victims of circumstances beyond their control. But Rowntree in particular advanced the discussion by his less impressionistic and more statistical approach. He introduced a measurement or poverty line on the basis of the cost of basic food and shelter for a family of five, which he put at just under 22 shillings a week. He also described the poverty cycle commonly experienced: the young married couple were well off when in work, they fell into hardship as the number of dependent children grew, prospered when the children brought home extra income, and then fell unavoidably into poverty again in old age. This helped to direct attention towards certain aspects of the problem like childhood and old age, for which remedies were forthcoming.

It was not only the Poor Law but private charity that lost credibility in the late-Victorian period. Although large sums of money continued to be donated, they were increasingly recognized as inadequate in view of the scale of poverty and the difficulty of distributing resources rationally. Sudden slumps or disasters attracted philanthropic attention in the form of distribution of coal and blankets, but this left the long-term causes of daily poverty untouched. In recognition of this the Charity Organization Society had been founded in 1869. It tackled the problem by means of casework with individual families, not the indiscriminate distribution of relief, in this way pioneering modern social work. But it still reflected the traditional idea that the poor were responsible because of their personal failings, and remained largely blind to the underlying social causes.

It would clearly be an exaggeration to suggest that attitudes towards the poor altered radically during this period. Even the reformers retained some belief in the idea of personal responsibility. Rowntree, for example, distinguished between primary and secondary poverty; the latter he attributed to those who enjoyed an adequate income but who still experienced poverty as a result of excessive expenditure on alcohol or a very large family – factors held to be within the individual's control. Nor was the confidence in thrift, abstinence, industriousness and self-help confined to the middle class. Workingmen like Arthur Henderson and Keir Hardie argued that many a worker could quickly improve his condition of life by giving up drink. Moreover, the new thinking of Booth and Rowntree cannot be said to have penetrated throughout society; rather, it influenced an educated minority within the middle and upper classes. Consequently the impact of such reformers in terms of policy was limited, at least before 1906, and the old Poor Law survived until 1929.

Popular attitudes towards the state and self-help

Although many Victorians believed that their economic success was conditional upon minimizing the activities of government, their society was, in fact, characterized by a steady expansion of state interventionism. What concerns us here, however, is the extent to which this development reflected pressure from below. From the perspective of the post-1945 welfare state it is only too easy to take for granted the idea of government responsibility for the level of unemployment and standards of living; many have assumed – as did some mid-Victorian reformers – that once a popular vote had been granted, collectivist social policies designed to raise living standards and to redistribute wealth would become inevitable. Empirically, however, this appears not to have been the case. Gladstone's governments concentrated more on political, legal and religious reforms than on social; Disraeli's innovations made little impact; and from 1880 onwards the tendency was towards *less* social interventionism in spite of the increase in the electorate.

Why was social reform unpopular?

In the first place, some of the existing expressions of intervention in the lives of working-class people aroused a good deal of antagonism, which naturally blunted the appetite for more. Often the supposed beneficiaries felt themselves to be the targets or victims of those who would improve them, regulate their behaviour, or extract taxes from them. The most persistent object of working-class hostility was the poor-law system. But the move towards universal elementary education after the 1870 Forster Act constituted a growing provocation. Parents often felt less than convinced that able-bodied children should be detained in school until twelve years old when they might be earning extra wages for the family. Compulsory attendance meant visits from the inspectors to chase up the parents of truants, and resulted in 86,000 prosecutions in 1892. Indeed, much of the state's activity in connection with children – vaccination, medical inspection, school meals, arrangements for taking them into care – was resented by parents as an infringement of their role.

A second explanation for popular scepticism is that, while some collectivist measures seemed acceptable in theory, the practical effects greatly diminished their significance in the eyes of the working classes. For example, the 1875 Artisans Dwellings Act may loom large in the long-term development of public-housing policy, but all it did in the 1880s and 1890s was to facilitate the demolition of slum property by local authorities. Since the slums were frequently not replaced, the effect was to exacerbate overcrowding. Understandably, then, many workingmen placed less importance on social reforms than on wage rates, conditions of employment, and unemployment, which were largely, though not entirely, regarded as beyond the control of the government. The most welcome benefits were often those obtained by their own initiatives through membership of Cooperative Societies, Friendly Societies and trade unions. By 1900 approximately five million Friendly Society policies were held, which, in return for small weekly contributions, offered the 'death benefit' and sometimes sickness benefits and treatment by a doctor. Understandably, these forms of self-help, which gave each family some choice as to the most appropriate scheme, seemed preferable to solutions imposed by the state.

Taxation

Finance was the third reason for negative attitudes towards collectivist policies. The working-class radicals of the 1860s and 1870s largely endorsed Gladstone's belief in retrenchment and minimal taxation. They appreciated that the bulk of the government's revenue was derived from indirect taxes and duties on consumption and relatively little from the direct taxation of income and wealth. This meant that the burden fell disproportionately upon poor people. At the same time, a high proportion of state expenditure benefited comparatively well-off people because it was devoted to the armed forces, the civil service, interest on the National Debt, pensions for former state employees, and the civil list, which grew steadily on account of all the marriages and births amongst Queen Victoria's numerous offspring. John Bright's famous dictum about the British Empire and foreign policy as a gigantic system of outdoor relief for the upper classes rang true with many radical workingmen; hence their enthusiasm for the Gladstonian strategy of avoiding expensive entanglements abroad.

Thus when Gladstone's Chancellor of the Exchequer, Robert Lowe, cut both expenditure and taxation in 1869 and 1870, he was responding to the pressure of working-class voters. And Gladstone's pledge in 1874 to abolish the income tax altogether should be seen in the same context. For although liability for income tax did not begin until an annual income of £100, increases in money wages at that time were bringing some skilled workers into the net. Subsequent governments actually raised the threshold to £150, and to £160 by 1894, which effectively excluded manual workers. Thus the emphasis on retrenchment by both parties in the later nineteenth century has to be seen not simply as a wish to pander to the middle classes; many workingmen, too, regarded low taxation, free trade and non-interference as in their best interests.

When did a more positive view emerge?

Nonetheless, it is important not to exaggerate these negative attitudes towards the state. They commanded much less support in the early 1900s than they had in the 1870s. Even in the late-Victorian period *some* social reforms attracted a positive working-class response, notably Booth's idea for a non-contributory old-age pension. By 1898 the scheme was being canvassed by the National Committee of Organized Labour for the Promotion of Old Age Pensions. Also, some workers showed more interest in reform than others; the low-paid frequently found it impossible to afford self-help schemes or to join trade unions, and therefore stood to gain from greater government intervention. Women in particular tended to be neglected under existing arrangements and were, correspondingly, the beneficiaries of state welfare. Moreover, the reliance upon self-help strategies, which had always had shortcomings, looked increasingly unwise. The emphasis on payment of a death benefit by the Friendly Societies was a misdirection of resources which gave a man a respectable funeral but did nothing for his family. Moreover, many of the policies of both Friendly Societies and insurance companies lapsed when members found themselves unable to keep up the payments, and all their contributions were lost. Also, by the 1890s the finances of many societies were in a precarious state. As

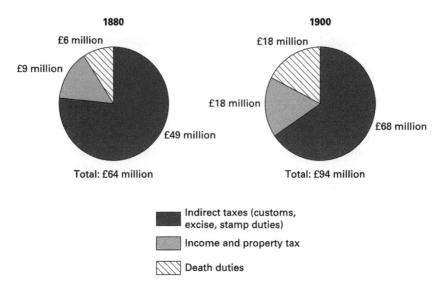

1880

£6 million

£9 million

£49 million

Total: £64 million

1900

£18 million

£18 million

£68 million

Total: £94 million

■ Indirect taxes (customs, excise, stamp duties)

▨ Income and property tax

▧ Death duties

Figure 3.1 Sources of state revenue (£ million).

members lived longer they were making more demands for benefits during old age when they found themselves too ill to work; consequently the societies' incomings failed to match their outgoings, and bankruptcy threatened. They therefore looked with growing interest to the state pension as a means of relieving them of their burdens. By 1900, then, confidence in the traditional remedies had been considerably undermined and the ground prepared for the innovations of the Edwardian period.

The growth of local government

However, this is by no means the only explanation for the strengthening of pressure for collective action to improve living standards. On the whole, Westminster and Whitehall adopted a rather high and mighty attitude towards local government in the nineteenth century, regarding it as chaotic and tending towards jobbery and corruption. A typical expression of this view was the New Poor Law of 1834, intended to impose uniform policies on the local boards of guardians who commonly evaded or defied pressure from the centre. On the other hand, Victorian governments increasingly wanted local bodies to assume responsibilities they themselves shirked, and so, in spite of their misgivings, they significantly extended local democracy after 1870. Up to that point the chief elective authorities were the municipal councils created in some of the large towns, excluding London, in 1835, and the boards of guardians. Annual elections were held in November. After 1870 school boards were also elected and added their own education rate. But county government remained in the grip of unelected landowners serving as Lords Lieutenant and Justices of the Peace. Since the radicals made no secret of their wish to sweep away this bastion of privilege, Salisbury's government decided to forestall a Liberal bill by introducing elected county councils in 1889. However, they attempted to limit the damage and scope for radicalism by restricting the electorate and including a bench of nominated aldermen in the new authorities. The next stage came in 1893, when the Liberals created elected urban district, rural district and parish councils. Again, Conservative fears about the threat to landed power led the House of Lords to impose severe limits on the legal expenditure of the new councils. Finally, the Conservatives were so upset by Liberal control of the London County Council that in 1899 they tried to weaken the London County Council by introducing a lower tier of elected borough councils in London.

Local democracy

All this amounted to a major extension of democratic participation in Britain. Although the local electorate was based on the ratepaying heads of households, which excluded some of the men eligible to vote in parliamentary elections, it did include some unmarried and widowed women who, after 1869, composed 10–15 per cent of the local electorate. There was also some change in the composition of local councillors. Although a number of aristocrats took the field and held on as chairmen of the new county councils, many of them withdrew or suffered defeat as the Liberals won majorities in the early elections. Workingmen also won places on the new councils, and some agricultural labourers came forward to serve on the parish councils. The abolition of the property qualification for guardians in 1894 brought fresh recruits like George Lansbury onto some poor-law boards and, with them, more progressive ideas. However, since meetings were largely held during working hours many workingmen experienced difficulty in serving, and often withdrew after one term in office. The male monopoly also came to a decisive end in this period. Apart from the county councils these local authorities were open to female candidates. By 1900 some 270 women sat on the school boards and 1,147 on poor-law boards as elected members. Taking all elective authorities together, by 1914 1,007 included some women, while 1,414 did not.

Expenditure, rates and loans

Perhaps not surprisingly, the expenditure of local authorities increased significantly from £36 million in 1880 to £108 million by 1905. The three most costly items of expenditure were highways, public lighting and poor relief, followed by education, the police, public utilities, water, sewage and refuse collection, hospitals and asylums. This was financed by three means – rates, loans and grants from the national exchequer. Although the two latter sources clearly rose absolutely, it is noticeable that rates increased at least as fast, so that by the turn of the century they formed as high a proportion as in 1875 – around 40 per cent. This is why aggrieved local ratepayers looked askance at new legislation that added to the burdens of local authorities, and demanded higher subsidies. Conservatives, who were sensitive to the complaints of the gentry and landowners now suffering from falling agricultural prices, favoured the relief of local taxation by grants-in-aid from national revenue. For example, between 1887 and 1892 they doubled local authority support from £4 million to £8 million; and in the 1890s they granted £1.5 million in relief of agricultural land. Liberal governments were much more reluctant to raise grants-in-aid, however. For them the remedy lay in reforming local finance by widening the sources of direct income. As things stood the burden fell heavily on tenants, while the owners of land and premises, who were often much wealthier people, largely escaped taxation. Many of the radicals adopted the idea of site-value rating as a means of tapping the huge increase in the value of urban land; they felt that landowners made large and unjustified profits from sales of land to municipalities or for commercial development when they had done little or nothing to bring about the rise in value. However, any reform of local finance would have been both complicated and controversial, and so nothing was done; Britain entered the new century with an archaic rating system which was propped up by increasing resort to exchequer grants.

As an alternative many municipalities resorted to loans from the late 1870s onwards. Birmingham led the way by taking on loans of £1 million in both 1877 and 1878. From a total of £137 million in 1880, local authority loans rose to £448 million in 1903. On the whole central government found this an alarming trend, in spite of the beneficial effects of slum clearance and town improvement schemes. The fact was that municipal policy ran counter to the spirit of Gladstonian finance, which placed the emphasis on reducing the National Debt. Between 1875 and 1900, when the National Debt was being cut, municipal indebtedness doubled.

However, the local authorities found themselves trapped between contradictory pressures. New legislation invariably involved additional expenditure; yet the rates fell heavily on persons of modest means like clerks, artisans and small shopkeepers. A further complication was the Local Government Board, created in 1871. It sometimes exercised its power to refuse to allow local authorities to raise loans for new projects, or imposed repayment terms that made it too expensive. Conservative governments especially disapproved of the larger school boards because they extended their role by providing secondary and adult education. Eventually this was checked by a challenge in the courts – the 'Cockerton' Judgement of 1899. In the 1902 Education Act the Conservatives abolished the school boards and gave their responsibilities to the county councils. It was also open to the Local Government Board to institute official investigations into poor-law boards suspected of exceeding their remit, as was done in the case of Poplar in 1906.

Ideas and experiments in social welfare

Since local government was generally regarded as the most appropriate level at which to handle poverty, it became unavoidably involved in a number of experiments and innovations stimulated by the social investigations of the 1880s and 1890s. Some bodies, like the parish councils which had been expected to promote allotments and smallholdings, simply lacked the resources to do very much. Some school boards initiated schemes to provide meals for needy children. The better-endowed boards of guardians built hospitals, as they had done in the past. But they increasingly resorted to outdoor relief for deserving elderly people, in which they were encouraged by the Report of the Royal Commission on the Aged Poor (1893–5) and by the Local Government Board. This was tantamount to providing an old-age pension. In Bradford the guardians even built houses for the elderly. Some socialist guardians like George Lansbury in Poplar wanted to tackle unemployment by setting up farms to which the surplus urban workforce could be transferred, though this was severely inhibited by lack of resources. In 1886 Joseph Chamberlain, then President of the Local Government Board, urged the municipal councils to organize public-works schemes to relieve unemployment. Although widely attempted throughout the 1890s, this strategy usually provided only unskilled work on road-repairing and snow-clearing which was unattractive to artisans. In any case, since unemployment was concentrated in the poorest boroughs, it was never possible to mobilize enough resources to make a major impact. One important advance was the establishment of a direct labour department by the London County Council. As the council undertook to pay the wage rates and to observe the conditions of employment negotiated by the local unions, this met with working-class approval, though the competition attracted criticism from private employers.

Women, poverty and the Poor Law

As consumers and as household managers, women had a particularly close interest in social policy. They experienced at first hand the fluctuations in prices and housing standards; they often took responsibility for self-help strategies in the family; they had a natural interest in promoting temperance; and they made up a majority of the recipients of poor relief. Although officially treated by the Poor Law as dependants, women were frequently instrumental in keeping their families out of poverty by their additional earnings. Their habit of sacrificing their own diet in order to feed husbands and children, and the debilitating effects of repeated pregnancies, undermined the health of many working-class women; yet they were the least likely to enjoy any form of health insurance or professional medical treatment.

Victorian women were highly vulnerable to poverty because they were so frequently widowed or deserted and left with young, dependent children. From 1846 the guardians could grant outdoor relief to widows, but some chose not to do so because they believed the children would be better off brought up in the workhouse. The poor-law authorities were usually reluctant to support a wife if they believed her husband was still alive, though not maintaining his family, because the expectation of relief would diminish fathers' sense of responsibility. If her husband refused to enter the workhouse a woman might be refused help, even if she were destitute; and conversely, while a woman's husband remained inside the workhouse she, too, would be confined. From 1876 wives enjoyed a legal claim to maintenance if legally separated from their husbands, but obtaining it was not easy. From the 1870s the local guardians were officially advised to treat single women as if they were able-bodied men, which meant no relief, on the grounds that they had a duty to take work. Between 1871 and 1892 the number of women receiving outdoor relief fell from 166,000 to 53,000. This, however, was not necessarily the result of central direction, rather of local pressure over rising rates. Clearly the treatment meted out to women varied, as it did for men, according to the attitudes and finances of each board. But mothers who received support were likely to get 2s. to 3s. weekly plus ls. to ls. 6d for each child. In spite of the falling cost of living, this obviously fell far below the poverty line as calculated by Rowntree.

Women's charitable and political work

During the late nineteenth century women also began to play a new managerial role in the field of poverty. This grew from their traditional activities in charitable organizations, which led naturally to participation in the extended local government system after 1870. By the 1850s women had already gained an unofficial footing in many poor-law unions as workhouse visitors, a role promoted by Louisa Twining's Workhouse Visiting Society. From 1869 middle-class ladies involved themselves in social work under the aegis of the Charity Organization Society. Perhaps the best known of these was Octavia Hill, who carved out a role as the manager of private tenement housing in London; she undertook to collect rents regularly so as to ensure a fair return on capital, but also to repair and improve the properties. As more women attended higher-education courses, they were drawn into the activities of university settlement houses in London and other conurbations, where they endeavoured to improve the moral and educational lives of girls and women. For the more academic, like the young Beatrice Webb, there was ample opportunity for scientific investigation of poverty under the auspices of the Fabian Society. Those who relished a more public role participated as 'Hallelujah Lasses' in General William Booth's Salvation Army.

However, the major step towards a formal public role for women came with the grant of a local government vote in 1869. Women proved to be especially successful in winning election to the school boards and poor-law boards – perhaps because these were regarded as a natural extension of women's domestic functions – but they also sat on municipal councils, rural district, urban district and parish councils. Only from the county councils were they effectively barred until 1907. Female representatives made a distinctive contribution because as women they were aware of and able to look into matters of which the men chose to remain ignorant. They encouraged the fostering of children as an alternative to long-term institutionalization. Annie Besant, an early recruit to the London School Board, scored a triumph by persuading her colleagues to initiate the provision of school meals. Although they often stood as independents, many of these women were Liberals and Socialists, and as such they prepared the ground for the adoption of the revisionist thinking in social policy of both New Liberalism and Fabianism at national level after 1906.

Nor was the female contribution exclusively a middle-class one. The formation of the Women's Co-operative Guild (WCG) under Margaret Llewellyn Davies in 1883 brought the working-class wife's view to bear on social policy. In particular the WCG advocated maternity benefits, home helps, the 'endowment of motherhood' (family allowances) and school meals. Such issues began to attract more interest in political circles as a result of growing concern about the decline in the birth rate and the rising infant mortality rates in the 1890s. Although it was tempting simply to blame mothers for neglect and ignorance about child-rearing, a more constructive approach also manifested itself. Some local authorities began to supply hygienic milk and employ health visitors. Civil servants and politicians now became anxious to raise the status of motherhood and to ease the mother's burden; they looked with more sympathy upon the prescriptions of the WCG than the demands of middle-class feminists, and the introduction of the maternity benefit in 1911 and local maternity clinics in 1914 were among the first fruits of WCG pressure.

Municipal Socialism

Ultimately, however, interventionist ideas in the field of poverty and welfare ran up against prevailing moral ideas about self-reliance and assumptions about the operation of the economy. Very broadly, Victorian thinking emphasized the virtues of the free market; competition between individuals tended to maximize production, profit and employment. The system operated 'as though by an invisible hand' to promote the interests of society as a whole. It followed that wise governments abstained from interference for the more that was absorbed by way of taxation the less was available for productive investment in the economy. If the effects of this policy upon those who became the victims of competition seemed unfortunate, the exponents of classical economics drew upon science for their rationale. Herbert Spencer in his *Man Versus the State* (1884) adopted the fashionable Darwinian view that, if the state diverted its resources to protecting the weak, the result would be to drag down the whole of society and check progress.

In practice, however, the bracing notions of classical economics were less respected than some of the rhetoric of Victorian England suggests. The whole era was characterized by a series of interventionist initiatives by governments; and some argued that around 1870 the tendency to infringe rather than reflect *laissez-faire* grew decisively. Many Victorians had become aware of the shortcomings of free enterprise but the challenge to convention was highlighted by the emergence of various Socialist organizations in the 1880s and 1890s. The most conspicuous deviation from reliance on market forces took the form of 'municipal socialism'. Fabian Socialists such as Sidney Webb argued that this offered a gradual path towards Socialism along which the country had already advanced largely through the work of local authorities in London and the provincial cities. They increasingly adopted a collectivist approach by financing street lighting and paving, public parks, libraries, art galleries and hospitals. They also ventured further into municipal enterprise by buying out privately owned water, gas, electricity and tram companies. The motive behind such policies was not necessarily ideological. Water companies, for example, were often felt to be charging a high price for a poor-quality service and it could be argued that every person was morally entitled to a supply of clean water. But it also proved to be more efficient and economical to run these services under municipal control, for, while the initial costs might be high, councils often made a profit which helped to subsidize the rates. Moreover, experience of municipalization strengthened the view that other industries, notably the railways, were really utilities that should properly be subject to some form of regulation and control in the public interest. Politically it proved advantageous that as measures of municipal Socialism were, as the Fabians perceived, comparatively small and non-ideological they could be undertaken by those who were not themselves Socialists.

National efficiency

By the 1880s, therefore, when increasing numbers of middle-class intellectuals began to join the new Socialist societies, the strict individualist notions of Herbert Spencer already looked increasingly irrelevant. It was apparent that an excessive reliance on voluntarism or the 'hidden hand' was handicapping Britain in some ways. This was underlined by an awareness of the rapid economic and social progress being made by Germany. Under Bismarck, Germany conspicuously developed a system of state social welfare in the 1880s, not to mention a superior educational system. The Royal Commission on Technical Instruction commented in 1884: 'Our industrial empire is vigorously attacked all over the world. We find that our most favourable assailants are the best educated people.' This emphasis on promoting what came to be called 'national efficiency' was typical not only of late-Victorian Socialists but of Liberals and Conservatives too. Consequently state interventionism came to be justified not simply out of humanitarian concern for the poor, or from a desire to expropriate wealth, but as a means of promoting the efficiency of the nation. Unfettered private enterprise seemed to be a wasteful and inefficient use of resources; guided by short-term profits it resulted in excessive investment in some areas and the neglect of others.

Origins of the New Liberalism

By the 1890s a good deal of collaboration had grown up between middle-class Socialists and constructive Liberals, especially under the aegis of the Progressive majority on the London County Council. But there was also a sustained effort to revise traditional thinking across the whole range of social and economic policy through organizations like the Rainbow Circle, founded in 1893, which involved Fabian Socialists like Ramsay MacDonald and New Liberals such as Herbert Samuel, Charles Trevelyan and J.M. Robertson. The common starting-point was that British capitalism had evidently failed to reduce poverty. Although conventional Liberalism held a negative Gladstonian belief that free trade and industrial development would suffice, New Liberals argued that state interventionism was consistent with Liberalism where it was designed to promote the greater freedom of the individual; it was insufficient to bestow political, legal or religious rights on the individual if he remained trapped by his material conditions of life.

From this the authors of the New Liberalism – J.A. Hobson, L.T. Hobhouse, Charles Masterman – urged that the state had a duty to promote the social-economic side of the individual's development. In education and temperance this was already widely accepted. But extending this to social welfare meant a new approach to taxation. The New Liberals proposed that government should move away from its reliance on indirect taxation towards the direct taxation of income and wealth. It had long been considered by radicals that sources of wealth like land ought to be more effectively taxed, especially as the income derived from it was often *unearned* and thus could properly be used for the benefit of the community. Increasingly they argued that taxes paid should reflect the ability to pay; this was reflected in Sir William Harcourt's death duties of 1894, which were based on a graduated scale which began at 1 per cent on property worth £500 and rose to 8 per cent on property worth £1 million. By extracting a fair contribution in this way, the government would not damage productive investment and would leave private ownership basically intact. Some radicals like Hobson went a stage further by suggesting that the underlying weakness in the economy lay not in investment but in underconsumption, that is, insufficient demand for the goods produced. If extra government revenue were redistributed via social policies to relatively poor people, this would have the effect of increasing the consumption of goods and thus stimulating the economy.

Why was change slow?

During the 1890s these views were as yet far from being typical of provincial Liberalism. But as Gladstonianism lost impetus and the older generation of radicals were defeated and dropped out, those with more advanced views and different assumptions about the scope of political action gradually rose up through the party. Ultimately the force of circumstances gave more credibility to the novel ideas about poverty and the state's responsibility. Back in the 1850s there had been some grounds for confidence that the continued spread of factories and workshops would generate enough employment for all those willing and able to work. By the 1890s this was evidently not so. With the fading of mid-Victorian optimism, the findings of Booth and Rowntree in the 1890s could not be overlooked as easily as those of Mayhew in the 1850s. Gloomy prognostications about Britain's position in the international economy undermined any claims that poverty would diminish in the future. The national interest clearly provided an added force to the collectivist rationale by 1900. As one Liberal, T.J. Macnamara, observed in connection with social welfare reforms for children: 'All this sounds terribly like rank Socialism. I'm afraid it is; but I am not in the least dismayed, because I know it to be first rate imperialism.'

Nonetheless, in spite of the shocking revelations about poverty and the revisionist views about its causes, it cannot be said that any radical change in the methods of handling the problem had occurred by the turn of the century. Why was this? The immediate explanation lies in local government, which was the scene of most attempts to grapple with the problem. In spite of the experiments, the new elective authorities, and the changes of personnel, reform was handicapped by the constraints of local finance; the burden of rates fell too narrowly so that local authorities lacked the resources they needed. The obvious solution lay in a complete overhaul of local government finance, but with the Liberals largely out of power this was repeatedly postponed. The chief positive conclusion to emerge was that advanced especially by the Fabians – that the functions of the Poor Law should be separated and redistributed to county councils; and that the intractable problems of unemployment should become a *national* responsibility under a separate ministry, which would provide either employment or relief. Other schemes such as pensions also waited upon a national government initiative, because it was clear that, to be of real value, a pensions scheme would have to be non-contributory; otherwise those most in need, like women, would fail to benefit.

The second part of the explanation lies at the parliamentary level. Though increasingly aware of social problems, politicians were slow to adjust their priorities. Any idea that a working-class electorate would necessitate a radical modification of the agenda proved baseless, as we have seen. An alternative argument suggests that the politicians were moved not by votes but by the threat of physical force, as manifested in 1886 and 1887 by the demonstrations and marches of unemployed workers. However, these were not in fact signs of an anti-parliamentary movement, nor were they sustained. In Westminster and Whitehall priorities proved slow to change. Those departments most closely involved with social questions – the Local Government Board, the Board of Trade and the Board of Education – enjoyed a low status in the Cabinet hierarchy. As late as 1905 the young and ambitious Winston Churchill disdainfully rejected the Local Government Board: 'I decline to be shut up in a soup kitchen with Mrs Sidney Webb!' Under the Conservatives legislation in the later years of the century was limited to such matters as grants for allotments (1887), smallholdings (1892) and free elementary education (1891) – a concession to Chamberlain. The Liberals' brief 1892–5 ministry showed signs of radical thinking with the death duties scheme and the grant of compulsory purchase powers to local authorities; but several measures, including an employers' liability for accidents bill, were emasculated by the House of Lords. A number of official inquiries marked the progress of ideas. In 1885 a Royal Commission on Housing made new proposals, but Lord Salisbury refused to move beyond purely permissive legislation for local councils. The Royal Commission on the Aged Poor (1893–5) and the Parliamentary Select Committee on the same subject (1899) strengthened the case for old-age pensions. But, again, Salisbury's governments stuck to the traditional nostrums of classical liberalism: the budget should be balanced, the National Debt reduced, revenue confined to indirect taxes needed to maintain basic services like the armed forces, civil service and police.

The final part of the explanation for the pattern of change lies in personnel and party fortunes. The thinking of Booth, Rowntree, the Webbs and others largely influenced an interested minority of middle-class politicians, intellectuals and social investigators. They were in a position to draw up schemes and to proffer policy options to the politicians, but lacked the power to implement them. Not until the Edwardian period did young reformers like Charles Masterman, Herbert Samuel and William Beveridge climb up the ladder to become MPs, ministers and civil servants. Eventually the huge change in the composition of Parliament brought about by the 1906 election accelerated this process and opened the way to a sustained extension of the role of the state between 1906 and 1914.

Further reading

On living standards and poverty see:

J. Burnett, *Plenty and Want: a Social History of Diet from 1815 to the Present Day* (1966)

H. Fraser, *The Coming of the Mass Market* (1973)

M.A. Crowther, *The Workhouse System 1834–1929* (1981)

M. Rose, *The Relief of Poverty 1834–1914* (1972)

G. Stedman Jones, *Outcast London* (1971)

Pat Thane, 'Women and the Poor Law in Victorian and Edwardian England', *History Workshop Journal*, 6, 1978

Carl Chinn, *Poverty Amidst Prosperity: The Urban Poor in England 1834–1914* (1995)

There are several classic contemporary accounts:

Robert Roberts, *The Classic Slum* (1971)

B.S. Rowntree, *Poverty: a Study of Town Life* (1901)

Charles Booth, *Life and Labour of the People in London* (1902–04)

M. Pember Reeves, *Round About a Pound a Week* (1913)

Some light is thrown on popular attitudes in:

Henry Pelling, 'The Working Class and the origins of the Welfare State', in *Popular Politics and Society In Late-Victorian Britain* (1979) – makes the negative case.

Pat Thane, 'The Working Class and State Welfare in Britain 1880–1914', *The Historical Journal*, 27/4, 1984

Martin Pugh, 'Working-Class Experience and State Social Welfare 1908–1914: Old Age Pensions Reconsidered', *The Historical Journal*, 45/4, 2002

Flora Thompson, *Lark Rise to Candleford* (1939)

Robert Tressell, *The Ragged Trousered Philanthropists* (1914)

On the role of women see:

Patricia Hollis, *Ladies Elect: Women in English Local Government 1865–1914* (1987)

Jane Lewis, *Women and Social Action in Victorian and Edwardian England* (1991)

F.K. Prochaska, *Women and Philanthropy in Nineteenth Century England* (1980)

M. Llewelyn Davies, *Life as We Have Known It* (1931)

On policy and political ideas see:

H.V. Emy, *Liberals, Radicals and Social Politics 1892–1914* (1973)

A. McBriar, *Fabian Socialism and British Politics 1884–1918* (1962)

G.C. Peden, *British Economic and Social Policy: Lloyd George to Margaret Thatcher* (1985)

Jose Harris, *Unemployment and Politics* (1972)

Jose Harris, *Private Lives. Public Spirit: Britain 1870–1914* (1993)

G.R. Searle, *A New England? Peace and War 1886–1918* (2004)

B.B. Gilbert, *The Evolution of National Insurance in Great Britain* (1966)

4

Victorian Values: Myth and Reality

During the 1980s the Prime Minister, Margaret Thatcher, resurrected the idea of 'Victorian values' which were understood to include thrift, hard work, self-improvement, family life, morality and religion. This was a reaction against an anti-Victorian tradition which had been articulated by Lytton Strachey in a famous book, *Eminent Victorians* (1918) in which he questioned the virtues of several iconic nineteenth-century figures including Florence Nightingale and General Gordon. Thatcher's comments triggered several reassessments by historians. Her notion of Victorianism was flawed in many ways. It was, of course, politically inspired, but she did not understand that to a large extent the values and triumphs she believed in were associated more with pious, mid-Victorian Nonconformist Liberalism, whereas Conservatism drew its strength and character from different traditions, being more populist, less concerned about self-improvement and more indulgent towards leisure, drink, sport and gambling.

Above all, historians recognize that many of the virtues and values later associated with Victorian society arose to a considerable extent from *prescriptive* literature; they indicated what Victorians *wanted* but were not a good indication of actual behaviour. In particular they largely represented the aims and notions of middle-aged, middle-class men, rather than women, who felt conscious of both a frivolous upper class above them and a dissolute working class below them. The unregenerate sections of society shared obvious common interests; the slowness of the political elite to tackle the problem of drunkenness, for example, was not unconnected with its own fondness for alcohol. In spite of this, however, it must be conceded that in some ways the trend was towards approved middle-class forms of behaviour and the idea of improvement commanded wide sympathy, but this involved a ceaseless struggle between 'virtue' and 'vice' in the late-Victorian period.

The expansion of the state

Victorians believed strongly in the idea of progress and their society resounded to the triumphs of improvement through individual endeavour. Samuel Smiles, author of the best-selling *Self-Help* (1859), and science, in the person of Charles Darwin, underlined the message that the progress of society – and its decline – reflected the vigour of its individual members. As chancellor during the 1860s, Gladstone had declared himself in favour of leaving money 'to fructify in the pockets of the people', and in 1894 when he finally left politics he claimed: 'of one thing I am, and always have been, convinced – it is not by the state that man can be regenerated, and the terrible woes of this darkened world effectually dealt with.'

Yet despite these expressions of confidence Victorians increasingly found themselves driven to accept that their society and economy were too complex to be left to run themselves; one of their characteristic achievements was to chart a route that led out of the chaos of competitive individualism towards the sophisticated modern state. A crude measurement of the expanding state is government expenditure. However, for a truer perspective expenditure must be seen in the context of the total output of the British economy. The growth of production, population and consumption enabled governments to raise more revenue without taking a higher proportion at least up to the 1880s. The twenty years from 1890 to 1910 marked the beginning of a long-term trend towards a bigger state. It will be noted that this did not *precede* the start of Britain's relative industrial decline, and cannot be seen as a cause.

Some indication of the development of government responsibilities may be detected in the establishment of new ministries, including the Local Government Board (1871), the Scottish Office (1885), the Board of Agriculture (1889) and the Board of Education (1899). Expenditure on education from central funds rose from £750,000 in 1870 to £7 million in 1895. However, the bureaucracy remained surprisingly small; for example, in 1876 the Home Office consisted of a mere thirty-six permanent officials. In all, the number of civil servants increased from 42,000 in the 1850s to 50,000 in 1881 and 116,000 in 1901. The major growth in state employment occurred in the Post Office and in local government notably in such occupations as teaching. Throughout the mid- and late-Victorian period, a wide range of interventionist legislation required the employment of additional clerks, accountants, administrators, inspectors and experts. Moreover, all this interventionism infringed the rights and freedom of individual property-owners and entrepreneurs. The ten-hour working day was enacted in 1847. A succession of Acts dealing with food and licensing

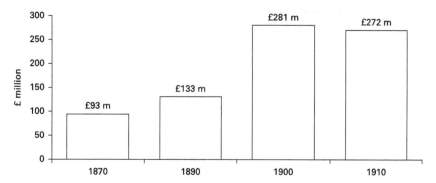

Figure 4.1 Total government expenditure (£ million, at current prices).

regulated the sale and production of consumables. Compulsory education brought an unending list of restrictions. In Ireland and parts of Scotland the legislation of 1881 and 1886 deprived landlords of the right to set rents; and local authorities won powers of compulsory purchase. In the 'Congested Districts' of Ireland the government intervened to subsidize a range of economic functions from light railways to seed potatoes. Public Health Acts were passed in 1848, 1866 and 1875, and during the 1860s the state financed the construction of a vast sewage system for London.

Public ownership

As early as the 1840s it became clear that in the matter of water supplies private enterprise had failed; as a result, by the 1870s nearly half the local authorities supplied their own water, and by 1900 two out of three water authorities were publicly owned. Cleanliness may have been next to godliness, but was an integral part of municipal Socialism too. Provision of gas followed a similar pattern; and by 1900 two-thirds of the electricity companies were also under municipal ownership. The railways, which had always been regarded as a kind of public utility, found themselves regulated in terms of safety and price controls, and in 1870 the government empowered itself to run the entire system, which it did in 1914–18. During the late nineteenth century, governments also became increasingly concerned about industrial relations; this resulted in the 1896 Conciliation Act, which empowered the Board of Trade to inquire into the causes of strikes and appoint conciliators at the request of the parties involved. This proved to be a modest but important step towards regular government intervention after 1905, usually designed to persuade recalcitrant employers to recognize trade unions. Of course, this catalogue of interventionist and collectivist measures did not indicate the demise of *laissez-faire* as a general principle; Britain continued to be basically a market economy. But the infringements of *laissez-faire* were so common that the trajectory was clearly away from Gladstonianism and towards collectivism.

The angel in the house

Nowhere are the perils of the prescriptive literature more apparent than in connection with the role of women. Victorians evidently considered work to be a great virtue, but not for women. Coventry Patmore summed up the ideology of the separate spheres in a famous poem entitled *The Angel in the House* that praised the ideal woman as not only a wife and mother, but as one who was confined to the domestic sphere where she could be decorative, a comfort and support to her husband, and a moral influence on the children; this would be all the better accomplished, so the argument ran, if she remained free from the distractions of the rough world of employment and public affairs.

All of this amounted to an absurd travesty of the life experience of most Victorian women. For one thing, women constituted nearly 32 per cent of the total British labour force in 1871, though this figure fell slightly to 29 per cent by 1901. Put another way, 55 per cent of single women worked outside the home, as did 30 per cent of widows and 10 per cent of married women. The geographical pattern of employment varied according to the local economy. For example, women made up 60 per cent of the labour force in the Lancashire cotton textile industry; by contrast, regions like the northeast, dominated by coal, iron and shipbuilding, offered far fewer employment opportunities for women.

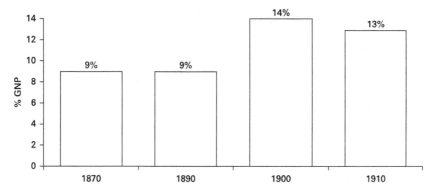

Figure 4.2 Government (central and local) spending as a percentage of gross national product.

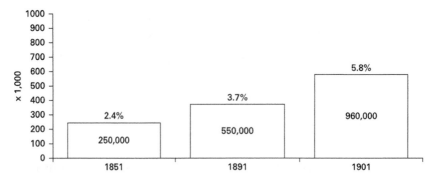

Figure 4.3 Employment in the civil service, local government and the armed forces (as a percentage of the working population).

From the mid-nineteenth century onwards there was a tendency for employment, especially among married women, to diminish. This may reflect the gradual shift of male workers into higher or more regularly paid jobs, which reduced the pressure on wives to work outside the home. Certainly the oral evidence has shown that many women preferred to stay at home provided that their husbands earned enough to support the family. A degree of coercion was also at work. For trade unions increasingly adopted the 'family wage' as their target, and to that end they attempted to exclude women from industrial employment on the grounds that their readiness to accept low wages depressed the general level of pay. To some extent Parliament co-operated in this by legislating to restrict working hours or to bar women and children from certain types of work, ostensibly for humanitarian reasons.

Women's employment

Notwithstanding male pretensions, most working-class women took up employment from their mid-teens until the early years of marriage; but thereafter they were periodically driven by necessity to work outside the home. Moreover, beyond the range of the official census lay a multitude of expedients adopted by women to earn extra money while based at home. This included taking in washing, accommodating lodgers, child-minding and selling items of food and drink; this latter sometimes developed into a small shop in a woman's own front room. While no firm figure can be put on this activity, it is clear that countless families were saved from hardship by the vital income earned by housewives. Even among the middle classes, many wives and daughters maintained a charade, pretending to be purely decorative and leisured ladies. Yet on a lower-middle-class income it was impossible to employ more than one servant to take over the heaviest work of carrying coal, cleaning fires and washing, which left a good deal of time to be spent on cooking, cleaning and needlework by the ladies of the house.

Far and away the most important paid occupation for women was domestic service, which employed 1.5 million by the 1870s: after this came textiles, with around 700,000, and the clothing trades, with nearly as many. The food and drink industries offered a growing number of jobs to women, while in agriculture their role diminished sharply. They benefited most from the expansion of white-collar employment as shop assistants, typists, civil servants in the Post Office and elementary schoolteachers. From the 1870s these were all growing sectors. Women teachers increased from 80,000 in 1862 to 171,000 by 1901, and women clerks from 279 in 1861 to 57,000 by 1901. Taking female teachers, nurses, clerks, civil servants and shop assistants together, the total rose from 184,000 to 562,000. None of these offered high-paid employment, but most represented an improvement in status and conditions for young women whose mothers had been restricted to agriculture, the 'sweated trades' and domestic service. In most cases the key to entry lay in elementary education, which was imposed equally upon both sexes. Women profited more than men from this, for in terms of literacy they had traditionally lagged behind: by 1900 both sexes enjoyed a literacy rate of around 95 per cent.

Although middle-class women were less likely to work for money some undertook low-paid employment as governesses and others wrote novels, but more typically they entered the public sphere, and thus challenged the conventional wisdom, by participating in a multitude of charitable, philanthropic and political activities involving the Poor Law, prison visiting, emigration schemes or missionary work abroad. Their significance should not be disparaged, for it turned women into organizers, trained in the techniques of conducting meetings, taking minutes, raising funds, keeping accounts and learning to speak in public. The Women's Co-operative Guild also coached working-class wives in similar skills thereby enabling them to enter elective local government as new opportunities arose.

Marriage and the family

However contemporaries commonly disregarded the facts of female employment, holding marriage and motherhood to be the overriding object of a woman's life. Yet the emphasis on marriage reflected the *weakness* not the strength of the institution, for the imbalance of the sexes put the marital state beyond reach for many people. Higher mortality among baby boys, earlier death among adult males, and the emigration of thousands of marriageable young men every year left women in a majority, and many doomed to spinsterhood. The problem was exacerbated, especially in the middle classes, by the belief that a man should not marry until he was sufficiently established in his career to be able to support a wife and employ servants, thereby delaying marriage until his thirties. As a result, by 1871, out of every thousand women aged 20–25 years 652 were unmarried, as were 294 of those aged 25–35. Marriage, quite simply, was a markedly *less* common experience than it was to become in the twentieth century. Moreover, it appears to have been losing ground during the late nineteenth century; by 1901 single women accounted for 726 per thousand in the 20–25 years age group.

Mid-Victorian feminists felt that society had only itself to blame for the reluctance of girls to marry. In law the position of the married woman was abysmal: she did not exist. The male marriage vow – 'with all my worldly goods I thee endow' – was a bad joke, for the wife's property and income became her husband's; even after a separation he could legally claim any money earned by her. Divorce was both difficult and costly even for men, and almost impossible for women. The separated wife usually lost access to her children. To cap it all, the unmarried female municipal elector lost her vote when she married!

Although most women put up with the legal inequalities in marriage a number of reforms were achieved by the Victorian feminist campaigners. In 1857 divorce became a much simpler and somewhat less expensive business, though the law continued to discriminate: whereas a man might obtain a divorce for adultery alone, a wife had to prove adultery plus cruelty or desertion. The 1886 Guardianship of Infants Act gave women some rights over their children, subject to the view of the courts. And the Married Women's Property Acts of 1870 and 1882 secured for a wife both the property held before marriage and any subsequent income. Nonetheless, there is some impressionistic evidence from the autobiographies of educated Edwardian women that they saw life in terms of a choice between domesticity and dependence on the one hand and a career and independence on the other. As a result male anti-suffragists often argued that giving women a vote would undermine marriage even further.

Social class and marriage

In fact the great majority of women actively sought marriage, though this may have been because the life of a single woman was so difficult. At all events, the feminist campaigners represented very small middle-class pressure groups. This reflects the fact that in practice the legal inequalities had little bearing on the lives of most married women. Among the upper classes it was customary to use the law of equity to settle money on a daughter which her husband could not touch. Moreover, such women enjoyed enough wealth to pursue a range of personal, social and public interests and activities. They had separate bedrooms from their husbands (and relatively small families) and often enjoyed extramarital affairs or platonic relationships with other men. It was a fairly liberated lifestyle.

At the other end of the spectrum the law was largely irrelevant to working-class wives. Amongst the respectable working class, marriage, a settled home and a husband who brought home a regular wage were cherished ambitions. For the less respectable, wives frequently found themselves deserted or not supported because husbands spent too much on alcohol. They themselves often abandoned husbands or faced life as widows. In each case questions of custody or property rarely arose, and there was no resort to formal divorce or separation because it was too expensive. Whether deserted or widowed the working-class wife often headed her family, and she was in many ways the dominant figure because she managed the money and made the decisions while her husband remained rather a marginal presence. It was consequently in middle-class households that wives felt deprived of a satisfying and influential role.

Home and family life

The emphasis on home and family life which is so characteristic of Victorian propaganda about marriage also gave a misleading impression. The physical house was much less secure and stable than might be supposed. For example, home-ownership was by no means a Victorian practice even amongst quite well-off people; over 90 per cent of homes were rented. The wealthier constantly moved house, while in poor urban districts 20–30 per cent of families moved every year because they had fallen behind with the rent. Nor has the notion of the big, happy Victorian family of grandparents, parents and children survived the scrutiny of modern research. Most families comprised just two generations. Moreover, male mortality and desertion resulted in a very high proportion of single-parent families led by women. The working-class home was often a crowded, noisy and uncomfortable place from which men escaped to the pub. Parents routinely farmed out their children to relations or neighbours, and they dispatched girls of thirteen years to distant towns to work as domestic servants. Moreover, the middle classes took a dim view of working-class family life. On entry to the workhouse, husbands and wives and parents and children were split up. At the slightest pretext the children of the poor were removed from their families in favour of institutional care, control by employers or even export to the colonies. Higher up the social scale Victorians placed a great value on family life – but only in a tightly controlled and sanitized form. Once childbirth was over, children were routinely entrusted to nurses, nannies and governesses. The parents might then enjoy their offspring for half an hour a day between tea and bedtime when children were presented in a clean condition for inspection. But they did not invade their parents' space or inhibit their social lives. In due course they were packed off to boarding schools, to endure all manner of ill-treatment and undernourishment, and were only fully received back into the family when old enough to be useful; daughters in particular were often kept at home to be unpaid secretaries and housekeepers to their mothers.

Population and sex

Men were also concerned that women did their duty by bearing the nation's children. From only 10.5 million people in 1801 the population of Britain grew to 20.8 million by 1851 and to 37 million by 1901. This was one of the highest growth rates in Europe, and it naturally resulted in a distinctly young population; in 1871, for example, one person in every two was under 21. Up to the late 1870s the birth rate remained consistently high at 32.5 per 1,000 population. Death rates changed little in spite of developments in medical science and public health; indeed, by the end of the century life expectancy, at 44 years for men and 48 for women, was only slightly better than that in the early-Victorian period.

Fears about birth control

However, by the 1880s population growth had begun to slow down because of a fall in the birth rate which proved to be the start of a long-term trend. From 35 per 1,000 in the 1870s, the birth rate dropped to 29 in the late 1890s. What caused this change is a matter of some argument. At least part of the explanation lies in the tendency to marry later in life. But some couples had deliberately chosen to limit the size of their families. The census suggests that they were concentrated in certain middle-class occupations, and it has been argued that they were reacting to the growing financial burden of children in terms of the wages of nannies, governesses and

Table 4.1 Population of the United Kingdom, 1871–1981 (England, Wales, Scotland and Ireland)

Year	Population in millions	Average annual percentage increase
1871	30.5	1.32
1881	34.9	1.44
1891	37.7	1.17
1901	41.5	1.22
1911	45.3	1.09
1921	44.0*	0.49
1931	46.0*	0.55
1951	50.2	0.48
1961	52.7	0.52
1971	55.4	0.26
1981	55.7	0.01

* Before 1921 the figures include the total population of Ireland; in 1921 and 1931 no census was taken in Northern Ireland and therefore an estimate of 1.2 million for the province is included.

domestics, and the fees for private education. This, however, seems more plausible for groups like clerks who aspired to middle-class status on inadequate salaries; for them, family limitation was an obvious means of maintaining their standard of living. The methods adopted at this time are also a matter of speculation. Traditional expedients included abstinence from sexual relations – comparatively easy for partners who enjoyed separate bedrooms – withdrawal, and prolongation of breastfeeding. As yet the more sophisticated methods made little impact. In the 1870s rubber sheaths for men became available, and women used a variety of pessaries, sponges and douches; but these were costly and not easy to use. In addition the sheath, which was used chiefly to protect men from venereal disease, was damned by association with extramarital sex.

Female health and sexuality

Women themselves had the most compelling motive for adopting birth control for in all social classes many women died in childbirth and thousands had their health ruined by repeated pregnancies. The existence of a demand for birth control is underlined by the advertisements in women's magazines and the wide variety of substances recommended as abortifacients. Birth control also received huge publicity as a result of the trial of Annie Besant and Charles Bradlaugh in 1877 who were prosecuted for obscenity when they republished an old pamphlet of advice on the subject. However, in view

Table 4.2 Crude birth rates in England and Wales, 1866–1915

Year	Birth rate per thousand population
1866–70	35.7
1871–75	35.7
1876–80	35.4
1881–85	33.5
1886–90	31.4
1891–95	30.5
1896–1900	29.3
1901–05	28.2
1906–10	26.3
1911–15	23.6

of the couple's own unmarried status and their association with such causes as atheism and republicanism, the publicity may have done as much to hinder as to promote birth control amongst respectable couples.

Indeed, at this time many middle-class women, including feminists, regarded artificial methods of avoiding pregnancy as inherently immoral, for their use was calculated to encourage men to indulge their sexual appetites without fear of the consequences. In this they reflected a widely expressed belief that physical desire was chiefly a male characteristic; ladies were not thought to enjoy sex, or if they did this was a sign that they had been dragged down to men's level. It is extremely difficult for the twenty-first century, which has such different assumptions, to know what to make of this. Of course, many of the unfavourable comments made by Victorian women on the subject of sex were made in the context of concern about the consequences. During the Edwardian period, evidence accumulated from wives who badly wanted to be able to enjoy physical relations with their husbands but who were inhibited by the fear of pregnancy and poor health. The limited studies we have of the married life of upper- and upper-middle-class couples suggests that they generally married for love, tempered by suitability, and that their relations were sensual and emotional, not cold and distant. Even Queen Victoria is nowadays recognized as having had a very healthy interest in the opposite sex, in spite of her complaints about the burdens of motherhood.

Male sexuality

For the majority of people family limitation was not yet on the agenda. It ran up against the prevailing assumption that no man should be denied his conjugal rights. Even in cases where a husband had contracted venereal disease, doctors usually refrained from advising the wife about the need to avoid sex. Edwardian feminists were to use this peril as a major argument against marriage. One victory was won in 1891 when a Mrs Jackson, who had been confined by a husband with whom she did not wish to live, was set free by the Court of Appeal. Public opinion, however, seemed to show itself more sympathetic to Mr Jackson.

However much evangelicals urged the merits of self-control and abstinence, most Victorians seem to have accepted the absolute necessity of sexual outlets for men. Gladstone claimed that, of the eleven prime ministers he had known, seven were adulterers. The postponement of marriage among middle-class men until they were able to support a wife and family led many to resort to prostitutes. The most striking recognition of male sexuality was provided by the notorious Contagious Diseases Acts of the 1860s, which reflected the army's view that the men in the lower ranks could not possibly control themselves, whether married or not. The Acts in effect licensed prostitutes in and around army barracks, and allowed the authorities to confine to hospital those women found to have venereal disease. This antagonized feminists, the Churches and many respectable working-class families, and in any case the Acts were not effective in limiting the disease. A huge and protracted campaign led by Josephine Butler embarrassed politicians and resulted in abolition in 1886. Another success was won by W.T. Stead, who exposed in the *Pall Mall Gazette* the existence of a traffic in young girls; as a result the age of consent, which had been raised from 12 to 13 in 1871, was put at 16 in 1885. These, however, were only minor dents in the double standards of sexuality which characterized Victorian Britain.

First-wave feminism

It was during the 1850s and 1860s that an organized women's movement emerged led by Barbara Leigh Smith, Bessie Rayner Parkes, Jessie Boucherett, Maria Rye, Lydia Becker and Frances Power Cobbe who were known as the 'Ladies of Langham Place'. Challenging the idea of separate spheres they organized the Society for Promoting the Employment of Women and the Women's Local Government Society as well as a series of single-issue campaigns including opening higher education to women, entry into the medical profession, gaining property rights for married women and the abolition of the Contagious Diseases Acts. Analysis of these first-wave feminists shows that they were largely middle class, often from an evangelical Christian or a Liberal family background, and, contrary to anti-suffragist propaganda, they were not hostile to men. Many had been helped into education and careers by their fathers and over half were married; indeed a feature of late-Victorian campaigning was the collaborative action of such couples as John Stuart Mill and Harriet Taylor, Annie Besant and Charles Bradlaugh, Richard and Emmeline Pankhurst, Josephine and George Butler, and Henry and Millicent Fawcett. This movement was not as fragmented as it appears because the various pressure groups enjoyed a common membership and published several journals including *The English Woman's Journal* (1858), *The Englishwoman's Review* (1866) and Lydia Becker's *Women's Suffrage Journal* (1870).

First-wave feminists battled against conventional thinking that saw women as endowed by God with certain qualities that fitted them for lives of marriage and motherhood. But in *The Subjection of Women* (1869) John Stuart Mill argued that women were so restricted by artificial rules prescribing what they must do and could not do that it was literally impossible to know what women were capable of. By 1900 they had already extended their role considerably. Traditionally much of the writing about this Victorian women's movement portrays it as a failure. However, this is mistaken and is unduly influenced by the better-known Edwardian suffragette campaigns. In fact these feminists won the local government vote as early as 1869, a series of Married Women's Property Acts (1870–92) and the abolition of the Contagious Diseases Acts in 1886. Women had already gained a footing in higher education through the foundation of Queen's College and Bedford College, London and this was extended via the foundation of Girton College, Cambridge and Newnham and St Hugh's Colleges in Oxford. All this was achieved even without the vote. However, feminists felt that progress was slow and the wall of prejudice still high, and increasingly it seemed that the best way forward lay in focusing on the parliamentary vote. Women were conscious that since 1874 male trade unionists had begun to win direct representation in parliament and gained more attention as a result.

Votes for women

From 1870 onwards local groups in Manchester, London, Bristol and elsewhere campaigned for the vote, but in 1897 they largely amalgamated in the National Union of Women's Suffrage Societies under Millicent Fawcett. The issue was tested in parliament in 1867 when John Stuart Mill proposed an amendment to Disraeli's reform bill which was defeated by 196 to 73, but thereafter backbenchers repeatedly introduced women's suffrage bills. Most of these proposed to enfranchise single women on the basis that they paid rates and taxes and therefore were qualified just as men were. However, this suffered from a major flaw in that members of parliament felt reluctant to reward women for remaining unmarried; on the contrary they were anxious to promote marriage and motherhood. Many feared that behind the modest demand to enfranchise a few women lay huge social changes. A female electorate might encourage women to avoid marriage and motherhood in favour of careers which would undermine Britain's role as a great industrial and imperial power. Anti-suffragists initially took their stand on Biblical arguments that men and women had been designed to fill different roles and equipped with different qualities; women were widely seen as unsuited for the public sphere as being intellectually inferior and prone to hysteria. They were supposed to be morally superior, a quality that would be fatally undermined by participation in elections which were associated by drink, violence and disorder. These anti-suffragist arguments were all the more difficult to refute because they were endorsed by some able and successful *women* including Mrs Humphry Ward, the novelist, and Beatrice Webb, the Fabian Socialist. They claimed that the vote was irrelevant to women as sufficient opportunities were already open to them. Most women, according to the 'Antis', did not really want a vote anyway.

Why did the suffragists win the argument by 1900?

However, an excessive focus on the dramatic campaigns of the suffragettes after 1906 has often obscured the success of the Victorian suffragists in winning the argument over several decades. How did this come about? First, women benefited by the extension of elective local government that enabled them as voters and as councillors to demonstrate that they possessed the qualities necessary for public life. Second, they worked within the political parties, undertaking canvassing and even public speaking, again proving their interest and aptitude. The Women's Liberal Federation, founded in 1887, was ostensibly an organization of volunteers to help the party, but its members were feminists, using it as a Trojan Horse to push the party towards adopting the vote for women. The Primrose League had a similar effect among Conservatives. Third, many of the extreme claims made by anti-suffragists about the results of votes for women were exploded when New Zealand enfranchised all its women in 1893; from 1894 onwards the

Australian states did the same, and in America eleven states granted the vote between 1869 and 1914. Fourth, some anti-suffragist women such as Beatrice Webb recanted their opposition. She pointed out that the agenda of British politics was changing. As national governments involved themselves in health, education and living standards the old distinction between local government (the women's sphere) and national government (the men's sphere) broke down; in effect women had become part of British politics with or without the vote.

As a result support for women's suffrage grew in parliament with Conservatives joining the original Liberal promoters of reform. The turning-point came in 1897 when MPs voted by 230 to 159 in favour of a backbencher's bill. Once again Victorian thinking had been decisively overthrown. This, of course, did not settle the issue. Politicians had to decide how many women would vote and on what terms. This mattered because of the fear that a limited franchise would give an advantage to one party. Consequently the parties avoided adopting an official policy leaving it to backbench legislation which was unlikely to pass. The suffragists were also unlucky in that several prime ministers, notably Gladstone and Asquith, were personally anti-suffragists even though their party was favourable.

Victorian indulgences

The gradual improvement in living standards enabled many Victorians to divert their extra income into indulgencies of all kinds thereby, in the process giving birth to the modern consumer society. For example, tobacco had long been used by men, but after 1883, when James T. Bonsack invented a machine capable of mass-producing cigarettes, smoking became very popular. Cheap cigarettes displaced pipes and cigars among men and by the 1900s women who wished to signify their emancipation also smoked in public. Expenditure on tobacco rose sharply from £3.5 million in 1870 to £42 million by 1914. As a result, by the 1930s 80 per cent of men and 40 per cent of women in Britain smoked.

Drink and drunkenness

By comparison with the twentieth century, Victorian society was given over to excessive drinking. In London in the 1860s there were 17,000 arrests for drunkenness each year – the largest category of offences – and one house in every seventy-seven was a public house or beershop; small country towns had literally dozens of drinking places. It was possible to drink practically

24 hours a day. Over-indulgence had been exacerbated by government policies designed to free the trade by lowering the duty on spirits and making it easy to obtain a licence under the Beer Act of 1830. Consequently consumption rose through the late 1860s to reach a peak in 1876, fuelled by higher money wages. Men commonly spent their extra money at the pub rather than passing it on to their wives. Thereafter, the check to money wages and the wider availability of other consumables led to a small drop in consumption to 1881 and a fairly stable level of drinking to 1900. Even so, observers like Booth and Rowntree believed that working-class families commonly spent anything between a sixth and a third of their income on alcohol. Household finances were also affected by the development of mass gambling on horses and dogs during the 1880s, promoted by the national press and the telegraph system.

Temperance campaigns

Not surprisingly, the evils of drink stimulated the growth of a temperance movement from the early nineteenth century onwards. The leading pressure group was the United Kingdom Alliance (UKA), founded in 1853, whose object was to enact a bill to give the 'Local Option' or 'Popular Veto', that is, the power to prohibit sales of alcohol by a referendum of local ratepayers. Many of the less extreme reformers like the Church of England Temperance Society aimed instead at moral persuasion and encouraging people to 'take the pledge' to abstain rather than legislative remedy. Yet although persistent and well-funded, these organizations seem to have failed. Why? In the first place the upper and middle classes were in no position to influence behaviour by example, and they hesitated to use their political influence to initiate a process that might be difficult to stop. Indeed, the temperance movement was handicapped by the feeling that interfering reformers were trying to deny the workingman pleasures which their own class freely enjoyed. Many workers did, of course, take the pledge to abstain, though many soon lapsed and little progress was made in the long run. Secondly, drinking was sustained by a variety of social pressures. The public house offered men a welcome escape from the home, a valuable indoor meeting-place for clubs and societies, and was sometimes the place chosen for the payment of weekly wages. In time the building of temperance halls and hotels and the replacement of music halls by the expansion of cinemas were to undermine this social function. Thirdly there was the question of health. Manual workers commonly considered that the consumption of a pint of beer first thing in the morning and at intervals during the day was necessary in order to keep their strength up. Drinking was also seen as a sign of masculinity. Even doctors often advised their patients to take fortified wines and spirits, either as nourishment or to deaden pain.

Popular consumption of drugs

In addition to alcohol, many Victorians relied on drugs for medical-cum-social purposes. This often began in babyhood, when opium, in the form of laudanum, was administered to keep them quiet. A popular mixture for this purpose was Godfrey's Cordial, a blend of opium, treacle, water and spices. Opium became so cheap and so freely available that the majority of working-class families are thought to have used it for a wide range of ailments while the middle classes commonly resorted to morphia to relieve pain. Furthermore, from the 1880s cocaine began to be imported by the ton. Regarded as fairly harmless, it became popular among middle-class men and among the many women who enjoyed ill-health. Invalids kept supplies available for routine use when they felt the need of a pick-me-up. 'It works like magic,' explained Mrs Humphry Ward, the highly productive novelist.

While this kind of drug addiction was scarcely recognized as a problem, the prevalence of drunkenness was taken seriously by politicians. But they regularly disappointed the temperance fanatics by drawing a careful line between drunkenness and drinking. Gladstone, for example, was prepared to check adulteration of beer, impose licensed hours and have premises inspected. But by making drinking a little more respectable he only antagonized the temperance reformers, who saw that removal of the worst excesses would only make total prohibition more difficult. To increase pressure on the politicians the temperance groups often intervened in by-elections in order to secure the defeat of government candidates, but the huge expansion of the electorate after 1867 made this a futile strategy. Instead they concentrated on influencing the Liberal Party by working within the National Liberal Federation to commit the party to the suppression of licensed premises by means of a local veto bill. Although Gladstone refused to accept this policy, he could not prevent the Conservatives making political capital out of the link between Liberalism and temperance. Not surprisingly, many of the commercial interests in the form of brewers and publicans threw their support behind the Conservatives. Thus, although the UKA greatly increased its support among Liberal MPs, it was never possible to pass a local option bill. When Sir William Harcourt made the policy a key plank in the Liberal programme in the 1895 election it proved to be a dead weight, dragging him and his party down to defeat. Under Conservative governments the most that could be achieved was to reduce the number of licensed premises by offering financial compensation for loss of business. But none of this made much impact on the drinking classes before the First World War.

Work, leisure and improvement

As the example of women suggests, the Victorian belief in the virtues of hard work was shot through with inconsistencies. Its significance certainly varied from one social class to another. When writing about the landowning and aristocratic class, historians often dwell upon their political and economic role; but for many of these men the possession of a substantial income from rents, royalties and investments simply enabled them to enjoy a life of leisure and indulgence. This could take the form of riding to hounds, gambling on horse racing, shooting game, playing cards, cultivating gardens and grounds, or collecting art and furniture, according to taste, pocket and season. Most of the year could be devoted to a busy social round, beginning with London dinners and receptions from Easter onwards, taking in such highlights as Henley and Ascot, followed by shooting in August and prolonged house parties in various parts of the country. Improvements in travel by sea and by train encouraged the rich to take the waters in the German and Austrian spa towns, to escape the London smog with winter holidays on the French Riviera or in Italy, and, for the more adventurous, to visit Africa, India and the United States.

Admittedly a life given over to leisure at a time of dwindling agricultural rents resulted in considerable indebtedness in the late nineteenth century. Nonetheless, living within one's means was not the style for a gentleman, and only the most financially embarrassed were prepared to give up their lifestyle altogether. Traditionally the younger sons of aristocratic and gentry families were denied more than a bare annual allowance; they fell into debt, married into wealth, and took a career in the army, the Church, the law or politics, though these often proved expensive options. It was taken for granted that at his public school and college a youth would pile up large debts in the hope that his father would eventually settle his gambling losses and the bills of irate tradesmen. Nor did youthful irresponsibility end with money. Life at public schools was characterized by an obsession with sport, fighting, fagging and brutal punishments, rather than with the development of good working habits or a love of scholarship. Oxford colleges were often essentially good rowing clubs, and students commonly left without a degree through idleness. Lord Rosebery was instructed by his college to give up horse racing but refused and simply abandoned Oxford without damage to his political career.

The middle class and improvement

It is not difficult to see why successful middle-class Victorians often took a dim view of the upper class, and why they believed that their own industry, thrift and self-control were the foundation of British prosperity in the Victorian period. Admittedly the immensely long hours worked by most middle-class men were made bearable by the supporting army of servants and assistants so freely and cheaply available. The period from the 1870s to 1914 represented a golden age for the professional and business classes as their salaries bought the services of nurses, nannies, governesses, cooks, maids, valets, gardeners and chauffeurs. Tradesmen were anxious to deliver provisions to their door, and they enjoyed the services provided by railways, the telephone and post office three times a day. In addition, large homes were available at modest prices, country houses could be taken for holidays in the Lake District or Scotland, while substantial villas in Italy could be rented cheaply.

Faced with growing opportunities to enjoy life, the middle classes often preferred to speak of rational or improving recreation rather than leisure. This might involve activities in the church or philanthropic bodies, reading, singing, the piano, poetry, sketching, needlework and collecting things. However, there are many signs that after the 1850s the influence of evangelicalism diminished, and that more middle-class people determined to enjoy, if not indulge, themselves in the manner of the rich. The pretext of spending more time with the family helped justify such light-hearted pursuits as charades, summer holidays and elaborate celebrations at Christmas made respectable by Queen Victoria and Prince Albert. Adults also increasingly indulged themselves with bridge, tennis, golf and attendances at the theatre and concert hall to hear Gilbert and Sullivan, Oscar Wilde or G.B. Shaw. The later Victorian period also saw a huge demand for fiction which was satisfied by such prodigious novelists as Mrs Humphry Ward. With her best-selling books *Robert Elsmere* and *Hellbeck of Bannisdale*, Mrs Ward broke the stranglehold of the circulating libraries and opened the way to the rapid publication of cheap editions of new novels for a popular market. The middle classes liked to think that seaside holidays were good for children because of the constructive interests to be pursued on the seashore.

But, with the aid of Thomas Cook and his son John, they increasingly ventured further afield, to Paris, the Rhine, Switzerland, Italy, and, by the 1880s, to Egypt, though they continued to patronize Bournemouth, Eastbourne, Torquay and Southport too. In many respects the middle classes were now following the pattern of their social superiors; a higher standard of living almost inevitably involved a fuller life of leisure and entertainment, notwithstanding their religious and political scruples.

Working-class leisure

What did concern many Victorians was the role of leisure in *working-class* society. In theory there was not much time for relaxation. The Ten Hour Day Act of 1847 did not apply to all workers by any means; servants, for example, commonly had to get up at five o'clock and be on call most of the day. Also, many workingmen spent several hours on the journey to and from work. On the other hand, in many occupations employment was by the day not the whole week, or was subject to seasonal and cyclical fluctuations which inevitably created periods of enforced leisure. Thousands who resented regular work six days a week in factories or mines traditionally coped by taking Monday off, and many declined to turn up for work while they still had money in their pockets from the previous week. The mid- and late-Victorian periods saw a trade-off between the employers, who wished to replace irregular and informal holidays with official ones, and the workers' own desire to lighten the wearing round of toil. Consequently the opportunities for leisure were extended by commercial policy and government intervention. From the 1850s employers in Lancashire textiles began to treat Saturday as a half-day, and to organize excursions by train for their men. As this was gradually copied it undermined the resort to 'Saint Monday'. In 1871 and 1875 Bank Holidays were introduced and spread rapidly to most workers. By the 1880s some northern mills and factories had begun to close for an entire week at a time, thereby promoting the modern summer holiday, though workers were not yet paid for this time off and it was decades before the practice became general. Nonetheless, seaside holidays clearly grew popular in this period; Blackpool, for example, attracted 850,000 visitors in the early 1870s and nearly 2 million by 1890.

Social control?

But to what end was all this extra leisure for workingmen? Historians have devoted much energy to considering whether the middle classes were successful in imposing a degree of social control over the leisure activities of the workers. Contemporaries were undoubtedly anxious to influence their behaviour. The Bishop of Winchester expressed a typical opinion when he declared that it was 'that they may in their leisure hours raise their own physical force ... then their family, then their intellectual, and above all their spiritual being'. Yet whether middle-class notions about rational recreation influenced popular behaviour seems doubtful. At all events, church-going continued its decline. Several factors also conspired to prevent improvement. In the first place, workingmen enjoyed the capacity to organize their own leisure activities, whether improving or not. Some of these were, of course, approved by their social superiors, including cycling, choral singing, allotments, leek clubs, horticultural shows, pigeons and whippets. Secondly, the improvers found themselves frustrated by the growing commercial element in leisure. The increase in real wages gave many workers the option to choose to take advantage of professional entertainment such as music-hall which spread rapidly from the 1860s onwards. Though not in any obvious way improving or rational, the music-hall did become more respectable. By the 1880s the introduction of fixed rows of seats led to much less drinking and more attendance by women. As a result, working-class audiences were usually reported as perfectly well-behaved by the end of the century.

Working-class initiatives

Perhaps the biggest obstacle to improving leisure was the capacity of the workers for taking over activities and changing their character to suit themselves. The simplest example of this was the railway excursion, which reformers naively regarded as a route to respectable seaside leisure; but such trips routinely ended in drink and dissipation, however soberly they had begun. Then there was the case of the workingmen's clubs. Back in 1862 the Workingmen's Club and Institute Union had been founded as a middle-class initiative for improving purposes. Yet by the 1880s the rank-and-file had asserted itself by insisting on having alcohol on the premises. This was accepted as clubs could make a 30 per cent profit on beer sales, and without it their membership collapsed. Team sports were favoured by churchmen on the grounds that they improved health, fostered an acceptance of rules and discipline, and brought the different classes together for a common purpose. To this end the rough, traditional game of football was taken in hand by middle-class amateur enthusiasts who set up the Football Association in 1863. They introduced a common set of rules to facilitate regular competition between clubs from all parts of the country and in 1871 established the FA

Cup. However, the effects of these good intentions left much to be desired. Football soon became so popular that it turned into a mass spectator sport. It was the debilitating effects on whole generations, who merely watched, that provoked Kipling's famous outburst in the aftermath of the Boer War:

> Then ye went back to your trinkets,
> Then ye contented your souls
> With the flannelled fools at the wickets
> And the muddied oafs at the goals.

In addition, it rapidly transpired that the working-class footballers of the northern town clubs could not afford the travel and time off work unless they were subsidized. This undermined the amateur status of the game; and during the 1880s the Football Association failed in its attempt to ban professional players. The working-class players were too good to be excluded. This lesson was underlined by the famous victory of Bolton Olympic over the Old Etonian team of amateurs and gentlemen. From this time the upper classes retreated, to leave football as a proletarian sport. Not only did football fail to unite the classes, but the working-class professionals routinely declined to 'play the game'; kicking the man as much as the ball and disputing the referee's decisions became an integral part of British football. On the other hand, cricket did succeed in crossing the class divide both among players and spectators, and the tight grip of the higher classes on the organization of the game ensured respect for rules and less emphasis on professionalism.

Respectability and order

The more historians have studied Victorian patterns of leisure the clearer it has become that most people declined to be guided into improving activities. This is not to deny that recreation lost some of its rough and rowdy behaviour. But the chief trend was simply towards a fuller and more elaborate pattern of leisure; the middle classes clearly became more relaxed and self-indulgent, while the working classes took advantage of shorter working hours and higher real wages to enjoy life outside the factory and mill. But social control by the higher classes looks improbable. Drink, as we have seen, proved fairly resistant to pressure for change. Religion remorselessly declined. As early as 1851 the census found only 40 per cent attending a Christian service, and as little as a quarter of the population in the big northern cities. Gradually, in spite of the spread of Sunday schools, the churches were edged out of their role in education and became a marginal factor in the lives of most people.

One characteristic Victorian strategy for social improvement was the development of a system of police forces. There are some grounds for thinking that law and order prevailed more generally by the 1890s than in, say, the 1830s. After a long-term rise, crimes against property and persons began to fall in the second half of the century. However, it is not clear how far, if at all, the police were responsible. Arrests for offences such as drunken and disorderly behaviour or for prostitution were easy to make, and all the statistics tell us is that the more police were employed the more crime was reported. Many crimes were opportunistic, the outcome of poverty, and it seems likely that, even without the new police forces, the improved wages would have had a beneficial impact. In some areas, such as music-hall and elections, the evident reduction in rowdy behaviour owed a good deal to the growing role of the respectable working class and to the wider entry of women into the public arena.

The impact of education

In some ways the most striking manifestation of improvement is to be found in education. In an earlier era education had been suspect in the eyes of the wealthy because of the association between literacy and political radicalism. But by 1870 the radicals had won their battle for a free and cheap press, and the emphasis of public policy shifted to educating the new voters. As a result, compulsory school attendance after 1880 pushed up literacy rates to around 95 per cent for both sexes. The most conspicuous indication of the increase in writing was the expanding work of the Post Office, which delivered 704 million letters in 1870 and 2,827 million in 1913. Commercial lending libraries catered to the middle class and the number of public libraries increased from 60 in 1875 to 438 in 1918 in England alone. The public taste for light romantic and adventurous fiction was eventually satisfied by the speedy production of cheap editions of new novels by the 1890s. By then reading was much easier during the evening, owing to the spread of gaslight to the majority of homes. Most people contented themselves with one of the mass-circulation Sunday newspapers like the *News of the World* or *Lloyd's News,* and the family papers, including *Titbits* (1881), *Answers* (1888) and *Pearson's Weekly* (1890). There also occurred a major expansion in women's magazines, with 48 new titles between 1880 and 1900 including *Housewife* (1886), *The Mother's Companion* (1887), *Forget-Me-Not* (1891) and *Home Chat* (1895). These papers would not have enjoyed as great a success had they not served as a means for advertisers to reach a more prosperous lower-middle- and working-class market. The *Daily Mail,* which reached a sale of half a million by 1900, after its foundation in 1896, was the foremost example of the advantages of advertising revenue; it soon led to imitations like the *Daily Express*. In a way the *Daily Mail* encapsulates the whole phenomenon of popular culture in the late-Victorian era. The upper classes did not exactly warm to it – a paper, as Lord Salisbury reputedly said, that was written for office-boys by office-boys. But at the same time, even a population reared on the *Daily Mail* represented a considerable improvement over the earlier years of the nineteenth century.

Further reading

There are several critical evaluations of Victorian values:

Matthew Sweet, *Inventing the Victorians* (2001) – argues the Victorians were much less moral than we think.

James Walvin, *Victorian Values* (1987)

G. Marsden ed., *Victorian Values: Personalities and Perspectives in Nineteenth Century Society* (1990)

Several volumes explain the emergence of the feminist movement and its early recruits:

Barbara Caine, *English Feminism 1780–1980* (1997)

Barbara Caine, *Victorian Feminists* (1992)

Olive Banks, *Becoming a Feminist: the social origins of first wave feminism* (1986)

Olive Banks, *Faces of Feminism* (1981)

Susan Kingsley Kent, *Gender and Power in Britain, 1640–1990* (1999)

Christine Bolt, *Feminist Ferment: the Woman Question in the USA and England 1870–1940* (1995)

Jane Rendall, *The Origins of Modern Feminism* (1985)

On the Victorian suffrage movement see:

Martin Pugh, *The March of the Women: a Revisionist Analysis of the Campaign for Women's Suffrage 1866–1914* (2000) – argues that the suffragists largely won the debate by *c*.1900.

D. Rubinstein, *Before the Suffragettes: Women's Emancipation in the 1890s* (1986)

Julia Bush, *Women Against the Vote* (2007)

Brian Harrison, *Separate Spheres: The Opposition to Women's Suffrage in Britain* (1978)

Paula Bartley, *Votes for Women 1860–1929* (1998)

Harold L. Smith, *The British Women's Suffrage Campaign 1866–1928* (1998)

Aspects of women's lives are discussed in:

Jane Lewis, *Women in England 1870–1950* (1984)

Elizabeth Roberts, *Women and Work 1840–1940* (1988)

Martha Vicinus, *Independent Women: Work and Community for Single Women 1850–1920* (1985)

Joan Perkin, *Women and Marriage in Nineteenth-Century England* (1989)

Jeffery Weeks, *Sex, Politics and Society* (1981)

Lucy Bland, *Banishing the Beast: English Feminism and Sexual Morality 1885–1914* (1995)

R.A. Soloway, *Birth Control and the Population Question in England 1872–1930* (1982)

Helen Mathers, *Patron Saint of Prostitutes: Josephine Butler and a Victorian Scandal* (2014)

On leisure and sport see:

R. Holt, *Sport and the British* (1989)

Derek Birley, *Sport and the making of Britain* (1993)

James Walvin, *Leisure and Society 1830–1950* (1978)

J.M. Golby and A.W. Purdue, *The Civilisation of the Crowd: Popular Culture in England 1750–1900* (1984)

P. Bailey, *Leisure and Class in Victorian England* (1978)

Matthew Hilton, *Smoking in British Popular Culture 1899–2000* (2000)

P. Haydon, *Beer and Britannia* (2001)

Brian Harrison, *Drink and the Victorians* (1971)

R.I. McKibbin, 'Working-Class Gambling in Britain 1880–1939', *Past and Present*, 82, 1979

Attitudes to work and respectability are discussed in:

F.M.L. Thompson, *The Rise of Respectable Society* (1988)

Jose Harris, *Private Lives, Public Spirit: Britain 1870–1914* (1993)

Robert Gray, *The Aristocracy of Labour in Nineteenth Century Britain 1850–1900* (1981)

Paul Johnson, 'Credit and Thrift and the British Working Class 1870–1939', in Jay Winter ed., *The Working Class in Modern British History* (1983)

Henry Pelling, *Popular Politics and Society in Late Victorian Britain* (1979)

5

British National Identity: Unity and Division

Between the mid-Victorian and the interwar period the British enjoyed a secure sense of their national identity, so much so that they did not find it necessary to define it or celebrate it as much as other nations. It was founded not just on British success in the industrial and imperial sphere, but on a belief that Britain was pre-eminently the nation of freedom; the British did not imprison people without bringing charges in open court, they allowed free criticism of governments, tolerated all kinds of religions, and did not pay taxes unless they were approved annually by an elected parliament. As a result the British appeared a remarkably cohesive nation politically and even geographically. They enjoyed a compact territory and an admirable system of internal communications. By 1870 when the railway branch lines extended as far as Cornwall and the west and north of Scotland 300 million rail journeys were undertaken every year.

However, the country was less united than this suggests for Britain was actually a *state* comprising four distinct *nations,* the English, Scots, Welsh and Irish, the latter three having been brought under English dominance by a mixture of armed force and pressure. The Union was also unbalanced; in 1881 England had 24.5 million people, Ireland 5.2 million, Scotland 3.7 million and Wales 1.5 million. Logically Britain should have had a federal structure to reflect this but was in fact a highly centralized state. Economic and political success kept the lid on discontent but society contained divisions over religion highlighted by migration and immigration, resentment over London's treatment of the Celtic fringe, and struggles between a declining aristocracy, an ambitious middle class and an increasingly organized and assertive working class.

The Union with Scotland

By the middle of the nineteenth century the Union of 1707 between Scotland and England appeared to meet with general acceptance north of the border. As *The Times* rather complacently put it: 'the separate nationalism of Scotland is happily in these days an anachronism'. It was mistaken; in London the newspaper's editors could not see that most Scots found their Scottishness compatible with an overall Britishness. One reason for this was that the Union had left intact some of the institutions in which Scotsmen took pride, notably the legal and educational systems. Scotland boasted four distinguished universities, and outstanding achievements by her middle class in medicine, science, engineering, literature, economics and philosophy. The country enjoyed a higher literacy rate than England, and the separate Education Act of 1872 inaugurated a much more sweeping reform than that of 1870 in England. In Scotland the school boards were not hindered by religious disputes; they moved rapidly towards compulsory education up to 13, and were permitted to provide secondary education. In contrast to the decadent and elitist ancient universities of England, those north of the border were more academically orientated and relatively open to talent. Five times as many Scots as English attended universities. Nor had the Union involved the imposition of an alien Church. Scotland's controversies here were purely internal; in 1843 the Presbyterian Church of Scotland had suffered a breakaway by the Free Church, and after 1847 was also challenged by the United Presbyterian Church.

The Union also worked at an economic level. Scotland had become a major element in the Victorian success story by taking advantage of the wider market for her coal, iron, ships, textiles and chemicals. Scots entrepreneurs and workers also moved south to take up new opportunities, and thus became key participants in the wider expansion of the British Empire. This affected several levels of society. At one end aristocratic figures like Dalhousie, Elgin and Minto occupied grand roles as Indian viceroys and colonial governors, while at the other, poor Scots were recruited into the

Table 5.1 Religious allegiance in Scotland (in thousands), 1871–1901

	Episcopal	Church of Scotland	Free Church of Scotland	United Presbyterian Church	Roman Catholic	Methodist, Baptist and Congregationalist
1871	56	436	253	163	326	35
1881		528	312	175		
1901	116	662	350	194	450	55

Highland regiments created by the Westminster government as a means of turning the martial qualities of the people to useful purposes. Moreover, thousands of Scotsmen emigrated to become farmers in Canada, tea-planters in India, missionaries in Africa, as well as doctors, merchants, shippers and bankers. Of the latter, the greatest was the Jardine Matheson firm, whose interests stretched to India, China and Japan. Scotland was, in fact, so bound up with empire that great imperial crises like the Boer War generated powerful political support for the British cause north of the border. Not for nothing did Glasgow style itself 'the second city of the empire'.

Scottish nationalism

Despite this a distinctive Scottishness survived. It expressed itself more in cultural than in political forms. One manifestation consisted in the romantic revivalism associated with the Highland games, clan tartan and the wearing of the kilt, stimulated by the writings of Sir Walter Scott, dignified by Queen Victoria's decision to purchase Balmoral in 1847, and sustained by the tourist trade. However, it remained very much the culture of the Anglicized Scottish aristocracy and gentry, and left ordinary people, especially the majority living in the urban Lowlands, unmoved.

Indeed, Scotland in the nineteenth century was a society deeply divided by social class; and the workers of the central industrial belt found in sport a different medium for expressing a sense of national consciousness. This was something much stronger than the friendly competitiveness in rugby between middle-class, public-school Scots and their English counterparts. Among workingmen, professional football aroused a fanatical loyalty which crystallized into anti-Englishness in the late-Victorian era. The continued drain of top players to English clubs underlined the growing self-image of Scotland as a poor, semi-colonial territory, and made victory over the English on the football field a vital means of bolstering national pride. However, the nationalist implications of Scottish sport were limited. Football reinforced divisions within Scottish society as much as it united them against the English. The influx of Irish Catholics and Ulster Orangemen into the Lowland cities led to the emergence of teams backed by Protestants (Rangers and Hearts) and teams backed by Catholics (Celtic and Hibernian). Nor was the popular obsession with football closely linked to political nationalism, as it was in Ireland. Although some Scottish Labour leaders like Keir Hardie sympathized with Home Rule, it never became an important objective for them. Ultimately, sport was more of a safety valve than a destabilizing element in Anglo-Scottish relations in this period.

Political integration through Liberalism

In many ways Victorian Scotland was very well integrated into British politics, especially if measured by the role of the leading figures. Gladstone, with his Scots parentage and his Midlothian constituency, became a revered figure. Scotland also supplied a number of other prime ministers, both Liberal (Rosebery and Campbell-Bannerman) and Conservative (Balfour and Bonar Law). Rosebery was typical in combining a romantic Scots nationalism with a staunch British imperialism. The incorporation of such men into Westminster politics probably blunted separatist sentiments, though the habit of planting English carpetbaggers in safe seats north of the border (H.H. Asquith, John Morley, Winston Churchill) was probably counter-productive in the long run.

Scotland had given up her separate government for 72 Westminster MPs (after 1885) elected by 560,000 voters. By the 1860s Scottish politics had become woven into English through the allegiance first to Liberalism (and later to Labour) firmly rooted in a popular Liberalism based on land reform, free trade and a general hostility to the feudal class. In 1878 half of Scotland was owned by 68 men including great magnates like the Dukes of Buccleuch, Atholl and Sutherland. But even in the Highlands these figures lost some of their influence, and by 1885 the Liberals had captured 62 of the country's 70 constituencies. Of course, Scottish Liberalism was as subject to division as other Scots institutions. Five rebel crofter candidates won Highland seats in the 1880s against the conventional Whig-landlord figures. Here the accumulated grievances since the time of the clearances were exacerbated by poor crops and evictions. This produced a serious breakdown of law and order. After the famous 'Battle of the Braes' on Skye, which was an attempt to stop evictions, the government granted the crofters the right of rent reviews, compensation and security of tenure previously given to Irish tenants. At the same time, Whig magnates like the Duke of Argyll were already leaving the Liberal Party on account of its radicalism. The 1886 split had major consequences in Scotland because of the Irish Protestant community which resulted in the election of 17 Liberal Unionist MPs.

Scots Home Rule?

Although Scotland participated in mainstream British politics, from the 1860s onwards there were growing signs of dissatisfaction with the Union. Both Gladstone and Rosebery appreciated that the Westminster administration seemed remote and overbearing, and accepted the case for giving the country a separate administration rather than treating it as a subdivision of the Home Office. In fact, it was Salisbury who appointed the first Scottish Secretary in

1885 and an administration based in Edinburgh. But the Irish example inevitably had a stimulating effect on Scots nationalism, and 1886 saw the establishment of a Scottish Home Rule Association. From that time onwards, Liberals on both sides of the border increasingly supported the idea of a Scottish parliament; even Gladstone saw the advantage in a scheme of devolution-all-round which would free Westminster from a number of troublesome domestic issues. However, although a bill was introduced in 1892 it aroused very little interest. After 1906 the question of Scottish Home Rule revived again, to some extent as a result of the Irish controversy. In 1907 the Liberals set up a standing Grand Committee so that Scots legislation might receive proper attention and in 1908 the census was transferred to Edinburgh to help the implementation of old-age pensions. Bills to introduce a Scottish parliament were introduced on seven occasions between 1906 and 1914, and in 1913 the Commons gave a majority on second reading.

The integration of Wales with Britain

By comparison with Scotland, Victorian Wales was culturally cohesive, but hardly any national institutions survived. For 600 years the country had been administered from London like any region of England. Yet Wales was much more than a geographical expression. According to the census of 1891, the Welsh-speaking population composed 54 per cent, and was still 50 per cent in 1901. In the north-western counties of Anglesey, Caernarfon, Merioneth and Cardigan, some 48–51 per cent of the people spoke *only* Welsh. The other side of the coin was that in the whole of the country three-quarters could speak English, and for many years able and ambitious Welshmen had happily used the English language to obtain better employment. By 1891 228,000 natives of Wales resided in England, notably in Liverpool, Manchester and London. The Victorian railway system helped to integrate Wales with England, for the main routes ran east–west, linking the north with Manchester, mid-Wales with Shrewsbury and Birmingham, and the south with Bristol and London. But the migration was not all one way. In economic terms Wales comprised two regions, a rather depressed, agricultural north and a south made buoyant by coal, steel and shipping. By the 1880s eight of the thirteen counties were losing population, while Glamorgan, which contained a third of the total population, grew by two and a half times between 1861 and 1891. Its immigrants came initially from rural Wales, but also from the west of England; in fact, by 1870 four out of

Table 5.2 Religious allegiance in Wales (in thousands), 1871–1901

	Calvinistic Methodists	Baptists	Congregationalists	Wesleyan Methodists	Anglicans
1871	93	70	90	26	86
1901	160	109	149	44	144

ten were English people attracted by the employment available in the ports and mines of Monmouth and Glamorgan.

Welsh national culture

Although this English immigration diminished the role of the Welsh language, the country nonetheless retained its distinctive culture. This was partly a reflection of the dominance of the Nonconformist churches, which claimed over 80 per cent of all worshippers by the 1850s. In contrast to the Scots, the Welsh could boast a culture that crossed the class divide. It found expression particularly in the music and poetry that were the glories of the national eisteddfod. This culture permeated the political groups as well as the different social classes. Thus a leading Liberal like Tom Ellis MP could participate in the eisteddfod alongside the union leader William Abraham from the Rhondda. The sport of rugby also had a unifying effect. Whereas in England rugby was exclusive, in Wales it became a genuinely popular sport which helped to draw the non-Welsh-speaking immigrants into national life.

But in some ways Welsh politics echoed that of Scotland. It revolved around the grievances of small tenant farmers against landowners and the hated tithes to which was added a campaign against the Anglican Establishment and a demand for improved education. The 1867 Reform Act undermined the influence of the Conservative gentry, and the increase in the county electorate from 75,000 to 200,000 in 1885 completed the process. By 1880 the Liberals already held 29 of the 33 seats. Wales became the most consistently Liberal region of the British Isles; even in a poor year like 1900 the party retained 28 of 34 constituencies, and in the local elections of 1904 639 Liberals were elected against only 157 Conservatives.

Wales: an early case of multiculturalism?

With its strong basis in popular culture, Welsh radicalism had the potential to create a serious rift in British politics. The demand for Disestablishment developed into a nationalist cause, which made Gladstone's prevarication over the issue rather dangerous. Welsh radicals also felt rather tempted to emulate the Irish Land League. Indeed, by 1886 a Welsh Land League had appeared, under the leadership of Thomas Gee, committed to securing fair rents, security of tenure, abolition of tithes and graduated taxation. Yet the Welsh radicals remained notably loyal to the Liberal leader even in 1886; Liberal Unionism enjoyed nothing like the kind of support it won in Scotland. The explanation is that well before the split in the party the Welsh Liberal MPs had settled down under the leadership of Stuart Rendell, who refused to allow Welsh grievances to be used as a vehicle for separatism. This loyalty to British Liberalism cannot be ascribed to patronage. Indeed, in the late nineteenth century Tom Ellis, a junior whip, was the only MP to obtain promotion from the back benches; no one reached the Cabinet until Lloyd George in 1905.

However, the Welsh radicals clearly felt that it was worth staying under the aegis of the Liberal Party. In 1881 they achieved the first distinctively Welsh item of legislation: the Welsh Sunday Closing Act. Other Liberal reforms such as the Church Burials Act were of considerable importance to Welsh Nonconformists. In the long run they also capitalized on Gladstone's sympathy with the culture and education of Wales. The new college at Aberystwyth, formed in 1872, received a state subsidy, and it subsequently joined with the university colleges at Cardiff and Bangor to form the University of Wales in 1893. Moreover, as a result of their victories in the post-1870 school board elections and in the post-1888 county council elections, Welsh Nonconformists managed to seize control of elementary and secondary education. In 1905 the National Library of Wales was established at Aberystwyth, while two years later the Liberals created a Welsh Department at the Board of Education with the object of promoting Welsh language-teaching in schools. In effect Victorian Wales was evidence of successful multiculturalism in Britain; there was no inconsistency between being Welsh and being British.

Church Disestablishment

On the land question there was nothing comparable to the special legislation granted to Scottish crofters, though in 1891 the Conservatives made tithes payable by landowners, not the occupants, which helped to defuse the issue. However, the question of Disestablishment generated serious resentment as an example of English/Anglican dominance over Wales. From 1891 onwards the National Liberal Federation included Welsh Disestablishment in its programme, and even Gladstone abandoned his opposition. Nonetheless, his 1892 government failed to pass a bill into law, and it was left to the Edwardian Liberal government to try again. Although the House of Commons enacted the Welsh Disestablishment Bill three times during 1912–14, thereby overcoming the veto of the House of Lords, the outbreak of war caused the measure to be suspended so that it did not finally become law until 1920.

It was during the 1890s, when frustration over Disestablishment reached its height, that Welsh separatism looked dangerous. The emergence of a new organization, the Cymru Fydd, founded in London in 1886, provided a vehicle for some of the younger and more impatient Welsh radicals. Under the leadership of Lloyd George, Cymru Fydd took over the North Wales Liberal Federation in the cause of Home Rule, and threatened to create a break from British Liberalism. But there was to be no Welsh Parnell. The initiative broke down on the opposition of the South Wales Liberal Federation, and the nationalist leaders realized that there was not enough general enthusiasm for Home Rule. By 1896 Cymru Fydd was fading and Lloyd George had settled his course in the mainstream of British politics. The only other challenge to the political status quo came from a new generation of labour leaders based in the valleys of South Wales. Keir Hardie led the way with his victory at Merthyr Tydfil in 1900, and in his wake came James Griffiths, Vernon Hartshorn, Arthur Cook and Frank Hodges, all leaders of the coal mining community. Yet although they posed a serious threat to Liberal hegemony after 1906, they were not interested in Home Rule and so their rise consolidated the effect of Liberalism in integrating Wales into the broader pattern of British politics.

Ireland: the threat to the Union

In complete contrast Ireland was never really integrated into the British state. Ireland in the 1860s was a country of 4 million people governed by a Viceroy in Dublin and a British Cabinet minister, the Chief Secretary, who divided his time between London and Dublin. The Irish were also represented in Parliament by 103 MPs. Over two-thirds of the population were Roman Catholics who dominated the provinces of Leinster, Munster and Connaught, though in Ulster about 60 per cent were Protestant. The chief links with England, other than political institutions, were the industry of Ulster, which benefited from access to mainland markets, the Established Church, which was Anglican, and the Anglo-Irish landowning class. Magnates such as the

Marquis of Lansdowne, the Duke of Devonshire, the Duke of Abercorn, Lord Fitzwilliam and the Marquis of Bath occupied influential positions in society on both sides of the Irish Sea. Over the decades these landowners had let land to small peasant farmers; but the combination of the subdivision of plots and a wet, mild climate dictated a heavy reliance on the cultivation of potatoes.

Irish nationalism

The chief catalyst of change in the Victorian period was the famine of the 1840s, which resulted in the death of a million people, the emigration of a million, and the loss of a further million by emigration between 1851 and 1861. Much of the country continued to be depressed; the 1870s and 1880s saw poor harvests, falling agricultural prices and consequent pressure for reductions in rents. The new element in the situation was the Irish emigrant community in the USA which had founded the Fenian Brotherhood. By the 1860s they were capable of promoting violent anti-British activities both in Ireland and on the mainland of Britain, where attempts were made to free Fenian prisoners from jail.

British politicians showed themselves slow to grasp the gulf that was beginning to separate them from the Irish people, and to appreciate the seriousness of the challenge to the Union. As Prime Minister, Gladstone was reluctant even to accept that he required constant police protection from the 1860s onwards. He did, however, at least adopt a constructive approach towards the Irish Question. Though rather ignorant of the people and of the country, which he rarely even visited, Gladstone diagnosed two major problems – religion and land – and he attempted to conciliate the Catholic majority by disestablishing the Church in 1869 and giving the cultivators some help through his first Land Act in 1870.

However, the inadequacy of these measures became fully apparent at the election of 1874, when the recently formed Home Government Association returned 59 MPs committed to the restoration of an Irish parliament in Dublin. These Home Rulers, acting under the leadership of Charles Stuart Parnell from 1878, became a fixed and sometimes crucial element in British politics down to 1918. By largely eliminating Liberal representation in Ireland, they immediately began to alter the configuration of party politics at Westminster. The Irish Home Rulers benefited greatly from the franchise reform of 1884, which increased the electorate in the counties where their support was strong. But at the same time Gladstone deliberately excluded Ireland from the redistribution of constituencies in order to avoid obstructionism by the Irish members. This left Ireland markedly over-represented with 103 MPs. From 1885 onwards, between 81 and 85 of these were Home Rulers; they held the balance of power in the Commons in 1885, 1892 and 1910.

British governments found the Irish Question difficult to handle because the nationalist campaign operated on two levels – as a respectable political party at Westminster and as a violent mass movement in the Irish countryside. They therefore oscillated between conciliation and coercion. In 1879 the Irish Land League was founded under the leadership of Michael Davitt to protect tenants from high rents and evictions. Its campaigns resulted in widespread violence, including the murder of the Chief Secretary for Ireland, Lord Frederick Cavendish, in 1882. Meanwhile, Gladstone embarked on a radical reform in the shape of a second Irish Land Act in 1881, which established tribunals to revise the rents of the tenant farmers. This represented an unprecedented interference with the rights of property-owners, and was to have profound consequences. In the short term, however, Gladstone obtained no relief from the dispiriting round of conflict and repression; by 1886 he had determined to break the deadlock by conceding a parliament in Dublin and new legislation to buy out the Irish landlords.

Home Rule and the Liberal split

Gladstone's scheme for Home Rule went a long way to meeting the tangled needs of the situation but their frustration by Conservative and Unionist forces had tragic long-term consequences. He proposed a Dublin parliament with extensive internal powers over the whole country but retained the link with Westminster which would continue to control defence, foreign policy, trade and currency. Ireland would contribute one-fifteenth of the imperial revenue. By removing Irish representation at Westminster, the scheme pleased those who resented the disruption of the parliamentary timetable. Above all, Parnell accepted Gladstone's proposals. Thus, 1886 offered a chance of both preserving the Union, satisfying nationalist demands, and averting decades of violence and misery in Anglo-Irish relations. However, the first Home Rule Bill was defeated by 30 votes when the Conservatives combined with 93 rebel Liberals who subsequently withdrew to form the Liberal Unionist Party. In fact Home Rule did not cause the flight of the Whigs, which was already under way, but it certainly accelerated the process. The split precipitated a general election in 1886, which put the Conservatives in office for most of the next 20 years. In his brief ministry from 1892 to 1894, Gladstone managed to push a second Home Rule Bill through the Commons, only to see it rejected in the House of Lords by 400 votes to 40.

Conservatives defend the Union

For the Irish this was a sobering statistic. The new Prime Minister, Salisbury, had little liking for democracy even in England, and had declared the Irish to be as fit for self-government as the Hottentots – a newly 'discovered' tribe of Southern Africa. Initially the Conservatives reacted as the party of landed property to a threat to their self-interest. However, this is not a sufficient explanation as they subsequently abandoned the landed interest. They also feared the eventual result would be complete separation of the two countries which would weaken Britain's strategic position, especially in an era of naval rebuilding and invasion scares. There were other possible ramifications from Home Rule. Concessions to the Irish might stimulate the disintegration of the Empire; 1885 was, after all, the foundation year of the Indian National Congress, whose active London office enjoyed the support of some of the Irish members. More immediately, Home Rule provided a useful supply of material for Tory Party propaganda designed to damn the Liberals as weak and unpatriotic.

The flaw in all this was that the Irish people had emphatically voted for Home Rule, continued to do so consistently, and were becoming ungovernable. Moreover, in the three southern and western provinces Protestant supporters of the Union constituted only 10 per cent of the population, and in time they reconciled themselves to the inevitability of Home Rule. In 1886 the Protestant majority in Ulster belatedly organized itself in support of the Union, stimulated by Gladstone's bill and the notorious visit of Lord Randolph Churchill who proclaimed that 'Ulster will fight and Ulster will be right', thus initiating a tradition of Conservative support for violent resistance to the will of Parliament. However, by securing the election of 17 Unionists from Ulster's 33 constituencies, they gave the British Conservatives a firmer basis for their resistance to Home Rule.

Irish land reform

Under Salisbury's premiership Arthur Balfour made his political reputation as Chief Secretary by restoring a degree of calm to the Irish countryside. This involved repressing the violence, which was dwindling anyway, and offering a number of expensive concessions. As the Conservatives left Gladstone's 1881 Land Act intact, the tenant farmers began to benefit from substantial reductions in rents. In addition they passed a series of measures in 1885, 1888, 1891 and 1903 which allocated Exchequer revenue to buy up Irish estates, which were then split up and sold on generous terms to small farmers. The irony in all this was that the Conservatives were implementing the policy of Davitt's Land League! The long-term effect was to leave Ireland as a country of small Catholic farmers – a recipe for a conservative society. Only outstanding incompetence on the part of British governments could have made such a society the home of terrorism. For although Balfour and Salisbury congratulated themselves in the 1890s on having subdued the subversives, they actually made no impact on the strength of Irish nationalism. The Home Rulers maintained their grip on the Irish constituencies and waited for their opportunity to come round again. By 1900, then, the Union with Ireland had become an artificial imposition which dangerously divided the British state and could not be expected to last.

Religion and national identity

As the examples of Wales and Ireland suggest, the Anglican Church of England was not entirely satisfactory as a British national Church. It was seen as an alien imposition by many people. In fact, by 1800 Anglicans comprised only 46 per cent of active church-goers against 43 for Nonconformists and 10 per cent for Catholics. Although the Church of England enjoyed the status of a national or Established Church whose bishops sat in the House of Lords, its centrality in national life was gradually eroded; in 1857 Church courts were eliminated from divorce, and the Church was disestablished in Ireland in 1869 and finally in Wales in 1920. As the Nonconformists argued, its spiritual role was undermined by its close relationship with the political establishment.

The Nonconformists

Most of the religious and racial groups in late-Victorian society were regarded as 'minorities'; Nonconformists resented this description, however, as they felt they had already drawn level with the Church of England by mid-century. By the 1870s they were beginning to move from the periphery to the centre of British politics by integrating themselves into the structure of the Liberal Party. A number of essentially symbolic reforms, beginning with the abolition of religious tests at Oxford and Cambridge in 1871, helped to remove the body of discriminatory legislation. This process continued up to 1898, when the Marriages Act removed the requirement for a civil registrar to be present at weddings in Nonconformist and Catholic Churches. But as early as 1880, when the Church Burials Act was passed, the momentum behind political Nonconformity began to wane. This may seem surprising because the great issue of Disestablishment still remained to be tackled, and, according to the Liberation Society, the number of MPs who supported the cause had risen to 171 by 1885. But in fact, the resolution of most of the immediate Nonconformist grievances and the steady absorption of Nonconformist politicians into the political establishment blunted the sense of alienation among the Free Churches generally. Outside Wales the campaign for Disestablishment had lost momentum by the late 1880s, as is indicated by the dwindling funds and membership of the Liberation Society. Some of the more affluent Wesleyans had already migrated to the Conservatives. Thus, although the number of Nonconformist MPs was still to reach its peak – 210 in 1906 – Nonconformist issues were not quite as central as they had once been. In 1908 H.H. Asquith became Britain's first Nonconformist Prime Minister, and David Lloyd George was to be the second; but both regarded Welsh Disestablishment as essentially a necessary concession to the party faithful, and did not even place English Disestablishment on the agenda. As Nonconformists moved into the mainstream so religious controversies became less divisive.

The Catholic community

On the other hand English Catholics, who were concentrated in Lancashire, Cheshire, Durham, Northumberland, Warwick and Staffordshire, continued to be seen as subversive and alien. Politically they were forced into a marginal role for most of the Victorian era and continued to be the target of vitriolic 'No Popery' campaigns in elections. Although the emancipation legislation of 1829 allowed Catholics to sit in Parliament, they returned only 36 MPs by 1868. However, both Gladstone and Disraeli showed a willingness to incorporate Catholics into the system, and in 1871 the Liberal leader lifted the penalties imposed upon Catholic bishops by Lord John Russell in 1851. Meanwhile as the Liberals moved increasingly towards radicalism there was a temptation for English Catholics, a naturally conservative community, to gravitate towards the Conservatives; however, the party's association with the most rabid Protestantism deterred them for many years. Eventually doctrinal prejudice was overcome by a combination of electoral expediency and social class. A number of titled and gentry Catholic families, led by the Duke of Norfolk, found an alternative avenue into Conservative politics via the Primrose League. The Duke himself was awarded the Garter, became Chancellor of the League, and joined the Cabinet as Postmaster-General in 1895. In the context of their Irish policy it was advantageous for the Conservatives to be able to avoid looking like an exclusively Protestant organization. Moreover, there were votes to be won, especially in school

Table 5.3 Estimated Roman Catholic population, 1851–1911

	Roman Catholic population	Number of churches	Attendance at Mass
1851	900,000	597	482,000
1891	1,357,000	1,387	726,000
1911	1,710,000	1,773	915,000

board elections in the North of England, by defending the voluntary Catholic schools. At the 1885 election Cardinal Manning urged Catholics to oppose the advocates of secular education. Consequently the community had clearly moved in from the periphery by the 1890s. It was also hugely expanded as a result of Irish immigration.

Migration and immigration

Britain enjoyed a long and honourable tradition as a haven for immigrants fleeing from religious and political persecution especially in the autocratic regimes in Russia, France, Italy and Germany for much of the nineteenth century. This tradition was reinforced by Liberal and free-trade opinion which held that free movement of people was as valuable as the movement of goods. In 1895 the Home Secretary, H.H. Asquith, brushed aside a trade union deputation complaining about alien immigration: 'Who is it who had gained most from the free circulation and competition of labour? The English.' Not until 1905 were any controls imposed on entry into Britain. Of course most of the movement of people involved internal migration by the Irish driven by economic hardship in the decades after the famine. By 1871 the Irish in England and Wales numbered 566,000 and in Scotland 207,000; however, by 1900 the numbers had fallen by a fifth as many migrants moved on to the United States. Irish migrants were concentrated in Lancashire, Clydeside and London, but steadily spread to most industrial towns in search of employment.

The impact of the Irish

How far did Irish migrants become integrated into English and Scottish society? Many were always more attracted by the material opportunities available in America, and viewed England as a purely temporary refuge. Traditionally many Irish people had also found seasonal jobs in agriculture on the mainland, but the permanent immigrants largely undertook semi- or unskilled work as dockers, porters or building labourers. Like the Highland Scots they were recruited into the British army, where they accounted for 14 per cent by the 1890s. In view of the surplus of unskilled labour the Irish presence attracted a good deal of criticism on the grounds that they depressed wages, caused overcrowded housing, imposed severe burdens on the poor rate, and added to the drunkenness and criminality of urban society. Not surprisingly, they rapidly became segregated by residence for mutual support, and relied upon the assistance of the existing Catholic network, which was much stimulated by the arrival of so many co-religionists. Some resentment was caused when employers resorted to Irish labour for purposes of breaking strikes; but Irish participation in the great dock strike of 1889 helped to integrate them into the Labour Movement. In time the Irish community produced major union leaders, including James Connolly and James Larkin.

However, Irish migrants caused polarization in communities in Merseyside and Clydeside between Catholics and Protestants as was indicated by the emergence of Catholic-Irish football teams such as Everton, Celtic and Hibernian. This cultural divide was translated into long-lasting political allegiances as Conservative and Unionist propaganda against Home Rule and Irish terrorism fed a Protestant backlash. For their part, the Nationalist leaders, T.P. O'Connor, who became the MP for Liverpool Scotland, and John Denvir, set up the Irish National League of Great Britain and the Home Rule League of Great Britain with a view to mobilizing the Irish vote. Though not large, it was frequently crucial in shoring up Liberal majorities in urban constituencies.

Attitudes towards immigrants

Immigration brought many other nationalities to Britain in this period. There were small but longstanding groups of Chinese, Indians and Africans, most of whom arrived as seamen, merchants or students. Two of the wealthier Indians served as MPs: Dadhabhai Naoroji (Liberal) in 1892 and M.M. Bhownagree (Conservative) in 1895. But the most widely dispersed nationality were the Germans, who numbered 33,000 by 1871. Many of them worked as waiters, musicians and pork butchers, but some were employed as clerks, attracted by the experience and better wages available in England. Though seen as efficient and well-qualified, they caused much resentment among English clerks struggling in an oversubscribed occupation. Several German Jews who followed careers in finance or the professions achieved a considerable reputation and left a lasting impression on British life: Charles

Table 5.4 Immigration, 1870–1919

Year	Number of people immigrating to Britain
1870–79	744,000
1880–89	1,089,000
1890–99	1,567,000
1900–09	2,287,000
1910–19	2,224,000

Hallé, Edgar Speyer, Sir Ernest Cassell and Sir Ernest Oppenheimer are examples. The entrepreneurs were originally attracted by the relatively tolerant climate of Britain as well as by the greater economic opportunities.

During the 1890s the Germans were overtaken by Poles, Lithuanians and others driven from the western districts of Russia by a combination of persecution and inadequate economic opportunities. The Lithuanians gathered in Scotland, while the Poles, who numbered 82,000 by 1901, concentrated in Stepney, Manchester and Leeds. Many of them were Jewish, and their arrival helped to swell the total number of Jewish immigrants into Britain between 1870 and 1914 to 120,000. In addition, the Italian community increased from 5,000 in 1871 to 20,000 by 1911. They had originally migrated from rural Italy to the towns of the north, but failed to find work there. In Britain Italians often worked as cooks, waiters, hairdressers and musicians, or set up businesses in confectionery, ice-cream and catering. British attitudes towards these immigrant communities varied widely. At one end of the spectrum, Italians evoked sympathy and respect partly because of their recent struggle for freedom and because they did not compete as directly for employment as some other groups. Many of the wealthier Indians met with tolerance and friendliness in Britain, in marked contrast to the racial prejudice they encountered in India and South Africa. Attitudes towards Germans, on the other hand, deteriorated markedly during the 1890s and 1900s as a result of the growing commercial rivalry, the naval race and German support for the Boers.

Jewish immigration

Most controversy over immigration focused on the Jewish community which increased to 160,000 in the 1890s as Jews fled from persecution in Tsarist Russia and to 300,000 by 1914 concentrated in the East End, Manchester and Leeds. In effect there were two communities, one of poor refugees who did not always speak English, and another wealthier, long-established one already advancing into the political mainstream. Back in

1847 Lionel de Rothschild had been elected an MP, but had been prevented from taking his seat because the parliamentary oath taken by all members referred specifically to the Christian religion. The House of Commons abandoned this rule in 1858 leading to the election of nine Jewish MPs by 1900, 17 by 1929 and 28 in 1945. In 1885 Nathan Rothschild became the first practising Jew to gain a peerage through Gladstone's recommendation. Under the Parliamentary Oaths Bill of 1885 confessed atheists were also enabled to take their seats, and in 1892 some 40 members chose to affirm rather than take the traditional oath.

For politically ambitious Jews the real obstacle lay in the reluctance of the parties to nominate them. Their obvious strength lay in the East End of London though only a minority of them were actually voters. The Liberals, who were the more tolerant party, returned the influential spokesman for the Jewish community, Samuel Morley, for Whitechapel. Several Jews also sat as Conservatives in such seats as Stepney and Limehouse, though they felt obliged to advocate restrictions on immigration – which meant Jewish immigration. Perhaps the most telling sign of the integration of Jews into British politics was the success of younger men including Herbert Samuel, Edwin Montagu and Rufus Isaacs in winning elections in constituencies where the Jewish vote was negligible, and in holding high office in the Edwardian Liberal governments.

Anti-Semitism

Nonetheless, anti-Semitism remained widespread in all levels of society and in all political parties. At the top of society Jews were often described as clever but disloyal and cowardly; and the ministerial careers of the three Liberals suffered from the prejudice of colleagues and opponents alike. In popular debate Jews endured crude, stereotyped attacks. On the one hand they were portrayed as exploitative capitalists and blamed for dragging Britain into the South African War in 1899. Conversely the Liberals usually defended them as models of enterprise and industry. On the other hand Jews in the East End were depicted as a burden on the community because of the destitute condition in which immigrants arrived, and they were also suspect because of their role as opponents of Tsarist Russia which gave them a reputation as dangerous socialists or even anarchists. Jews also attracted prejudice on the grounds that they introduced 'sweated labour' into the clothing trade and cabinet-making, and thus undermined existing businesses. In fact, their enterprises did no more than exacerbate problems of low wages and overcrowding that already existed; but with their growing numbers and their shops and synagogues the Jews were a conspicuous target. As a result the period from the 1880s onwards saw sporadic campaigns against alien immigration led by Tory MPs such as Sir Howard Vincent and Major W.E. Evans-Gordon. Under pressure the government eventually set up a Royal Commission on Immigration in 1903; the Conservatives had, so far, benefited from an anti-immigrant reaction without doing anything about the problem. The result was the 1905 Alien Immigration Act, which attempted to exclude undesirable and destitute immigrants. It required immigrant ships to dock at certain specified ports, and empowered the authorities to expel unwanted aliens, though appeals could be lodged by those fleeing political or religious persecution. After 1906 it fell to the Liberals, who had opposed the Act, to administer or to repeal it; they chose to operate it humanely by giving immigrants the benefit of the doubt.

Energetic efforts to counter anti-Semitism were undertaken by wealthy Jews who organized charities to assist new immigrants and start new businesses. The Jewish Board of Deputies and the *Jewish Chronicle* actively promoted the idea that the community was an integral part of British life: 'The reign of Queen Victoria has assumed an almost sacred character to English Jews for it marks the era of their complete emancipation.' In 1885 the *Jewish Chronicle* claimed that voters saw Jews 'as Englishmen who are only differentiated from themselves by religious creed' and in 1900 and 1914 it urged Jews to show gratitude by making donations and volunteering for the war effort. Though optimistic in view of the popular prejudice, this view reflected the contributions Jews were making to economic and political life in Britain.

Monarchy and national identity

As the Crown gradually lost its political power during the nineteenth century, its function as a personalized symbol of the British nation became much more important. For the ordinary citizen the King or Queen offered a tangible link with the state and a channel for the expression of loyalty through a series of visits, tours, pageants and celebrations. Queen Victoria has sometimes been thought to have played this role particularly successfully partly because, as a wife and mother, she embodied the Victorian ideal of family life, and because her Jubilees crystallized the popular feeling for empire towards the end of the century, when external threats encouraged the instinct to rally round the flag. However, we have no real way of measuring the popularity or otherwise of the monarchy in this period and historians have often exaggerated the significance of Queen Victoria's reign. The Queen was remote from most of her subjects who would have been shocked to hear that when she spoke English, rather than the preferred German, it was with a strong guttural accent. Despite royal visits to Ireland accompanied by displays of enthusiasm the monarchy had no effect in stemming the growth of separatism and nationalism there. Also, many of the features of the monarchy during the last two decades of the Queen's reign actually pre-dated her. Under George III the monarchy had already come to personify the national cause, and provided a good deal of pageantry and spectacle. It may be that in late-Victorian times the public display was more splendid and more widely appreciated because of improvements in communications, but it was not fundamentally different from the earlier period.

Republicanism

Any assessment is also complicated by the sharp fluctuations in attitudes towards royalty. In 1837 Victoria enjoyed an easy popularity as a young wife and mother following several disreputable old Kings. However, her withdrawal from public life following the death of Prince Albert in 1861, which was aggravated by stories about her extraordinary reliance upon her Scots servant, John Brown, reduced her standing to a low point for about a decade. As a result an organized republican movement sprang up, and in Parliament criticisms were voiced by as many as 64 MPs, including Sir Charles Dilke, Joseph Cowen, John Morley and Joseph Chamberlain. However, their attacks focused largely on the expansion of the civil list for the support of the Queen's growing number of relations, which amounted to £358,000 by the 1870s. They missed the real target, which was her interference in politics.

Even at its height the republican movement, with around 6,000 members, was not especially strong. Possibly because she was a woman, the critics underestimated the resilience of the Queen; certainly when she began to appear in public again the attacks on the civil list faded quickly. In the eyes of many middle-class Victorians, the Queen's withdrawal indicated a proper sense of the importance of mourning. In 1871 when the Prince of Wales nearly died from typhoid, a good deal of sympathy was quickly generated, and this is usually considered a turning-point in the recovery of popularity by the royal family. While the Prince's dissolute personal life was disapproved of by some, his patronage of popular sports and entertainments undoubtedly endeared him to many sections of the population. The recovery of popularity by the late-Victorian monarchy was also promoted by the press. By contrast with earlier periods, the radical republican press had become marginal, outflanked by the mass-circulation newspapers which relied heavily on the royal family for copy. Both the national dailies and the expanding women's magazines promoted popular interest in the monarchy with the extra advantage of photographic illustrations.

Admittedly the Queen herself proved to be uncooperative in the face of efforts to advise her. She stuck to her widow's weeds for forty years and clung to the seclusion of Windsor and Balmoral. She obstinately refused Gladstone's well-meant requests to give the Prince of Wales a major public role, for example as Irish Viceroy, a position which, because of the dignity and the danger attached, would have done much to assist his national standing. She was too stubborn and opinionated to accept the role of a constitutional monarch above politics, but fortunately for her the public never realized how politically biased she had become.

Eventually, however, Victoria was rescued by her sheer longevity, admired for bearing the burdens of a wife, mother and head of state for six decades. Women's suffragists cited her as proof that women could play a public role without undermining their domesticity, much to her irritation! The more Britain seemed to be challenged by foreign powers, the more people felt inclined to rally around a figurehead. This sentiment reached a climax with the Silver Jubilee of 1887 and the Diamond Jubilee of 1897 which effectively symbolized the people's pride in British achievements under Queen Victoria and legitimized the British system of government.

The Victorian class struggle

Nineteenth-century observers of Britain's social-class system ranged all the way from Karl Marx, who detected a steady polarization of two antagonistic classes, to Lord Palmerston, who believed that wealth and rank were open to everyone. But the existence of class was not in doubt. By the 1830s the use of class terminology had become common. Victorians referred to the 'landed interest' which they equated with an upper or ruling class, the 'middling or industrious classes', and the 'working classes', though they distinguished the latter from the 'residuum' at the bottom of the pile. Although Marx was wrong in predicting that Britain would experience the first proletarian revolution to overthrow capitalism, he was correct to see the Victorian era in terms of a three-way struggle between classes. Middle-class reformers and working-class radicals forced the landed aristocracy to concede parliamentary reform in 1832 and free trade in 1846. But subsequently middle and upper classes combined against the workers; in the last twenty years of the century propertied interests united in fear of a threat from Irish nationalism, trade union militancy and land reformers.

The peerage

At the tip of the social pyramid stood the landed aristocracy, who were probably at the height of their political and economic success between the 1850s and the 1870s. In this period they comprised between 500 and 600 peers, of whom 430 sat in the House of Lords. To maintain the dignity of his position a peer was thought to require a minimum of around 3,000 acres of land, though most owned far more – the Duke of Devonshire had 200,000 acres and the Duke of Northumberland 166,000, for example. The landed class also included the 4,250 gentry families listed by Burke's *Landed Gentry*, many of whom were knights or baronets. According to convention a country gentleman or squire should possess at least 1,000 acres. Traditionally these families enjoyed a near-monopoly of power in the House of Lords, the Cabinet and in the Commons, and at local level as JPs and Lords-Lieutenant. In 1865 around three-quarters of the MPs came from aristocratic and gentry families. Their position was clearly entrenched by the remarkable concentration of land-ownership in Britain; 80 per cent of the entire British Isles was in the possession of 7,000 families.

Moreover, in some ways this was a rather rigid and exclusive elite as recruitment into the British peerage was much more restricted than in other European countries. Although many peers enjoyed income from commerce, mining royalties and urban property, mere wealth was not the key qualification; a stake in the land mattered most of all. Queen Victoria rejected Gladstone's original proposal to ennoble Nathan de Rothschild with the words:

> she cannot think that one who owes his great wealth to contracts with foreign governments, or to successful speculations on the stock exchange, can fairly claim a British peerage ... This seems to her not the less of a species of gambling because it is on a gigantic scale.

On the other hand, economic vicissitudes certainly caused both upward and downward mobility in the landed class. Successful farmers could elevate themselves by accumulating landholdings, withdrawing from labour, building fine houses and marrying their daughters into established county families. Conversely, the younger sons of peers, who were denied a share of their fathers' landed property, usually found themselves obliged to establish professional careers in the army, the law, the Church or banking, thereby sustaining regular traffic between the landed and the middle classes.

Aristocratic decline?

The 1880s marked a turning-point in the fortunes of Britain's landed class. From this decade onwards their status, power and wealth began to be undermined, though not as extensively as contemporary comment suggested. Some squires and aristocrats suffered from sharply declining rents as a result of the agricultural depression, though this was not characteristic of all regions. Henry Chaplin lost heavily in arable Lincolnshire, as did the Duke of Atholl on his huge but unproductive Perthshire moors. This resulted in the sale of millions of acres up to 1914 at very low prices. The upper classes also took alarm from the radical campaigns for the imposition of taxation on landed wealth although as yet they had only a limited impact. Many Irish estates were dispersed, the Crofters' Act impinged upon Highland owners, and Harcourt's 1894 death duties began a more effective system of taxation. It was doubtless this last that prompted Oscar Wilde's Lady Bracknell to lament: 'land has ceased to be either a pleasure or a profit; it gives one position and prevents one from keeping it up.' But the real threat to landed wealth was to come with Lloyd George's budget of 1909 and the First World War.

By the 1880s the political role of the peerage began to suffer serious attack. Undermined by the expansion of the county electorate in 1884, which resulted in the defeat of many county families, a number of the magnates retreated to safer seats in suburbia. Some were content to abandon what had only ever been a dilettante interest in national politics in order to devote themselves to other pursuits or to local government. Even there, some suffered the indignity of defeat in county council elections, though many peers continued to play a major role as county council chairmen. To some extent their personal loss of influence was cushioned by the dominance of the Conservatives and by Lord Salisbury's premiership down to 1902. It was not then obvious that he would be the last peer to serve as Prime Minister. Here, too, the real crisis was to come in the Edwardian period, when the House of Lords lost its veto and was held up to derision by the Liberals.

Diluting the peerage

What gave many peers an uneasy feeling about the decline of their order were internal changes rather than external attacks. Its members were conscious of the onward march of some extremely rich men who owed their position to industry rather than land. This fear was expressed in the Tory attacks on the 'radical plutocrats' who supported the social and political reforms of the Edwardian Liberals with generous donations. But well before that time the status of the peerage had been undermined by the entry of non-landed figures. Symptoms of the change could be observed in the Prince of Wales's friendship with Jewish financiers, and in the growing number of marriages between impoverished aristocrats and American heiresses; the families of the Duke of Marlborough and Lord Curzon each made several such American alliances in this period. But most alarming was the dilution of the peerage from the 1880s onwards, as the result of a faster rate of ennoblement and the inclusion of many non-landed men. Prominent examples were Lords Armstrong (armaments), Joicey (coal), Inverclyde (shipping), Glenesk (newspapers), Leverhulme (soap) and Ashton – known as 'Lord Linoleum'. Altogether, of the 200 new peers created between 1886 and 1914, one-third were plutocrats and one-third professional middle-class men, while only a quarter came from traditional landed families. In effect the peerage was being devalued by the political parties, who used ennoblements to attract large donations to their funds and to manipulate members of parliament. At the same time, hundreds of extra knighthoods were created and new honours were awarded, including the Order of the British Empire, the Royal Victorian Order, the Order of Merit and the Imperial Service Order. From 1888 onwards, the New Year, as well as the Queen's Birthday and her Jubilees, produced lavish distributions of these distinctions. A generation before Lloyd George took a hand, the honours system had already been diluted and partly discredited.

Who were the middle classes?

Although they made up only about 15 per cent of the population, the Victorian middle classes have usually been regarded as the key element in nineteenth-century society; they were at the heart of Britain's economic success and vigorously propagated their values and ideals – enterprise, self-help, domesticity, religiosity – among those above and below them. However, there were two obvious flaws in this. The *prescriptive* literature which carried the middle-class message was a misleading guide to the actual behaviour of Victorians. They were, for example, on the retreat from religion. Neither upper-class nor working-class women were confined to the domestic life that middle-class males thought proper. Nor can we speak of a cohesive middle class at all for the term covers everyone from merchants to small shopkeepers, clerks and farmers, the professions, financiers and manufacturers. The incomes enjoyed by these different groups varied greatly. While the secure centre consisted in those families with an annual income of £300–£1,000, this was a very long way from the position of the millionaire banker at one extreme or the insecure clerk on £100 or less at the other. There was a major distinction between businessmen on the one hand and professionals and those who depended upon the state for their employment. Politically, too, they were split down the middle. Whereas the Home Counties professional man was likely to be a Conservative, his counterpart in Wales, Yorkshire and the north-east was typically a Liberal. Even the lower middle class comprised two distinct elements. On the one hand were the pre-industrial small entrepreneurs and shopkeepers, and on the other the low-paid white-collar employees such as clerks, civil servants, elementary schoolteachers, journalists, insurance collectors and travelling salesmen. Many of these people found their incomes scarcely adequate to support conspicuous forms of middle-class behaviour like servant-keeping.

Social mobility

In effect the middle classes comprised a series of social layers, some of which overlapped with the classes above and below them; there were elements of conflict and of collaboration in these relationships. Throughout the century political controversy often took the form of a debate between members of the middle classes and the aristocracy. 'We are a servile, aristocracy-loving, lord-ridden people', complained Richard Cobden, who was a foremost exponent of the view that the landed class was merely parasitic upon the industrious classes. Joseph Chamberlain in the 1870s and Lloyd George in the 1900s employed similar language. These radicals forged alliances with workingmen in order to challenge the political power of the idle rich by reviving the question of land taxation. On the other hand, there is evidence to suggest that this type of conflict diminished by the 1890s. This was an inevitable consequence of the success of the middle classes in joining the political establishment by becoming voters, local councillors, MPs and even Cabinet ministers. From the 1860s such men as John Bright, Henry Fawcett and John Morley on the Liberal side, and W.H. Smith and Richard Cross on the Conservative side, were achieving ministerial status. However, this must not be exaggerated for most ministers continued to be drawn from the upper classes. Not until 1908 did Britain get a middle-class Prime Minister in H.H. Asquith.

However, the most important sign of the *rapprochement* between the middle and landed classes was the concentration of propertied interests in the Conservative camp especially after 1886. This shift at parliamentary level was reinforced by other, economic pressures upon the middle ranks of society; small shopkeepers felt antagonized by the rise of the Co-operatives, and many employers reacted against the steady growth and militancy of trades unions. In short, middle-class behaviour was increasingly defensive and conservative in character. They were no longer, if they ever had been, boldly imposing their own entrepreneurial values upon the rest of society. In some ways they appear to have been subject to the downward spread of aristocratic habits and behaviour.

Moreover, in a period of falling land values it was easy for businessmen to acquire country houses and estates. This might not make the manufacturer an accepted figure in landed county society immediately, but in the next generation it was difficult to distinguish his from the older families. In this connection the rapidly expanding public schools played an important role, for they provided a common education for sons of middle- and upper-class men, though it seems that the professionals were more attracted than provincial manufacturers. Of course, some of the vehicles for interaction between the two social levels were of quite long standing. For example, middle-class families employed in the public service in India had long enjoyed an aristocratic style of life, and found it comparatively easy to fraternize with those immediately above them. The women of the two classes enjoyed extensive opportunities for mingling by means of the huge network of charitable activities. Among middle-class girls it became increasingly common to ape their superiors by indulging in coming-out parties, presentations at court and marrying into gentry or titled families.

Class consciousness and the trade unions

Approximately eight out of ten Victorian people were working class in the sense that they had manual occupations. Marx and Engels confidently expected that, as Britain was the most developed industrial society, manual workers would increase as a proportion of the population, would become increasingly immiserated, and would thus become more class conscious. After winning the vote it seemed likely they would levy taxes on the rich as Victorian society was characterized by huge and growing inequalities of wealth and income; in 1867 the top 10 per cent of income-earners enjoyed 52 per cent of all income, while the bottom 40 per cent had only 15 per cent of income. Some feared that the agent of wealth taxation would be the trade union movement, whose membership had increased to 2 million by 1900 and to over 4 million by 1914. The incorporation of semi-skilled workers was gradually making it less exclusive and more Socialist. In spite of the economic depression, trade unions became involved in between 500 and 900 separate strikes every year during the 1890s, and anything from 3 million to 30 million working days were lost. Gradually the small workshops which inhibited the development of class consciousness were giving way to large-scale industrial organizations in which employer and employees found themselves separated into two conflicting camps.

Prosperity and respectability

However, these developments, though consistent with the predictions of Marx and Engels, fell well short of their expectations. Large sectors of the working class such as domestic servants remained impossible to organize, and many men continued to enjoy close relations with employers. As Britain's capitalist economy matured, it led to a growth of 'white-collar' employment in the service sector and to the relative decline of the proletariat. Far from being immiserated, from the mid-Victorian period onwards sections of the working class enjoyed greater prosperity, which in the short run accentuated the divisions within the working-class community. Rather than a simple consolidation around a common proletarian objective, there was something of a scramble for sectional advantage. Moreover, the changing occupational structure permitted a certain amount of mobility between working-class families and the social groups immediately above them. Traditionally many skilled artisans aspired to become small employers. However, by the later-nineteenth century this was becoming less feasible. Many men still pursued this objective by becoming shopkeepers, builders, plumbers, joiners or painters and decorators, though such enterprises frequently failed and the proprietors remained in the ranks of the working class. A much more important form of mobility lay in the expanding opportunities in such occupations as teaching or in banks and local government where clerks were required. Many of the recruits to such jobs were drawn from working-class families. The key lay in improved elementary education, which equipped the late-Victorian generation with the necessary grasp of English and mathematics for this employment. As in other social classes, women often played a key role in upward mobility. Their work as domestic servants, for example, made them more familiar than men with middle-class habits, and sometimes led them to aspire to a different style of life; men, largely because of their different experience of work, were more inclined to want to maintain class boundaries. Their experience and attitudes sometimes led mothers to encourage their sons to use education as a vehicle for upward mobility. But for many, marriage offered a direct route; in some areas it has been found that up to 30 per cent of the daughters of skilled workers married into the lower middle class, thereby blurring the lines of demarcation between them.

A labour aristocracy?

Even within the ranks of the working class there remained some major divisions. Contemporary investigators like Booth and Rowntree identified six subclasses within the urban community. But Victorian Marxists focused on one major division, that between the majority and what they called a 'labour aristocracy' at the top. This section composed around 10 per cent of the working class, largely the better-paid or skilled men. It was tempting to regard the labour aristocracy as an obstacle to the development of class consciousness, because its members aped the middle classes and tried to maintain differences between themselves and other manual workers. However, it is far from clear that the labour aristocracy really corresponded to the distinctions understood within the community at the time. The income earned by a single male head of household now seems a very inadequate criterion for assessing status within the working class. One problem is that a man's wages frequently fluctuated during the course of his working life according to age, fitness or changing skills. Consequently the labour aristocracy would not have represented a fixed body of men but a category whose composition changed over time. In the long term the migration of men into the higher and more regularly paid occupations steadily widened the section at the top of the scale. In any case the status of a working-class family depended upon a much wider range of factors. Even its income was frequently the joint result of the wages of wives and children, not just of husbands. Above all, the way in which the housewife spent the income would determine whether a family was seen as part of the respectable working class. The type of house one rented, the use made of the pawnbroker and credit, the regularity of school attendance by the children, drinking habits, the possession of suits of Sunday clothes – these were all criteria by which a family's status might be measured. An important sign of respectability was the adoption of self-help strategies such as friendly societies and the Co-operative stores; clearly this was by no means confined to a 10 per cent minority but, on the contrary, had become fairly typical by the end of the century.

Nor should respectability be interpreted as a sign that workers had become conservative, or unduly keen to emulate the habits of the middle classes. On the contrary, the better-off, literate and socially mobile workingmen often took the lead in organizing the workers and joining Socialist societies. In contrast, the depressed residuum were too ground down by the daily struggle for survival to find the confidence and optimism necessary to be able to challenge the political status quo. Thus, while the emerging movement of unions, the ILP and other societies was not the vanguard of a revolutionary proletariat, it undoubtedly represented a powerful sense of pride and independence within the working-class community. Conventional politicians appreciated that they were no longer threatened by the kind of class conflict characteristic of the 1830s and 1840s; rather, the workers posed a challenge broadly within the limits of the political and economic system. To that extent, the Victorians had achieved a relatively stable class society.

Further reading

On the making of national identity see:

Paul Ward, *Britishness since 1870* (2004)

Martin Pugh, *Britain: Unification and Disintegration* (2012)

R. Samuel ed., *Patriotism: the making and unmaking of British national identity* (1989)

Helen Brocklehurst and Robert Phillips eds, *History, Nationhood and the Question of Britain* (2004)

On Scottish nationalism and integration:

Tom Devine, *The Scottish Nation 1700–2000* (1999)

Tom Devine, *To the Ends of the Earth: Scotland's Global Diaspora 1750–2010* (2011)

Ewen Cameron, *Impaled Upon a Thistle: Scotland since 1880* (2010)

C. Harvie, *Scotland and Nationalism (Scottish Society and Politics 1707–1977)* (1977)

Michael Fry, *A New Race of Men: Scotland 1815–1914* (2013)

Allan Massie, *The Thistle and the Rose* (2005)

On Wales see:

K.O. Morgan, *Rebirth of a Nation: Wales 1880–1980* (1982)

K.O. Morgan, *Wales in British Politics 1868–1972* (1991)

D.W. Howell and C. Baber, 'Wales', in F.M.L. Thompson ed., *The Cambridge Social History of Britain 1750–1950*, vol. I (1990)

J. Davies, *A History of Wales* (1990)

The Irish Question and the impact of the Irish is discussed in:

Alan O'Day, *Irish Home Rule 1867–1921* (1998)

Lawrence J. McCaffrey, *The Irish Question* (1995)

G.R. Searle, *A New England? Peace and War 1886–1914* (2004)

R. Swift, *The Irish in Britain 1815–1914* (1990)

S. Fielding, *Class and Ethnicity: Irish Catholics in England 1880–1939* (1993)

On religion, immigration and the Jewish community see:

Hugh McLeod, *Religion and Society in England 1850–1914* (1996)

Robert Winder, *Bloody Foreigners: the story of immigration to Britain* (2004)

Colin Homes, *John Bull's Island: Immigration and British Society 1871–1971* (1988)

Anthony Julius, *Trials of the Diaspora: A History of Anti-Semitism in England* (2010)

G. Alderman, *Modern British Jewry* (1992)

T. Kushner ed., *The Jewish Heritage in British History: Englishness and Jewishness* (1992)

On the role of the monarchy:

William M. Khun, *Democratic Royalism: the Transformation of the British Monarchy 1861–1914* (1996)

Frank Prochaska, *Royal Bounty: the Making of a Welfare Monarchy* (1995)

David Cannadine, 'The British Monarchy 1820–1977', in E. Hobsbawm and T. Ranger eds, *The Invention of Tradition* (1983)

Andrzej Olechnowicz ed., *The Monarchy and the British Nation: 1780 to the Present* (2007)

Tom Nairn, *The Enchanted Glass: Britain and Its Monarchy* (2011)

A.W. Purdue and J. Golby, *The Monarchy and the British People* (1988)

Walter Arnstein, *Queen Victoria* (2003)

Aspects of social class are dealt with in:

Mike Savage and Andrew Miles, *The Remaking of the Working Class 1840–1940* (1994)

Alastair Reid, *Social Classes and Social Relations 1850–1914* (1992)

G. Stedman Jones, *Languages of Class* (1983)

G.E. Mingay, *The Gentry: Rise and Fall of a Ruling Class* (1976)

David Cannadine, *The Decline of the Aristocracy* (1991)

G. Crossick, *The Lower Middle-Class in Britain* (1977)

G. Anderson, *Victorian Clerks* (1976)

R. Gray, *The Aristocracy of Labour in Britain* (1981)

Brian Harrison, 'Traditions of Respectability in British Labour History', in *Peaceable Kingdom* (1982)

W.D. Rubinstein, *Men of Property* (1981)

6

Isolation and Expansion

In common with other nationalities, the British drew much of their sense of unity from essentially negative and external factors – a mixture of superiority over foreigners and fear about the threat they posed. In the three decades after 1870 the latter emotion began to predominate in Britain, though xenophobia did not reach its peak until the Edwardian years as fears about foreign spies and a German invasion reached their height.

The defence of the realm

In spite of her resources, Britain remained essentially a peripheral power in European terms for most of the nineteenth century because she lacked a substantial regular army, and her governments, regardless of political complexion, showed themselves reluctant to increase expenditure. In the 1870s the British had 0.25 million soldiers compared to 3.5 million in France and Germany and 4 million in Russia. This was not an indication that the British were a particularly peaceable people; rather, they continued to channel their aggression and expansion into colonial skirmishes, where the costs were usually modest. Instead, Britain concentrated on maintaining a superior navy. Its purpose was to protect the British Isles from invasion, to maintain imports of food, to pressurize backward states to engage in trade, to transport soldiers to the colonies in an emergency, and to blockade the enemy's ports during a major war.

Splendid isolation

Victorians often boasted that the essential British policy was one of isolation, dignified as 'splendid isolation'. Of course, in the ordinary sense of the word Britain was the least isolated country in the world, for her myriad commercial interests involved her in the politics of innumerable other states. But Britain could claim to be isolated in a special sense: she avoided binding treaty obligations to give military support to the other European powers. Her geographical position made this a relatively easy option but it required the maintenance of the two-power standard for the Royal Navy. With control of the Channel and the North Sea, Britain had little to fear from the Continent and little reason to become entangled in standing alliances. Both Liberals and Conservatives favoured the so-called 'Blue Water' school of national defence, in the belief that it was cheaper and less provocative than the alternatives. This was underpinned by a good deal of expert writing in the late-Victorian period which held that the key to victory lay in command of the sea attained by decisive battles between big capital ships.

However, Britain's relations with the European powers were more complicated than these principles suggest. For one thing, Britain did undertake certain obligations to foreign states. For example, a series of treaties with Portugal went back several hundred years, but were useful only as a pretext for warning other powers away from territory in Africa claimed by the Portuguese. Britain had also given a guarantee of the territorial integrity of Belgium going back to 1839 and reaffirmed in 1870. This reflected a material British interest in preventing the occupation of the Low Countries by a major military power. But Britain was not the sole guarantor and could, if she wished, decline to act except in conjunction with others. In addition, Britain acquired a formal involvement with Turkey in the form of the Cyprus Convention of 1878, which bound her to maintain Turkey's Asiatic territory but did not involve any obligation to fight a European war in her support. In any case this was rejected by Gladstone and the Liberals which underlined a widely held view that Britain's parliamentary system rendered participation in standing alliances impossible; commitments entered into by one government could be repudiated by its successor. In fact this was an exaggerated view. As in most countries, foreign policy reflected a good deal of continuity regardless of changes of regime. All of these commitments were held rather lightly by British governments. 'Our treaty obligations', as Salisbury put it, 'will follow our national inclinations and will not precede them.'

The rise of Continental threats

British isolationism was also complicated after the 1870s by the acceleration of colonial expansion which brought Britain increasingly into dispute, and sometimes collaboration, with other European states, thereby exposing the limitations of her diplomatic position. Eventually this led to a formal breakdown of isolation. The other disruptive factor was the Franco-Prussian War, which made the British much more concerned about the security of the British Isles. Since 1815 the absorption of the European powers in their internal problems and the isolationism of the USA had left Britain remarkably free to pursue her own interests. But after 1870 this situation changed fundamentally. The triumph of the Prussian armies in three successive wars marked the emergence of the kind of Continental power not seen since Napoleonic times. It was not just the size of the new European armies but their capacity to mobilize quickly that alarmed the British. Although the sea made a direct threat unlikely, the build-up of the French and Russian navies and the introduction of ships built of steel and powered by steam undermined confidence in naval protection. Though still the largest single navy, the Royal Navy suffered from poor gunnery, training and tactics, and it was lucky not to have been challenged by a serious rival in this period. Moreover, Britain's growing dependence upon imported food rendered her highly vulnerable to enemy fleets.

For much of the century the underlying weakness of Britain's position had been obscured by the absence of opponents in Europe, the pre-eminence of the navy, and the patriotic bombast associated with Lord Palmerston. But when a serious challenge arose, as with Russia in the Crimean War in the 1850s, Britain managed to deal with it only by means of an ad hoc alliance with other powers; victory in the Crimea brought dubious and temporary gains, and it would have been impossible without French troops, which made up the majority of the allied forces. Even this expedient could be adopted only exceptionally. During the 1860s, for example, when the Prussians engaged in three Continental wars Britain stood on the sidelines. She strongly disapproved when Bismarck grabbed the duchies of Schleswig and Holstein in 1864–5, but in the absence of an ally even Palmerston had to swallow his pride. A similar but more serious dilemma arose over Prussia's defeat of France and the annexation of Alsace-Lorraine by the new German Empire in 1871. Gladstone was appalled by this, but since Austria and Russia were both unable or unwilling to co-operate, intervention was out of the question.

Moreover, foreign policy now began to damage Gladstone domestically, because the Russians took advantage of the crisis caused by the Franco-Prussian War to renounce the Black Sea Clauses which had been part of the settlement at the end of the Crimean War. These forbade Russia to keep warships in the Black Sea. This area was of strategic importance to Britain because the Black Sea offered Russia a warm-water route via the Bosphorus and the Dardanelles into the eastern Mediterranean, through which much of Britain's trade with India and the Far East passed. Although the government managed to convene a conference in London in 1871, it failed to win the backing of France or Germany; as a result, Gladstone was blamed for allowing the Russians to reverse the verdict of the Crimean War, although the only alternative would have been a declaration of war by Britain alone, a foolish and impractical step.

Should Britain fight for Turkey?

During the 1870s the Eastern Question became important in polarizing opinion between the two political parties. As premier after 1874, Disraeli quickly grasped the opportunity to play the patriotic card as Palmerston had traditionally done. The chance arose when Russia went to war with Turkey in 1877, following the massacres of Christian Slavs in the Balkans. Since the Turkish Empire straddled the European and Asiatic shores of the Bosphorus, it provided a convenient buffer to Russian expansion. Disraeli was not alone in believing that the Russians exploited Slav nationalism in order to undermine Turkey and justify intervention against her. However, his concern led Disraeli dangerously close to war with Russia, much to the dismay of his own colleagues; his Foreign Secretary, Lord Derby, actually resigned. What saved Disraeli was the unease of the other powers about Russia's territorial aggrandizement; as a result they convened the Congress of Berlin in 1878, which modified Russia's gains and left Britain in possession of the island of Cyprus.

But this triumph for Disraelian diplomacy proved to be an empty one. Cyprus, which lacked an adequate harbour, was of little use in protecting British trade routes. And the establishment of Bulgaria, in whatever form, marked another step in the disintegration of Turkey. Although Gladstone's opposition was expressed in moral-humanitarian terms, it was also much more *realistic* than Disraeli's policy. It may have been wrong to prop up Turkey, but it was also futile; in the long run the creation of nation states in the Balkans offered a better prospect of checking Russia's advance. Moreover, it was Gladstone who subsequently did most to secure Britain's strategic interests in the Mediterranean by the occupation of Egypt in 1882, which enabled her to control the Suez Canal. In fact, by the 1890s the Conservative leader, Salisbury, came to the conclusion that Gladstone had been right and that Britain had backed the wrong horse in Turkey.

The burdens of empire

The Egyptian question proved to be only one of a series of military and colonial worries during the 1880s. By 1882 there was alarm over reports that the French were digging a tunnel under the English Channel. This gave way to better-founded evidence of a major French naval building programme. Gladstone felt obliged to devote an extra £5.5 million to the navy. But this went against the grain for both parties, who believed that Britain was already reaching the limits of her resources, so that further state spending would damage her capacity to create new wealth. In the event, Britain did fail to maintain her position: whereas in 1883 she had 38 capital ships to 40 for France, Russia, Germany, Italy, the USA and Japan combined, by 1897 the ratio was 62 to 96.

In the absence of adequate physical force, the British government's preferred alternative was negotiation, but this was only likely to be effective in concert with another power. In fact, the annexation of Egypt had been planned as a joint intervention with France, who had dropped out at the last minute, leaving Britain exposed to charges of imperialism. It was more usual in the 1880s for Britain to seek co-operation with Austria, Italy and Germany, simply because they had less reason than France or Russia to dispute her colonial interests. However, by the 1890s Bismarck, who had often worked with Britain, was no longer in power; and the strain of perennial colonial disputes began to tell. In this decade Britain experienced problems with Russia on the northern frontiers of India, opposition from France and Russia to expansion in Nigeria, hostile collaboration by France, Russia and Germany in China, where Britain had a valuable trade at risk, as well as a verbal clash with the American President over British Guiana. The year 1896 brought the notorious Jameson Raid in the Transvaal, which was condemned by the German Kaiser; 1898 saw France and Britain close to blows at Fashoda near the headwaters of the River Nile; and after 1899 the outbreak of war in South Africa drew hostile reactions to Britain from all the Great Powers. Britain, in Joseph Chamberlain's words, was like 'a weary Titan staggering under the too-vast orb of his own great weight'.

Co-operation with Germany?

In these circumstances Britain's diplomatic isolation looked increasingly like weakness; she had neither the military nor the naval strength to defend her far-flung interests. She had remained aloof from Europe at a time when the other powers had gradually committed themselves to two alliance systems: the Dual Alliance of France and Russia against the Triple Alliance of Germany, Austria and Italy. Now, neither of these had been formulated with Britain in mind; they reflected Franco-German enmity over Alsace-Lorraine and Austro-Russian antagonism over Balkan nationalism. Yet in practice the alliance system operated to Britain's disadvantage for whenever a new problem arose Britain had no regular ally to back her up, and she could not afford to use physical force to defend all her interests.

As a result, the feeling grew among statesmen like Joseph Chamberlain that Britain ought to seek an ally. The crisis in the Far East during 1897–8, when China became the victim of pressure, especially from Russia, brought matters to a head. On balance Germany appeared to be the best prospect; partly because Britain had co-operated with her in the past, and because she could bring pressure to bear on Britain's most acute problem: Russia. While Britain alone lacked the strength to warn Russia off when she tried to expand in the Far East, the combined influence of Britain and Germany would be a more serious deterrent. But the drawback for Germany was obvious. By antagonizing the Russians she would encourage the French to invoke their alliance and force Germany at some stage into a war in the east and the west simultaneously. Could Britain offer Germany anything to make the risk worthwhile? France remained Germany's most immediate concern. Britain's navy, her proximity to French coasts, and her ability to threaten French colonies would amount to a powerful deterrent if she allied with Germany. Yet the government hesitated. Though an irritation in the colonial sphere, France was not a problem in the European context. Increasingly, Germany seemed to be the dominant Continental force. The British instinct had always been to promote coalitions against the biggest Continental power; an alliance with Germany entailed a risk of encouraging a future German government to provoke the French into another war and an inevitable defeat, which would further exacerbate the imbalance of forces.

Consequently by 1901 the prospects for an Anglo-German alliance had broken down. The failure was rendered more decisive because negotiations had coincided with the new German naval laws of 1898 and 1900, by which Germany announced her intention of building a navy capable of challenging Britain in the North Sea. But the problem that had stimulated ideas for a deal with Germany remained. Her failure made Britain all the quicker to acquire an alternative Far Eastern ally: Japan. The treaty signed in 1902 bound each country to remain neutral if the other were at war with a single power, but to give active support if the other were engaged with two opponents. Strictly speaking this treaty was designed to meet a local problem, and its immediate effect was to allow Britain to withdraw some of her ships from the Far East. But the firm pledge did represent a break with the tradition of diplomatic isolation. Moreover, the alliance proved to have profound effects upon the European situation in the years before 1914 as the Japanese intended to fight Russia.

The new imperialism

By the 1860s Britain's imperial possessions comprised three distinct elements: the white dominions, the huge Indian Empire, and a scattering of protectorates and colonies in Africa, the Far East, the Pacific and South America. Though already large, this Empire was to grow at a remarkable rate in the 1880s and 1890s. It is not altogether clear why, because Britain never had a long-term plan of expansion. To complicate matters, there is even evidence of anti-imperial sentiment among politicians in the mid-Victorian period. Governments of all shades shared the irritation voiced by Disraeli when he referred to colonies as 'millstones around our neck'. All too often, British settlers got into difficulties with native peoples or other Europeans and had to be bailed out at great cost by the home government. But few went as far as free-trade radicals like Richard Cobden, who argued that the only useful part of empire was trade, and that formal political-military control was an unnecessary cost.

In practice British imperial policy, if it can be so described, lurched between neglect and recklessness. As long as they could get away with it, governments avoided imposing formal control, but where British commercial interests were threatened they invariably stepped in, however reluctantly. Very often the Westminster government found itself unable to control events; rather, it was led by the men on the spot. In India a succession of Governor-Generals had ignored instructions and grabbed new territories, though by the 1870s the improvement in communications with London and the tendency to make party-political appointments reduced the scope for freelance imperialism. Even the supposedly anti-imperial mid-Victorian era witnessed considerable expansion – Sind and the Punjab in the 1840s, Oudh, Burma and Hong Kong in the 1850s. This pattern of expansion clearly reflected local pressures and strategic objectives; a new acquisition could invariably be justified as a source of revenue, as a buffer to protect an existing territory or as a key point on a trade route although these claims were usually exaggerations or misrepresentations.

Imperial aggrandizement in Afghanistan and South Africa

During the late 1860s party politics increasingly entered into imperial questions because the Conservatives attacked Gladstone for seeking to dismember the Empire but despite such charges, colonial policy continued to be largely a bipartisan affair. There was, however, some basis for controversy.

After 1868 Gladstone's ministers attempted to make economies, partly by withdrawing some of the troops scattered around the world. In particular, by pulling them out of New Zealand in 1869 they intended to serve notice on the settlers to cease provoking the Maoris by encroaching on their land. When in office the Conservatives supported this policy. In the long term Gladstone envisaged that the Empire would evolve into something like the institution that in the twentieth century was called the British Commonwealth, but he had no intention of dismembering the empire as the Conservatives claimed. By 1870 it was already accepted that the provinces of Canada and Australia were entitled to internal self-government, preferably under a strong federal system. The example of the American colonies served as a warning against attempting to retain British control for too long.

However, some Liberals looked further than the white dominions to India. Although obviously autocratic and alien, British rule in India was not an unmixed autocracy. The British people there took it upon themselves to criticize official policy in quite extreme terms in the 1880s, thus offering Indians an excellent example of British politics at work. Moreover, for much of the nineteenth century Indians also enjoyed rights like freedom of the press which in Europe were seen as a key aspect of a liberal system. By establishing an English educational system, Britain had helped to produce a generation of Indians well-versed in the political principles of Western liberalism who were anxious to obtain for India the benefits of British parliamentary government. Indian independence was not on the agenda; but a Liberal Viceroy like Lord Ripon (1880–4) accepted that it was both right and necessary to give educated Indians greater participation in their government. The formation of the Indian National Congress in 1885 was an indication that Indians appreciated that concessions could be won from the politicians in London, who often showed more sympathy than the British residents in India.

After 1874 Disraeli's ministry seemed to mark a reversion to a forward policy in imperial affairs which culminated in wars in South Africa and Afghanistan. In 1878–9 Lord Lytton, the Indian Viceroy, embarked on Britain's second invasion of Afghanistan. As with every invasion it proved easy to send a Western army to Kabul and to replace the Amir with a pro-British ruler, but after that the enterprise collapsed as the country could not be controlled and the British withdrew. In his Midlothian campaigns, Gladstone condemned the Afghan war as reckless aggrandizement which cost money and achieved no good. 'Remember this', he told one audience, 'that the lives of those poor savages, as we may call them, in their humble homes amid the winter snow, are as precious in the eyes of Almighty God as are your own'. This attitude was not mere sentimentality, but was consistent with British interests. Since a Russian invasion of Afghanistan was scarcely practical at this time, there was no point in Britain going forward to meet her in central Asia; Afghanistan was best left as a natural buffer zone.

However, despite the controversy the difference between the policies of the parties was somewhat exaggerated as the wars were driven by local representatives rather than the home government. In South Africa the conflict with the Zulus was a typical product of the pressure exerted by the white settlers for land, and the initiative came from the High Commissioner, Sir Bartle Frere, acting contrary to his instructions from London. In India Disraeli had deliberately appointed the reactionary Lord Lytton as a party-political Viceroy, and Lytton adopted policies, such as arbitrary control over the Indian press, which were subsequently reversed by the Liberals. But Lytton exceeded his brief in plunging into an invasion of Afghanistan; Disraeli and Salisbury wanted more influence over Afghan foreign policy with a view to excluding Russian influence, but a reckless war was another thing.

Qualifications must also be made about other forward moves under Disraeli, including the establishment of protectorates over the Gold Coast, the Malay States and Fiji. He in fact took no interest in these, leaving matters to his Colonial Secretary. Moreover, in the Gold Coast and the Malay States the policy was simply a continuation of initiatives begun under Gladstone. It is true that after his return to office in 1880 Gladstone checked Tory policies in South Africa and India. But he soon felt obliged to intervene militarily to safeguard British interests in Egypt. As so often, he found himself subsequently caught up in the strategic-political consequences. Egypt's own security was considered to depend upon control of the River Nile, which stretched all the way to Sudan and East Africa. By 1885, when these areas were experiencing Muslim nationalist rebellions, Gladstone lost patience and ordered a withdrawal from the Sudan. In a classic case of imperial insubordination, General Charles Gordon refused to carry out his instructions by pulling out and soon found himself besieged and then massacred by the rebels at Khartoum. As usual, the home government felt obliged to send another force to rescue their representative; it simply arrived too late.

Was there a 'new imperialism'?

The Egyptian invasion of 1882 was widely held to have inaugurated a new phase of imperialism which *The Times* memorably described as the 'Scramble for Africa'. At first sight, all that was novel about the expansionism was the involvement of new imperial powers (Germany and Italy), the concentration on Africa, and the remarkable speed at which territory was acquired. Britain herself absorbed Egypt in 1882, Somaliland, Bechuanaland and Nigeria in 1884–5, the Rhodesias in 1889, Kenya, Zanzibar, Uganda and Nyasaland in 1890, and the Transvaal and Orange Free State after the war of 1899–1902. Whether this frenetic activity really amounted to a new policy on Britain's part is, however, not obvious. Expansion traditionally reflected economic motivation; the search for cheap raw materials and markets for British goods formed a thread running through all her colonial ventures. It can, however, be argued that after the 1870s the consciousness of the loss of markets, the reintroduction of tariffs, and the lack of employment at home underlined the urgency of finding fresh economic opportunities, and thus accelerated the process of colonization.

However, much depends upon who was actually responsible for imperial expansion: private entrepreneurs or governments. Several leading politicians did identify an economic rationale behind empire. Lord Rosebery supported British expansion in Uganda in the 1890s, and claimed that Britain was engaged in 'pegging out claims for the future'. Joseph Chamberlain also showed himself aware of the material gains; for example, he saw British control of South Africa in terms of the region's mineral wealth and the opportunities for emigration by British workers. These politicians shared a broader vision of 'imperial federation' which implied drawing the British possessions together into a single economic community protected by tariffs, so as to give Britain a large and secure 'domestic' market for her products, and developing a common defence policy for the empire. The successful developments of great continental-scale economies in the USA and Germany seemed to suggest that large units held the key to future prosperity. On the other hand, it is significant that nothing substantial came of the idea of imperial federation; it remained a minority cult in Britain and aroused little support even in the white colonies.

In 1902 J.A. Hobson, a left-wing critic, argued in *Imperialism: A Study,* that colonial expansion was driven by an urgent need to find outlets for the surplus capital generated by European industry. Recently the idea of empire as the work of a keen, dynamic, economically driven British imperialism has been resurrected by a right-wing historian, Nial Ferguson, in *Empire* (2003). Yet Ferguson's approach seems rather old-fashioned and certainly does not reflect the research of specialist imperial historians who have increasingly questioned the material value of empire and its impact especially in the newly-acquired African territories. Moreover, the statesmen who usually determined British policy – Salisbury and Gladstone – did not think primarily in terms of economics. Britain notoriously failed to use her network of diplomats abroad to promote British commercial interests. Where Britain did enjoy a large trade, as in China, the instinct of governments was to try to preserve free trade, not to impose formal control. In Africa, Salisbury and Gladstone cheerfully ceded huge territories to the other European powers, which suggests that they often had considerations other than economic ones in mind. There was, of course, good ground for scepticism about the contemporary claims made about the material value and opportunities of the new territory. In Africa only the Royal Niger Company, dealing in the cocoa and palm oil of the western states, proved to be really profitable. The British East Africa Company never paid a dividend to its shareholders, and, in spite of the fanfare attending its launch, Cecil Rhodes's South Africa Company only occasionally paid one. Contrary to Hobson's claims two-thirds of British investment went either to old-established colonies or to countries outside the Empire altogether, notably the USA and Argentina. Beyond the Gold Coast and Nigeria the African territories attracted little attention from cautious British investors. Vast areas like the Sudan, Kenya, Bechuanaland and the Rhodesias were thinly populated and often semi-desert, lacking the communications necessary to exploit whatever resources they might have had. They were consequently unattractive to Western capitalism.

Whatever the reason, British ministers remained doubtful about the value of new territory. For example, Salisbury attracted criticism from patriotic Conservatives when he allowed the tract of territory between Lakes Victoria and Nyasa to become German East Africa. Enthusiastic imperialists noted that its incorporation into British territory would have given Britain a continuous empire stretching from Cairo to the Cape. But Salisbury was not impressed: the land at issue had little intrinsic worth. Clearly the Prime Minister thought in different terms when partitioning the African continent. Sometimes, as in Egypt, strategic motives came to the fore. But increasingly in the 1880s and 1890s Salisbury simply regarded colonies as useful weapons in the more important game of European diplomacy. It was, for example, desirable for Britain to retain the goodwill of Bismarck, and if this meant helping Germany acquire an African empire, so be it. To some extent all the Great Powers used the partition of Africa as a safety valve to reduce tensions in Europe. The disputes that arose over colonies were bearable if they helped avert a really serious conflict in Europe.

Was the Empire popular?

If there was anything new about empire in this period it may have been its impact on the public. During the later 1880s and the 1890s, the pace of expansion was so rapid and the eruption of imperial issues so frequent that it seemed as though the Empire had come to occupy a much more central part in British life than hitherto. Controversy subsided for a time, as both parties accepted that expansion was a desirable thing. Liberals like Rosebery and Liberal Unionists like Chamberlain found common ground with Conservatives, while propagandists like Rudyard Kipling articulated the moral justification for empire in terms of extending the benefits of Western rule to backward peoples in his poem, *The White Man's Burden*. Yet it is less clear how far these sentiments spread beyond the political elite. How popular was the Empire in British society?

There is no easy way to measure popular imperialism. A wide variety of evidence can be adduced to suggest a considerable and growing enthusiasm for almost anything connected with empire. Since the 1850s the popular imagination had been stirred by the heroic explorations of David Livingstone, H.M. Stanley and Richard Burton. In their wake came narratives of adventurers in exotic locations, ranging from fiction like Rider Haggard's *King Solomon's Mines* to first-hand reports such as Winston Churchill's *The Malakand Field Force* and *The River War*. Schoolchildren learned a patriotic version of history and geography based on British achievements; and the success of the *Boy's Own Paper* (1879), which attracted sales of a million copies, underlined the growing market for patriotic adventure. From 1896 onwards the new *Daily Mail* tapped similar sentiments among adults. This period also saw a number of very popular Imperial Exhibitions and a great expansion of music-hall, in which patriotic-imperial songs formed a staple element. In addition, the development of advertising by the suppliers of cheap consumables often served to emphasize the close connection between better living standards and supplies of empire products.

A key element in all this was the improvement in technological methods of representing the Empire in tangible and visual forms to millions of people. In addition to the press, books and entertainment, the magic lantern was employed by large organizations like the Primrose League to portray the cause of empire in crude but colourful images. Among the examination questions set for juvenile members of the Primrose League were: 'What would be the advantages of European supremacy in China?' and 'Give a short sketch of the war in South Africa, its cause and progress. What good is expected to result from it?' Clearly, many late-Victorian children grew up in a climate of opinion that was unambiguously imperial.

Imperial myths and the Boer War

However, there are good reasons for doubting how much these manifestations tell us about the popularity of imperialism. Some can be seen as propaganda by commercial interests or by middle- and upper-class leaders, rather than as genuine reflections of the attitudes of ordinary people. It has been argued that the higher social classes were consistently more enthusiastic about empire than the working classes. Also, many of the expressions of imperialism were so vague and generalized that it is difficult to know what they meant; on occasions of national triumph or disaster in the colonies popular sentiment merged into patriotism, xenophobia, racism and monarchism which makes it difficult to define as strictly imperialist.

Another complication is that imperialist fervour was apt to fluctuate sharply over time as is suggested by the South African War (1899–1902), better known as the Boer War. Its origins lay in the struggle between the British colonies in Natal and Cape Colony and the Dutch settlements in Transvaal and the Orange Free State. The discovery of diamonds at Kimberley in 1868 and gold in the Transvaal in 1886 attracted settlers and major financial interests as well as ruthless apostles of expansion including Cecil Rhodes, who founded the British South Africa Company, and Lord Milner, Britain's High Commissioner, who aimed to incorporate the Boers into a British South African Federation. Although there was no excuse for a war, Milner pressurized the Boers into one, backed by the London government who mistakenly believed Britain would enjoy an easy victory. For a year or so the war engendered widespread support enabling Salisbury to win a general election in 1900. However, this reflected the mood of national crisis as British troops were defeated and British communities besieged at Kimberley, Ladysmith and Mafeking. As the war dragged on and the sense of crisis passed, a reaction set in. Britain's use of concentration camps for the civilian population attracted criticism including that from the Liberal leader, Campbell-Bannerman who condemned the 'methods of barbarism'. By 1902 it had become clear that a costly war had left a damning legacy of high taxation and inflation while none of the promised gains had materialized. In fact, the defeated Boers were as strongly entrenched in South Africa as ever. The extravagant claims made by Milner and Joseph Chamberlain about employment for British workers in the mines of South Africa were hopelessly discredited when Milner imported Chinese indentured labourers instead. As a result the enthusiasm collapsed, and popular backing for empire never really recovered from the setback.

Emigration

On the other hand, there was more to empire than Africa and the imperial message penetrated deeply into all levels of British society in other ways than conquest. The late-Victorian generation enjoyed a tangible link with

Table 6.1 Emigration, 1870–1919

Year	Number of people emigrating from Britain
1870–79	2,149,000
1880–89	3,570,000
1890–99	2,680,000
1900–09	4,404,000
1910–19	3,526,000

empire that was probably of greater significance than the mere propaganda. Between 1870 and 1914 approximately 10 million people emigrated from the British Isles. Many of these were Irish and Englishmen on their way to the USA, but many workingmen looked to Canada, Australia and New Zealand for better economic opportunities than those enjoyed at home. Amongst groups like agricultural labourers and dock workers, where surplus labour kept wages low, emigration seemed so desirable that some trade unions promoted emigration schemes in order to strengthen the bargaining power of those who remained at home. In addition there were extensive programmes by charitable bodies like Dr Barnardo's to send children from poor families to Canada. Also some Victorian feminists were keen to promote female emigration because of inadequate employment opportunities at home, while anti-feminists urged the same policy in order to redress the sexual balance of the population.

Empire as safety valve

For workingmen emigration constituted an important safety valve for domestic unemployment and discontent, for Britain's economy was patently unable to generate enough jobs to absorb its growing labour force. Consequently, the Labour Movement thought of empire in terms of the colonies of white settlement, Canada, Australia and New Zealand, rather than Africa or India. The traffic in people also had political implications. In rural districts, for example, those who left home were invariably the more discontented, able and ambitious, but their departure deprived such areas of their natural leadership, and deepened the passivity which so frustrated the radical politicians. One of the ironies of emigration was the role of Scottish crofters and others driven out by pressure and poverty. Though highly critical of the British establishment in the home context, in Canada the Scots came to occupy a central place in government, and emerged as a highly loyalist, pro-British element against the pressures exerted by both French and Americans.

The most obvious effect of extensive emigration was to leave most British families with close relatives working in the Empire, while others were involved in its defence through the army or the navy. This made for pride and a sense of common interest which was demonstrated by the response of the volunteers to crises in 1899 and 1914. But empire was not all adventure and war. A multitude of other interests linked the home population with those overseas. For some the colonies offered a field for moral endeavour, notably in missionary work. Another interest lay in gathering the horticultural riches of the tropics, the rhododendrons of South Asia, the buddleias of China and the eucalyptus of Australia, to mention but a few that graced English gardens. Another characteristically British interest was sexual opportunity, which the tropics offered in abundant variety. To a large extent, indeed, the British Empire can be seen as the work of homosexuals, active and passive, who found life more congenial there than at home, particularly after the tightening up of the law in 1886.

Sport, social class and empire

But perhaps the most characteristic form of interaction lay in sport. The advantages of organized sport – fitness, discipline, teamwork and loyalty – were regarded as vital in the imperial context and as expressions of the classic British qualities. Rugby, cricket and athletics served to foster local pride, but also underlined links with the mother country. Australians, for example, derived pleasure from taking on upper-class English cricket teams, but the development of institutions like the Ashes in the 1880s symbolized the mixture of competition and friendliness. White settlers often wished to foster and celebrate their British cultural roots, and this became especially important in regions where a non-British element existed, such as the French in Canada or the Dutch in South Africa. Cricket also offered a bridge between the British and native peoples in the West Indies and India. Prince Ranjitsinhji actually played in the English Test team and captained Surrey. 'The Game of Cricket', declared Lord Harris in 1880, 'has done more to draw the mother country and the colonies together than years of beneficial legislation could have done'. In post-Mutiny India, where the British were anxious to cement the loyalty of the princes to the Raj, the involvement of the males of the two races was regarded as serving an important political purpose.

Many of those involved in the higher levels of imperial affairs obviously did not emigrate but became semi-permanent residents of the colonies, often moving from one to another as administrators, policemen, lawyers and merchants. As such groups were closer to the politics of empire, they expressed their imperialism in terms of public policy and principle. But it would be misleading to think that they did not share with the lower classes a material and self-interested approach to empire. Indeed, without the opportunities it offered there would have been an employment crisis for middle-class families at home. The leading public schools sent a high proportion of their boys to the Indian civil service or the colonial service, which provided prestigious and well-paid work. Once abroad, many men who came from relatively modest middle-class backgrounds discovered that one could live a charmed existence equivalent to that of the aristocracy in Britain. In the twentieth century the colonies were, in fact, increasingly to serve as a dignified dumping-ground for distressed landed figures, as well as for politicians to whom the government owed a debt or whom it wished to remove from the domestic scene.

British militarism

During the nineteenth century the British regarded themselves as a patriotic but not an aggressive nation. Although foreigners, noting the remarkable expansion of the Empire and the use of force it entailed, felt understandably unconvinced, this self-image was not without foundation. What contemporaries really meant was that Britain, in contrast to other European powers, was not *militarist*. Gladstone's attacks on Disraeli reflected the view that a reckless use of force to win territory was alien to British traditions. Not only did Britain's army remain comparatively small, but she showed very little enthusiasm for it. Below officer rank army life was barbarous, the men being confined to dismal barracks and becoming vulnerable to all kinds of immorality. They invariably joined up out of desperation or to escape something in their civilian life.

In reality dislike for the army as an institution did not indicate that the British were a pacific people; their militarism simply took different forms. For example, as a result of the military problems of the 1850s – the Indian Mutiny, the Crimean War and the fear of an attack by Napoleon III – the authorities cast around for ways of improving Britain's capacity for home defence that would not lead to great expenditure or a large standing army. In 1859 an expedient was found in the Volunteer Movement. This involved part-time training for voluntary rifle corps. Volunteering brought with it some pride and satisfaction in defending one's country, an attractive uniform, and the social prestige conferred by the patronage of the Lords-Lieutenant without the drawbacks of the regular army. Between the 1860s and the 1880s recruitment fluctuated between 224,000 and 288,000. Initially, middle-class and lower-middle-class men came forward, but by 1900 70 per cent were workingmen, mainly artisans. These 'Saturday soldiers' gradually helped to change attitudes towards the army in general in the late-Victorian and Edwardian period. Their influence spread to youth organizations such as the cadet corps of the public schools, which were attached to Volunteer Units. Members of the Volunteers also founded the Boys' Brigade in 1883 and the Church Lads' Brigade in 1891.

After 1870 the renewed sense of an external threat also began to make an impact as the relatively relaxed British patriotism gave way to a more shrill and aggressive nationalism. The shock of Prussia's swift defeat of the French triggered the publication of a famous fictional account of the 'Battle of Dorking', based on the idea of an enemy landing on the south coast which caught the British unprepared and led to an advance on London. The Battle of Dorking was to be fought many times on paper and on the platform in the years before 1914; it served to keep the subject of national defence high up the agenda, and prepared several generations of British people for the need to defend the country against a surprise invasion. What also changed gradually during this period was the perceived source of the external threat. Traditionally it was almost taken for granted that the enemy would be the French or the Russians who posed a threat to overseas territories; but this made less sense in the European context.

Attitudes to Germany

For some years British attitudes towards Germany had been relatively favourable. The two countries largely operated in different spheres; moreover, British statesmen regarded it as perfectly proper for so civilized a state as Germany to assume a number of colonial responsibilities. The two countries were seen to share a common culture and religion, and to have connections through the royal family. There was much admiration in Britain for German achievements in philosophy, music, science and education. Many German Liberals saw the British parliamentary system as a model. Unfortunately Bismarck did not, and the steady decline of the Liberal forces in Germany was one sign that the sympathies between the two countries were ebbing. Relations deteriorated because of claims that the Germans were dumping goods at below-cost prices in the British market. However, the significance of economic rivalry should not be exaggerated; commercial relations between the two countries were highly profitable for Britain, and Germany was only one of a number of industrial competitors. By the 1890s Germany was still a lesser irritation than France or Russia, though incidents like the

Kaiser's telegram of support to President Kruger of the Transvaal over the Jameson Raid in 1896 severely damaged relations. However, around the turn of the century things deteriorated further with the realization that, for the first time, Germany was building a fleet capable of threatening Britain in the North Sea. The combination of the German army and a first-class navy represented a nightmare, and Germany's transformation into Britain's national enemy was rapidly accomplished in the Edwardian period.

Invasion fears

Meanwhile, the Boer War had the effect of exposing Britain's lack of friends in Europe and her military vulnerability; if another challenge had occurred during the South African conflict it would have been extremely difficult to meet. Thus, in spite of the disputes over the origins of the war and the methods adopted by Lord Kitchener to overcome the Boers, there was widespread agreement that it had exposed alarming deficiencies in Britain's military, political and social systems. This provided the stimulus to the movement for National Efficiency and, after 1903, to Chamberlain's tariff-reform campaign. The reformers attacked British party politics as incompetent in the planning and management of war. One modest innovation was the establishment of the Committee of Imperial Defence, which was designed to bring more expertise and less politics to bear upon strategic problems. Critics also looked for more professionalism in the army; the Officers' Training Corps (1902) and the General Staff (1904) were steps in this direction. More generally, they looked to more extensive forms of military training, higher educational standards and improvements in the physical condition of children; hence the support for compulsory training of midwives, the provision of school meals, and the medical inspection of schoolchildren, much of which was recommended by the Inter-Departmental Committee on Physical Deterioration which reported in 1904.

Although National Efficiency as a movement was soon overtaken by normal party warfare, both the ideas and the general sense of external threat remained; they left a legacy in the form of several right-wing pressure groups whose object was to pressurize the government and to arouse popular support for a more robust national defence. One of these, the Navy League, had been in existence since 1895, but it had greater success after 1900 in pushing the government into extra naval rebuilding programmes. The most interesting yardstick of public concern over an invasion was the National Service League (NSL), formed in 1901 to campaign for universal male conscription. Although it became a substantial body in British terms, the

NSL was never comparable in size or influence to similar organizations in Germany at this time. In spite of the Boer War, or perhaps because of it, the NSL had only 4,000 members by 1906: it took the prestige of Britain's foremost military hero, Lord Roberts of Kandahar, who became its President, to push up membership to 98,000 by 1912, though the mounting fear of invasion must have helped a good deal. However, the NSL failed to convince the political parties of the need for peacetime conscription. Even the Conservative leaders thought this a bridge too far. It was widely believed that workingmen would simply not accept compulsory training, and the distaste for the Prussian approach to national defence was clearly deep-rooted. The British took pride in their own distinctive militarism, based on the voluntary system of recruitment. The huge popular response in 1914–15 proved the wisdom of this policy, and underlined the extent of patriotic sentiment.

* * * *

During 1870 to 1902 Britain began to take the measure of various challenges to Victorian thinking and conventional practice, raising in the process issues that were to dominate the new century. Aware of the challenge posed by powers such as the United States and Germany, with larger populations and greater resources, she also recognized the difficulty of maintaining her superpower status with a poorly-educated and unhealthy population; hence the growing feeling that huge inequalities of wealth and income were dysfunctional and that the state could not afford to stand aside in the hope that the market would resolve any weaknesses. These questions were promoted by relatively novel movements including feminism, Socialism, trade unionism and National Efficiency, but the conventional parties also played their part. Although the political system was subject to severe challenge, notably from Irish nationalism, it remained stable, legitimate and flexible enough to take the strain by holding out the prospect of reform and improvement. Political stability continued to be underpinned by a society effectively sustained by vigorous regional economies, freedom of trade, immigration of labour and extensive emigration.

Further reading

There are some excellent general accounts of empire:

John Darwin, *Unfinished Empire: the Global Expansion of Britain* (2012)

Bernard Porter, *The Lion's Share: a Short History of British Imperialism 1850–1950* (1975)

P.J. Cain and A.G. Hopkins, *British Imperialism 1688–2000* (2002) – argues that expansion was driven not by industrialists or politicians but by financial interests.

R.E. Dumett ed., *Gentlemanly Capitalism and British Imperialism* (1999)

C.C. Eldridge, *Victorian Imperialism* (1978)

N. Ferguson, *Empire: How Britain Made the Modern World* (2003) – a triumphalist account out of touch with modern work.

A major challenge to the significance traditionally placed on empire is: Bernard Porter, *The Absent-Minded Imperialists* (2004)

Other discussions of the popularity of empire include:

A. Thompson, *The Empire Strikes Back? The Impact of Imperialism on Britain from the Mid-Nineteenth Century* (2004)

J.M. Mackenzie, *Propaganda and Empire: the Manipulation of British Public Opinion 1880–1960* (1984) – takes virtually the opposite view to Porter.

R. Price, *An Imperial War and the British Working Class* (1972)

J. Springhall, *Youth, Empire and Society: British Youth Movements 1883–1940* (1977)

P.A. Duane, 'Boys' Literature and the Idea of Empire 1870–1914', *Victorian Studies,* 24, 1980

Henry Pelling, 'British Labour and British Imperialism', in *Popular Politics and Society in Late-Victorian Britain* (1979)

L. Senelick, 'Politics as Entertainment: Victorian Music Hall Songs', *Victorian Studies,* 19, 1975

On the Boer War see:

Andrew Porter, *The Origins of the South African War: Joseph Chamberlain and the Diplomacy of Imperialism 1895–99* (1980)

Bill Nasson, *The South African War 1899–1902* (1999)

David Omissi and Andrew Thompson eds, *The Impact of the South African War* (2002)

Britain's military and diplomatic rearrangements prior to 1914 are discussed in:

Paul Kennedy, *The Rise of the Anglo-German Antagonism 1860–1914* (1980)

Zara Steiner, *Britain and the Origins of the First World War* (1977)

David French, *The British Way in Warfare 1688–2000* (1990)

E. Spiers, *The Army and Society 1815–1914* (1980)

F. Coetzee, *For Party or Country: Nationalism and the Dilemmas of Popular Conservatism in Edwardian England* (1990)

I.F. Clarke, *Voices Prophesying War 1763–1984* (1970)

Anne Summers, 'Militarism in Britain before the Great War', *History Workshop Journal,* 2, 1976

R. Samuel ed., *Patriotism: the Making and Unmaking of British National Identity* (1989)

Part II

The Reorientation: The Emergence of the Interventionist State, 1902–18

7

The State, Social Welfare and the Economy

During the twenty years before 1906 Britain had seen debates triggered by the revelations about the extent and causes of urban poverty and by growing fears about the performance of the economy in the face of competition from Germany and the United States. However, while the debate had resulted in a good deal of experimentation at local level the real breakthrough in terms of policy did not come until after 1906. It involved a significant change in the agenda and scope of politics which proved long-lasting and broke with Victorian traditions of permissiveness and localism in social and economic affairs and took the state into areas of its citizens' lives it had previously avoided. Although this inevitably generated controversy it is worth recalling that to some extent all three political traditions contributed to this process, although as the Liberals were in power they were the major players. Why was the Edwardian era so formative a period for these changes?

National decadence and national efficiency

The domestic crisis engendered by the South African War came as a shock not only because of the military setbacks but because of revelations about the poor quality of the urban population. In some towns as many as six out of ten volunteers had been judged physically unfit for military service, findings later confirmed in 1904 by the Inter-Departmental Committee on Physical Deterioration. The question began to be asked whether Britain could sustain herself as a major industrial-imperial power on the basis of a poorly fed, educated and trained domestic population. The effect was to foster a mood of pessimism and self-doubt around the turn of the century. It became fashionable to diagnose the phenomenon of 'national decadence' and to examine the causes behind the decline of other great empires in history; Darwinian thinking suggested that in human affairs, as in the animal world, only the most vigorous and adaptable would survive. The death of Queen Victoria was taken to symbolize this turning-point in British history.

As a result there was much criticism of British politics and political parties for fostering amateurism and incompetence and a feeling that in all aspects of life a greater role should be given to experts and businessmen. The immediate target of this was the discredited Salisbury government which seemed to epitomize the lackadaisical, aristocratic tradition. Advocates of 'national efficiency' in all parties argued for cutting down on parliamentary government, rationalizing elective local government, imposing universal military training, extending state education and legislating for social reform at national level. Politically these ideas were important because they gave some Conservatives a justification for state social welfare in terms of promoting the national interest rather than helping the poor or redistributing wealth.

Admittedly the disintegrating effects of the Boer War left Salisbury's successor, A.J. Balfour, struggling over taxation and internal division up to 1905. Although Chamberlain had promised state old-age pensions, nothing was done. However, Balfour's premiership saw several initiatives to improve military efficiency and initiatives in social policy including the 1902 Education Act, which made county councils, not school boards, responsible for education. The inflation and consequent fall in real wages resulting from

Table 7.1 Money wages, the cost of living and real wages, 1899–1914 (1914 = 100)

Year	Money wages	Cost of living	Real wages
1899	89	86	104
1900	94	91	103
1901	93	90	102
1902	91	90	102
1903	91	91	99
1904	89	92	97
1905	89	92	97
1906	91	93	98
1907	96	95	101
1908	94	93	101
1909	94	94	100
1910	94	96	98
1911	95	97	97
1912	98	100	97
1913	99	102	97
1914	100	100	100

the war led the government to introduce an Unemployed Workmen's Act in 1905. In a sense this represented the final fling of late-Victorian experiments with public-works schemes by local authorities. The interesting thing about the Act was the way in which contemporaries interpreted it as a commitment by the government to provide employment for respectable workingmen. But Balfour intended nothing so radical; the 1905 Act was purely a temporary expedient. Balfour handled the political problem by setting up a Royal Commission on the Poor Laws, which reported in 1909 and gave further publicity to the Fabian Socialists' case for breaking up the poor-law system and shifting responsibilities for unemployment to central government on the grounds that local authorities lacked the necessary resources.

1906: the political breakthrough

The immediate explanation for Edwardian social reform lay simply in the dramatic general election of 1906 which returned a huge Liberal majority and raised expectations. The majority of Liberal members elected had committed themselves to major social reforms, and the emergence of a substantial Labour Party in parliament strengthened their hand. This became clear when scores of Liberal backbenchers joined with Labour MPs in support of amendments to the King's Speech demanding old-age pensions and the Right to Work Bill. In fact, the new Chancellor of the Exchequer, H.H. Asquith, had already begun to set aside resources for the introduction of pensions, so the reformers were pushing at a half-open door.

This is a reminder of the importance of accidental factors such as political personnel in explaining the timing and character of social reform. Asquith played a vital role, first as Chancellor in preparing pensions and taxation reforms, and then as Prime Minister by giving support to Lloyd George's controversial budget. The Local Government Board, in some ways the most likely vehicle for social reform, failed to contribute much, largely because of the negative and conservative attitude adopted by its President, John Burns. Not until 1914, when he was succeeded by Herbert Samuel, did the board help to promote welfare policies. In contrast the Board of Trade emerged as a key ministry under the leadership of a succession of radical Presidents, Lloyd George, Winston Churchill and Sydney Buxton. Though Lloyd George's contribution to taxation and social policy is often seen in terms of his comparatively humble origins, this is clearly far from sufficient explanation, as the record of Burns, a working-class leader, suggests. Lloyd George's characteristic asset lay in his unorthodox methods. Lacking the patience for the usual committee-led route to legislation, he preferred to use advisers and assistants in whom he had confidence and with whom he could talk through the solutions unhindered by conventional civil servants. A typical decision was the dispatch of William Braithwaite to Germany to draw up a quick report on the operation of state welfare schemes there. He noticeably ignored the proposals in the reports of the Royal Commission on the Poor Laws, much to the chagrin of the Webbs, and relied on politicians like Charles Masterman who were outside his ministry but politically sympathetic.

Winston Churchill emerged as another unorthodox collaborator in these discussions. In 1905 Churchill's only Liberal credentials were his support for free trade. When offered a post at the Local Government Board he evidently saw it as a backwater. But Churchill was a man of sudden enthusiasms. By 1908 he was, in Masterman's words, 'full of the poor whom he has just discovered', and with Lloyd George he mapped out the series of reforms that became the centrepiece of the government's programme. Churchill brought to government a Tory paternalist's confidence that the power of the state should be freely employed to improve efficiency and promote the stability of society. Asquith deliberately promoted Churchill in the face of jealousy amongst other Liberals towards this rather suspect newcomer to the party; but after 1911, when he had gone on to the Home Office and the Admiralty, Churchill found new fields for his restless energy.

It is also noteworthy that, as in the nineteenth century, social reform owed something to the role of civil servants and experts. Though Sidney and Beatrice Webb enjoyed much less influence than they expected to have, they managed to get the young William Beveridge taken on at the Board of Trade to prepare the scheme for unemployment insurance. At the Board of Education Sir Robert Morant, a more orthodox figure, worked successfully, under three transient ministers who were preoccupied with the politics of education, to introduce a scheme of school medical inspection in 1907. Morant understood that this would generate so much evidence of ill health amongst children that it would be comparatively easy to extend inspection into a school medical service.

Liberal social reform

The early reforms of the Liberal government in 1906–8 concentrated on children: school meals, medical inspection, compulsory registration of births and the Children's Act of 1908. This reflected the current consensus expressed in the 1904 report of the Inter-Departmental Committee on Physical Deterioration – a mixture of humanitarian concerns and Bismarckianism. However, these measures provoked some controversy. Even the modest bill which allowed local authorities to feed necessitous schoolchildren was interpreted in some quarters as subversive for whereas those who received poor-law relief were disenfranchized, there was to be no such penalty for parents whose children enjoyed free school meals. 'Why a man who first neglects his duty as a father and then defrauds the State should retain his full political rights is a question easier to ask than to answer', complained A.V. Dicey, the eminent jurist. The more important change actually came in 1914 when the government made the provision of school meals *compulsory*, one of the several indications that the reforming impulse was still going strong when war broke out.

The significance of old-age pensions

The scheme for old-age pensions, introduced in Lloyd George's first budget in 1908, also infringed traditional thinking in several ways. The means-tested pension of 5 shillings per person at the full rate was available to elderly people who were 70 years old and had an annual income not above £21, or a little over 8 shillings a week; the pension decreased by stages from 4 shillings to 1 shilling a week for those with an income between £21 and £31 a year. In effect, the state pension supplemented pensioners' existing incomes, leaving many with a total income of around 13 shillings. The radical aspects in the scheme were the absence of any contributory element and the retention of voting rights by the recipients. In the event, the original estimate of 572,000 eligible pensioners turned out to be too low, for 668,000 qualified in the first year and 968,000 by 1913–14; the cost rose from £8.6 million in 1909–10 to £12.5 million in 1913–14. Initially those in receipt of poor relief had been excluded, but this restriction was abandoned in 1911. The government also decided to give married couples the full rate of 10 shillings. As the government sensibly used the existing post offices to pay out pensions the administrative costs were minimal, almost all the money going to the beneficiaries.

Health and unemployment insurance

Subsequent reforms proved much more complicated, largely because so many vested interests had to be squared or outfaced. Lloyd George's health insurance programme, which was embodied in the 1911 National Insurance Act, took a long time to produce because of opposition by commercial and professional bodies, and was less radical than he would have liked. In one sense the scheme was rooted in the Victorian practice of making contributions in return for benefits at a later stage. In return for weekly payments of

3 pence by the worker, 2 pence from the state, and 4 pence from the employer, the insured person received 10 shillings for each of 13 weeks and 5 shillings for each of 13 subsequent weeks in any one year; in addition, he enjoyed free treatment from a doctor. The boldness of the scheme lay in the fact that it replaced the multiplicity of local and optional policies with a compulsory, national one. This is why it attracted criticism from trade unions, whose members already subscribed to their own forms of insurance, and worried the Friendly Societies and commercial insurance companies, who feared competition from the state. In fact the policies paid out by Friendly Societies were largely worthless as they usually involved a 'death benefit' to cover the costs of a funeral. Eventually many of them were appeased by the option of being incorporated into the health insurance provisions as approved societies through which benefits could be paid.

The British Medical Association (BMA) also objected to state intervention. As the spokesman of wealthy professionals it instinctively disliked the prospect of doctors becoming employees of the state; the health of the people came low down the BMA's priorities. It threatened to make the Act unworkable by refusing to treat insured people whose income was under £2 a week. However, it transpired that the complacent BMA leadership was out of touch with ordinary GPs, who commonly received only 4 or 5 shillings per patient per year under existing schemes. Lloyd George offered 6 shillings. Thereupon the doctors agreed to participate and the BMA had to climb down. In a way this was unfortunate, for it meant that Lloyd George did not carry out his threat to create a state medical service by offering a salary of £350 per annum to 12,000 young doctors to run his scheme. The obvious weakness of health insurance was that it did not include children or the majority of women. Lloyd George was acutely aware of this, though he did introduce a maternity benefit of 30 shillings which was at least a recognition by the state of the vital contribution of women as mothers, and of the hardship endured by them.

Unemployment, an even more complicated problem, was tackled in several stages. The first came in 1908 with the introduction of labour exchanges, and the second in 1911, in the form of unemployment insurance. The latter was, again, based on contributions from worker, employer and the state in return for benefits of 7s. 6d. for each of fifteen weeks in any one year. This was a distinctly cautious scheme, both in the sense that the unemployment fund was intended to be self-supporting and in the sense that only engineers, shipbuilders and building workers were covered. These groups included some highly paid men, who were relatively well placed to afford the contributions. Also, their occupations were notoriously subject to sudden cyclical slumps. The motive here was to save skilled, respectable workingmen from being forced onto the Poor Law. Because these proposals for the unemployed ignored the recommendations of the minority report of the Royal Commission on the Poor Law they provoked criticism from the Webbs, who considered that attendance at labour exchanges ought to be compulsory, not voluntary, in order to enable the idlers to be distinguished from those genuinely seeking work. But Lloyd George and Churchill understood working-class politics better than the Webbs. They knew that, as it would take time to overcome the suspicion of labour exchanges, a voluntary approach was wiser. Nor was it feasible for the state to take over wholesale responsibility for the unemployed from the poor-law authorities, as the Webbs advocated. The potential costs were huge and the political complications considerable. Neither workers nor the government were keen to adopt a complete system of state regulation of labour.

Not a welfare state?

Taken as a whole, the Edwardian social reforms were in no sense a welfare state, although they shared an important link with the post-1945 system in the shape of the insurance principle. The Liberal measures were not intended as a comprehensive or uniform system of welfare provision. Rather, they involved targeting certain discrete parts of the problem of poverty; those not included continued to require a safety net, which meant that it was necessary to leave the Poor Law in being, though it clearly had a diminishing role to play.

However, any weaknesses in detail do not detract from the overall, long-term significance of the innovations. They represented a marked departure from the principles governing welfare and poverty in the Victorian era, and they led the state into a position of responsibility from which no political party was subsequently able to remove it. At the time, the Conservatives became anxious to deny any intention of abandoning old-age pensions; and in spite of their attacks on the 1911 National Insurance Act they claimed only that they would improve the schemes if returned to office. By 1911 a Unionist Social Reform Committee had emerged, with a view to recovering the initiative for the party in this field. They favoured a break-up of the Poor Law and transfer of its functions to the county councils; they advocated the *compulsory* adoption of slum clearance, school meals and medical treatment by local authorities; and they believed the necessary finance should take the form of grants-in-aid from central government, supported by direct taxation. This was a synthesis of Fabian socialism and Toryism, at once interventionist and nationalist. Although the party leadership avoided taking up these proposals, the fact that the committee included much of what was to be the interwar leadership of the party – Stanley Baldwin, Edward Wood, Samuel Hoare, F.E. Smith, L.S. Amery and William Joynson-Hicks – was an indication that social policy was to occupy a central place in British politics in the future.

Finally, it is now clear that the Liberal programme was not a brief expedient that had gone as far as it could by 1914 but part of a strategy whose momentum was being maintained right up to the outbreak of war. Ministers were very conscious of the shortcomings of their programme. For example, it was always intended to extend unemployment insurance once the viability and acceptability of the scheme had been established. The war and its aftermath influenced the timing of this, and it was 1920 when the majority of workers were incorporated. Similarly, Lloyd George had been frustrated in his wish to include widows' pensions in his 1911 reforms, and the money could not be found until 1925. Other innovations were, however, being introduced in 1914. Herbert Samuel pioneered a new policy for women in the shape of local-authority maternity clinics which were backed by a 50 per cent grant from the government. Subsequently this policy became obligatory for local councils, as did school meals in 1914. The Liberals were also anxious to tackle housing, especially as some Conservatives began to take up the issue. In 1914 Lloyd George made loans of £4 million available for local-authority building, and under the Land Campaign he proposed direct state intervention to build cheap rented housing. Edwardian reform was thus an ongoing programme, required by the political logic of the situation and made possible by the new approach to public finance adopted by the Liberals.

Popular attitudes to state welfare

In 1912 Hilaire Belloc denounced state welfare on the grounds that the workers were being made to give up political freedom for servility. In one sense this was absurd; as we have seen, it was a characteristic of the Edwardian reforms that they involved no loss of political rights for the recipients. Pensions, in the words of the *Nation*, were 'a right conferred by citizenship, rather than a boon conferred by poverty alone'. As the extensive reforms of 1918–19 were to show, wider political rights now began to go hand in hand with social legislation. Thus commentators like Belloc and Dicey were fighting in the last ditch to resuscitate the ideas of mid-Victorian individualism. It was no longer seen as enough to exhort the working classes to stand on their own feet, for many who lived industrious, thrifty and abstemious lives were still liable to fall into poverty through circumstances beyond their control. However, if contemporary propaganda designed to discredit the social reforms lacked credibility, we should not, on the other hand, assume that the innovations were automatically popular. We know that working-class communities traditionally regarded state intervention in their lives with suspicion and hostility. The Edwardian years are therefore interesting for the way in which they reflect the transition from negative Victorian attitudes towards the post-1945 views of the state.

Not surprisingly the response varied according to the effects of each particular measure on families and individuals. Old-age pensions were already widely advocated in the working class by 1908, and Asquith's scheme attracted emphatic support. This was because it involved no cost to the beneficiaries and none of the indignity associated with seeking relief from the poor-law guardians; recipients collected pensions at the post office which was already a familiar institution. The only bureaucratic impediment was the necessity to establish one's claim by producing a birth certificate; but thereafter Post Office staff were under instruction to assist with filling in the two-page forms. Staff themselves had an incentive in that they were paid an extra shilling for every successful application; they were also paid according to the number of pension coupons they handled each week. Historians have often underestimated the significance of the 1908 pension as a result of the apparent lack of evidence to show the reactions of the beneficiaries and the operation of the scheme at the grass roots. However, evidence in Post Office archives and the local newspapers offers a valuable corrective. Applicants queued up enthusiastically at post offices before opening times. For the majority of pensioners, for whom visits to the post office were not intimidating, this was the only contact they had with administration of the scheme.

The provincial newspapers, which sent journalists to gather reactions outside the post offices, reported that the pensioners were delighted, the only reservation being a fear that the money would surely run out! That it never did was an important lesson that helped to modify popular perceptions about the state and in particular encouraged ordinary citizens to understand that the state enjoyed more power to assist them than they had thought. Newspaper headlines on 1 January 1909 announced the start of the scheme in ecstatic terms: 'PENSION DAY: HAPPY VETERANS: NATIONAL HONOUR REDEEMED: CROWNS FOR FROSTED HEADS.' This language is a reminder that the old-age pension became a mark of respectability and citizenship, as something to which an elderly person became entitled rather than as a concession awarded grudgingly by the poor-law authorities; it conveyed a measure of independence and status upon the recipients, especially as they retained their right to vote. When the disqualification for receiving poor-law relief ended in 1910, another 160,000 people became pensioners, bringing the total to 968,000 by 1913–14 – in effect this meant that pensions were being paid to a wider section of society than simply the very poor.

Negative reactions

At the other extreme, reforms involving children continued to create some friction and resentment. The 1908 Children's Act allowed local authorities to take children into care, and made parents liable to prosecution for neglect; medical inspection exposed parents to embarrassment and criticism; and even school meals were problematical because it was open to the authorities to try to recover the costs from those parents deemed able to pay. Clearly, not every reform was welcomed at first. But some writers have followed contemporary propaganda by concentrating on the initial criticism of, for example, the 1911 National Insurance Act, and failing to see how this reform won acceptance in time. Though some employers and union leaders attacked the contributory element in the 1911 Act, this was to overlook the fact that most families were already accustomed to the idea of contributory insurance in one form or another. The question was whether one got value for money, hence Lloyd George's 'ninepence for fourpence' claim. Part of the problem lay in the fact that contributions began to be collected in 1912, though the benefits were not paid until 1913. But by that time the controversy had subsided; for most workers the state scheme marked an improvement over the failing benefit schemes traditionally available.

It is fair to say that one potential drawback to state welfare was the involvement of the recipients with an unsympathetic official bureaucracy. For example, unemployment insurance benefits were paid at labour exchanges. However, the government was quite well aware when launching its scheme in 1908 that many workingmen regarded labour exchanges with suspicion because in the past they had been used to supply labour to break strikes or to offer work at below union rates. These problems were effectively tackled partly by making attendance voluntary and by allowing men to reject any jobs which seemed to undermine the terms and conditions for which the unions were contending. Churchill sought to reassure them further by employing trade unionists in many of the minor posts in the labour exchanges. This practice extended higher up the civil service too.

Indeed, some Conservatives accused the Liberals of trying to shackle the Labour Movement by jobbery. *The Times* claimed in 1913 that 374 known activists in socialist and labour organizations were employed in government departments, notably in National Insurance, the Board of Trade and the Home Office. The best known was David Shackleton, formerly of the Weavers' Union and a Labour MP, who was taken on by Churchill as a labour adviser at the Board of Trade. In this context, it is not surprising that the new labour exchanges attracted rapidly rising business, and the fears expressed about the men's attitudes were at least partly overcome by familiarity and the tangible benefits available.

Who benefited?

Another important qualification to be made about the social reforms is that they were naturally of more relevance to some sections of the working class than others. Historians have often underestimated their value because they have neglected women's interests. Yet nearly three in five pensioners were female. Women had a compelling interest in improvements in health and Lloyd George was alive to this, as is indicated by the introduction of the maternity benefit and his losing fight for widows' pensions. Certainly these were the reforms advocated by the Women's Co-operative Guild, which sought to focus attention on the poor health endured by working-class women as a result of excessive child-bearing. The introduction of local maternity clinics in 1914 was the next step in this direction and helped to generate support for further expenditure on subsidized milk, family allowances and even birth control during and after the war.

Attitudes towards the state also varied according to the employment experience of different groups. The unskilled and low-paid were less likely to enjoy trade union membership benefits or to be able to maintain Friendly Society policies, and so incorporation into a state scheme could represent a real gain. Similarly, in very poorly paid occupations where surplus labour held down wages, trade union action was never very effective, and the intervention of the state offered the prospect of improvement. Thus, for example, the Trade Boards Act affected men and women in the 'sweated trades' after 1909; in chainmaking there followed a 50 per cent wage rise between 1911 and 1914, which still left wage levels comparatively low but nonetheless represented a gain that was unattainable by any other means. Women stood to benefit because of their concentration in low-paid occupations. Trade unions also derived some indirect benefits from state intervention. The effect of trade boards in tailoring and chainmaking was to stimulate membership recruitment in these traditionally difficult sectors. There were similar advantages for unions which acted as approved societies for payments under the National Insurance scheme, notably among railwaymen and shop assistants.

Ultimately, popular reactions to state interventionism were determined by the perceived effectiveness of the new schemes. Some clearly took time to make an impact. By 1911, for example, only four in ten local authorities were actually providing school meals; hence the scheme was made obligatory in 1914. However, some of the criticisms made by historians about the shortcomings of the reforms are misleading, for example the claim that health insurance did nothing for those most in need, namely women and children. The key purpose of the scheme was to replace the income lost when the family's breadwinner became too ill to work, so that the indirect advantage for wives and children was very important. It is probably true that the free medical treatment proved less attractive, largely because working-class families were unconvinced about the value of doctors and hospitals and preferred to rely upon patent pills purchased at chemists. Unemployment insurance was, initially, limited to relatively well-paid men, though the 2.5 million covered represented a considerable part of the workforce. Four-fifths of these men had previously enjoyed no insurance against unemployment, and in the first year of the scheme 23 per cent made a claim. However, the fact that national insurance operated for only a year before the outbreak of war disrupted the pattern of employment makes it difficult to assess the impact. The official figures issued by the poor-law authorities offer an inadequate measurement of poverty because they excluded the majority of the poor. However, they do reveal something of the impact of the reforms. Between 1910 and 1914 those assisted by the guardians diminished from 916,000 to 748,000. This was largely due to the disappearance of men and women over seventy years old, previously on outdoor relief and now receiving pensions. Workhouse visitors commented on the sudden absence of elderly people, though some 50,000 who needed institutional care did remain.

Of course, one should not exaggerate the material benefits arising from state welfare. For many families, the cheap food which was perceived to be the result of free trade was the most tangible advantage of Liberal policy. Moreover, many workingmen naturally placed full employment and high rates of pay at the top of their agenda. But they also appreciated how vulnerable they were to the vicissitudes of the economy. Unemployment fluctuated from only 3.7 per cent in 1907 to 7.8 per cent in 1908, but was down to 3.0 per cent by 1911 as the Edwardian economy enjoyed its last boom. Social welfare could only be a supplement to the 'family wage' to which trade unionists aspired. But it was one that even the best-paid workers needed at several stages in their lives. Increasingly they could look to the state, in preference to the anachronistic poor-law system which had cast such a long shadow over the lives of their Victorian predecessors.

The taxation revolution

The Boer War had had the effect of increasing the National Debt to £640 million by 1901 and to £800 million by 1904. By way of response orthodox economists and politicians advocated retrenchment in government spending to enable this sum to be reduced. But the conflicting pressures to service the debt and to cut taxation meant that Chamberlain's hopes for the introduction of old-age pensions were strangled once again. Asquith, the new Liberal Chancellor, managed to redeem £41 million of the National Debt; but despite this concession to orthodoxy, his chief role was to lay the foundations for a drastic shift in the basis of government finance. Faced with evidence of widespread evasion of income tax, in 1907 he introduced compulsory returns of all classes of taxable income, and obliged employers to make returns of their employees' wages and salaries. Also in the 1907 budget he adopted the principle

Image 4 Conspicuous consumption: a party arrives at Derby Day, Epsom, 1914.

of differentiation by setting the tax on earned incomes at 9d. in the pound and that on unearned incomes at 1s. Asquith was coming round to the idea that taxation should be graduated according to ability to pay, the case for which had been recently argued by Leo Chiozza Movey, a Liberal MP, in his book *Riches and Poverty* (1905). In particular Asquith committed himself to the introduction of a supertax levied on a rising scale on all incomes above £5,000. He also insisted that it was no longer realistic to 'treat each year's finances as though they were self-contained; the Chancellor ought to budget, not for one year, but for several years'. This heralded a long-term commitment to fund new social-welfare policies, which made inevitable some broadening of the basis of taxation and a greater reliance upon direct taxation.

The 'People's Budget'

Lloyd George's celebrated budget of 1909 was built on the foundations laid by Asquith, though the pressures of an anticipated budget deficit of £16 million to £17 million drove him to adopt an unexpectedly radical catalogue of measures, or at least gave him an excuse: 'I have got to rob somebody's hen roost next year.' In all he proposed to raise an extra £13 million to £15 million revenue. Income tax on unearned incomes over £700 was increased from 1s. to 1s. 2d.; on earned incomes up to £2,000 it remained at 9d. but went up to 1s. in the £2,000–£3,000 range. A supertax was introduced on incomes over £5,000, payable at 6d. at £3,000. Additional sums were levied on death duties, stamp duty and liquor licences. There were also two novel sources of revenue: a tax on petrol and a motor-car licence proved excellent ways of taxing conspicuous wealth especially as motor-car owners were few in number and were not popular. And, most controversially, Lloyd George proposed a half-penny in the pound levy on the value of undeveloped land, excluding agricultural land, and a 10 per cent duty on benefits gained by a lessor on the termination of a lease. Land taxation was justified as a levy on the rising value of land – a form of unearned income.

The key feature of these measures was that they affected only a small number of rich people. At this time income tax liability, which began at £160, included only one million people in all. But most of them were unaffected by the new levies: for example, there were only 25,000 taxpayers above the £3,000 level. In addition, as a further safeguard the Cabinet persuaded Lloyd George to assist those on modest middle-class incomes by introducing tax relief of £10 for each child under sixteen years to those below £500 annual income. The only aspects of the budget which affected the working class were the extra purchase taxes on spirits and tobacco.

The redistribution of income

The 1909 budget proved to be of very considerable significance, both immediately and in the long term. It established the principle that taxation ought to be related to capacity to pay. This was reflected both in the system of graduation and in the shift from indirect taxes on consumption, which were largely paid by the poor, to direct taxes on income and wealth. By 1914 around 60 per cent of all government revenue was derived from direct taxation, compared to 44 per cent in the late 1880s. Much of the extra revenue was now spent on social welfare which stood at £33 million in 1913 as against £5 million in the late 1880s. Thus the effect of this combination of social and taxation policies was unquestionably to redistribute the nation's income from rich to poor, albeit very slightly. In fact, the Edwardian reforms inaugurated a trend in British public finance which lasted for many decades. The modest redistribution of income continued until the 1979–92 period, when reactionary governments reversed the pattern by transferring income from poor to rich via the tax system.

Moreover, the People's Budget created a momentum which was still carrying the Liberal government forward in 1914. Despite some internal dissent, Lloyd George actually extended his innovations in the last peacetime budget. Incomes above £2,500 were subject to a tax rate of 1s. 4d. in the pound. The supertax limit was lowered from £5,000 to £3,000 and a maximum rate of 2s. 8d. was applied. Death duties were again raised to 20 per cent on estates worth over £1 million. And the tax relief for children was doubled to £20. Clearly, the vigorous application of the redistributory elements in the 1909 budget prepared the way for even more drastic measures during the war.

The state and the economy

In the heat of the Edwardian political debate, Conservatives sometimes accused the Liberals of introducing socialism by which they implied the expropriation of individual wealth and ownership and the creation of a huge central bureaucracy. Government was undoubtedly becoming a bigger employer: between 1901 and 1911 the number of jobs in the civil service, local administration and the armed forces rose from 960,000 to 1,270,000. The administration of the new schemes of national insurance and land valuation created a further 5,000 permanent and 10,000 temporary posts up to 1914. However, while happy to justify a proper role for the state, the

Liberals indignantly rejected the imputation of socialism. Their tax policies still left private wealth and individual ownership intact; the economy would continue to be governed largely by freemarket forces – it could hardly be otherwise for a party wedded to free trade. Indeed, it is only comparatively recently that historians have recognized that the Liberals had discovered, perhaps by luck as much as by judgement, a viable mixture of collectivism and individualism. The balance in policy reflected, in an approximate fashion, the blend in their support in the country. For, vital as their working-class vote was, the Liberals clearly remained a party with significant backing among the middle classes too.

Although a number of employers jibbed at the radical taxation policies, 37 per cent of Liberal MPs were still businessmen in 1906, which represents only a modest reduction over the 1890s. Indeed, some of the country's most successful entrepreneurs in manufacturing and finance, including William Lever, Sir John Brunner, George Cadbury, Joseph Rowntree and Lord Swaythling, were major contributors to Liberal funds as well as supporters at elections. Yet their role should not be exaggerated. They were not typical businessmen; rather, they were sufficiently well established in business to be able to indulge their own interest in political and social causes. Also, apart from Walter Runciman and J.A. Pease, there were no businessmen in Asquith's Cabinet, though this is not particularly significant since the same is true of the late-Victorian cabinets of both parties.

Why did a number of employers remain Liberal supporters when the party's policy was moving to the left? For some, free trade continued to retain its importance; it helped to maximize export markets, maintain cheap raw materials and reduce the pressure for higher wages. Some clearly remained Liberal for non-economic reasons or simply out of habit. But a number of the more successful and enlightened businessmen broadly accepted the diagnosis of the progressives. They were increasingly concerned about Britain's failure to educate and train her labour force, and to improve the health and housing of her people. Some employers had already pioneered welfare schemes which were subsequently overtaken by the state. Above all, they recognized that, if simply left to itself, private enterprise did not work efficiently in all areas; in particular it failed to generate the necessary investment for the utilities and services on which all producers depended. Thus, if the adherence to free trade and the involvement with capitalists placed limits upon Liberal collectivism, it did not stop, and in some sense actually promoted, moves away from an unqualified *laissez-faire* approach.

Why did the state intervene?

State intervention was seen as appropriate by the Edwardian governments in three broad areas. First, and most simply, there were problems or sectors in the economy where an acute national interest overrode a private interest. For example, since 1870 the government had enjoyed the legal power to take over the operation of the railways, which it did promptly on the outbreak of war in 1914. During the Edwardian period ministers intervened drastically, following the outbreak of foot-and-mouth disease, to force farmers to co-operate in checking the spread of the disease. But the most striking case of intervention, which involved a change of ownership, not simply of control, came as a result of Churchill's decision to authorize a switch from coal to oil-fired battleships. Oil was more efficient but brought the danger of dependence on foreign supplies. Consequently the Cabinet agreed to his request to purchase the Anglo-Persian Oil Company for £2 million. This proved a highly profitable investment for the government and the taxpayer over many decades until, in the 1980s, it was disposed of by the Thatcher government. Churchill, of course, was no socialist, but regarded the state's participation as an owner as justified where an important national interest was at stake.

The second area of state intervention consisted in promoting the rights and the efficiency of the labour force. This proceeded from the belief that trade unions had a legitimate role to play in the marketplace in seeking improved wages and conditions. This led governments beyond efforts to promote arbitration and conciliation to direct interference with the rights of employers and owners. In 1909 the Trade Boards Act imposed minimum wages in a number of 'sweated trades' where the surplus of labour, the presence of women workers, or the lack of skills had the effect of holding pay at very low levels. In 1912 the government eventually resolved the industrial dispute in the coal industry by legislating for an eight-hour working day. Even as an ad hoc measure, this was not to be undertaken lightly by a government committed to private enterprise. During 1913–14 the momentum was maintained by Lloyd George's Land Campaign. It emerged that six out of ten agricultural labourers earned less than 18s. a week, which put them below the poverty line as defined by Rowntree. The Chancellor proposed to tackle this by appointing regional wage tribunals, which would impose minimum wages in each area.

The third aspect of the government's interventionism centred around the problem of unemployment and inadequate growth rates of the economy. A first step towards a solution had been the labour exchanges, which were a recognition that the free market in labour was not efficient and as a way of improving the mobility of labour and, eventually, reducing the incidence of casual employment. During the first five months of the scheme, the exchanges filled 900 vacancies a day, but by the first six months of 1914 they were filling over 3,000 a day. Thus, although the economic boom sharply reduced unemployment, men were increasingly being drawn into the system.

But in his 1909 budget Lloyd George pointed the way to a more radical approach to unemployment and investment in the form of the Development Commission. He proposed to set aside £200,000 a year, plus any surplus revenue, for a Development Fund which would promote scientific research, exploit resources not presently being used, and finance land reclamation, afforestation, transport and experimental farming. The bill actually defined the scope of the Commission's work to include 'any other purpose calculated to promote the economic development of the United Kingdom'. Conservatives attacked this chiefly on the grounds that it allowed governments to bribe voters or industrialists with Exchequer funds, was likely to be wasteful of public money, and would result in a swarm of new officials. But the Development Commission was in effect a recognition of the need to invest more in certain sectors of the economy where private enterprise had failed to serve the national interest vigorously enough. Progressive industrialists believed there to be a role for government to play by complementing private business rather than competing with it. But the fund was also a sign that government expenditure might usefully be regulated according to the state of the labour market. The minority report of the Royal Commission on the Poor Laws called for public spending to be raised in those years when the economy was depressed so as to stabilize the level of employment. In the event, little was done to realize this objective because during the last years of peacetime the economic boom in coal and shipbuilding largely removed the need to stimulate employment. Significantly, the Land Campaign included proposals for state-subsidized rural house-building which would have been a useful countercyclical measure if applied. Even in the Treasury the notion of public works designed to modify the trade cycle was under discussion. In this way the ground was prepared to some extent for wartime interventionism, and for the economic strategy associated with J.M. Keynes between the wars.

Further reading

The ideas and divisions affecting the Conservatives are discussed in:
Alan Sykes, *Tariff Reform in British Politics 1903–1913* (1979)
P. Cain, 'Political Economy in Edwardian England: the Tariff Reform Controversy', in Alan O'Day ed., *The Edwardian Age* (1979)

G.R. Searle, *The Quest for National Efficiency* (1971)
E.H.H. Green, *The Crisis of Conservatism* (1995)

Liberal welfare policy is analysed in:
D. Gladstone, *The Twentieth Century Welfare State* (1999)
H.V. Emy, *Liberals, Radicals and Social Politics 1892–1914* (1973)
Jose Harris, *Unemployment and Politics* (1972)
J.R. Hay, *The Origins of the Liberal Welfare Reforms 1906–1914* (1975)
J.R. Hay, 'Employers and Social Policy in Britain: the Evolution of Welfare
     Legislation 1905–1914', *Social History*, 2, 1977
Pat Thane, *The Origins of British Social Policy* (1978)
Pat Thane, *Old Age in English History* (2000)
K.D. Brown, *Labour and Unemployment* (1971)

On popular attitudes to social welfare Vincent is negative, Pugh positive, the
others more neutral:
Pat Thane, 'The Working Class and State Welfare in Britain 1880–1914',
     Historical Journal, 27, 1984
D. Vincent, *Poor Citizens: the State and the Poor in the Twentieth Century*
     (1991)
Martin Pugh, 'Working-Class Experience and State Social Welfare 1908–1914:
     Old Age Pensions Reconsidered', *Historical Journal*, 45, 2002
Paul Thompson, *The Edwardians; the Remaking of British Society* (1992)

On changes in taxation and economic policy see:
B.K. Murray, *The People's Budget 1909–1910* (1986)
Frank Trentmann, *Free Trade Nation: Commerce, Consumption and Civil
     Society in Modern Britain* (2008)
M. Daunton, *Trusting Leviathan: The Politics of Taxation in Britain 1799–1914*
     (2001)
G.C. Peden, *British Economic and Social Policy from Lloyd George to Thatcher*
     (1985)

8

The Liberal–Labour Alliance

The Edwardian era marked a watershed in the scope and substance of British politics which set the pattern for the twentieth century. The performance of the economy, the level of unemployment, the standard of living and social welfare all began to occupy a central role in political debate and in the work of governments. Gladstone and Salisbury had largely contrived to avoid this by concentrating on the traditional politics of the constitution, the law, the Church and foreign policy. But who gained from this shift? The politics of Edwardian Britain have generated a good deal of argument among historians involving different types of evidence and different ways of interpreting the evidence. Although the Liberals retained office after three election victories the traditional view saw this as the final fling of Liberalism, reflecting the Victorian issues of retrenchment, temperance, free trade, disestablishment and education, now becoming outflanked by the Labour Party. However, the traditional view has been comprehensively challenged by revisionist research. On the positive side this emphasizes that Liberalism adapted, indeed led the new agenda and re-invented itself as the party of social reform, redistributive taxation and interventionism. On the negative side close research into the pre-1914 Labour Party suggests that it was outflanked by the Liberals if anything, that its electoral support and organizational base were quite weak, and that its electoral success reflected its client relationship with the Liberal Party. In short there was nothing inevitable about Labour replacing the Liberals. Yet the revisionism, too, has been challenged. Much depends on which sources of evidence one uses. It is argued that Liberal success rested on a limited pre-war electorate that did not fully reflect the working-class support that Labour would enjoy especially when it had tapped the resources of an expanding trade union movement.

The politics of the People's Budget

In spite of the changes in Edwardian politics, it would be an exaggeration to suggest that the new agenda dominated throughout the period. Indeed, between the end of the Boer War and the general election of 1906 some very traditional issues held sway. The effect of the war in increasing the national debt and taxation gave the Liberals an opportunity to steal the Conservatives' clothes and advocate retrenchment. A.J. Balfour's 1902 Education Act reactivated Liberal Nonconformity because it abolished the school boards and obliged Nonconformists to contribute towards the cost of Anglican schools in some areas. This led to a passive resistance campaign involving non-payment of rates, and to a selective application of the new legislation by county councils in Wales under Liberal control. As this coincided with a religious revival in Wales, it was as though the spirit of Victorian politics had been restored. Above all, after 1903 the tariff-reform campaign allowed Liberals to sink their differences in defence of free trade. But although Balfour's government hung on, a number of Tory free-traders, including Winston Churchill, decided to quit in order to join the Liberals.

1906: the Liberal landslide

By December 1905 Balfour had decided to resign. The new premier, Sir Henry Campbell-Bannerman, won a landslide victory in January 1906 with 401 Liberals against 157 Conservatives, 83 Irish Nationalists and 29 Labour. In the light of the Liberals' decline and downfall during and after the First World War this election has sometimes been seen as a freak result, the last fling of Victorian radicalism. Clearly the high profile of free trade, retrenchment and Nonconformity gives some grounds for this view. In reality the 1906 election showed that the Liberals were a changed party. Half of the MPs had never sat in parliament before. The majority of them were committed not only to the traditional causes but to old-age pensions, poor-law reform and graduated taxation. In any case, even if the election had been no more than the last gasp of Victorianism, 401 seats would still have been an extraordinarily robust death rattle!

The defeated Tory leader professed to see in the rejection of his party and the emergence of a substantial Labour Party an echo of the revolutionary currents affecting some European societies. This seems a far-fetched analogy for Ramsay MacDonald, Philip Snowden and Arthur Henderson, all men deeply committed to the parliamentary system. But their election in 1906 was a portent of change. Labour's initial breakthrough resulted from some careful tactics designed to make the most of the new party's limited resources. The alarm amongst trade unionists over the Taff Vale decision encouraged more affiliations to the Labour Representation Committee, which boosted its funds and its authority. At the same time the success of its candidates in by-elections at Clitheroe, Woolwich and Barnard Castle in 1902–3 raised expectations.

However, the lesson MacDonald drew was that Labour could prosper in partnership with the Liberals because its candidates could expect to be elected only by winning over the votes of Liberal workingmen. This was the logic of the 1903 electoral pact between MacDonald and the Liberal Chief Whip, Herbert Gladstone. Thus Labour fielded 50 candidates of whom 31 were not opposed by the Liberals; since 24 of the 31 were elected in 1906, MacDonald's tactics appeared to have been fully vindicated.

From the Liberals' perspective the pact also had advantages, for they stood to lose from any split in the non-Conservative vote. In the short run Labour's willingness to finance candidates, especially in areas such as Lancashire where the Liberals had been weak, saved Gladstone a good deal of money. In addition, Liberals like Gladstone regarded the Labour politicians as similar to the existing Lib–Lab trade unionist MPs, that is, as essentially working-class Liberals, not Socialists. By maintaining co-operation with them, it would be possible to preserve the balance within Liberalism which was otherwise liable to be tipped to the right by the growth of Liberal Imperialism and by the recruitment of Tory free-traders.

In retrospect it is easy to see the 1903 pact as an historic error for Liberalism: it had taken a cuckoo into its nest. But although the Liberals would have won the 1906 election even without the pact, this was not obvious in 1903. Even after the landslide, it was wise to avoid alienating Labour and unrealistic to think that the new party could simply be crushed.

Table 8.1 General election results, 1900–10

	Conservative		Liberal		Labour		Irish	
	Percentage vote	Seats	Percentage vote	Seats	Percentage vote	Seats	Percentage vote	Seats
1900	51.5	402	44.6	184	1.8	2	2.5	82
1906	43.6	157	49.0	401	5.9	29	0.6	83
1910 J	46.9	273	43.2	275	7.7	40	1.0	82
1910 D	46.3	272	43.8	272	7.2	42	2.5	84

Note: J = January; D = December.

In by-elections in 1907 Labour won Liberal seats at Jarrow and Colne Valley, while also making modest gains in municipal elections. For a time it appeared as though the rising expectations in the working class might give Labour a sustained boost in popularity. Briefly after 1906 the party began to influence the political agenda with its bills for school meals and trade union reform, which were taken up by the Liberal government. Keir Hardie also embarrassed ministers with the 'Right To Work' Bill, based on the ideas of the Webbs, which made central government responsible for providing either a job or relief for the unemployed worker. As this could not be accepted, the campaign highlighted the shortcomings of Liberal policy on unemployment.

1908: the turning-point

Labour successes during 1906–7 coincided with the deflation of Liberal hopes in Parliament. Refusing to be overawed by the huge Liberal majority in the Commons, the House of Lords amended a series of bills on education, land and plural voting. For a time it seemed as though the Liberals were back in the dilemma faced by Gladstone and Rosebery in the 1890s. There was a danger of disappointing the expectations of both the traditional party activists and the working-class voters. However, by 1908 the tide had begun to turn and the government regained the initiative. The introduction of old-age pensions heralded this recovery. It is significant that at the 1910 elections Liberal agents offered to help pensioners fill in their application forms. When Asquith took over the premiership and Lloyd George became Chancellor, it was inevitable that the government would tackle the questions of finance and the House of Lords. Lloyd George struck a blow at both with the 'People's Budget' of 1909.

Behind this famous budget one may detect three distinct motives. The immediate one was the need to meet a budgetary deficit resulting from falling tax revenues during the trade depression, and the extra expenditure of £8 million on pensions and £3 million for the naval estimates. Second, the budget was designed to deal with the loss of morale consequent upon rejection of Liberal legislation by the peers. Banking on the convention that the upper chamber could not amend financial legislation, Lloyd George planned his budget as a Trojan Horse which incorporated increases in licence duties and proposals for land valuation which had been thwarted as ordinary legislation. This would amount to an effective repost to the arrogant peers, and was an indication that Lloyd George did not anticipate outright rejection. The third motive was more fundamental. For some years politicians had faced growing pressure to tackle the issue of poverty, but had backed away from the financial implications for local and national government. Conservatives calculated that the Liberals' commitment to free trade would leave them unable to finance social reform and thus squeezed between protectionism on the one side and Labour on the other. The 1909 budget demolished these calculations at a stroke by demonstrating that one could retain the advantages of free trade while raising additional tax revenue to pay for pensions and new Dreadnoughts for the navy. This freed the Liberals from their dilemma and forced their opponents back onto the defensive. Since Labour was bound to welcome measures damned as 'socialism' by the Conservatives, the effect of the budget controversy was to reinforce the loyalty of Labour to the electoral pact and thus maintain the government's base.

'Peers versus the people' in the 1910 elections

Although Lloyd George had believed his budget to be politically shrewd, even he did not at first appreciate just how central it was to become. This is because he underestimated the strength of the Tory reaction. Within days the protectionists, seeing how the new taxes had checkmated them, began to assert the right of the peers to reject the budget. Many peers felt tempted to do so because of the implications of the scheme for land valuation; though Lloyd George expected to raise little revenue from the land taxes in the first year, it was clear that once he possessed comprehensive information about land-ownership he would be in a position to realize a long-standing aim of Victorian radicals: effective taxation of the vast landed wealth of Britain. Soon the opposition organized a Budget Protest League, and Lloyd George set about provoking the Conservatives into adopting an intransigent position. At famous meetings held in Limehouse and Newcastle-upon-Tyne, he derided the Tory peers as selfish rich men who wanted Britain to rebuild the navy but refused to contribute a fair share towards it. He resurrected the old radical attack on landowners as parasites living off the hard work of employers and workingmen:

> The question will be asked whether five hundred men, ordinary men chosen accidentally from among the unemployed, should override the judgement . . . of millions of people who are engaged in the industry which makes the wealth of the country. That is one question. Another will be: who ordained that a few should have the land of Britain as a perquisite? Who made ten thousand men the owners of the soil, and the rest of us trespassers in the land of our birth?

Even before these words had been uttered, Balfour had decided to acquiesce in the wish of the extremists to reject the budget in the House of Lords.

Although this was an immensely dangerous step in view of Lloyd George's challenge to the class interests of the peers, to back down at that stage would have been divisive and demoralizing for the party and exposed the leadership to attack. As a result, the peers threw out the budget by 350 votes to 75. 'At last, with all their cunning, their greed has overborne their craft', declaimed Lloyd George; 'we have got them at last.' He was essentially right. Faced with no alternative but to seek a popular mandate to override the peers, the government dissolved Parliament. At the election in January 1910 the Liberals lost many seats, but that was inevitable after the landslide of 1906. The return of 275 Liberals, 82 Irish and 40 Labour MPs meant that the Conservatives had been heavily defeated. Not only were they obliged to swallow the budget, but they had also put reform of the House of Lords at the top of the Liberals' agenda. However, reform could be accomplished only if the new King, George V, agreed to create hundreds of new Liberal peers. Obviously reluctant, he appealed for an attempt to find a compromise, which led to a constitutional conference between representatives of the two sides in the summer of 1910. But the Conservatives were still too angry or too arrogant to see that they would have to back down, and the conference failed. The King could not afford to reject the advice of his elected government without involving the Crown in party-political controversy, and so he undertook to create peers on condition that Asquith won a second election. The December campaign concentrated on the House of Lords issue and produced a repetition of the January result.

Thereupon Asquith introduced the Parliament Bill, which abolished the power of the peers over financial legislation; other bills could be delayed for up to two years, but would become law if approved in the Commons in three successive sessions; finally, Parliament's lifetime was reduced from seven to five years. Eventually enough peers backed down for the bill to pass. In detail the Parliament Act of 1911 was something of a mistake for the Liberals as they had left the hereditary membership of the upper chamber intact and undermined the power of the Commons by shortening its life. But the whole episode clearly represented a triumph for the Liberals. Through serious misjudgements the Conservatives had put themselves in the position of

Table 8.2 Edwardian governments

1902–05	Conservative/Liberal Unionist	(A.J. Balfour)
1905–08	Liberal	(Sir Henry Campbell-Bannerman)
1908–10	Liberal	(H.H. Asquith)
1910	Liberal	(H.H. Asquith)
1910–15	Liberal	(H.H. Asquith)

opposing financial and social policies that commanded popular support; as a result they had largely destroyed the bulwark against radicalism used by Salisbury and opened the way to further innovations such as disestablishment and Home Rule. Not surprisingly, a by-product of all this was the infliction of bitter internal divisions on the party for some years.

The Conservative dilemma

In three successive Edwardian elections the Conservatives failed to devise any way of returning to power. The immediate cause lay in the launch of Chamberlain's tariff reform campaign in 1903 which activated tensions that had been simmering for years. Throughout the 1890s the National Union of Conservative Associations had debated tariff reform at annual conferences, so the ground was well prepared. Chamberlain's immediate motive was to lift the party out of the toils of the Boer War and give it fresh momentum. By offering protection to British producers tariffs guaranteed more jobs for British workers. The policy appealed to empire enthusiasts because tariffs could be varied so as to favour British colonies and thus foster trade amongst them. And it offered a source of revenue to a government otherwise trapped by a swollen National Debt and inflated income tax. At first the protectionists seemed to carry all before them and the Tory free-traders were reduced to a small minority in 1906, partly by the election but also by defections and pressure in their constituencies. As a result a majority of the parliamentary party became committed to tariffs although Balfour prevaricated, not wishing to alienate the free-traders.

However, the strategy suffered from many problems. Much of British commerce benefited too much from free trade to want to abandon it; even manufacturers were divided between those who prospered by the free exchange of goods and those in steel or cutlery who suffered from foreign competition. Protectionist support also fluctuated according to the health of the economy. In the trade depression of the early Edwardian years its appeal to the unemployed naturally strengthened; but by 1909, as the economy began to boom again, the momentum was lost. Above all, popular fears of higher food prices, which were fully exploited by the Liberals in 1906, deterred voters and gradually sapped the resolve of the Conservatives themselves. Defeat in 1906 had seemed unavoidable, but the failure to recover sufficiently in 1910 caused Conservatives much more concern. Balfour decided to try to take the sting out of tariff reform by offering to hold a referendum before abandoning free trade and subsequently it was

Table 8.3 Affiliations to the Labour Party, 1900–14

Year	Trade union members	Constituency parties (670)
1900–01	353,000	7
1901–02	455,000	21
1902–03	847,000	49
1903–04	956,000	76
1904–05	855,000	73
1905–06	904,000	73
1906–07	975,000	83
1907	1,049,000	92
1908	1,270,000	133
1909	1,450,000	155
1910	1,394,000	148
1911	1,501,000	149
1912	1,858,000	146
1913	–	158
1914	1,572,000	179

decided to exclude food from the new policy. But such concessions failed to rescue the party in the 1910 elections. Increasingly tariff reform appeared to be too great a handicap. Worse, it had led the party into the decision to reject the 1909 budget, thereby precipitating a constitutional crisis and the loss of safeguards against radical legislation. Consequently, the more pragmatic Conservatives began to water down the commitment to tariff reform after 1910. This left the party in disarray over its future economic policy and casting around desperately for alternatives.

'Balfour must go'

Repeated defeat generated extreme reactions on the far right of the party and encouraged the critics to blame Balfour for not giving a clear lead. After losing three elections, Balfour had become highly vulnerable. While the traditionalists felt he had failed to stand up to Chamberlain, the reformers blamed him for prevaricating over tariffs and for failing to back the majority line. Eventually the parliamentary party asserted itself, and in 1911 Balfour became the first of a long line of twentieth-century Tory leaders to be driven out by their own followers. When the party divided evenly between Austen Chamberlain and Walter Long, a compromise candidate emerged in Andrew Bonar Law. With his modest middle-class background, Bonar Law initiated the twentieth-century tradition of taking Conservative leaders from outside the ranks of the landed elite. Even Asquith – sprung from a West Riding woollen manufacturer, though polished by Balliol College – referred to the

Tory leader as 'a gilded iron-merchant with the mind of a Glasgow baillie'. Many Conservative dignitaries were equally dismissive of the bourgeois and relatively inexperienced new leader.

In the event, Bonar Law proved to be a success in party terms. A crisper and more aggressive leader of the opposition than Balfour, he adopted a simple, negative solution to the Conservative dilemma. He concluded that it was futile for Conservatives to attempt to compete with the Liberals over social reform as some wished to do; the more the debate concentrated on such issues the more advantage the radicals would enjoy. Instead, Bonar Law determined to rally the party around opposition to Irish Home Rule. This at least had the merit of uniting the fractious Conservatives, and allowed them to portray the Liberals as mere tools of John Redmond, desperately clinging to office by buying the votes of the Irish MPs. However, the Orange card had been played before. If there were no votes for the Liberals to win on the issue, neither were there many for the Conservatives. The British electorate was no longer moved by the Irish Question, and the Conservatives privately admitted that their campaign fell flat in the country. Moreover the Conservatives' irresponsible role in encouraging armed resistance to the Home Rule policy made them highly vulnerable. In the event, their strategy proved self-defeating for every extreme stance they adopted only had the effect of keeping Labour in alliance with the Liberals and thus maintaining the electoral pact. The party was also unnerved by the growth of trade unionism and militancy among the working class such that many doubted its ability to control the industrial situation in the event of its return to office. In short, the Edwardian period left the Conservatives badly shaken and demoralized. In this light it is an historiographical eccentricity that the period was characterized as *The Strange Death of Liberal England*, a book written in the 1930s. For it is clear that it was nothing of the sort. Rather, it was the Conservatives' world that had collapsed because they had clung too long to the strategies of the Salisbury era. It was to take a world war to rescue the party from its dilemma.

Labour's turning-point

Historical research on the Edwardian period has cast much doubt on the strength of popular support enjoyed by Labour, and on the assumption that it outflanked Liberalism by offering a more radical alternative. As we have already seen, the policies of the two parties largely converged on a progressive formula of social welfare and taxation reform; moreover, as the Labour leaders were the products of the same Victorian era as the Liberals, they were equally enthusiastic about the traditional radical programme of free trade, Home Rule and temperance. However, this made it difficult for Labour to establish a distinctive position except by advocating Socialism, which was neither particularly popular with the working class nor supported by most of the Edwardian Labour MPs.

However, policy was only one aspect of the question. The other was the electoral strategy. The growing organization and political awareness of the working class inevitably threatened the Liberals' ability to maintain a cross-class alliance, more especially when a rival party could offer workingmen much more direct representation. Yet the elections of 1910 give grounds for thinking that it was indeed feasible for the Liberals to maintain their electoral position. Although they lost many of the seats gained in 1906, these did not go to Labour; rather, they were rural and residential middle-class seats recaptured by the Conservatives. The Liberals held onto their industrial, working-class strongholds in the Midlands, the north, Wales and Scotland. In fact the social-geographical pattern of modern elections was already in place by 1910. Most of the territory north of a line from the Wash to the Bristol Channel was Liberal and Labour; south of it the Conservatives predominated except in parts of London, East Anglia and the West Country. Class-based politics had substantially arrived in Britain before 1914, and thus pre-dated the rise of Labour as one of the major parties.

Within the confines of the electoral pact the Labour Party performed strongly. But while their candidates usually won if the Liberals stood down, in three-cornered contests they invariably came third or, at best, second. When a local pact broke down the Liberals regained seats from sitting Labour MPs, and they also recovered the seats lost in by-elections in 1907. This electoral weakness on Labour's part was obscured by gains and losses between 1906 and 1910. The party lost eight of its existing seats and gained three. But the decision of the miners' federation to affiliate to the party meant that technically most of the Lib–Lab MPs were now 'Labour'. Hence the official total rose from 29 to 40. In practice, however, many of these MPs remained Liberals both at Westminster and in their constituencies.

Labour's regional strength

The electoral pact obviously restricted Labour's growth, but it was not the only explanation for the party's patchy development. The other is more fundamental, the result of the political culture of the working-class community. Conventional histories used to see the rise of Labour in terms of winning a unified working-class electorate. But it was much more complicated and protracted because working-class politics varied from one region to another. Consequently Labour was forced to vary too. In the West Riding of Yorkshire and the north-east local Labour organizations had arisen early on based on self-help groups such as friendly societies and trade unions, advocating temperance and free trade, and influenced by Nonconformity. Here they competed with local Liberalism. But in Scotland Labour was often more Socialist as is clear from the absence of the electoral pact there. Conversely in Liverpool and Merseyside, Birmingham and the West Midlands and parts of London's East End working-class culture was different, reflecting a popular Conservatism which was less religious and improving, hostile to temperance, and pro-imperialism. Where, as in Lancashire, working-class Catholics were numerous, local Labour often adopted the Conservative defence of religious education and many of the recruits of the Independent Labour Party came via a Conservative not a Liberal background. As a result Labour took on different characteristics according to the regional culture; it was early to advance in some industrial districts but later to develop in others, a feature that persisted even in the 1920s under universal suffrage.

This patchy geographical performance was reflected in the weakness of Labour's organization in the country. By 1909 the number of affiliated constituency organizations stood at 155, and it was only 158 by 1913, about a quarter of the total. Thus, the party's modest total of parliamentary contests – 50 in 1906, 78 in January 1910 and 56 in December 1910 – was not simply the result of the pact but a reflection of limited local organization. Even among the seats that were fought, the candidates sometimes had to rely upon the Liberals or a trade union to run an election. The federal structure of the party represented a weakness here, for membership was largely indirect, that is, it consisted in the membership of unions or socialist societies which affiliated to the party; there was little direct membership as such.

Was it time to abandon the pact?

Despite this many local activists in the ILP felt that the party would grow if the leadership adopted a bolder strategy. MacDonald and Snowden were accused of collaborating with the government in order to save their own seats. In 1908 Ben Tillett wrote a famous denunciation characterizing them as 'flunkeys to Asquith' in *Is the Parliamentary Labour Party a Failure?* Victor Grayson, briefly the MP for Colne Valley, argued that by adopting a real Socialist policy they would attract the working-class vote from Liberalism. But the party leadership believed this to be nonsense, and they largely disapproved of attempts by ILP activists to increase the number of candidates where there was little organization. But they could not entirely prevent wildcat or propagandist candidates in by-elections, and as a result, the 1911–14 period saw many three-cornered by-election contests. But in the process Labour lost all four of the seats it was defending and made no gains. MacDonald appreciated that excessive provocation of the Liberals would only result in the loss of Labour seats at the next general election; but he also feared the wider effect of splitting the non-Conservative vote, which would simply restore the Tories to power. In 1910 the Conservatives won 46 per cent of the poll, more than enough to give them a majority under the first-past-the-post system in the absence of the electoral pact. Thus, by 1914 Labour was expected to contest 37 seats already held plus 18 others in which the national executive had agreed to a contest. In addition, 22 constituencies had selected candidates without approval by the National Executive Committee (NEC). Even this modest total of 77 was not out of line with the December 1910 candidacies, and was likely to be cut back as the election drew near.

Trade union militancy

Understandably, party activists were also inspired by the mood of militancy among working-class communities which manifested itself in the strikes and expanding union membership of these years. From 2 million in 1900, the unions had grown to over 4 million by 1914. Ever since the formation of the ILP, the goal of tapping the funds and resources of trade unions for Socialist politics had proved rather elusive. However, during the last years of peacetime success appeared to be much closer. Liberal–Labour relations were complicated in 1908 when a Liberal trade unionist official in the Society of Railway Servants, W.V. Osborne, successfully took his union to court to stop it using its funds for party-political purposes. As a result, Labour suffered a loss of income estimated at £30,000 during 1909–14. Many workingmen regarded this as patently unfair, since the wealthy were free to spend huge sums on political causes.

Eventually the Liberal government tackled the financial grievances of the Labour Movement. In 1911 MPs received a salary of £400 per year for the first time. In 1913 the Trade Union Act made it legal to raise a separate fund for political purposes subject to two qualifications: every union must first hold a ballot to obtain members' consent to a fund, and any member might opt out of the political levy while retaining his membership. In the long run the scheme proved advantageous to Labour, since many men paid the levy without realizing it. The ballots conducted by most unions in 1913 produced a majority in favour of the political fund, though the minority was substantial and the turnout low. Here was at least a potential gain of major proportions for those who wanted Labour to break out of the electoral pact. But as the new funds were only being established in 1914 when the war broke out, it is difficult to estimate their effect. During the spring and summer of 1914, MacDonald seemed intent on working with the Liberals up to the next election. There was not sufficient evidence either of Labour strength or of Liberal weakness to justify any major change.

The franchise factor

Another question mark over Labour strength vis-à-vis the Liberals consists in the restricted nature of the pre-1914 electorate which enfranchised six out of ten men. Some historians argue that this under-represented the working class and consequently that Edwardian elections understated Labour support. However, the impact of the electorate was less simple than it appears. Although four out of ten men were not on the voters' register at any one time it was not the *same* four each year. Because of the need for twelve months continuous residence for a household voter many men who moved house passed on and off the voting lists. There is no obvious reason for thinking that the unenfranchised workingmen were more likely to vote Labour than enfranchised ones, other than the fact that some of them were young men living with their parents. Also, we know that young *middle-class* men often failed to qualify because they were not householders, which means it is not certain that the system was so biased against the working class.

One concludes that Labour had not reached the point where it could replace the Liberals by 1914. Asquith's party seemed entrenched in office and retained the initiative. Conventional claims that Liberal radicalism had been checked by 1914 because of the fear of alienating the middle class is simply not borne out by the facts. In fact in 1914 new social reforms were being introduced, graduated taxation and income redistribution was being pushed further ahead, and Lloyd George had seized the initiative with the Land Campaign which promised tribunals to raise agricultural wages and schemes to build rural houses. A prospective peacetime election late in 1914 or 1915 would probably have brought another Liberal victory.

Further reading

The case for Liberal adaptation and viability is argued in:
P.F. Clarke, *Lancashire and the New Liberalism* (1971)
Martin Pugh, *The Making of Modern British Politics 1867–1945* (2002)

Duncan Tanner, 'The Parliamentary Electoral System: the Fourth Reform Act
    and the Rise of Labour in England and Wales', *Historical Research*, 56, 1983
N. Blewett, *The Peers, the Parties and the People* (1972)

Neutral accounts are:
G.R. Searle, *The Liberal Party: triumph and disintegration 1886–1929* (1992)
David Dutton, *A History of the Liberal Party* (2004)
Michael Freeden, *The New Liberalism* (1978)
A.J.A. Morris ed., *Edwardian Radicalism* (1974)

There are many biographies:
Paul Addison, *Churchill on the Home Front 1900–55* (1993); *Asquith* by Roy
    Jenkins (1964) and S.E. Koss (1976); *Lloyd George* by K.O. Morgan (1974),
    Martin Pugh (1988), Chris Wrigley (1992), Stephen Constantine (1992), Ian
    Packer (1998), and a multi-volume study by John Grigg (1973, 1978, 1985)

On the significance of land reform see:
Ian Packer, *Lloyd George, Liberalism and the Land 1906–14* (2001)
Paul Readman, *Land and the National in England: Patriotism, National Identity
    and the Politics of the Land 1880–1914* (2008)

The case for Labour displacing the Liberals is advanced in:
R.I. McKibbin, *The Evolution of the Labour Party 1910–24* (1974)
H. Matthew, R.I. McKibbin and J.A. Kay, 'The franchise factor in the rise of the
    Labour Party', *English Historical Review*, 91, 1976
K. Laybourn, 'The Rise of Labour and the Decline of the Liberals: the state of
    the debate', *History*, 80, 1995

For neutral accounts of Labour's development see:
A. Thorpe, *A History of the British Labour Party* (1997)
Martin Pugh, *Speak for Britain! A New History of the Labour Party* (2010)
Duncan Tanner, Pat Thane and Jim Tomlinson eds, *Labour's First* Century (2000)
D. Marquand, *Ramsay MacDonald* (1977)
K.D. Brown ed., *The First Labour Party 1906–14* (1985)
Gordon Phillips, *The rise of the Labour Party 1893–1931* (1992)

Some authors have demonstrated the regional character of Edwardian politics:
Duncan Tanner, *Political Change and the Labour Party 1900–1918* (1990)
Henry Pelling, *A Social Geography of British Elections 1885–1910* (1967)

On the internal divisions among Conservatives see:
J. Ramsden, *The Age of Balfour and Baldwin 1902–40* (1978)
R.J.Q. Adams, *Bonar Law* (1999)
Alan Sykes, *Tariff Reform in British Politics 1903–13* (1979)
Richard Rempel, *Unionists Divided: Arthur Balfour, Joseph Chamberlain and the
    Unionist Free Traders* (1972)
E.H.H. Green, *The Crisis of Conservatism* (1995)

9

Crisis and Controversy in Edwardian Britain

In *The Strange Death of Liberal England,* published in 1935, George Dangerfield painted a graphic picture of a society in the first stages of breakdown and about to be engulfed in the greater chaos of world war. The violent challenges to law and authority posed by strikes, suffragettes, Ulstermen, Irish Nationalists and even the antagonists in the constitutional struggle over the House of Lords, were seen as aspects of a single crisis that threatened to make Britain ungovernable. However, the book was a piece of journalism not a serious work of history and has long been eclipsed. It was written with hindsight reflecting the interwar period when liberal democracy was in decline in several European societies. Before reaching apocalyptic conclusions about Edwardian Britain we have to pose two questions. First, did the various challenges to authority really reflect a violent rejection of law and constitutionalism? Second, were the different controversies connected as parts of a general malaise of British society?

Class struggle and class collaboration

Some contemporaries were alarmed by the growth of trade unions and the assertiveness of the working-class movement in the Edwardian period. A simple measurement of this is the pattern of annual strikes which rose from 300–400 a year in 1902–6 to 800–900 a year in 1911–14; the peak came in 1913, with 1,459 separate strikes, though the largest number of working days – 41 million – was lost in 1912, when the miners struck. Since many of these strikes proved to be successful they gave a fillip to union membership, which had doubled to reach 4.1 million by 1914. However, whether this phenomenon amounted to a threat to parliamentary government depends less on the size than on the character and motivation of the Labour Movement. Did the workers' struggles with their employers indicate greater class consciousness and a rejection of the parliamentary system? There is some evidence for a qualitative change, for example, the attempts made to unite men previously divided by skills or jobs into single unions. There was also a certain amount of sympathetic strike action. For example, in 1911 the seamen's strike led to supportive stoppages and thus to the emergence of the National Transport Workers' Federation under Ben Tillett. During the London dock strike of 1912 the men agreed to stay out until the grievances of every group of workers had been resolved. The culmination of this trend came with the formation of the so-called Triple Alliance of miners, transport workers and railwaymen in 1914. A joint stoppage by these groups would have paralysed the economy and thus been tantamount to a general strike – a challenge to the government as much as to the employers. Emotions were also heightened by several clashes between workers and the police and troops. In 1910 two miners lost their lives at Tonypandy in South Wales, when troops were ordered out to restore order by the Home Secretary, Winston Churchill. The authorities misjudged the situation when they arrested several syndicalist leaders; for example, Tom Mann was prosecuted for encouraging the troops not to fire on strikers in 1912, and in the following year Jim Larkin of the Irish Transport Workers received a seven-month sentence for sedition. In fact, although Mann and Larkin were inspiring orators and figureheads they were not really leading the Labour Movement and official heavy-handedness only gave them more prominence and credibility than they would otherwise have had. Some unionists advocated syndicalism, the idea that workers should be united with a view to holding a general strike, thereby forcing the elected government to resign and replacing it with industrial democracy. However, ordinary workingmen came out on strike for largely pragmatic reasons rather than from ideological motives. In the late 1890s falling prices had given way to a renewed period of inflation, and for several years money wages failed to keep pace. Inevitably the men wished to recover lost ground when circumstances changed. After 1908 the economy began to expand again, and by 1911 unemployment had fallen to 3 per cent, which gave workers more bargaining power. In addition unions had become legally liable for the costs of strike action to their employers as a result of the Taff Vale decision of 1901; but after 1906 the Trades Disputes Act removed this restraint, and the accumulated grievances of the men inevitably prompted more widespread industrial action.

Table 9.1 Trade union growth and strikes, 1895–1914

Year	Total union membership in millions	Number of strikes	Working days lost in millions
1895	1.5	728	5.7
1896	1.6	906	3.5
1897	1.7	848	10.3
1898	1.7	695	15.2
1899	1.9	710	2.5
1900	2.0	633	3.1
1901	2.0	631	4.1
1902	2.0	432	3.4
1903	1.9	380	2.3
1904	1.9	346	1.4
1905	1.9	349	2.3
1906	2.2	479	3.0
1907	2.5	585	2.1
1908	2.5	389	10.8
1909	2.5	422	2.7
1910	2.5	521	9.9
1911	3.1	872	10.1
1912	3.4	834	40.9
1913	4.1	1,459	9.8
1914	4.1	972	9.9

The workers and the system

Of course, it is possible that, however moderate and pragmatic the original objectives behind the Edwardian strikes, in the course of struggling against stubborn employers the men's sense of class consciousness increased, and they began to become more politically motivated. This period certainly saw a good deal of interaction between workers and government. But it does not follow that they were necessarily antagonistic. We have already noted how workingmen benefited from government intervention over minimum wages and working hours, from the employment available in labour exchanges, and from the indirect advantages of the national insurance scheme for the unions. Government also impinged directly upon the industrial situation. Since 1896 it had been empowered to offer arbitration in disputes if the two sides agreed. Under the Liberals, the Board of Trade soon became very active in all major strikes. Lloyd George, Churchill and Sydney Buxton were all keen on intervention, and from time to time other ministers, including Sir Edward Grey, John Burns, Herbert Samuel and Charles Masterman, also participated. Their mediation was not entirely even-handed, for they frequently felt exasperated at the refusal of employers to recognize the union leaders and exerted pressure on them to engage in regular collective bargaining.

Taken together, the various government measures dealing with industrial relations, union law, wages, hours and social welfare amounted to a formidable catalogue of concessions. Not surprisingly, most union leaders and Labour MPs recognized this. Increasingly they were putting their money into parliamentary politics. For them, the lesson of the Edwardian years was that, by a combination of organization in the country and steady pressure in Parliament by both Liberal and Labour MPs, it was now possible to use democratic elections and the power of the state to the advantage of workingmen. This does not mean that the unions were wholly satisfied with official policies, but it made it highly improbable that the Labour Movement in general would become alienated from the British parliamentary system in these years; on the contrary, the underlying significance of events, both industrial and political, was that they gave working-class men a foothold within the apparatus of the state that they had not hitherto enjoyed.

The challenge of feminism

To upper-class Edwardian men, the campaigns of the suffragettes represented one of the most alarming symptoms of the underlying malaise in British society. Although founded in 1903 by Emmeline and Christabel Pankhurst, the Women's Social and Political Union (WSPU) failed to attract much public notice until 1905 when it adopted militant tactics. Militancy began mildly enough, with the questioning and heckling of Cabinet ministers at public meetings over their reluctance to introduce a women's suffrage bill. Thereafter it gathered pace, with attempts to rush into the lobby of the House of Commons and interrupt debates in the chamber itself, though the WSPU also used traditional methods, including huge rallies and marches, to demonstrate their support, and organized campaigns in by-elections designed to demoralize the government by securing the rejection of its candidates. However, the Pankhursts found that, despite the interest the newspapers took in these activities, the novelty quickly wore off. Since publicity was the best way of attracting new funds and members, it was necessary to keep the movement in the public eye. This meant finding new forms of militancy capable of evading the successful counter-measures taken by the authorities. In July 1909 Marion Wallace Dunlop initiated a new phase by hunger-striking in prison and after 91 hours she was released. Subsequently 37 suffragette prisoners were released before the authorities, calculating that it would be unwise to allow them to starve, resorted to forcible feeding. However, although the new technique failed to change government policy, it was a gift to suffragette propaganda. As a result, by 1913 the government had introduced a Prisoners Temporary Discharge Act, better known as the 'Cat and Mouse' Act, which allowed the prison authorities to release suffragettes, usually for periods of one or two weeks, to recover their health, and then re-arrest them to continue serving their sentences.

Militancy and the Establishment

The other militant tactic involved attacks on property. This dated from June 1908 when Mary Leigh broke the windows in Downing Street in protest at Asquith's refusal to receive a deputation. But it did not become a regular tactic until November 1911, after the collapse of a truce, when suffragettes smashed the windows in government ministries, West End shops, newspaper offices and the National Liberal Club, leading to the arrest of 223 women. In December, Emily Wilding Davison set fire to letter boxes, a tactic that was to be repeated using targets such as country houses, bandstands and sports facilities, in addition to the dispatch of packages containing incendiary materials through the post. However, the arson campaign had the effect of alienating public opinion, so much so that the police often had to protect suffragettes from hostile crowds when they appeared in public.

Whether these militant methods amounted to a subversive or revolutionary threat to British politics and society is open to question. The Pankhursts' migration from Manchester to London reflected a leap up the social scale as much as a geographical move. The key to the WSPU's success after 1905 lay in its skill in tapping the resources and support of wealthy upper-class ladies and the patronage of the West End stores, which was retained even when their windows were broken. Though militant, suffragism stood squarely within the British radical tradition; moreover it was based within the British Establishment and it aimed to gain entry into the system for women rather than to change it fundamentally. This is why left-wing suffragettes such as Sylvia and Adela Pankhurst became marginalized and were eventually expelled from the organization because Christabel and Emmeline disapproved of the way they presented votes for women as a means of winning higher wages for low-paid female workers. Moreover, suffragette attacks on property were not sustained by an anarchist or a Socialist antagonism towards the institution of private property. Their targets were of little economic significance being mostly private houses and leisure facilities; consequently, although the violence attracted considerable publicity, it represented a law-and-order problem rather than a subversive threat.

To the more extreme anti-suffragists, these escapades were shocking proof of their claims about the unfitness of women to be voters and also about the unrepresentativeness of those women who were demanding the vote. In a notorious letter published in *The Times* in 1912 a leading doctor, Sir Almroth Wright, resurrected the commonly held but unspoken assumptions that women were prone to nervous hysteria as a result of the menstrual cycle:

> these upsettings of her mental equilibrium are the things a woman has most cause to fear; and no doctor can ever lose sight of the fact that the mind of woman is always threatened with danger from the reverberations of her physiological emergencies.

In the case of the militant suffragettes Wright alleged that they were 'sexually embittered', that is, unmarried, women 'in whom everything has turned into gall and bitterness of heart and hatred of men. Their legislative programme is licence for themselves or else restrictions for men.' To some extent Christabel Pankhurst played into the hands of the anti-feminists by publishing her pamphlet *The Great Scourge and How to End It* (1913), which urged that, since the majority of men had contracted venereal disease, women should avoid marriage altogether. However, Wright's prejudices no longer commanded much serious attention. Indeed it is easily forgotten that extreme anti-suffragist propaganda alienated opinion, including opinion among women who had previously opposed the vote. By the Edwardian period many of the Victorian 'Antis' had died and the anti-suffrage movement was in decline in the country though leaders like Lords Curzon and Cromer still collected funds from wealthy men in gentlemen's clubs. Significantly, however, their requests were now refused by those who told them it was not women's suffrage that posed a threat but Socialism.

Revisionist views on the suffrage campaign

Modern research has radically changed perspectives on Edwardian suffragism. By the time the Pankhursts adopted militancy Parliament had become converted to the principle of votes for women. The real difficulty was now to find a precise formula, defining how many women would have the vote and on what qualifications, which could be embodied in a parliamentary bill. In this situation the significance of militancy was more complicated than it appears. Like earlier radical movements such as Chartism and Irish

Image 5 Crowds gather in London's Regent Street after suffragettes smash the windows of Swan and Edgar, 1912.

Nationalism, women's suffrage developed two, ostensibly antagonistic, methods – physical force and moral force, or militancy and non-militancy. But in some ways the two complemented each other. For example, the suffragettes initially attracted huge publicity which was valuable especially as the 1906 general election and the subsequent controversies would otherwise have marginalized the issue among the politicians. Moreover, although most women felt reluctant to participate in militant activities, many were naturally deeply moved by the suffering of suffragettes in prison. This led a growing number to join the non-militant National Union of Women's Suffrage Societies (NUWSS), whose membership increased to over 50,000 by 1914. By 1913 the NUWSS had 460 branches, compared with only 90 for the WSPU and 61 for the Women's Freedom League.

This is a reminder that the phenomenon of militancy has been greatly exaggerated. In fact, the bulk of the suffragist movement was always non-militant in character. The official list of suffragette prisoners for the entire period from 1905 to 1913 includes only 1,097 names, though as some arsonists were never caught this underestimates the total. Nevertheless, it underlines the point that even within the WSPU only a minority were actively involved in militancy, the rest subscribing to funds or undertaking conventional propagandist work. In any case, after 1912 the WSPU declined and the initiative passed to the non-militant campaign.

On the other hand, militancy also damaged the cause. It alienated a number of Liberal and Labour MPs, who felt it unreasonable to attack them rather than anti-suffragist Conservatives at by-elections. Also, men in all parties were antagonized by the suffragette violence. The effect became obvious in the House of Commons when a pro-suffrage vote of 255–88 in 1911 turned into an anti-suffragist vote of 222–208 in 1912. Even within the women's movement the Pankhursts were a highly divisive element; this was not so much because women disliked their militancy as because of their autocratic style of leadership, which was so much at odds with the democratic cause for which they were fighting. The Pankhursts forced no fewer than three splits from the WSPU, first the Women's Freedom League in 1907, then the United Suffragists led by the Pethick-Lawrences in 1911; finally Sylvia Pankhurst was driven out, to establish her own group in East London. This left the WSPU as a dwindling band of Pankhurst family loyalists based on a scattering of groups in London and the Home Counties. The idea that such an organization possessed the moral influence to compel a well-entrenched government to back down was totally unrealistic.

Moreover, the WSPU went into a steep decline during the last two years before war. Thus, in spite of its embarrassment, the government continued to use the full force of the law against the suffragettes. The Home Secretary, Reginald McKenna, closed WSPU headquarters, intercepted its mail, tapped its telephones, largely suppressed its journal and by 1914 was about to prosecute its financial benefactors for the costs of militant actions. In doing all this the government was confident that the suffragettes had alienated public opinion by their violence. The Pankhursts themselves threw away their opportunity when they left Manchester for London and severed connections with the Lancashire working-class women in order to concentrate on cultivating well-to-do ladies in south-east England. This, ultimately, explains why the suffragette movement never posed a serious threat to parliamentary government. It was entirely dwarfed by the big battalions of trade unionism and Ulster Unionism.

The suffragist pact with Labour

Politicians did, in fact, show themselves more susceptible to female pressure where it seemed to reflect the social and economic grievances of ordinary working-class women. Thus, the greatest progress in the Edwardian period was actually made by conventional methods. Several trade unions were persuaded to drop their opposition to women's suffrage, and the NUWSS began to forge links in working-class communities. Their electoral pact with the Labour Party in 1912 contributed strongly to this, for it brought middle-class and working-class radicals together and put pressure on the Liberals by promoting new Labour candidacies in seats held by anti-suffragists. Since Liberal–Labour co-operation was crucial to the government's survival this was shrewd tactics. Combined with the alienation of many women Liberals and the defection of some of them to Labour, it sounded a warning to Prime Minister Asquith, about the consequences of his obdurate resistance to women's suffrage. On the eve of war he had been forced by a mixture of internal and external pressures to accept the need to enfranchise women on terms that would include the wives of workingmen – the solution that was in fact to be adopted in 1917.

The Irish Question

However, the authority of government was challenged in other ways during the Edwardian period. The first act of defiance took the form of the 'passive resistance' to the 1902 Education Act offered by some Nonconformists who refused to pay rates to maintain Anglican schools. However, the campaign was not widely supported by Nonconformists and soon petered out. The central controversy of the period developed out of the dispute over the 1909 budget. This was complicated by the absence of a written constitution. The Liberals took their stand on the *convention* that the peers did not amend money bills, and the lower house pronounced the House of Lords action to be 'a breach of the constitution and a usurpation of the rights of the Commons'. However, the peers undoubtedly enjoyed the right to amend and reject ordinary legislation. Yet there was no satisfactory way of resolving a dispute when the peers rejected a bill passed by a large majority in the Commons, which had become a regular occurrence since the 1870s, when the peers had acquired a large Conservative majority. In practice, Liberal governments simply hoped that the expansion of the electorate after 1867 would overawe the Tory peers. Lord Salisbury's response to this had been to invent the notion of the mandate: if the elected government was held to lack a popular mandate for a particular measure the Lords were entitled, indeed morally bound, to delay it until the people had spoken at a general election. This preposterous principle was applied only under Liberal governments, and it threatened to make general elections an annual occurrence if the government were to pass its legislation.

The Parliament Act of 1911 only partly resolved this problem. Though limiting the veto powers of the House of Lords, it left intact the anomaly of its hereditary membership and its extraordinary political bias. As the preamble to the Act had included a promise of further reform, the Conservatives insisted that the British constitution was now in suspension while the pledge went unredeemed; the country, they argued, was subject to single-chamber government. After 1914 the role actually played by the House of Lords certainly diminished, and the constitutional question languished on the margins of political debate for decades. Although Tory peers produced a plethora of schemes for further reform, their leaders steadfastly declined to live up to their own professed intention of restoring the role of the upper chamber. In effect they acquiesced in what the Liberals had done.

Ulster and the Home Rule Bill

However, the immediate ramifications of the Parliament Act proved more dramatic. As a result of the 1910 elections the Liberals became dependent upon the 82 Irish MPs for an overall majority. In these circumstances the Nationalist leader, John Redmond, naturally expected a new Home Rule Bill, more especially now that the removal of the peers' veto made it practical politics. Thus in April 1912 the third Home Rule Bill began its passage through the Commons, and by May 1914 it had been passed three times as required by the Parliament Act. However, the Conservatives and Unionists exploited the two-year interval to foment resistance to the measure in Ulster. Led by Captain James Craig and Sir Edward Carson, the Unionists argued that a Dublin parliament for the whole of Ireland would be oppressive towards the Protestant minority, politically radical, likely to jeopardize the advantages Ireland enjoyed through free trade with England, and certain to open up a weakness in Britain's defences. As Westminster would have retained control of foreign affairs and defence this was obviously untrue. In effect, as the dominant elite in Ulster, they feared a loss of power and status. However, the government refused to be overawed. They saw that the Unionists' cause had already been abandoned by the English Unionist landowners who had taken government money and surrendered their territorial interest in Ireland. In spite of their concentration in Ulster, the Unionists could hardly expect to veto indefinitely the wishes of the majority. Four-fifths of the Irish constituencies had consistently voted for a Home Rule parliament, and from 1910 onwards their representatives held the balance of power in the House of Commons.

On the other hand, Asquith underestimated the depths of Ulster resistance and the lengths to which English Conservatives were prepared to go in order to thwart the policy of the elected government. The campaign began with a dignified declaration of adherence to the Union known as the Ulster Solemn League and Convenant, to which a quarter of a million people put their signatures. But the rebels also established an Ulster Volunteer Force of some 90,000 men, which gained a measure of respectability as a result of the irresponsible pledge given by Bonar Law to support the Ulstermen even if they resorted to violence. The government continued to regard this as bravado until January 1914, when a number of gun-running episodes occurred. Before long the Ulster Volunteers possessed 35,000 rifles, landed from Germany, and the Nationalists countered by organizing the Dublin Volunteers. The emergence of these private armies raised the prospect that civil war would erupt when the Dublin parliament was set up. That seemed even more likely after the notorious Curragh Mutiny of March 1914 when some 57 officers, stationed in Ireland, offered to resign rather than enforce the Home Rule policy in Ulster. They had been encouraged in this action by senior army officers in London, who placed loyalty to party above their duty to the government. The failure to court martial those responsible suggested that the government could not wholly rely upon the army to carry out orders. Although this clearly represented the most serious challenge to parliamentary government, it remains a matter of speculation as to what the consequences of civil war would have been. Asquith could not risk retreating from the Home Rule Bill because he would have lost his parliamentary majority, and because to do so would have caused chaos in the three nationalist provinces. A civil war in Ireland might have led to some violence in Liverpool and Glasgow, but most of the population of the mainland would almost certainly have remained indifferent. They did, after all, subsequently witness a virtual civil war in the early 1920s. These events undoubtedly aroused the political elite, especially the far right, but there is no indication of a similar degree of concern in the country at large.

Plans for war

Meanwhile Home Rule was eclipsed by the far more serious conflict abroad. The Anglo-Japanese Alliance had set in train a series of events that exacerbated the existing tensions in Europe. It immediately alarmed the French because of the possibility that, if Russia and Japan became involved in a war, they might involve their respective partners, France and Britain, who had no interest in such a conflict. But Russia's stunning defeat by Japan in 1904–5 put a different perspective on the alliances as it dramatically exposed the weakness of the Dual Alliance. If this was France's immediate problem, it was one that increasingly concerned Britain. For not only did she feel threatened by the German navy, she was equally worried about the prospect of another French defeat at the hands of the German army.

The Anglo-French Entente

As the security of the British Isles loomed larger in the minds of the strategists and politicians, it seemed necessary to downgrade Britain's extensive colonial obligations. Since these could not be met through force, the alternative was diplomacy and compromise. The first step in this direction came in the form of the Anglo-French Entente of 1904. While this dealt with certain specific disputes over Egypt and Newfoundland fishing rights which had complicated relations for years, the underlying rationale behind the entente was the appreciation that the two countries faced a common threat in Europe. Moreover, although the entente fell far short of an alliance, Germany chose to interpret it, correctly, as more than simply a settlement of disputes. She therefore tested the strength of the new relationship, putting pressure on the French by challenging their attempt to take over Morocco. The Germans calculated that in a crisis the British would abandon France, leaving her aggrieved and isolated again. Up to a point this proved correct, for the French were checked in North Africa. But in reality the German government had seriously miscalculated, for its clumsy intervention proved to London and Paris how necessary it was to co-operate against the bully. The immediate effect was to prompt Sir Edward Grey, the new Liberal Foreign Secretary, who had entertained suspicions of German ambitions since the 1890s, to move closer to the French. This took the form of conversations between the two navies. The move took place in the context of an existing redeployment of the British fleets. Squadrons in Pacific and Canadian waters had already been withdrawn, and others were reduced or amalgamated in order to concentrate on an Atlantic Fleet based at Gibraltar, and a Channel Fleet. As the relationship with the French developed, this resulted in further concentrations of British ships in the Channel and the North Sea, where Britain undertook to defend France's northern coast, while in the Mediterranean Britain could rely upon French naval support in protecting her trade routes.

Invasion scares

As yet all this was not widely known in the country, or in the Cabinet for that matter. What caught the public attention was the launching of the Dreadnought battleship in February 1906. With a speed of twenty-one knots and ten twelve-inch guns, the Dreadnought outclassed all existing competitors. On the other hand, it rendered Britain's existing fleet obsolete and vulnerable if another power were to build more rapidly to Dreadnought standard. In this situation scares about invasions, spies and internal subversion flourished. Erskine Childers (*The Riddle of the Sands*, 1903), William Le Queux (*The Invasion of 1910*, 1906) and H.G. Wells (*The War In The Air*, 1903) were among those who pandered to the fashion. Following the precedent of the fictional 'Battle of Dorking', Le Queux collaborated with Lord Roberts of the National Service League and Lord Northcliffe of the *Daily Mail* to focus attention upon the likely route chosen by an invading army; it followed towns in which Northcliffe was anxious to boost sales of the *Daily Mail*, thereby enabling him to mix profit and patriotism in a rather satisfying way! Soon, however, it became difficult to separate fact from fiction. It was well known that thousands of Germans and other aliens lived in Britain working as waiters, servants, barbers and clerks. They were now alleged to be mostly spies, plotting acts of subversion to facilitate the landing of an enemy force. Reports of suspicious activities from members of the public provided useful copy for the *Daily Mail* and other papers and the excitable mood prompted the Navy League to foment panic over the navy in 1909, on the basis of information that the Germans planned to build 14 Dreadnought-type ships. At that time Britain possessed six, and the Admiralty planned to add to these at the rate of four a year. The League, the Northcliffe press and the opposition in Parliament demanded eight new ships immediately.

Although these scares about spies, invasions and the German navy were baseless propaganda, they were not without some political influence. Many of those in high places wanted to believe the rumours, as did the general public. In addition to becoming amateur spy-spotters, many Edwardians undertook first-aid training, especially under the Voluntary Aid Detachments organized by the Red Cross, so as to be useful when the invasion came. The Cabinet could not afford to be outflanked either. It established a regular secret service, introduced registers of aliens to enable the authorities to control their movements, and made arrangements to have strategic buildings properly guarded. In 1910, on a quiet Friday afternoon, the government squeezed a new Official Secrets Bill through the House of Commons; this was intended to enable the police to check subversion by prosecuting any person who was considered to be suspicious but without producing any

Table 9.2 British strength relative to other Great Powers in 1914

	Britain	France	Russia	Germany	USA
Population	45 million	40 million	164 million	65 million	92 million
Military expenditure	£50 million	£37 million	£67 million	£60 million	£30 million
Soldiers	711,000	1,250,000	1,200,000	2,200,000	150,000
Battleships	64	28	16	40	37
Submarines	64	73	29	23	25

evidence that he was a spy or had actually spied. Though this was a scandalous piece of legislation in a liberal society, the Act was accepted without serious question because of the climate of fear. Once war had broken out the authorities immediately arrested 21 'spies'; and it was widely believed that the British forces would have done much better had they not been betrayed by the network of spies ensconced in Britain. John Buchan's famous novel *The Thirty-Nine Steps* (1915) caught the mood very neatly.

Meanwhile Asquith defused the naval scare in 1909 by undertaking to build eight new Dreadnoughts if the rate of building in Germany appeared to warrant it. In fact, the Germans never regarded an invasion of Britain as feasible. By 1911 they had only six Dreadnoughts, and Britain retained a comfortable lead right up to 1914. However, the scares helped to lock the two countries into the naval race, and obliged the Chancellor of the Exchequer to fund the higher naval estimates. Although Lloyd George offered some resistance to this, he had come to agree fundamentally with the new trend in Britain's foreign and defence policy; consequently he always found the money for new Dreadnoughts.

The British Expeditionary Force

While such signs of determination on the naval front were reassuring to the French, the situation in Europe remained very worrying. After all, Britain had given no firm or public commitment to support France. In the event of war, the Royal Navy would play no part in resolving the immediate strategic problem; for the German armies were expected to cross the frontiers of France and Belgium in a series of arcs which would envelope Paris. In a matter of weeks the French government would collapse, and the war might be effectively over before the Russian forces had swung into action. Increasingly, therefore, the French wanted to know whether Britain would put any real weight behind her new friendship in the early stages of a war. Reluctantly Grey concluded that Britain must do so because a further defeat of France could lead to her being seriously weakened as a great power; once the Germans gained control of northern France they would be in a strong position to threaten the British Isles and the empire. This was Britain's rationale for war in 1914.

The plans designed to give effect to this intention emerged from the discussions of the Committee of Imperial Defence and the Army's General Staff, which had been created as recently as 1904. Faced with Britain's chaotic efforts to raise a substantial army for the South African War, the new Secretary of State for War, Richard Haldane, chose to reorganize his forces by amalgamating the regulars, the militia and the volunteers into two. The Field Force, basically the professional army, was to be capable of mobilization within 15 days and thus to be available for use abroad in an emergency, while the Home Force or Territorial Army, consisting of partly trained men, would be ready for action six months after the outbreak of war. At the time the authorities avoided saying that the Field Force, or British Expeditionary Force (BEF), was to be deployed in Europe. Since the memory of the Boer War and apprehensions about the Russian threat to India's North-West Frontier were very much alive, the army was conveniently seen in terms of colonial emergencies. Indeed, as the Russian railway system reached Tashkent in 1904 it became feasible for the first time to convey a substantial army to within striking distance of the Indian Empire. But the British government had no intention of giving the Commander-in-Chief in India the extra forces he believed he required. It followed that a Russian threat must be tackled and defused by diplomatic means, as the French had been. This was accomplished by the Anglo-Russian Entente of 1907. The Russians agreed to communicate with the Amir of Afghanistan only through Britain, and to keep their agents out of his country – a remarkably favourable deal considering how vulnerable Britain's position was. In Persia the two powers agreed to confine themselves to separate spheres of interest, the Russians to the north around Teheran, the British to the south-east around Bandar Abbas. The rationale for this was identical to that underlying the Anglo-French Entente: both powers considered the threat of war in Europe as the greater priority.

The 1907 Entente virtually completed the diplomatic revolution. It allowed the Committee of Imperial Defence to plan for the dispatch of 120,000 men of the BEF to reinforce the left flank of the French forces in Europe, with a view to checking the German advance towards Paris. For a time the Admiralty prevaricated over this, because it did not wish to be downgraded to become a transport service for the army. But the navy's own ideas about the war simply failed to address the key strategic problem, and by 1911 it had been overruled; Britain was effectively, though not formally, committed to fighting a Continental land war.

Misunderstandings over British entry into war

As a result, Britain was better prepared for the First World War than for almost any war in her modern history; consider by comparison the chaotic approach in 1854, 1899 and 1939. This is worth emphasizing as some writers continue to suggest that Britain was unprepared for war in 1914. In fact she had diagnosed the strategic threat posed by German plans, rationalized her forces and adapted her planning to meet it. In the event she successfully implemented her policy: Paris was saved, and the Allies won vital time in which to mobilize both Russian manpower and British industrial might.

Yet this has not been always been recognized in received accounts of the period partly because, in spite of her planning, Britain gave no binding promise to join France and Russia in war with Germany. This was to some extent due to political inhibitions. In the Cabinet half the ministers tended to oppose participation in a Continental war. Much of the Liberal and Labour forces in the country and in Parliament strongly disapproved of the naval race, felt that more should be done to maintain good relations with Germany, and abhorred the entanglement with the oppressive Tsarist regime in Russia. Yet even if such pressures had not existed, it is not clear that an *alliance* with France would have been wise or efficacious. Grey rightly felt that any firm pledge to the French would have made them all the more willing to risk a war with Germany. Since above all things he hoped to maintain peace, Grey saw the wisdom of keeping the other powers in some doubt about Britain's course of action in a crisis.

However, contemporary criticism had little effect on the development of government policy. The radicals found it impossible to deny the necessity for some naval building, especially since, in spite of several overtures from the British, Germany refused to modify her own programme. In addition, the government took some of the sting out of the criticism by saving money on the army reorganization and by managing to finance its social policies in spite of the swollen naval estimates. After 1910, when the Liberals lost their independent majority and party passions were inflamed by the House of Lords and Home Rule issues, the critics felt reluctant to upset the boat over foreign policy. This still left a serious charge against Grey over the secrecy in which British policy was being made; the radicals correctly suspected that the Foreign Secretary was committing Britain to more than he was prepared to admit in public. This concern was shared by Cabinet ministers, who were largely excluded from policymaking. The issue came to a head as a result of the second crisis over Morocco in 1911, when the German government again tried to bully the French and demanded compensation for the French occupation of North Africa. This provoked a famous warning to Germany not to treat Britain as though she were of no account in international affairs delivered by Lloyd George in his speech at the Mansion House. In Cabinet John Morley spoke for many when he complained that Grey seemed to be giving unauthorized promises of support to the French. As a result the ministers formally decided that no communications should take place between British and French forces that committed Britain to intervention, and that any talks must first be approved by the Cabinet. This, however, was shutting the door after the horse had bolted.

During the next three years fears among the political elite were, if anything, diminished by Grey's successful diplomacy. He had succeeded in containing regional wars in the Balkans and when a crisis erupted in late July 1914 following the assassination of the Austrian Archduke at Sarajevo, the initial expectations were of yet another *regional* war, albeit one involving Austria and Serbia. However, such expectations were dashed by the decision of the Russians that they could no longer stand by and allow their interests in the Balkans to be trampled upon. Since Germany intended to back up Austria, France was unavoidably involved too. Faced with the prospect of war between the great powers, the British Cabinet initially declined to commit itself to either intervention or neutrality. But on 2 August the ministers took a crucial half-way step by authorizing Grey to assure France that Britain would not allow Germany to use the Channel for hostile purposes. The doubters in Cabinet appreciated that Britain had entered into some obligations to the French for mutual naval defence and were tempted to see Britain's role in the forthcoming conflict as primarily a naval one. But news of the violation of Belgian territory helped to bring the waverers into line behind an ultimatum demanding Germany's withdrawal and eventually all but two Cabinet ministers, John Burns and John Morley, accepted the decision. However, British entry into the war was not essentially bound up with the Belgian issue, even though this provided a respectable legal and moral cause. Rather, Britain calculated that her own security was now closely linked with the maintenance of France as a great power.

An ungovernable society?

Was the Cabinet's fateful decision to take Britain to war connected with domestic considerations? Was it a desperate ploy to save a turbulent society sliding into chaos? It is fair to say that for Asquith the international crisis came as a timely diversion from domestic troubles. War had the immediate effect of producing a party-political truce and the suspension of the controversial bills to give Ireland Home Rule and to disestablish the Church in Wales. Strikes and suffragette campaigns were swiftly abandoned. John Redmond gave a remarkable pledge of loyalty to the British cause and the warring parties in Ireland withdrew from confrontation.

However, the deep loathing with which the Liberal ministers committed the country to war leaves no room for suspicion that they opted for it as a way out of domestic difficulties. Indeed, they saw war as the ultimate triumph of Toryism which would probably check, if it did not destroy, all the progress that had recently been made. This represented a contrast with the situation prevailing elsewhere. For the unstable regimes of Germany, Austria and Russia there was always a temptation to use external conflict to manufacture unity and silence domestic opposition. But the British parliamentary system remained strong and viable, and the Liberal government was well entrenched in spite of the controversies surrounding it. At worst Asquith had been weak towards the Ulster Unionists, whose leaders ought to have been arrested, and he had been foolishly stubborn in resisting the claims of women to enfranchisement. But bit by bit the various challenges facing the government were all being surmounted. Asquith had consolidated his position by twice winning elections in which first 86 per cent and then 81 per cent of the electors had voted. Above all, the particular configuration of parties meant that social class was never the source of acute disunity and instability that it became in some other countries. To Lloyd George's opponents it naturally appeared that he employed the language of class war against the dukes, but in fact the rationale behind his radical rhetoric was to shore up the alliance of workingmen and the middle class. The economic boom of the last years of peacetime made this all the easier to achieve. Neither the Labour Movement nor the women's movement was really anti-parliamentary for their aim was to join the system rather than to overthrow it. Nor were there any significant links between the various extraparliamentary movements. They were coincidental controversies rather than symptoms of a common malaise.

If a sense of frustration and alienation existed at all in these years, it was characteristic of the right wing of the political elite. Some Conservatives found it hard to accept their protracted exclusion from office, and the landed class could see that it was being marginalized politically. Above all the Edwardian period was characterized by bitter attacks by the 'radical right', including such men as Leo Maxse, Sir Henry Page Croft and Willoughby de Broke. Much stirred by Britain's poor showing in the Boer War, they espoused simplistic conspiracy theories to explain the country's decline. They diagnosed an enemy within in the form of Irish Nationalists, Liberals, Socialists, Jews, aliens and 'radical plutocrats'. The latter group comprised wealthy cosmopolitan businessmen who remained outside the Conservative Establishment and chose to promote Liberal causes such as land reform. The radical right also felt betrayed by its own party leaders, who now attracted criticism as an effete, upper-class elite inherited from the Salisbury era. Balfour was the obvious victim of this mood. The outbreak of war made these Tory rebels even more neurotic and suspicious of their own party leadership, and even the return to office failed to heal the divisions that had developed in the party. Their anger represented a problem but was not indicative of a general crisis.

Further reading

The question of governability and the political crisis is discussed in:
David Powell, *The Edwardian Crisis: Britain 1900–1914* (1996)
George Dangerfield, *The Strange Death of Liberal England* (1935) – a piece of journalism, lively but not serious history.
Alan Sykes, *The Radical Right in Britain* (2005)
G.R. Searle, *Corruption in British Politics 1895–1930* (1987)
G.R. Searle, *A New England? Peace and War 1886–1918* (2004)

On industrial relations and working-class militancy see:
Keith Laybourn, *British Trade Unionism 1770–1990* (1991)
Henry Pelling, 'The Labour Unrest 1911–14', in *Popular Politics and Society in Late Victorian Britain* (1979)
Henry Pelling, *A History of British Trade Unionism* (1987)
H. Clegg, A. Fox and A. Thompson, *A History of British Trade Unions since 1889* (1964)
Paul Thompson, *The Edwardians: the Re-making of British Society* (1992)
S. Meacham, *A Life Apart: The English Working Class 1880–1914* (1977)

New thinking on Edwardian women's suffrage campaigns is advanced in:
S.S. Holton, *Feminism and Democracy: Women's Suffrage and Reform Politics in Britain 1900–1918* (1986)
Martin Pugh, *The March of the Women: A Revisionist Analysis of the Campaign for Women's Suffrage 1866–1914* (2000)
Martin Pugh, *The Pankhursts* (2001)
Julia Bush, *Women Against the Vote* (2007)
Mynam Boussahba, *Suffrage Outside Suffragism: the Women's Vote in Britain 1880–1914* (2007)
Andre Rosen, *Rise Up Women! The Militant Campaign of the Women's Social and Political Union* (1974)

Angela V. John and Claire Eustance eds, *The Men's Share: Masculinities, Male Support and Women's Suffrage 1890–1920* (1997)

Richard Symonds, *Inside the Citadel: Men and the Emancipation of Women 1850–1920* (1999)

On the Irish Home Rule crisis see:

Alan O'Day, *Irish Home Rule 1867–1921* (1998)

Ronan Fanning, *Fatal Path: British Government and Irish Revolution 1910–22* (2013)

Lawrence J. McCafferty, *The Irish Question* (1995)

F.S.L. Lyons, *Culture and Anarchy in Ireland 1890–1939* (1979)

The centenary of the outbreak of war in 1914 produced many new books but no new ideas on the causes and origins:

Margaret Macmillan, *The War That Ended Peace* (2013)

Keith Wilson ed., *Decisions for War, 1914* (1995)

Zara Steiner, *Britain and the Origins of the First World War* (1977)

Paul Kennedy, *The War Plans of the Great Powers 1880–1914* (1979)

Paul Kennedy, *The Rise of the Anglo-German Antagonism 1860–1914* (1980)

F.H. Hinsley ed., *The Foreign Policy of Sir Edward Grey* (1977)

10

Politics and Society in the Great War

In Britain the conflict that broke out in August 1914 was quickly dubbed 'the Great War'. The British people had experienced nothing on the scale since the Revolutionary and Napoleonic Wars a century earlier. Since then war had been a matter of minor colonial skirmishes; even the Crimean War, which did involve three Great Powers, was peripheral by comparison. This was the sense behind Sir Edward Grey's famous remark: 'The lamps are going out all over Europe; we shall not see them lit again in our time.' By comparison with the regimes of Germany, Russia, Italy and even France, Britain was to emerge remarkably unscathed by the ordeal. Yet during the 1920s and 1930s contemporaries saw the war almost wholly in negative terms – the loss of 750,000 British males, a collapse of moral standards, high income tax and new threats to the empire. However, after 1945, influenced by the aftermath of a second great war, historians increasingly emphasized the constructive effects of the First World War. It began to be seen as one example of a new kind of war – 'Total War' or 'Mass War'. Previous conflicts, especially for Britain, had usually involved quite small numbers of fighting men and thus made only a limited impact on society. During 1914–18, on the other hand, over 5 million British men enlisted in the armed forces; moreover, the support and maintenance of the troops required a huge civilian effort by both men and women. The necessity for mass participation led historians to argue that the political elite had no option but to grant a succession of concessions or rewards including social-economic ones, such as council housing, and political ones, notably the vote, which had the effect of levelling some of the inequalities in British society. In this perspective mass war was a major progressive force for change in the twentieth century.

The Continental commitment

At first the war was widely expected to resemble the Franco-Prussian War; it would involve swift mobilization, rapid flanking movements, decisive battles and thus reach a speedy conclusion. In a famous phrase, it would all be over by Christmas. Britain's role would be primarily naval and economic in that her industrial and financial resources would enable the French and Russian armies to overcome the Central Powers. In order to prevent an early knockout blow against Paris by the advancing German armies, the British Expeditionary Force, commanded by Sir John French, was conveyed across the Channel to reinforce the left flank of the French. At Mons the BEF, which found itself directly in the path of much larger German forces, quickly joined in the general retreat south but a counter-attack at the Battle of the Marne in September checked the German advance and movement rapidly ceased. The rival forces then raced to the coast to prevent flanking attacks, and dug elaborate lines of trenches protected by rolls of barbed wire. By January 1915 the prospect of rapid advances and frontal attacks had nearly disappeared and four years of stalemate on the western front had begun.

Although British strategy had already scored a major success – the defeat of the Schlieffen Plan – this was not widely recognized at the time or since. Yet Britain had won the time needed to bring her industrial might and Russian manpower into play. But though Paris had been saved she remained, throughout the war, only a few precarious miles from enemy forces and thus vulnerable to a sudden attack. In this situation the man who did most to develop British strategy beyond the first stage was Lord Kitchener, whom Asquith appointed Secretary of State for War. Kitchener quickly perceived that the struggle would be prolonged, and that Britain would have to play a greater role on the Continent than had been anticipated. Ignoring the pre-war Territorial Army, he proceeded to create an entirely new British army from the mass of eager volunteers.

The volunteer armies

The popular response to the crisis is one of the most remarkable features of the whole war. The authorities were swamped by the numbers of men who came forward voluntarily to serve in the forces. Recruiting figures ran at 300,000 in August, 450,000 in September, 137,000 in October, 170,000 in November, 117,000 in December, and 156,000 in January 1915. Explanations for this response vary. Even though there was no specific territorial issue at stake for Britain, people had grown to expect a war and to regard the

Table 10.1 Armed forces personnel, 1913–18

Year	Army	Navy	Air force
1913	247,000	139,000	
1914	1,327,000	201,000	
1915	2,476,000	251,000	
1916	3,344,000	328,000	
1917	3,883,000	368,000	
1918	3,838,000	407,000	290,000

Germans as a threat to British interests. For many, the most concrete issue was Belgium, which was presented by the press and government propaganda as the innocent victim of the German bully. Tales of German atrocities, almost wholly unsubstantiated, and the arrival in Britain of Belgian refugees helped to reinforce this view and to give a high moral tone to the British cause. The Liberal government enlisted liberal writers like H.G. Wells and John Galsworthy to present Britain's case in idealistic terms. Those who sought comfort from the appalling situation were attracted by the idea that this was a 'war to end wars', not one for territorial aggrandizement. However, most people were more moved by fear and hatred of Germany. Economic motives for volunteering were not particularly important as unemployment was not high at this time, and the rush of recruits clearly went far beyond any particular class or industry. Many young men were swept up in the excitement, felt vaguely patriotic, were attracted by the status conveyed by a uniform, and anticipated a brief adventure in foreign parts in the company of fellow workers. Hence the popularity of the 'Pals Battalions' based on particular occupations and companies.

Controversy over British strategy

Consequently, by early 1915 an unusually large British army was undergoing training for service abroad. The question arose: exactly what use should be made of it? Britain's planning did not go beyond the original commitment to France. Kitchener, in common with almost all other generals, adopted the view that, since the war could be lost very easily on the western front, Britain had no option but to concentrate her forces there and seek a decisive victory over Germany. This view gained force from the demands made by the French that Britain must relieve the pressure on them by taking over more of the front line.

Against this were ranged a number of arguments and interests. The Royal Navy, never happy at being downgraded by the Continental commitment, enjoyed a good deal of political support, especially from those Liberals who wanted a limited war. Up to a point the traditional naval strategy was implemented. Enemy ships were soon cleared from the oceans, Germany's foreign trade was largely stopped, the British Isles protected from invasion, and the navy prepared for a decisive battle with the German High Seas Fleet. However, this was far from being a recipe for overall victory in the war. Apart from the Battle of Jutland in 1916 the Germans avoided major naval actions, and it was far too dangerous for Britain to attack close to the enemy's home waters; battleships were very vulnerable to mines, submarines and torpedoes. After all the controversy of the Edwardian years, the navy proved something of a disappointment and was by no means the key to Britain's war effort.

But critics of the army's strategy including Lloyd George and Winston Churchill contended that over-concentration on the western front simply dissipated Britain's precious manpower for no strategic gain. Instead, they wished to use the flexibility offered by the navy to transfer the new armies to other theatres in which the Central Powers were more vulnerable. To some extent this strategy was implemented in the campaigns in the Dardanelles, Salonika, Mesopotamia and East Africa. By thus 'knocking away the props' in the shape of Turkey, Austria and the German colonies, Britain, it was argued, would isolate Germany. Unhappily these territories turned out not to be props for Germany at all. In any case, it proved almost as difficult to achieve victories in these campaigns as on the western front, and the military authorities were never willing to release enough resources to attain decisive results. East Africa alone offered a definite victory but it was of no significance for the wider war.

Military incompetence?

The politicians were generally reluctant to overrule expert military advice, even when it failed to produce positive results. Both wartime prime ministers found themselves exposed to charges that they had failed to provide either munitions or troops in sufficient quantity and thereby hampered the army's efforts. This was to have important political consequences. For example, when Sir John French's spring offensive of 1915 failed he blamed Asquith rather than admitting his own incompetence, arguing that if he had had more high-explosive shells the breakthrough would have been achieved. This situation contributed to Asquith's decision to replace his Liberal government with a three-party coalition in May 1915. It also led to the creation of the Ministry of Munitions under Lloyd George, which generated huge quantities of armaments, albeit at great cost, and made his reputation as a war minister when others were being discredited.

As the generals lost one excuse they sought another. By the start of 1916 debate had come to focus on the supply of men necessary to sustain an offensive on the western front. Now that the number of volunteers had dwindled, the generals, supported by most Conservatives and some Liberals, argued that the time had come to adopt conscription like the other belligerents. This was resisted in Cabinet partly on the grounds that compulsion was morally wrong, that it would antagonize the Labour Movement, and it was essential for Britain to maintain her industrial output so as to sustain the allied war effort for a long period; frittering men away on futile offensives would achieve nothing except a German victory. But in 1916 the government eventually opted for conscription first of single and then of married men. This made possible Sir Douglas Haig's disastrous offensives of 1916 and 1917, first the Battle of the Somme, which produced 60,000 British casualties on the first day alone, and then the prolonged Passchendaele campaign. Neither achieved any significant territorial or strategic gain and the offensives actually wore down British forces more than German.

However, recent years have seen sympathetic biographies and a measured defence of British military tactics. This consists of three main arguments: that the generals were right about the western front, that they learnt from their mistakes, and that they maintained the army in a sufficient state to be able to inflict defeat on Germany in 1918. Yet no one claims that Britain produced brilliant generals in the Great War. Ultimately it was the much-abused politicians, through the supply of munitions, the maintenance of food imports, the mobilization of resources via loans and taxation, and the creation of national consensus by means of coalition and concessions to the workers, who won the war rather than the generals.

In spite of Haig's repeated assurances that his offensives had worn down and demoralized the enemy, in the spring of 1918 the Germans launched a major attack which very nearly brought them victory. It broke up the British Fifth Army, forced the allies into a headlong retreat, and almost divided the British forces from the French. This military setback created a political crisis for Lloyd George, who was accused of deliberately withholding troops from Haig as a means of deterring him from embarking on fresh offensives. This came close to destroying the government, but Lloyd George managed to bluff his way out, largely because even his critics thought his government the best one available. When the allied forces, now strongly reinforced by American troops, resumed the attack in the summer of 1918, they were surprised to find the Germans in retreat. Although never comprehensively defeated, the German leaders agreed to an armistice in November and the war came to an unexpectedly sudden end. At last it was the turn of the politicians to seize some advantage from military events. Lloyd George lost no time in holding a general election in December 1918, while his prestige as the 'man who had won the war' was at its height.

State intervention in the economy

The adoption of a Continental policy involving the recruitment of mass armies had major implications for wartime economic policy because of the demands it imposed upon industry. From the very beginning, substantial numbers of skilled men in engineering, mining and steel, who were essential to the war effort at home, joined the armed forces. To some extent their loss was checked by exempting key workers from military service, and in 1917 Lloyd George introduced a National Service Department with the intention of distributing manpower rationally between the various industries and the armed forces. But this proved impossible, largely because the army had already distorted the labour market and it was politically difficult to force it to disgorge its recruits.

Instead, the government introduced large numbers of unskilled men, women and boys into the jobs previously done by the men at the front. At first many war workers felt grateful to have a full week's work and escape occupations like domestic service which suffered from low pay and status. In time, however, they realized that they were being exploited by the government and by employers, who were making huge profits guaranteed by government contracts. Not surprisingly, trade union membership increased from 4 million to 6.5 million by 1918. The number of strikes, which had been running at a high level, dropped sharply in 1915 and 1916, but then rose again in 1917 and 1918. Workers, angered by the rising cost of food and housing, appreciated that they were in a strong bargaining position. Many companies were making assured profits from war orders and paying unskilled rates for skilled work. Since the government was desperate to avoid any interruption to the flow of production, it encouraged the employers to grant substantial increases in wages during the second half of the war and in the immediate aftermath.

The other pressure at work was inflation. Since Britain depended heavily on imported food some substantial price rises were inevitable, especially when German submarines attacked merchant shipping indiscriminately. An equally serious problem arose over accommodation, which was almost wholly rented at this time. The diversion of workers from the building industry meant that there could be no improvement in the housing stock during the war. Moreover, the major migration of workers to such areas as Clydeside, Newcastle and Sheffield, where munitions factories were concentrated, created severe shortages and led to much higher rents.

State controls

Wartime governments could not ignore the resulting tensions as they needed munitions desperately. Originally the Liberals had expected the war to have the effect of disrupting industry and creating mass unemployment. However, they soon realized that the huge demands of the war machine would lead to a shortage rather than a surplus of labour. They particularly feared that, as the initial euphoria wore off, civilian discontent would offer opportunities both to syndicalists and to pacifists, who were campaigning for a negotiated peace, to disrupt industry. The result was a barrage of interventionist measures to regulate the economy and ensure the free flow of vital goods. Landlords tried to take advantage of munitions workers by increasing rents, thus provoking rent strikes and forcing the government to pass the 1915 Rent Restriction Act to peg rents to pre-war levels. From the beginning of the war the government began to buy food supplies on the world markets and release them so as to check price increases. Propaganda designed to achieve the more economical use of food and appeals for voluntary rationing largely failed, and by 1917 a compulsory rationing system had been introduced. Key items like bread and potatoes were subsidized, and 80 per cent of all food was purchased by the Food Controller. Draconian steps were also taken, in the form of the 1917 Corn Production Act, to impose precise output targets upon farmers.

Industry also came under extensive official control. In August 1914 the government invoked its powers under an act of 1870 to take over the operation of the railways during the war. Thereafter the state intervened as and when shortages, bottlenecks or industrial unrest created a threat to production. Between 1915 and 1917 the coalfields were brought steadily under official control. Under the auspices of the Ministry of Munitions, the government became the owner of 250 factories and supervised the work of a further 20,000 involving 2 million employees. The cost of the war meant that government expenditure accounted for nearly 60 per cent of gross national product by 1917 compared to 7 per cent in 1913. Although 70 per cent of the cost of the war was met by loans, the remaining 30 per cent was financed by taxation, which meant an increase in income tax from a maximum pre-war rate of 2s. 8d. to 6s. in the pound. In addition the tax net was greatly extended because the threshold was lowered from £150 to £130 and rising wage rates made millions of workingmen liable for income tax for the first time.

Image 6 Official propaganda designed to engage women in the war effort.

Table 10.2 Standard rate of income tax

Year	Income tax as a percentage
1914	6
1915	8.5
1916	15
1917	25
1919	30
1923	25
1926	20
1931	22.5

The stimulus to Socialism

Of course, all this did not mean that Liberal and Conservative politicians had suddenly become Socialists. By and large, wartime economic innovations resulted from ad hoc responses to a succession of crises; they were expedients rather than considered strategies. Consequently, most were quickly reversed, though there was to be no return to low income tax. But an important precedent for sweeping state intervention had been set, and the inability of unfettered private enterprise to meet national needs had been demonstrated. Both trade unions and employers appreciated how much they had to gain from the closer involvement of the state in the economy. For example, wartime experience strengthened the pressure among the miners for the nationalization of the coal industry. But some socialists noticed how beneficial state control could be for the owners because it helped them to reduce strike action. Although limits were placed upon profits, this was a small price to pay for the certainty of large profit margins resulting from government contracts. Industrialists, now increasingly organized in such bodies as the Federation of British Industry, determined to maximize their influence on government in the future so as to obtain a range of policies, from lower taxation to tariff protection, to help maintain their wartime grip on the domestic market. In this sense the war marked the start of a 60-year retreat from traditional capitalist enterprise in favour of a more corporatist approach.

Coalition politics

Asquith demonstrated great skill in taking Britain into war by restricting ministerial resignations to two and by creating a wide consensus in the country. A truce with the suffragettes was declared and controversial Bills for Welsh Disestablishment and Home Rule were suspended. The addition of Lord Kitchener as Secretary of State for War was another astute move. However, in the absence of any conspicuous naval or military successes and scurrilous attacks in the press, government fortunes soon deteriorated. Many Liberals had misgivings about wartime policies, the Defence of the Realm Act and the infringement of free trade in the 1915 budget, for example. However, this would never have become a serious problem but for a major miscalculation in May 1915, when Asquith invited the Conservatives and Labour to join him in a coalition; neither he nor Bonar Law had consulted more than a handful of their colleagues beforehand. In the short run coalition had the advantage of enabling the politicians to avoid holding the general election due in 1915. The Conservatives, who might have won an election, shrank from governing alone because they did not command the loyalty of the industrial workers that was now so necessary for the war effort.

Liberal decline

However, for the Liberals the coalition was seriously flawed because it reversed the logic of their pre-war political strategy which pointed to co-operation with Labour and with the Irish Nationalists. A coalition with the Conservatives was destructive of the rationale that had underpinned the Liberals' position since 1906. It immediately alienated the Irish who, though invited in, refused to serve with the Conservatives. As the implementation of the Home Rule Bill seemed increasingly unlikely, the Nationalists' own position in Ireland began to be undermined. The Easter Rebellion of 1916 greatly accelerated the process, so that by 1918 Redmond's party was largely ousted by supporters of Sinn Fein, exasperated by the failure of the parliamentary strategy for achieving Home Rule.

More immediately damaging to Liberal morale was the perception that alliance with the Conservatives had led to the adoption of conscription and committed the country to the total defeat of Germany – the 'knockout blow', in Lloyd George's phrase. Many Liberal and Labour politicians who had had misgivings, especially over co-operation with Russia, now began to conclude that pre-war policy, including the arms race and the entanglement with France, had been mistaken; in view of the horrendous casualties suffered in 1915 and 1916 it seemed wiser to seek a negotiated peace. The attractions of this admittedly minority view were strengthened when President Woodrow Wilson expressed similar sentiments; and the evident inability of the government to define Britain's war aims in anything but vague terms only exacerbated fears that the government, influenced by Tory imperialists, would drift into a vindictive peace and a protectionist policy.

The alternative lay in a compromise settlement which respected the wishes of the various national groups, general disarmament, and a new method of conducting international diplomacy – the League of Nations. Such policies were advocated by the Independent Labour Party and the Union of Democratic Control, a new pressure group which included Socialists like Ramsay MacDonald and such Liberals as Charles Trevelyan and Arthur Ponsonby. By 1916 such groups were gaining recruits among Liberals who felt that the war was no longer being pursued by liberal methods or for liberal objectives; consequently, there seemed less necessity to maintain Asquith as Prime Minister. Although many Liberals greatly disliked the Lloyd George coalition which replaced Asquith in December 1916, there was little attempt to organize an effective opposition to it, partly because this would have appeared unpatriotic and might well have provoked a wartime general election. Consequently during 1917–18 the Liberals found themselves divided between two leaders, one acting as Prime Minister and the other as leader of the opposition; the party inevitably lost its sense of purpose once it had abandoned the strategy that had served it so well up to 1914. As this division between Asquith and Lloyd George lasted until 1923 it handicapped the Liberals at a crucial stage when Labour challenged it as the alternative party of government.

The rise of the Labour Party

Conversely, the war gave a renewed sense of purpose to the Labour Party. Unexpectedly its status was raised as it became a party of government; in 1915 Arthur Henderson entered cabinet and George Roberts and William Brace were junior ministers, while under Lloyd George Labour ministers included Henderson, Roberts, Brace, George Barnes, John Hodge, Stephen Walsh and George Wardle. Moreover, the trade union movement, especially leaders such as Jimmy Thomas of the railwaymen, rapidly emerged as central to the war effort. In this way Labour succeeded on the one hand in being patriotic and supportive while also adopting a critical view of government policies. From the start the majority of the movement was highly pro-war, but several MPs, including Ramsay MacDonald and Philip Snowden, argued it was a mistake for Britain to join. However, there were no splits or expulsions, and members largely put aside their differences over the war to concentrate on defending the interests of working-class families over wages, pensions, wartime allowances, prices and rents. Moreover, the enactment of new social policies such as state-subsidized housing after the war enabled the party to seize the initiative from the demoralized Liberals at the grass roots.

Surprisingly it took several years of war before Labour realized that, with the collapse of Liberal organization in the country, the time had come to abandon the Edwardian electoral pact and run candidates of its own in a majority of constituencies. In 1918 388 candidates stood compared with a maximum of 75 previously. This strategy became feasible because the unions were gaining members and building up their funds, as was permitted under the 1913 Act. Above all, the 1918 Representation of the People Act gave further encouragement by enfranchising an extra five million men creating a large working-class majority; it also helped Labour by reducing some of the costs of fighting elections. Prompted by these favourable circumstances, the party took a series of initiatives between the autumn of 1917 and the autumn of 1918. It produced new statements of party policy in both domestic and external affairs. The party also devised a new constitution which included the famous Clause 4, committing it to Socialist objectives for the first time. Most important in this scheme were the arrangements for individual party membership, which complemented the much larger indirect trade union membership, and the establishment of a local Labour Party in every constituency; between 1914 and 1918 the affiliated constituency associations rose from 179 to 389. The 1918 constitution effectively placed central power in the hands of the trade unions by allowing their block votes to determine the membership of the NEC at each annual conference. This had the effect of undermining the role of the small socialist societies and the ILP, who had been so influential under the original party constitution. In this way Labour equipped itself to challenge the Liberals for their role as the chief alternative to the Conservatives in 1918.

The Coupon Election, 1918

The outbreak of war found the Conservatives in a highly fractious condition as a result of their prolonged spell out of office. In collaboration with their allies in the press, they accused their opponents of lacking patriotism and being unqualified to run the war. Yet at the same time the Conservative leaders also sensed that, with the rise of the Labour Movement, conditions were still moving against them. They proved reluctant to risk forming a purely Conservative government in 1915 and in 1916, for fear that they would be unable to obtain the co-operation of the working class in maintaining the war effort. Coalition, however uncomfortable, was the best they could hope for.

On the other hand, the crisis of war and the threat to the empire helped to give the Conservatives a renewed sense of purpose. Particularly under Lloyd George's premiership, Bonar Law, Balfour, Austen Chamberlain and Lord Milner found a very satisfying role to play. Victory, however, raised in an acute form the underlying problem of the party's future strategy. It had not won an election since 1900. Now the concatenation of working-class enfranchisement, the growth of the Labour Party, and the prevailing mood of radicalism which seemed to be affecting all European countries by 1918, threatened to create a left-wing landslide at the post-war general election. In these circumstances the Conservatives decided to swallow their dislike of Lloyd George, maintain the coalition, and fight an election under his leadership. In this way they could hope to prosper by association with military victory, benefit from Lloyd George's personal popularity, and also keep the Liberals divided.

In the event, this plan worked even better than expected. Following the armistice in November Lloyd George called a sudden election as 'The Man Who Won The War'. At the election of December 1918 the supporters of the Coalition, who received a 'Coupon' or endorsement from the Prime Minister, won 541 seats, including 478 Conservatives and 136 Lloyd George Liberals, on the basis of 54 per cent of the vote. Against them were ranged 73 Sinn Feiners, who did not take their seats, 63 Labour, and a mere 28 Liberal MPs. This was the result partly of the way in which Asquith had been discredited and partly of the split between Labour and the Liberals which divided the non-Conservative vote. But it also reflected the unexpectedly emotional circumstances in which the election was conducted. It was fought so soon after the end of hostilities that wartime feeling ran high. Politicians discovered that voters had not yet re-orientated themselves to domestic politics; rather, they showed themselves anxious to make Germany pay for the war and to hang the Kaiser. The coalitionists simply pandered to the hysteria. One government minister made the notorious promise: 'We will squeeze Germany like a lemon; we will squeeze her until you can hear the pips squeak.' It thus proved all too easy to condemn the more restrained Liberal and Labour candidates as weak and unpatriotic, and as responsible for obstructing Britain's victory in the war. By 1918, then, the war years had effectively destroyed the left-wing alliance that had dominated Edwardian politics, and ushered in an era of Conservatism.

Structural changes in government

In addition to the party-political effects wartime had the effect of greatly extending the reach of government. Under the Defence of the Realm Act the authorities enjoyed broad but ill-defined powers to control British citizens and to arrest anyone considered to be undermining the war effort. This coercive power was complemented by the official propaganda machine and the unofficial co-operation of the press which largely abandoned its responsibility to report truthfully to the public about the war. Under Asquith innovations in government machinery were limited to the new Ministry of Munitions, extra cabinet committees and War Cabinets that debated military strategy. But in December 1916 Lloyd George by-passed the twenty-member cabinet with a five-man War Cabinet, comprising himself, Bonar Law, Lord Milner, Lord Curzon and Arthur Henderson, which met daily free from departmental duties to make quick decisions on war issues. Its efficiency was enhanced by the Cabinet Secretariat under Sir Maurice Hankey who circulated minutes for the first time. Lloyd George also by-passed the civil service with his personal secretariat of experts and advisers. Apart from the War Cabinet these innovations largely survived the war and helped promote the dominance of the Prime Minister at the expense of the cabinet. Lloyd George also increased his powers of patronage by creating new departments for Labour, Pensions, Food, Health (which included housing), Shipping, Air, Information and National Service. He imported non-party figures, like an American President, including Sir Eric Geddes (a railway engineer), Sir Joseph MacClay (a shipowner) and Lord Devonport (a grocery magnate). Many of these ministries failed to survive the war but Labour, Pensions and Health became long-term fixtures, reinforcing the trend to a larger civil service; although suspect to the Treasury as spending ministries, the emergence of a mass electorate and the rise of Labour made it risky to abolish them.

Social reconstruction

Although the war did not fundamentally change the Edwardian system of state-financed social welfare, it helped to expand it and strengthened its political foundations in the long term. As a result of the mass enlistment of young men, many of whom left wives and children behind, it became necessary early in the war to pay allowances and, as casualties mounted, pensions to civilian dependants. This experience had some long-term significance in that it convinced some feminists that payments made directly to mothers were a highly cost-effective means of relieving poverty. At the time the idea was referred to as the 'endowment of motherhood', though subsequently it became better known as family allowances. Under Eleanor Rathbone and others, a campaign began to persuade the state to recognize that the role of the wife and mother was of equal importance to other occupations and should therefore receive remuneration in the form of a direct payment. During the Edwardian period, politicians had become more susceptible to pressure on behalf of married women, with the result that in 1914 Herbert Samuel had offered local authorities grants to set up maternity health clinics. The huge loss of young men during the war made governments even more concerned to promote the health of infants and to make motherhood less burdensome. The result was a considerable extension of existing policy, but not the adoption of the more radical ideas of Rathbone. The number of clinics increased from 350 to 1,290, and health visitors from 600 to 1,350, by 1918. This policy culminated in the 1918 Maternity and Child Welfare Act, one of the few enduring wartime reforms, which compelled local authorities to implement nationally determined standards of care.

Addison's Housing Act, 1919

Another by-product of wartime concern about the younger generation was H.A.L. Fisher's 1918 Education Act, which made secondary education compulsory to the age of fourteen, proposed a complete system from nursery education to higher education, and offered a 50 per cent grant to local authorities. But the main reconstruction debate concentrated on the deterioration of the housing stock during the war. It was officially estimated that 300,000 extra houses would be required after the war. The result, much delayed, was Dr Addison's 1919 Housing Act. This measure was based on the idea that each local authority should prepare a house-building programme reflecting local needs, be responsible for carrying out the scheme, and offer homes to rent to working-class families. It was housing that assumed the highest profile among social reforms, then and subsequently, because the Lloyd George government promised to build half a million 'Homes For Heroes' in 1918. However, the shortage of labour and the uncooperative attitude of builders made the housing targets initially difficult to meet. Eventually, additional government subsidies helped to achieve a total of 170,000 new houses. Although this fell a long way short of the promises made, it represented a major advance on previous housing policies, and was important not least for setting a higher standard for working-class housing. Unfortunately, the higher cost made the housing programme very vulnerable to post-war expenditure cuts in 1920; by 1921 the Addison Act had been abandoned and its author driven from office. Similarly, the education reforms were severely curtailed by financial retrenchment. This speedy reversal of large parts of the reconstruction programme clearly suggests that it is at least an exaggeration to claim that the mass participation in the war effort had a fundamental impact on official thinking; in many ways the rhetoric of reconstruction proved an ephemeral feature, designed to serve a temporary political need.

Votes for women – and men

In some ways the most solid concession granted in wartime – because it could not be withdrawn even when circumstances changed – was political reform. Up to 1914 only six out of every ten men, and no women, enjoyed a parliamentary vote, and the Liberal government had been severely embarrassed by the consequences of its failure to effect some reforms. Initially wartime governments avoided tackling the franchise and the votes-for-women campaign largely subsided. However, it returned to the agenda during the war simply because many men lost their place on the electoral register as a result of leaving home for war work in the armed forces. Fearful of holding an election from which large numbers of patriotic war workers were actually excluded, the political parties agreed in 1916 to appoint an all-party conference under the Speaker of the Commons, to devise a compromise scheme of reform. The conference started with small matters and left women's suffrage to the end, on the assumption that having agreed on many changes no one would want to kill the compromise by disagreement over one issue. The resulting Representation of the People Bill of 1917 enfranchised virtually all males over the age of 21 and women over 30 years who were themselves, or were married to, local government voters. This transformed the pre-1914 electorate of just under 8 million into one comprising 13 million men and 8.4 million women.

However, it is very doubtful whether this reform can be explained in terms of fundamental changes in attitude brought about by popular participation in the war. Politicians certainly paid tributes to patriotic war work, implying that the vote was a reward or, in the case of women, a recognition that they had proved their capability as war workers. But in fact most politicians continued to disapprove of women as paid employees. They had no hesitation about forcing them out of their new jobs, and they deliberately withheld the vote from the young women who had worked in the vital munitions factories. War had clearly failed to alter traditional ideas about the role of the two sexes. In fact it strengthened traditional thinking by encouraging politicians to focus on the birth rate and marriage; this explains why they were happy to enfranchise wives. Also, the sweeping nature of reform broke the log-jam on women's suffrage and thus solved the party political problems; enfranchising 8 million rather than 1 million single women (which the pre-war suffragists Bills had done) seemed too wide to give an advantage to any one party. A democratic reform that included votes for men as well as women was simply more realistic than the narrow Bills confined to women for which the Pankhursts had fought. Though the Conservatives had given most away in the all-party compromise, they took comfort from the wartime patriotism shown by the working classes, the redistribution of the constituencies in their favour, and their alliance with Lloyd George.

The Lost Generation

In the 1920s and 1930s the most pervasive view of the war, fostered by anti-war literature, was that it had swept away the cream of British youth and manhood, thereby blighting the lives of a whole generation. Yet without in any way minimizing the physical and psychological damage caused by the conflict, subsequent historians have largely revised this bleak view of the social impact of the war period. This is especially true for the majority of the population who occupied civilian roles. War accelerated the move out of low-paid occupations, gave many workers a full week's employment, increased union membership and raised wages. The rationing system went some way to ensuring that the diet of poorer people did not deteriorate. The results of this were improved life expectancy for civilians, and in particular a reduction in infant mortality rates during and after the war.

On the other hand, the war left an indelible mark in the shape of three-quarters of a million British male deaths, another 200,000 from the colonies and a large number of men too crippled or shell-shocked to be able to readjust to a normal, civilian life. Many men who had gained status by becoming officers suddenly found themselves unable to gain appropriate employment and they resented their fall in the social scale. Careful study of the casualty rates among the social classes has gone some way to corroborating the idea of a Lost Generation in that the losses were highest among junior army officers because they were required to be first out of the trenches to lead their men into the attack. Since the junior officers were largely drawn from men in their late teens and twenties often from public schools and universities, they were clearly concentrated in a very limited social range. It is this loss that was to be reflected so vividly in post-war literature.

However, the broader implications so famously depicted in such works as Vera Brittain's *Testament of Youth* (1932) are not borne out by the evidence.

Table 10.3 British casualties in the First World War

Civilians	Army	Navy	Air force	Wounded	Prisoners of war
1,414	673,375	43,244	6,166	1,676,037	163,242

At the time it was natural to assume that thousands of young women would be deprived of husbands, which would not only blight a generation but also undermine the British state by weakening family life and reducing its supply of manpower through the lower birth rate. In fact the husband shortage proved to be a complete myth, although that has not stopped several books being written about it! While war led directly to male deaths, it also had the indirect effect of checking emigration which regularly removed several hundred thousand, largely male, persons from Britain each year. Consequently the supply of marriageable men did not diminish in relation to the female population; in fact, it improved because after 1918 emigration never returned to its traditional levels except in Scotland. Moreover, the desire to marry appears to have grown quite markedly perhaps because young men felt the need for some stability and security after the disruption of wartime. By the later 1920s a higher proportion of men, and especially of women, were marrying, and the trend gathered pace throughout the 1930s. Though interrupted temporarily by the Second World War, the marriage rate in Britain continued to rise until the 1970s.

Continuity rather than change?

This is a reminder that the significance of the war for women was complex and contradictory. On the one hand, there is some evidence that it had a liberating or emancipating effect. The number of women in paid work outside the home increased by 1.2 million net, a change that encompassed the withdrawal from domestic service of 400,000 young women. They escaped the long hours and low status of servants and were reluctant to return in the 1920s. Hence the contemporary newspaper criticism of the so-called 'flappers' who were thought to be using their new incomes to enjoy an irresponsible and immoral lifestyle, while capitalizing on their new political power to avoid marriage and motherhood. In some ways the war proved more significant for middle-class women because it opened the way to a freer social life. They had more money, fewer chaperones, and opportunities to mix with the opposite sex in cinemas and at dances. It began to be accepted that they should establish a career, if only temporarily, before marriage.

In fact there was more continuity than change in women's lives in this period. Before the war had come to an end they were already being pushed out of their new jobs in munitions, trams and offices so that soon there were *fewer* women in the labour force than there had been before 1914. The census of 1911, 1921 and 1932 actually shows almost no change in the proportion of women in employment, which makes the drama of wartime seem a huge exaggeration. By and large women's work continued to be a matter of temporary, low-paid jobs, undertaken as necessity and opportunity dictated. For the majority of women domesticity determined the pattern of their lives just as it always had. In all social classes girls aspired to marriage and motherhood. The fact that family size was falling only helped to make domesticity more attractive than hitherto. Indeed, the most significant portent of this period was not women's war work but rather the publication in 1918 of Marie Stopes's book *Married Love*, which evidently caught the mood of the ordinary woman perfectly. In this Stopes argued that, if married couples deliberately spaced pregnancies rather than allowing them to follow rapidly after one another, this would lead to an improvement in the health of both babies and mothers. By freeing sexual relations from the perpetual fear of pregnancy, she claimed, husbands and wives would enjoy married life much more. For many couples this was the advice they wished to hear, and the widespread adoption of birth control led to a sharp fall in family size during the 1920s to around 2.2 babies as opposed to six for Victorian women.

Mass war and popular participation

Such evidence calls for considerable qualification about the effects of the war. Many of the trends and innovations attributed to the Great War turned out to be not so much the direct product of war as the outcome of long-term developments whose origins lie in the pre-1914 period. The long-running campaign for female enfranchisement is perhaps the foremost example of this. The war also extended existing patterns of change, in some cases strengthening or accelerating the process. The extension of the Edwardian innovations in taxation is a case in point. Several social reforms such as the 1911 unemployment insurance scheme and the 1914 provisions for infant and maternal welfare were also extended as a result of the war but did not originate in war. Similarly, the cause of tariff reform gained force from the war years because the seizure of German markets generated demands for the protection of several growth industries; the 1915 budget marked a significant infringement of free trade.

Conversely in several respects the war interrupted the pattern of development, and even caused a reaction against change which persisted for many years. For example, the war created a huge increase in the National Debt which severely limited the scope of government policy in the 1920s. The great increase in government resources engendered during 1914–18 stimulated a backlash in favour of lower taxation and retrenchment which seriously disrupted existing social policies and delayed the implementation of others. State economic intervention was very rapidly reversed, so that by 1921 industry had been restored to private control and proposals for nationalization of coal and the railways were abandoned. For a time the object was simply to return to unfettered free enterprise and remove government from the economy; it was some time before it was generally appreciated that this was a wholly unrealistic objective. Finally, as we have seen, the liberation of women during the war years was ephemeral and had the effect of making men anxious to force women back into domesticity. During the 1920s women workers were invariably sacked when they became married on the grounds that, as they were supported by their husbands, they ought not to deprive a man of a job. This was to ignore the fact that many women supported their families from their earnings.

On the other hand, not all the innovations of wartime perished in the post-war reaction. Both the Ministry of Labour and the Ministry of Health survived to keep alive the interventionist spirit in Whitehall. Amongst the social policies, those for mothers and children's welfare continue to gain resources even in the 1920s. And although Addison's Housing Act was abandoned, the policy of state-subsidized building was revived in 1924 by the first Labour government. Equally important in the long term was the fact that rent restrictions were never entirely given up (until the 1980s), and from 1918 there was a steady decline in the role of rented accommodation in favour of private ownership and council housing.

One lasting effect of the war was the way in which it disrupted the Edwardian pattern of politics. By destroying the progressive alliance it paved the way for two decades of Conservative predominance in Britain. Yet the huge expansion of the electorate placed definite limits upon the kind of policies the Conservatives felt able to pursue; indeed, in many ways it forced them to embrace the interventionist and redistributive Edwardian social policies they had once criticized. Conversely the war promoted continuity, not only in terms of detailed policies but also in the survival of the parliamentary system and the constitutional monarchy in Britain. The very fact of the country's victorious conclusion to the war served to strengthen her institutions and to foster pride in her empire; by contrast defeat disrupted and discredited regimes in Russia and Germany and in Italy even victory undermined her democratic regime paving the way for fascism in 1922. In this perspective war fostered a somewhat unrealistic impression that Britain could retain her traditional practices and even her role in the world, an assumption that was to be only gradually undermined in the 1920s and 1930s.

* * * *

Throughout the 1902–18 period many Victorians felt that British society had been subject to radical and subversive threats, not only the obvious political ones but novel forms of social behaviour and thinking. The very idea of Victorianism fell into disrepute among intellectuals such as Lytton Strachey in *Eminent Victorians* (1918) in which he debunked the reputation of Victorian heroes including Florence Nightingale and General Gordon. In particular the period saw bitter controversies over whether to abandon free trade, whether to grant Ireland Home Rule, whether to enfranchise women and how far to extend the role of the state in peacetime. However, not for the first time the British Establishment compromised notably by the incorporation of women into the system and the wider democratization of politics. This was a calculated risk at a time when millions of men and women had enjoyed new experiences that challenged received opinions and raised aspirations. In the heady mood created by victory in 1918 the optimists believed that concession would help legitimise and stabilize the British system but no one could as yet be confident.

Further reading

For analysis of the relationship between mass war and social change see:
Rex Pope, *War and Society in Britain 1899–1948* (1998)
Adrian Gregory, *The Last Great War: British Society and the First World War* (2008)
A. Marwick, *The Deluge: British Society and the First World War* (1965)
J.M. Winter, *The Great War and the British People* (1985)
David Reynolds, *The Long Shadow* (2013) – a corrective to negative views of the war; emphasizes that Britain's experience differed from that of other countries.
G. Braybourne and Penny Summerfield, *Out of the Cage: Women's Experiences in Two World Wars* (1987)
Gerard De Groot, *Blighty: British Society in the Era of the Great War* (1990)
J. Bourne, *Britain and the Great War 1914–1918* (1989)
S. Constantine, M. Kirby and M. Rose eds, *The First World War in British History* (1995)

The impact of war on the political parties is discussed in:
G.R. Searle, *The Liberal Party: Triumph and Disintegration 1886–1929* (1992)

Trevor Wilson, *The Downfall of the Liberal Party 1914–35* (1966) – the author did not intend to argue that war was the cause of Liberal decline though his book is often read that way!

R.I. McKibbin, *The Evolution of the Labour Party 1910–24* (1974)

Martin Pugh, *Speak for Britain! A New History of the Labour Party* (2010)

J.M. Winter, *Socialism and the Challenge of War* (1974)

N. Keohane, *The Party of Patriotism: the Conservative Party and the First World War* (2010)

Martin Pugh, *The Making of Modern British Politics 1867–1945* (2002)

G.R. Searle, *Country Before Party; the Idea of National Government in Modern Britain 1885–1987* (1995)

John Turner, *British Politics and the Great War 1915–18* (1992)

Ronan Fanning, *Fatal Path: British Governments and Irish Revolution 1910–22* (2013)

Charles Townshend, *The Republic: the Fight for Irish Independence* (2013)

On state interventionism see:

J.E. Cronin, *The Politics of State Expansion* (1991)

Keith Grieves, *Sir Eric Geddes* (1989)

K. Burke ed., *The War and the State: the Transformation of British Government 1914–18* (1982)

Rodney Lowe, *Adjusting to Democracy: The Role of the Ministry of Labour in British Politics 1916–39* (1986)

Military aspects are dealt with in:

J.P. Harris, *Douglas Haig and the First World War* (2008) – the hostile view.

Gary Sheffield, *Forgotten Victory: the First World War Myths and Realities* (2001) – good example of recent military historians who defend the generals and British strategy.

Ian Becket, *The Great War 1914–18* (2001)

Peter Simkins, *Kitchener's Army: the Raising of the New Armies 1914–16* (1998)

M. Middlebrook, *The First Day on the Somme* (1971)

John Keegan, *The Face of Battle* (1976)

David French, *The British Way in Warfare 1688–2000* (1990)

Joanna Bourke, *An Intimate History of Killing* (1999)

There are some interesting volumes on opposition to war and reactions to the casualties:

Martin Ceadel, *Pacifism in Britain 1914–45* (1980)

John Rae, *Conscience and Politics: the British Government and the Conscientious Objection to Military Service 1916–19* (1970)

Keith Robbins, *The Abolition of War: the Peace Movement in Britain 1914–19* (1976)

Adrian Gregory, *The Silence of Memory: Armistice Day 1919–46* (1994)

J.M. Winter, *Sites of Memory, Sites of Mourning* (1995)

Part III

The Period of Confusion: Collectivism versus Capitalism, 1918–40

11

The Failure of *Laissez-faire*

The Edwardian period had ended in a boom enjoyed by the traditional staple industries – coal, textiles, shipbuilding and steel, which was overtaken by the emergency expansion and interventionism during wartime. But when the dust had settled the underlying problems of the Edwardian economy resurfaced in more acute form: the narrow base of the export industries, poor investment, low productivity and the stranglehold of the Bank of England.

The legacy of war

The war exacerbated the existing imbalance of the British economy by shifting resources away from consumer goods into sectors whose output was desperately needed for the war effort: coal, steel, engineering, shipbuilding. Consequently Britain ceased to supply many of her foreign markets with textiles and coal – key elements in the Edwardian balance of trade. Other countries, notably the USA and Japan, stepped in to supply Britain's former customers, while several of the less industrialized states, such as Canada, India, Brazil and Argentina, became more self-sufficient during the war. India for example doubled her cotton textile production, which contributed to a huge fall in British post-war exports. Admittedly, the war did give a boost to chemicals, electrical goods and motor vehicles, in which production had lagged for some time. But overall the effect of the war was to bequeath a deteriorating balance of trade in the 1920s.

Restoring the pre-war economy?

Of course, a deficit on visible exports and imports was by no means new, but it had previously been covered by invisible earnings from foreign investments, shipping and insurance. However, these were much more elusive after 1918.

The prevailing depression between the wars restricted the scope for such income, which is why many economists and politicians believed so strongly in the necessity of restoring international trade to its pre-war level as soon as possible. Unfortunately, this was now largely beyond Britain's power. In the first place, the war triggered the spread of protectionism – even Britain had infringed her free-trade principles in 1915 – and many of the fragile, newly created states adopted tariffs thereby limiting world trade. Moreover, during the war Britain had liquidated a high proportion of her overseas assets, and she had borrowed extensively from the USA to whom she owed debts of £1,150 million. As a result she found it difficult to recover her former role as the leading creditor nation and could not, therefore, effectively stimulate the general level of economic activity. The USA, which might have occupied this role, tended to recall her loans and retreat into protectionism. Finally, a severe fall in the price of food and raw materials between the wars impoverished many of the less developed countries, who were consequently unable to purchase manufactured goods from Britain as they had traditionally done. Hence, in spite of periods of growth, especially in the later 1920s, the world economy was never fully restored to the buoyant condition which had been the key to Britain's former prosperity.

The National Debt

At home the war also bequeathed problems for the government's finances. Even when the huge military costs of the war had been scaled down, governments were still left with expensive commitments in terms of expanded social policies. In the early 1920s government expenditure consumed 24–29 per cent of gross national product, compared with around 12 per cent before 1914. This put post-war governments in a strong position to influence the level of output and income, but they generally saw the negative rather than the positive side of state expenditure. They concerned themselves chiefly with the need to balance the budget and to deal with the National Debt, which had risen from £650 million to £8,000 million. Annual interest payments on the debt increased from £20 million in 1913 to £325 million by 1920, and remained around £300 million until the 1930s. Naturally these payments absorbed a substantial part of the government's expenditure: 24 per cent in 1920 and as much as 40 per cent later in the decade. Consequently, governments felt that they had little room for manoeuvre; while servicing the National Debt, reducing income tax from the 6s. in the pound levied during the war, scaling down military estimates and curtailing social spending without endangering their political position, they felt they must somehow continue to end up with a balanced budget.

Table 11.1 United Kingdom balance of payments, 1911–38 (in £ millions)

Year	Balance of visible trade	Balance of invisible trade	Net balance
1911–13	−140	+346	+206
1920–24	−258	+419	+161
1925–29	−398	+481	+83
1930–34	−328	+301	−27
1935–38	−356	+332	−24

This was not an insuperable problem, but it was tackled with a lack of vision and imagination. For much of the time the government's budgetary policy was so deflationary as to have an inhibiting effect on economic growth. The policy amounted to a rather traditional mixture, in which academic economic ideas were often overlaid by fundamental moral beliefs and by simple political prejudice. For example, the restoration of the pound to its pre-war value could scarcely be justified by economic considerations, but really reflected an emotive and irrational belief in sterling as a patriotic symbol of British strength; as such, it was adhered to when it no longer made much sense. Similarly, after 1918 ministers often felt they had been led morally astray by the financial irresponsibility of Lloyd George, both before and during the war. The reaction against his interventionist and inflationary style was accelerated by the political necessity for the Conservatives of giving their supporters some relief from income tax. On the whole they attempted to return to Victorian policies, only to be frustrated eventually by the scale and persistence of the interwar depression.

The return to gold

British policymakers were overwhelmingly anxious for a return to the pre-1914 era, when Britain had been central to the world's trade and the pound was the leading medium of exchange. But this involved backing the currency with gold. This was never sound because Britain's gold reserves were not adequate. During wartime the government had been forced to abandon the gold standard and to issue paper pound and ten-shilling notes for the first time. After 1918 it was seen as a matter of urgency to return to the gold standard. Indeed, the Cunliffe Committee of 1918 pronounced this to be the overriding object of British policy, a view fully accepted by the governments of the period. This reflected their essentially internationalist, Victorian view of British interests; to them it seemed self-evident that the country's prosperity lay in the traditional staple industries on which the industrial revolution had been based; and since these relied upon export markets it was necessary to restore the smooth functioning of the pre-war world system. Until this was accomplished, it was inevitable that unemployment would remain high.

A flawed policy

However, there were several practical flaws in this strategy. The first has already been noted – that Britain lacked the capacity to influence the international economy that she once had. Second, even when the level of world trade did begin to return to pre-1914 levels, as it did in the mid-1920s, Britain proved unable to recover her former share of it. Third, there was a crucial judgement to be made as to what value should be put on the pound when she did return to the gold standard. The Cunliffe Committee had not so much as considered anything lower than the pre-war rate; and most orthodox economists, civil servants and politicians made exactly the same assumption. This meant valuing the pound at \$4.86. Yet since 1914 the actual value commanded by the pound had fallen far below this level. The politicians understood fully that to maintain the higher level required deflation and wage cuts in Britain. This is why they hesitated to return to gold until 1925, fearful of popular unrest over falling wages.

However, in the deflationary climate after the war the advocates of a return to gold felt encouraged by the upward trend of the currency. From \$3.40 in February 1920, the pound rose to \$4.63 dollars by the end of 1922. After 1924 it rose to \$4.79 and Treasury officials felt convinced that the time for a return to gold had come. The decision, taken in 1925, was probably the most important single act of economic policy between the wars – and the worst mistake. The Chancellor, Winston Churchill, who was somewhat out of his depth in economics, made a point of hearing both sides of the argument. J.M. Keynes and Reginald McKenna, the former Liberal Chancellor, explained

Table 11.2 Exports of cotton piece goods – annual average per decade, 1910–49

Year	Cotton in millions of yards
1910–19	5,460
1920–29	4,239
1930–39	1,970
1940–49	621

why a return to gold at $4.86 was undesirable, but Churchill followed the Treasury's advice – and later admitted he had been wrong.

The results of currency overvaluation

The drawbacks to the policy were twofold. The obvious one was that by increasing the value of the pound the government immediately made British goods more expensive abroad, which checked economic growth and employment. Keynes put the overvaluation of the pound at 10 per cent, but it is nowadays thought to have been 20–25 per cent. The decision reflected the excessive influence of City of London financiers, who stood to benefit from an overvalued pound, at the expense of manufacturers whose interests suffered; the latter were of much more importance for the overall health of the economy.

Even worse were the domestic implications of the return to gold. In order to defend the pound at its new, high level it was necessary to attract and retain foreign funds; this meant raising the bank rate and keeping interest rates high. Meanwhile industry had to cope with its uncompetitive prices by reducing its domestic costs, especially wages. Thus the government's policy imposed a phase of deflation on the economy in which businessmen were inhibited from investing and in which domestic demand was restricted. One immediate effect was to arouse trade union fears about general wage cuts, a situation which produced the General Strike in 1926. Moreover, while other industrial countries began to enjoy substantial economic growth in the second half of the decade, Britain's economy continued to be sluggish. By throwing away the chance for a real economic recovery, the Baldwin government of 1924–9 proved itself the most incompetent of the interwar period.

To make matters worse, the government's persistence with the policy of deflation and the gold standard ultimately failed even on its own terms. For in spite of the debacle of the General Strike, money wages did *not* generally fall to any significant extent. Consequently, as the 1920s wore on the attempt to hold the pound at its 1925 level, in the face of a balance-of-payments deficit, was increasingly unrealistic. Yet politics and national pride prevented both Conservative and Labour governments from devaluing the currency, even in the face of evidence that France and Belgium had successfully stabilized their currencies by accepting a lower rate. Fortunately for Baldwin, his government was defeated at the 1929 election, largely as a result of his failure to reduce unemployment, thus leaving Ramsay MacDonald to face the consequences of his misjudgements. But policy continued as before. Philip Snowden, the Labour Chancellor, fully accepted the Bank of England's right to determine interest rates with a view to maintaining foreign investments in Britain. 'Parliament', he declared, 'is not a competent body to deal with the administration of such highly delicate and intricate matters.' As a result of this attitude the Labour government faced huge pressures to balance the budget by reducing expenditure which eventually split the Cabinet and destroyed the government. It was replaced in 1931 by a National Government which was established expressly to maintain the pound. However the new government was rapidly driven to abandon the gold standard and to adopt devaluation. A decade had been wasted in a vain attempt to sustain an unrealistic objective.

Unemployment

Despite these failures it would be misleading to think of the interwar economy as a period of unrelieved depression. In 1919–20, for example, the high family incomes engendered by wartime produced a considerable demand for consumer goods that had been unavailable for four years. Businessmen enthusiastically abandoned war production and attempted to switch resources into domestic goods once again; there was rapid restocking and some unwise speculation. But in the summer of 1920 the boomlet collapsed suddenly, as industry realized it had put too many goods on the market and had not recovered its foreign customers. By 1921 unemployment had leapt to 2 million or 17 per cent of the insured labour force. The subsequent recovery proved to be slow, leaving unemployment between 1 million and 1.5 million throughout the 1920s. After the 1929 Wall Street Crash the economy deteriorated again, and unemployment reached 3 million by 1932. A period of modest and uncertain economic growth from 1933 to 1937 brought unemployment down to 2 million in the mid-1930s.

Table 11.3 Total shipping completed in the UK, 1913–39 (in thousands of tons)

Year	Thousands of tons
1913	1,950
1920	2,400
1925	800
1930	950
1935	680
1939	1,000

However, the national figures concealed considerable fluctuation, over time and also geographically; indeed, the concentration of certain depressed industries in the north and west of the country made unemployment a largely regional problem. In 1921, for example, when national unemployment stood at 17 per cent, it rose to 27 per cent in engineering and 36 per cent in shipbuilding. In 1932, London and south-east England reported 13.7 per cent out of work compared to 27 per cent in the northern counties of England and 36 per cent in Wales. By 1934 St Albans, typical of the towns around London attracting light industry, had only 3.9 per cent unemployment while Jarrow, dependent on a collapsed shipbuilding industry, had 68 per cent.

Cyclical or structural unemployment?

The regional concentrations of unemployment were held by the Treasury to be proof that the problem was structural. This was true to the extent that the staple industries – cotton, coal and steel – had been experiencing declining productivity for decades. However, much of the unemployment reflected cyclical problems; even in the depressed areas, unemployment fell in response to a general improvement in the economy. With a less deflationary policy and a more competitive exchange rate, far fewer jobs would have been lost. Insofar as the governments of the 1920s accepted that unemployment was cyclical in nature, they believed that it reflected a purely temporary imbalance in the economy. After a short period of depression, certain adjustments were thought to operate so as to restore full employment. Wages would fall and businesses would employ more workers. However, in the 1920s this process was evidently not working properly. For one thing, the government itself inhibited business activity by maintaining high interest rates to support its exchange rate policy. But at the time politicians, businessmen and civil servants widely believed that the crucial adjustment – falling wages – was being checked; wages had to drop significantly before the economy would recover.

In addition, the government's budgetary policies contributed to depressing the level of domestic demand for the products of industry. It worked on the traditional assumption that each year its revenue and its expenditure ought to be in balance; any surplus should be used to redeem the National Debt or reduce taxation. As a result of huge wartime spending, the balanced budget had been temporarily abandoned. But now the problem was firmly taken in hand. In 1921 a committee under Sir Eric Geddes recommended sweeping cuts in government expenditure, and as a result the budget deficit of £300 million was turned into a surplus of £200 million which made possible a cut

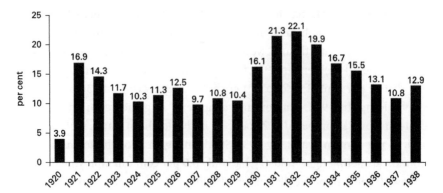

Figure 11.1 Interwar unemployment as a percentage of insured workers.

Note: Unemployment was lower amongst uninsured workers; if they are included, the annual figure for unemployment is 2–3 per cent lower.

in income tax from 6s. to 4s. in the pound. Yet the cuts were counter-productive because they slowed the recovery. Any budget surplus was devoted to repaying the National Debt but this meant diverting it to relatively wealthy people who had loaned money to the government rather than directing it to less well-off people whose spending would boost the demand for goods and services. Government deflationary policies, in short, helped to keep the economy sluggish during the 1920s thereby delaying recovery.

Unemployment insurance

In spite of this the government continued to believe it was spending too much on social welfare. In particular, it regretted the cost of unemployment insurance. The original scheme of 1911 had been extended to cover 12 million workers in 1920; domestic servants and agricultural labourers were the only major groups still omitted. Lloyd George's system had worked well enough while unemployment remained low. But in an era of mass, long-term unemployment, more was paid out by the Unemployment Insurance Fund than was paid in, forcing the Treasury to subsidize it. Much rhetoric was expended by politicians and the press on the alleged extravagance of this system after 1918. The government appeased its critics by withdrawing benefits from women, even when they had made contributions, if they refused to accept jobs as domestic servants; and from 1921 applicants were obliged to meet the requirement that they were 'genuinely seeking work' before receiving benefit. But in spite of such efforts the costs remained high, because genuine unemployment continued to rise. In 1930 the Labour government withdrew the 'genuinely seeking work' condition. This, combined with the rapid deterioration in the economy, pushed the fund further into deficit, so that its debt stood at £100 million by the end of the year.

The crisis of 1931

The dual threat of a budget deficit and a balance-of-payments deficit prompted Ramsay MacDonald to resort to the traditional device of a special committee to investigate government spending. Sir George May's Committee estimated the budget deficit for 1931–2 at £120 million and recommended £97 million of expenditure cuts, including lower unemployment benefit and salary reductions for public employees. There were, in fact, alternatives, including the use of a revenue tariff and devaluation of the pound. Even the object of balancing the budget need not have created a crisis; no less than £60 million in the 1931 budget was devoted to repayment of the National Debt, a wholly unnecessary item which no other major country paid at this time. But the Labour government accepted the need to balance the budget by retrenchment; it disagreed only on the means to that end. Its successor, the National Government, eventually imposed cuts, thereby weakening the level of demand for goods and worsening the depression.

Capitalism, Socialism and Keynesianism

From the tone of political debate between the wars one would expect policies to have fluctuated sharply between free market Conservatism and state Socialism. Conservatives warned about the threats to private wealth, and demanded that individual enterprise be freed from government interference. Labour politicians advocated a levy on capital, coal nationalization, investment and welfare reforms, while some socialists even praised the centralized economic planning of the Soviet Union.

Yet on both sides much of this was empty rhetoric, designed essentially to arouse party supporters. In practice, as we have noted, bipartisan policies prevailed on all fundamentals during the 1920s and 1930s. Philip Snowden was every bit as orthodox a Chancellor as Austen and Neville Chamberlain. Conservative governments maintained historically high levels of income tax and social-welfare spending; Labour retreated from radical ideas about the capital levy and land reform, and never prepared a precise scheme for nationalization of industry. They disagreed only over tariffs, where Labour remained loyal to free trade, and the level of unemployment benefits. But this hardly separated a party of capitalism from a party of socialism.

The Keynesian alternative

This, however, does not mean there were not real divisions over economic issues. The alternatives to the Treasury orthodoxy adhered to by both Conservative and Labour governments were propagated by an assortment of individuals and groups, including J.M. Keynes, Lloyd George and his Liberal inquiries, the Independent Labour Party, Sir Oswald Mosley, younger Tory MPs such as Robert Boothby, Oliver Stanley and Harold Macmillan, and the 1930s pressure groups, Political and Economic Planning and the Next Five Years Group. Although they cannot be equated with one another, their remedies had a great deal in common. Essentially they shared a scepticism about the orthodox belief that the solution to unemployment lay in a restoration of the international market and the role of sterling. Instead, they looked to the domestic market and emphasized the capacity of governments to stimulate production and consumption at home. To this end they advocated varying combinations of tariff protection, public works, cheap money, central control over banks and investment, and devaluation of the pound.

Keynes offered much the most comprehensive and well-thought-out alternative economic programme beginning in 1918 with his warning about the effects of reparations payments in *The Economic Consequences of the Peace*. By 1923 he had begun to argue against deflationary policies in his *Tract on Monetary Reform*, and he totally condemned the return to gold at $4.86 in *The Economic Consequences of Mr Churchill* (1925). His famous collaboration with Lloyd George and others involved abandoning attempts to balance the budget and to reduce wages, and instead using the government's resources constructively to raise the level of demand for British-made goods. Keynes found it frustrating that the government actually maintained a fairly high level of expenditure, but wasted too much of it on the National Debt instead of boosting the incomes of those who would increase spending. In 1929 the scheme propagated by Lloyd George involved an expenditure of £251 million on public works over two years. Bearing in mind that Britain's depression was comparatively mild the Keynesian solution was quite realistic; between 1929 and 1932 gross domestic product fell by 30 per cent in the United States, but by only 5.5 per cent in Britain.

However, the Treasury rejected the Keynesian/Lloyd George programmes on the grounds that public-works schemes would take much longer to put into operation than they anticipated, that the budget must be balanced, and that since there were no unemployed financial resources any further state investment would merely have the effect of reducing the funds available to private businesses. There was no validity in these objections except for the first one; Keynes's policies would have been slower to achieve their cumulative effect than he realized, though this was hardly an argument for not applying them.

It is often suggested that Keynes's ideas came too late to have any real impact between the wars. He himself once described his work as 'the croakings of a Cassandra who could never influence the course of events in time'. But although his most celebrated work, *The General Theory of Employment, Interest and Money*, did not appear until 1936, it is clear that he had subjected conventional economics to a continuous attack since 1918. The case for countercyclical public-works schemes was widely accepted in the 1920s among both economists and left-wing politicians. By the early 1930s the TUC and key unionists like Ernest Bevin had been won over to Keynes's programme. And when in 1938 Harold Macmillan published *The Middle Way* it was clear that he, too, had now absorbed Keynesian thinking. The post-1945 agenda had begun to take shape.

State intervention in industry

The other novel feature of interwar economic policy was the bipartisan move towards state collectivism in industry. Labour had put nationalization in its 1918 constitution, but did little to turn this into a practical policy until the 1930s. More remarkably, the Conservatives showed a growing appreciation that it was not always in the national interest to leave industry to the free play of market forces. Several Tory ministers in the Lloyd George coalition, as well as Churchill who was still a Liberal, had been ready to support nationalization of the railways – an obvious example of a key industry losing efficiency because it was divided into too many competing private companies. In the event, nationalization was killed in the post-war reaction and the companies were amalgamated into larger units instead. There was a similar but even stronger case for nationalization or rationalization in the coal industry, which was divided into 1,400 separate colliery companies, many of them small and inefficient. Although the majority on the Sankey Commission accepted the case for a change of ownership, the report was ignored for political reasons. Eventually in 1930 the Labour government intervened to set total output, apportion quotas for each pit and fix prices, thereby propping up the less efficient parts of the industry. Subsequently the Conservatives continued this policy, and took a further step in nationalizing the royalties of the coal-owners in 1938, a policy long advocated by radical critics of the landowners.

However, Conservative collectivism went much further than this. It really began under the post-war coalition with the establishment of the Forestry Commission (1920). This was a recognition that, as Lloyd George and the radicals had long claimed, private enterprise simply neglected to invest in forests and woodland. The war had underlined the danger to national security of being too dependent on imported wood, and in the 1920s extensive investment was undertaken to repair the deficiency. An even more important example was electricity. In 1919 the government allocated £20 million for new investment and divided the country into districts, each under a Joint Electricity Authority with responsibility for extending the supply. In 1927 Baldwin created the Central Electricity Generating Board to own and operate the national grid: the national interest required an efficient electricity supply which could only be achieved by economies of scale.

Subsequently the National Government also recognized the inadequacies of private enterprise in several sectors. In 1933, for example, it adopted a bill prepared by Herbert Morrison to establish a London Passenger Transport Board, thereby creating a state monopoly over all the transport services in the capital. By 1938 it had decided that the competition between Imperial Airways and British Airways had been disastrous, and so the two were merged into a state company, British Overseas Airways Corporation, under Sir John Reith. But in some ways the most significant, and certainly the most expensive, aspect of interventionism under the Conservatives was in agriculture, even though it involved no change of ownership. As a result of wartime food shortages the farming industry had expanded, and in the 1920s many men were assisted to establish themselves in smallholdings. But in 1921 the government withdrew the subsidies that had been designed to maintain a minimum price for corn; and during the 1920s and 1930s food prices fell drastically, driving many farmers out of business. The second Labour government offered a solution in the shape of Dr Addison's 1931 Agricultural Marketing Bill. The idea was to impose quotas on imports of food, to give farmers guaranteed prices, and to establish marketing boards to buy up and resell the farmers' crops. By 1933 the National Government had adopted and extended this policy to cover milk, potatoes, pigs, wheat, sugar and hops. The effect, as with coal, was to protect the inefficient, but it certainly stimulated an increase in agricultural output of around 16 per cent between 1931 and 1937, though at an annual cost of between £30 and £40 million.

It can, of course, be argued that each case of state interventionism was a special one, not part of an overall plan or philosophy. But by 1939 the list of special cases had become rather too long for such a view to be satisfactory. State collectivism was becoming a habit for both parties. The Conservatives in particular had breached *laissez-faire* principles so deliberately that there could be little doubt that their leaders, at least, had abandoned the old confidence in an unfettered free-enterprise economy.

Economic recovery in the 1930s

The National Government began by imposing £70 million of expenditure cuts and increases in taxation designed to balance the budget and restore confidence which had the effect of inhibiting recovery and increasing unemployment during 1932–3. However, by 1934 clear signs of recovery manifested themselves as unemployment began to fall and output exceeded the 1929 level. Indeed between 1932 and 1937 unemployment fell from 3 million to 1.5 million while industrial production increased by 46 per cent. This improvement has given rise to a much more optimistic view of the 1930s than has traditionally been held. As with all claims in economics, much depends on which periods are chosen for comparison; but the basis for the optimistic view rests on the evidence that, whereas national income increased by only 10 per cent from 1921 to 1929, it rose by 17 per cent from 1929 to 1937.

Admittedly this growth was rather patchy in geographical terms. It was associated with a limited range of industries largely dependent on the domestic market for consumer goods rather than on a recovery in exports. The building industry was the major example. Whereas in the 1920s 150,000 houses were built on average each year, after 1934 well over 300,000 were being built annually. This meant a rapid increase in employment, since small firms were able to take on extra labour quickly, and a stimulus to companies supplying bricks, pipes, glass and paint. Typical of the expanding consumer-goods industries was vacuum cleaners, whose production rose from 37,000 in 1930 to 409,000 in 1935. The aircraft industry, transformed by rearmament after 1935, generated (on one estimate) around a million extra jobs by 1938. Motor cars manufactured in Britain increased from 212,000 in 1928 to 445,000 by 1938 and employed two million workers, the second largest industry in the country. The leaders were Alfred Austin, who marketed the Austin 7 for £165, and William Morris whose Morris Cowley fell from £465 in price to £225. But few British manufacturers managed to emulate them by mass producing motor cars. The famous firm of Bentley manufactured glamorous cars that were a feat of engineering and won races, but their price increased from £750 to well over £1,000 and by 1931, when the firm collapsed, they had made a mere 3,037 cars since 1919!

The role of the National Government

How far can the limited recovery from the depths of depression be ascribed to the policies of the National Government? This is a complex question; many different pressures were at work simultaneously. The government was by no means as orthodox as the Chancellor, Neville Chamberlain liked to pretend. He abandoned the policy the government had been established to defend by quitting the gold standard and devaluing the pound. By March 1932 the pound had fallen from $4.86 to $3.40. Devaluation had the effect of reducing the cost of borrowing, making it cheaper to service the National Debt, stimulating exports, checking the fall in Britain's share of world trade, and boosting domestic employment. But the greatest benefit was that monetary policy had been freed from external pressures, and it thus became possible to cut the bank rate from 6 per cent to 2 per cent in 1932. Interest rates remained low for the rest of the decade, thereby sustaining house-building. All this represented a victory for Keynesian thinking and a defeat for the Treasury and the government. Unfortunately, the government failed to use cheap money as a countercyclical weapon as Keynes wished for the Treasury was more interested in simply reducing the cost of the National Debt. However Chamberlain soon abandoned his financial orthodoxy. From 1932 onwards his budgets were mildly inflationary and by the 1935 election income tax had been reduced and the expenditure cuts of 1931 largely abandoned. He resisted pressure to increase spending on rearmament but eventually gave way.

However, other policy innovations of the 1930s were of more marginal significance. For example, the government passed an Abnormal Importations Act in November 1931 which empowered it to levy 50 per cent tariffs on certain goods, and an Import Duties Act in 1932 which imposed a general 10 per cent duty, with exemptions for British Empire products. In this way free trade came to an end at last. However, tariffs made little impact on exports as productivity remained poor, and raised only £23 million revenue in the first year. Certain industries benefited from protection; imports of vacuum cleaners fell off sharply, for example, and fresh investment in steel led to new plant at Ebbw Vale, Corby, Shotton and Workington. But other run-down industries were not easily restored. The government's attempts to foster Empire trade by means of the Ottawa Agreements also had only a marginal effect, because India and the dominions insisted on protection for their own industries. After decades of controversy tariff reform was not the solution.

The government recognized the depth of the problems in the old industrial districts by a belated and half-hearted attempt at a regional economic policy. The first stage was the appointment of commissioners to investigate the 'Distressed Areas' – South Wales, Tyneside–Durham, West Cumberland and Scotland. They identified schemes including improvement of water and sewage supplies, harbour repairs and hospital building, but the meagre £2 million allocated for this scarcely reflected the extent of the problem. From 1936 the government offered to remit rent, rates and taxes for companies which moved into distressed areas, which fostered the development of trading estates. But even in 1938 only 17 per cent of newly opened factories were in the special areas, compared to 40 per cent in Greater London, though this at least represented a major improvement on previous years. If the effects were marginal they were a pointer to post-1945 economic planning.

The limits of recovery

Consequently suggestions about a recovery from the depression must be heavily qualified. Unemployment remained at nearly 11 per cent on the outbreak of war in 1939. The growth industries had failed to make a major impression on the worst of the problem partly because growth was concentrated in the south-east and Midlands. Factors such as coal, iron or water that had influenced the original location of industry no longer applied. By the 1930s electricity was available everywhere, and the London market made the south attractive to businessmen. It has been claimed that the unemployed workers failed to migrate to the new industries because they were cushioned by unemployment benefits. But this is doubly untrue. In fact considerable movements of population took place; boom towns like Slough absorbed large numbers of men from South Wales, for example. But there were real obstacles to migration. Most of the jobs lost in the old industries were for skilled men, whereas in the growth industries employers wanted women, and particularly young workers, for unskilled production-line work because they would accept low wages and were unlikely to be union members. Older men with families could not easily move to areas of low wages and relatively expensive housing.

Apart from being limited in extent, the recovery also proved to be fragile. In 1937 it collapsed into another brief slump from which it was saved largely by the rearmament programme. Even in 1939, only 68 per cent of cotton-weaving capacity and 76 per cent of spinning capacity was being employed. Britain had a balance-of-payments deficit each year from 1937 to 1939. The truth was that the growth industries flourished in the home market but were unable to compete abroad while the structural problems of British industry remained unresolved. Ultimately it was the Second World War that resolved the problem of mass unemployment rather than Neville Chamberlain.

Further reading

Roderick Floud and Paul Johnson eds, *The Cambridge Economic History of Modern Britain vol. II 1860–1939* (2004)

Martin Daunton, *Wealth and Welfare: an Economic and Social History of Britain 1851–1951* (2007)

J. Tomlinson, *Problems of British Economic Policy 1870–1945* (1981)

G.C. Peden, *British Economic and Social Policy: Lloyd George to Margaret Thatcher* (1985)

D. Winch, *Economics and Policy* (1969)

A.S. Milward, *The Economic Effects of the Two World Wars on Britain* (1970)

W.R. Garside, *British Unemployment 1919–39* (1990)

John McIlroy, Alan Campbell and Keith Gildart eds, *Industrial Politics and the 1926 Mining Lockout* (2004)

Rodney Lowe, *Adjusting to Democracy: The Role of the Ministry of Labour in British Politics 1916–39* (1986)

F. Trentmann, *Free Trade Nation* (2008)

S. Glynn and A. Booth, *Modern Britain: An Economic and Social History* (1996)

For discussions of Keynesian ideas see:

P.F. Clarke, *The Keynesian Revolution in the Making 1924–36* (1988)

G.C. Peden, *Keynes, the Treasury and British Economic Policy* (1988)

A. Marwick, 'Middle Opinion in the Thirties: Planning, Progress and Political Agreement', *English Historical Review*, 9, 1965

On Labour's ideas see:

N. Thompson, *Political Economy and the Labour Party* (1996)

J. Tomlinson, 'Labour and the Economy', in D. Tanner, P. Thane and N. Tiratsoo eds, *Labour's First Century* (2000)

R.I. McKibbin, 'The Economic Policy of the Second Labour Government', *Past and Present*, 36, 1975 – a defence of the 1929–31 government.

J. Callaghan, *Socialism in Britain since 1884* (1990)

National Government policy is discussed in:

Nick Smart, *Neville Chamberlain* (2010)

Nick Smart, *The National Government 1931–40* (1999)

Robert Self, *Neville Chamberlain: A Biography* (2001) – argues that Chamberlain has been under-rated.

B.W.E. Alford, *Depression and Recovery? British Economic Growth 1918–39* (1972)

12

Mass Democracy in an Age of Decline

By the end of 1918 it seemed that the war had obliterated many of the familiar landmarks of Edwardian politics. Each of the four political parties had suffered some division since 1914, and two of them were now in headlong decline. The country was now firmly in the grip of a coalition government from which, it was widely predicted, a new centre party would shortly emerge. Yet in the end many of the expectations of radical change failed to materialize, or at least proved to be exaggerated. In spite of the severe social problems generated by the economic depression, the enfranchisement of millions of new voters, and the emergence of a major working-class party the political system remained remarkably stable; the forces making for change were somehow absorbed and assimilated.

National identity between the wars

Victory in 1918 had the effect of consolidating support for British institutions – Parliament, monarchy and empire – in contrast to the impact of war in discrediting and destroying regimes in Russia, Germany and Italy. In this George V played a key role not just as a symbol of wartime unity but by avoiding political partisanship afterwards. In 1932 he instituted the tradition of Christmas broadcasts and attained his Silver Jubilee in 1936 amid national celebrations. A sense of national identity was also complemented by a novel institution: the BBC. Founded in 1922 and run by Sir John Reith, the BBC consciously adopted a propagandist strategy, defining its role in terms of fostering Britishness, marginalizing regionalism, championing the English character, celebrating the empire and promoting the royal family. The media, including newspapers, women's magazines and cinema, energetically projected the royal family as a model of family life for millions of people.

Domesticity combined with the fashionable retreat into a celebration of the English countryside offered interwar society a comfort zone at a time of economic insecurity caused by mass unemployment and political disruption following the collapse of European democracies. In many ways British national identity appears very secure in this period.

Ireland, Scotland and the war

On the other hand, a wider perspective reveals some flaws in national identity. The war accelerated the trend towards a more secular society partly through the development of a mass leisure industry that competed with the Churches. More fundamentally it undermined the Church of England whose clergy were widely considered to have made themselves the mouthpiece for the official patriotic propaganda that sent young men to their deaths during the war. Leading bishops also discredited themselves by taking the government's line in the general strike in 1926 and over the abdication of Edward VIII in 1936. In effect the Church had become too close to the Establishment.

Nominally the major blow to the unity and integrity of Britain came with the end of the Union with Ireland in 1921. Admittedly this loss proved much less traumatic than expected perhaps because it was long-anticipated and because of the continuing loyalty of Ulster. In fact Westminster politicians largely wanted to forget Ireland, Scotland and Wales. In this spirit they created a Northern Ireland parliament at Stormont. This was perverse as the Ulstermen had always argued that they wanted nothing but to be under the Westminster parliament, but London preferred to free itself from Irish controversies. The results were eventually disastrous as the dominance of Ulster politics by the Unionists and discrimination against Catholics generated another violent separatist movement in a later generation.

Historians have also largely neglected the destabilizing effects of the war in Scotland where it radicalized politics, stimulated pessimism and provoked anti-English sentiment. The mortality rate for Scots troops had reached a horrendous 26 per cent, compared with 12 per cent for the British army as a whole. The Scots economy, focused on shipbuilding, textiles, steel and heavy engineering, was devastated by the post-war depression leaving the country with higher unemployment than England for a century to come. To some extent the depression undermined the English regions too. Lancashire, which traditionally took enormous pride in being the greatest textiles producer in the world, went into a long-term decline which made it a target for the British Union of Fascists in the 1930s; and from this time the economic and cultural vigour of the English regions, which had been a notable feature of the Victorian era, dwindled as resources and status gradually became focused narrowly on London.

For Scotland one immediate result was that emigration ran very high, up to 400,000 in the 1920s, a trend that became aggravated by migration from Ireland which fostered a gloomy belief that Scotland was a society in irremediable decline. After two hundred years of success the Union with England was ceasing to work. This generated some anti-Englishness which was reflected in a Scottish literary revival. However, political nationalism appeared weak as yet. The decline of the Liberals largely killed the idea of a Scottish parliament as both Labour and the Conservatives adopted a rigidly Unionist approach, opposing almost all forms of constitutional reform. To fill the gap new nationalist parties were formed in 1928 and 1932, amalgamating in 1934 to form the Scottish National Party (SNP). Although the SNP enjoyed very modest success for the next thirty years, the seedbed for modern Scottish separatism had been established.

Structural changes in politics

The Representation of the People Act (1918) involved enormous potential for change as it replaced the Edwardian electorate of 8 million with one of over 21 million. The new voters differed in three ways. Many were young and politicians regarded them as politically ignorant, unattached to party and easily swayed. Forty per cent were now female and thus considered to be unpredictable. Fears were compounded by the fact that around 80 per cent of voters were now working-class; had their wartime experience made them patriots and imperialists or had the impact of rising prices and rents left them disaffected? Just as significantly, 1918 involved a drastic redrawing of the constituency boundaries, extending the trend towards equal-sized, single-member seats, giving Labour more seats dominated by working-class voters and the Conservatives more suburban seats where they faced no effective competition. Conservatives also gained from the events in Ireland, notably the refusal of the Sinn Fein members to attend Westminster and the withdrawal of the Nationalist majority after 1921 leaving only the Ulster members. It was thus much easier for them to win a majority than before 1914.

Organizing the working-class vote

The Labour Party now aspired to represent the interests of the working-class majority. Under the guidance of the Party Secretary, Arthur Henderson,

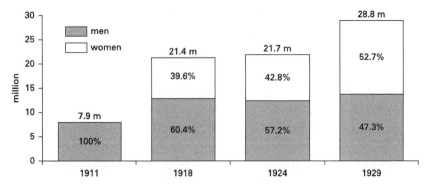

Figure 12.1 Parliamentary voters in the UK, 1911–29.

Labour built up a formidable organization during the 1920s helped by as many as 3.5 million trade union members who paid the political levy to the party. A former union official of moderate Liberal views, Henderson was ideally placed to win the full co-operation of the unions; in 1920 he even obtained a 50 per cent increase in the political levy. Additionally the unions sponsored large numbers of parliamentary candidates by offering financial subsidies to the constituency associations that adopted them. The number of constituency Labour parties affiliated at headquarters increased from 397 in 1918 to 626 by 1924, a process accelerated by the frequency of general elections in 1922, 1923 and 1924. By 1928 the party's individual membership stood at 215,000; but much of the local work was done by the 1,800 women's sections, who claimed approximately 300,000 members by 1929.

There were, however, limitations. Labour was by no means as wealthy as the Conservatives, financed by business and the honours system. Also, Labour's resources remained concentrated in a limited band of very safe constituencies, not in the marginals where they were needed. One sign of this was the deficiency of full-time paid agents, who numbered little more than 100 in the 1920s. Nor did the individual membership seriously rival that of the Conservatives. However, the result of improved organization and extra candidates was a steady increase in the party's vote to 37 per cent by 1929. Clearly, Labour had not yet mobilized the majority of the working-class vote, otherwise it would have done much better than this. However, this performance was quite sufficient to establish Labour as the second party from 1918 onwards, and as the Opposition in Parliament. This, though it ruffled feathers at the time, did not pose any fundamental challenge to the political system, for Labour politicians were dedicated to parliamentary methods and traditions. Yet Labour was, of course, different; the product of extraparliamentary forces, it had virtually no representation in the House of

Lords; and as an avowed class party it appeared to threaten to polarize politics between the representatives of capital and those of labour.

The impact of women

The novel element after 1918 consisted in the 8.4 million female voters. In 1928, when Stanley Baldwin enacted the Equal Franchise Act, a further 5 million women became enfranchised, and as a result women became a majority of the total British electorate. However, the impact of this was not as great as contemporaries anticipated. Women proved slow to come forward as parliamentary candidates, and the parties showed reluctance to give them winnable seats. By 1935, after seven general elections for which women had been eligible, only 5 per cent of candidates were female, and after the election of Nancy Astor in 1919 the number of female members reached a maximum of 15 in 1931.

How far did the new voters influence the character and the agenda of politics? Paradoxically, the larger electorate proved to be much quieter and better-behaved than its Victorian predecessor. Women's participation contributed to this change. Fewer people attended big public meetings, and politicians increasingly communicated with the voters by radio broadcasts, doorstep canvassing and cinema newsreels. In the Edwardian period, political debate had already begun to focus on social-economic issues and Labour had some reason to feel that unemployment, pensions, housing and health would dominate the political agenda after 1918. This was corroborated by the Conservative leaders who concluded that the combination of a new electorate and the rise of Labour made it dangerous for them to neglect questions of social welfare and standards of living. The Conservatives also gave much less emphasis to imperial issues than they had traditionally done, preferring a bipartisan approach to a polarization of views.

Table 12.1 Women in interwar parliamentary elections

	Women candidates	Total MPs	Women MPs
1918	17	707	1*
1922	33	615	2
1923	34	615	8
1924	41	615	4
1929	69	615	14
1931	62	615	15
1935	67	615	9

* Countess Markievicz was elected as a Sinn Fein candidate in Dublin but did not take her seat.

Image 7 Nancy Astor harangues the voters of Plymouth where she was elected the first woman MP, December 1919.

This, however, did not mean that the party was simply obliged to echo its rivals in social reform. It took the initiative in tackling questions such as widows' pensions in 1925. On the negative side, the Tories sought to discredit Labour by equating it with Socialism, which in their view implied atheism, hostility to the family, state appropriation of private property, and Stalinist autocracy. All this was so far-fetched that it made little impression on the working class, though it probably helped to frighten some of the middle classes. The Conservatives also emphasized the need to protect British industry, and thus British jobs, with tariffs. It also proved advantageous that mass enfranchisement had coincided with the movement of many working-class men into the income-tax net. This gave them a direct interest in keeping taxation low, and thus limited their willingness to support expensive social policies. Overall the enfranchisement of women reinforced the existing trend for politicians to concentrate upon economic management, living standards and welfare. Most politicians chose to believe that women's interests were largely confined to domestic matters. As one party agent predicted in 1921:

> The women's vote is having a narrowing effect upon politics, making them more parochial and is, at the moment, reducing them to bread and butter politics and the cost of living . . . their votes will probably be given on purely home questions . . . while Imperial and foreign issues will leave them cold.

The Liberals and Labour felt sure that women's role as household managers made them keen free-traders, fearful of the effects of tariffs on food prices; and when the Conservatives lost heavily over this issue in 1923 they blamed the supposedly volatile female electors.

The interwar feminist movement

The attainment of the vote in 1918, and especially equal suffrage in 1928, posed questions for feminists. Should they modify their aims and agenda, and was it appropriate to change their tactics and methods now they were inside the system? The equal-rights feminists correctly saw that in the 1920s politicians were more susceptible to pressure, resulting in much legislation including the Sex Discrimination (Removal) Act (1919) which opened the professions to women, the Matrimonial Causes Act (1923) which gave women equal grounds for divorce, Widows Pensions (1925), and the introduction of equal guardianship of infants (1925).

Conversely other women argued that there was now less momentum behind the equal-rights agenda and that feminism must extend its appeal amongst women not previously involved. Advocates of 'New Feminism', led by Eleanor Rathbone, who was elected as Independent MP for the Combined Universities seat in 1929, campaigned for family allowances and providing advice on birth control to married women. However, politicians largely refused to tackle these issues and other feminist causes such as equal pay. Consequently, by the late 1920s legislation for women had virtually come to a stop, in spite of their new standing as the majority of the electorate. Their cause was hindered by the depression which strengthened the traditional assumption that the available jobs should be reserved for men while women returned to domesticity; one symptom of this thinking was the 'marriage bar' which meant the sacking of married female employees by local authorities.

Feminists abruptly dropped militant tactics in the 1920s and the Pankhursts withdrew from the movement. However continuity was provided by the National Union of Women's Suffrage Societies, now renamed as the National Union of Societies for Equal Citizenship (NUSEC), which continued to employ parliamentary methods. Several new feminist organizations also emerged including the Women's Citizens Association (1918), the Six Point Group (1921), the Open Door Council (1926) and the Townswomen's Guilds (1928); the latter, an attempt to extend Women's Institutes, had recruited 54,000 members by 1939.

However, some feminists believed that as women were now voters it was appropriate to work through the political parties. All three parties developed an organizational hierarchy for women and recruited members so that by 1928 the Conservatives had around a million in 4,000 branches of the Women's Unionist Association, Labour about 250,000 in 1,800 Women's Sections, and the Women's Liberal Federation 88,000 members. But as few women became MPs, and only a handful of them were really feminists rather than party loyalists, many feminists thought it necessary to keep an independent women's movement alive. Despite this, the new organizations were quite small and NUSEC's branches had dwindled to 222 in 1920 and 90 by 1929, dwarfed by comparison with 300,000 in the WIs and 700,000–900,000 female trade unionists. By the 1930s the movement was in decline.

The first Labour government

After his stunning victory in 1918, Lloyd George appeared likely to dominate British politics for the foreseeable future: 'he can be prime minister for life if he likes,' declared the Tory leader, Bonar Law. In fact the golden aura of

Table 12.2 Interwar governments, 1918–40

1918–22	Coalition	(Lloyd George)
1922–24	Conservative	(Bonar Law Oct 1922; Stanley Baldwin May 1923 to Jan 1924)
1924 Jan to Nov	Labour	(J. Ramsay MacDonald)
1924–29	Conservative	(Stanley Baldwin)
1929–31	Labour	(J. Ramsay MacDonald)
1931–35	National	(J. Ramsay MacDonald)
1935–37	National	(Stanley Baldwin)
1937–40	National	(Neville Chamberlain)

victory evaporated swiftly as the problems of peacetime loomed larger. Lloyd George's position was never as strong as it appeared for he remained a prime minister without a real party. His only chance in the long run was to create a new centre party before he lost office. In 1920 there was much talk of 'fusion' between Conservatives such as Austen Chamberlain and Lloyd George and Liberals such as Winston Churchill, but Bonar Law never backed it. In the event Lloyd George held the premiership for as long as the Conservatives, who comprised the bulk of his parliamentary majority, were prepared to tolerate him – a remarkable four years.

Up to a point Lloyd George fulfilled expectations by helping to keep the threat of Labour and class warfare at bay. Since the number of working days lost in strikes rose from 21 million in 1919 to 86 million in 1921, this mattered greatly to the Conservatives. Lloyd George steered a course through this phase by invariably granting big rises in wages; and he adroitly diverted the miners' pressure for coal nationalization by appointing the Sankey Commission in 1920. However, after this the Conservatives' grievances against Lloyd George steadily mounted. He made the mistake of continuing to govern like a wartime leader; his personal interference in foreign policy led him very near to another war with Turkey over the Chanak crisis in 1922. His success in reaching a settlement with the Irish Republicans also outraged some Tories, though the party leaders had by then reconciled themselves to the end of the Union. Others attacked the reckless sale of honours by the Prime Minister's henchmen, though this was in part because it deprived the Conservatives themselves of financial contributions!

By 1920 a reaction against high taxation had developed among rank-and-file Tories. This so-called 'anti-waste' campaign so alarmed the Conservative leaders that they insisted on policy changes. An official committee under Sir Eric Geddes in 1921 proposed economies in housing, education and the armed forces, which were followed by a placatory reduction in income tax. However, such retreats only undermined the Liberal wing of the coalition. Dr Addison was led to resign after the abandonment of his housing policy, and Edwin Montagu, who was bitterly attacked by the Conservatives over his Indian reforms, had been driven from office by 1921. The introduction of protective tariffs in 1921 and the brutal tactics used by the 'Black and Tans' in Ireland further embarrassed the coalition Liberals.

Baldwin and the overthrow of the coalition

However, these grievances only proved fatal when the electoral position of the government began to crumble. By-election gains by Labour and the

Independent Liberals led many Lloyd George Liberals to think about rejoining their old party. To the Conservatives Lloyd George no longer looked like an effective bulwark against the rise of Labour; instead he appeared increasingly a deadweight around the Conservative Party's neck. In the autumn of 1922 these misgivings were brought to a head by the realization that Lloyd George was contemplating another term of office. As a result the Conservative leader, Austen Chamberlain, who had succeeded Bonar Law after his retirement for health reasons, agreed to hold a meeting of the parliamentary party at the Carlton Club in October where many junior figures such as Stanley Baldwin voiced their dislike of Lloyd George. Baldwin spoke for the rank-and-file who surprised the leaders by voting 187–86 against fighting another election in association with Lloyd George. The immediate result of this was the Prime Minister's resignation and Chamberlain's replacement as party leader by Bonar Law, whose health

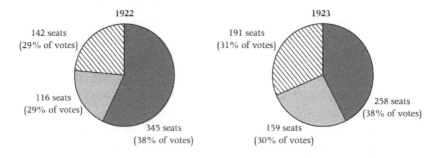

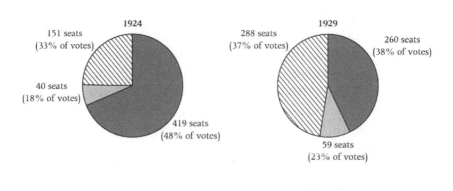

Figure 12.2 General elections, 1922–9.

had improved. After nearly eight years of multi-party governments, normal party politics had been restored at a stroke. Bonar Law held an immediate general election, which he won comfortably though with only a minority of the votes. The Conservatives had shrewdly severed their links with Lloyd George just when he had become a discredited figure. The party suffered some damage when a group including Chamberlain, Balfour and Lord Birkenhead, who opposed the breakup of the coalition, refused to join the new government. But this at least created a chance of high office for some junior figures, notably Stanley Baldwin, who became Chancellor of the Exchequer. It was not long before ill-health again led to Bonar Law's retirement. With the coalitionists still detached, there was little material to choose from. Lord Curzon, the obvious choice, found himself ruled out, ostensibly because he sat in the House of Lords, but in reality because his colleagues found him so obnoxious. As a result the choice fell upon the apparently undistinguished Baldwin.

Within months of succeeding to the premiership Baldwin astonished the political world by holding a fresh general election. Since he had a large majority and four years of his term still to run, this seems odd and historians have never agreed on how to explain his decision. He claimed that he wanted a popular mandate to introduce tariffs although this seems implausible as he soon dropped the idea and, in any case, the Conservatives had been elected in 1922 on a protectionist programme. In reality an election fought on this issue was expected both to reunite the Conservative Party and to drive Lloyd George back into the arms of the Liberals which is what Baldwin wanted. In effect the unnecessary election was an abuse of prime ministerial power to serve party purposes. Although both Baldwin's objects were accomplished he miscalculated in that in the election the Conservatives lost far more seats than expected, owing to fears that tariffs would lead to an increase in the cost of living, and the upshot was the first Labour government of 1924.

The evolution of Labour

'I wonder what dear Grandmama [Queen Victoria] would have thought of a Labour government', wrote George V in his diary. Most Labour politicians were equally surprised as they had not expected to come to power so soon. As recently as 1918 they had only 63 MPs, and the leading figures, including MacDonald, Snowden and Henderson, had all been defeated. Yet Labour's new status as the effective alternative to the Conservatives was quickly underlined by the municipal elections of 1919. The party made sweeping gains, especially in London, which proved to be the start of a trend that lasted throughout the 1920s and 1930s. Soon the Liberals and Conservatives began to be driven into an anti-Labour alliance in local government.

From the early 1920s onwards the Labour Movement enjoyed a powerful conviction that history was on its side now that the capitalist system had become discredited by depression and mass unemployment. By comparison with the tarnished Lloyd George and the uninspired Tory leaders, the party seemed fresh and idealistic. Ramsay MacDonald, who returned to the leadership in 1922, was an able parliamentarian who appealed across the lines of class to a wide public. Many working-class families now felt aggrieved about the profiteering of wartime; with the collapse of the boom in 1920 and the sudden increase in unemployment the fruits of victory were seen to have withered already. This created fertile ground for interventionist policies. In particular, the proposal for a special levy on capital to pay off the National Debt and thereby free government resources for more constructive purposes proved appealing, and not just within the Labour Movement.

However, under MacDonald and Snowden the tactics were to tone down the party's socialism and play up its respectability. To this end they distanced themselves from the capital levy and made no attempt to 'soak the rich' when in office in 1924 or 1929. Indeed, in many ways Labour's chief tactical triumph consisted in capitalizing on the continuity between its policies and traditional Liberalism. For example, the party staunchly upheld the free-trade cause, and sought to promote it by re-establishing commercial relations with Russia. By giving priority to housing, health, unemployment and education the party effectively took over the Liberals' role as the champion of social reform. Above all, MacDonald's principled stand against British entry into the war placed him and his party in a good position to benefit from the gathering reaction against the pre-war arms race. Labour carried more credibility as an advocate of disarmament and the League of Nations in the 1920s than either of its rivals. This goes a long way to explaining the attraction Labour exercised over many former Liberals, disillusioned by their party's pre-war and wartime policies and divisions. In many ways Labour had become the effective heir to the radical tradition in both domestic and external affairs. As a result the party's ranks were swollen by middle- and upper-class recruits such as Charles Trevelyan, Christopher Addison, Arthur Ponsonby and Richard Haldane.

Conservative recruits to Labour

Recent research shows that Labour's expansion in the 1920s also embraced distinguished figures from *Conservative* family backgrounds, including

Susan Lawrence, Stafford Cripps, Hugh Dalton, Hugh Gaitskell, Lord Sankey, Oswald Mosley, Cynthia Mosley (the daughter of Lord Curzon), Oliver Baldwin (the son of Stanley Baldwin) and Lord Chelmsford (the former Indian Viceroy) among others. The significance of this can hardly be exaggerated. It endowed the untried party with many experienced and well-connected people when forming its first government. Moreover, far from diluting Labour's socialism, the ex-Conservatives were often intellectually formidable people who had thought hard about the failings of free enterprise and concluded that state interventionism had become necessary; consequently they wanted Labour to take its socialism more seriously. Also, the ex-Conservatives were widely employed as candidates in areas such as the West Midlands to combat the traditional populist Toryism. Mosley, for example, drove Neville Chamberlain from his Birmingham constituency and himself represented Smethwick for Labour from 1924 to 1930 while his wife won Stoke-on-Trent for Labour. Thus, in spite of its reputation as the working-class party, Labour actually developed into a representative national party during the 1920s; arguably it was more national than the Conservatives, who still depended upon a very narrow section of society for their candidates and MPs.

Liberal division and revival

Despite this there was no irresistible force carrying Labour to power in the 1920s, and one must take account of the large element of contingency in the party's rise. But for Baldwin's extraordinary decision to call an election in 1923, for example, the first Labour government would have been much delayed. Similarly, errors committed by the Liberals played an important part in Labour's fortunes. Even after the disaster of 1918 there was nothing inevitable in the continued Liberal decline. During the 1920s they generated radical new policies to deal with the economic depression and effected a revival in their fortunes; even under a mass electorate they ran Labour neck-and-neck, with 29–30 per cent of the popular vote in 1922 and 1923. In addition, free trade remained a popular cry. Traditional Liberal causes such as Nonconformity, temperance and Home Rule had clearly lost some of their prominence, though the real problem was that many of the advocates of these issues found it more electorally efficacious to vote Labour.

On the other hand, the Liberals were immensely handicapped because for five years after the 1918 election they continued to be riven by squabbles between the followers of Asquith and Lloyd George. Indeed, even after the formal reunion of 1923 the infighting was maintained by Sir John

Simon, Walter Runciman and others who detested Lloyd George. Asquith stubbornly held on to the leadership until 1926, though he was barren of ideas; in this way he deprived the party of abler leadership until it was almost too late. In addition, the Liberals suffered badly from the erratic and unrepresentative workings of the electoral system. This system now delivered big majorities to the Conservatives on the basis of only 38 per cent of the vote, and in 1929 nearly did the same for Labour on 37 per cent. But the Liberals' support was not concentrated except in rural Wales, Highland Scotland and parts of the West Country. Labour's growth in urban-industrial seats fatally undermined them, while in the Conservative areas the Liberal vote was split by the additional Labour candidates who came forward. As a result, the Liberals never obtained representation in proportion to their high vote. The failure to include proportional representation or the alternative vote in the 1918 reform bill proved to be a crucial error. As one election succeeded another, the non-Conservative voters increasingly concluded that Labour was better placed to defeat the Conservatives, and voted tactically. This process gradually left the Liberals as a party of the right looking to attract protest votes from middle-class Conservatism; this was somewhat at odds with their traditions and with many of the parliamentarians' instincts which pointed to a restoration of Liberalism's radical, reformist strategy.

A minority government

After the 1923 election the Liberals had to make a crucial decision because no party enjoyed a majority. Since the Conservatives already held office and remained the largest party, they declined to resign at once. Yet as they had clearly lost the election, Asquith joined with Labour to vote them out of office. As the leader of the second largest party, though with only 191 MPs, MacDonald was invited to form a minority government. Some authors erroneously assume that this involved an alliance between Labour and the Liberals in 1924. On the contrary, MacDonald deliberately refused any arrangement with the Liberals either to join the government or even to support an agreed programme of legislation for to do so would have been inconsistent with his long-term strategy. He preferred to keep them at arm's length so as to underline Labour's higher status as a party of government. Nonetheless the Liberals inevitably bore much of the blame, in Conservative eyes, for the MacDonald government.

Moreover, his lack of a working majority scarcely worried the new Prime Minister. It gave him a good excuse for not attempting to introduce a socialist programme which he did not, in fact, possess. Instead, he filled his Cabinet with a mixture of former Liberals and Conservatives with experience of high office and worthy trade unionists unlikely to frighten anyone but the most extreme Tories. For the experiment was intended to be *reassuring*, to prove Labour's competence as a governing party. As Foreign Secretary, MacDonald played a constructive role in getting the French to withdraw from the Ruhr. At the Exchequer Philip Snowden produced a cautious budget which reduced some indirect taxes on food but involved nothing novel or radical.

This was sound tactics, in that it denied the Conservatives the opportunity to claim that Labour government was a disaster. But the caution was probably overdone. MacDonald could have achieved something solid, but he missed the opportunity to introduce several widely expected measures, such as widows' pensions and equal votes for women, which would have had Liberal backing and been feasible for a minority government. He thus allowed Baldwin to gain the credit for these reforms after 1924. The greatest achievement was John Wheatley's Housing Act which re-instated subsidies to local authorities and resulted in 520,000 new council houses by 1935. Ironically, MacDonald was reluctant to give Wheatley, a Clydeside Socialist, a ministry but calculated that some concession should be given to the left. He deliberately excluded another Socialist, George Lansbury, as being a class warrior. However, after nine months in office Labour's own supporters grew critical about the failure to tackle unemployment. As chancellor, Snowden cut taxes by £29 million, balanced the budget and backed the pound – highly orthodox policy. There were ominous signs here of MacDonald's incapacity as an executive leader. In the event he was relieved to be defeated in the Commons in September 1924, whereupon he resigned and held yet another general election after only nine months in office. Although this produced a big Conservative victory, Labour increased its share of the vote, and the real losers were the Liberals, whose seats fell from 158 to 40; in effect MacDonald had engineered a return to two-party politics. The 1924 election was marked by the release of the 'Zinoviev Letter' by the *Daily Mail* four days before polling. It purported to be an incitement to class war and chaos from the Communist International though it was almost certainly a forgery. Most voters took little notice. The significance of the Zinoviev Letter was, rather, that it gave the Labour Movement proof of trickery by reactionary forces in the press and the Establishment to deny them power, and to that extent it diverted attention from the shortcomings of MacDonald's policy in office.

The General Strike and the 1929 election

For the next five years it fell to a Conservative government to tackle unemployment; Lloyd George took over from Asquith as Liberal leader and engineered a fresh revival, while MacDonald escaped significant criticism from his own party over the inadequacies of the 1924 government and built up the movement for another victory in 1929.

Baldwin and Conservatism

As Conservative leader from 1923 to 1935 Stanley Baldwin was the most skilful and influential single politician of the interwar period, in terms of both his own party and the wider evolution of politics. He made a distinct break with previous Conservative leaders and tactics in his refusal to adopt a confrontational stance. Baldwin believed that as the war had shown that the British working class was loyal, patriotic and imperialist, it was now sensible for his party to adapt to the rise of Labour and mass enfranchisement rather than to retreat into reaction. In effect this meant accepting Labour as the alternative party of government and even learning from Labour in some ways by relying less on wealthy men as Conservative candidates for example. Baldwin wanted to pursue social reform, he vetoed demands for anti-union legislation, and he adopted a bipartisan approach to the empire. He also showed himself a remarkably modern leader in his adaptation to the new, quieter techniques required by radio broadcasts and in his appeal to the middle ground. He was alive to the need to attract the new women voters and to persuade middle-class Liberals to come over to the Conservatives; to this end he made Winston Churchill, who had rejoined the party in 1923, Chancellor of the Exchequer. This was the strategy that made the Conservatives the dominant electoral force for decades to come. Baldwin also complemented his abandonment of the traditional aggressive Tory endorsement of the Union with Ireland and imperial expansion with a subdued and sentimental celebration of Englishness and the English countryside, which probably reflected popular feeling after the war when people were retreating from the wider world into a more domestic frame of mind. Admittedly much of this proved unpalatable to right-wing Tories, who regarded Baldwin as a liberal and a traitor to his party's principles. They had welcomed his decision to seek a mandate to introduce tariffs in 1923 but were subsequently angered when this led to defeat, to the first Labour government and to the abandonment of protectionism.

The causes of the General Strike

However, Baldwin's undoing was the failure of his 1924–29 government to tackle unemployment effectively. When the Chancellor, Churchill, revalued the pound in 1925 it was plain that this implied general reductions in wages to sustain the currency at its new high level. This was the prelude to the General Strike of May 1926. Although the proximate cause lay in the decision of the coal-owners to cut miners' wages, the other trade unions recognized that they now shared a common interest with the miners in staving off reductions in their own pay. To this end they empowered the TUC to lead a General Strike, a decision that threatened to derail Baldwin's economic and political strategy by provoking a bitter clash between workers and employers. But Baldwin tried to avoid the crisis. Defying his right-wingers who complained that the Prime Minister was being too weak in resisting the unions' threat, he granted a subsidy to maintain existing wage levels for miners while a commission under Sir Herbert Samuel investigated the industry's problems. Baldwin undoubtedly hoped that in the interim either Samuel would come up with a compromise solution or the other unions would decide not to join the miners in a strike; either way he wanted to avoid a General Strike.

However, after nine months he could not extend the subsidy any further and neither side accepted Samuel's proposals, hence the strike occurred in May 1926. For several years governments of both parties had been preparing emergency plans to ensure that food and essentials were available during a major strike involving regional committees supported by around 80,000 volunteers who joined the Organization for the Maintenance of Supplies to keep the basic services running. In fact, these arrangements were not especially effective because the volunteers lacked the necessary skills to be able to drive trains and other sophisticated operations and the strike was solidly supported by industrial workers; as a result, the economy suffered a huge loss of production. However, the government was saved because after only nine days the TUC decided to call off the strike even though the workers were happy to continue and the miners themselves stayed out for a further six months.

Was the strike a success or a failure?

Conventional accounts of the General Strike follow contemporary propaganda in painting it as a failure for the unions. However, it is now apparent that this is simplistic and misleading. Accounts based on London, the political elite and the metropolitan press distort the reality. Admittedly the miners suffered wage cuts and their union split in two, but beyond that the effects were minimal; for example the decline in union membership pre-dated the strike by five years, reflecting the rise in long-term unemployment. The swift end gave Baldwin a triumph in the short term, but thereafter his political and economic strategy largely collapsed. It is easily forgotten that most ordinary people sympathized with the strike because of the fear of wage cuts. Where local elections coincided with the strike Conservative canvassers encountered great hostility from voters as they reported to headquarters. In effect the strike undermined the conciliatory approach towards the working class that Baldwin had tried to adopt because he felt obliged to give way to pressure within his Cabinet and in the party to take coercive steps to try to prevent another general strike by means of the 1927 Trade Union Act. This measure outlawed sympathetic action by the unions and it changed the system by which union members contracted out of the political levy to one of contracting in. The effect was that fewer paid the levy, thereby reducing the Labour Party's income by a third.

MacDonald and the Labour leaders had not supported the General Strike because they felt it threatened their control and would alienate support at elections. However, this turned out to be a complete misunderstanding for they turned out to be the beneficiaries. The government's punitive reaction

Image 8 Armoured cars escort a supply convoy through Aldgate, London, during the General Strike, 1926.

encouraged the political and industrial wings of the Labour Movement to unite to return another Labour government. Finally, although the General Strike lasted only nine days the miners' strike lasted six months and public sympathy was aroused by the suffering of the miners' families. Many working-class voters had not yet been won over to Labour but the loyalties of many union members who had hitherto voted Conservative and Liberal had been strained by the strike, and as a result some changed allegiance; as a result Labour began to make extensive gains in the local elections at the expense of the Conservatives.

Moreover Baldwin's economic strategy was severely damaged by the strike because, contrary to expectations, wages (outside coal-mining) did *not* fall significantly afterwards, and to this extent the strike should be regarded more as a success than a failure. Consequently the government's attempt to maintain the pound at its new high level failed. Unemployment remained fairly high at 1.1 million or 11 per cent in 1929 when the general election took place. Meanwhile, in 1928 Lloyd George received the report of the Liberal Industrial Enquiry 'Britain's Industrial Future', the fruit of collaboration between politicians and distinguished economists including J.M. Keynes, Walter Layton and William Beveridge. This enabled him to offer an unusually detailed and coherent programme of state investment in capital projects designed to stimulate the sluggish economy and reduce unemployment by half a million. Although this helped Lloyd George to engineer a Liberal revival and score some by-election victories during the late 1920s, his pledge at the 1929 general election – 'We Can Conquer Unemployment' – probably did more to benefit Labour. This was because voters assumed, incorrectly as it turned out, that Labour would implement his proposals and because voting Labour seemed a more effective way of defeating the Conservatives. In the event, the Liberal vote rose to 23 per cent but yielded only 59 MPs, while the Labour vote increased from 33 per cent to 37 per cent, resulting in the return of 288 Labour MPs against 260 Conservatives.

The National Governments

The second Labour government lasted two-and-a-half years. Labour was still short of a parliamentary majority though was much closer than in 1924. However, as unemployment rose inexorably from 1.1 million in June 1929 to 2.5 million by December 1930 MacDonald's apparent inability to get to grips with the problem undermined his parliamentary support, leading to revolts by the ILP members from Clydeside, and also weakened Labour morale in the country, as was indicated in poor by-election results. MacDonald's record has been defended on the basis that there was little to be done in the circumstances of an international depression and that he was handicapped as leader of a minority government. But the lack of a parliamentary majority was no real obstacle to bringing forward new policies; the problem was excessive caution and lack of ideas. Yet alternatives were available. Lloyd George repeatedly engaged in private talks designed to produce an agreed programme in return for regular Liberal support in the Commons. By February 1930 one frustrated junior minister, Oswald Mosley, drew up his own programme including tariffs, control of the banks, rationalization of basic industries, and a development plan for agriculture, a scheme similar to those of the ILP and Lloyd George. But it was rejected by Cabinet ministers still overawed by the Chancellor, Snowden, who adhered rigidly to the Treasury's views about balancing the budget and defending the pound. The Cabinet appears to have been handicapped by a mixture of ignorance and naivety; when, after the fall of the government, the gold standard was abandoned and the pound devalued, one ex-minister ruefully commented: 'No one told us we could do that.'

The Cabinet split of 1931

As the economic and political situation deteriorated, MacDonald gradually succumbed to the logic of the situation, which was to reach an agreement with Lloyd George though he was reluctant to do so. For a long time MacDonald engaged Lloyd George in talks without trying to reach a conclusion but by the summer of 1931 they were co-operating; the government had introduced a bill for the Alternative Vote, to please the Liberals, while the latter were propping up the government's majority in Parliament. However, the Prime Minister had allowed matters to drift for too long. By 1931 the costs of mounting unemployment had exacerbated the budgetary deficit; deteriorating world trade and the overvalued pound had resulted in a serious balance-of-payments problem. This inevitably created fears that the pound would be devalued, which provoked withdrawals of money from London. There was consequently strong pressure to restore confidence in the pound amongst investors, which, it was argued, could best be done by balancing the budget. Consequently, in August 1931 a committee under Sir George May was appointed to recommend cuts. It estimated the deficit at £120 million and advised expenditure cuts of £97 million, including a 10 per cent reduction in unemployment benefit. Eventually the Cabinet split 12–9 in favour of these proposals; but in view of the opposition of the

TUC it was clear that the government could not go on in this divided state. Yet there was nothing inevitable in this breakdown. The financial interests had been anxious, not to destroy MacDonald's Cabinet, but to persuade it to take the necessary measures.

In the circumstances the normal response would have been for Baldwin, as the leader of the opposition, to form an alternative government. But against expectations the Labour government was succeeded by a National Government under MacDonald's premiership, including the Conservatives, the Liberals and a few Labour members. This was entirely the result of an intervention by George V, who liked MacDonald personally despite his obvious failure as premier since 1929. It was a stark indication of the power still residing in the monarch in circumstances when no one enjoyed a clear majority. Initially Baldwin was far from enthusiastic about this. He had been a major critic of coalition under Lloyd George and retained vivid memories of its disruptive effects upon the party. However, it was awkward to refuse the King's offer especially as Herbert Samuel, the acting Liberal leader while Lloyd George was conveniently in hospital, had agreed, so he reluctantly decided to serve in a National Government.

Why did the National Government last so long?

The remarkable feature of the National Government was that, though designed as a purely temporary expedient to defend the pound, it lasted up to 1940, killed only by the Second World War. As so often with coalitions the explanation lay with the Conservative leadership and their management of the party. Baldwin had suffered during 1929 to 1931 as the target of attacks by fellow Tories who favoured empire free trade, that is tariffs designed to protect Britain and her empire from foreign trade. Backed by Lord Beaverbrook of the *Daily Express* and Lord Rothermere of the *Daily Mail*, this campaign involved running candidates against official Conservatives, and in 1930 it almost succeeded in forcing Baldwin from the leadership in favour of Neville Chamberlain. However, the right-wing rebels could be marginalized within a much larger coalition. Within the National Government Baldwin would have more scope to pursue his original aim of making his party more centrist and liberal. Moreover, in the short term the Conservative leaders rapidly began to see the advantages of keeping the National Government together to fight an early general election *before* the economic crisis had been dealt with. They feared that any delay in holding an election would allow Labour the chance to recover and capitalize upon the unpopular decisions taken by the government. It was clearly going to take longer than anticipated to resolve the economic problem, and the measures would be more complicated than a mere balancing of the budget. In particular, the Conservatives saw the opportunity to introduce the protectionist policy they had so long advocated; but in view of voters' reaction to tariffs it seemed wiser to get an election out of the way first. Hence the decision to appeal for a vague 'Doctor's Mandate' to put the economy right. MacDonald had no objections to this for once his former colleagues had repudiated him there was no way back to the Labour Party. It was the Liberals, who had hoped to postpone an election, who were the most reluctant, especially as Lloyd George had stayed outside the National Government. But they hesitated to withdraw so soon, particularly as their participation in the government would at least guarantee short-term protection at the election.

The elections of 1931 and 1935

As a result, a snap election took place in October 1931 in which the National Government won an overwhelming mandate with 67 per cent of the votes and 554 MPs. Labour's impossible position was not improved by incompetent leadership by Arthur Henderson. At least half of the ex-ministers supported measures of retrenchment, and Henderson failed to offer any clear opposition to the new government's policy. Consequently the party found itself confused and vulnerable to the accusation of Snowden and MacDonald that it had run away from the economic crisis and was not fit to govern.

A myth developed to the effect that in spite of the party's difficulties, Labour's support held up at the election. In fact, while the turnout was as high as in 1929, Labour's share of the vote fell sharply, from 37 to 30.5 per cent, and only 52 MPs held their seats. To some extent this reflected the loss of the advantage Labour had enjoyed in 1929, when it had won many seats on a minority vote in three-cornered contests. Now the non-Labour vote was concentrated on a single National candidate in most constituencies, and three out of five former Liberals seem to have switched to the government. Women voters were particularly ready to desert the Labour Party; since far fewer of them enjoyed the institutional links, such as union membership, which helped keep the men loyal, they were always a more volatile element.

The year 1931 also proved important as a turning-point for free trade. Though both Labour and the Liberals believed it was still a popular cry, they lost votes equally heavily. After their success the Conservatives naturally wished to press ahead by introducing tariffs, and as a result the Samuelite Liberals withdrew from the government in 1932, leaving behind the National Liberals under Sir John Simon, who no longer supported free trade. Consequently by 1932 the Liberals had lost their foremost unifying cause, and they had also discredited themselves by remaining even for a year in the ranks of a government with whose policy they disagreed. Thereafter the Liberals were too closely associated with the right wing to be credible as a radical force. At the 1935 election they ran only 161 candidates, won 6.4 per cent of the poll, and returned 20 MPs. The events of 1931 had entirely destroyed the revival of 1926–9.

The election thus gave the National Government a five-year lease in office, but in the event it remained in power until 1940. Although ostensibly formed in order to defend sterling the new government soon abandoned the gold standard and accepted a substantial devaluation. Bank rate fell to 2 per cent by June 1932, and in due course a slow economic recovery began. This was the key to political survival. Cheap money proved especially helpful in stimulating the building industry; a million houses were constructed between 1931 and 1935. By 1934, when unemployment at last began to fall, there was a sense that Britain had emerged from the depression. The cuts in unemployment benefit were restored, and new income tax relief was offered in the 1935 budget. The combination of deflation and lower taxes meant rising real incomes for middle- and working-class people if they had a job. This paved the way for a second general election in 1935.

The Labour Party, bereft of its leaders after the holocaust of 1931, chose the elderly George Lansbury as its leader until 1935, when he resigned and was replaced by Clement Attlee. It was, however, still difficult to rebut the accusation that Labour's return to office would bring with it an economic crisis. In spite of that, Labour pushed up its vote to 38 per cent, a little higher than in 1929. But this produced only 154 MPs, by comparison with 288 in 1929. The electoral system was now working to the advantage of the National Government, which, with 432 seats, enjoyed a majority of 249 over all other parties. Baldwin, now at the height of his popularity, took over the premiership from the failing MacDonald.

The rejection of Churchill

It suited Baldwin to project the National Government as the epitome of moderation at a time when other countries were succumbing to the extremes of Fascism and Communism. For him personally it assumed the role of an air raid shelter against his domestic rebels. Their leading figure was Winston Churchill, who had left the shadow Cabinet in 1930 in order to be free to attack his Indian policy at a time when Lord Irwin, a Conservative Viceroy, was making concessions to the Indian nationalists; consequently Churchill was not invited to join the new government. However, Churchill was widely regarded as an opportunist and many of the 470 Conservative MPs elected in 1931 preferred Baldwin's conciliatory, middle-of-the-road line, for they appreciated they were less likely to retain their working-class vote if the party lurched to the right. With its huge parliamentary majority the government could afford to shrug off revolts by the diehard elements on the Tory back benches. Thus although Churchill led a bitter onslaught on the Indian reforms during 1931 to 1935, even the 50 or so MPs who supported him were insufficient to make the government back down. Churchill was, in any case, widely regarded as disloyal and as a careerist by orthodox Conservatives. Having been brought out of the wilderness by Baldwin, who made him Chancellor of the Exchequer in 1924, he was now apparently bent on overthrowing his leader.

This view of Churchill's Indian crusade coloured reactions towards his next cause – rearmament and appeasement. Although his complaints about the poor state of British defences were well-informed and often well-received, he was seen as an incorrigible warmonger, and never attracted more than a handful of supporters in Parliament. Also, he suffered from the charge of inconsistency, for as Chancellor after 1924 he had been partly responsible for *reducing* military expenditure. It also seemed odd that one who had been so vitriolic in his attacks on the Bolsheviks in Russia in the early 1920s should now be willing to co-operate with them in order to check the Nazi regime in Germany. Admittedly, by 1938 opinion had begun to move against the appeasement policy of Baldwin and his successor, Chamberlain. The resignation of Sir Anthony Eden as Foreign Secretary in that year over Chamberlain's pro-Mussolini policy provided a more respectable figurehead for the critics. Yet Eden and his allies continued to keep aloof from Churchill for fear of damaging their cause. In any case, Eden himself failed to keep up a sustained attack on government policy, partly because he had been so closely associated with it, and he never mobilized more than a small group of followers. Setbacks for National Government candidates in by-elections in 1938 and 1939 heralded a collapse of public support for appeasement, although right up to the outbreak of war contemporary opinion still expected the government to win a third general election in 1939 or 1940.

The Labour revival, 1935–9

Conventional accounts of the 1930s suggest a gloomy decade of decline and divison for the Labour Movement. However recent research suggests a much more positive view, pointing to significant ways in which Labour reformed and prepared for its victory in 1945. While the war accentuated Labour's landslide, it was by no means the entire explanation for it. Although Labour had suffered a humiliating reverse in 1931, the party comfortably retained its position as the alternative government, and effected a considerable recovery. In 1932 it gained 458 seats in the local elections, and in 1934 it won control of the London County Council. This was the achievement of Herbert Morrison who organized London Labour like a Continental Socialist Party, building up membership, regular canvassing to keep in touch with members, a programme of social events and the organization of women and younger voters. Morrison's system enabled Labour to win in the socially mixed constituencies that were politically marginal as opposed to the union strongholds. Meanwhile national party membership increased by 100,000 to 380,000 in 1933, and reached 419,000 in 1934. The 94 gains at the 1935 general election, though disappointing, at least made Labour a powerful parliamentary force again.

Keynesianism and Socialism

But the traumatic events of 1931 had affected the party in more profound ways. MacDonald was almost universally condemned as a traitor by Labour activists, who remained suspicious of anyone who was merely using the movement for personal advancement. Inevitably the question was raised as to how the party had reached the dilemma of 1931. It had preached socialism but neglected to produce a socialist policy, thereby leaving itself with the task of ameliorating the effects of a failing capitalist system rather than changing it. In 1932 the ILP voted to dissafiliate from the party, but within a year a third of its branches folded and the membership dropped from 16,000 to 7,000 by 1934, many members simply joining Labour instead. Some critics argued that socialism would never be attainable because, even if Labour won a majority of seats, the Establishment would manage to frustrate its policies. However, parliamentary traditions ran so deep that the bulk of the movement resisted the temptation to opt for an extraparliamentary strategy. Indeed the movement continued to show little interest in constitutional reform of any sort. Socialists like Harold Laski recognized that once Labour had won a parliamentary majority the centralized British system would be very serviceable for the implementation of a Socialist programme.

Indeed, amid the controversies and divisions on the left during the 1930s it is easy to overlook the fact that the foundations were being laid for Labour's post-1945 success. Although Clement Attlee, who succeeded George

Lansbury as leader in 1935, offered uninspiring leadership, he allowed several of his talented subordinates to change the direction of the party during the mid to late 1930s. On the domestic front, union leaders such as Ernest Bevin were increasingly impressed by the success of Keynesian methods for boosting employment in the United States; for him it was no use waiting for capitalism to collapse, there must be a constructive interim programme. Bevin and others encouraged the Party to adopt what was fashionably called 'economic planning', which in effect involved a combination of demand management along Keynesian lines, a regional policy designed to concentrate new industries in the depressed areas, and an extensive programme of nationalization of the failing industries. During the 1930s the party committed itself to a long list of industries ready to be taken into state ownership, and for the first time adopted a realistic procedure for implementing the policy. This was the achievement of Herbert Morrison, who had produced a model for nationalization in his London Passenger Transport Bill based upon compensation to the former owners and a small board of experts to run the industry. As a result by 1945 Labour had a much clearer idea of what it wanted to do in office.

Anti-fascism and the popular front

In external affairs, the strategy was influenced by Hugh Dalton, who succeeded in persuading the party to abandon its pacifism, accept rearmament, vote for the military estimates and support a policy of collective security designed to check the fascist dictators. This shift coincided with, and was reinforced by, a similar change in the balance of the press which had previously been largely hostile to Labour. During 1935–39 the *Daily Mirror*, originally a pro-Conservative newspaper, withdrew support from the National Government in protest against its appeasement policy and gradually aligned itself with the Labour Party, endowing it with a major advantage during the Second World War and the post-war era.

Meanwhile, in the country despair about the National Government's betrayal of the League of Nations, its cultivation of Mussolini and Hitler, and the emergence of yet another fascist power as a result of the civil war in Spain led to a widespread feeling that the progressive forces should combine to promote a popular front, as they had done in elections in France and Spain in 1936. However, as much of the impetus behind anti-fascist and pro-Spain campaigns came from the Communists and the ILP, the Labour leadership regarded the whole idea with great suspicion, seeing it as a ploy to enable Communists to infiltrate the Labour Party. As a result Labour members were officially banned from participating in popular front activities, a policy that culminated in an NEC decision to expel the leading advocate of a popular front, Stafford Cripps, from the party in January 1939.

However, in practice rank-and-file activists did co-operate with Communists, ILP-ers and also Liberals to promote a popular front, notably through by-elections where they opposed the appeasement policy of National Government candidates. At two famous by-elections, at Oxford and Bridgwater in the autumn of 1938, the Labour and Liberal parties backed independent candidates; their victory at Bridgwater offered dramatic proof that by raising the turnout, a popular front strategy could defeat the National Government even in its strongest seats. However, historians have usually overlooked many similar campaigns and the extent of co-operation between Liberals and Labour activists leading to Labour gains with Liberal support at Derby (1936) and West Fulham (1938). As Labour's leadership was so out of line with rank-and-file opinion, the NEC slightly diluted its resistance to the popular front to the extent of allowing local Labour parties to stand down in favour of Liberal candidates at St Ives (1937) and even an anti-appeasement Conservative at Kinross and West Perth (1938). The popular front idea was also being promoted in circles beyond the Labour Party by the Left Book Club, which was formed by Victor Gollancz in 1936 and had 57,000 members, and also by the *News Chronicle*, a Liberal, anti-appeasement newspaper that was read by many Labour supporters frustrated by the orthodoxy of the *Daily Herald*. The by-election victories demonstrated that Labour had little to fear and much to gain by adopting a bold anti-fascist line. Although the caution and obduracy of Attlee and his parliamentary colleagues hindered the progress of the popular front, the effect of local campaigns combined with the National party's new support for rearmament and sanctions against the dictators helped to put the party in touch with the progressive voters it had lost since 1931. The more its candidates and speakers adopted an anti-appeasement line, the more the party gained the patriotic high ground at a time when Chamberlain was steadily losing it through his failure to stand up to the dictators. However, the full impact of these changes was not to be realized until the Second World War.

Why was Britain so stable?

By comparison with many other European states, Britain weathered the economic and social strains of the interwar period fairly successfully. While parliamentary regimes collapsed in the face of both left- and right-wing autocracies, the British soldiered on under their parliamentary system and constitutional monarchy. Political divisions were, if anything, less acute than they had been in the Edwardian era. There are several contributory reasons for this surprising stability. The most obvious explanation is that the tradition of parliamentary politics and respect for political institutions was more deeply rooted in Britain because it was older. It is interesting that even a further influx of new voters in 1929 resulted in high turnouts at general elections: 76.1 per cent in 1929, 76.3 per cent in 1931 and 71.2 per cent in 1935.

A constitutional Labour Movement

In the 1920s, however, some right-wing propagandists argued that Britain was destabilized by the rise of Labour which threatened to open Britain to subversive Bolshevik influences. Militancy was at its height around 1919–20 as the economy collapsed and the reaction against the war set in. 'Direct Action' became fashionable for a time and gained prestige when the dockers resisted Lloyd George's attempt to support the anti-Bolshevik forces in Russia by refusing to load the *Jolly George*, a ship believed to be carrying arms. Yet Ramsay MacDonald and most Labour leaders remained very hostile to direct action, and it was indicative of their control that Labour conferences voted to ban Communists from holding Labour Party membership. Similarly, although the General Strike in 1926 offered an opportunity for syndicalists to challenge parliamentary government, it was motivated by straightforward concerns about wages rather than ideological objectives; and again neither the TUC nor the Labour leaders sympathized with syndicalism. No doubt there was an element of luck here for had the strike lasted more than nine days the government would have made more use of troops with more violence as a result.

On the whole militancy declined after the early 1920s and by the 1930s the response to depression was surprisingly subdued. The classic expression of protest was the Jarrow March of 1936, a deliberately small scale, well-behaved affair of respectable married men backed by clergymen; after delivering a petition at Westminster the march returned home. Although Ellen Wilkinson MP joined it, Jarrow attracted no public backing from the Labour leaders. It was a dignified protest not a portent of revolution. After 1931 some Socialists, including Stafford Cripps and Harold Laski, claimed that capitalism had overthrown a properly elected government and would always frustrate democracy; consequently Labour in future should take emergency powers to control the House of Lords and civil service. However, party conferences rejected such thinking and union leaders like Ernest Bevin dismissed Cripps and Laski as silly intellectuals. The Labour mainstream never lost confidence in constitutional methods despite the setback of 1931.

This restraint was echoed by some leading Conservatives. Although party propaganda portrayed Labour as unfit to govern, Baldwin had little time for such extremism. His privately-held view was: 'the main ambition of my life is to prevent class war becoming a reality'. His bipartisanship was reflected in policies of domestic reform and liberalism towards the empire as well as his desire to avoid the General Strike. There was an element of contingency in all this, for a Conservative Party led by Austin Chamberlain, Curzon or Churchill would have adopted a harsher view of Labour and polarized the country.

However, the positive view of the 1930s is qualified by the evidence that the parliamentary system became the target of attack by reactionaries from the right. The *Daily Mail* argued that the vote had been given in 1918 to many people who should not have had it. Turnout at elections remained consistently lower than before 1914 though this was partly because the reforms of 1918 and 1928 brought into the political system large numbers of new young voters who were much less committed to the conventional political parties and rather more open to alternative movements. This was compounded by the presence of many disillusioned ex-servicemen who felt let down as a result of post-war unemployment. In the 1930s some of them were attracted by the British Union of Fascists. The politicians were so worried about demobilized troops that several attempts at organizing them had been made in the immediate aftermath of war. The Comrades of the Great War was formed by extreme right-wing figures, the National Federation of Discharged and Demobilized Soldiers had links with Liberal politicians, while the National Union of Ex-Servicemen was attached to the Labour Movement. However, in each case these organizations dwindled after the initial surge of enthusiasm, and even the British Legion, which was established with a view to keeping former soldiers out of the clutches of either the right or the left, never managed to recruit more than 10 per cent of the eligible men. Thus, in spite of their grievances, the ex-servicemen appeared to be no more likely than the population in general to be attracted into radical or revolutionary movements that were fundamentally opposed to the British system of government.

Popular monarchism

Part of the explanation may be that even when the conventional parliamentary politicians became discredited, as many of them clearly were, the public continued to place its faith and loyalty in the figure of the monarch, King

George V. For many people the King provided a focus for national pride and loyalty above and beyond the political parties and untainted by their failings. However, there was nothing inevitable about the success of the interwar monarchy. During the war the Royal Family had felt so vulnerable on account of its German connections that it decided to deflect criticism by changing its name to Windsor. George V's success also reflected several shrewd judgements. For example, after the Bolshevik Revolution he decided not to offer sanctuary in Britain to the deposed Tsar and his family, understanding how offensive his repressive regime was to liberal opinion in Britain and how fervently the revolution had been welcomed by the Labour Movement. He wisely allowed his children to marry British commoners rather than choosing from the dwindling pool of discredited Continental royals. And although fearful of the left, the King handled it tactfully. In January 1924 he lost no time in inviting Ramsay MacDonald to form the first Labour government, without conditions, even though he had only 191 MPs. His acceptance of Labour gave legitimacy to the untried party and consolidated the already strong monarchism in the Labour Party. In 1923 the annual conference debated a republican motion for just fifteen minutes before rejecting it by 3.69 million votes to 380,000.

The depth of support for the monarchy in Britain was highlighted by the abdication crisis following George V's death in 1936. His successor, Edward VIII, was equally popular but also an unsuitable King. Ostensibly the problem arose from his determination to marry an American divorcee, Wallis Simpson, but the underlying objection was caused by the new King's insistence on interfering in political matters, notably by promoting Anglo–German friendship, and his indiscreet visits to the depressed areas where he appeared to criticize government policy. Baldwin refused Edward VIII's request for legislation to allow him a morganatic marriage with Mrs Simpson. As Attlee backed Baldwin by indicating that he would decline to form an alternative government – further proof of Labour's orthodoxy – it looked as though the politicians had effectively boxed the King in. However, their scheme began to collapse when a King's Party emerged led by Churchill, Beaverbrook and Rothermere and widely supported in the press. Although traditional accounts of the abdication crisis suggest that the royal marriage was unpopular, it is now clear that it enjoyed huge support in the country; angry crowds descended on Downing Street and letters flooded into the newspapers condemning Baldwin for forcing the King into abdication. Had the King kept his nerve, the prime minister would have been obliged to resign or climb down, but Baldwin was saved when he opted for a quick abdication in December 1936. The new King, George VI, was widely seen as an inferior substitute for his brother, but by adopting the same constitutionally correct approach as his father he avoided controversy and re-established the monarchy in the people's affections. Significantly Edward VIII, now Duke of Windsor, who had left the country in 1936, was never permitted to return by the National Government.

The impact of the depression

On the other hand, much of the most important explanation for the relative stability of the interwar period lies in the social impact of economic developments. In Britain the depression was neither as severe nor as protracted as it was in much of Europe and North America. Deflation meant that many middle- and working-class people enjoyed rising real incomes, had access to a growing range of consumer goods, and could make savings without risk. Of course, improving material conditions do not necessarily guarantee political stability; rising expectations often constitute the greatest danger to governments. This is why one must take account of contingent elements including political leadership.

It was not until 1931 that the ingredients for a major crisis in liberal democracy seem to have been present in Britain: a deepening economic depression, long-term unemployment, a declining trade union movement, discredited political leadership and millions of young voters. In these circumstances it is scarcely surprising that extremist movements of the right

Table 12.3 Trade union membership and strikes, 1918–33

Year	Trade union membership in millions	Number of strikes	Working days lost in millions
1918	6.5	1,165	5.9
1919	7.9	1,352	35.0
1920	8.3	1,607	26.5
1921	6.6	763	85.9
1922	5.6	576	19.9
1923	5.4	628	10.7
1924	5.5	710	8.4
1925	5.5	603	7.9
1926	5.2	323	162.2
1927	4.9	308	1.2
1928	4.8	302	1.4
1929	4.8	431	8.4
1930	4.8	422	4.4
1931	4.6	420	6.9
1932	4.4	389	6.5
1933	4.4	357	1.1

and left attempted to make capital at the expense of conventional politics. Critics of the TUC alleged that it had presided over a fall in membership from over 8 million in 1920 to 4.3 million in 1933, and was doing very little to organize the men. For a time the National Unemployed Workers Movement (NUWM), led by Wal Hannington, stepped into the vacuum. It mobilized 50,000 members in 1930–1, organized demonstrations and hunger marches, and presented petitions. Its especial objects were the abolition of the hated Means Test and the restoration of the cuts in unemployment benefit. Yet this was scarcely subversive. The NUWM reached a peak in 1932 with a 25,000-strong rally in Hyde Park, but then petered out.

Many contemporary critics assumed that these protest movements were organized by Communists with a view to reducing Britain to chaos and fomenting class war. The British Communist Party had been formed in 1920, but despite receiving subsidies from Russia it remained a small organization, riven with internal divisions. Its exclusion from the Labour Party marginalized it for most of the period, so much so that by 1930 membership stood at around 6,000. However, by taking the initiative in opposing fascism and in supporting the Republican cause in Spain by sending volunteers and by raising funds for the victims of war, the Communists gained considerable influence and credibility – by 1939 membership had risen to 18,000, though much of this was thought to be from middle-class intellectuals rather than manual workers.

The challenge of British fascism

A more serious threat to conventional politics was posed by interwar fascism. This has traditionally been misunderstood because fascism was seen through the Churchillian perspective in terms of German Nazism. In fact, British fascism pre-dated the Nazi seizure of power in 1933. From 1923 onwards several organizations, including the British Fascists, the National Fascisti and the Imperial Fascist League, had appeared, inspired not by Germany but by *Italian* fascism. In the 1920s many British people admired Mussolini's achievements and hoped to emulate them. They were reacting against the new mass democracy, industrial militancy, the rise of Labour, the impact of the war and the retention of control by the older generation of politicians. During the General Strike of 1926 fascists looked forward to stepping in to save the country from chaos and subversion. They also found it easy to appeal to ex-servicemen, unable to find a satisfying role in post-war society, and to landowners undermined by falling land values and higher taxation.

Fascism regained momentum after the crisis of 1931 which left the parliamentary leaders of both left and right discredited, thereby generating a fashionable demand for strong, patriotic leadership in Britain of the sort that was being adopted on the Continent. By forming the British Union of Fascists (BUF) in 1932, Sir Oswald Mosley went some way to filling this need. It is often forgotten that much of what the fascists advocated was not distinctively fascist but appealed to people whose allegiances usually lay elsewhere. In particular, Mosley's apparent grasp of the economic situation and his positive programme for tackling unemployment impressed many on both sides of politics. His refusal to relax British control in the Empire, his advocacy of tariffs to protect industry and agriculture, and his attacks on conventional parliamentary democracy as a proven failure rang bells with many people who felt alienated or marginalized from British politics.

Between 1932 and 1934 it appeared to many people that Mosley might well be the only alternative as the National Government was not managing to reduce unemployment or to defend the pound. When Lord Rothermere used the *Daily Mail* and the *Sunday Dispatch* to promote the BUF in 1934, the movement gained thousands of members and a good deal of respectability, especially among disillusioned Conservatives who resented Baldwin's liberalism. This support was to some extent dissipated by the violence used by fascists, notoriously at their Olympia Rally in 1934. However, while many left the movement, others were attracted to it, and Conservative politicians defended Mosley's militarist methods as a necessary defence against Communist disruption. Significantly, the government proved very reluctant to intervene to stop the illegal drilling and arming of members by the BUF. A Public Order Act eventually came into effect in 1937, but made little practical difference to fascist activities.

During the latter part of the 1930s the BUF became notorious for its anti-Semitic campaigns in the East End of London where it gained support by exploiting the fears of small businessmen and shopkeepers. But it took on a different appearance in other parts of the country. In the declining textile districts of Lancashire the BUF held out the prospect of rejuvenating local industry by suppressing imports from India, while in agricultural areas Mosley attracted enthusiastic – and non-violent – audiences by offering hope to failing farmers. In fact, the most dangerous aspect of Mosley's campaign was not its violence but the extent to which his movement acquired respectability, which he saw as a prelude to being invited into office in the next political crisis just as Mussolini and Hitler had been. In fact, his closest brush with power came in 1936 during the abdication crisis when the fascists campaigned for the King; had Edward VIII refused to quit, the 'King's Party' led by Churchill would probably have invited Mosley to join. As another war loomed during the late 1930s, Mosley adopted a new tactic by campaigning for peace and blaming the Jews for trying to drag Britain into an unnecessary conflict with Germany. This, too, was very appealing and it attracted large numbers of respectable people to his meetings up to the outbreak of war in September 1939. Even after war began Mosley was allowed to continue his anti-war propaganda for a further nine months, a reflection of the influential support he and other Nazi sympathizers enjoyed within the British Establishment, and it was not until May 1940 that Churchill finally decided to arrest and intern 700 of the leading fascists.

Further reading

Aspects of national identity are discussed in:
Paul Ward, *Britishness since 1870* (2004)
Thomas Hajkowski, *The BBC and National Identity in Britain 1922–53* (2010)
H. Brocklehurst and R. Phillips eds, *History, Nationhood and the Question of Britain* (2004)
Frank Prochaska, *Royal Bounty: the Making of a Welfare Monarchy* (1995)
T.M. Devine, *The Scottish Nation 1700–1900* (1999)
Richard Finlay, *Modern Scotland* (2004)

Liberal decline is analysed in:
John Campbell, *Lloyd George: the Goat in the Wilderness 1922–31* (1977)
K.O. Morgan, *Consensus and Disunity: the Lloyd George Coalition Government 1918–22* (1979)
G.R. Searle, *The Liberal Party: Triumph and Disintegration 1886–1929* (1992)
David Dutton, *A History of the Liberal Party in the Twentieth Century* (2004)

For the post-war aims and organization of feminism see:
Martin Pugh, *Women and the Women's Movement in Britain since 1914* (2015)
Brian Harrison, *Prudent Revolutionaries: British Feminists Between the Wars* (1987)
Deidre Beddoe, *Back to Home and Duty: Women Between the Wars 1918–39* (1989)
Susan Pedersen, *Eleanor Rathbone and the Politics of Conscience* (2004)
Cheryl Law, *Suffrage and Power: the Women's Movement 1918–28* (1997)

Labour's rise and decline is discussed in:
David Howell, *MacDonald's Party: Labour Identities and Crisis 1922–31* (2002)
Martin Pugh, *Speak for Britain! A New History of the Labour Party* (2010) – emphasizes how the party grew by region and social class by recruiting ex-Conservatives.

D. Tanner, P. Thane and N. Tiratsoo eds, *Labour's First Century* (2000) – twelve essays on all aspects.

The only study of the first Labour government was published in the 1950s by Richard Lynam before archive sources became available. It is now replaced by: John Shepherd and Keith Laybourn, *Britain's First Labour Government* (2006) – a competent account which does not change the existing picture.

There are also three chapters on the government in:
David Marquand, *Ramsay MacDonald* (1977)

Matthew Worley, *Labour Inside the Gate: A History of the British Labour Party Between the Wars* (2005)
Pamela Graves, *Labour Women: Women in British Working-Class Politics 1918–39* (1994)
Patrick Renshaw, *The General Strike* (1975)
Keith Jeffrey and Peter Hennessy, *States of Emergency: British Governments and Strikebreaking since 1919* (1983)
Andrew Thorpe, *A History of the British Labour Party* (1997)
Ben Pimlott, *Labour and the Left in the 1930s* (1977)

The 1931 crisis, the Conservatives and the National Government are discussed in:
Robert Skidelsky, *Politicians and the Slump* (1967)
Andrew Thorpe, *The British General Election of 1931* (1991)
G.R. Searle, *Country before Party: The Idea of National Government in Modern Britain 1885–1987* (1995)
Nick Smart, *The National Government 1931–40* (1999)
John Ramsden, *The Age of Balfour and Baldwin 1902–40* (1978)
S. Ball, *Baldwin and the Conservative Party: the Crisis of 1929–31* (1988)
P. Williamson, *Stanley Baldwin: Conservative Leadership and National Values* (1999)
Tom Stannage, *Baldwin Thwarts the Opposition: the British General Election of 1935* (1980)
M. Francis and I. Zweiniger-Bargielowska eds, *The Conservatives and British Society 1880–1980* (1996)
Martin Pugh, *The Making of Modern British Politics 1867–1945* (2002)
Nick Smart, *Neville Chamberlain* (2010)

On British fascism see:
T. Linehan, *British Fascism 1918–39* (2000)
Richard Thurlow, *Fascism in Britain: A History 1918–85* (1987)
Martin Pugh, *'Hurrah for the Blackshirts!' Fascists and Fascism in Britain Between the Wars* (2005)
Robert Skidelsky, *Oswald Mosley* (1975)

13

The Era of Domesticity

The traditional view of interwar Britain as a period of depression, despair and unemployment is not without a good deal of empirical support, especially if it is contrasted with the happier decades after 1945. However, it does represent an exaggerated and partial picture of life between the wars. Indeed, in some respects the 1930s saw the beginning of social changes more usually associated with post-war Britain; we should think in terms of a period of continuity from the 1930s to 1950s interrupted by war.

The rising standard of living

For most of the time most of the British people enjoyed paid employment; but what mattered to them was essentially how much their wages and salaries would buy. Here we have to distinguish contemporary rhetoric from fact. Unquestionably politicians, civil servants and employers regarded substantial wage reductions as an economic necessity in the 1920s; and the government's whole strategy for restoring the pre-war value of the pound assumed that this could be achieved. But one must remember that the strategy was frustrated. Between 1920, when the boom collapsed, and 1923, money wages fell sharply, though at the same time prices began to fall. Union fears about a general attack on wages, especially after the return to gold in 1925, led to the General Strike of 1926. Yet by 1929 wage rates were still at the 1923 level, despite the fact that retail prices had fallen by 6 per cent. After 1926 there appears to have been some kind of mutual understanding between employers and unions – formalized in the Mond–Turner talks of 1928 – about maintaining stable wages. This meant that the unions did not resist employers' attempts to cut costs by reducing their labour force, while the owners abstained from cuts in wage rates. As a result even in the depression of 1929–32 wages fell by only 4 per cent on average. In the same period wholesale prices dropped by

Table 13.1 Wages in the UK, 1920–38 (1930 = 100)

Year	Annual money wages	Annual real wages
1920	143.7	91.2
1921	134.6	94.1
1922	107.9	93.2
1923	100.0	90.8
1924	101.5	91.6
1925	102.2	91.7
1926	99.3	91.2
1927	101.5	95.8
1928	100.1	95.2
1929	100.4	96.7
1930	100.0	100.0
1931	98.2	105.1
1932	96.3	105.7
1933	95.3	107.6
1934	96.4	108.1
1935	98.0	108.3
1936	100.2	107.7
1937	102.8	105.4
1938	106.3	107.7

25 per cent and the Ministry of Labour's cost-of-living index by 12 per cent. From 1934 wages were rising again, as was the cost of living. Thus, although workers in hard-hit industries like coal and cotton suffered badly, on the whole employees enjoyed rising real wages in the 1920s and 1930s. One estimate suggests a 17 per cent improvement in real wages between 1924 and 1935.

Interwar consumerism

This was obviously of considerable political and economic importance. Rather than being crushed by poverty and hopelessness, many people entertained gradually rising expectations. Improved family incomes opened the way to a wide range of inexpensive consumer goods and minor luxuries characteristic of this period: cinemas, dances, the radio, women's magazines, football pools, cigarettes, cosmetics and mass-produced copies of fashionable clothes. Clearly, the expansion of the consumer-goods industries would not have been possible without the capacity of millions of middle- and working-class families to enjoy a small surplus left over from their essential expenditure. Throughout the interwar period consumers benefited from significant reductions in the price of food as a result of a resumption of large-scale imports and improvements in supplies from the Empire as well as countries such as Denmark, Ireland and Argentina. As a result, consumption of key items including fruit, especially bananas, vegetables, eggs and fresh milk rose substantially, improving the diet in the process. The 1930s saw innovations such as Milk Bars, which helped to make milk fashionable with the young. The government, anxious to help farmers, also assisted by requiring pasteurization of milk from 1922 onwards, while the big commercial dairies introduced bottled milk and doorstep deliveries. Canned and tinned food, though dating from the late-Victorian era, also became a central part of British eating habits in this period; firms such as Heinz and Crosse and Blackwell offered canned peas, beans, ham, pilchards, meat loaf, peaches, pineapples, pears and apricots to housewives who found them an economical and convenient way of feeding their families. Other labour-saving items became popular, including Birds Custard Powder, instant coffee from Nestlé, and Kellogg's Cornflakes, which rapidly displaced porridge as the staple breakfast dish. Nothing, however, disturbed the majority of British gastronomic traditions. Daily consumption of 'red' meat became almost universal (chicken was a rarity for most people), the consumption of sugar continued its inexorable rise via cups of tea, jam and sweets, and fish-and-chips reached its peak with between 30,000 and 35,000 fish-and-chip shops by the 1930s; at 4 pence a head it remained a nourishing meal eaten at least once a week in working-class families.

Improved health and longevity

The effects of gradual improvements in living standards showed up in improved health and longevity between the wars. Life expectancy for women increased from 55 to 66 years between 1910 and 1938, and from 52 to 61 years for men. The figures for infant mortality also continued to fall. However, the national statistics conceal much unevenness. In 1935, for example, infant mortality rates stood at 47 in south-east England but 68 in the north of England. Poverty meant that the working classes were much more likely to die young. Death rates per 1,000 in 1937 varied from 73 in Harrow and 80 in Oxford to 134 in the Rhondda and 138 in Wigan. A major study, *Food, Health and Income* by Sir John Boyd Orr, in 1936 suggested that 10 per cent of the population was badly fed, including one in five schoolchildren. But this evidence of poor diet for some should be seen in the context of notable improvement in society as a whole. By comparison with the pre-1914 period there had been major increases in the consumption of fruit, vegetables and eggs. When B.S. Rowntree repeated his famous study of York in 1935–6, he found only 3.9 per cent of the population in absolute poverty. However,

Table 13.2 Motor cars produced in Great Britain, 1908–38

Year	Cars produced in thousands
1908	10
1913	34
1923	95
1928	212
1933	286
1938	445

Table 13.3 Private motor cars in use in Great Britain, 1905–39

Year	Private cars in use in thousands
1905	16
1910	53
1915	139
1920	187
1925	580
1930	1,056
1935	1,477
1939	2,034

Rowntree revised his original poverty line and argued that a family of five required a weekly income of 43s. 6d. On this basis 17.7 per cent of the population were below the poverty line. He found that low wages and casual labour were greater causes of poverty than either unemployment or old age.

Improved health and longevity reflected a mixture of trends and changes: better diet, a municipal water supply piped to virtually all homes, preventive measures against such diseases as tuberculosis and typhoid, and the long-term effects of Edwardian state welfare policies such as the school medical service. Contemporary fears about the declining birth rate helped to sustain social policies for mothers and children during and after the war. Typical of this thinking was the 1918 Maternity and Child Welfare Act, which required local authorities to set up infant welfare centres and antenatal clinics and to appoint health visitors; it also allowed them to provide home helps, day nurseries and food for expectant mothers. By 1928 these services cost nearly £1 million per annum.

However, there were huge gaps in the system. The 1911 health insurance scheme covered 15 million people by 1921 and 20 million by 1938. But this left around 15 million, largely women and children under five, without assured help. The provision of hospitals was also patchy, involving a mixture of voluntary, municipal and poor-law hospitals. Much concern focused on

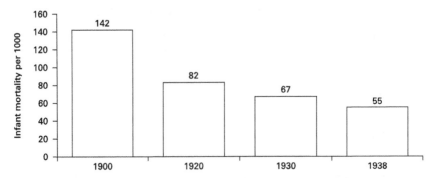

Figure 13.1 Infant mortality rates per 1,000 live births in Great Britain.

the failure to reduce the incidence of maternal mortality; the rate per 1,000 stood at 4.82 in 1923, rose to 5.94 in 1933, and fell to 3.25 by 1939. The Women's Co-operative Guild and several other women's organizations which campaigned for improvements in female health established a Women's Health Committee Inquiry in 1933, which studied 1,250 working-class women and published the results as *Working-Class Wives*, edited by Margery Spring Rice, in 1939. In the sample no fewer than 46 per cent of the women suffered from 'bad' or 'grave' ill-health, while only 22 per cent were in 'good' health. In general it was abundantly clear that women's health was neglected, partly because wives minimized their own ailments but also because they lacked access to professional advice and treatment.

Feminists advocated the extension of health insurance to all women regardless of whether they were in employment, the introduction of family allowances, and the provision of advice on birth control. None of these remedies was adopted, with the partial exception of the third. However, the politicians were susceptible to pressure on behalf of women and children. Under the 1929 Local Government Act, the local authorities were allowed to take over the poor-law hospitals; they increased the number of maternity beds, and by the 1930s it was becoming usual to give birth in hospital. From 1934 they were also permitted to distribute free or subsidized milk in schools; by 1937 3.2 million children were benefiting from this. In 1936 the Midwives Act compelled local authorities to train midwives. All these ad hoc measures took Britain half-way to a national health service by 1939. Those who were not covered by insurance could always pay for private treatment, but in practice those most in need, such as women, did not do so. Private medicine was no answer to the problems of ill-health, but it would take another war to create a consensus in favour of a comprehensive state system.

The housing revolution

Another important aspect of improving living standards between the wars was the higher standard of housing; but this also coincided with radical changes in housing *tenure*. Before 1914 scarcely 10 per cent of homes were owner-occupied, almost all the rest being privately rented. However, most landlords were small property-owners and lacked the resources to maintain or improve their houses. They were not a popular class, and during the war the government lost little time in imposing restrictions on rents. Thereafter some form of rent restriction remained in place, and the private rented sector entered a protracted period of decline.

One alternative was the construction of municipal council houses for rent. By the end of the war the government felt very concerned both about the inadequate supply of housing and about the poor quality of the existing stock. Not only did it enact the Addison Housing Act, under which 170,000 council houses were built between 1919 and 1921, it also set up the Tudor Walters Committee, whose 1918 report recommended the provision of indoor toilets and bathrooms, larger separate kitchens, proper light and ventilation, and extra bedrooms. The policy of state subsidies for council housing was reintroduced in 1924 by John Wheatley, which led to another 520,000 houses being built by 1933. Arthur Greenwood's 1930 Housing Act subsidized slum clearance and boosted the municipal housing stock further. Altogether 1,100,000 council houses were built between the wars, representing nearly a third of the total number of new houses. Municipal housing set a high standard which private builders often failed to match, but with which they had to compete. Unfortunately, the benefits for working-class families were not as great as they might have been, partly because the rents charged were fairly high and also because the Conservatives disliked municipal housing on grounds of the cost and because of the competition it posed to private builders. They therefore cut off subsidies in 1933 and so checked the expansion of council housing.

The rise of home-ownership

On the other hand the National Government's cheap-money policy helped to reduce mortgage rates to only 4.5 per cent; in combination with rising real incomes this generated a fast-growing demand for owner-occupation. As a result, by the end of the decade 1.4 million people held building-society mortgages. Two-and-a-half million houses were built for sale between the wars, and by 1939 31 per cent of all houses were owner-occupied. By the

1930s a semi-detached house could be purchased for £400 with a deposit as low as £25. This soon produced miles of suburban roads filled with three-bedroomed semi-detached houses adorned with mock-Tudor beams and identical front and back gardens. In retrospect, suburbia has attracted a good deal of disdain. It is true that the properties were often inferior in quality to municipal houses; inadequate planning controls led to 'ribbon development'; and the developments suffered from an absence of community facilities. On the other hand the houses represented a major improvement in the living conditions of millions of families now able to enjoy proper drainage, toilets, baths, hot water and private gardens. The reduction of overcrowding, especially in bedroom accommodation, made for happier home life.

Above all, women were the beneficiaries of the housing revolution. They spent more time in the house than other family members, and traditionally suffered most from the inconvenience and drudgery involved in keeping decaying property clean. The Women's Co-operative Guild and the Labour Party Women's Organization urged the authorities to take notice of women's own needs in terms of separate kitchens and internal bathrooms, and this was one of the few questions on which the authorities were really prepared to listen to women. As a result, the new housing was easier to keep clean and warm; between the wars working-class homes enjoyed twice as much floor space as they had had in the mid-nineteenth century; above all, two-thirds of all homes had been wired for electricity by 1939. Admittedly none of this made women's domestic lives easy. The new equipment – cookers, vacuum

Table 13.4 Housing tenure in England and Wales, 1914–85 (as a percentage)

Year	Rented from private landlords	Rented from local authorities	Owner-occupied
1914	89	1	10
1939	55	14	31
1951	52	17	31
1966	27	26	47
1977	14	32	54
1985	12	26	62

Table 13.5 House-building, 1913–39

Years	1913–17	1918–22	1923–27	1928–32	1933–37	1938–39
Annual average of house-building	30,000	38,100	169,700	200,900	339,700	307,400

cleaners, washing machines – were comparatively expensive and did not reduce the time devoted to housework. They were chiefly useful for middle-class wives, who now found it difficult to find and retain domestic servants.

Leisure and consumerism

Women were also among the major beneficiaries of the huge expansion of leisure activities after the war and they became instrumental in the growth of what is now recognized as a consumer-oriented society. This was the product of several trends, notably the rise in real incomes, the fall in average working hours from 54 to 48, the reaction against the privations suffered during wartime, the influence of American popular culture in the shape of jazz, dancing, cinema and cocktails, and the role of commercial interests which invested in dance halls and cinemas as well as novel leisure activities including football pools and holiday camps. The craze for dancing rapidly became the symbol of the 'Roaring Twenties' as a result of the arrival of the tango, the jog trot, the black bottom, the Charleston and many other new dances, most of which provoked criticism for causing a moral decline through their suggestive and erotic movements. Dancing was also a major attraction, along with drugs, in the nightclubs, some 11,000 of which flourished in London alone by 1925. Sir William Joynson-Hicks (Home Secretary, 1924–9) vowed to suppress them, but beyond limited regulation and police raids, which resulted in prosecutions for selling alcohol without a licence, he made little impression.

Respectability and leisure

In fact, dancing represented part of the move away from the traditional, male-dominated British patterns of leisure, involving drunkenness, rowdyism and violence, towards more respectable and domesticated behaviour. This was partly because women attended dances either with men or in search of men. Dances helped to divert people away from pubs and as a result the interwar period saw a major fall in prosecutions for drunkenness which had been such a feature of Victorian society. Only 10 per cent of men and 20 per cent of women abstained from alcohol, but consumption had become more moderate. This had nothing to do with legislation, for Britain wisely avoided the disastrous experiment with prohibition that was attempted in America. But the decline in consumption, which had been evident since the 1880s, accelerated during the war. Wartime governments had lowered the alcoholic content of beers and spirits, drastically shortened licensed hours and imposed higher taxes. Remarkably, this interference with the rights of the drinking classes was not retracted after the war. The result, in combination with wider leisure opportunities, led to a fall in beer consumption from an average of 26–27 gallons in 1900 to 13–14 gallons by the 1930s. Some of the expenditure was diverted to smoking, which enjoyed its heyday in the 1920s and 1930s. In this period there was no objection on health grounds; indeed, smoking was recommended for its associations with masculinity and fitness, and was seen as a rite of passage into adulthood. It became a universal leisure activity, popular at all levels of society; King George V, usually a strict parent, gave his sons cigarettes when they reached 16. As a result, by the 1930s 80 per cent of men and 41 per cent of women smoked.

The idea of leisure for women was something of a novelty in 1918, but it soon became an important social phenomenon. Women took full advantage of one of the iconic interwar innovations, the 'wireless' or radio, largely because they spent so much of their time in the home. By the 1930s a radio could be bought for £1 10s., and as a result the number of licence-holders rose from 36,000 in 1922 to a remarkable 8.8 million by 1939. Women also comprised the majority of cinemagoers in this period. During the war middle-aged people had condemned cinemas because they encouraged the young to consort together in the dark. Yet cinema was another symptom of the growing respectability of British leisure activities. By 1939 there were 5,000 cinemas, many of them newly built, capable of seating 2,000 people and decorated in art deco, Egyptian, Mexican or Spanish style. They offered luxurious surroundings, including plush seats, wall-to-wall carpeting, marble staircases and ladies' powder rooms, a programme of films, cartoons and newsreels lasting up to three hours, and all for a ticket that cost anything between 6 pence and 2 shillings a head. Not surprisingly, by 1939 23 million British people attended the cinema every week, some several times.

Popular motoring

Cinema and radio were hallmarks of a more family-oriented pattern of leisure between the wars, along with seaside holidays and motoring. The idea of *paid* holidays, which were available to only 1.5 million people in 1925, became a major objective of the trade unions and as a result of the Holidays With Pay Act of 1938 some 11 million people were entitled to one by the end of the period. This encouraged a huge investment designed to improve the attractions of holiday resorts by building lidos, ballrooms, concert halls, bandstands and gardens. Meanwhile, as the traditional desire for a fair complexion gave way to the cult of the suntan, British holidaymakers exposed larger areas of their bodies to the sun by adopting cut-away bathing suits for women and topless bathing trunks for men.

While most people travelled to the seaside by train, charabanc and motor coach, growing numbers used their own motor cars. After the war motoring ceased to be a hobby for aristocrats, plutocrats and eccentrics and became increasingly seen as a necessity for ordinary families. Motoring remained controversial with many people, however, because of the dangers it posed to

Image 9 A 1930s traffic jam on Blackfriars Bridge, London.

pedestrians and cyclists through the combination of untrained drivers who routinely ignored speed limits, ill-maintained vehicles, and dangerous, potholed and unlit roads. In 1930 alone deaths in road accidents reached 7,000 and accidents 150,000. Yet no politician was prepared to take motoring in hand until 1935 when Leslie Hore-Belisha introduced road safety into schools, built the famous Belisha Beacons at pedestrian crossings, imposed a compulsory driving test on new drivers and banned hooting in silence zones after 11.30 at night. Unfortunately none of this made much impression on the number of accidents or on behaviour as Britain's motorists resented any interference with their rights. The number of private cars on the road increased from 132,000 in 1914 to 1,477,000 by 1935 largely because average car prices had dropped from £308 in 1912 to £259 in 1924 and to £130 by 1935. This reflected the introduction of popular small cars such as the Morris Minor in 1928 and the Austin 7 in 1922, variously known as the 'Baby Car', 'The Mighty Miniature' and 'The Bed Pan'!

Women, family and marriage

After the war the public image of young women changed abruptly. Where papers like the *Daily Mail*, *Daily Express* and *Daily Sketch* had recently portrayed the patriotic munitionette, now they saw the 'flapper'. 'The social butterfly type has probably never been so prevalent as at present,' complained the *Mail*: 'It comprises the frivolous, scantily-clad, "jazzing flapper", irresponsible and undisciplined.' Young women were widely accused of lowering moral standards in their pursuit of an exciting social life, while men, as usual, were regarded as innocent victims. Part of the problem was that the war had unbalanced the population even more than usual. 'Our Surplus Girls', in the *Mail*'s words, outnumbered men by 1.9 million. It was feared that as a result of their wartime employment women would want to retain jobs now needed for the returning servicemen, though in the event they were almost all sacked. The refusal of many women to go back to poorly paid lives of drudgery as domestic servants was taken as a worrying sign in the servant-employing classes that women were getting ideas above their station. It seemed possible that their new political influence and their entry into the professions was attracting women away from marriage and motherhood. Indeed, according to Barbara Cartland, then a young journalist and self-appointed authority, the physical condition of the flappers was so changed by their lifestyle – dieting, dancing, masculine clothes, narrow hips, small breasts – that many would be unable to give birth to healthy babies anyway.

The rise of marriage

Not for the first time, nor the last, the popular press had things more or less completely wrong. There is some evidence that between the wars the younger generation was more likely to engage in sexual relations before marriage; but this should be seen in the context of a major decline in two of the great vices of Victorian and Edwardian England – prostitution and alcoholism. British society was actually becoming more moral between the wars, and its route lay through the spread of domesticity, not in a retreat from it. The participation of women in the labour force hardly changed between the Edwardian period, the 1920s and the 1930s. Moreover, despite fears that the war had blighted the marriage prospects of younger women or distracted them from traditional roles, the fact is that during the 1920s the Edwardian decline in marriage rates was reversed; among women in their late teens and twenties a higher proportion now married. The proportion continued to rise through the 1930s and, indeed, in every decade up to the 1970s, with a brief interruption in the Second World War. It is an unavoidable conclusion that most of the rising generation of British women regarded marriage and motherhood as the major goals in life. Even amongst younger feminists like Vera Brittain, marriage was seen in a very positive light; to some extent they were able to take political rights and access to careers for granted; the new challenge was how to *combine* employment with marriage and motherhood, not choose between them. It is only fair to note that while marriage rates rose, so too did divorce rates. The reform of 1923 equalized divorce so that women need prove only adultery, and A.P. Herbert's 1937 bill added a number of additional grounds for divorce including desertion, which was especially important for women. However, in spite of the increase only 6 per cent of all marriages ended in divorce in the late 1930s. In view of the fact that marriages had to last longer as a result of greater longevity, it can be concluded that interwar marriage was a remarkably stable institution.

The falling birth rate

One key consideration affecting women's view of marriage between the wars was the belief that pregnancy and child-rearing need not be as great a burden as it had been in the past. The trend towards smaller families among certain middle-class groups had been clear since the late 1870s, but now it spread throughout society. By the late 1920s married women experienced on average 2.2 live births, by comparison with five or six in the Victorian period. One of the remarkable aspects of this profound social change is that it was accomplished in the teeth of much propaganda designed to deter couples from restricting family size. The women's magazines resolutely avoided the subject of birth control. The National Baby Week Council co-operated with the politicians in upholding the view that childbirth was a duty owed by women to the state. Governments offered few material inducements to have big families beyond increased tax allowances for second and subsequent children; but the *News of the World* continued to present free willow-pattern plates to all proud mothers of ten! In the 1920s the medical profession, the Church of England and all the political parties condemned birth control, though many members of each of these institutions actually practised it. Indeed, those who printed birth-control literature were still liable to prosecution for obscenity.

In spite of all this, behaviour clearly changed markedly, though it is not easy to explain why. Over a long period of time the effect of rising standards of living and declining infant mortality invariably had the effect of encouraging married couples to reduce family size. In Britain many women wanted to avoid pregnancy, but were ignorant of the ways of doing it. Traditionally, couples either avoided sexual relations or attempted coitus interruptus. In addition large numbers of women obtained abortions or miscarriages by one means or another. As late as the 1930s it was estimated that 100,000 to 150,000 women died each year as a result of abortion. By the 1900s some improvements in the mechanical methods of birth control had been achieved. Condoms had become cheaper, more reliable and familiar as they had been distributed to the troops during the war. However, they were not widely approved of, and reformers like Marie Stopes recommended caps, pessaries and diaphragms. The drawback was that these required some co-operation from doctors, which was not generally forthcoming.

The key to change lay less in the adoption of any particular method of birth control than in a growing determination to make the attempt. The mood was well caught by Marie Stopes's famous little book, *Married Love*, which sold 400,000 copies between 1918 and 1923 and a million by 1939. Stopes's contribution was to make the idea of birth control respectable. She argued that frequent pregnancy was not in the national interest any more than the mother's; it simply ruined women's health and led to high infant mortality. By deliberately spacing births, a couple could ensure a healthy generation of mothers and children. But in addition Stopes addressed a very clearly felt need amongst married couples. Many women were anxious to be able to enjoy sexual relations with their husbands free from the perpetual fear of another pregnancy. Above all *Married Love* was a tract in praise of a modern marriage of equals, in which it was recognized that women enjoyed sex as much as men.

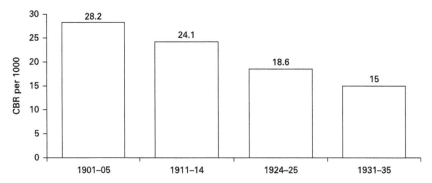

Figure 13.2 Crude birth rates (per 1,000 population) in England and Wales.

Marie Stopes followed up her literary success in 1921 by establishing a clinic dispensing advice on birth control in Holloway. Twenty or so voluntary clinics were operating by the late 1920s, but successive ministers of Health claimed that it would be illegal for local authority clinics to give any such service. This view was not abandoned until 1930, the year in which both the Church of England and the British Medical Association backed down on the issue. The doctors were moved less by concern for women's health than by the fear that they were gradually losing business as women went elsewhere for medical treatment. However, as late as 1937 only 95 of 423 local authorities were actually providing birth-control advice, and then only to married women for whom pregnancy would be detrimental to health. There were around 70 voluntary clinics also in operation by this time. Thus the emergence of the two-child family continued to be largely a matter of private endeavour, achieved without professional assistance.

Social welfare and income distribution

As a result of political pressure to reduce taxation and the attempts to balance the budget, government spending on social welfare fell between 1921 and 1924, though by 1929 it had regained its former level. In general pensions, housing and unemployment benefit tended to expand their share and education and health to contract. As unemployment mounted, total expenditure rose, much to the government's dismay, with the result that by 1930 11.1 per cent of gross domestic product went on the social services; by 1932–3 the figure had risen to 13.1 per cent, though by 1935–6 it had slipped slightly to 12 per cent. But this compares with only 4 per cent in 1913. Actual expenditure rose from £100 million in 1913 to nearly £600 million by 1938.

As we have seen, governments showed some sympathy for measures designed to promote the health of women and children, though they tended to put the responsibility onto local authorities. However, they resolutely avoided the one innovation that would have made a significant impact on mothers and children: family allowances. This idea was propagated by Eleanor Rathbone, among others, as a result of experience during the war which had shown that quite modest allowances, paid directly to mothers, were a very cost-effective way of keeping children out of poverty. However, the cost would have had to be borne by the national revenues, and none of the parties was yet willing to include this in its programme. The major initiative was Neville Chamberlain's 1925 Widows, Orphans and Old Age Contributory Pensions Act. This extended the 1908 pensions scheme to those aged 65, but only in return for contributions by employers and employees. The most important part of the legislation was the 10s. weekly pension for widows. This was a long-awaited and widely advocated measure which brought relief to thousands of hard-pressed women now able to save their children from the workhouse.

Education, by contrast, was not a priority for either Conservative or National governments between the wars. The school-leaving age had been raised to 14 in Fisher's 1918 Education Act, but other innovations succumbed to the 'Geddes Axe' in 1921. After 1924 Lord Eustace Percy, the minister responsible, imposed further economies on staff which meant that classes of 50 children were common. At this time three children in every four received their entire education in the *elementary* schools. The Hadow Report of 1926 sought to address the problem of Britain's inadequate secondary education. It recommended raising the leaving age to 15 and dividing schools into primary and secondary, the transition occurring at age 11; at the secondary stage children would go either to 'modern' schools to receive a non-academic education or to grammar schools. By 1938 two-thirds of children were attending modern schools. Grammar and direct-grant schools charged fees, although a number of free places were available for pupils from poorer families who won scholarships. The National Government dropped the promise to raise the leaving age to 15, cut teachers' salaries in 1931, and began to charge fees after a family means test even for formerly free places. As a result British education, already well behind that in Western Europe and North America, continued to be a serious impediment to national economic development.

Controversies over unemployment benefit

The most controversial area of social policy concerned the provisions for the unemployed. Basically, interwar governments used Lloyd George's 1911 scheme in which workers, employers and the state made contributions to the Unemployment Insurance Fund from which benefits were paid. However, this ceased to be financially viable because from 1920 onwards the scheme was greatly extended to cover 12 million workers and unemployment was consistently high. The fund had therefore to be subsidized by the Exchequer. There was also a growing problem concerning workers who had not paid enough contributions to qualify for normal benefits due to long-term unemployment; they either received 'uncovenanted' benefits or simply applied to the poor-law guardians. One result of the pressure on the fund was a series of dismal expedients designed to reduce the costs. Conservative ministers imposed a means test in 1922–4 and 1925–8. Large numbers of women applicants were driven away by the requirement that they must accept work as domestic servants. Also, applicants were obliged to demonstrate to the local employment committees that they were 'genuinely seeking work'; this led to 3 million people being refused benefits during the 1921–30 period.

The other major controversy arose out of the treatment of those unemployed workers who, because of their ineligibility for benefits, were forced to apply to the poor-law guardians. Around 450,000 received relief from this source each year in the mid-1920s, and three times that number in the aftermath of the General Strike. As a result of the advance of the Labour Party in local government after the war, many of the guardians were sympathetic to the plight of the unemployed, and were often willing to provide relief at higher rates than those approved by the Ministry of Health. This incensed Conservative ministers, and rekindled their longstanding hostility to the spread of elected local authorities during the later decades of the Victorian era. In that period Conservatives had particularly objected to the policies of the London County Council and many of the school boards, partly because of the increase in rates and partly because they felt that it was dangerous to provide too much education for the working classes.

Between the wars this suspicion of local government as a hotbed of radicals and socialists resurfaced in connection with the board of guardians in Poplar, where George Lansbury was mayor; the Poplar guardians paid above local minimum wage rates, applied no household means test, and supported men engaged in industrial disputes. In 1921 some of the Labour councillors there ended up in prison as a result of their financial policies. By 1926 Neville Chamberlain, the Health Minister, had taken powers to suspend and replace the guardians in West Ham, Chester-le-Street and Bedwelty for paying excessive relief. Conservatives were not impressed by the fact that the boards had been elected to pursue the policy of which they disapproved. On the contrary, Conservatives believed it to be wrong that people who were dependent on welfare should be able to vote in the elections for the administering bodies. By 1929 Chamberlain had concluded, like his predecessors, that the only course was to abolish the poor-law boards, which he did under the Local Government Act.

Their functions were transferred to committees of county and county borough councils, known as Public Assistance Committees (PACs). They were instructed not to exceed the payments that applicants would have received under unemployment insurance. But democracy was not so easily suppressed, and the PACs often paid more generously. The 10 per cent cut in unemployment benefit imposed in 1931 only exacerbated the tension between national policy and local practice. Moreover, the PACs were required to apply a stringent means test, which meant basing relief not on the individual applicant but on the family's income. As a result, fathers and husbands could be refused relief because of the earnings of sons, daughters and wives. This inevitably caused friction within families and led some to leave the family home. So resented was the inquisition that it had the effect of deterring many from applying for relief; around a quarter of a million were removed from the registers, and another half a million had their payments reduced.

However, the payments were still insufficiently uniform for the government and so they intervened again in 1934, with a new Unemployment Act which fixed new national scales and transferred the work of the PACs, which now dealt with 928,000 applicants, to Unemployment Assistance Boards. In the event the new rates turned out to be significantly lower than existing PAC payments, which led to massive popular demonstrations by the unemployed in January 1935. The National Government, now contemplating a general election, suspended the new scales and introduced more generous ones in November 1936. The actual level of unemployment benefit stood at 23s. a week for a family of five in 1922, at 29s. in 1931–5, and at 36s. from 1937. This should be compared with the estimate made by Rowntree in the 1930s that 43s. was required to keep a family of five above the poverty line.

These shifts in official welfare policies, combined with the collapse of traditional industries and communities, made for a heightened sense of class consciousness and conflict between the wars. Critics of British society could truly say that income and wealth continued to be very unevenly distributed after the war, as it had been before 1914. On the other hand, the slight redistribution of income begun in the Edwardian period was sustained between the wars. There are broadly four explanations for this pattern. First, working-class wages tended to grow faster than middle-class salaries – five times faster between 1911 and 1938, though this was mostly concentrated into the war and immediate post-war years. Second, many of the largest incomes, especially those derived from land, agricultural rents and incomes from abroad, fell quite markedly. Third, the transfer of income via government social welfare to poorer people continued, albeit at a modest pace. Fourth, the taxation of incomes continued to make a major impact. The period from 1916 to 1918 had forced the wealthy to get used to what were historically very high rates of taxation. Even after cuts in the early 1920s, the basic rate of tax was 4s. in the pound by comparison with 1s. 4d. just before 1914 and 8d. in the 1890s. In fact, the use of tax allowances in respect of children helped to keep many middle-class people with modest salaries out of the tax net, but the unmarried, the childless and those on large incomes were comparatively heavily taxed. The effect of taxation alone was to reduce the share of income enjoyed by the top 1 per cent of the population from 29 per cent to 24.4 per cent between 1914 and 1938. While great inequalities clearly remained, the long-term trend was towards a more equal distribution of income in British society.

Further reading

Overall accounts of the period:

Martin Pugh, 'We Danced All Night': A Social History of Britain Between the Wars (2008) – puts the subject in a more positive light than is traditional.

Richard Overy, The Morbid Age: Britain Between the Wars (2009) – focuses on pessimistic contemporary views of the period.

F. Carnevali and Julie-Marie Strange eds, 20th Century Britain: Economic, Cultural and Social Change (2007)

Paul Johnson ed., 20th Century Britain: Economic, Social and Cultural Change (1994)

John Stevenson, British Social History 1914–1945 (1984)

R.I. McKibbin, Classes and Culture: England 1918–1951 (1998)

S. Glynn and A. Booth, Modern Britain: an Economic and Social History (1996)

On standards of living specific aspects are discussed in:

J. Benson, The Rise of Consumer Society in Britain 1880–1980 (1994)

M. Hilton, Smoking in British Popular Culture 1800–2000 (2000)

K. Laybourn and D. Taylor, The Battle for the Roads of Britain: Police, Motorists and the Law 1890–1970 (2015)

P. Hayden, Beer and Britannia (2001)

Pat Thane, *Old Age in English History* (2000)

C. Webster, 'Health, Welfare and Unemployment During the Depression', *Past and Present*, 109, 1985

S. Constantine, *Unemployment in Britain Between the Wars* (1980)

A. Crowther, *British Social Policy 1914–1939* (1988)

G.C. Peden, *British Economic and Social Policy: Lloyd George to Margaret Thatcher* (1985)

M. Daunton, *A Property Owning Democracy? Housing in Britain* (1987)

J. Burnett, *A Social History of Housing 1918–1970* (1978)

There are many stimulating accounts by contemporaries but watch for the bias:

William Woodruff, *The Road to Nab End: An Extraordinary Northern Childhood* (2002)

Margery Spring Rice, *Working-Class Wives* (1939)

George Orwell, *The Road to Wigan Pier* (1937) – one of the Left Book Club's commissioned volumes.

Ellen Wilkinson, *The Town That Was Murdered* (1939)

For women's interwar experiences see:

D. Beddoe, *Back to Home and Duty: Women Between the Wars* (1981)

Elizabeth Roberts, *A Woman's Place: An Oral History of Working-Class Women 1890–1940* (1984)

Carol Dyehouse, *Feminism and Family Planning in England 1880–1939* (1989)

Jane Lewis, *The Politics of Motherhood* (1980)

Jeffery Weeks, *Sex, Politics and Society* (1981)

Diana Gittens, *Fair Sex: Family Size and Structure 1900–1939* (1982)

14

Imperial Climax and Decline

From the perspective of the Second World War it is very tempting to see interwar Britain as a great power already in headlong decline. No doubt she had come close to military defeat in 1918 and had been fortunate to receive American financial and military aid. In the post-war world relative power had clearly shifted in favour of the United States, while Britain continued to be hampered by a sluggish economy, a vulnerable empire, extensive international obligations and a failure of political leadership.

Yet while this pessimistic view is not without foundation, it greatly exaggerates British weakness. Although Britain undoubtedly suffered from her old dilemma of inadequate resources and extensive obligations, her relative position, especially as far as the 1920s are concerned, was much stronger than the defenders of appeasement have admitted. This was largely because of the special circumstances affecting the other powers. The USA simply failed to play the influential role in economic and diplomatic affairs that her underlying strength would have allowed. Germany and the Soviet Union were largely consumed by internal turmoil. France and Japan were strong and showed a propensity to take initiatives, but essentially within limited regional spheres. Britain alone could claim to be a global power in the 1920s. Thus in the aftermath of the Treaty of Versailles the two allies, Britain and France, could view the world in general, and Europe in particular, from a position of great strength. This situation obviously changed over time. But it is a caution against the assumption that interwar Britain was obliged to adopt a policy of appeasement out of sheer physical weakness. In a 20-year period, appeasement was more appropriate at some stages than at others; further, its value as a policy depended very much on the skill – or the incompetence – with which it was implemented.

Defence and disarmament

From a purely British viewpoint the post-war peace settlements were largely satisfactory. The German navy had been sunk at Scapa Flow; the German military threat to France and the Low Countries had been eliminated both by enforced disarmament and by the demilitarization of the Rhineland; the Empire had been preserved and even extended by the acquisition of mandates over former German colonies; and Britain's strategic position in the eastern Mediterranean had been strengthened by the dismantling of the Turkish Empire, the creation of buffer states, and the British occupation of Palestine, Transjordan and Iraq.

On the other hand, the Tsarist regime in Russia had given way to a Bolshevik one preaching international revolution and the overthrow of imperialism. Japan and Italy were anxious to grab new territory in the Pacific and North Africa respectively. In Europe a large number of new, weak states had been established, creating much potential for conflict and instability. France had to be restrained from further intervention against Germany. And finally, there was little confidence in any new methods for dealing with these problems; the League of Nations, set up to satisfy President Woodrow Wilson, was largely resented by British Conservatives, who thought it might undermine British sovereignty and the Empire.

Demobilization

After November 1918 the government embarked on a major and hasty demobilization. Inevitably the army suffered from a reaction against the massive commitment that had been made to a Continental strategy and from the wish to avoid a repetition of such a costly conflict. It was tempting to believe that Britain no longer needed an expeditionary force. In 1919 her defence policy was based on the 'Ten-Year Rule', an assumption that she would not be engaged in a great war for the next decade. To a large extent, all the governments of this period believed it desirable to avoid an arms race of the sort that had characterized the Edwardian period; and they felt that beyond a certain level expenditure on armaments would hinder the growth of the economy. To this end conscription was abandoned in 1920, and the army, which had been 3.5 million strong in 1919, was reduced to 370,000 by the end of 1920. Its chief role now was to police the Empire; some 60,000 troops remained in India, and others were kept busy in Ireland and the Middle East.

From 1919 onwards the Treasury began to press for severe cuts in the defence estimates, proposing a total annual expenditure of £110 million

Table 14.1 Armed forces personnel, 1918–39

Year	Army	Navy	Air force
1918	3,838,000	407,000	290,000
1919	1,064,000	268,000	
1920	435,000	133,000	28,000
1924	207,000	99,000	31,000
1929	194,000	100,000	31,000
1934	195,000	91,000	31,000
1939	241,000	129,000	113,000

which was less than that in 1913–14. Yet the Treasury did not get its own way by any means. The views of the Foreign Office, the Admiralty, the War Office, the India Office, the Colonial Office and the new Air Ministry had also to be considered. From 1923 the chiefs-of-staff subcommittee of the Committee of Imperial Defence also contributed to the debate. But by 1920 expenditure on the armed forces, which had been £600 million, was cut to under £300 million. The pressure of the Geddes Committee made for further reductions from 1922 onwards, which pushed costs down to £110 million, but this was partly because certain problems had now diminished and Britain was less committed in Ireland, Afghanistan, Persia, southern Russia, Egypt, Transjordan and Mesopotamia. Once down to £110 million, British defence spending remained fairly constant until 1935, but there were limits below which disarmament could not be taken.

The novelty of air power

Moreover, even the economies of the 1920s left some scope for rearmament of which the chief beneficiary was the Royal Air Force. The growing emphasis on air power is readily explicable. The raids by German planes and airships on London and the east coast during the war had made a deep psychological impression because of their novelty. Sir Hugh Trenchard, the Chief of Air Staff, capitalized on this to establish the RAF's independence from the two senior forces; he won a separate ministry and, thus, some political influence for the RAF. It was widely believed that a future war would begin with a massive air attack which would deprive Britain of the advantage hitherto conferred by her island position; her population, concentrated in a few major conurbations, would be highly vulnerable, and massive loss of life and destruction of industry seemed inevitable. The demoralizing effects of such an attack might oblige Britain to sue for peace. 'The Bomber', in Baldwin's notorious words, 'will always get through.'

Thus Trenchard argued that the creation of a British bomber force capable of deterring hostile powers was essential to British defence. But he also used other reasons to justify an expansion of the RAF. By comparison with the army, an air force could be an economical means of meeting some of Britain's obligations. In the Middle East, where Britain had to police large areas but preferred not to become too deeply involved, it was possible to withdraw some of the expensive infantry and rely instead on small numbers of aircraft. In Iraq, for example, where Britain was trying to maintain an unpopular regime, she used air squadrons to bomb the villages of the rebellious Kurds into submission; and similar tactics were adopted in Transjordan and Aden. Since the French air force was the only one capable of inflicting damage on Britain in the early 1920s, it was taken to be the national 'enemy'. French aggression in the Ruhr in 1923 prompted the government to examine carefully how large an air force Britain required. In 1922 she had 23 squadrons, of which 14 were bombers and 9 fighters. A committee under Lord Salisbury advised that Britain should have 52 squadrons by 1929, and as a result there was a 50 per cent increase in RAF estimates between 1923 and 1926. By 1935 the ratio of expenditure on the army, navy, and air force was 36:49:15.

The lack of a coherent strategy

To some extent the Royal Navy was being displaced as the politician's favourite peacetime force; it had lost its claim to be Britain's first line of defence to the RAF. However, as the navy still had a major role to play in keeping open Britain's worldwide trade routes and defending imperial communications, it maintained its share of resources more successfully than the army. For the navy, attention shifted from Europe, where there was no serious rival, to the Far East, where the rapid building by both Japan and the USA posed a challenge. In 1920 Lloyd George's government had decided to allow the Admiralty to build against the USA, but it was impossible for Britain to maintain a two-power standard against these formidable rivals in the Pacific. Several expedients were adopted to meet the problem. In 1921 it was decided to build a naval base at Singapore to which, in the event of war, a major fleet would be dispatched. Meanwhile the Anglo-Japanese Alliance of 1902 was abandoned. At the Washington Naval Conference in December 1921, the USA, Britain, Japan, France and Italy agreed to restrict their capital ships to the ratio 5:5:3:1.75:1.75, and thus to cease building capital ships for a decade. Taken together, these policies were probably unwise for Britain. They damaged her shipbuilding industry, which was now starved of orders. The Admiralty was dismayed at the decision to abandon the policy of maintaining superiority over any one rival navy. Above all, Britain had given up her pre-war policy of safeguarding her position in the Far East by co-operation with the Japanese. All the British government really had to put in its place was a vague conviction that it could rely on the Americans; but for many years that proved to be a baseless expectation.

The chief result of these modifications in the 1920s was to leave British defence in an incoherent condition. The three services each planned for a different war; the RAF with France, the navy with Japan, and the army – now that a Continental role was ruled out – concentrated on the defence of India's North-West Frontier. Yet none of these options was wholly realistic. Singapore was never adequately prepared, and in any case battleships on their own were far too vulnerable; the RAF was thinking about the wrong enemy altogether; and if India had ever faced a serious invasion Britain simply did not have the large number of troops that would have been required. Above all there was no equivalent to the co-ordination of planning and resources that Britain had undertaken before 1914.

Popular opposition to war

Not surprisingly, the interwar period in Britain saw a strong reaction against the huge casualties suffered in the Great War; there was also much criticism of the pre-war arms race and an unwillingness to pay high taxes to finance additional rearmament. But did this impose a check on the government's defence policies thereby forcing it to appease the fascist dictators? The origins of this view lie with some of the leading politicians closely associated with appeasement. Baldwin, for example, claimed that the public were wholly opposed to rearmament in the early 1930s and that the government could not obtain a mandate to change course until 1935. The Munich settlement of 1938 was, and still is, defended in part on the grounds that it bought an extra year or two of peace in which Britain could rearm. The implication is that the politicians were invariably waiting for public opinion to catch up before they could be tough towards Hitler.

However, this explanation originated as an excuse amongst discredited politicians, and must therefore be regarded with suspicion; it has never been demonstrated that at the time governments were influenced primarily by public opinion in determining their policies. Since all governments, in spite of party-political disagreements, actually offered rather similar policies on disarmament and the League of Nations, there is no obvious means of estimating public reaction, and none of the general elections from 1922 onwards can be said to have turned on foreign or defence policy.

When assessing the manifestations of popular opposition to war it is important to take account of both the extent of their support and the depth of feeling. The outright pacifist organizations, for example, were quite small groups of Quakers and Socialists, often of very long standing. On the other hand, several much larger bodies of opinion adopted an anti-war stance without necessarily being pacifist. The Labour Party Conference regularly voted in favour of complete disarmament, and in Parliament the party opposed the military estimates until 1937. However, it cannot be assumed that these decisions, taken on the basis of the block votes cast by big trade unions, necessarily reflected the views of the ordinary members. Politicians showed some concern about the views of women, who were often considered to be naturally inclined to oppose war, though the experience of 1914–18 provided very little basis for such a generalization. Among the women's organizations the Women's Co-operative League was the most important one which actively propagated the cause of peace. On armistice day each year its members distributed white poppies in protest against the slaughter of the Great War. However, this has to be set against the larger numbers of people who marked armistice day in the conventional way. Perhaps the most significant and typical pressure group in this period was the League of Nations Union (LNU). Founded in 1918, the LNU boasted 225,000 members by 1925, rose to a peak of over 400,000 in 1931, and then declined to under 200,000 in the later 1930s. It was not a *pacifist* organization, however; rather, it represented middle-of-the-road opinion in all classes and all parties which wished to avoid the mistakes of the pre-1914 era and was anxious for the British government to co-operate in helping the League of Nations to resolve disputes peacefully.

Interpreting the symptoms of pacifism

It is significant that many of the best-known symptoms of anti-war sentiment were concentrated in a fairly short period in the late 1920s and the early 1930s. These were the years of the 'King and Country' debate in the Oxford Union (1933), when the students voted in support of a proposal that 'this House will in no circumstances fight for its King and Country', the East Fulham by-election (1933), in which a Conservative majority of 14,000 was turned into a Labour one of 5,000 ostensibly because of the unpopularity of rearmament, and the so-called 'Peace Ballot' of 1934, in which 11 million people voted overwhelmingly in favour of further disarmament, even to the point of total disarmament. There was a flood of anti-war literature including Robert Graves's *Goodbye To All That* (1929), Siegfried Sassoon's *Memoirs of an Infantry Officer* (1930) and Vera Brittain's *Testament of Youth* (1933), all of which, judging by their large sales, appeared to catch the mood of the British people at the time.

However, the meaning of these manifestations is complex and easily misunderstood. For example, the Fulham by-election probably turned on domestic issues rather than on foreign policy. In any case the seat was normally a marginal one, so that a government defeat was not very startling. This was only one of 40 seats defended by the National Government, the majority of which were in fact retained even where candidates did support rearmament. In the case of the Peace Ballot, it is relevant to note that it was organized with the object of demonstrating to the government the extent of popular support for the League of Nations at a time when the withdrawal of Germany had placed a question mark over the future of both the League and the Disarmament Conference. Much the most significant question in the ballot was whether voters approved of the use of both economic and *military* sanctions against aggressor states; this was in fact *supported* by 6.7 million to 2.3 million. This was an indication that the public was not pacifist, and was in fact ready for an initiative, under the auspices of the League, to check the ambitions of the dictators. Consequently the title 'Peace Ballot' is a misleading one.

1935: the reorientation to war

What does seem clear is that public attitudes to war and peace fluctuated considerably during the interwar period. In 1918 voters were in a highly belligerent mood. In the early 1920s the anti-war organizations gained members but represented only politically active minorities. Later in the 1920s and in the early 1930s anti-war opinion apparently strengthened reflecting the heightened hopes and fears aroused by the Disarmament Conference at Geneva and its subsequent failure. However, the rise of Hitler and the emergence of the British Union of Fascists stimulated some rethinking amongst left-wing opponents of war, as well as confirming some right-wing critics of appeasement in their views. Then came a series of grave international crises, including Mussolini's invasion of Abyssinia in 1935, the remilitarization of the Rhineland, the outbreak of the Spanish Civil War in 1936, which severely weakened pacifism on the left, and the German advances into Czechoslovakia and Austria in 1938. The cumulative effect was to make war seem much more likely, and also a just and necessary risk to many people. One sign of the shift was the Labour Party's change of position during 1935–7; influenced by Ernest Bevin and Hugh Dalton, the party conference voted heavily in favour of 'collective security', which meant League of Nations sanctions against aggression, thereby precipitating the resignation of the pacifist party leader, George Lansbury. The moderate LNU lost membership at this time because some concluded that war was inevitable while pacifists were attracted by a new body, the Peace Pledge Union, formed in 1936; by 1937 it had obtained pledges not to participate in a future war from 120,000 people.

How far interwar governments allowed themselves to be influenced by public attitudes is unclear especially as the key decisions were the result of expert military and diplomatic advice. As we have seen, there was a limit to the extent to which they were prepared to disarm, whatever the public may have wanted. Neville Chamberlain was especially disdainful of popular opinion. Winston Churchill, who, as Chancellor of the Exchequer from 1924 to 1929, played a major role in keeping arms expenditure down, was not noticeably affected by popular views, any more than he was in the 1930s when advocating rearmament. It is abundantly clear that Lloyd George and the Conservatives paid lip-service to the League of Nations but had no intention of abandoning traditional methods in favour of open diplomacy. Baldwin's decision to appoint the popular Anthony Eden as Minister with responsibility for League affairs was a typically adroit move to keep on the right side of public opinion, but indicated no change of policy.

The government's contempt for popular opinion was strikingly indicated by its duplicitous policy in 1935 when Mussolini attacked Abyssinia. While Sir Samuel Hoare, the Foreign Secretary, had pledged Britain's support for the League, he then offered to partition Abyssinia to satisfy Mussolini's demands. The public, having been led to expect a very different response, were outraged. Baldwin saved his government by sacking the Foreign Secretary; but he applied only half-hearted sanctions against Italy and dropped them as soon as the controversy had subsided. The truth was that the National Government wished to appease Mussolini as a matter of *policy*, not because it thought the public opposed war. The whole episode suggested that the electorate was ready to take a tougher line with the dictators while the politicians were dragging their heels, not the other way around.

Later in the 1930s the government grew increasingly anxious to manipulate public attitudes as voters began to give support to anti-appeasement candidates in by-elections. At Bridgwater in 1938, a Conservative appeaser was defeated by an Independent critic of Chamberlain's policy. Conservative Central Office and the Whips applied intense pressure to rebellious MPs, threatening to withdraw the whip and encouraging their constituency associations to select new candidates. One arch-opponent of appeasement, the Duchess of Atholl, resigned her seat under this pressure and fought a by-election in December 1938. She was only narrowly defeated by the official Conservative, despite being branded a warmonger. These events signified that by the late 1930s much of the British public was prepared to face the possibility of war, not that it was holding the government back.

The Empire and nationalism

In many ways British imperialists derived comfort from the experience of the First World War. India and the dominions had contributed 2.5 million troops to the allied cause. The leaders of the white colonies had come to London to sit in the Imperial War Cabinet in 1917–18. Above all, the war not only strengthened imperial strategy by entrenching British control in the old Ottoman territory straddling the Mediterranean route to the East, it also extended imperial territory by the mandates over German East Africa, South-West Africa and New Guinea. This, however, merely created an illusion of imperial strength and security. In reality the interwar Empire was weakened by economic depression, by nationalist movements, and by the loss of will and divided counsels at home.

The dominions assert themselves

Although the white colonies had accepted Britain's right to declare war on their behalf in 1914, their subordinate status was resented by much of the population of South Africa, Canada and Australia. The effect of military participation was to strengthen their own nationalist pride as much as their loyalty to Britain. Australia, whose troops suffered heavy casualties in the Dardanelles, was inclined to be very critical of British military incompetence. Thus, in the aftermath of the war the dominions felt unwilling to pool their naval or military resources with Britain or to accept imperial federation. The most they would agree to was to meet at Imperial Conferences in 1921, 1923 and 1926. They insisted on being listed separately from Britain at the League of Nations; and their common refusal in 1922 to support Britain when she seemed about to plunge into a war with Turkey was a sign that they intended to pursue independent foreign policies in the future.

Consequently the British government accepted the necessity for a formal clarification and reassessment of the constitutional relationship between the dominions and the mother country. A new Dominions Office was established in recognition of the different status enjoyed by dominions by comparison with colonies. At the 1926 Imperial Conference Baldwin conceded self-government in external as well as in domestic affairs. The dominions were henceforth defined as 'autonomous communities within the British Empire, equal in status, in no way subordinate one to another in any aspect of their domestic or external affairs, though united by a common allegiance to the Crown'. In future the Crown would be represented by a Governor-General, and the dominion governments would deal with each other through high commissions. These changes were embodied in the Statute of Westminster in 1931.

This redefinition of the meaning of 'dominion status' had important repercussions: while it pleased the white colonies, it greatly complicated the question of constitutional reform in India. Elsewhere nationalism began to have disintegrating effects upon British control. In the Middle East, for example, where Britain had acquired responsibility over large tracts of territory, she had given undertakings to the Arabs of independence from the Turks, and in 1917 had made the famous Balfour declaration promising a 'national homeland' for the Jews. Consequently she found herself obliged to station troops to deal with the insurrections by nationalists whose ambitions had not yet been satisfied. In 1922 Britain granted Egypt a strictly limited independence which left her in control of Egyptian defence and the Suez Canal.

Irish Republicanism

However, for British politicians much the most traumatic episode of the early 1920s was the renewed challenge of nationalism in Ireland. As a result of the Easter Rebellion of 1916, the Irish Home Rulers and their parliamentary strategy had been discredited, and in the 1918 elections Sinn Fein swept the board outside Ulster. A Dáil or parliament for the 'Irish Republic' had been established under the presidency of Eamon de Valera, and from 1919 the Irish Republican Army (IRA) waged a terrorist campaign against the British army and the Royal Ulster Constabulary. Lloyd George felt obliged to employ an irregular force known as the 'Black and Tans' to counter the IRA's guerilla tactics, and while his own Tory diehards refused to abandon their opposition to Irish demands the Prime Minister became hopelessly enmeshed in a bloody conflict. It was not until 1921 that Lloyd George accepted that physical force was never going to settle the problem of republican Ireland. By this time the Tory leaders had also come to accept the inevitable loss of

Ireland. In December, agreement was finally reached on the establishment of the Irish Free State, which was granted the status of a Dominion under the Crown. Power was formally transferred in March 1922. In effect the bulk of Ireland now became an independent country, though there was still 'common citizenship' and Irish Free State citizens were allowed to vote in UK elections. Although the immediate repercussions were very limited many imperialists felt embittered and could not help seeing this victory for nationalism as the start of a policy of 'scuttle'; they were consequently all the more sensitive to the challenge now being posed by nationalism in India.

Gandhi and Indian nationalism

Although a nationalist organization in the form of the Indian National Congress had existed since 1885, most British officials regarded it, with some justification, as an anglicized elite with little following in the country. They comforted themselves with the thought that India comprised too many religious, social and regional communities ever to be capable of generating a united movement for self-government. However, from the First World War onwards, this assumption was to be thoroughly undermined. During 1916 and 1917 Hindus and Muslims began to collaborate in order to pressurize the British, and fresh popular interest was aroused by the Home Rule Leagues. This development stimulated a major concession by the Liberal Secretary of State, Edwin Montagu. In 1917 he offered to involve Indians more closely in the administration 'with a view to the progressive realization of responsible government in India as an integral part of the British Empire'. This historic declaration was subsequently translated into the Montagu–Chelmsford reforms, which greatly extended elected Indian representation in provincial governments and gave them effective control over a limited number of departments. The new system was to be reviewed after ten years with a view to introducing further reforms.

This strategy was intended to encourage the moderate nationalists to continue their co-operation with the British government. However, it failed for two main reasons. First, Montagu's statesmanlike approach was undermined both by British officials in India and by reactionary politicians at home, who chose to believe that the British Raj would last forever if only a firm policy were pursued. During 1919 official overreaction to popular unrest in the Punjab led to the imposition of martial law and thus to the notorious 'Amritsar Massacre', when troops under the command of General Reginald Dyer shot and killed nearly 400 Indians who were not engaged in political activity. This was an unnecessary blunder, for which Dyer was quite properly sacked. Unfortunately a great deal of support was shown for him in Britain, which served to antagonize Indians and to weaken the credibility of those who wished to co-operate with the British.

Meanwhile a remarkable transformation of Congress was underway under M.K. Gandhi's inspired leadership in the early 1920s. Gandhi shrewdly focused Indian attention upon specific, material grievances, successfully engineered collaboration between Muslims and Hindus, and effectively created a mass movement for the first time. Nationwide campaigns including Non-Cooperation in 1920–2 and Civil Disobedience in 1930–1 severely shook the morale of the British officials, and gave Congress a mass membership and an organization in every part of India. As a result from 1920 onwards Congress was able both to organize massive campaigns of disruption and to win elections all over the country, twin tactics similar to those used by the nationalists in Ireland.

Internal self-government for Indians

The crucial stage in the struggle came in 1928–31, under Lord Irwin's viceroyalty. Congress was by now pressing for dominion status which, as a result of the 1926 Imperial Conference, effectively meant independence. Gandhi led a Civil Disobedience campaign which eventually ended when Irwin took the initiative by releasing Congress leaders from jail and negotiating directly with Gandhi. This led to a series of compromises, including an undertaking by Gandhi to attend the Round Table Conference in London. On balance the deal seemed to represent a gain for the British side. However, British official opinion was outraged and demoralized by the Gandhi–Irwin Pact because, by treating Gandhi as the effective spokesman for India, the Viceroy had raised his status greatly. Moreover, although nothing came of the Round Table Conference, Baldwin and the National Government accepted the necessity to grant further constitutional reform. Eventually in 1935 Sir Samuel Hoare succeeded in enacting the Government of India Act, which gave Indians effective self-government at the provincial level and majority representation in the central government. This measure proved to be of major importance. It led to fresh elections in 1937, which Congress won allowing it to form governments in the majority of provinces.

In Britain, however, the Act was the object of a bitter and prolonged campaign in which liberal Conservatives like Baldwin, Hoare and Irwin were attacked by the diehards led by Winston Churchill. The Tory critics argued that Congress was unfit to govern and unrepresentative of India, a claim that was soon exploded. They also contended that once Britain ceded control in India she would rapidly fall from the ranks of the Great Powers. Yet while Churchill and his allies enjoyed considerable support within the rank-and-file of the Conservative Party, they failed to deflect the National Government from its objective. This was a decisive defeat for the defenders of the British Empire. There was never to be so stern a struggle again.

The interwar period also witnessed more subtle challenges to Britain's position in India. One symptom of the declining will to rule was the publication of E.M. Forster's famous novel, *A Passage to India,* in 1924. At the time this was regarded as a thoroughly subversive work because of its depiction of friendship between British and Indian people. In 1934 George Orwell, himself in official employment, wrote *Burmese Days*, which frankly suggested that many of the British themselves now detested their system of rule. Indeed, beneath the public controversy over reform important changes were taking place in the administration of India. During the war a high proportion of the members of the Indian Civil Service (ICS) had left the country. Thereafter it proved difficult to recruit young men into what had once been a most prestigious career. Thus, during the 1920s and 1930s Indians joined the service in growing numbers, such that by 1939 they comprised almost half of the ICS. As a result new British recruits often worked under Indian officers or alongside them. In this situation they inevitably adjusted their attitude, if they had not already done so. The old confidence that Britain's role would last forever steadily dwindled. Taken in conjunction with Congress rule under the 1935 Act, the changes in the ICS meant that Indians were to a considerable extent actually governing themselves before the Second World War. The ground for full independence was thus well prepared.

This period also brought important changes in the economic relationship between Britain and India. For example, the costs of both British and Indian troops in India had traditionally been met from the Indian revenues even if the troops were used outside India. By 1918 the British government was already paying for Indian troops when involved outside their own country; but from 1933 it also subsidized the cost of British soldiers stationed in India. In this way India was ceasing to be an asset to Britain, and after 1940 it became a huge military liability. More importantly, during the 1930s the advantages Britain had traditionally derived from trade with India dwindled. The war itself had greatly stimulated Indian manufacturing industries; then, as a result of the interwar depression she became increasingly self-sufficient, introducing protective tariffs and gaining control over her exchange rates. Consequently, by the 1930s India was exporting more to Britain than she was importing from her. In the economic sphere she had already moved towards a position of independence.

Decline of empire?

Faced with these developments in India, British imperialists like L.S. Amery cast around for a fresh strategy. Amery always felt that Winston Churchill and his followers were too sentimental and narrowly political in their approach, failing to appreciate the underlying *economic* potential of the colonies. For Amery Africa not only held extensive mineral and agricultural resources, it offered opportunities for emigration and was not beset by troublesome nationalist movements. As Colonial Secretary under Baldwin after 1924 Amery took initiatives designed to strengthen the economic basis of the empire. An Empire Marketing Board was created to encourage the public to buy more produce from the colonies; there was an Empire Settlement Act (1928) and a Colonial Development Act (1929) whose object was to promote the construction of the railways and harbours needed if Africa's economic potential was to be effectively exploited.

But what effect did all this have? The popularity of the great British Empire Exhibition at Wembley in 1924 and 1925 suggested that the British were still a vigorously imperial people. But this was only superficially true. In spite of the depression at home and the official encouragement, only 130,000 people per annum emigrated on average during the 1920s, which was well below the pre-1914 level. By the 1930s more British people were returning than were emigrating. Those that did leave went largely to the white dominions, and only a few thousand to Kenya, Rhodesia and South Africa, where Amery hoped to build up a large British population so as to ensure the long-term future of the Empire. Falling prices made it very difficult for those who emigrated to establish profitable plantations in Africa. Nor was the British government willing to devote resources on the required scale to these territories. Even in the Conservative Party, Amery was increasingly a peripheral figure leading a failing cause. Like the country as a whole, the politicians turned inwards to concentrate on domestic problems rather than striking out boldly for colonial development.

This is borne out by another colonial stratagem. In pursuit of the appeasement of Hitler, Chamberlain, Baldwin and Lord Halifax (the former Irwin) made it clear that they were willing, indeed anxious, to restore Germany's colonies to her. Clearly the mandates were not regarded as particularly valuable by Britain; but extensive territories were involved and their cession would have been another blow to the imperial cause. Though the policy was not implemented, it provides a telling indication of government priorities; colonies were assets to be disposed of if they could serve the more important object of improving Britain's relations with the Great Powers in Europe.

Appeasement and rearmament

Although the appeasement of Germany is indelibly associated with Neville Chamberlain's premiership after 1937, this was only the climax of a policy pursued throughout the interwar period. It originated in the conviction, shared by Lloyd George himself, that the Treaty of Versailles had been too harsh on Germany. During the 1920s all governments engaged in acts of appeasement. For example, German reparation payments were steadily reduced before being abandoned, she was assisted with her currency problems, and the British helped to reverse the French occupation of the Ruhr in 1923. In 1925 Germany became a signatory to the Locarno Agreements which, by guaranteeing the boundaries of Western Europe while conspicuously ignoring those in the East, virtually invited a further revision of Versailles. Then in 1926 the allied powers made an early withdrawal from the Rhineland, and Germany was admitted to the League of Nations.

These expressions of appeasement were widely seen as an enlightened policy pursued from a position of strength, founded on the expectation that if Germany's humiliation was expunged and her economy restored, the new parliamentary regime under the Weimar Republic would survive; consequently the causes of war would not arise. However, it is by no means certain that the limited forms of appeasement undertaken in the 1920s really satisfied even the respectable politicians of Weimar Germany. Appeasement stopped well short of restoring Germany to her former military strength or of permitting the political unity of the German people. Consequently German grievances continued to fester and the Weimar regime was undermined. Thus the question arose whether appeasement should be taken further.

Ramsay MacDonald, who became Prime Minister for the second time in 1929, recognized that the growing discontent in Germany over the low level of her armed forces imposed on her by the Treaty of Versailles called for some response. The hope was that, if the Western powers took their own disarmament further, the situation would stabilize. At the 1930 London Naval Conference, it was agreed to extend the moratorium on capital ships to 1936 so that by the mid-1930s the ratio of British to Japanese capital ships would be only 15:9, a further deterioration from Britain's point of view. For fear that the Germans might renounce the military clauses of the Treaty of Versailles, a fresh initiative was taken in the form of a Disarmament Conference which met at Geneva from 1932 to 1934. This crucial period coincided with the Foreign Secretaryship of Sir John Simon, widely considered the least effective occupant of that office in the twentieth century. The congenitally indecisive Simon had the misfortune to be in office when events began to move fast. In autumn 1931 Japan flouted the League of Nations by invading Manchuria and then withdrawing from both the League and the Disarmament Conference. Britain did nothing, but the chiefs of staff advised the government to restart work on the base at Singapore and to abandon the Ten-Year Rule.

Appeasement from strength?

Concern increased when Hitler came to power in 1933, and soon afterwards took Germany out of the League and the Disarmament Convention. It was now clear that Germany would try to accelerate the process of revising the Treaty of Versailles which the Western powers had already implicitly accepted at Locarno. Most British politicians took the view that the fall of Weimar required a more urgent application of appeasement, not that it had destroyed the logic of the policy. However, their strategy was intended to be a combination of appeasement and rearmament. Britain now faced potential challenges from Germany, Italy and Japan, each in a different part of the world; for the chiefs of staff it was now urgent that Britain's diplomacy be properly matched by military plans and resources. The result was the establishment of a Defence Requirements Committee under Sir Maurice Hankey in November 1933. It concluded that Germany, not Japan, must be regarded as Britain's most serious enemy. The scheme recommended to meet the danger involved recreating an expeditionary force of five regular divisions and expanding the RAF to 1,736 first-line aircraft, the majority of which would be bombers. The idea was to stop Germany seizing Belgium and Holland and using airfields there from which to bomb Britain; at the same time, Britain would be capable of threatening the Germans with a counter-offensive in the air.

If adopted this might have enabled Britain to pursue a strategy of responding to Germany's grievances from a position of strength. The leading appeasers claimed that the purpose of their policies in the later 1930s was to buy time in which Britain could rearm effectively. This was not, however, consistent with their practice. For several years the government was most reluctant to finance rearmament, and Neville Chamberlain, as Chancellor of the Exchequer, strongly resisted the Defence Requirements Committee proposals on the grounds that extensive government borrowing would jeopardize the fragile economic recovery. He largely got his way; the extra £97 million of expenditure proposed was cut back to £59 million. British defence spending rose from 2.7 per cent of gross national product in 1933–4 to just 2.8 per cent in 1934–5 and 3.0 per cent in 1935–6. In the circumstances this was little more than a token effort; serious rearmament did not begin until 1936–7. However, the important thing was not the amount of money spent but the strategy. While willing to expand the RAF, the government remained adamantly opposed to a new expeditionary force. The result was a dangerously unbalanced form of rearmament which had the effect of undermining British diplomacy in the later 1930s. The French and the Russians were dismayed that Britain still lacked the capacity to put an army on the Continent; this inevitably made them much more cautious about resisting Hitler's demands. For his part, Hitler was fortified by the knowledge that there was unlikely to be any effective intervention by Britain. The point was underlined in 1936 when he remilitarized the Rhineland. It was vital for the Western powers to maintain the strategic advantage of a demilitarized zone on France's vulnerable eastern frontier. Its loss weakened Britain's capacity to negotiate still further, and seriously demoralized the French.

During 1935–6 a second element of the government's appeasement policy also disintegrated. Britain and France had hoped to capitalize on Italian fears about German designs on Austria by drawing closer to Mussolini, thereby keeping Hitler isolated. Unfortunately, they were so friendly towards Mussolini that he concluded it would be safe to pursue his long-standing ambition to seize Abyssinia. His judgement proved correct in the sense that the initial reaction of the British and French was to offer the Hoare–Laval Pact, a scheme to partition the country in Italy's favour. Only a popular outcry against this forced the governments into an embarrassing retreat, and into the application of very lame sanctions against Italy. This simply had the effect of antagonizing Mussolini and further discrediting the League of Nations. In addition, the Abyssinian crisis had major repercussions for British diplomacy. The joint front of Italy, Britain and France collapsed, and Mussolini was drawn into the Rome–Berlin Axis; as a result Hitler

Table 14.2 British strength relative to other Great Powers in 1939

	Britain	USSR	France	Germany	Italy	Japan	USA
Defence expenditure as a percentage of national income (1937)	5.7	26.4	9.1	23.5	14.5	28.2	1.5
Soldiers in millions	0.154	1.3	0.7	1.5	0.85	1.00	0.166
Aircraft	2,800	1,500	2,500	4,500	2,000		2,500
Battleships	19	4	5	5	4	9	15
Submarines	71	38	76	36	82	60	84

calculated that he could now take the risk of moving his troops into the Rhineland. The effect of all this was to shift the military-strategic balance in Germany's favour. France, recently so strong, saw her position threatened by two fascist powers on her frontiers followed by a third in Spain after 1936. Appeasement, in theory a viable policy, had been applied incompetently by its exponents.

Chamberlain's delusions

This was the rapidly deteriorating situation facing Neville Chamberlain on becoming Prime Minister in 1937. By comparison with the lackadaisical Baldwin and the indecisive MacDonald, he seemed to represent a marked improvement. Chamberlain took the view that the German leadership had a strictly limited list of outstanding grievances; the sooner these were resolved the sooner the tension in Europe would be lowered. If this involved an extension of German control in central-eastern Europe this was a price well worth paying, for it would restore stability to a region of undesirable little states now vulnerable to Soviet expansion. Contrary to the traditional view, Chamberlain was by no means ignorant of foreign affairs; but he was arrogant, never understood Hitler, suffered from an inflated view of himself and found it difficult to abstain from interference in the work of his colleagues. Consequently he came to rely upon a narrow group of colleagues who shared his opinions – Hoare, Halifax, Simon and the Ambassador in Berlin, Sir Neville Henderson. Those who differed, such as Sir Robert Vansittart, the Permanent Secretary at the Foreign Office, were pushed out. Chamberlain began to pursue his own foreign policy because he considered that Sir Anthony Eden and the Foreign Office were too hostile to Mussolini; but he failed to grasp that his cultivation of Mussolini looked to Hitler like undermining the Rome–Berlin Axis and was thus counter-productive to his main aim!

In effect Chamberlain led Hitler to believe by both political and diplomatic communications that the British government would never ultimately resist him, and would even help him towards further territorial gains. Thus, when he occupied Austria in March 1938 Britain adopted the view that the German people there were fully entitled to join their fellow nationals, and the sooner the *Anschluss* was accomplished the better. Hitler next demanded the Sudetenland districts of Czechoslovakia, populated by 3.5 million Germans. Now Chamberlain took the initiative in bringing pressure to bear on the Czechs and on the French, who had treaty obligations to defend Czechoslovakia, by warning that they could expect no support from Britain if they chose to resist. In this way he threw away any bargaining power. Hitler's aggression brought Britain close to war in the summer of 1938 but Chamberlain was determined to avoid it: 'How horrible, fantastic, incredible it is that we should be digging trenches and trying on gas-masks here because of a quarrel in a far-away country between people of whom we know nothing.' His famous visits to negotiate directly culminated in the Munich Settlement in September 1938 and effectively legitimized the partition of Czechoslovakia.

At the time, the case for another act of appeasement looked strong. It was argued that Britain had no vital national interest at stake in a war over the boundaries of Czechoslovakia or, indeed, any of the other East European states which were so disliked by British statesmen. Britain was said to lack the effective military means to intervene even if she wanted to; nor were the Czechs, the French or the Russians able and willing. Both arguments had been used on every occasion when the question of resisting the dictators came up. It was all too easy to minimize the importance for Britain of any individual act of aggression and fail to see the cumulative effect. The appeasers backed their case by systematically exaggerating the strength of Britain's opponents and minimizing that of her potential allies. In 1938, for example, the Air Ministry claimed that Germany had 2,909 front-line aircraft to Britain's 1,550; in fact they were nearly equal in number.

On his return from Munich claiming 'peace with honour', Chamberlain enjoyed a fleeting popular triumph. But this collapsed in March 1939, when Hitler moved his troops into Prague and dismembered even the non-German parts of Czechoslovakia. By now the futility of Chamberlain's policy was widely recognized; he had been attempting to appease an opponent who was not really appeasable. Yet although the Prime Minister made a radical departure by proceeding to give guarantees to Poland and Romania, the next victims of Hitler's demands, he evidently continued to believe that further deals would obviate the need for war. When Hitler began to put pressure on the Poles the old argument was wheeled out: was it worth shedding British blood for Danzig? However, by this time Lord Halifax, for one, had recognized the folly of further appeasement and Chamberlain could not afford to lose a second Foreign Secretary. Even so, he prevaricated. When he addressed the House of Commons on 2 September 1939, by which time German troops had spent several days on Polish soil, he amazed MPs by failing to announce a declaration of war. Only the combination of dissension in the Cabinet and rebellion among the MPs forced him to do so the next day.

*   *   *

1918 to 1939 proved to be a remarkable period. Amid the collapse of regimes, monarchies and empires under the impact of war and the destabilizing effects of mass unemployment, British society remained relatively stable and her institutions appeared resilient. By the 1930s the dire warnings issued by sections of the press and the political Establishment about social and political change had proved to be exaggerated if not wholly baseless. The new democracy had bedded in. The Labour Movement had risen rapidly to power but without trying to overthrow, or even reform, the existing system. Women had been absorbed into the system but the earlier fears of anti-suffragists about the threat to marriage and motherhood had failed to materialize. On the other hand, optimistic accounts by some historians about the government's success in resolving the economic depression in the 1930s are also much exaggerated; Britain entered the Second World War with 10 per cent unemployment. Throughout the period she suffered from serious failures of economic management and from poor political leadership. Moreover, Britain's role as a great imperial power had no sooner reached its peak than it came under question, partly because of her inadequate resources and partly because her liberal society was developing doubts about the moral case for maintaining alien rule over Asian and African peoples indefinitely; consequently the first withdrawals from empire were made during this period. However stable things appeared in 1939 the new domestic and external agenda was clearly in sight.

Further reading

Paul Doerr, *British Foreign Policy 1919–39* (1998)
Margaret Macmillan, *Peacemakers* (2003) – a revisionist view of Versailles, challenging critics of Lloyd George.
David Reynolds, *Britannia Overruled: British Foreign Policy and World Power in the Twentieth Century* (1991)
C. Bartlett, *British Foreign Policy in the Twentieth Century* (1989)
G. Schmidt, *The Politics and Economics of Appeasement* (1986)
Martin Ceadel, *Pacifism in Britain 1914–45* (1980)
A. Adamthwaite, *The Making of the Second World War* (1977)

On the controversy over appeasement:
R.A.C. Parker, *Churchill and Appeasement* (2000) – avoids hero-worship; asks whether Churchill could have stopped Hitler.
R.A.C. Parker, *Chamberlain and Appeasement* (1993) – hostile to Chamberlain.
Nick Smart, *Neville Chamberlain* (2010) – hostile to Chamberlain.
David Dutton, *Neville Chamberlain* (2001) – sympathetic to Chamberlain.

John Charmley, *Chamberlain and the Lost Peace* (1989) – argues that Chamberlain was right.

On British preparations for war see:
Brian Bond, *British Military Policy between Two World Wars* (1980)
David French, *The British Way in Warfare 1688–2000* (1990)
David French, *Raising Churchill's Army: the British Army and the War Against Germany 1991–45* (2000)
M. Smith, *British Air Strategy between the Wars* (1984)
R.P. Shay, *British Rearmament in the Thirties* (1977)

On empire and imperial policies see:
Bernard Porter, *The Lion's Share: A Short History of British Imperialism 1850–1983* (1984)
A. Thompson, *The Empire Strikes Back: the Impact of Imperialism on Britain from the Mid-Nineteenth Century* (2004)
J. MacKenzie, *Propaganda and Empire: the Manipulation of British Public Opinion 1880–1960* (1984) – argues that the British were heavily influenced by imperialism.
Bernard Porter, *The Absent-Minded Imperialists* (2004) – argues that the influence of empire was really superficial.
M. Havinden and David Meredith, *Colonialism and Development: Britain and Its Tropical Colonies 1850–1960* (1993)
Judith Brown, *Modern India: The Origins of an Asian Democracy* (1985)

Part IV

Consensus: The Age of the Benign State, 1940–70

15

The People's War

When Neville Chamberlain addressed the House of Commons on 2 September 1939, it was widely anticipated that he would announce a British declaration of war upon Germany. Commitments recently given to Poland and Hitler's fresh aggression against that country appeared to leave the Prime Minister with no choice. His failure to declare war shocked Parliament, and was taken as a sign that his heart was not in the cause. As a result, the remaining months of Chamberlain's premiership became known as the 'Phoney War'. It seemed possible that, if Britain avoided drawing German fire in the west, Hitler's success in Eastern Europe might bring the whole affair to an end without the necessity for major conflict on her part especially as Germany lacked the resources to sustain a long war. The leading appeasers continued to entertain such hopes for some time, and within the British Establishment there was widespread defeatism underpinned by a feeling that Britain should be fighting Russia not Germany. However the effect was to undermine confidence in Chamberlain's capacity as a war leader. While the country and most politicians were united about the justness of the war against fascism, the Labour Party remained bitter towards Chamberlain as a result of his earlier policies, and his arrogance, narrowness and insecurity made him seem unsuitable as a unifying national leader.

Breaking the mould

The first indication of a breakdown of the interwar pattern of politics came with the refusal of the Labour and Liberal Parties to join Chamberlain in a coalition government, although, following the precedent of the First World War, they agreed to a by-election truce. However, some steps were taken to put the government onto a war footing. New ministries appeared for Home Security, Economic Warfare, and Food and Shipping, and Winston Churchill accepted the prominent – but vulnerable – post of First Lord of the Admiralty. Yet the leading appeasers, Simon, Hoare and Halifax, remained in office, while the nine-member War Cabinet soon became bogged down in arguments. The situation was not unlike that faced by Asquith's 1914 administration, in which a peacetime system was marginally adapted for war.

Before long, Chamberlain's plans for damage limitation were disrupted by two unpredictable protagonists: Hitler and Churchill. Within a matter of weeks the Poles had succumbed to German invasion from the west and Russian advances from the east. Meanwhile neither the French army nor the British Bomber Command took the opportunity of German absorption in the east to seize the initiative. Four infantry divisions were dispatched to France, the Royal Navy began to apply a blockade, and the RAF scattered propaganda over the German mainland. But it was all an anticlimax. By the beginning of 1940 the situation at home and abroad was beginning to deteriorate. Chamberlain made the mistake of removing a popular War Minister, Leslie Hore-Belisha, which provoked the criticism of the press, already restless for lack of good copy. The Gallup polls began to record a slide in the Prime Minister's popularity. Churchill alone generated an air of purposefulness and excitement, but as in the previous war he showed a propensity for inventing wild military schemes. Chamberlain may well have calculated that he would discredit himself in this way. Such a prospect rapidly materialized as Churchill grew enthusiastic about sending troops to the Norwegian port of Narvik and mining Norwegian waters, with a view to checking German access to iron-ore supplies. This was both politically and militarily unrealistic, but eventually Churchill overcame his colleagues' opposition to the idea. In the event the campaign was incompetently managed, and Hitler moved in quickly to overrun the country. Although large amounts of German shipping were destroyed, Allied forces suffered heavy casualties and had been driven back from Norway by April.

Three-party coalition

Although Churchill deserved to be blamed for this fiasco it was Chamberlain who suffered. In parliament Conservatives including L.S. Amery and Lord Salisbury, and the Liberal Clement Davies, joined forces, backed from outside by the *Daily Mirror*. The Labour opposition tabled a motion on the Norwegian campaign for debate on 7–8 May. Several weighty figures from the past, including Lloyd George and Admiral Sir Roger Keyes, joined the condemnation. Amery resurrected some famous words of Oliver Cromwell: 'You have been sitting here too long for all the good that you have been doing. In the name of God, go!' In the vote, the government's majority sank from well over 200 to 81. Even so, Chamberlain might have saved his premiership if the Opposition had agreed to enter a coalition; but they refused, and he had to resign. In this situation Lord Halifax was the man most generally acceptable to the Conservative Party, the Labour Party and the King. But his reputation as an appeaser left him with less standing with the public, and Halifax chose to use the excuse of his membership of the House of Lords to back down in favour of Churchill. Thus at the age of 66 Churchill suddenly saw his fading career given a new lease of life. His elevation proved to be a turning-point, both because it destroyed the hegemony of the National Government and restored Labour to power, and because it coincided with disastrous events abroad which were to leave a deep impression on the public mind.

In a way, Churchill's political position resembled that of Lloyd George in 1916; for as Prime Minister he was not the leader of a party, and had come to power only over the ruin of his leader's reputation. Like Lloyd George, he formed a three-party coalition and established a small War Cabinet. But at first the break was not too sharp; Chamberlain, Halifax and Simon retained high office. Several anti-Chamberlain Tories, including Eden, Kingsley Wood, Lord Lloyd, L.S. Amery and Duff Cooper, joined the government, as did non-party figures such as Sir John Anderson (Home Office) and Lord Woolton (Food). From the Labour ranks Attlee and Arthur Greenwood became ministers without portfolio, Ernest Bevin became Minister for Labour, Herbert Morrison Minister for Supply, Hugh Dalton Minister for Economic Warfare and A.V. Alexander First Lord of the Admiralty. The effect, by 1945, was to re-establish Labour as competent and patriotic in government after the damage done to the party's reputation in the 1930s.

Churchill enjoyed an advantage over Lloyd George in his relationship with the military authorities. He did not suffer sustained opposition from the generals, though this largely reflected the fact that Germany's sweeping success on the Continent left the British with far less room for manoeuvre than in the 1914–18 war and fewer casualties. Moreover, Churchill made himself Minister for Defence, thereby subordinating the three service chiefs. And although the chiefs of staff found him exhausting and unpredictable, they recognized the value of his own experience at both the War Office and the Admiralty, and contented themselves with restraining his wilder notions. For his part, Churchill was somewhat sobered by the reflection that with his previous record of military setbacks he could easily become the victim of the next fiasco.

Churchill's entry into office certainly coincided with a rapid deterioration of the military situation. Although the 400,000 troops of the British

Expeditionary Force, combined with the French, Belgian and Dutch, were roughly equal in numbers to the German armies facing them, their quality and staff work were inferior. The Allies also misjudged German intentions. Following a main attack through the Ardennes, a breakthrough in the Allied line caused them to retreat towards the coast; by the end of May Britain was planning an evacuation from Dunkirk. This was well chosen, because it was close enough to be within range of fighter planes based in England. Some 200,000 troops were evacuated on 2 and 3 June alone, and eventually 338,000 made their escape. But by the end of the month the French had been forced to capitulate, leaving much of the north and west of the country in enemy hands and thereby exposing Britain to an acute danger of invasion. 'Personally', noted the King, 'I feel happier now that we have no allies to be polite to and pamper.'

Public morale and the Churchill myth

However, the government now prepared for the worst. Male enemy aliens were interned, Sir Oswald Mosley and 700 BUF members, though not the aristocratic pro-Nazis, were imprisoned, and men aged between 17 and 65 were recruited into a Local Defence Volunteer Force. But in spite of the military crisis, there was little sign of demoralization except among some leading politicians. The conventional view has been that public morale was boosted by firm official action and by Churchill's inspiring broadcasts. 'I expect the Battle of Britain is about to begin,' he declared on 18 June, 'Let us brace ourselves to our duty, and so bear ourselves that if the British Empire and its Commonwealth last for a thousand years, men will still say, "This was their finest hour".' In fact, public opinion was quite mixed. The surveys conducted by Mass Observation suggested that Churchillian rhetoric had a limited impact, particularly on women. As a group women were more resigned, less involved and less optimistic about the war than men. This may have been partly because they bore the brunt of the conflict in terms of its disruptive effects on normal family life; they resented the evacuation of children, food queues, the blackout, the deterioration in the housing stock and the loss of a social life. Certainly much of the population became indifferent or cynical towards the massive propaganda effort of the Ministries of Information, Food and Labour. Official advice about the danger of giving away vital information by gossiping was regarded as ridiculous, and material on the economical use of food was either unread or ignored. The propagandists clearly had difficulty in judging the response to their message. When the Ministry of Information issued a poster bearing the slogan 'Your Courage, Your Cheerfulness, Your Resolution Will Bring Us Victory' it attracted so much hostility that it had to be withdrawn.

In a sense, the authorities were suffering not simply from their current policies but from accumulated resentment over their pre-war incompetence. The most famous manifestation of this was the book *Guilty Men*, published in 1940 and reprinted ten times in that year alone. A satirical attack on the leading appeasers, Chamberlain, Hoare and Simon, it struck a chord with the public and continued to be discussed up to 1945. In the short term *Guilty Men* contributed to the feeling that the country was still in the grip of the kind of men who had called for sacrifices in 1914–18 and let the country down subsequently. The view that in the current war sacrifices ought to be equally shared amongst the population was echoed in J.B. Priestley's radio broadcasts and in the pages of the *Daily Mirror*, a newspaper then coming into its heyday on a timely blend of patriotism and social radicalism. One immediate effect of this critical mood was to facilitate interventionist policies, such as food-rationing, which would introduce an element of equality into wartime experience. In this way the crisis helped to dissipate the political resignation typical of the 1930s and restore a spirit of irreverence which eventually ushered in a more left-wing agenda.

Mass war and social change

The Second World War focused attention upon civilians and their living standards even more effectively than the Great War had done. This was partly the result of military events. By the summer of 1940 Allied forces had been chased out of Europe so that for some time Britain's direct military participation was very limited. Consequently the defence of the British Isles and the morale of the population at home moved to centre stage. Pre-war propaganda had prepared people for a massive bombardment from the air, hence the evacuation of 1.5 million children from vulnerable urban areas to the countryside. When the Blitz began in September 1940 2.5 million Anderson shelters, capable of holding 10 million people, had been distributed to homes with back gardens; others used communal shelters including 177,000 who squatted in the London Underground. In fact pre-war propaganda about bombing proved to be wildly exaggerated though 60,000 civilians were killed and 4 million houses, representing about a third of the total housing stock, suffered damage. In time people became inured to regular bombing raids. As the attacks fell on the West End as much as the docks and East London the misery appeared to be shared, a feeling reflected by the Queen after a raid that damaged Buckingham Palace: 'Now we can look the East End in the face'. But as one MP shrewdly observed, had the Germans simply concentrated on the East End 'there might have been a revolution in this country'.

Civilian mobilization

The war also impinged upon civilians by stimulating the demand for labour, and succeeded at last in pushing unemployment below 10 per cent. Indeed, by the beginning of 1941 the government's Manpower Requirements Committee advised that an extra 2 million workers were required. Clearly, they would not materialize simply on the basis of the exhortation and propaganda used so far. Both politicians and trade unions showed as much reluctance as in 1914–18 for the obvious solution: the recruitment of more women. But by 1941 Bevin could see no alternative. Women were required to register in successive age groups at their local labour exchanges, where they would be allocated employment. As a result by 1943, 46 per cent of all women aged between 14 and 59 were doing paid work for the war effort. The conscription of women was a striking achievement, not matched by either Nazi Germany or Stalinist Russia, and made a material impact on the war by enabling Britain to mobilize a higher proportion of her economic resources. It underlined the superiority of a liberal parliamentary system over autocracy in rallying the people around the national interest. The success of this policy is underlined by the evidence that on the whole women, outside the younger age groups, were not enthusiastic about being conscripted. To some extent, however, the authorities responded to women's problems by providing day nurseries and adjusting shifts so that housewives could fit in their shopping. Some 470,000 young women also joined the three armed forces during the war, while thousands more served in the Auxiliary Territorial Service, the Land Army, Air Raid Precaution and Auxiliary Fire Service. As in the First World War, the uniform was widely seen as a form of emancipation in itself.

Table 15.1 Casualties in the Second World War

	Civilians	Army	Navy	Air force	Merchant navy	Wounded	Prisoners of war
Number of casualties	60,284	144,079	50,758	69,606	30,248	277,077	172,592

Declining moral standards?

For many men this sudden rise in status for women proved to be as disorientating as in 1914–18. They reacted against the appearance of large numbers of young, independent women, with money in their pockets, in public houses and other public places. This led inexorably to claims about deteriorating moral standards during wartime for which women were blamed. The government maintained its own double standard by distributing free condoms to soldiers to protect them against venereal disease, while leaving uniformed women unaided to risk pregnancy. Of course some married women, who faced lonely separation from their husbands, did pursue affairs, while many young women enjoyed brief relationships with American or Canadian troops. The result was a number of hasty marriages and a doubling of the illegitimacy rate to 9 per cent of all births by 1945. Five times as many people sought divorces after the war as before, and 58 per cent of divorce petitions were now lodged by men.

However, middle-aged males were alarmist in interpreting all this as a collapse of traditional moral values. Extramarital affairs resulted from the boredom and loneliness of wartime life but they did not signify a revolt against marriage. Indeed, the Mass Observation surveys at the time underlined that for the majority of women marriage and motherhood remained their overriding goals. Though the marriage rate fell during 1941–5, thereafter it swiftly rose above pre-war levels and continued to rise until the early 1970s. This helped to keep the birth rate buoyant and led to the 'baby boom' of 1946–8. By the end of the war men and women were anxious to return to a settled family life. In particular, Mass Observation reported that three-quarters of women workers wanted to drop their employment as soon as possible.

Concessions in social policy

The coalition government recognized that the central part played by civilians virtually dictated not just promises about future social improvement but considerable innovation in social policy during the war. This manifested itself in four main ways. First, a system of rationing was applied to most food items except bread and potatoes, and free or subsidized milk, orange juice and cod-liver oil was supplied to young children and expectant mothers, thereby helping to improve the health of the most vulnerable groups. Second, the government paid pensions and allowances to families whose income had been lost through war service by the head

Image 10 Munitions workers, Newcastle-upon-Tyne, 1943.

of household, and in 1941 they abolished the unpopular family means test. By 1945 a bill to introduce family allowances was going through Parliament. Third, they created the Emergency Medical Service from the existing patchwork of hospitals – a step towards the National Health Service. Fourth, as a result of pressure from Bevin, wage levels were raised for certain low-paid groups, including agricultural and railway workers. The general effect of labour shortages and the availability of overtime was to drive average weekly wages up from around 53s. in 1938 to 96s. by 1945. An 80 per cent increase in wages, in the context of a 31 per cent rise in the cost of living, left most families better off.

Much the most striking indication of the mood engendered by the external crisis came in the response to the famous report of Sir William Beveridge in December 1942. By the time he was appointed to chair the government's Committee on Social Insurance in June 1941, Beveridge knew that the idea of a general reconstruction of social-welfare provisions enjoyed wide support amongst political, professional and academic circles. In many ways his report was a consolidation of 'middle opinion' of the 1930s. For example, Political and Economic Planning pre-empted him with proposals for a national minimum wage, family allowances and a national health service. Beveridge enunciated a sweeping plan to conquer the five giants – Want, Ignorance, Squalor, Idleness and Disease. Government would be responsible not only for social insurance 'from the cradle to the grave', a health service and family allowances, but also for maintaining the economy such that unemployment would not exceed 8 per cent.

If the scope of this was sweeping, its character was not revolutionary. Beveridge's ideas, after all, were moulded by Edwardian and Victorian National Efficiency ideology. His plan was based on the principle of *insurance*; contributions would bring entitlement to a national minimum income, but for those who fell outside the range of guaranteed benefits there was to be a scheme of National Assistance. And though Beveridge's proposals were to be of great advantage to women, his scheme recognized women essentially as wives and mothers. Though not a feminist he adopted the feminist idea of family allowances because it was now an urgent national interest, in view of falling birth rates, to promote larger families.

Beveridge's report crystallized opinion half-way through the war; it sold 100,000 copies in the first month and 630,000 in all. In this way it encouraged politicians to recognize the force of public opinion, thereby ensuring that the Second World War would have lasting effects rather than the largely ephemeral impact of the 1914–18 war. Churchill and Kingsley Wood, the Chancellor, became worried about the popularity of the Beveridge Report, because it seemed likely to raise excessive expectations and distract the public from the tedious necessity for continued privations and discomforts. However, though cautious over the cost of the programme, they judged it expedient to show their commitment to social improvement. One sign of this was R.A. Butler's 1944 Education Act. In the same year Beveridge published his *Full Employment in a Free Society*, and government white papers appeared on Social Insurance, a National Health Service and the famous one on Employment Policy which committed the government to Keynesian techniques for adjusting the level of public spending so as to maintain a high rate of employment. The following year brought legislation for family allowances which offered 5s. a week for second and subsequent children. By excluding the first child, this scheme departed from the feminist idea of the payments as a recognition of the value of every mother's work; moreover, the government's scheme proposed to make the payments to *fathers*, though Eleanor Rathbone forced them to back down on that point. Taken as a whole, the reforms achieved during the war, and the momentum building up for further reform by 1945, ensured that social change would be underpinned by political change and thus sustained into peacetime in a way that had not been true after 1918.

The origins of the post-war consensus

The experience of the First World War made the adoption of state controls designed to mobilize national resources less controversial during 1940–45. The civil service expanded from 387,000 to 704,000; the Ministry of Labour used draconian powers to direct workers to needy sectors; and the government used the radio and the press as vehicles for official propaganda, though stopping just short of formal censorship. Inevitably, government expenditure rose enormously, from £1.4 million in 1939–40 to £6.1 million by 1944–5, of which £5.1 million was for defence. But as early as 1941 Britain was exhausting her resources. Lord Lothian, the ambassador in Washington, had cheerfully told American reporters in 1940: 'Well boys, Britain's broke; it's your money we want.' The US government co-operated by agreeing to a series of 'lend-lease' arrangements to enable Britain to maintain her war effort until 1945, though they extracted a high price for this assistance. By the end Britain had practically exhausted her reserves of gold, dollars and overseas investments, and her debt had grown from nearly £500 million in 1939 to £3,500 million. However, though lend-lease was a useful expedient, its importance should not be exaggerated; Britain largely financed the war effort from her own resources. The first war budget had raised income tax from 5s. in the pound to 7s. 6d., and it subsequently rose to 10s. In 1943 the Pay As You Earn system was introduced.

The Keynesian revolution

The war crisis helped to discredit the retrenchment philosophy in British economic policy. The war budget of 1941 is usually regarded as marking the adoption of a Keynesian approach to public finance. Even before 1939, Keynesianism had been establishing its influence in the civil service and Parliament, and the necessity to mobilize the country's economic resources completed the defeat of orthodox *laissez-faire* attitudes. During 1939–43 some 3 million additional men and women entered paid employment, thereby removing at last the stubborn unemployment that had dogged the interwar period. As a result Britain's rearmament advanced very rapidly, so much so that she was soon outproducing Germany in tanks and aircraft.

In the 1980s, however, this remarkable success came under attack by some right-wing historians including Corelli Barnett (*The Audit of War, 1986*) hostile to all forms of state involvement in the economy and society. They criticized the wartime coalition on the grounds that industrial production was inefficient and thus shored up sectors that should have been radically reorganized; they also felt that the high-minded liberal establishment imposed an expensive welfare commitment upon post-war Britain. This is largely invalid. In the crisis it was inevitable that the extra output desperately needed in munitions was obtained at a heavy cost and with lower productivity because new workers were hastily enrolled. Industry operated with the advantage of firm orders; it could charge the actual costs of production plus a guaranteed rate of profit. The idea that in the desperate situation faced by the government it could restructure industry, squeeze manufacturers' margins or obtain workers' full co-operation without safeguarding their living standards is quite unrealistic.

Moreover the costs of new social policies were from the start conditional on the performance of the economy; Beveridge argued that a high level of employment must be maintained specifically so that the burden of state welfare would not become too great. Moreover, the assumption that governments entered into new social policies during the war *unnecessarily* seems very dubious. After the experiences of 1914–18 and the interwar period, much of the British population was unwilling to make great sacrifices except on the basis of current and future social improvement. During the war trade union membership rose from 6.25 million to 8 million and, as in the Great War, only the first two to three years saw a reduction in militancy. By 1942 strike activity was growing again, and continued to do so to the end of the war, largely because men feared that peace would once again bring higher unemployment and lower wages. In these circumstances, concessions were no more than a realistic means of achieving the measure of co-operation in the war effort that was so crucially necessary; it represented a hard-headed strategy, not an optional luxury for the liberal establishment.

Finally, any 'audit' for the Second World War must recognize the positive economic effects, not merely the negative ones. No doubt the conflict gave an artificial stimulus to traditional sectors like coal and steel by driving resources into them which might have been better employed elsewhere in peacetime. But this was scarcely avoidable. The war gave a valuable boost to innovation in agriculture, chemicals, electronics, aircraft and the motor industry, due to developments in radar, jet propulsion, antibiotics and atomic power. This greatly strengthened science-based industry after 1945, and contributed to the usually high rate of economic growth achieved in the aftermath of war.

The survival of the coalition

In retrospect the aura of victory tends to make the Churchill coalition appear much more secure than it was; certainly in the summer of 1940 many observers thought it unlikely to last the duration of the war. However, by the autumn, with Britain winning the Battle of Britain, the prospect of a German invasion dwindled and the standing of the government naturally improved. Chamberlain's retirement for health reasons necessitated a ministerial reorganization and the selection of a new Tory Leader. The first task was accomplished by expanding the War Cabinet to eight members and appointing Herbert Morrison Home Secretary and Minister for Home Security. Churchill could have avoided the party leadership, but that would have left him in a vulnerable position comparable to Lloyd George's in 1918. He not only became leader but also removed his main rival, Halifax, by making him ambassador to the United States shortly afterwards. This allowed Eden to return to the Foreign Office.

In the House of Commons the government's position looked, on the face of it, impregnable. The absence of many MPs on wartime work weakened Parliament, while the absorption of the bulk of the Labour leadership into the government inevitably inhibited the usual role of the opposition. But new critics emerged, taking the government by surprise. War had an energizing effect on the back-bench women members, and drew Labour and Conservatives together in defence of women's interests. The leading figures in this were Edith Summerskill (Labour), Mavis Tate and Irene Ward (Conservatives), Eleanor Rathbone (Independent) and Megan Lloyd George (Liberal). In the early months of war they felt the government was slow to find employment for women, and deputations urged a greater use of women in the civil service and the abandonment of the marriage bar. The government made a concession by setting up a Womanpower Committee, which led to a debate in March 1941 in which Bevin came in for much criticism. The women MPs also demanded equal compensation for injuries suffered by women in the war, which resulted in a heavy defeat for the government by 229–95 votes in November 1942. They also surprised ministers during the passage of the 1944 Education Bill by obtaining a narrow majority – 117 to 116 – for an amendment to give equal pay to women teachers. The Cabinet overthrew this only by threatening to resign and seeking a vote of confidence.

Why did Labour benefit under the coalition?

Although Labour was an integral part of government it also sustained an opposition led by figures such as Emmanuel Shinwell and Aneurin Bevan. In May 1941, after the failure of the campaign in Greece, the House debated a confidence motion, but the coalition defeated it overwhelmingly despite being attacked by Lloyd George. In July 1942 there was another back-bench protest demanding higher pensions. Although Churchill's personal popularity remained consistently high, opinion polls showed sagging confidence in the government; by January 1941 support had fallen to 58 per cent, and by July 1942 to 41 per cent. Ironically, the entry of the USA and the Soviet Union into the war, and the British success in North Africa during 1942, stimulated criticism because it raised the prospects of an end to the war. In this situation the Labour Party benefited by being both patriotic and critical at the same time. By abstaining from by-election contests the party felt it was making a considerable sacrifice, because a number of safe Conservative seats were lost to Independents and the new Commonwealth Party. However, the Conservatives complained that Labour was nonetheless maintaining normal party propaganda. There was some truth in this. The Conservatives' local associations held no party conferences until 1945 and Churchill neglected the party organization which had been his enemy throughout the 1930s. After their defeat in 1945 Conservatives argued that they lost the advantage organizationally because many of the agents were away in the forces. By 1944 163 of their 384 agents had left for other work. However, as Labour was down to 65 agents the Conservatives still retained an advantage. In any case organization was more a symptom than a cause of success at the election.

Both parties lost members during wartime. Labour's individual membership fell from 408,000 in 1939 to 265,000 in 1944, although indirect union membership increased from 2.2 million in 1939 to 2.5 million by 1945. Labour also continued to hold annual conferences and Attlee and the other parliamentary leaders kept in touch with the MPs and party members. Though loyal to the election truce, Labour never treated it as a *political* truce and so local parties were free to campaign on the Beveridge Report for example. The greatest signs of revolt came in February 1943, when 121 MPs supported an opposition motion critical of the negative response of the Chancellor to the Beveridge Report. By that time the backbenchers were reflecting the mood of rising expectations in the country and the trade unions' apprehension about the economic effects of an end to the war. Yet it is easy to be misled by evidence of internal controversies. The Labour Party never split because it was completely committed to winning the war and it saw evidence that its pressure was extracting concessions for working people from the government. In October 1944, Labour's NEC decided that the party must abandon the coalition as soon as Germany had been defeated in order to concentrate on the general election now overdue.

The collapse of British power

The Second World War made a reality of the nightmare long feared by the chiefs of the armed forces. Britain found herself simultaneously engaged in defending the British Isles from invasion, meeting the challenge of the Italian navy in the Mediterranean, and fending off Japanese aggression in the Far East. Her resources were hopelessly overstretched. This dilemma had been obvious since the 1890s, but before 1914 it had been dealt with by a mixture of diplomatic and military expedients; by 1939 Britain was relying more on bluff. However, the situation was never quite as bad as it appeared in the early stages of war. Fortunately, Hitler never regarded the military defeat of Britain as an urgent matter; he had not prepared for it, and in any case the Luftwaffe lacked the capacity for a major attack. Once Britain had begun to outbuild Germany it became increasingly unlikely that Hitler would attain the necessary air supremacy over southern England to justify risking an invasion. Britain's strength in fast fighter planes – Hurricanes and Spitfires – combined with the radar early-warning system enabled her to take a heavy toll of the relatively slow German bombers during 1940, and thus to remove the prospect of an enemy landing.

In the emergency, Churchill's instinct was to try to capitalize upon what he called 'the natural Anglo-American special relationship'. Half-American himself, Churchill devoted much of his time to cultivating President Roosevelt with a view to eventual entry by the USA into the war. Meanwhile, his greatest contribution to the war effort was to secure the lend-lease deals and the use of American cruisers when Britain was at her most vulnerable. Even so, the relationship was not without its complications. The American government wanted Britain to announce withdrawal from India, and to give up Imperial preference and the sterling area, which Churchill saw as essential props to Britain's position in the world. There was also some disagreement over strategy. Britain wished to delay the opening of a western front against Germany, and preferred to tackle Italy, which closely affected her Mediterranean communications. It suited the USA to concentrate on the Pacific, and thus postpone the landings in France until 1944. This delay crucially affected relations with the Soviet Union, whom the Allies failed to relieve during her time of greatest need. By July 1943 the Russians had turned the tide of war against Hitler's forces by themselves, which meant that they were able to begin an advance into Eastern Europe well before the British and Americans were able to bring effective power to bear on that area. In this way, Allied strategy was to lead to major problems in the post-war era.

Imperial breakdown

Even in the worst days of the war Britain had not stood quite alone against Hitler. Altogether 5 million colonial troops, including 2.5 million from India, fought on her side. The Empire was retained – but only just. The entry of Japan into the conflict in 1941 exposed the crippling weaknesses in Britain's world position. For neglecting the proper defence of Singapore against a long-expected attack, and for underestimating the capability of the Japanese, Churchill was as culpable and as misguided as all the other politicians of his generation. In 1941 two battleships, HMS *Repulse* and *Prince of Wales*, were dispatched to Singapore without the necessary air cover, to be promptly sunk by Japanese attack. Then, during 1942, Singapore, Hong Kong, Malaya and Burma rapidly fell to the advancing Japanese forces, leaving India itself exposed to invasion.

These events helped to seal the fate of British India especially as British prestige was fatally undermined in the eyes of many colonial peoples in Asia and Africa. Moreover, the war finally turned India from what had once been a military asset into a huge liability. Nineteenth-century statesmen had spent years worrying about a possible attack on India via the North-West Frontier which had never materialized. Now the threat had come across the north-east border, and scarce military resources had to be dispatched to the south Asian theatre to meet it. Inevitably this military crisis impinged upon the internal stability of India. In September 1939 Lord Linlithgow, a tactless and mediocre Viceroy, had declared the country at war with Germany with no pretence of consultation. Since at this time Congress was ruling most of the provinces of India, and Nehru fully accepted the necessity for defeating the menace of fascism, this was a unforced error on Linlithgow's part. He gave the radicals within Congress a good opportunity to withdraw their co-operation from the government and return to confrontation.

Back in Britain, the new Prime Minister ringingly declared, 'I have not become the King's First Minister in order to preside over the liquidation of the British Empire.' But for all his bluster, Churchill had been obliged by the need for American support to accept the Atlantic Charter which, among other things, encompassed the break-up of empire. Concessions did, in fact, begin to come thick and fast in several parts of the Empire during the war. Jamaica achieved adult suffrage, an elected majority was introduced into the Gold Coast legislature, and promises of self-government were given to Malta and Ceylon. In India itself Britain ceased to be in effective control. In view of the need to maintain some internal co-operation, the government decided to send Sir Stafford Cripps to India in March 1942 with a new offer to the effect that a post-war assembly should draw up a constitution for a self-governing India. But the Indian National Congress was not unduly impressed. Some thousands of captured Indian soldiers, under Subhas Chandra Bose, were already undergoing training with the Japanese with a view to joining in the expected invasion of India. In this situation Congress could not lightly agree to support the British in resisting an enemy whose forces included their own Indian nationals. The Cripps offer, therefore, had to be an attractive and watertight one. Unfortunately, the British had not grasped how important it was to Congress to avoid a Balkanization of the subcontinent, and Cripps's proposals seemed to allow for the splitting up of India into its provincial territories. In the end Gandhi dismissed the offer as 'a postdated cheque on a failing bank', fully conscious that the proximity of the Japanese would maintain the pressure on the British authorities. As a result, Congress went on to organize the 'Quit India' movement, its last great campaign against the British Raj, and the remainder of the war was a frustrating period of deadlock between Congress, the Muslim League and the new Viceroy, Lord Wavell. Although the British took comfort from the gradual retreat of the Japanese, they lost control internally in the face of Hindu–Muslim rioting, widespread industrial strikes, mutinies in the armed forces, demoralization amongst the police force, and a major famine in Bengal. By 1945 it was unrealistic to expect British power to survive more than a couple of years.

1945: the Labour landslide

Before 1939 British politics had apparently been firmly fixed in the mould established by the National Government in 1931. In spite of a handful of gains at by-elections in the late 1930s there was no obvious indication by the outbreak of war that the opposition was within striking distance of winning a majority. Even after the traumatic events of wartime the political world was thus shocked by the scale of Labour's victory in 1945: almost 48 per cent of the poll and 393 seats, compared to barely 40 per cent and 213 seats for the Conservatives. In fact, the opinion polls had pointed to a big Labour lead since 1943, but such polls were still a novelty. Politicians preferred to rely on intuition and experience, which told them that polls and by-elections represented an ephemeral protest. There was a reliable precedent in Lloyd George's sweeping victory at the head of a victorious coalition in 1918 which pointed inexorably to the return of Churchill to power.

Yet despite the superficial similarities, the circumstances of 1918 and 1945 were not fully comparable. An obvious point for comparison lay in the structural changes in the electorate which affected both of these elections. In 1945 there had been no legal reforms, but since ten years had elapsed since the last election, a considerable number of voters had died and many new ones had joined the registers. One-fifth of electors were voting for the first time in 1945, and subsequent studies suggest that around six out of ten of them supported Labour. This reflected the making of a distinct political generation amongst voters who had been dismayed by the poverty and unemployment of the 1930s and were aroused by the experience of wartime to repudiate those responsible. The turnout in 1945 was much higher than in 1918, which meant that the anti-Conservatism among the troops made itself felt in the ballot box. This was sometimes attributed to the activities of the Army Education Corps and the Army Bureau of Current Affairs, whose bulletins helped to promote debate on topics which tended to reflect badly on pre-war governments. However, the leftward drift in the army would probably have occurred even without such activities.

This highlights a second part of the explanation for 1945. As the party in power before the war, the Conservatives were bound to suffer some blame for the country's unpreparedness, as Asquith's Liberals had done after 1914. However, the effect was compounded by the close association of most leading Conservatives with the appeasement of the dictators; this sharpened the distinction between Churchill himself and his party. Many Tory MPs were exposed for Fascist sympathies, one of them, Captain A.H.M. Ramsay was interned while Sir Thomas More was damned in the press as 'Hitler's Friend'. At the election some Labour candidates printed pictures of Tory opponents embracing Mussolini. 'It was not Churchill who lost the 1945 election', said Harold Macmillan, 'it was the ghost of Neville Chamberlain.' In

Table 15.2 General election results, 1931–51

Year	Conservative		Labour		Liberal	
	Seats	Percentage of vote	Seats	Percentage of vote	Seats	Percentage of vote
1931	521*	60.7	52	30.5	37+	7.7
1935	432**	53.7	158	38.6	21	6.7
1945	213	39.8	393	47.8	12	9.0
1950	298	43.5	315	46.1	9	9.1
1951	321	48.0	295	48.8	6	2.5

* includes 3 National Liberals and 13 National Labour.
+ includes 4 Independent Liberals.
** includes 33 National Liberals and 8 National Labour.

contrast, the pre-war record of the Labour leaders had been blotted out by their prominent, patriotic service as war ministers. Whereas in 1918 many Labour and Liberal candidates had been attacked for being soft on Germany, by 1945 Labour expressed the general feeling that the Nazi regime must be eradicated and that Nazi leaders should be brought to trial for their crimes. As it was impossible to accuse the opposition of lacking patriotism, therefore, Churchill's political position could never be as strong as that of Lloyd George in 1918.

Opinion moves leftwards

The third explanation for the Labour landslide is that the election was fought over different kinds of issues from the 1918 election. In the Great War the British had not been expecting victory in 1918, and the sudden turn of events leading to the armistice in November 1918 meant that the December election had been held while the emotions of wartime remained at their height; voters had by no means readjusted to peacetime politics. In the Second World War, however, the public had begun to take victory for granted by 1942. Over a period of several years thoughts had time to focus on the post-war situation; hence the centrality of the Beveridge Report, for example. By the summer of 1945 the polls suggested that the electorate was chiefly concerned about housing, unemployment and the implementation of Beveridge's proposals – issues on which Labour carried far more credibility than the Conservatives. The party's programme, 'Let Us Face the Future', and its propaganda, 'Ask Your Father', chimed with the public mood and reminded voters they had been let down before in the aftermath of a great war. Labour's policies had not been significantly altered since 1935; what had changed was the public perception of them. In particular the proposals for nationalization had lost their association with extremism. This did not indicate a wholesale conversion to socialism; but it reflected wartime experience in which government was seen to have involved itself in the economy to good effect. As a result, there was relatively little objection to extending into peacetime interventionist policies that had worked well during the war.

The final element in the situation was timing and the tactics of Churchill himself. After Germany's surrender in May 1945, the Labour leadership came under strong pressure to withdraw from the coalition government. Churchill thereupon offered Attlee either a continuation of the coalition until the defeat of Japan or a general election in July. Attlee had no confidence of winning an election because Churchill's popularity was obviously high, the register was out of date, and it was possible that many of the soldiers would not participate. But as he did not wish to split the party he accepted the early election. In the event, Churchill handled the election as if the country was still at war; though it was, the voters showed little interest in the fact. He also relapsed into the tactics of the 1930s, by labelling Labour as a party of extremists unfit to govern, resurrecting the old argument that socialism could never be introduced without some form of autocratic government. But in view of the record of Attlee and his colleagues in office, such attacks carried no credibility. Nonetheless, Churchill's tours around the country became a triumphal progress in many areas, but voters evidently made a clear distinction between him and his party.

In spite of this, Churchill's personal standing almost certainly helped his party up to a point. Labour's lead in the opinion polls had been as wide as 16 per cent, but narrowed to 8 per cent in July 1945. In effect the election had been decisively lost by the Conservatives two to three years before the actual poll, and the campaign only served to modify that a little. The result represented a watershed, for Labour had now extended its reach into many middle-class areas. For example, in London the party won 48 of the 62 constituencies. Elsewhere the remains of nineteenth-century loyalties were swept away; in Liverpool, 8 of 11 seats went to Labour, and in Birmingham, 10 out of 13. In this sense 1945 proved to be the culmination of the ambitions of the MacDonald–Henderson generation of leaders, who had aspired to unite a broad swathe of working- and middle-class people around a programme of social and economic interventionism. This forced the Conservatives into a reconsideration of their past record, and made them more ready to accept some of the goals and priorities of their rivals. The centre of politics had shifted to the left, so that objectives such as full employment and state social welfare became common to the majority of politicians, not the distant expectations of a few idealists.

Further reading

The war is now considered in wider terms than is traditional, including its social impact on the men and British military performance:

John Buckley, *Monty's Men: The British Army and the Liberation of Europe* (2014) – argues that the British military record has been unfairly criticised.

Jeremy Crang, *The British Army and the People's War* (2000)

Max Hastings, *Finest Years: Churchill as Warlord 1940–45* (2009)

Geoffrey Best, *Churchill and War* (2005)

S.P. Mackenzie, *The Home Guard: A Military and Political History* (1995)

For the political impact of the war see:

K. Jeffries, *The Churchill Coalition and Wartime Politics 1940–45* (1991)

Paul Addison, *The Road To 1945* (1975) – a classic analysis of how war experience changed opinion to prepare the ground for the 1945 election.

Robert Crowcroft, *Attlee's War: Second World War and the Making of a Labour Leader* (2011) – high politics approach that emphasizes Attlee's strengths.

Martin Pugh, *Speak for Britain! A New History of the Labour Party* (2010) – shows how Labour managed effectively under a coalition; critical of Attlee as party leader.

Stephen Brooke, *Labour's War: The Labour Party During the Second World War* (1992)

Jose Harris, *William Beveridge* (1977)

Paul Addison, *Churchill: The Unexpected Hero* (2005)

S. Fielding, P. Thompson and N. Tiratsoo eds, *England Arise! The Labour Party and Popular Politics in 1940s Britain* (1995) – emphasises apathy and disengagement among the public.

Paul Ward, *Britishness Since 1870* (2004)

Studies of the impact of war on British people are numerous:

Mark Roadhouse, *Black Market Britain 1939–1955* (2013)

Ina Zweiniger-Bargielowska, *Austerity Britain: Rational, Controls and Consumption 1939–1955* (2000)

Juliet Gardiner, *Wartime Britain 1939–1945* (2004) – enjoyable anecdotes but no analysis.

H.L. Smith, *Britain in the Second World War: A Social History* (1996)

Tom Harrison, *Living Through the Blitz* (1976)

G. Braybourn and Penny Summerfield, *Out of the Cage: Women's Experiences in Two World Wars* (1987)

James Hinton, *Nine Wartime Lives* (2010) – examines nine of the Mass Observation diarists.

Geoffrey Field, *Blood, Sweat and Toil: Remaking the British Working Class 1939–45* (2011)

Alan Allport, *Demobbed: Coming Home After World War Two* (2009)

Angus Calder, *The People's War* (1971)

16

The Keynesian Era

'But this is terrible,' expostulated a diner at the Savoy Hotel in July 1945, 'they've elected a Labour government, and the country will never stand for that.' In fact the Attlee government, backed by 393 MPs and over 48 per cent of the vote, was unusually in tune with the popular mood in the aftermath of war. It has some claim to be the most successful government of the post-1945 period, and arguably of the twentieth century, both because of its record of concrete achievements and because it left the country stronger than it had been when it took over. Traditionally historians have emphasized how far the government fell short of Socialism, but since the 1990s that perspective has changed; it now appears bolder and more ideological by comparison with the retreat of a later generation from Socialism. The new administration had an unusually clear idea of its objectives and how to accomplish them. No fewer than 75 Acts were passed during 1945–6 alone. The ministers also benefited from their experience of administration obtained during the war, and from the quiet efficiency with which Attlee managed his talented Cabinet. The result was the enactment of a programme from which there was to be no major deviation for thirty years. 'Mr Attlee's consensus', as it has been described, commanded the respect of the Conservatives and the loyalty of Labour at least until the 1970s.

Planning and the mixed economy

In 1945 all parties accepted that it would be a mistake to abandon wartime controls rapidly as had been done in 1919–20. It was, of course, a matter for debate as to how many controls should be retained and for how long. But for Labour, the success of wartime policies in mobilizing the nation's resources underlined the efficiency of state control. In the country, food rationing and price controls commanded wide support down to the late 1940s. Import restrictions were also necessary in order to check the shortage of dollars in the immediate post-war years. Investment was another aspect of state interventionism; the Labour government used its powers to promote a regional economic policy to counter the high unemployment in the 'Development Areas'. As a result, 51 per cent of all new factories established during 1945–51 were sited in these regions. Unemployment was never above 2 per cent in the post-war period, a huge improvement over the 1930s; it was this that enabled ministers to manage the huge deficit inherited from wartime. But planning brought other benefits too. From 1947 farmers enjoyed fixed prices for two-thirds of their output. In 1949 the first National Parks were established for Snowdonia, the Lake District and the Peak District. New towns including Basildon, Bracknell, Crawley, Harlow, Hatfield, Hemel Hempstead, Stevenage and Welwyn Garden City were built in the south-east alone.

However there were limitations on the government's ability to plan. The trade unions were never co-operative about the planning of labour resources in peacetime. Instead the government resorted more to moral and political influence to mobilize more workers where needed and to restrain wage claims; as a result, wages rose on average by only 2.8 per cent per annum up to 1949. Meanwhile in 1948–9 a number of wartime controls had been abandoned as unnecessary; the young President of the Board of Trade, Harold Wilson, tried to pre-empt Conservative criticism by announcing a 'bonfire' of controls in 1949. Despite this the government was slow to abandon wartime controls. One legacy from war were the national identity cards. In 1950 one Clarence Willcock refused to produce his card for the police but, when prosecuted, was acquitted by the High Court, a decision that led to their abandonment in 1952.

Nationalization

Against this, however, the government had embarked upon a major extension of state intervention in the form of the nationalization of key industries. This programme began in 1946 with the Bank of England, civil aviation, and cable and wireless, moved on to coal and railways in 1947, electricity, gas, and long distance transport in 1948, and ended in 1951 with the steel industry. With the exception of steel, about which the Cabinet itself was very divided, the takeover by the state engendered little controversy. This was partly because several utilities like gas and electricity were already municipalized. Further, there existed an acceptable model for nationalization in the form of the London Passenger Transport Board. This involved running the nationalized industries through small boards of experts appointed by the relevant minister. The takeover could be justified in terms of national efficiency as much as by socialist ideology, for industries like coal and railways had become seriously run-down under private ownership; the free-enterprise system was clearly not going to provide the investment required, and the former owners were lucky to receive generous compensation for the loss of their wasting assets.

The politician who best grasped the role of the nationalized industries in the context of overall economic planning was Sir Stafford Cripps, who served successively as President of the Board of Trade, Minister for Economic Affairs and Chancellor of the Exchequer. It could not simply be left to the market, especially in the aftermath of a war, to see that scarce resources were sensibly allocated. Unless essential sectors like coal, the railways and steel, upon which the rest of the economy depended, were put on a sound footing, industry as a whole would be held back. In many ways, this limited approach to Socialist economic planning proved to be a success; it enabled the government to boost exports, restrain inflation and maintain full employment simultaneously – a combination of achievements that eluded all subsequent governments. In the years up to 1948 retail prices, for example, rose by only 3.3 per cent per annum, and by only 2 per cent from 1949. Nationalization left about one-fifth of the economy under state control – enough for planning purposes but not enough to undermine free enterprise where it was more appropriate.

There were, however, several flaws in the nationalization programme. By concentrating on obviously failing industries and public utilities, it seemed to set natural limits upon the extension of the policy. There was a strong case for nationalizing consumer-goods industries, like sugar, which operated as virtual monopolies against the public interest. But the government shrank from the political consequences of such a move. In this connection it was probably a mistake to exclude any workers' co-partnership in the state industries. This reflected the arrogance of the bureaucrat-intellectuals of Fabian socialism, who regarded the workers as incompetent, but by creating an unresponsive bureaucratic structure, they denied nationalization a broader base of support in the country.

Devaluation of the pound

The other major factor which weakened the government's capacity to plan the economy was simply the force of events beyond their control. The first Labour Chancellor, Hugh Dalton, inherited horrendous economic problems in 1945. With the end of the war, the lend-lease arrangements came to an abrupt stop. Britain's exports in 1945 stood at only 46 per cent of their

1938 level because of the diversion of resources to war production. The sale of £1,000 million of investments during the war further weakened the balance of payments; altogether, 28 per cent of Britain's wealth had been wiped out. Moreover, the country's liabilities had risen to £3,500 million by 1945.

The first step taken to deal with this situation was to raise a loan of $3,750 million from the USA and $1,250 million from Canada for a three-year transition period while the British economy adjusted to peace. Though a necessary expedient, the loan came with stringent conditions attached. The Americans insisted on making sterling convertible into other currencies, and on the maintenance of stable exchange rates – a practical impossibility. Moreover, the value of the loan was reduced by US inflation and by a movement of the terms of trade against British goods. As a result, Britain suffered a severe dollar shortage by 1947.

However, the government managed to concentrate resources into the manufacturing industries most capable of selling goods abroad such as textiles. As a result, it achieved something rarely accomplished by governments – an export-led boom. Exports increased by 77 per cent between 1945 and 1950 and imports by only 14.5 per cent. This notable success would have been greater but for the diversion of vital labour resources into the armed forces; Labour's defence policy was clearly detrimental to its economic strategy. The other factor that hampered growth was the coal shortage, especially in the winter of 1946–7. The Minister for Fuel and Power, Emmanuel Shinwell, bore the blame for not recognizing the shortage quickly enough, and for failing to divert more coal from domestic use to industry.

However, the recovery of industrial output by 1948 made it appropriate to take another beneficial step – a devaluation of the pound; the growth industries could now take full advantage by expanding exports. In fact, the Labour government was extremely reluctant to do this. All parties regarded devaluation in emotional terms as an unpatriotic act, rather than as a technical adjustment. However, by 1948 the recession in the USA had reduced Britain's dollar earnings, undermined the balance of payments, and thus led to increasing speculation against sterling. Eventually in 1949 the decision was made by Hugh Gaitskell, Douglas Jay and Harold Wilson to devalue the pound from $4.03 to $2.90. This was a perfectly sensible readjustment. It not only improved Britain's balance of payments but in the longer term led to a beneficial trade balance between the dollar economy and the non-dollar world.

However, as the government accepted the conventional wisdom that regarded devaluation as a defeat rather than as rational management, it failed to capitalize on it politically; indeed, the decision set Labour on the course that ended its term in power in 1951. There were several distinct explanations for this defeat. Labour did not, in fact, lose popular support, rather it gained, but Attlee, never an inspiring tactician or party manager, threw away the party's position. Devaluation required a deflationary policy for the last two years of the government's life, but Attlee blundered by holding an early election in February 1950 before the beneficial effects of devaluation had become apparent. The Chancellor, Cripps, astonishingly high principled by later standards, thought it improper to introduce a spring budget just before an election and offered nothing to attract voters. As a result of this mistiming and an improvement in the Conservative vote, the Labour majority was reduced to five at the 1950 election.

The election of 1951

Several further mistakes followed. Hugh Gaitskell, now Chancellor, put excessive strain on the economy by financing a huge rearmament programme, and Attlee, who had now lost his grip, then called a second election in 1951. He should have been replaced by a more vigorous leader who would have held on longer, for with benefit of the economic improvements that materialized in 1952 the government would almost certainly have been returned to office. The second election found the Liberals short of resources; they ran far fewer candidates, allowing the Conservatives to attract much of their vote. The third, and arguably key, factor in Labour's defeat lay in the behaviour of the female vote in 1951. Although women were not congenitally Conservative, there were already indications that they favoured the party, partly because they were, as a group, older than men, but also because they were less subject to the influence of workplace and trade unionism that fostered Labour voting. Moreover, the Conservatives devoted great attention to women as housewives, tapping into their resentment over austerity and food rationing which was tightened in 1946. By contrast Labour continued to be a very male-dominated party insufficiently aware that women had run out of patience with austerity. By overdoing rationing Labour played into the hands of the British Housewives League, a new pressure group designed to mobilize the female vote.

In the event, whereas men backed Labour by 51–46 per cent in 1951, women voted Conservative by 54–42 per cent, which, as they were a majority, was crucial. Despite this, Labour did well by winning 48.8 per cent of the vote which exceeded the Conservatives at 48.0 per cent. However, the first-past-the-post electoral system misrepresented voters' intentions by giving the minority party 321 seats and an overall majority of 17 to Labour's 295. Consequently Labour lost office more by ineptitude than popular will, and at the time it was widely expected to return at the next election.

The welfare state

The creation of the welfare state was the greatest and the most enduringly popular of the achievements of the Labour governments. It involved a willingness by the community to accept responsibility for insuring its citizens against the perils of sickness, unemployment, injury and old age, as well as for providing adequate housing and education. By comparison with earlier state systems, the post-1945 scheme was intended to offer benefits that were comprehensive and acceptable to the entire population without stigma. How far the welfare state provisions actually met this ideal is a matter of debate. Inevitably, the chief architect, Beveridge, left the mark of his Edwardian Liberal creed upon Labour's programme in the form of the insurance principle. There was obviously an element of continuity with interwar policies such as the 1925 pensions scheme and subsidized council housing. But there was also a definite socialist contribution in the work done by the Socialist Medical Association, for example, in promoting the idea of free treatment and unifying the Poor Law, municipal and charitable hospitals into one national hospital system. No doubt, wartime innovation by the coalition government made some impact too, but one can easily exaggerate the continuity. It is unlikely that the Conservatives would have been as radical as Aneurin Bevan in insisting on nationalizing the hospitals, or that they would have given priority to raising the school-leaving age.

The measures that composed the welfare state were enacted largely by two eloquent and effective Welsh politicians, Jim Griffiths and Aneurin Bevan, between 1945 and 1948. Strictly speaking, the Family Allowances Act was already on the statute book when the new government took office. It was, however, an important measure, which brought weekly payments of 5s. for all children, after the first, to nearly 3 million families; it was a cost-effective means of adding to family income where it could do most good by direct payment to mothers. 1946 brought the Industrial Injuries Act and the National Insurance Act. A payment of 26s. for a single person per week was adopted; this represented an increase over existing provisions of 2s. a week for unemployment, 8s. for sickness and 16s. for the old-age pension. This last is a reminder of the major impact of the reforms upon the elderly, who had been chief victims of poverty in the past. In 1948, when the new National Health Service (NHS) came into operation, the whole population enjoyed for the first time free medical treatment, medicines, spectacles and false teeth, and a national system of hospital provision incorporating the various voluntary and local-authority hospitals. Access to medical services was now based upon need, not on ability to pay. Women, whose health had traditionally been neglected because many were not wage-earners and because they sacrificed themselves to their families' needs, gained more than any other section of the population.

How radical was it?

The NHS has been described as the most beneficial reform ever enacted in Britain. However, the welfare programme attracted some contemporary criticism for not going far enough towards the ideal of a welfare state; and conversely, in the 1980s it was regarded by some on the extreme right as having gone too far. Clearly the innovations suffered from some shortcomings. Bevan admitted that housing was not his first priority although 1.35 million new homes were constructed between 1945 and 1951. Pensions were not linked to the cost of living. At first this did not matter while the government held down price rises, but in time the payments began to lag behind inflation. As a result, many people had to apply for National Assistance, which involved benefits assessed after a personal means test. By 1955 over a million people were receiving National Assistance. For socialists it was also a matter of regret that the welfare state failed to create a completely classless system of provision in education and health. Ellen Wilkinson suffered criticism for implementing the 1944 Education Act and leaving public schools intact. However, in 1945 no great political pressure had been generated to remove the private sector, and it was not until 1951 that Labour became committed to 'comprehensive' schools. In fact there was a good deal of Labour support for the traditional grammar schools, and the new system, based on the eleven-plus examination, did in fact facilitate the passage of many able working-class children into higher education. Wilkinson's other achievement was to raise the school-leaving age from 14 to 15. In health provision, the doctors were allowed to continue in private practice while working for the NHS, and a number of 'pay-beds' were retained in public hospitals. This compromise resulted from the resistance Bevan encountered from the vested interests of the medical profession. As in 1911, the British Medical Association played an obstructive role; as late as 1948 doctors were, by a margin of eight to one, opposed to working the NHS system. But as Bevan said, 'I stuffed their mouths with

Table 16.1 Defence and social services expenditure as a percentage of central government expenditure

Year	Defence	Social services
1890	44	10
1913	54	22
1924	19	27
1930	16	40
1937	32	34
1950	24	40

gold' thereby winning reluctant co-operation. The maintenance of a private sector introduced an element of inefficiency which later became serious as private medicine expanded and fed off the resources of the NHS.

From the opposite perspective, some critics claimed that the welfare state was a hugely expensive burden which damaged the British economy in the long term. This was, however, misleading propaganda. Expenditure on health increased from £275 million in 1948–9 to £464 million in 1950–1 because of extra staff, the cost of drugs and rising demand. This was about five times the 1938 level but simply signified that a great deal of ill-health had previously gone untreated with damaging effects on the economy. Any genuine audit of welfare policies would have to include some assessment of the economic gain from a more fit and healthy labour force. After 1948 a number of studies of the NHS were undertaken including American ones and all concluded that it was a more efficient way of spending money on health than the reliance on private suppliers. Other welfare spending such as family allowances were also cost-effective ways of relieving hardship. When the famous Rowntree study of poverty in York was repeated in 1950, the conclusion it reached was that only 2.77 per cent of the working class suffered from poverty. If the welfare state did not abolish poverty altogether, it represented the most effective single campaign against it.

Table 16.2 Registered unemployment in Great Britain, 1940–70

Year	Number registered unemployed
1940	963,000
1945	137,000
1950	314,000
1955	232,000
1960	360,000
1965	329,000
1970	579,000

Finally, it is important to remember that any suggestion that state welfare expenditure got out of control has no basis in fact. Beveridge himself had prepared his programme on the basis that it would be sustainable provided that unemployment did not exceed 8.5 per cent; beyond this the costs of welfare would be excessive. The government aimed to meet this requirement by using Keynesian techniques to maintain a high and stable level of employment. It succeeded in this. In 1947 unemployment was only 1.6 per cent, and indeed, it rarely exceeded 2 per cent in the post-war period; to a large extent the people paid for their welfare. Nor did the government neglect economic considerations in order to meet its social objectives. It deliberately ensured that resources went into the construction of new factories at the expense of hospitals, schools and house-building, for example. In any case, the level of welfare payments in the 1940s was far from generous, hence the resort to National Assistance. It was not long before other European states developed more costly welfare programmes than Britain, but their liberal provisions did not appear to damage the economic efficiency of countries like West Germany and Sweden. The Labour Chancellors of the Exchequer, Dalton, Cripps and Gaitskell, were all rather severe about keeping expenditure within bounds, rather more so than their Conservative successors, who beguiled voters with giveaways before elections in 1955 and 1959. The most obvious sign of this was the imposition of charges on false teeth and spectacles in 1951 by Gaitskell. In fact, the money actually saved in this way was negligible, and since the decision precipitated the resignation of Aneurin Bevan and Harold Wilson it was scarcely worth the trouble it caused. However, if this showed poor political judgement on Gaitskell's part, it indicated his determination to keep tight control over welfare spending.

The politics of consensus

The experience of a coalition government in mobilizing national resources for the war effort had helped to generate a broadly based consensus in British politics by 1945. Something similar had appeared during the First World War, but that had been a superficial and ephemeral mood. The post-1945 consensus reflected enduring agreement about the substance of the main social and economic policies. Moreover, controversies over constitutional issues had largely disappeared after declining since 1914. The nearest Attlee's government came to a constitutional issue was the decision to trim slightly the House of Lords veto by allowing the Commons to overrule the peers by passing a disputed bill in two sessions rather than three.

Limitations of consensus

Despite this the parties did not agree on everything. There were five major areas in which Labour and the Conservatives adopted the same approach. First, the welfare state was consistently respected. Second, full employment was accepted as a legitimate and central aim. Third, the mixed economy, involving a much larger state sector than before 1939, became an established fact. Fourth, it was considered that the participation of the trade unions by consultation and conciliation was as necessary in peacetime as it had been in war. Fifth, it is often forgotten that the fundamentals of foreign, defence and imperial policy were also common to both parties in this period. This involved commitment to NATO, the nuclear deterrent, the gradual run-down of Empire, and enthusiasm for the Commonwealth. The external dimension is a reminder that the consensus was not simply a matter of concessions by the Conservatives; for, if they moved to the left in social and economic policy, Labour moved to the right in external affairs.

The idea of consensus is, of course, somewhat embarrassing to partisans of both the main political parties who felt obliged to enthuse supporters by making aggressive speeches from time to time. Naturally there are some qualifications to be made about consensus. It does not imply complete agreement and there were differences in detail and in priorities between successive governments. Nor does it mean that the *whole* of each party embraced consensus policies. In the Labour ranks there were those who campaigned against nuclear weapons; while on the Conservative side a right-wing section was to form the League of Empire Loyalists in protest against their leaders' decolonization policies. There was clearly more opposition to consensus policies among rank-and-file Tories than among the parliamentary elite; however, as the right-wingers were largely excluded from office by Churchill, Eden and Macmillan the critics enjoyed little effective leadership.

Table 16.3 British governments, 1945–70

1945–50	Labour	(Clement Attlee)
1950–51	Labour	(Clement Attlee)
1951–55	Conservative	(Winston Churchill)
1955–56	Conservative	(Anthony Eden)
1956–59	Conservative	(Harold Macmillan)
1959–63	Conservative	(Harold Macmillan)
1963–64	Conservative	(Sir Alec Douglas Home)
1964–66	Labour	(Harold Wilson)
1966–70	Labour	(Harold Wilson)

Conservatives and consensus

The main test for the consensus view of post-war politics consists in the response of the Churchill government after its return to power in 1951. It is easy to be misled by the party rhetoric designed to rally the activists by exaggerating the difference between the two parties. Labour freely predicted a return to extreme and divisive policies if Churchill regained office while Conservative propaganda tempted voters with 'good red meat' after years of austerity, proposed to 'set the people free', and described Britain as a 'socialist state monopolizing production'. Yet the reality was more prosaic. The new government cut income tax a little and reduced subsidies on food; it continued the abolition of controls begun by Harold Wilson; it moved more resources into house-building, and it spent less on defence. But when all these are added together they made no more than a marginal difference, at most, to the Labour programme. In the 1970s, when the supporters of Margaret Thatcher investigated the record of the Churchill Cabinet, looking for a truer Conservatism, they were rapidly disillusioned with what they found. Churchill's party pledged itself to full employment. It made no attempt to dismantle the welfare state; in fact, by 1955 the real value of pensions and other benefits had increased since 1951. There was no denationalization except in steel in 1953 and road haulage in 1954, industries about which Labour itself had been rather uncertain. It was thus scarcely surprising that at the 1955 election Labour found some difficulty in attacking the Tory government. Both parties were beginning to find themselves in the position of claiming not that they would make fundamental changes, but that they would manage the existing policies more competently than their rivals. By 1951 Labour had already moved the emphasis of its economic policy away from planning and physical controls towards Keynesian management. Hence the famous characterization of the policies of Hugh Gaitskell and R.A. Butler as 'Butskellism' by *The Economist*. Butler cheerfully accepted the Keynesian label for himself, while Gaitskell was to be active, if unsuccessful, in attempting to remove the famous Clause 4, which committed Labour to state ownership of the means of production, from his party's constitution. The most important indication of the shift in Labour thinking was Anthony Crosland's *The Future of Socialism* in 1956. In this he argued that capitalism had been reformed, and that governments enjoyed sufficient means of control over the economy without resorting to further measures of nationalization.

Why did the Churchill administration sustain the consensus? One reason is simply fear of the electoral consequences of rejecting it. 1945 had been a shock, and the party appreciated that it would not have been returned to power if it had proposed to undo Attlee's reforms; Labour had won more votes than the Conservatives in 1951, and was thought likely to recover power at the next election. The second explanation is that many of the new ideas had already influenced Conservatives since the 1930s. After 1951, men of the liberal or 'one-nation' Tory school, like Butler and Macmillan, achieved high office, while another generation of progressives, including Reginald Maudling and Iain Macleod, was being advanced via the party's research department. Under its director, Butler, the department produced fresh statements of party thinking, notably *The Industrial Charter*, designed to educate the rank-and-file and bury the legacy of the 1930s. Third, Churchill himself was responsible for consolidating consensus politics within the party. As an old man still basking in the role of wartime leader of the nation, he doubtless wished to avoid spending his last years as Prime Minister beset by controversies; he wanted to promote peace and reconciliation. Moreover, Churchill, married to a good Liberal, had never entirely forgotten his Edwardian record as a Liberal social reformer. By marginalizing the right-wing critics and promoting the conciliatory figures to ministerial posts, he helped to ensure the continuation of one-nation Toryism for some years, under the premierships of Eden and Macmillan. The latter was a pronounced liberal who had advocated state interventionism on unemployment throughout the interwar period. As housing minister Macmillan made his reputation by presiding over the construction of 300,000 houses annually in 1952, 1953 and 1954. As premier he determined 'to keep the Tory Party on modern and progressive lines' and followed an interventionist and Keynesian line in the later 1950s and early 1960s when prices and incomes policies came into vogue. But the ultimate proof of the Conservative attitude was its use of state resources. In 1950, under Labour, government expenditure accounted for 39 per cent of gross national product; by 1960, after nearly a decade of Conservative rule, the figure stood at 41 per cent. The post-war consensus had been sustained, and was to survive into the 1970s.

The affluent society and the stagnant society

For most British people the 1950s and 1960s were decades of rising living standards and an expanding economy. To a considerable extent this reflected developments outside the control of British governments. From 1952, the winding down of the Korean War contributed to a resumption of economic growth and facilitated a reduction in British defence expenditure. R.A. Butler's 1953 budget set the tone by taking 6d. off the standard rate of income tax. Britain benefited greatly from the rapid expansion in economic activity in the Western world generally, particularly as a result of the reduction in trade barriers by the General Agreement on Tariffs and Trade and the development of the European Economic Community. The terms of trade also moved in Britain's favour, thereby enabling her to consume more of her own output at full employment. Finally, British industry was, by 1951, well placed to take advantage of the improved conditions, as a result of the diversification of manufacturing under the stimulus of the war and the concentration of resources in manufacturing under the Attlee government. Attlee's successors, Churchill, Eden and Macmillan, led administrations dominated by pragmatic, conciliatory Conservatives, anxious to keep on the right side of public opinion and re-establish their credentials as a party of government. This concatenation of domestic political motives and broader economic forces made the period one of unusual affluence. Throughout the years 1945–69, unemployment hardly ever touched 3 per cent, and then only briefly, typically standing at 2 per cent or less. Inflation was on average 4 per cent per annum in the 1950s and 1960s. Average money wages rose from over £8 in 1951 to over £15 per week in 1961. By comparison with the high unemployment of the 1930s, and of the 1980s, this was unquestionably a golden age for the British people.

Consumerism

Naturally enough, the further the war receded, the more the population demanded access to consumer goods and an end to sacrifice and austerity. The Conservatives were quick to exploit this mood and consistently promoted consumerism by relaxing credit and lowering taxes during the 1950s. Hence Macmillan's famous claim in a speech at Bedford: 'Let's be frank about it. Most of our people have never had it so good.' However, the underlying explanation for higher spending on consumer luxuries lay in the capacity of the economy to generate extra unskilled and part-time jobs for women, thus making possible the rise of the two-income family. As a result this period saw a huge increase in the number of motor cars from 1.5 million in 1945 to 11.5 million by 1970 when more than half of all households possessed one. Shopping patterns were transformed following the appearance of the first supermarket in Croydon in 1950; by 1960 there were 367 supermarkets, 3,000 by 1967 and 5,000 by 1972. Leisure time became dominated by television; the proportion of the population with a set rose from 4 per cent in 1950 to 82 per cent by 1960, while cinema audiences collapsed by over two-thirds. Another conspicuous sign of affluence was the fashion for foreign holidays, particularly in Spain, though this was still more a middle-class habit; whereas in 1955 Britons took just 2 million holidays abroad, by 1971 they enjoyed 8 million. But perhaps the most conspicuous form of private consumption was housing though this was not new; by 1939 home-ownership had risen to 35 per cent, compared to barely 10 per cent in 1914, and it continued to grow, reaching 59 per cent by 1981. The new Churchill government and the flamboyant Housing Minister, Harold Macmillan, deliberately made housing a priority. The 1950 Conference had pledged the party to build 300,000 new houses a year. In 1953 this target was reached when 318,000 were built, though four out of five were local-authority homes for rent, not sale. Nonetheless, the 1950s saw a major expansion of building societies which offered cheap mortgages, so that home-ownership came well within the reach of many working-class families; 35 per cent of manual workers were buying their own homes by 1959, in effect making a reality of the Conservatives' aim of creating a 'property-owning democracy'.

Table 16.4 Motor cars produced in Great Britain, 1948–85

Year	Motor car production in thousands
1948	500
1960	1,353
1965	1,722
1970	1,641
1975	1,648
1979	1,479
1985	1,311

Table 16.5 Private motor cars in use in Great Britain, 1945–85

Year	Private cars in use in thousands
1945	1,487
1950	2,258
1955	3,562
1960	5,526
1965	8,917
1970	11,515
1978	14,069
1985	16,453

What was wrong with British society?

Yet this mood of optimism was qualified by contemporaries who identified some serious flaws in British society. It was in 1953 that A.J.P. Taylor coined the phrase 'The Establishment' to define the narrow circle of men governing Britain incompetently. Another reason for scepticism was that the rising living standards of the 1950s and 1960s were by no means justified by the record of the British economy. Annual rates of economic growth averaged around 2.2 per cent, which were, in historical perspective, respectable, but well behind those of other Western countries: 4.6 per cent in France and 4.9 per cent in West Germany. Symptomatic of the need for modernization was the £68 million loss made by the railways in 1960 which resulted in the notorious report by Dr Richard Beeching. The result was a reduction of rail track from 18,000 miles to 12,000 miles and of stations from 7,025 to 3,002 between 1961 and 1969, with the loss of 160,000 jobs.

The governments of this period enjoyed an advantage over their predecessors in possessing Keynesian techniques for moderating the pattern of booms and slumps in the economy. However, two things detracted from this advantage. One was the incompetence of the advice given by the Treasury over a long period; its data and forecasts were so unreliable that governments found themselves reflating the economy when unemployment was about to fall, or deflating when it was about to rise. The second general problem lay not in the Keynesian methods as such but in the systematic misuse of them by a succession of Conservative Chancellors for political purposes. The first guilty politician in this series was R.A. Butler who pursued an erratic economic strategy influenced heavily by the fact that the government had a small majority and a Prime Minister (Churchill) whose powers were obviously failing. When Eden took over in the spring of 1955, he capitalized upon his own novelty by holding a general election in May. Butler's April budget lowered taxes and thus helped the Conservatives to extend their majority to a comfortable 70 seats. But Butler's blatant election giveaway simply boosted consumer spending, stimulated inflation and weakened the balance of payments; after the election the boomlet had to be dampened down – the start of what was to be a depressing stop/go pattern in the economy.

Eden's short premiership was chiefly notable for the Suez affair which abruptly ended the comfortable, soporific mood of the early 1950s by introducing deep and bitter divisions into politics. The Suez crisis was widely credited with reviving the Labour opposition under Gaitskell and alienating much of the intellectual middle class from the Conservatives, to the benefit of the Liberal Party. However, the impact seemed rather ephemeral at the time. This was partly due to the diplomatic skill of Eden's successor, Harold Macmillan; but it also seems likely that Suez affected only the politically aware minority. Initially 37 per cent of the public supported the invasion and 44 per cent opposed, but patriotic opinion soon rallied and most voters showed little concern about the immorality of their government's policies; as the 1959 election suggested they were more interested in material matters.

However, Suez proved to be a turning-point in that it brought home to the politicians the extent of Britain's decline as a world power, especially her economic weakness. In 1957 Britain suffered a big fall in her gold and dollar reserves and a £500 million balance-of-payments deficit. Suez also destroyed Eden and, by bringing Macmillan to power, helped to accelerate a readjustment in British policy. Macmillan initiated three shifts of considerable long-term importance: he began serious economies in defence spending in 1957; he appointed Ian Macleod to accelerate the policy of decolonization; and he made the first British application to join the EEC in 1961. In all this Macmillan played with great skill the classic role of the twentieth-century Tory leader, in gently but firmly trying to educate his party to accept the adjustments necessary now that Britain was no more than a second-rate and declining power. Macmillan's smooth Edwardian style, and his shrewd forays on the international stage, helped him to soften the blow and minimize the right-wing reaction. In a famous phrase, Lord Salisbury denounced Iain Macleod, the reformist Colonial Secretary, as 'too clever by half', which may not have helped his career, but amounted to a mere expression of frustration that the party was so firmly in the hands of liberal-minded Tories.

Despite this Macmillan was an old-fashioned premier. Thirty-five of his eighty-five ministers were his own relations, including seven of sixteen Cabinet members! In domestic affairs he showed himself stronger on style and presentation than on substance; he gave way too easily to short-term electoral pressures. By 1957 it was clear that incomes were rising much faster than output, and the Chancellor of the Exchequer, Peter Thorneycroft, wanted to check inflation by holding expenditure for 1958–9 down to the level of 1957–8. He warned the Prime Minister: 'With relatively few assets and large debts, we continue to live upon the scale of a great power.' However, ministers in charge of the spending departments unanimously opposed the proposed check on their programmes, and Macmillan conspicuously sided with them against his Chancellor. Eventually Thorneycroft resigned along with his junior ministers, Nigel Birch and Enoch Powell, the first shots in the battle for monetarist policy in the Conservative Party.

Macmillan suavely dismissed the whole episode as 'a little local difficulty', and proceeded to put pressure on his new Chancellor to come up with more tax cuts with a view to preparing the scene for an election. Both the 1958 and 1959 budgets included some tax cuts, the latter to the tune of £370 million, the largest single giveaway ever recorded. The British voters were once again lulled into a false sense of security by all this. With the memory of 1956 safely expunged, they returned Macmillan with an increased majority of over 100 at the 1959 general election. But by 1960 the precariously contrived boom had collapsed; excessive credit and spending produced inflation and increased imports which the Chancellor felt obliged to curb by raising the bank rate to 6 per cent.

Poor economic performance

As a result of the erratic and opportunistic economic policies of the 1950s, something of a reaction set in around 1960. Critics emphasized that economic growth was much faster in the countries of the European Economic Community than in Britain. But they also began to look more deeply into British politics for explanations. A typical critique of this period was Michael Shanks's *The Stagnant Society* (1961), which identified the rigidity of the social-class system as central to the problem; this resulted in poor industrial relations and insufficient opportunities for people of ability, but low social origins, to rise to positions of influence. By comparison with the successful West German economy Britain experienced more friction between employers and workers. Critics argued that the level of strikes, survival of restrictive practices, and wage-driven inflation seriously hampered the output and efficiency of British industry and dated these problems to 1951, when Churchill deliberately appointed the conciliatory Walter Monckton as Minister for Labour with instructions to avoid antagonizing the unions. In major strikes in the public sector, such as the 1954 railway dispute, the government frequently intervened, or appointed an inquiry which invariably led to the concession of the unions' demands. Churchill firmly closed the door to any legislation designed to interfere with picketing, the closed shop or the political levy. On the other hand, it is easy to exaggerate the unions' responsibility. Wage demands were driven by inflation, often arising out of government policies; when union leaders tried to restrain the pressures, they could be undermined by shop stewards and unofficial strikes. Also, the employers as a group showed very little capacity to put industrial relations on a sound footing; they failed to follow the German example by instituting co-partnership schemes designed to break down the barriers between workers and management. Both the main political parties were bereft of constructive ideas in this area.

Industry in general suffered from poor productivity due to inadequate investment, which was already an established feature of the British economy. Governments did little to help; indeed, by diverting excessive resources into house-building, and by providing financial inducements to take on large building society mortgages, they exacerbated the drift of investment into housing at the expense of manufacturing industry. In addition the banks and the City of London continued to play an unhelpful and inadequate role in industry. Those companies that invested heavily in long-term research and technological improvement tended to find their share value marked down by the stock market while conversely a short-term bid for profits at the expense of training and investment was rewarded with rising share prices. In this area, market forces could not be relied upon to promote the national interest.

The governments of the period clearly weakened the productive economy by their concentration on short-term expedients. They invariably found that full employment led to inflation, an inflow of imports and a balance-of-

Table 16.6 Trade union membership and strikes, 1950–72

Year	Trade union members in millions	Strikes	Working days lost in millions
1950	9.3	1,339	1.4
1951	9.5	1,719	1.7
1952	9.6	1,714	1.8
1953	9.5	1,746	2.2
1954	9.5	1,989	2.4
1955	9.7	2,419	3.8
1956	9.7	2,648	2.1
1957	9.8	2,859	8.4
1958	9.6	2,629	3.4
1959	9.6	2,093	5.2
1960	9.8	2,849	3.0
1961	9.9	2,701	3.0
1962	9.9	2,449	5.8
1963	9.9	2,068	1.7
1964	10.2	2,524	2.2
1965	10.3	2,354	2.9
1966	10.2	1,937	2.4
1967	10.2	2,116	2.8
1968	10.2	2,378	4.7
1969	10.5	3,116	6.8
1970	11.1	3,906	10.9
1971	11.1	2,228	13.5
1972	11.3	2,497	23.9

payments crisis. This put pressure on the exchange rates, because investors rightly judged that in view of the weakness of the economy there was a danger of a devaluation, and sold sterling accordingly. Every British government, however, chose to regard devaluation as anathema. In order to avoid it, they repeatedly raised interest rates and imposed a dose of deflation to dampen consumers' demand for imports. But these measures undermined manufacturing industry by adding to its costs, deterring investment and making long-term planning difficult. The maintenance of the pound as a major international currency thus became a serious handicap as industry's interests were sacrificed to maintain it. By 1961 Macmillan had accepted that the best way of attaining sustained economic growth and the exports that had eluded Britain was to enter the European Economic Community and share in its buoyant economy; but this aim was not achieved until 1973, by which time it was too late to arrest Britain's decline as a manufacturing power.

In the meantime, the government was impressed by the success of economic planning in France which achieved rapid growth without the problems of inflation. As a result, in 1961 Macmillan strongly backed the National Economic Development Council (NEDC), whose object was to bring together employers, the TUC and ministers to hammer out an agreed strategy; the NEDC set a target of 4 per cent annual growth for 1961–6. The unions, however, refused to co-operate in restraining wage demands. Therefore the Chancellor, Selwyn Lloyd, imposed an eight-month pay pause on the public sector in 1961, and asked employers in the private sector to co-operate. Subsequently he indicated a guideline of 2 or 2.5 per cent for wage settlements, on the understanding that they would be matched by productivity agreements. These efforts at imposing a policy for prices and incomes did have a measure of success. However, by 1962 the stop/go cycle had attracted a great deal of criticism of the government as a result of the increase in unemployment. In 1963 Lloyd was replaced as Chancellor by Reginald Maudling, whose preference for a Keynesian expansionist policy was reinforced by the need to prepare the ground for a general election in 1964. Yet with rapid inflation and a balance-of-payments deficit that was to reach £800 million, there was a strong case for dampening down consumer spending. In the event the election was postponed until the last possible moment, and Maudling made yet another irresponsible bid to expand consumers' spending power for fear of losing votes. The result was to exacerbate the balance-of-payments problems and to bequeath to his successor an unavoidable dose of deflation. It was a depressing conclusion to 13 years of missed opportunities.

Adjusting to decline

The three successive election defeats suffered by the Labour Party in the 1950s inevitably created a mood of pessimism and frustration on the left of politics. In fact the party's loss of votes was modest, from 48.8 per cent in 1951 to 43.8 per cent in 1959, but magnified by the electoral system. But it began to appear that Labour was too old-fashioned in the eyes of the electorate, too closely associated with the unpopular trade unions, and insufficiently in touch with the aspirations of a property-owning democracy. For a time, a fashionable thesis held that much of the working class had been seduced by the consumerism of the 1950s and now aspired to middle-class aims and values, among which was Conservative voting. However, this analysis did not survive serious investigation, which showed that the marginal shifts by affluent working-class voters were ephemeral and that there was no real change in class allegiance.

However, Labour devoted much effort to diagnosing its problems. After the 1955 election, an investigation into party organization pointed to the drop in individual membership since 1952 and the lack of professional agents, especially in the marginal constituencies. Little had been done to remedy the deep seated failings of the party organization. Labour also devoted much time to internal controversies between left and right, though this was largely a personal fight between Nye Bevan and Hugh Gaitskell. These divisions were mismanaged by Attlee who failed to give Bevan the promotion he deserved to both the Exchequer and the Foreign Office. The movement was also split over nuclear weapons culminating in the 1960 conference vote for unilateral disarmament, a humiliating defeat for Gaitskell and further proof of his unsuitability as leader.

The rise of Harold Wilson

However, Labour's gradual decline was interrupted by short-term political factors in the early 1960s. First came the untimely death of Hugh Gaitskell and his replacement by Harold Wilson. Though admired and respected as a man of intellect and integrity, Gaitskell had proved to be a poor tactician, unduly rigid, and a divisive leader. He became embroiled in major internal controversies over the removal of the socialist commitment in the party's constitution and over unilateral nuclear disarmament. However, from 1963 Harold Wilson brought a very different style of leadership. He had an exaggerated reputation as a left-winger, largely because he had resigned along with Nye Bevan in 1951 over NHS charges; but this reassured the left, who were more co-operative in the 1960s than they had been, especially as Wilson promoted their leading figures. In fact Wilson showed himself a very pragmatic politician, whose chief formative influences were his Liberal background and his wartime civil service experience. He succeeded in conciliating the various interest groups within the party and in maintaining a degree of unity throughout the 1960s. Indeed Wilson became the most successful leader of the opposition in the twentieth century. He cultivated the press very successfully, took advantage of the difficulties of the Macmillan government, and deftly exploited the pervasive concerns about British national security during 1963–4 and the feeling that Macmillan's government was old-fashioned and out of touch. Macmillan himself was panicked by bad opinion polls in 1962 into sacking a third of his Cabinet, which only undermined his credibility.

The atmosphere of suspicion about security in official circles began in October 1962 with the resignation of an Admiralty clerk, John Vassall, who was convicted of spying for the Soviet Union; this led to the resignation of the responsible minister. Then in 1963 it became known that another of the many traitors within the Foreign Office, Kim Philby, had fled to the USSR. In June came the resignation of the Secretary of State for War, John Profumo. He had had an affair with a call-girl, Christine Keeler, who had also been involved with a Russian diplomat, Captain Ivanov. The intrinsic importance of this affair by no means justified the sustained public debate that it generated, for there was no significant threat to British security. But Profumo had lied to the House of Commons and the Prime Minister had been made a fool of. The political effect of the Profumo affair was thus to keep the government on the defensive for a long time and to demoralize Macmillan, who appeared to be seriously out of touch.

Wilson undoubtedly presented a fresh and more attractive image than either Macmillan or his extraordinary successor, Sir Alec Douglas Home, who renounced his peerage in order to become premier, though it was only convention that a Prime Minister sat in the Commons. Many observers, then and since, gave great emphasis to Wilson's proposals to exploit Britain's scientific and technological skills in order to rejuvenate the economy. But the British voters were little interested in science and much more impressed by Wilson as a middle-class provincial who reminded them that he, too, had a mortgage to pay. In the event Wilson won the much-delayed election in October 1964, but with a majority of just three. This result has been described as 'one of the major upheavals of British democratic history'; but it is difficult to see the basis for this claim. The real significance of the 1964 election is that, in spite of all their problems since 1961 and in spite of the very favourable publicity won by Wilson himself, the Conservatives almost *won*. Labour's share of the vote rose fractionally from 43.8 per cent in 1959 to 44.1 per cent, with the Tories on 43.4 per cent.

Economic decline

In economic affairs the Wilson premiership showed a striking continuity with that of his Conservative predecessors. Economic growth rates during 1964–70 averaged 2.7 per cent per annum, respectable but much inferior to the record of Britain's rivals. As before, spurts of growth were regularly interrupted by balance-of-payments deficits and speculation against the pound; since Britain lacked the reserves necessary to defend the currency, there was mounting pressure for devaluation and futile deflationary policies on the government's part. As in the 1950s, wages rose faster than output. So, too, did public expenditure which absorbed an extra 5 per cent of gross domestic product by 1970. This reflected the new government's determination to raise benefits for needy groups like pensioners and to offer rate rebates to the very low-paid. But the Exchequer also came under financial pressure because of the steady increase in the number of elderly people in the population and the need to provide higher education for the post-war generation now reaching their late teens.

The Labour government inherited a serious problem in the shape of a balance-of-payments deficit of £800 million. This presented the Cabinet members with an opportunity to cut themselves free from the mess into which their predecessors had fallen by a quick devaluation of the pound. Wilson, however, was highly conservative, and seems to have been influenced by the political effects of the 1949 devaluation; he refused to countenance the idea. Instead James Callaghan, the Chancellor, opted for surcharges on imports and increases in taxation. However, this only led to a run on the pound and the raising of the bank rate to 7 per cent. In this way the new government swiftly destroyed the hopes for economic growth, and condemned the country to a phase of deflation and stagnation in order to maintain the value of the pound. This proved to be a crucial error from which the government never fully recovered. It was, moreover, a failure, since devaluation could not, ultimately, be avoided. The strategy made nonsense of the elaborate scheme that had been prepared for a major new ministry, the Department of Economic Affairs. It produced a grandiose National Plan which projected economic growth of 25 per cent during 1964–70. But this was window-dressing, for the plan had no teeth and was, anyway, torpedoed by the key decisions about defending the currency made in the Treasury. The new department served the purpose of setting the Prime Minister's chief rivals, Callaghan and George Brown, in competition with one another, but was of little practical relevance to the economy. It demonstrated that Wilson enjoyed the same skills of manipulation and presentation as Macmillan, but had little appetite for getting to grips with underlying economic problems.

The Wilson government was also unlucky in taking office at a time when it came to be realized that neither the welfare state nor full employment had eradicated poverty in Britain. A 1965 study by Peter Townsend and Brian Abel-Smith identified an underclass who had been by-passed by affluence. Between the mid-1950s and early 1960s poverty had increased from 8 per cent to 14 per cent. Much of this was attributable to the low level of old-age pensions and the failure of 3 million elderly people to claim the means-tested extra payments to which they were entitled – a hangover from the Victorian reluctance to rely on the state. Initially Wilson tried to help the poor by increasing pensions and widows' benefits, by abolishing prescription charges and by repealing the 1957 Rent Act and restoring rent controls. But thereafter the deflationary policy made things difficult.

Devaluation

During 1965 and 1966 the government sought to defend the pound by invoking the support of the USA. In September 1965 the Prime Minister

Image 11: Oliver Smedley, businessmen and politician, campaigning against entry into the EU, 1967.

reached a secret agreement with President Johnson under which, in return for American backing, Britain would resist pressure to devalue and would maintain her costly role east of Suez. To this extent British policies were dictated by the American president. Johnson also demanded active British involvement in the Vietnam War. Though Wilson drew the line at this, he continued to support American policy in South-east Asia. This humiliating deal simply locked Britain into two doomed strategies, external and internal, and ultimately damaged the government's standing at home. It meant that when there was a modest improvement in the balance of payments in 1966 which created favourable circumstances for a planned devaluation, Wilson again missed his opportunity. However, he was primarily influenced by political calculations and at the end of March 1966 he held the long-expected general election, which transformed his tiny majority into one of 98.

After this high point in the life of the Labour government, its central policies collapsed and it went into a prolonged decline up to 1970. The worsening of the balance of payments in 1967 led James Callaghan to raise the bank rate to 7 per cent again and impose a massive dose of deflation on the economy. This failed to defend the weakened currency, and in November the pound was devalued from $2.80 to $2.40. Once again a stubborn refusal to make timely adjustments had resulted in a panic devaluation and, more seriously, had led government to inflict prolonged stagnation upon the economy. Economic weakness also forced the government to abandon its east-of-Suez role and cut defence generally at this point. Moreover, Britain's second application to join the EEC in May 1967 was summarily rejected in November. To add to the problems, Labour now began to lose by-elections, even in very safe seats, both to the Conservatives and to the Welsh and Scottish Nationalists.

By the later 1960s the failure of Harold Wilson to fulfil high expectations on the economic front led much of the Labour Movement to rebel over other aspects of policy. His handling of the rebellion by white settlers in Rhodesia, who had illegally declared their independence in 1965, was a case in point. The rebels were fearful of direct British intervention, and would have backed down before a threat of military action. Wilson, however, disastrously undermined his position by letting the Rhodesian regime know that he would never resort to force. Instead, he imposed economic sanctions which he claimed would bring down the regime in weeks if not months. In fact the rebellion survived the sanctions comfortably. Wilson had been playing safe with the British public, who were not interested in the issue, but at the price of antagonizing many in his own party.

Even more divisive was Wilson's pro-American line in Vietnam. Foreign policy became far more important than economic issues in left-wing politics in the later 1960s, and by 1968 a large anti-war movement had emerged in protest at the destruction of life by the massive American force in South-east Asia, especially the use of CS gas. The anti-war movement was co-ordinated by the British Council for Peace which was overtaken in 1966 by the Vietnam Solidarity Campaign which advocated victory for North Vietnam. In March 1968 25,000 people gathered in Grosvenor Square to march on the American embassy, and 100,000 in October that year. But although Wilson dissociated Britain from American bombing of oil deposits in Hanoi and refused to send troops he dared go no further, thereby alienating a whole generation of young radical activists. They were driven outside the Labour Party into extraparliamentary pressure groups, while the disillusion and dismay within the constituency organizations resulted in a collapse of voluntary work for the party.

Trade union reform

The culminating failure of the Wilson premiership was the mishandling of trade union reform in 1968. It had become part of the conventional wisdom that the economy was hampered by excessive strikes. But although the number of working days lost did increase from the 1950s to the early 1970s, Britain was not unduly strike-prone; the rate of strikes was 50 per cent higher in France, three times as high in Italy and four times as high in America for example. However, Wilson, who had come to the Labour Party via Oxford and the civil service, had no base in the organized working-class movement. In 1964 he had tried to build bridges between government and unions by making Frank Cousins, leader of the Transport and General Workers Union, a Cabinet minister. But in 1966 Cousins resigned in protest against the introduction of the Prices and Incomes Board. Like many union leaders, he refused to countenance any legal interference in wages and industrial relations. Nonetheless, in 1968, when the report of Lord Donovan's Royal Commission on trade unions appeared, Wilson determined to act. He felt, correctly, that the public was beginning to blame union militancy for Britain's economic difficulties, and would probably support a bold move by the government. The new Secretary of State for Employment and Productivity, Barbara Castle, prepared an ironically titled white paper, *In Place of Strife*, in January 1969 in which she proposed to empower herself to require unions to hold pre-strike ballots of their membership, to insist on a conciliation period of 28 days before a strike took place, and to impose a settlement where an inter-union dispute led to an unofficial strike; an Industrial Board was to be set up to fine those who contravened the new rules.

The trade unions would have been wise to accept these proposals but they reacted with shock and anger. Yet the Prime Minister could probably have ridden out the opposition if the critics had not drawn support from both left and right of the party, and from the Cabinet as well as the rank-and-file. Since Wilson had always regarded the parliamentary left wing as the key prop to his leadership, he was very reluctant to alienate it over the white paper, and he had become paranoid about threats to his leadership from right-wingers, notably Roy Jenkins and James Callaghan. Up to a point he was justified as Callaghan deliberately used the issue to reinvigorate his fading career by making himself the unions' champion in Cabinet; he cynically argued that trade union legislation ought to be left to the Conservatives. Not surprisingly, the party's National Executive rejected the government's proposals by 16 votes to 5, and the Chief Whip advised that he would be unable to guarantee a majority in the Commons. In these circumstances Wilson accepted a humiliating defeat and dropped the proposed legislation. This was not the only such setback in 1969 as the government also abandoned its bill to reform the House of Lords under the pressure of internal opposition led by Michael Foot. It began to appear that in spite of its large majority the government was unable to govern.

At the Exchequer, meanwhile, Roy Jenkins imposed a stern deflationary strategy. His 1968 budget had taken £900 million out of the economy in indirect tax rises, and had imposed a 3.5 per cent maximum on wage increases. The 1969 budget continued the deflationary line, and by the autumn the balance of payments had greatly improved. However, all this was achieved at the expense of economic growth; Labour's original hopes of breaking out of the stop/go economy had come to naught. Wilson was misled by the improvement in Labour's standing in by-elections, local elections and opinion polls during the winter of 1969–70 into thinking that he could win an election in the spring. But when Jenkins failed to provide an electioneering budget the party was doomed. Consequently the Conservatives returned to office at the 1970 election in which the turnout dropped to 72 per cent. This was a sign of the apathy and disillusion amongst Labour supporters, who no longer saw the purpose in returning their party to power.

Although Harold Wilson managed to return as Prime Minister in 1974, he attracted a high level of criticism as Prime Minister incurring blame from both right and left. The younger generation of 1960s radicals experienced the high hopes and then the disappointment that Wilson aroused. On the other hand the right looked back to his premiership as part of the decadent phase of Keynesianism. It must, however, be remembered that by comparison with, say, the Thatcher governments of the 1980s, Wilson achieved a modestly impressive record in terms of higher economic growth, lower unemployment and a stronger balance of payments, though his greatest achievements lay in the field of education and social reform. Even sympathetic biographers found it difficult to exonerate Wilson on three charges. First, despite being technically better qualified to manage the economy than any other twentieth-century premier, he made major misjudgements and failed to arrest Britain's economic decline. Second, he gave way to the prevailing conservatism in his party and missed the opportunity to begin the modernization of the political system. Wilson largely failed to capitalize on the Fulton Commission's report on the civil service or on Richard Crossman's enthusiasm for reforming the House of Commons, and the attempt at updating the Lords was abandoned. Third, in spite of his considerable skill in managing the Labour Party and keeping it united, Wilson left it seriously demoralized, and consequently vulnerable to the lurch to the left which was to condemn the party to the wilderness from the end of the 1970s.

Challenges to the political system

One of the chief differences between Victorian-Edwardian politics and the twentieth century was the decline of the great debates over constitutional and electoral reform. After the House of Lords controversy of 1910–11 and the resolution of the suffrage question in 1918 and 1928, the parties largely neglected such topics. When Labour won power in 1945, there was little they wished to change in the system of government; to some extent, wartime experience in office and the feeling that the civil service was on their side strengthened the party's natural conservatism. Even the fact that Labour lost office in 1951 despite winning more votes than the Conservatives failed to stir interest in reform of the electoral system. On its return to power in 1964 the party showed itself to have become absorbed into the Establishment; it had no ambitions to implement fundamental change, aspiring instead to make the existing system work. As a result only two reforms of any importance occurred in the post-1945 era. In 1958 Macmillan introduced life peerages, a shrewd way of propping up the existing hereditary chamber which was an extraordinary anachronism in the second half of the twentieth century. The other change came in 1969, when Labour lowered the voting age from 21 to 18, thereby enfranchising 3 million extra voters. But this occasioned nothing like the debate which had traditionally attended a reform of the franchise.

The emasculation of Parliament

In these circumstances the parliamentary system in Britain suffered a prolonged decline during the entire period from the 1940s to the 1990s. Admittedly some features of this decline, such as the tightening grip of the party whips, had been evident since the 1880s. But by 1945 back-bench MPs were treated as obedient lobby-fodder, and a government, even with a small majority, was very rarely in danger of being defeated. The extensive use of patronage in the form of ever-increasing ministerial posts was one way of emasculating potential rebels. But in any case MPs were poorly equipped to do their job. Salaries remained low, working facilities very poor, and few were able to carry out the research or gain access to the information that would have been necessary to criticize government policies effectively. Parliament had, in fact, largely ceased to perform its traditional role of checking on government expenditure; debates on the estimates had deteriorated into largely ritual occasions for general political discussions.

Ministers increasingly took advantage of delegated legislation which, in effect, empowered them to take decisions without the need for parliamentary approval. When the Attlee government created the nationalized industries, it practically excluded any detailed parliamentary criticism on the grounds that this would impede efficiency. Both Attlee and Churchill kept the decisions over the development and testing of atomic weapons secret. Later in the 1950s, when the nuclear energy plant at Sellafield (Windscale) in Cumbria suffered a major accident which resulted in the widespread release of radioactivity, it was kept secret by Macmillan. But these were exceptional examples. More typically, governments presented Parliament with decisions too late for them to be effectively scrutinized. The worst area was defence, in which the government allowed itself to be regularly overcharged by the industries supplying its weapons and machinery. It rarely exercised any effective control over schemes to design and produce new aircraft. The development of the supersonic airliner, Concorde, was the classic case of a very costly piece of technology which never found a market sufficient to justify the huge investment of taxpayers' money.

Yet Parliament was by no means the only institution which became more decorative than functional. The Cabinet found itself increasingly reduced to rubber-stamping policies, as power concentrated around the Prime Minister. Although the actual power of the Prime Minister remained, as always, subject to the vagaries of events, especially on the economic front, and his influence seemed to fluctuate according to the temperament and aims of each incumbent, nonetheless there was a definite tendency for government to become more prime-ministerial. It became normal for each premier to retreat into a clique of personal advisers, and to introduce new policies through carefully controlled Cabinet committees. They also made increasing use of the press and television to strengthen their position. Attlee was, in this respect, the last of the old-style premiers who took little trouble with the media. But to later prime ministers such as Macmillan and Wilson, the manipulation of the media was a key factor in their retention of power. It became normal for them to leak information – for which others were liable to be prosecuted – in order to promote their policies or to undermine their rivals and opponents. Moreover, finding that Britain's economic problems were intractable, premiers increasingly succumbed to the temptation to cut a figure on the international stage, where it proved easy to earn plaudits and bolster their domestic prestige even though very little was accomplished. On the whole, the press and television acted as willing tools of their self-promotion strategy.

The Campaign for Nuclear Disarmament

Frustration with Parliament as a spectacle resulted in some important issues being debated outside under the aegis of pressure groups and protest movements. From 1958 the consensus among the main parties on the nuclear weapons policy came under attack by the Campaign for Nuclear Disarmament (CND). This was triggered by the events of 1956 and 1957, notably the Suez crisis and the Soviet invasion of Hungary, but it really reflected the conviction that the conventional politicians were too negative to be able to save Europe from an impending conflict. Though a classic middle-class, intellectual pressure group in its origins, CND rapidly reached far beyond this to mobilize a large section of British society. Its annual marches from Aldermaston in Berkshire to London became a major feature of the political year. In due course CND became divided between those who wished to remain above party politics and those who saw Labour as the best vehicle for achieving their aims. The triumph of the supporters of unilateral nuclear disarmament at the 1960 party conference marked a high point; that year was CND's peak with 100,000 gathering at Aldermaston. However, only 33 per cent of the public favoured disarmament and the Gaitskellite leadership soon overthrew the disarmers by mobilizing the votes of the trade unions. As a result, by 1961–2 CND suffered a decline, though it showed a capacity for revival during the next 20 years. After the resolution of the Cuban Missile Crisis in 1962 and the signing of the Test Ban Treaty in 1963, CND lost more of its momentum, but its supporters turned their attention to the campaign against American intervention in Vietnam. These peace-and-war issues were largely responsible for drawing university students into political activity in this period, and they also gave a stimulus to the emerging Women's Liberation Movement which regarded war as the peculiar result of a male-dominated political system.

Women's Liberation

During the 1950s the organized women's movement dwindled, the death of Eleanor Rathbone in 1946 symbolizing the passing of Edwardian feminism. The one significant achievement came in 1954–5 when R.A. Butler was persuaded to introduce equal pay for female teachers and civil servants. However, after this success the Equal Pay Campaign Committee dissolved itself, reflecting the assumption that there was insufficient support to extend equal pay to the private sector. This was consistent with the continued failure to make a political breakthrough; in 1945 just 24 women MPs were elected, and the total was still 27 by October 1974. The political parties treated feminist issues as marginal and ignored women members; for example, the efforts of Eirene White, one of the few feminist MPs, at divorce reform in the 1950s were frustrated by the Labour governments. The rising generation of women politicians, Barbara Castle, Shirley Williams and Margaret Thatcher, devoted themselves to mainstream party questions, assuming that they would marginalize themselves by concentrating on women's issues.

However, by the later 1960s and 1970s these politicians found themselves overtaken by a younger generation of university-educated, career-minded women with high expectations who launched Women's Liberation. On the fiftieth anniversary of female enfranchisement in 1968 they noticed how little had been achieved; although Wilson appointed four women to his Cabinet they felt that parties, like all organizations, became hierarchies dominated by men. Consequently Women's Liberation reflected disillusionment with the post-1964 Labour government, the experience achieved in the peace movement and a wider rejection of Parliament and the political parties; it took the form of devolved, localized groups and workshops from which men were often excluded. The movement was part of a wider rebellion common to educated youth in Western societies, though there were differences, the British being more pro-Socialist than the Americans. In Britain, 1960s student radicalism was a pale reflection of the activities in France and America, partly because the student body was still so narrow that the wider society felt less interest in its university oriented grievances.

The initial goals of Women's Liberation included equal pay, equal education, free contraception, abortion on demand and 24-hour free child-care. There were some differences between Socialist feminists who regarded marriage as another form of class oppression and radical feminists who condemned patriarchy and male violence, and argued that women should control their own sexuality. The movement also promoted the study of women's history both by amateurs and professionals and generated new publishing houses including Virago Press and The Women's Press and magazines including *Shrew* (1969) and *Spare Rib* (1972). Some tracts were published, notably Germaine Greer's *The Female Eunuch* (1971) which sold a million copies, hugely extending the influence of feminism. Among feminism's achievements were abortion reform (1967), the Equal Pay Act (1970) and the Sex Discrimination Act (1975). However, the absence of a national leadership and an effective parliamentary foothold handicapped the movement and as a result there was some shift in tactics in favour of electoral involvement, though this did not bear fruit until the elections of 1987 and 1992.

Liberal revivalism

During the 1960s the Labour–Tory dominance that had reached a peak in the 1950s began to be undermined in several directions. The Liberals had reached their nadir in 1951–5, ironically at a time when the influence of two great Liberals, William Beveridge and J.M. Keynes, was at its height. However, a turning-point came in 1956 with the election as leader of Jo Grimond, who abandoned the hopeless post-1931 role as a liberal-Conservative party in favour of its traditional progressive and radical brand of politics. The combined effect of the Suez crisis, stop/go economic policies and the high cost of mortgages attracted much fresh support from the Conservatives although most Liberal activists were more pro-Labour. A by-election victory at Torrington in 1958 was the party's first win for thirty years. It was eclipsed in 1962 by an even more dramatic gain at Orpington, a Kent suburban constituency. The Liberals built on this to re-enter local government, winning hundreds of seats in the early 1960s and re-establishing their organizational base. They also made a major impact on the political agenda with their advocacy of British entry into the European Union when the other parties were dragging their heels, devolution for Scotland and Wales, and reform of the House of Lords and the rating system. But although polling three million votes in 1964 the party won only nine seats, and twelve in 1966. It suffered from lack of money, neglect by the media, the first-past-the-post electoral system which left it hugely under-represented, and policies that made minimal impact on a materialist electorate. However, this was the first of a series of Liberal revivals that left the party steadily stronger.

Scottish and Welsh nationalism

During the 1950s Scottish and Welsh issues had barely figured on the political agenda. The welfare state and full employment satisfied most voters, thereby consolidating the Union, while the English, sustained by victory in the war, remained largely complacent about the political system and took their national identity for granted. Influential Welsh Labour politicians such as Bevan were contemptuous of nationalism and strongly centrist in their approach to government. But as a result Parliament had become increasingly out of touch with nationalist sentiment in Wales and Scotland and Labour's electoral domination led it to take them for granted, though it did create a Secretary of State for Wales on returning to power in 1964. However, as unemployment grew in the early 1960s and companies shifted their headquarters to south-east England the economic rationale for the Union with England began to lose credibility.

Yet since the foundation of Plaid Cymru in 1925 and the Scottish National Party in 1934 self-government had attracted the support of only a tiny minority. The conventional politicians were therefore completely taken by surprise by events in the mid-1960s. In 1964 the Liberals had already captured several Scottish highland seats by capitalizing on the sense of neglect felt by these far-flung districts. In both Wales and Scotland, the long-term decline in the regional economy and the tendency to suffer much worse unemployment than the south of England underlay the revival of nationalist support. Both Labour and the Conservatives had become remote, Westminster-based parties whose economic policies were failing. In Wales, opinion had been stirred by the decline of the Welsh language and by the flooding of several valleys to provide water for English cities. The nationalists managed to exploit the growing volatility of the electorate at by-elections notably in 1966 when Gwynfor Evans captured a Labour seat at the Carmarthen by-election; this was followed in 1967 by an even more dramatic upset in the Lanarkshire seat of Hamilton, when a large Labour majority fell to Winnie Ewing, the Scottish Nationalist. In local elections from 1968 onwards, the Scottish Nationalists made large inroads into Labour support in the central industrial belt where organizational decline and complacency had left it vulnerable to a populist challenge. Thus, although both Nationalist parties lost their by-election gains at the 1970 general election, their revival was a lasting achievement, for they capitalized on their advances to pressurize Westminster to recognize the demand for devolution in the 1970s.

Further reading

General accounts:

Paul Addison, *No Turning Back: the Peacetime Revolutions of Post-War Britain* (2010)

K.O. Morgan, *The People's Peace 1945–1990* (1992)

D. Kavanagh and P. Morris, *Consensus Politics* (1989)

David Dutton, *British Politics since 1945* (1992)

Analyses of Labour politics:

K.O. Morgan, *Labour in Power 1945–51* (1984)

R. Pearce, *Attlee* (1997) – a critical view that contrasts with the usual unqualified praise.

John Campbell, *Nye Bevan* (1987)

Peter Hennessey, *Never Again: Britain 1945–51* (1992)

Ben Pimlott, *Harold Wilson* (1992)

R. Coopey, K. Fielding and N. Tiratsoo eds, *The Wilson Governments 1964–70* (1993)

Clive Ponting, *Breach of Promise: Labour in Power 1964–70* (1989) – uses documents in President Johnson's papers to expose Wilson's deals with the Americans.

Lawrence Black, *The Political Culture of the Left in Affluent Britain 1951–64* (2003)

N. Thompson, *Political Economy and The Labour Party* (1996)

J. Callaghan, *Socialism and the Labour Party since 1884* (1990)

On the Conservatives see:

John Ramsden, *The Age of Churchill and Eden 1940–57* (1995)

Paul Addison, *Churchill on the Home Front 1900–55* (1992)

John Turner, *Macmillan* (1994)

David Dutton, *Anthony Eden* (1997)

D.R. Thorpe, *Supermac: The Life of Harold Macmillan* (2011)

M. Francis and I. Zweiniger-Bargielowska, *The Conservatives and British Society 1880–1990* (1996)

On the economy:

N. Crafts and N. Woodward eds, *The British Economy since 1945* (1991)

R. Millward and J. Singleton, *The Political Economy of Nationalization in Britain 1920–1950* (1995)

B.W.E. Alford, *British Economic Performance 1945–75* (1988)

Andrew Gamble, *Britain in Decline* (1986)

S. Pollard, *The Wasting of the British Economy* (1982)

G.C. Peden, *British Economic and Social Policy: Lloyd George to Thatcher* (1985)

On living standards and welfare see:

Rodney Lowe, *The Welfare State in Britain since 1945* (1993)

Ina Zweiniger-Bargielowska, *Austerity in Britain* (2000)

N. Timmins, *The Five Giants: a Biography of the Welfare State* (1995)
Charles Webster, *The National Health Service: A Political History* (1998)
D. Gladstone, *The Twentieth-Century Welfare State* (1999)
J. Benson, *The Rise of Consumer Society in Britain* (1994)

Critics of the system are discussed in:
Bruce Lenman, *The Eclipse of Parliament* (1992)
Michael Shanks, *The Stagnant Society* (1963)
R. Taylor, *Against the Bomb: the British Peace Movement 1958–65* (1988)
D. Bouchier, *The Feminist Challenge* (1983)
Martin Pugh, *Women and the Women's Movement in Britain since 1914* (2015)
B. Harvie, *Scotland and Nationalism* (1994)

17

The Permissive Society

By contrast with her economic failures, Britain enjoyed a notable success in cultural affairs during the 1960s. Her role as a world leader was captured when *Time* magazine hailed London as 'The Swinging City'. British achievement and self-confidence were especially conspicuous in music, fashion, design, photography, architecture and even in sport when England won the World Cup in 1966. Moreover, despite the association between cultural achievements and rebellious youth, it is easy to exaggerate the extent to which the arts became alienated from the Establishment. In many ways, not least because of its commercial success, cultural vitality became a cause for national pride. During the 1960s Britain generated a wealth of new novels, films and musical styles, while her theatres flourished and her television was widely regarded as the world's best. Newspapers alone experienced something of a decline as the middle-market press was emasculated by the growth of the disreputable tabloid papers; the demise of the *News Chronicle* in 1961 and the sale of the *Daily Herald*, which ended up as the *Sun*, left the national press politically unbalanced and intellectually enfeebled. The outstanding successes of the younger generation were the popular music industry, led by The Beatles and the Rolling Stones, and the design and fashion industry, which produced models like Jean Shrimpton, the clothes shops of Mary Quant, and the home furnishings of Terence Conran's *Habitat*. There was also a classless, or more accurately a working-class, quality to these cultural achievements which seemed to reflect a wider breakdown of Victorian class barriers. In 1963 cricket finally abolished the distinction between amateur (unpaid) and professional (paid) players, while in 1968 Wimbledon ceased to be a competition confined to amateurs.

The young achievers were symbolically embraced by the British Establishment in 1965 when Harold Wilson awarded MBEs to The Beatles. Like many of the successful performers of this era, The Beatles wrote their own music and were consequently taken more seriously than earlier singers.

Initially popular music had found its main outlets in off-shore, 'pirate' radio stations, but eventually these were closed down and replaced by BBC Radio One. A mixture of jazz, rock and roll and protest songs, the popular music of the 1960s had an almost universal appeal to Western youth, so much so that in May 1965 nine out of the ten top places in the American charts were occupied by British recordings. In that year political recognition of success in the arts was marked by the creation of a new Ministry for the Arts under Jennie Lee. A widely acknowledged success, Lee managed to increase the subsidies dispensed by the Arts Council from £3 million in 1965 to £9 million by 1971.

This record is a corrective to the impression that British society exhibited the symptoms of outright rebellion against conventional behaviour during the late 1950s and 1960s. Admittedly rebelliousness characterized a distinct generation of 'baby-boomers' who were born in the 1940s and brought the term 'teenager' into general use in the 1950s. Their revolt is usually explained in terms of a reaction by people who had been cushioned by material prosperity and thus felt able to reject adult society by developing alternative ideals. This was also a generation that had no direct experience of war, that benefited from the ending of national service in 1960, and that became more influenced by what seemed an impending nuclear catastrophe. It was also a secular generation as church attendance fell by half in the 1960s. Finally, the young were reputedly hedonistic in behaviour and liberal in their moral ideas. In fact, the rebels against bourgeois society were largely middle-class people whose protest took the form of Aldermaston marches and a counter-culture involving drugs. However, youth culture was made possible by affluence; by the early 1960s youth expenditure had reached £800 million a year. Teenagers as consumers attracted a good deal of market-research revealing that in 1959 they spent 20 per cent of their money on clothes, 17 per cent on cigarettes and alcohol, 15 per cent on coffee and sweets and the rest on entertainment. This resulted in the formation of several groups distinguished by their dress, music and general behaviour. During the 1950s 'Teddy Boys' acquired a reputation for violence, much encouraged by panic reporting in the newspapers. 'Rockers' rode motor bicycles and wore leather, while 'Mods' were more fastidious, fashionable and upwardly mobile.

On the literary front the so-called 'Angry Young Men' reacted against both the materialism of the consumer society and the political elite, discredited in the aftermath of the Suez crisis of 1956. Foremost among them were John Osborne, author of *Look Back in Anger* (1956), the theatre critic Kenneth Tynan and John Braine, who wrote *Room At The Top* (1957). By the early 1960s they were overtaken by an even greater irreverence towards authority in the shape of the political satire of the fortnightly *Private Eye* and, in 1962, the BBC revue *That Was The Week That Was*. Perhaps the greatest triumph for literary liberalism came in connection with the censorship of books and plays on grounds of obscenity traditionally implemented either by prosecution in the courts or by the Lord Chamberlain. In 1960 Penguin Books found itself up on just such a charge for publishing a paperback version of D.H. Lawrence's novel, *Lady Chatterley's Lover*, which had been officially proscribed since the 1920s. But the case exposed vividly the shift in attitudes that had occurred since that time. At one point prosecuting counsel notoriously demanded: 'Is it a book you would wish your wife or servants to read?' The jury lost little time in returning a not guilty verdict. As a result the role of the Lord Chamberlain was undermined and by 1968 it had been phased out altogether.

Liberal reform

The spirit of innovation that produced the characteristic economic and welfare reforms of the late 1940s did not initially extend to social and moral issues as the leading personnel of both main political parties were fairly conservative in their attitudes as was society generally, perhaps reflecting a backlash from wartime promiscuity. A stigma was still attached to sex outside marriage, to non-heterosexual sex and to divorce. Divorcees were not invited to royal garden parties, and Princess Margaret was forced to choose between marrying a divorcee, Group Captain Townsend, and renouncing her claim to the succession. Significantly, however, the public sympathized with her. Similarly, when the Archbishop of Canterbury, Geoffrey Fisher, told the Mothers Union that a real family must have at least three children, he underlined how out-of-touch the Anglican Church was becoming. Even in Parliament the 1945 generation of members gradually diluted the conservatism of the older politicians, though the tipping point did not come until 1966 and the return of a new Labour government with a majority of ninety which presided over major reforms of the law on capital punishment, divorce, abortion and homosexuality.

The myth of the 'permissive society'

However, there was nothing inevitable about social reform in the 1960s; but for the appointment of a comparatively liberal Home Secretary, Roy Jenkins, in 1965, few of the measures would have been enacted. Labour had made no mention of such reforms in its manifestos and regarded them as marginal at best. Consequently legislation relied on backbench

Image 12 Deptford teenagers sport the latest fashions, 1974.

initiatives, not on the government. At the grass roots Labour was still influenced by the traditional Nonconformist moral code, while Conservative politicians, though often personally liberal, were scared of the hostility of their local members to social reform. In 1964 the outgoing Tory Home Secretary made it illegal to cultivate cannabis, and Labour subsequently made no attempt to repeal the legislation. Conversely it has been argued that permissiveness pre-dated 1964, though the only definite evidence is the Conservatives' 1960 Betting and Gaming Act which legalized betting shops and gaming clubs.

Moreover, although the period was dubbed 'The Permissive Society' by a later generation of reactionaries who deplored the progressive changes of the 1960s, at the time the public was far from liberal. Wilson had said that homosexual law reform 'would cost us six million votes'. Whereas traditionally most people saw homosexuality as a sin, by 1963 93 per cent considered it an illness to be treated medically. Throughout the post-war period the Labour MP Sydney Silverman had regularly introduced bills for the abolition of capital punishment, but at least 60 per cent of people consistently supported hanging while only 23 per cent backed abolition in 1964. This reminds us that the reforms of the 1960s were unquestionably the achievement of an enlightened minority in the face of public conservatism.

In 1900 there had been 312 murders in Britain and the figure remained close to that right up to the 1960s. The case for abolishing capital punishment was threefold: it was seen as morally wrong for the state to take life; there was a danger of convicting the innocent; and the death penalty was not an effective deterrent. Up to the hanging of James Hanratty in 1962 Home Secretaries had invariably sanctioned the death penalty, but they grew increasingly uneasy about it. Eventually Silverman's bill obtained a large majority in the Commons, and it became law in 1966 with some assistance from Roy Jenkins. In subsequent years the opponents of abolition, who were conscious that the public still supported the death penalty, promoted further debates on the issue; but the abolitionist majority in Parliament remained large. MPs became increasingly reluctant to reintroduce capital punishment because of a collapse of confidence in the judicial system. Defendants were repeatedly convicted on what had previously been capital offences as a result of false confessions extracted by the police and other discredited types of evidence; it became clear by the 1980s that many innocent people would have been executed but for the 1966 Act.

Abortion was an even more emotive issue which most politicians avoided altogether. Yet very large numbers of working-class women, faced with the ruination of their health by frequent pregnancies and lacking the means to avoid them, sought illegal abortions that frequently resulted in death. Yet since the 1920s only a few organizations such as the Women's Co-operative Guild had been prepared to advocate the legalization of abortion. In the post-1945 period the increase in extramarital sex pushed the issue up the agenda, though, as with the birth-control issue in the 1920s, the political parties were reluctant to adopt a view on a question which attracted the wrath of the Catholic Church. In 1967 a Liberal backbencher, David Steel, used his place in the MPs' ballot to introduce the Abortion Law Reform Bill. This allowed women to obtain an abortion under the NHS within 28 weeks of conception; however, it required the consent of two doctors, which in many parts of the country was not forthcoming. As a result some 22,000 women had legal abortions in 1968, the total rising to 75,000 by 1970 and 128,000 by 1980. Though alarmingly high, the figure stabilized at around this level for some years; moreover, it was appreciated that the change saved thousands of women from the appalling risks entailed in illegal back-street abortions. For this reason the repeated efforts made by anti-abortionist MPs to modify the Act in the 1970s and 1980s were largely unavailing.

The question of homosexuality also came to the fore in this period. Since the Criminal Law Amendment Act of 1885, acts of 'gross indecency' between men had been punishable by up to two years' hard labour. This was the legislation under which Oscar Wilde had been prosecuted. It was in 1957 that the report of the Wolfenden Committee recommended changes in the law so that homosexual acts should not be illegal when committed in private between consenting individuals aged 21 or over. Subsequently the position of homosexuals in society began to be more freely discussed, partly as a result of the establishment of *Gay News* in 1962. In 1967 the Labour MP Leo Abse introduced a bill along the lines recommended by Wolfenden. However, this was an embarrassing issue for politicians. Only a few members such as Tom Driberg were known to be active homosexuals. Conservatives usually adopted particularly hostile attitudes on the subject of homosexual law reform; but this was probably a defence mechanism, whether conscious or otherwise, to divert suspicion at a time when public views were felt to be unsympathetic. In view of the habit of Conservative selection committees of choosing candidates who were unmarried men from public-school backgrounds, there seems little doubt that the Conservatives in Parliament included a relatively high proportion of members with homosexual experience. Whether attitudes began to change as a result of the passage of Abse's bill is hard to say, though 1970 saw the formation of the Gay Liberation Front and the start of a more assertive defence of gay rights. However, the late 1970s saw the ruin of a major political career, that of the Liberal leader Jeremy Thorpe, largely as a result of allegations that he had been involved in a homosexual relationship, and it was not until the 1980s that it become possible for public figures to admit their homosexuality without destroying their careers.

The family and marriage

Post-war discussion about the undermining of conventional behaviour and social institutions has to be seen in the context of the remarkable popularity of marriage for a quarter of a century after 1945. The war itself inevitably disrupted the normal pattern of married life, and during 1941–5 the marriage rate among women fell to 67.6 per 1,000. But war had done nothing to diminish the popularity of marriage. The rate rose to 75.7 per 1,000 during 1946–50, which was higher than the pre-war level, and thereafter it rose progressively, to reach 94.2 per 1,000 in 1966–70. The year 1972 marked the peak, after which a slight decline set in. The pre-1939 trend towards younger marriages was sustained, so that by 1971 60 per cent of all women in their early twenties were married, compared with 25 per cent before 1939.

Pessimists pointed to the increase during this period in the rate of divorce, which had become easier as a result of legal reforms in 1923 and 1938 which had put men and women on an equal footing. But divorce was still rare and not respectable. It was usually achieved only when one partner agreed to be the guilty party so that the other could prove a charge of adultery. Thus as late as 1951 only 7 per cent of marriages ended in divorce, and the reformers felt that couples often remained trapped in unhappy marriages because of their reluctance to admit to adultery. During the 1950s Eirene White MP attempted to introduce a bill to overcome this obstacle, but without success. It was not until 1969 that a new measure was enacted which introduced the principle that where a marriage had broken down it could be dissolved by mutual consent of both parties after three years. By 1974 19 per cent of marriages ended in divorce after ten years. However, this increase was not primarily due to the change in the law, for the rise in the rate of divorce preceded the 1969 Act. It was partly the result of the growth of marriage amongst the very young. But it also reflected the fact that as life expectancy increased, so the period through which marriages had to survive lengthened; before 1914 the typical marriage had been a briefer affair, terminated by the death of one partner.

The other long-term influence upon marriage was the prolonged decline in fertility which had made the two-child family typical by 1939. The Royal Commission on Population which reported in 1949 reflected interwar fears that the growing resort to birth-control techniques would result in a fall in population. This did not occur, but the increase levelled off in the 1970s and 1980s. By 1961 the total UK population had reached nearly 53 million. Low fertility and greater longevity combined to make for an ageing population; whereas in 1939 65-year-olds made up 9.2 per cent of the population, by 1981 they formed 15 per cent.

The key influence on family size was the use of contraceptive methods by 90 per cent of all couples in the 1950s. But because the birth rate was now so much within parental control it became rather volatile and was almost impossible for demographers to predict, though this did not stop them trying, often with unhappy results for government policies. During 1941–5 the birth rate per 1,000 population stood at 15.9, about the same as before

Table 17.1 Petitions filed for divorce in England and Wales, 1946–85

Years	Number of petitions filed
1946–50	194,500
1951–55	160,800
1956–60	137,400
1961–65	188,200
1966–70	284,400
1971–75	608,800
1976–80	812,400
1981–85	884,800

Table 17.2 Contraceptive methods in current use among ever-married women aged 16–40 years, 1970–83 (percentage of age)

Method	1970	1975	1976	1983
Pill	19	30	32	29
IUD	4	6	8	9
Condom	28	18	16	15
Cap	4	2	2	2
Withdrawal	14	5	5	4
Safe period	5	1	1	1
Abstinence	3	1	0	1
Total using at least one method	75	76	77	81
Not using any	25	24	23	19

the war. A dramatic 'baby boom' pushed it up to 18 per 1,000 during 1946–50. Thereafter the rate subsided to its former level, but demographers were surprised when it jumped again to 18.1 in the early 1960s before dropping back to 14.0 during 1971–5. Policies for school- and house-building were hastily modified in response to these fluctuations.

Limited emancipation for women

After the liberating experience of wartime, it might seem paradoxical that most women were keen to abandon employment to take up motherhood and domesticity once again. As a result the 1950s have often been seen as a missed opportunity for women. However, much depends upon what criteria are used to measure women's role and the changes affecting their lives. An interwar feminist like Vera Brittain saw the welfare state as proof of the emancipation of her sex. Moreover, the young women who cheerfully opted for a life of domesticity in the 1950s could expect a more attractive version of married life than their mothers and grandmothers had known. Birth control allowed them to enjoy sexual relations without the perpetual fear of pregnancy; their lives were much less dominated by childbirth; and after child-rearing there was a longer period in which to choose to return to paid employment or pursue other interests.

Women remained the targets of pressure to conform to the conventional roles. The commercial pressures manifested by women's magazines and driven by the need to attract advertising revenue continued to encourage women to devote themselves to the pursuit of consumer goods. As *Woman, Woman's Own* and the new *Woman's Realm* reached a peak in sales in the

1950s, five out of every six women read at least one such magazine each week. The political and religious leaders also urged women to stick to motherhood in the interests of the nation. 'The great majority of married women,' declared Beveridge, 'must be regarded as occupied on work which is vital but unpaid, without which their husbands could not do their paid work and without which the nation could not continue.' For this reason the welfare system was strongly biased in favour of married women; it neglected or discriminated against the woman who was single or separated, and, indeed, the married woman who took paid employment. Governments simply ignored feminist demands that the married but non-working woman should be allowed to claim benefit in her own right independently of her husband. Finally, during the late 1940s and 1950s women's role became the object of a good deal of propaganda by assorted experts who claimed some scientific authority for their views. Typical were Dr Benjamin Spock's famous book on *Baby and Child Care* (1947) and Dr John Bowlby's report, *Maternal Care and Mental Health* (1951). Such work was used to make women feel guilty of neglecting their children if they took paid employment, which was widely believed to lead to psychological problems, juvenile delinquency and crime. As a result of the evacuation of children and the general disruption of family life during the war, many parents were strongly influenced by such scientific propaganda during the 1950s and 1960s.

However, despite all the pressures, increasing numbers of women combined motherhood and employment. A typical post-war rationale for this strategy was expressed in *Women's Two Roles* (1956) by Alva Myrdal and Viola Klein; they saw it as a matter of *duty* for women to raise children and contribute directly to the nation's labour force. Both working- and middle-class women increasingly undertook jobs, often part-time, in order to enable their families to enjoy the higher standard of living now available. This was largely a by-product of the development of the economy rather than the result of pressure from feminists. By 1947 the government, desperate to boost output in the export industries, appealed to women, especially in the 35–50 age group, to return to work. As a result there were 800,000 more women in paid employment in 1947 than there had been in 1939. Subsequently they benefited from an expansion of the light engineering and electrical industries which produced consumer goods using unskilled, production-line methods. The steady growth of the clerical, administrative and lower professional sectors also continued to generate opportunities for women in shops, schools, hospitals and welfare services. As a result, by 1981 45 per cent of women enjoyed paid employment compared to 34 per cent in 1931. The major change was the rise in *married* women's employment.

For many decades only 10 per cent of married women had worked, but the figure rose to 22 per cent by 1951, 30 per cent by 1961, and 47 per cent by 1981.

The rise of an educated society

The neglect of education had been a distinguishing feature of British society throughout the nineteenth century; and in this respect the interwar years had merely continued the tradition. However, after the war the implementation of R.A. Butler's 1944 Education Act went some way towards improving educational opportunity, though it was soon recognized to be inadequate. Basically the Act proposed a system in which children would be transferred at the age of 11 to either grammar, secondary modern or technical schools according to their 'age, aptitude, and ability'. In practice this scheme suffered from several drawbacks. The secondary modern schools, which actually catered for about three-quarters of all pupils, had no clear purpose at all. Moreover, very few technical schools were ever built. As a result Britain failed, as in the past, to generate the supply of skilled workers that industry needed, in radical contrast to practice in Germany, where most children received vocational training. But the problem was more than a matter of educational policy: in Britain, businessmen largely failed to provide the apprenticeships for school-leavers that were normal in the more successful economies. In addition, the effect of the eleven-plus examination system was stultifying; it led what were regarded as the best primary schools to concentrate narrowly on the mathematics and English needed to pass the examination and to neglect many other aspects of education. Moreover, the number of children who actually passed into the grammar schools was often determined not by the pupils' ability but by the availability of grammar-school places, which varied from one part of the country to another. Above all, the examination at 11 was too early in the pupils' lives; it simply had the effect of channelling middle-class children into grammar schools and excluding many intelligent working-class ones. The overall result was that Britain continued to allow a high proportion of her pupils to drop out of school before they reached higher education. It is true that between the late 1940s and the late 1950s there was a 66 per cent rise in the numbers staying on into sixth forms, but Britain continued to lag behind other comparable countries. As late as 1969 only 13.7 per cent of 17-year-olds were in full-time education, compared to 16.9 per cent in Germany, 36.7 per cent in France, and 75.6 per cent in the USA.

The Labour government of 1964–70 tackled these problems in two ways. By 1962 90 of 146 local authorities had already agreed to go comprehensive so that all children would attend without need for an examination, but in 1965 Anthony Crosland announced an acceleration of the programme. By 1970 30 per cent of children attended comprehensive schools, and after 1970 Margaret Thatcher took it much further by approving all but 310 out of 3,426 schemes for comprehensives. The main flaw in the new system was that in some areas the retention of selective independent schools had the effect of depriving the local comprehensives of some able pupils. However, in spite of much fashionable criticism comprehensives proved to be a considerable success. Far from neglecting examination performance, as traditionalists and some middle-class parents claimed, the comprehensives achieved a steady increase in the proportion of their pupils who passed the GCE 'O' and 'A' level examinations. They were held back largely by the failure of successive governments to put sufficient resources into the recruitment of teachers qualified in foreign languages, sciences and mathematics. The lower pay and status of teachers in Britain by comparison with successful industrial states like Germany and Japan continued to be a crucial weakness in British society through to the 1990s.

The second major achievement of the Labour government was the expansion of opportunities in higher education. In 1939 only 50,000 students attended British universities. Many more possessed the academic qualifications for entry but were barred by lack of financial support and the total was still only 107,000 by 1961. Two sections of the population were especially severely handicapped. Only 3 per cent of the children of the working-class majority reached university. And while 5.5 per cent of boys attended, only 2.8 per cent

Table 17.3 School attendance in England and Wales, 1901–85 (percentage)

Year	12–14 years	15–18 years
1901	41.5	0.3
1911	57.5	1.5
1921	65.8	3.2
1931	73.0	6.0
1938	74.5	6.6
1951	93.1*	12.5
1961	99.1	19.6
1968	100.0	30.0
1976	100.0	36.0
1981	100.0	23.5+
1985	100.0	25.9+

* From 1951 the age group is 11–14 years.

+ These figures exclude students in further education and tertiary colleges.

Table 17.4 Students in full-time higher education, 1900–84

Years	Number of students
1900–01	25,000
1924–25	61,000
1938–39	69,000
1954–55	122,000
1962–63	216,000
1970–71	432,000
1980–81	482,000
1983–84	534,000

of girls did. The economy was being deprived of large resources of talent. However, in 1963 the Robbins Report recommended that university places should be increased to 197,000 by 1967–8 to cater for the post-war 'baby-boomers' who would be ready for higher education by that time. The Wilson government responded by building nine new universities in the 1960s; in addition, from 1966 onwards 21 polytechnics were set up under local authority control. Finally, in 1969 a charter was granted to the Open University which was designed to offer higher education to older students who had missed the conventional route to university but could undertake study by correspondence courses. The other key reform was financial. From 1962 local authorities were required to provide a grant for every student who was offered a place in higher education. But for this subsidy, the expansion would hardly have taken place. As a result Britain had just over 200,000 university students by 1968, which represented 6.3 per cent of the age group. She still lagged well behind her competitors in Western Europe and North America. Nevertheless, taken with the other reforms in schools, the university expansion helped to make education the greatest single achievement of the 1964–70 government. It was an irony that by 1970 that government had become the object of bitter attacks by many of the students who had benefited from its policies.

The reaction

Philip Larkin's famous quip that 'sexual intercourse began in 1963' reminds us what the social reactionaries thought about the period although the permissive society was never the radical turning-point its critics believed. British society remained largely conventional and conservative. Marriage, for example, was still the norm and had still to reach its peak in the early 1970s when a long-term decline set in. Although the Pill was marketed from 1963 onwards, it was not available to single women until 1967, and even the Family Planning Association began to advise unmarried women on contraception only in 1966. By the end of the decade surveys showed that just 12 per cent of people described themselves as tolerant towards homosexuals, far more regarding them with revulsion or with pity. Abortion reform had simply replaced unregulated with legalized abortion as the lesser evil; it had not given women the right to choose. And society was still male-dominated despite the Equal Pay Act; for example, women comprised only 28 per cent of university students by 1970.

Yet even the modest changes achieved by 1960s liberalism generated a backlash against sex outside marriage and the use of drugs especially by the young similar to the moral panics that had accompanied social change in the Edwardian period, in the 1920s and during the Second World War when middle-aged men simply equated behavioural changes with moral decline. These moral panics flourished in the face of evidence that British society had become *more* moral since Victorian times as a result of a massive decline in such traditional vices as prostitution and drunkenness, for example. A typical symptom of the supposed reaction to lower moral standards was the rise of Mary Whitehouse, who regarded the BBC as a source of moral pollution and campaigned to reduce the violence, sex and swearing on television from 1964 onwards. Above all the Profumo scandal generated a huge amount of speculation about moral standards fuelled by the official report by a distinguished judge, Lord Denning, who indulged in irrelevant material about sex-orgies among High Court judges rather than national security. The Establishment struck back by prosecuting an innocent osteopath, Stephen Ward, for living off immoral earnings because he had threatened to expose Profumo for lying to Parliament. One witness, Mandy Rice Davies, when asked by counsel whether she knew Lord Astor claimed to have had sex with her, famously replied: 'Well, he would wouldn't he?' A Labour Home Secretary, James Callaghan, endorsed the fashionable diagnosis saying it was 'time to call a halt to the advancing tide of permissiveness'. In this spirit the government closed down the pirate radio stations and the authorities prosecuted the Rolling Stones for drug use in the belief that they should be made examples of. Meanwhile, the BBC began to censor pop groups for using offensive words and referring to drugs.

Race and immigration

However, by far the main qualification to the reputation of the 1960s as a liberal decade lay in attitudes towards race and immigration. Britain had a long tradition of accepting immigrants, though she had been a net *exporter* of people up to the 1930s. Many of the 190,000 Poles who had fought for Britain in the war opted to stay afterwards. After 1945 governments were content to welcome immigrant labour as a means of boosting the output of the economy. Although the start of the influx is conventionally assumed to be in June 1948 when the SS *Windrush* docked at Tillbury bearing 492 passengers from Jamaica, there were already 75,000 black and Asian citizens living in Britain. During the 1950s large numbers amounting to 36,000 annually came from the Indian subcontinent, notably Punjabi Sikhs, Gujarati Hindus and Muslims from Pakistan. As Commonwealth citizens they enjoyed the right of entry into Britain under the 1949 Nationality Act. In the later 1960s many Asians were driven out of Kenya and Uganda by political persecution. By 1961 the black and Asian population reached had 337,000 and by 1971 650,000, less than 2 per cent of the total. Initially they largely comprised unmarried males who contemplated a temporary stay in Britain. Ninety-four per cent enjoyed regular employment; the immigrants were vital in sustaining public transport in London and many gravitated to towns with buoyant economics including Slough, Leicester, Nottingham and Bradford.

However, the newcomers faced discrimination, especially in housing and employment, and several extremist movements soon began to exploit prejudice towards them on grounds of their colour. In the 1950s Sir Oswald Mosley's Union Movement tried to use anti-immigrant propaganda as his fascists had done with regard to Jews in the 1930s; Colin Jordan organized the White Defence League; and in 1952 a Conservative MP, Sir Cyril Osborne, started a campaign to reduce immigration and repatriate immigrants on the grounds that the newcomers were diseased and criminal, an echo of the Edwardian attacks on Jewish communities in London. This activity conferred some legitimacy on resentment towards immigrants by less well-off English

Table 17.5 Population by ethnic group, 1984

Ethnic group	Population in thousands
White	50,894
West Indian	529
Indian	807
Pakistani	371
Bangladeshi	93
Chinese	109
African	109
Arab	63
Mixed	205

people and the result was a number of violent clashes between the communities in 1958 in the Notting Hill area of London.

Under this pressure governments considered placing limits on immigration, but they feared antagonizing the Commonwealth and appreciated the value of immigration for the economy. It was not until 1962 that the Conservatives introduced the Commonwealth Immigrants Bill; as by this time three-quarters of the public supported restrictions and the economy had become sluggish, reducing the need for extra labour, the political case seemed compelling. Although the Labour Party disliked the 1962 Act, it was handicapped by anti-immigrant prejudice among many of its working-class supporters. However, as an attempt to reduce coloured immigration, the Act proved a complete failure both because it provoked a rush of extra immigrants before it came into force and because it provided for the entry of relations of those already in Britain. This led to the development of complete communities and a larger permanent population.

Moreover the 1962 Act did nothing to reduce racial prejudice. On the contrary, some Conservative candidates felt able to exploit hostility to immigrants in local and parliamentary elections, the most notorious example being Smethwick, a Labour seat in the West Midlands, where the Conservatives defeated the incumbent MP against the national swing in 1964 on the issue. Racialism also gained a degree of respectability from non-political sources at this time, including the popular television comedy *Till Death Us Do Part*, in which routine expressions of racial abuse were associated with patriotic sentiment. 1967 saw the foundation of the National Front (NF), which campaigned for the repatriation of immigrants. Although the NF won only 3.5 per cent of the vote at the 1970 election, it spoke for a wider section of opinion. This was demonstrated by the extraordinary popular reaction to a controversial speech by Enoch Powell in April 1968. An obsessive reactionary, Powell had once advised Churchill that Britain could reconquer India with ten divisions! The 1962 Act had been followed by a party truce over immigration lasting several years, but Powell chose to break the truce by demanding voluntary repatriation, prophesying violence – and in effect legitimizing it – and employing inflammatory language by speaking about 'rivers of blood'; he could not accept that anyone with a black face could ever be British. Polls suggested that anything between 67 per cent and 82 per cent of people supported Powell's view and he became a hero in some working-class communities. Subsequently racists felt able to voice their opinions more openly and there was an increase in violent attacks on black and Asian people.

However, no other leading Conservatives adopted Powell's tactics and the party leader, Edward Heath, sacked him from the shadow Cabinet. The Wilson government had passed a Race Relations Act in 1965 which established the

Race Relations Board, which was strengthened with the Community Relations Commission in 1968. The idea was to give black and Asian people a legal means of seeking redress for discrimination over housing and employment. But Labour was now so fearful of losing votes over the issue that in 1968 Callaghan, then Home Secretary, was instrumental in restricting the entry of Kenyan Asians unless they could demonstrate a 'patrial' tie with a British resident. In effect, primary immigration now ceased and Commonwealth citizens could not enter Britain except on the basis of a temporary work permit. The problem shifted to the widespread racial prejudice within British society against which the legislation seemed ineffective, partly because victims of discrimination thought it a waste of time to complain. By the 1970s and 1980s a growing proportion of the Indian and Caribbean communities were not, in fact, immigrants but had been born in Britain, spoke with English accents and were better integrated into the community through education and popular culture than their parents had been. Many achieved success and prominence as businessmen, sportsmen and entertainers, and some entered local government and Parliament. However, prejudice was slow to disappear, especially among the older generations of white people. Those of Indian and Pakistani origin suffered violent attacks in several cities, while West Indians, especially young males, experienced harassment from the police and often sank into sub-communities dominated by crime and drug dealing.

Further reading

General accounts of the social history:
Mark Donnelly, *Sixties Britain: Culture, Society and Politics* (2005)
A.H. Halsey, *British Social Trends since 1900* (1988)
John Benson, *Affluence and Authority: A Social History of Twentieth Century Britain* (2005)
John Savage, *Teenage: The Creation of Youth Culture* (2007)
David Fowler, *Youth Culture in Modern Britain 1920–1970* (2008)

On morality and reform:
Jeffrey Weeks, *Sex, Politics and Society* (1981)
Frank Mort, *Capital Affairs: London and the Making of the Permissive Society* (2010)
John Campbell, *Roy Jenkins* (2013)
Mark Jarvis, *Conservative Governments, Morality and Social Change in Affluent Britain 1957–1964* (2005) – argues that permissiveness pre-dated 1964.
Callum Brown, *Religion and Society in Twentieth-Century Britain* (2006) – emphasizes the emergence of a popular hedonistic culture and theological doubt.

On women and liberation:
C. Bouchier, *The Feminist Challenge* (1983)
Jane Lewis, *Women in Britain since 1945* (1992)
Martin Pugh, *Women and the Women's Movement in Britain since 1914* (2014)
Elizabeth Wilson, *Women and the Welfare State* (1977)
Elizabeth Wilson, *Only Halfway to Paradise: Women in Post-war Britain 1945–69* (1980)
Sue Bruley, *Women in Britain since 1900* (1999)

On immigration see:
Robert Winder, *Bloody Foreigners; the Story of Immigration to Britain* (2004)
Paul Foot, *Immigration and Race in British Politics* (1965) – account of the 1964 Smethwick election.
Colin Holmes, *John Bull's Island: Immigration and British Society 1871–1971* (1988)
Rosina Visran, *Asians in Britain: 400 Years of History* (2002)

18

The Loss of Great Power Status

In foreign policy 1945 brought no shift to the left. This was partly the result of the wartime experience of the Labour ministers and partly the accident of personality. Post-war policy was dominated by Ernest Bevin as Foreign Secretary and by Clement Attlee, both old-fashioned patriots who remained keen that Britain should retain her status as a Great Power. 'There'll be no messing about with the British Empire,' Bevin reportedly said on entering the Foreign Office. However, these statesmen were the victims of circumstances, in particular the collapse of the wartime alliance and the development of the Cold War. It rapidly became clear that, instead of honouring the commitments given to Churchill at Yalta to allow democracy in Eastern Europe, the Soviet Union proposed to treat the territory as a buffer zone and an economic resource. She was also interested in extending her influence via the Black Sea into the Mediterranean, as had the Tsarist regime in the past. As a result, during 1946 the British government began to regard the Soviet Union as a greater problem than Germany. This came all too naturally to Bevin, whose experience as a trade union leader had left him with a rooted suspicion of Communists. His policy was founded on a belief that Russia intended to capitalize upon the weakness of Western Europe, the withdrawal of American forces, and dissension within the British Empire to spread the Communist revolution. He was therefore alarmed by the reduction in American troops in Europe from 3.5 million to 200,000 between 1945 and 1947, the absorption of President Truman in domestic affairs, and his government's decision to renege on previous undertakings to co-operate with Britain over the development of atomic weapons.

Cold War defence

These worries led the Labour government into several critical decisions in 1947. It decided that Britain should develop her own atomic bomb. This was partly the product of fears that without it Britain would lose status among the Great Powers, and partly a reflection of her vulnerability to Soviet military might; the case for an atomic bomb as a deterrent seemed attractive. The government also extended military conscription – an unprecedented policy in peacetime – which provoked 72 Labour MPs to vote against the government and a further 76 to abstain. As a result Britain had an army 900,000 strong by the early 1950s. Though huge by British standards, it compared with 4.75 million Russian and 3.25 million American soldiers. In effect Britain had embarked on a futile and debilitating policy of keeping up with the two superpowers, both of which were becoming active not only in Europe but in Africa, the Middle East, the Far East and South America. It was unrealistic to suppose that in the long run Britain could sustain such a worldwide role. This is not to deny the sound and even compelling reasons for Britain to maintain sufficient forces to be able to offer the USA serious support; she could hardly be expected to be responsible for defending Europe alone. Indeed, Bevin has won praise from several historians for the vigour with which he maintained British influence in those post-war years.

The Special Relationship

Unfortunately, Bevin adopted too narrow a view of foreign affairs and allowed British policy to be excessively cast in terms of American strategy, which in the longer term meant that Britain missed the opportunity to start readjusting her thinking for the post-colonial era. The Cold War made it all too easy for Britain to be beguiled by the traditional role that she had once enjoyed playing in the world by hitching a ride on the American juggernaut. In the short term Bevin's approach imposed an unnecessarily heavy burden on British public finance and inhibited the economic recovery the government was attempting, with some success, to bring about. Attlee showed more awareness of the dangers of saddling the country with an outmoded worldwide defence role, but the counter-pressure of the Chiefs of Staff and the Foreign Secretary carried the day. The year 1947 proved to be crucial. Impressed both by Soviet expansionism and by British decisions to withdraw from Greece, Turkey, Palestine and India, the USA prepared to step into the vacuum. The following year brought the Marshall Plan and 1949 the foundation of the North Atlantic Treaty Organization. As a result of the Russian blockade of Berlin and the Berlin airlift American aircraft returned to their former bases in East Anglia, and by 1950 the USA had committed four divisions to the defence of Europe. In supporting this initiative Britain steadily increased her own defence spending from £2.3 billion to £4.7 billion in 1951, representing no less than 14 per cent of gross national product.

This policy was seen by its practitioners in terms of a continuation of the 'special relationship' that had grown up during the war. Even at this stage, however, there were a number of causes of friction between Britain and the USA. The American government wished to accelerate the break-up of the Empire, at least in India, to destroy the sterling area and Britain's trading bloc, to deter Britain from the pursuit of an atomic bomb, and to promote the integration of Europe into a single economic unit. Since most of these aims ran counter to British policy, it must be doubted how much scope was really left for a special relationship. Moreover, there was no question of equality in the two countries' relations. Although by 1950 Britain had become extremely vulnerable as a result of her role as the USA's chief base in Europe, and as the point from which American planes carried atomic bombs, there was no real consultation between the two over vital questions of war and peace; even Churchill's return to office in 1951 made no difference in this respect. In a sense Britain had little room for manoeuvre because until her own atomic bomb and her long-range bomber force became available she was entirely dependent on America for her deterrent. In reality, Britain became a client of the USA: 'we are Greeks in this American empire', according to Macmillan. In time the special relationship became as much a matter of domestic politics as anything else. A succession of premiers, including Harold Macmillan, Harold Wilson, Margaret Thatcher and Tony Blair tried to exploit the relationship as a means of boosting their prestige and distracting attention from a record of failure on the domestic economic front. This had the unfortunate effect of inhibiting British governments from rethinking their relationship with their European neighbours and abandoning an essentially anachronistic role in world affairs.

The fragility of the special relationship was amply demonstrated by the war in Vietnam. As co-chairman of the Geneva Conference which brought an end to the war between the French and the Communists in 1954, Britain still enjoyed an independent foreign policy. However, in the 1960s when Labour MPs wanted to reconvene the Geneva Conference to obtain a ceasefire, American Presidents Kennedy and Johnson wished to involve Britain in the renewed war in Vietnam. Johnson simply refused to accept advice from Harold Wilson and demanded the support of British troops, a sign of how hollow the relationship really was. Although Wilson refused troops and dissociated Britain from American bombing in Vietnam in 1966, he was the last Prime Minister to follow an independent British policy.

The costs of the world role

Significantly the return of the Conservatives to power in 1951 saw a reduction in defence spending, a reflection partly of a lowering in international tension and partly of the excessive policies Labour had pursued under Bevin's regime. But the search for independent nuclear weapons continued. In October 1952 Britain tested her own atomic bomb, and in 1954 the government decided to develop the H-bomb, which, according to one Tory MP, Julian Amery, 'will make us a world power again'. Yet the practical significance seemed dubious, for the long-range V-bombers were not expected to be ready until 1955–7. Britain's defence rested ultimately on an American commitment to Europe, but it was politically difficult to recognize the fact. In spite of the economies made after 1951, Britain still devoted 8.2 per cent of her national income to defence in 1955, twice that of Germany. In 1956 Macmillan warned the Prime Minister, Sir Anthony Eden, that 'it is defence expenditure which has broken our backs'. The difficulty lay in the fact that Britain attempted both to become a leading nuclear power and to retain her conventional military role around the world, which eventually proved too costly. France, in contrast, was to demonstrate that it was feasible for a middle-rank power to achieve a genuinely independent nuclear capacity, but only if other defence commitments were reduced accordingly. In Britain the chiefs of the three armed forces enjoyed strong support in the Conservative Party, and lobbied successfully to slow down any cuts. In 1955 even the attempt to reduce national service from two years to eighteen months was defeated.

However, after the Suez incident in 1956 the new premier, Macmillan, his Chancellor, Peter Thorneycroft, and the Defence Secretary, Duncan Sandys, managed to introduce economies in the 1957 Defence White Paper. Conscription ended in 1960 and the army fell from 690,000 men to 375,000. Some troops and RAF forces were withdrawn from Germany. These reforms reflected the ministers' judgement that the economy could no longer sustain such a high defence burden. Increasingly the government justified its nuclear-deterrent policy on the grounds that it offered an economical alternative to conventional defence, and that it was, in any case, unlikely that future wars would involve the protracted use of ships, troops and planes. Britain's needs were thus twofold: a credible deterrent to the Soviet Union, and a modest but efficient force capable of tackling subversion in the Third World.

Yet even this proved a costly and unrealistic option because of the problems involved in delivering nuclear warheads. Already by the late 1950s the V-bombers were obsolescent. A new supersonic bomber perished in the Sandys economies. This left Britain with a new missile, Blue Streak, which was unlikely to be available until 1962–5; as its cost rose from £50 in 1955 to £300 by 1959 the Cabinet decided to cancel it in 1960. In March of that year, therefore, Macmillan visited the USA where the new President, Kennedy, agreed to sell Britain the Skybolt ground-to-air missile which would prolong the life of the V-bombers. In return Macmillan offered the USA a base at Holy Loch on the Clyde for submarines carrying the Polaris missile.

By the 1960s these hand-to-mouth efforts to maintain Britain as an independent nuclear power had become increasingly unrealistic, since she was wholly dependent upon the USA. The rationale for the policy was essentially political: to allay the dismay among Conservative MPs over the palpable loss of Britain's status as a great imperial power. But although Macmillan enjoyed a warm personal relationship with President Kennedy, Britain's true position was cruelly exposed by the Cuban missile crisis in 1962. If the USSR had not backed down and a war had followed, Britain would have been a leading target for Soviet attack. Yet her government was relegated to the sidelines, being denied influence and consultation about the use of American weapons based in Britain. British humiliation deepened in November 1962, when the American government abruptly cancelled the Skybolt programme on which she now depended. Again, the political pressures within Macmillan's party dictated that he should seek another lifeline from the USA, and a reluctant President agreed to provide a Polaris force on the grounds that it had become a 'political necessity' for Macmillan. Yet although the 1963 deal on Polaris was generous financially, it could be sustained only by squeezing the other armed forces, in particular the RAF, which now lost its strategic role to the navy, which did not want the Polaris submarines. However, while politics made it impossible for Macmillan to escape from the anachronistic nuclear policy, he had clearly become alive to the dangers of pursuing the goal of transatlantic interdependence with the USA; partly for that reason he initiated the first steps that were to lead Britain to Europe.

Decolonization

Neither Attlee nor Bevin had any wish to dismantle the British Empire. This was partly for reasons of national status and partly because they believed the standard of living in Britain benefited from colonial relationships. Empire provided markets for British goods and outlets for capital exports. In 1950 47.7 per cent of all British exports went to these territories. However, the new Labour ministers were also realistic enough to see that, as far as certain parts of the overseas territories were concerned, the liabilities had begun to outweigh the advantages. India had been helped half-way to self-government by 1939, and it was impossible to backtrack on the concessions made during the war. In any case, by 1946 the subcontinent was descending into disorder on a vast scale, and the government could not contemplate shouldering the military costs of maintaining the Raj. In fact, no British government ever had been willing to pay; they had never maintained more than a small number of British troops there, and had generally expected Indians to bear the costs. Morally the British had lost the will to rule India by 1939, the war simply accelerated the decision to quit.

What obstructed a final solution was the difficulty of deciding to how many successor states power should be surrendered. Eventually Attlee broke the deadlock by dispatching Earl Mountbatten of Burma as last Viceroy in March 1947, with instructions to hand over control by June 1948 at latest. Similar pressures in early 1947 led the government to renounce other British obligations. In particular, the burden of keeping 100,000 troops in Palestine to be the targets of Zionist terrorism, while Britain vainly tried to balance Israeli demands for free immigration against the Arabs' fears about losing their homelands, was no longer bearable. The Palestine problem was simply referred to the United Nations. Thus by 1947 India and Pakistan had received their independence, to be followed by Ceylon and Burma in 1948. Palestine was evacuated by 1949. 'Scuttle everywhere is the order of the day,' moaned Churchill.

Imperial continuity?

But how decisive were these initial steps towards the dismantling of the Empire? India's loss appeared crucial especially by comparison with the African colonies where British influence had been more superficial. In India there had been, for all the controversies, far deeper ties of pride and emotion. Once the British had wrenched themselves away from India they were never likely to dig in very deeply elsewhere. On the other hand, one cannot ignore the fact that, after the loss of the Indian subcontinent, there was no sudden collapse of the Empire. The chief phase of decolonization was not to come until the 1960s. Meanwhile, India's willingness to remain in the Commonwealth and retain Mountbatten as her first Governor-General conveyed a reassuring sense of continuity. There were several reasons for this situation. For one thing, although nationalist movements existed in other territories they were far less developed than that in India. Also, the Labour government tried to implement a positive policy, usually referred to as 'trusteeship', which implied eventual self-government when the circumstances in each territory were right. They were keen to promote economic development, especially in Africa, to which end £120 million was allocated over a ten-year period. It was hoped that after several decades of development a substantial middle class would emerge, capable of taking over the government. This would also enable Britain to entrust power to sympathetic, pro-Western regimes.

The sense of continuity was accentuated because even the loss of India left the strategic rationale for Britain's imperial role largely unimpaired. Indeed the elaborate system of overseas bases and communications was to remain until the late 1960s. In this respect the anti-imperial influence of the USA proved rather short-lived largely because the onset of the Cold War made Britain's worldwide connections useful assets not to be given up lightly, and the fact that her colonial peoples seemed vulnerable to Communist subversion only made the American government more supportive of Britain's role. The Middle East loomed especially large, partly because of the West's dependence upon its oil and partly because of its strategic role – the USSR could be threatened by aircraft stationed in the region. Whether these interests were sensibly pursued is another matter. When in 1951 Iran nationalized her oil refineries, including the British companies, Britain proved unable to intervene. Although she engineered a coup in concert with the USA, in 1953 Britain's subsequent share of Iranian oil fell from 53 per cent to 24 per cent. Egypt was similarly mishandled. In 1951 Britain still maintained 40,000 troops there. But the coup by Gamel Abdel Nasser in 1952 largely undermined what remaining influence Britain had. Even the Conservative government bowed to Nasser's determination to surrender the imperial role, and by 1954 Churchill had reluctantly agreed to withdraw British forces from the canal zone. The Western powers took comfort from the willingness of other states in the region, notably Turkey and Iran, to offer them bases now that Egypt had been effectively lost.

Rearguard actions

Britain also conducted a number of rearguard actions during the 1950s with a view to slowing down the loss of imperial control or ensuring that when power was handed over it would be granted to sympathetic successor states. These initiatives enjoyed mixed success. For example, between 1948 and 1955 Britain fought a war against Communist guerillas in Malaya in the belief that the local rubber supplies made the area too valuable to lose. Britain felt confident enough of success to grant Malaya independence in 1957, but continued to take an interest in the security of the area. She was to retain control of the foreign and defence policy of Singapore, and in 1963 promoted a federation between Singapore and Malaya. Similarly, Britain went to some lengths to retain influence in the East African territory of Kenya because Mombasa provided an important base on the Indian Ocean. During 1952–4 she waged a war against the Mau Mau or Kikuyu tribesmen. Self-government was then conceded by stages, and led to the eventual takeover by pro-Western forces.

Elsewhere, the rearguard actions enjoyed less success. In many African territories Britain attempted to use tribal chiefs as anti-nationalist bulwarks but as with the Indian princes, she found that this rarely worked. Thus elections in the Gold Coast and Nigeria in 1951–2 were won by the nationalists. The authorities allowed Kwame Nkrumah, the Gold Coast nationalist leader, out of prison in the belief that he would be a loyal collaborator. But after obtaining independence Nkrumah shocked the British by adopting a markedly anti-Western policy. An even worse mess was made by British initiatives in Northern Rhodesia, Southern Rhodesia and Nyasaland. It was hoped that the white settler population there might serve as the basis for long-term British influence. To this end the three territories became the Central African Federation in 1953. However, it lasted for only seven years. Even in Southern Rhodesia there were thirteen blacks to every one white, and 31:1 in Northern Rhodesia. Nationalist movements developed under Kenneth Kaunda in Northern Rhodesia and Dr Hastings Banda in Nyasaland, so that by 1962 Britain had conceded elective majorities in their legislatures. The Colonial Secretary, Iain Macleod, had recognized the impossibility of maintaining the Federation, though no government felt able to dissuade the beleaguered white community of Southern Rhodesia from holding out against African nationalism for some years to come.

One of the most unfortunate effects of the successful military initiatives was the misguided attempt to retain the island of Cyprus. It had never been of any practical use since the time Disraeli had acquired it from Turkey in 1878, but British governments chose to regard it as necessary to protect their oil interests. This led to the involvement of some 30,000 troops in a guerilla war against the forces of the majority Greek population during 1954–9.

The Suez fiasco

It was during the course of the Cyprus conflict that Britain suffered her greatest disaster, following Nasser's decision to nationalize the Suez Canal in

1956. Britain had consistently failed to understand Egyptian pride and aspirations to be completely free from the imperial relationship. She also became antagonized by Egypt's readiness to turn to the Soviet Union for arms, and by the dismissal of a British General, Sir John Glubb, by the Jordanian government in March 1956. Britain and the USA compounded the situation by refusing to finance the Aswan High Dam in the hope of bringing President Nasser to heel. To the general feeling that Western influence was slipping in the region there was added a powerful element of personal involvement by the new Prime Minister, Sir Anthony Eden, who felt he had been fooled by Nasser. The British government claimed that its vital trade through the Suez Canal would not be safe if the Egyptian government took over control, an absurd proposition to which none of the other trading nations who also depended on the canal subscribed. However, Eden insisted on treating Nasser as a latter-day Mussolini and determined that he should be removed. The result was a clumsy and misguided invasion plan. By the time the British troops arrived in early November the public opposition of the USA had led to a run on sterling, thereby exposing British weakness most acutely. Eventually Eden felt compelled to withdraw the troops because there was no other way of securing American support for sterling.

The significance of the Suez fiasco has generated some debate amongst historians. On the face of it, the consequences were considerable. It exposed graphically the limitations of British power and aroused almost universal opposition to her in the UN; indeed, only Australia and New Zealand were prepared to support her. In the Middle East the affair greatly weakened Britain's influence while strengthening Nasser's position in Egypt. His successful defiance of imperialism made Nasser a hero in the Third World, and helped to stimulate existing anti-imperial movements. On the other hand, Suez was an isolated example of imperial overreach. Other forward moves were either successful or, at least, less costly and demoralizing. Nor is it clear that the measurable effects of Suez were very great. Relations with the USA were quickly patched up under Macmillan's premiership. And it has been argued that the basic policies leading to decolonization were already in place by 1956. This, however, is rather dubious. It was clearly assumed in the 1950s that it would be several decades before most of Britain's colonies would be ready for self-government. In fact only three won their independence – Sudan in 1956, Malaya and the Gold Coast in 1957. Suez had a vital medium-term impact on this leisurely process in that it destroyed the premiership of Eden and, ironically, it brought to power the man who was almost as responsible for the disaster: Macmillan. He had failed to grasp

Table 18.1 Decolonization, 1947–74

Year	Country
1947	India, Pakistan
1948	Burma, Ceylon
1956	Sudan
1957	Gold Coast (Ghana), Malaya
1960	Somaliland, Nigeria, Cyprus
1961	Sierra Leone, Tanganyika
1962	Jamaica, Trinidad and Tobago, Uganda
1963	Singapore, Northern Borneo, Sarawak, Zanzibar, Kenya
1964	Nyasaland (Malawi), Malta, Northern Rhodesia (Zambia)
1965	Gambia
1966	British Guyana, Bechuanaland (Botswana), Basutoland (Lesotho), Barbados
1967	Leeward Islands, Windward Islands, Aden (South Yemen)
1968	Mauritius, Swaziland
1970	Fiji
1973	Bahamas
1974	Grenada

the American view of Suez and the consequences for sterling, and had misled Eden after his talks with President Eisenhower.

However, once in office Macmillan accelerated the process of decolonization, subject only to the check imposed by his own party. After his 1959 election victory, Macmillan felt more sure of his own position and appointed Iain Macleod as Colonial Secretary with a view to relieving Britain of what appeared to be her increasingly dangerous liabilities. Macleod told the 1961 party conference: 'I believe quite simply in the brotherhood of man', an indication of his bold liberal opinions. Ideas about trusteeship went out of the window as colonies were given up with little regard for the state of their political or economic development. This was not simply the result of a loss of nerve after Suez. Macmillan had already been conscious of the incongruity between Britain's imperial role and her economic weakness. As Chancellor he had drawn up a profit-and-loss account for every colony in order to determine where the balance of advantage lay. The result of this hard-headed approach was that no fewer than 27 colonies received independence between 1960 and 1969. By the mid-1970s all that remained were a scattering of islands too small for effective independence, plus a collection of troublesome oddities from the days of imperial greatness: Gibraltar, Hong Kong and the Falkland Islands. In the space of 25 years Britain had abandoned her imperial role but adopting a new one was to prove more uncomfortable.

For some years both Conservative and Labour politicians had placed high hopes on the Commonwealth as an alternative vehicle for British influence in the world. Although Burma had promptly left, most colonies followed India's example by remaining as members. Britain was keen to develop a common defence policy with a view to limiting Soviet influence over countries like India. But this failed to materialize, partly because the newly independent countries wished to be neutral in the struggle between communism and capitalism. Moreover, Canada looked to the USA for its security, while in 1951 Australia and New Zealand reached a defence agreement with their American neighbour without consulting Britain. In addition, the Commonwealth gradually divided along racial lines. In South Africa the defeat of the pro-British General Smuts by Afrikaner nationalists in 1948 paved the way for the imposition of the apartheid policy which culminated in the expulsion of South Africa from the Commonwealth in 1961. After 1965 Britain's failure to bring to heel the white settlers who declared unilateral independence in Southern Rhodesia attracted widespread condemnation from the black countries. At home, relationships with the Commonwealth also began to be adversely affected by large-scale immigration into Britain from the West Indies, India and Pakistan. The restrictions placed on immigration by the Conservatives and their exploitation of the issue attracted increasing criticism from Commonwealth leaders, with the result that by the mid-1960s the whole idea of the Commonwealth had largely lost its appeal for the right wing in Britain.

Reluctantly into Europe

As in the aftermath of 1918, so after 1945 Britain allowed her close relationship with France to lapse, and she showed herself slow to appreciate the significance of developments in Western Europe. This was partly because her own trade was, as yet, dominated by the sterling area, and because Europe, in its devastated condition, seemed likely to take years to recover fully. Moreover, British detachment reflected a very basic assumption that, in Bevin's words, 'Great Britain was not part of Europe' and had no wish to be. Thus, when Jean Monnet, one of the founders of the Common Market idea, visited Britain in 1949 to propose Anglo-French economic union he was rebuffed. But Monnet simply turned to Germany, and Britain missed the first of several opportunities to participate constructively and at an early stage in European co-operation. The first concrete initiative was the proposal for a European Coal and Steel Community (ECSC) in 1950. 'The Durham miners

Table 18.2 Geographical distribution of British trade, 1900–85 (percentage of total trade)

	North America	South America	Asia	Africa	Europe	Other
1900	25	8	12	3	44	8
1938	17	10	12	7	32	22
1970	20	5	12	10	25	28
1985	16	2	10	6	63	3

won't wear it,' announced Herbert Morrison, as though nothing more need be said on the matter. But by 1952 Britain was surprised to find that six members had joined the ECSC. By this time a new British government had taken over, but the consensus on external policy remained unaffected. Churchill saw no great relevance for Britain in the closer co-operation between France and Germany; he remained chiefly interested in consolidating the Commonwealth and in relations with the USA. Consequently he adopted a negative view of proposals for a European defence community in 1954, though eventually Eden pledged the permanent commitment of British troops to Europe.

Once again, however, the British were surprised to find that no rebuff by them ever finally killed off the momentum for greater unity. In 1955 six European states invited Britain to take part in talks on further European integration. This centred round a 'Common Market' involving the removal of internal trade barriers, a common external tariff, and the free mobility of labour and capital within the union. The Churchill–Eden governments took the view that such an arrangement might lead to political federalism and threaten the sovereignty of the member states. Moreover, it might damage Britain's advantageous commerce with the Commonwealth. In the mid-1950s it was easy for the government to convince itself that Britain had re-established herself as a Great Power on the basis of her nuclear capacity, her large army and her largely intact imperial role. For a time, therefore, Britain actually hoped to kill off the Brussels negotiations; but by early 1956 this had clearly failed, and the six states went ahead in March 1957 to sign the Treaty of Rome which created the European Economic Community. Meanwhile, Britain inspired a countermove in the form of a European Free Trade Association (EFTA) involving Denmark, Norway, Sweden, Austria, Switzerland and Portugal.

Britain had missed an opportunity, as soon became apparent. Already by the late 1950s Europe accounted for as large a proportion of British trade as the Commonwealth. Unfortunately, EFTA was not an adequate alternative to the EEC either economically or politically; indeed, far from being a bridge to Europe it only complicated Britain's subsequent application for membership. Had Britain agreed to play a constructive role in the formative phase of the EEC, she would have had no great difficulty in negotiating concessions to reflect her special interests in Commonwealth trade and her access to cheaper food. But the opportunity passed, and Britain was to be in a much weaker position in the 1960s.

Macmillan's attempt to join

By 1961 it had become clear that the government had miscalculated. The six states of the EEC were reducing tariffs, harmonizing their external duties, creating central institutions, and, above all, achieving substantially faster economic growth than Britain. The Prime Minister, Harold Macmillan, who had always been more favourably disposed towards Europe than Churchill or Eden, made the first application for membership in 1961. The case was widely expressed in terms of the economic advantages. In France and Germany economic growth was twice as high as in Britain; Western Europe offered the wealthy markets in which Britain could sell her manufactured goods; both EFTA and the Commonwealth were inadequate; her relatively sluggish economy would benefit greatly from the stimulus of EEC membership. However, for Macmillan and pro-Europeans of all parties, the economic arguments were to a large extent a way of popularizing the essentially *political* case for joining. As both the American and the Commonwealth props to Britain's worldwide status were now looking rather precarious, Europe seemed to offer a more realistic vehicle for maintaining her status as a Great Power.

Yet, though Macmillan recognized the force of international trends he could not take too many risks with his own party, which was seriously divided over Europe. Conservatives felt outraged in 1962 when the American former Secretary of State, Dean Acheson, made the perfectly reasonable observation that 'Great Britain has lost an Empire and has not yet found a role'. In view of this sensitivity, Macmillan took care to move pro-Europeans such as Edward Heath, Christopher Soames and Duncan Sandys into key positions. By September 1961 negotiations were under way under Heath's leadership. By 1962 considerable agreement had been reached, though largely because Britain simply accepted the common agricultural policy, the commercial policy and the external tariff. But the process was interrupted in 1963 by a veto on Britain's application delivered by President de Gaulle of France. He was much influenced by Macmillan's recent attempts, following the loss of Skybolt, to re-establish Britain's close defence relationship with the USA; he had seen this as an opportunity for Anglo-French defence co-operation instead. Clearly, there was some validity in de Gaulle's diagnosis. Up to this point Britain had changed her policy out of fear of losing her traditional role, rather than because of her enthusiasm for the European Community.

Wilson and the second application

The impasse in British external policy might have been broken by the change of government in 1964, for Harold Wilson, the new Prime Minister, was ostensibly dedicated to modernizing British society. In fact his policies in external affairs proved to be conservative and traditional. After Macmillan's fresh initiatives there came, for a time, something of a reversion to earlier patterns; Wilson seemed prepared to subject an ailing economy to the burdens of maintaining an increasingly anachronistic world role. Thus Britain's bases and troops 'east of Suez' were supported until, in the late 1960s, economic decline at last forced a reluctant government to withdraw. Wilson also held to the existing nuclear-deterrent policy, merely cancelling one out of five Polaris submarines as a political gesture. He was also keen to cultivate the special relationship with America. President Johnson clearly wanted Britain to uphold her role east of Suez, to maintain the value of sterling, and to back the USA in the war in Vietnam. Wilson loyally co-operated in all this for some years, though he gave moral rather than military support over Vietnam. Once again, Britain had returned to her client relationship. Wilson successfully obscured her demeaning position by deliberate appeals to national pride; 'our frontiers', he once claimed rather absurdly, 'are on the Himalayas'. However, this was not mere posturing on his part. He showed himself willing to devote scarce resources to the fight against subversion. In Malaya, for example, 68,000 troops and a third of the British fleet became engaged against Indonesia. On the other hand, when faced with a more minor challenge by the handful of white Rhodesian settlers who declared illegal independence in 1965, the government backed away from direct intervention.

As the 1960s wore on, however, mounting economic and political pressures forced the Labour government into revisions of its external policy. The Defence Secretary, Denis Healey, attempted to impose tighter control by abolishing the three separate armed-service ministries and amalgamating their interests under a single Ministry of Defence. Several expensive aircraft programmes were scrapped in favour of American substitutes purchased cheaply 'off the shelf'. Healey also began to reduce the navy's reliance on aircraft carriers. The flaw was that British commitments had not yet been reduced in line with costs. But in July 1967 the deterioration of the economy led Healey to decide to cut back British forces in Malaya and Singapore by half by 1970–1 as a step towards final withdrawal by 1975. In 1968 a reluctant Cabinet agreed to a complete withdrawal from the east-of-Suez role, with the exception of Hong Kong, by 1971. Coinciding as it did with the painful decision to devalue the pound, this represented something of a turning-point; one minister described it as 'breaking through the status barrier'.

This overdue reassessment had been facilitated by the gradual replacement of elderly Labour ministers and the promotion of the pro-European Roy Jenkins as Chancellor and the modernizing left-winger Tony Benn. Jenkins, like Heath on the Conservative side, had a clear conception that Britain's future lay in embracing the European option and giving up the old imperial role so dear to his colleagues. In 1966 the Prime Minister had announced Britain's intention to make a second application for membership of the EEC provided that the right terms could be negotiated. As in 1961, the fundamental reasoning behind this seemed to be political – there was no other feasible way for Britain to maintain her influence in the world in the long run – though the issue was largely discussed in terms of economics. In 1967 the Cabinet decided to make a second bid for membership, in the belief that Britain's decline would otherwise become precipitate. But, as before, de Gaulle perceived the application more as a matter of expediency than conviction, and he vetoed it in November.

British entry under Heath

The election of 1970 brought into power for the first time a genuine enthusiast for Europe in the person of Edward Heath. Although the public at large and many members of the two main parties continued to be indifferent or hostile towards the EEC, the determination amongst ministers plus the enthusiasm of some Labour and Liberal leaders gave the European cause fresh momentum. In the mood of disillusion and decline that had set in by the end of the 1960s, Europe seemed to offer the only constructive response to Britain's dilemma. The resignation of de Gaulle in 1969 also helped matters. French fears about the growing economic dominance of Germany began to make Britain's participation as a counterweight more attractive to her.

Britain herself had clearly declined as a manufacturing power when compared with Germany. Heath correctly saw that in American eyes Germany was becoming the more important power, and to that extent the USA was less interested in the special relationship with Britain. As Britain's negotiator in 1961–2, Heath also had a clear grasp of the difficulties ahead, especially the weakness of Britain's position; in applying to join what was no longer an experiment but a proven success, she could do little to modify the rules of the club or to influence moves to advance from the original customs union towards a more politically coherent community. When negotiations began in January 1970, Heath reassured the French President, Pompidou, about his government's attitude, and by June 1971 the terms for entry had been settled. Once again, the government chose to emphasize the material advantages to the British people, in terms of a higher standard of living, in spite of the higher food prices and large contributions to the EEC budget that membership entailed. In October 1971 the House of Commons approved British entry by 356 votes to 244, and Heath signed the treaty of accession in January 1972. As a detailed bill had still to be passed through Parliament, it was not until January 1973 that Britain actually joined the EEC.

It quickly became plain that Heath saw the move as part of a wider change in Britain's role in the world. For example, in negotiations with the USA Britain now joined her eight partners by adopting a common position in place of the old one-to-one talks. A deterioration in Anglo–American relations was underlined by the Arab–Israeli war of 1973, when Britain refused to allow NATO bases in Britain to be used to airlift supplies to Israel. The two countries appeared to be, in Henry Kissinger's words, 'at a turning point in Atlantic relations'. However, the British never quite embraced their new role in the world. This was partly because the European project remained the idea of an elite which had never fully persuaded the public. For some years Britain's relations with her new European partners were also strained, partly because the terms for entry into the EEC had been very unfavourable. A high proportion of the EEC budget was devoted to the common agricultural policy, which subsidized farmers and imposed levies on the cheaper imported food from which Britain had benefited in the past. Moreover, with a smaller and more efficient farming sector, Britain received relatively few benefits from the policy while contributing disproportionately to it. By 1978 she paid 20 per cent of EEC income but received only 8.7 per cent of its spending. The timing of British entry also proved unfortunate. From late 1973 the Arab–Israeli war led to an oil crisis; a 400 per cent increase in the price of oil checked economic growth in Western Europe for the first time in a quarter of a century. Britain experienced recession and inflation, rather than the stimulus she had hoped for after joining Europe.

The economic crisis destroyed the government of Edward Heath in 1974 and restored Wilson to office. This placed a question mark over Britain's role in Europe because the new premier treated Europe chiefly as a matter of party management. Since the Labour Party remained badly divided over the EEC, the Prime Minister decided to maintain unity and protect his own leadership by embarking upon an elaborate process of renegotiating the terms of entry and offering the public a referendum on EEC membership; he hoped thereby to appease Tony Benn and the left and keep the party united. Wilson achieved no more than marginal modifications in terms of a rebate on Britain's contributions and easier access for Commonwealth products. But on this basis a national referendum took place in June 1975 which produced a vote of 67.2 per cent to 32.8 per cent in favour of membership. Though the result was very clear, only 64.5 per cent had turned out to vote. The verdict reflected a fear that things might be even worse if Britain left the EEC, rather than a positive conviction about the merits of staying in. Continued inflation, unemployment and a deteriorating balance of payments during the 1970s did nothing to improve British attitudes towards Europe. On the whole she proved to be an uncooperative member, invariably opposing changes and resisting the application of common policies. Traditionalist leaders like Wilson and his foreign secretary, James Callaghan, regretted the loss of the close relationship with the USA and went some way to restoring the Atlantic Alliance. This took the form of nuclear co-operation in which the Polaris submarine system was updated. In this way the momentum generated by the Heath government was checked in the later 1970s, and the ground was laid for a further retreat from Britain's new role under Margaret Thatcher.

* * * *

In many ways the years from 1940 to 1970 represented a golden era for the British people. They enjoyed full employment, rising living standards, reduced inequality of incomes, more home-ownership, comprehensive state welfare and extended educational opportunities. On the downside British prosperity was precariously based on poor productivity and relatively slow economic growth. Moreover, despite some efforts to redefine her role the country began to lose the fundamentals that had sustained national identity and purpose before the Second World War. Absorbed by consumerism Britain failed to reform her institutions and to assess her values and traditions. She largely forgot that Britain was an artificial four-nation state. Northern Ireland was quietly left to drift away from the more liberal values of the mainland and to consolidate an unpleasant sectarian form of government. Although she executed a fairly uncontroversial retreat from empire she failed to adjust fully to being a post-imperial power. One symptom of this was the reaction to Commonwealth immigration. Another was the irrational attempt to cling to great-power status and the reluctance to embrace an alternative role in Europe. The failure by both politicians and by Treasury economists to chart an early path into the European Union represented, arguably, the most serious policy failing of the twentieth century. Britain decisively missed her opportunity to exercise a major influence on the new Europe.

Further reading

Foreign policy is dealt with in:

Sean Greenwood, *Britain and the Cold War 1945–91* (1991)

D. Sanders, *Losing an Empire, Finding a Role: British Foreign Policy since 1945* (1990)

D. Reynolds, *Britannia Overruled: British Foreign Policy and World Power in the Twentieth Century* (1991)

Jeffery Pickering, *Britain's Withdrawal from East of Suez* (1998)

R. Holland, *The Pursuit of Greatness: Britain and the World Role 1900–1970* (1991)

C.J. Bartlett, *British Foreign Policy in the Twentieth Century* (1989)

Alan Bullock, *Ernest Bevin: Foreign Secretary* (1983)

David French, *The British Way in Warfare, 1688–2000* (1990)

Paul Kennedy, *The Realities Behind Diplomacy: Background Influences on British External Policy 1865–1980* (1981)

On withdrawal from empire see:

John Darwin, *Britain and Decolonisation* (1988)

John Darwin, *The End of the British Empire* (1991)

Philip Murphy, *Politics and Decolonisation: the Conservative Party and British Colonial Policy in Tropical Africa 1951–64* (1995)

J.D. Hargreaves, *Decolonisation in Africa* (1988)

David Carlton, *Britain and the Suez Crisis* (1988)

David Dutton, *Anthony Eden* (1997)

Wendy Webster, *Englishness and Empire 1939–65* (2005)

B. Porter, *The Lion's Share: A Short History of British Imperialism* (1975)

Britain's entry into Europe is discussed in:

J.W. Young, *Britain and European Unity 1945–92* (1993)

M. Frankel, *Britain's Future in Europe* (1990)

A. Horne, *Harold Macmillan, 1957–1986* (1989)

John Campbell, *Edward Heath* (1993)

Part V

The Era of Reaction and Decline, 1970–2015

19

The Breakdown of the Post-war Consensus, 1970–9

Although the 1960s had witnessed a preoccupation with Britain's economic weaknesses, this made little impression upon most people because standards of living continued to improve on the whole. In the 1970s, however, there was an undeniable deterioration. Inflation, the balance of payments, unemployment, strikes, all became serious matters of concern. Increasingly governments scarcely seemed to be in control; both a Conservative and a Labour government broke down over major policies, and within each party an extremist wing began to gather strength. In this brittle and adversarial climate the longstanding political consensus dissolved.

This was also the decade in which the flaws in British national identity made themselves apparent. To add to the sense of decline engendered by economic problems, the empire had finally gone and Europe had arrived but most British people were reluctant to embrace a new role and status. National institutions including parliament, the civil service, the Church and the Union with Scotland were losing their credibility. A multi-racial society was born and a more liberal society gradually emerged. But all this found the English at best complacent and at worst negative. In some ways the crisis of national identity took the form of a crisis of *Conservatism* personified by two leaders, Heath and Thatcher, the first ready to adapt and the other essentially reactionary, but neither able to restore a positive sense of national identity in the long run.

Heath and the crisis of Conservatism

The surprise election result of 1970 brought Edward Heath to the premiership. Although drawn from more modest origins than most Tory leaders he was, in fact, an insider. He had risen smoothly via Oxford and the army to Parliament, where he spent only 18 months as a backbencher before moving on to the whips' office and the Cabinet. Heath stood squarely in the 'One-Nation' tradition of Conservatism; like Macmillan, who promoted him, he believed in maintaining state social services and was detached from the world of business. His most famous remark was an attack on disreputable commercial practices as 'the unacceptable face of capitalism'. Heath was also fairly liberal in his attitudes on such issues as capital punishment, South Africa and immigration, demonstrating his feelings about racial prejudice by sacking Enoch Powell from his shadow Cabinet in 1968 for a racially provocative speech. Above all the new Prime Minister was an ardent modernizer, determined to drag a reluctant Conservative Party into the twentieth century. Under a previous government he had been responsible for the abolition of resale price maintenance which antagonized small shop-keepers. Heath's greatest achievement as premier was to take Britain into the EEC, but he also restructured government departments, set up the Central Policy Review Staff or 'Think Tank' under Lord Rothschild, and imposed a sweeping local-government reform which caused much controversy by changing historic boundaries and abolishing some counties. In short, Heath proved to be a twentieth-century Peel. More a civil servant than a politician, he appeared too cold and arrogant ever to be popular with the rank-and-file; ultimately his inability to master the arts of party management was to destroy his career.

Continuity or change?

In 1970 Heath's arrival in power seemed to represent a clear break with the drift and deviousness of his predecessor. In retrospect some commentators interpreted the new government's strategy as a repudiation of consensus politics and a first instalment of Thatcherism which did not quite come off. Though this is not a valid view, it seemed plausible because Heath appeared to offer a sharp change in style from Wilson; and he was, for a Conservative, unusually concerned with detailed policy planning before entering upon office. In January 1970 he had gathered his shadow Cabinet at the Selsdon Park conference to discuss their future policies in some detail. There was much talk about curtailing state intervention, withdrawing subsidies from industrial 'lame ducks', and reforming the trade unions. To a large extent, however, this was simply the usual rhetoric adopted by Conservatives after a lengthy period in opposition. The sense of change was exaggerated when Harold Wilson attacked the emergence of 'Selsdon Man' as proof of a shift to the right. There were, undoubtedly, some initial indications of a break, though the policies were quite typical of incoming Conservative governments. Expenditure was cut in 1971, income tax was lowered, subsidies on council housing were reduced, free school milk was abolished, and both the Prices and Incomes Board and the Land Commission were wound up.

However, Selsdon Man enjoyed a very short life. By 1971 the government began to reconsider its policies as it was confronted simultaneously by high inflation and unemployment approaching one million. It rapidly became clear that the government could not simply stand aside and allow prices and wage negotiations to go the way market forces dictated. By 1971 employers were surrendering to pressure by raising the wages of manual workers by 15 per cent. The tendency to make concessions was increased by the irresponsible policy of the Chancellor of the Exchequer, Anthony Barber, who tried to thrust the economy into a growth phase by tax cuts and higher expenditure. This only boosted inflation, stoked up a consumer spending spree, and drew imports into the country. In the past Conservative Chancellors had repeatedly done this in order to cultivate a sense of well-being among voters before an election. But this time the boom was mistimed: it merely fed the appetite of the trade unions, and the strategy blew up in the government's face. In particular, Heath appeared to reverse his original policy in two striking ways. First, he increased expenditure on education, the NHS and housing, so much so that the annual average rise exceeded that under Labour during 1964–70. Second, he accepted that major industries could not simply be allowed to succumb to market forces if a national interest was at stake. Thus in 1971 Rolls-Royce was nationalized, the Upper Clyde Shipbuilders received a £35 million subsidy to safeguard 3,000 jobs, and British Steel also obtained extra investment from the state.

The clash with the miners

But the government's most distinctive initiative was its attempt to control escalating wage demands and check unofficial strikes by means of the Industrial Relations Act. Among other things, this required pre-strike ballots and allowed for the imposition of a 60-day cooling-off period. However, the trade unions determined to defy the law and the TUC threatened to expel any union that registered under the new Act. In the event, 1972 brought the loss of no fewer than 23 million working days in strikes, the highest since 1926. The Act was only rarely invoked, and when it was, as over the railwaymen's dispute in 1972, the workers simply voted in favour of a strike under the terms of the legislation. Several individual leaders of unofficial strikes received prison sentences, but this was subsequently ruled to be illegal and only exacerbated the government's political difficulties. The most dramatic challenge came when the coal miners rejected an 8 per cent wage offer in the winter of 1972. A well-organized system of 'flying pickets' operated by Arthur Scargill effectively checked the movement of coal, and as a result industry found itself restricted to a three-day week. But the real weakness in the government's position lay in the fact that the more moderate miners' leaders, Joe Gormley and Lawrence Daly, commanded considerable public sympathy for their cause. This led to a retreat, in the form of a Commission of Inquiry which offered the miners a massive 21 per cent rise. However, the offer was rejected by the NUM, and the strike did not end until February 1973, when miners won increases worth between 17 and 24 per cent.

The effect of the industrial militancy was extremely serious. It undermined the authority of an elected government, the law and the police. Moreover, the success of militancy encouraged extremists to rely increasingly upon direct action. The position of moderate union leaders became so insecure that they found it difficult to co-operate with the government over a voluntary pay policy. Conversely, the prestige of militants such as Scargill, who took over as the NUM President in 1973, rose considerably. Within the Labour Party, too, leading figures like Tony Benn were increasingly tempted to support the extraparliamentary forces and their methods. By the winter of 1972–3 the Heath government had been driven to adopt a statutory prices and incomes policy. Initially this involved a complete freeze on wages for three months. By November 1973 this threatened another confrontation with the miners. In fact the government consciously sought to avoid another clash by offering a 13 per cent rise, but by this time the workers' self-confidence and expectations were too high for them to respond rationally. The NUM refused even to ballot its members on the offer, and imposed an overtime ban.

The 1974 election

In spite of the collapse of its economic policies, the Heath government believed it could afford to weather the storm. It still had several years of its term of office, and although it was losing by-elections to the Liberals, it took confidence from the inability of the lacklustre Labour leadership to offer an effective challenge. As the Labour left gained influence, the party appeared divided and unable to recover public support. However, the political cycle was overtaken and disrupted by external factors in the shape of the Arab–Israeli War, resulting in a huge increase in the price of oil which exacerbated Britain's already pronounced inflation and, in turn, brought industrial relations to their nadir. By December 1973 Heath had declared a state of emergency and a three-day working week in view of the shortage of both coal and oil. At the same time the balance-of-payments deficit for the year reached £1.5 billion – the worst so far recorded.

It was understandably tempting to try to break out of the government's dilemma by holding an early election on the question 'Who Governs Britain?' There was a presumption that voters would be willing to overrule the unions and that Labour would be caught in an awkward position. As a miners' strike loomed in February, some ministers urged the prompt adoption of this course. But Heath hesitated. To go to the country was an admission of defeat on the government's part. Nor was it clear how far the public blamed the miners rather than the government. In the event Heath delayed a little too long, and eventually gave way to pressure to hold an election which took place on 28 February. The uninspired campaign fought by the Conservatives reflected their lack of confidence in their policies and record. Even so, they won more votes than Labour. But the eccentric British electoral system played another of its tricks upon the politicians. With more votes, the Conservatives won *fewer* seats than Labour – 296 to 301 – and Heath's government was destroyed.

Heath had certainly been unlucky in the circumstances of his premiership, but he had also shown a lack of political skill. His was the last attempt to make the post-war consensus work. The early 1970s ushered in several new elements in British politics, notably entry into the EEC which was to become a key problem for all successor governments. The spectre of a trade union movement swollen with power posed a serious threat to the economy and to Parliament. Finally the Heath years generated an angry backlash among Conservatives who felt betrayed by their leaders and alienated by the Keynesian-collectivist formula in economic policy, and who were determined to avenge their humiliating defeat at the hands of the miners.

Multi-party politics

The heyday of the two-party political system in Britain was between 1945 and 1959. During the 1960s the Conservative–Labour dominance diminished slightly, but the 1970s decisively marked the passing of the old pattern. Only the electoral system propped up the two big parties by over-representing them in the House of Commons. This trend was in part the result of repeated failures in economic policy by Tory and Labour governments, and a reflection of the drift towards what was dubbed 'adversarial politics'. The electorate found the debate between the Tory right wing and the Labour left increasingly sterile leaving the Liberals as the beneficiaries.

Liberal revival

At the grass roots the Liberals began to rival the older parties by contesting many more constituencies – 517 in the election of February 1974 and virtually every seat in October of that year. This restored the party as a national one and marked a reversal of its historic decline. Since the 1920s the Liberals had largely lacked the constituency organization and membership needed to capitalize on their parliamentary initiatives. But in the 1970s they successfully employed the methods of 'community politics', which involved links with radical pressure groups outside the party and concentration on involving the electorate in campaigns over local issues. This paid dividends by boosting Liberal representation in local government, and gave the party a strong base in large urban districts like Liverpool, Leeds and Birmingham that it had not enjoyed since the nineteenth century.

The Liberals also benefited from able and attractive leaders in Jeremy Thorpe and his successor, David Steel. Thorpe proved to be an asset on television and led his party to a remarkable revival at the February 1974 election, in which 19.8 per cent of the vote was won by the Liberals followed by 18.8 per cent in October 1974 and 14.1 per cent in 1979. In view of the unfavourable circumstances of the 1979 election, this was a surprisingly good performance and kept the party at a higher level than it had enjoyed during the 1950s and 1960s. When Heath lost his majority in 1974 he offered the Liberals a coalition but this was refused, largely because Heath was so unpopular that it would have been very damaging to the Liberals' radical credentials to have kept him in office. But the whiff of power was itself flattering to a party so used to the back benches. From 1976 the new leader, David Steel, concentrated on a parliamentary breakthrough. His opportunity came in March 1977, when the Labour government under James Callaghan lost its majority. A Lib-Lab pact was devised to provide Labour with the vital extra votes it needed. In return the Liberals had regular talks with ministers about government policy, but they got very little in the way of concrete concessions out of the arrangement. In particular, they failed to insist on any firm advance towards proportional representation. In a sense, the real virtue of the pact was to begin the process of educating the British public about coalition governments, which were a normal feature in most European countries but seen only as wartime expedients in Britain. However, by the summer of 1978 the pact had been abandoned. Although at the time it seemed that the Liberals had been the losers, it was the government that ultimately suffered. They went on to a deal with the Nationalist parties which led them to the electoral defeat of 1979.

Ulster sectarianism

It was also during the 1970s that the problems of the Irish, Welsh and Scottish parts of the United Kingdom returned to the forefront of politics after many decades of neglect by Westminster, compounding the problems facing the two old parties as a result of the rise of the Liberals. The Irish problem was most troublesome for the Conservatives. Since the 1920s Ulster had been governed by the Unionist-Protestant majority in the Stormont Parliament while the Catholics were excluded permanently from power and suffered severe discrimination particularly in housing and employment. Yet for decades Westminster governments simply turned a blind eye to the situation. In this way they created problems for themselves, for by the 1950s the Catholic population had become sympathetic to the IRA, and by the early 1960s there was enough support for a renewed campaign against British rule in Northern Ireland. The dissatisfaction took the form of a civil-rights movement, inspired partly by a similar campaign in the USA, which organized marches and demonstrations in the province. The resulting clashes between demonstrators and the police led the Home Secretary, James Callaghan, to send in troops in 1969.

Initially the British troops were welcomed by the Catholic community as a neutral force. But the central political problem – the Unionists' abuse of power – remained unresolved. Labour was not particularly interested and the Conservatives were traditionally allies of the Ulster Unionists – hence the absence of a Conservative organization in the province until the 1980s. Thus in time the violence of the campaign began to be turned upon the troops, and in 1971 the first British soldier was killed in Northern Ireland. On 30 January 1972 a demonstration that had been pronounced illegal resulted in the death of 13 people at the hands of the troops in Londonderry. 'Bloody Sunday', as the incident became known, was a fatal error by the authorities because it completed the alienation of the Catholics.

The response of the Heath government to these events was to abolish the Stormont Parliament in 1973 and impose direct rule upon the province. Though seen as a temporary expedient, this soon became a permanent policy. It proved very costly in terms of resources and the horrendous loss of life; 1,100 people died between 1969 and 1974 alone. Moreover, the move was politically unfortunate in that it moved the British government firmly into the IRA's sights and enabled them to present the Union with Britain as the source of the troubles. The Northern Ireland policy enjoyed bipartisan support in Britain for the next 20 years, but was nonetheless an unmitigated failure in that by the 1990s a solution was as far away as ever. The conflict made remarkably little impression upon the British public, even when the violence came to the mainland, and was treated with a stoical disdain as though it took place in a different country rather than within the UK. However the Ulster problem had one significant domestic political result, for the imposition of direct rule alienated the Unionists from the Conservative Party. When, in 1974, Heath lost his majority in Parliament, his bid to retain office was crippled by his inability to rely on the votes of the Unionist MPs.

Nationalist revival in Scotland

While the majority in Northern Ireland wished to stick resolutely to Westminster, the problem in Scotland and Wales was increasingly a disenchantment with control from London. After the Nationalist by-election gains in 1966–7 the government had thrown them a concession in the shape of the Kilbrandon Commission in 1968, which examined the question of a devolution of power from Westminster. Most Conservatives were wholly opposed to devolution though Heath sympathized. Labour traditionally adopted a conservative attitude towards all constitutional reform, opposing devolution on three grounds. First, socialists regarded Welsh and Scottish self-government as irrelevant and parochial; it would only detract from effective economic planning from the centre. Second, the experience with a regional parliament in Ulster was not very encouraging. Third, there was an element of political expediency. Since the 1920s Labour had largely dominated the Welsh and Scottish constituencies, and believed it could disregard nationalist criticisms despite the dramatic by-election losses suffered by Labour in industrial Scotland and Wales in the 1960s.

However, Kilbrandon made devolution respectable and accelerated the pressure by recommending an elected parliament in Edinburgh and a Welsh assembly. The Scots Nationalists in particular benefited from a new confidence in self-government engendered by the exploitation of rich deposits of oil off their country's coasts. Campaigning under the slogan 'It's Scotland's Oil', they could now argue credibly that an independent economic policy might enable the Scots to capitalize on their material resources and human skills, whereas under London's control they had suffered years of economic decline and unemployment. In the election of October 1974 eleven Scottish and three Welsh Nationalists were elected – a significant number for a government hanging on by a majority of just six. Thirty per cent of Scottish electors had voted Nationalist, only 6.4 per cent behind Labour. It was undeniable that the traditional mould of political loyalties had been broken. The Union no longer commanded the full approval of the people, and only the undemocratic electoral system had denied the nationalists fair representation in Parliament.

For Labour, political expediency dictated a concession to deprive the nationalists of their momentum. However, it went against the grain as the Secretary of State for Scotland, William Ross, was a diehard anti-devolutionist. The result was a half-baked compromise that pleased no one. A parliament in Edinburgh would be established, with no revenue-raising powers or real influence over industry and agriculture. An effective veto power was to be left with the Secretary of State. The Welsh proposals were even more paltry. In effect the country would be given a large county council responsible for allocating a central block grant to the social services. To make matters worse, the government had not really thought out the implications of devolution for Scotland and Wales. Should it lead to a reduction in the number of Welsh and Scots MPs sitting at Westminster? Was it a final solution, or would it pave the way for regional government in the English provinces? There was so much doubt in the Cabinet's mind that when the Bill passed through Parliament in 1976–7 it allowed crucial amendments to be made. One of these provided that, before the new institutions were established, not only must there be a referendum, but at least 40 per cent of all those on the register – not of those who actually voted – must vote in favour. This was extraordinary to the point of absurdity in the context of British electoral practice; but it seemed at the time a neat expedient to ensure the survival of the Bill. In the event it proved fatal to the government.

The campaign over the devolution referendum took place during the winter of 1978–9. By that time the Prime Minister, Callaghan, had lost his pact with the Liberals but relied instead upon the co-operation of the Nationalist MPs. In spite of this relationship, the Labour Party in South Wales largely turned its back on the referendum policy, and not surprisingly the Welsh voted 4–1 against devolution. In Scotland the strategy appeared to be working in that Labour regained some ground from the Nationalists. But the vote in favour of devolution was very narrow: 51.6–48.4 per cent; and it clearly failed to carry the required 40 per cent of the electorate. This failure left the Scottish Nationalists somewhat discredited and losing their earlier momentum. However, the devolution question had not been defused by the Westminster Establishment. On the contrary, it led the Nationalists to withdraw their support, which deprived the government of its majority and thus forced it into a disastrous election at the worst possible moment.

The decline of Labour

From its peak at the general election of 1966, when Labour polled 48 per cent of the vote, the party went into a long-term decline; by the 1970s its share had sunk to the level of 1929–35, and in the 1980s below even that. The seriousness of the decline was obscured by the period in office between 1974 and 1979; but in February 1974 Labour polled half a million *fewer* votes than in 1970. Heath and Wilson fought what was aptly described as an 'unpopularity contest' which Labour had not expected to win. The Labour leaders of the 1970s, Wilson and Callaghan, faced the same dilemma Gladstone had faced in the Liberal Party a hundred years earlier; they were caught between the general public, which seemed to be moving against radicalism, and the party activists, who were growing increasingly radical. In the event they handled the problem with considerable skill, and the surprising thing is not that they were eventually defeated but that they survived so long on borrowed time. In retrospect Wilson has been widely blamed for his party's misfortunes; but it was not so much for what he did in the 1970s as for what he failed to do in the 1960s that he was culpable. For by 1970 the party was so disenchanted that membership was collapsing; it continued to dwindle to around 600,000 officially by 1979, though it was probably less.

The Campaign for Labour Party Democracy

Not surprisingly, after the economic failures and the right-wing external policies pursued up to 1970, the party's rank-and-file activists began to reassert themselves in the 1970s. Their leader was Tony Benn, now playing Joseph Chamberlain to Wilson's Gladstone. He advocated wider state ownership, unilateral disarmament, withdrawal from the EEC, abolition of the House of Lords, reform of the Official Secrets Act, and greater democracy within the party involving wider participation in the election of the leader and shadow Cabinet. It would be a misrepresentation to portray these issues as simply the fads of an extremist minority as several clearly enjoyed wide support beyond the Labour Party. The radicals' position was all the stronger because several major union leaders including Jack Jones and Hugh Scanlon also felt strongly critical of the record of the 1964–70 governments. The National Executive of the party also asserted itself by adopting a more socialist policy, including the proposal that the state should acquire a controlling interest in 25 major companies. Although Wilson and Callaghan repudiated this and largely emasculated Benn's ideas, they could no longer

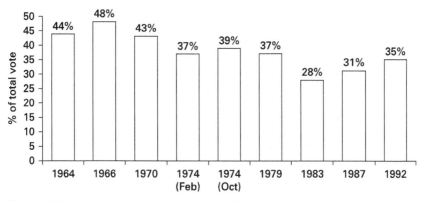

Figure 19.1 Labour share of the vote, 1964–92.

control the party beyond Parliament. By resisting the left's policies they provoked the establishment of the Campaign for Labour Party Democracy and the NEC's decision to lift the long-standing proscription on Communists within the organization. This, combined with the drop in membership, meant that the party was vulnerable, in both the constituencies and local government, to participation by small groups of radical activists of which the best-known was Militant. By the beginning of the 1980s local Labour parties, especially in London and other major towns, had become associated with a number of unpopular causes involving feminism, homosexuality and republicanism in Northern Ireland, as well as the more conventional left-wing causes, which enabled their opponents to condemn the party as a whole as extremist.

In this situation Harold Wilson scored some successes. The first was simply to consolidate his government during 1974. Labour's strongest card was the 'Social Contract', agreed with the unions in 1973, which offered the prospect that it would be better able than Heath to handle the industrial problem. In 1974 Wilson brought the left-wing rebel, Michael Foot, into office as Employment Secretary. This paved the way for a concession to the miners of the high wage rise they had been demanding, which led to the ending of the state of emergency and a reduction of tension. The promotion of Foot was an inspired move, for as leader Wilson found himself in a much weaker position in managing the party than his predecessors had been because he could no longer rely on the support of the major unions. The alliance with Foot helped to restore relations between government and the unions. Wilson capitalized on his success in defusing the sense of crisis by holding another election in October 1974. However, this did not quite work, for Labour emerged only slightly stronger, with 319 seats and an overall majority of three which was obviously vulnerable to by-elections. In most Western parliamentary systems this situation would have been resolved by a coalition without the need for a second election, but Wilson shared traditional Labour fears about coalitions.

Europe and the SDP breakaway

Thus, although Wilson returned to office he had no mandate and, in fact, little idea about what he wanted to do. In the event he devoted much time to questions of party management. Herein lay his second major achievement. He largely succeeded in defusing the issue of Britain's position in Europe which seriously threatened Labour unity: 'My one job is to keep the party united'. Wilson made a point of incorporating into his Cabinet both right-wing pro-Europeans such as Roy Jenkins and Shirley Williams, traditional left-wing critics like Michael Foot and Barbara Castle, and the new generation of radicals represented by Tony Benn who had changed his position over Europe. It was Benn's idea to hold a referendum over British membership of the EEC which seemed a likely route to withdrawal but eventually provided a lifeline for Wilson and party unity. In January 1971 119 Labour MPs voted against joining Europe, as did the NEC by 16–6. In this situation Wilson made a point of moving a little closer to the anti-Europeans, on the grounds that he could not afford to cut himself off from the left of the party. Although he was basically pro-Europe, Wilson placated the left by agreeing to hold a referendum on the question. This led Shirley Williams to announce that she would leave politics if the referendum went against the EEC. In a parliamentary division in October 1972 69 Labour members defied the whip to support Heath on entry while another 20 abstained. Though this was a substantial number of MPs, it did not conceal the fact that the leading Europeanists, Jenkins and Williams, were becoming rather isolated in the party. The proof of this came in the ballot for the leadership following Wilson's resignation in 1976, when Jenkins received only 54 votes. In the short run the referendum policy provoked resignations from the shadow Cabinet by a number of pro-Europeans, including Jenkins.

In these developments lay the origins of the subsequent split in the party leading to the formation of the Social Democrats in the 1980s. In this sense Wilson's referendum tactics were ultimately a failure. But after his return to office in 1974 he appeared to have brought off the difficult trick of maintaining the unity of the party. In the referendum held in June 1975, Wilson posed as a moderate who believed that on balance Britain should remain in the EEC, while other members of his Cabinet freely campaigned in both 'pro' and 'anti' camps. But the 67 per cent vote in favour of membership satisfied the right while also subduing the left. For the time being the Prime Minister could bask in another triumph of management.

On the economic front Wilson had, once again, inherited a serious mess from the Conservatives. During 1974 prices rose by 17 per cent and wages by 22 per cent. The oil shortage and the impact of EEC membership in raising food prices contributed to inflation of 27 per cent in 1975. The Social Contract seemed useless to restrain wage demands. Thus the new Chancellor, Denis Healey, determined to check excessive pay settlements by a combination of higher unemployment, extra taxation and expenditure cuts. 1975 saw economies of £3 billion in social spending. Wilson and Healey were clearly in retreat from the policies of the 1960s and heading towards monetarism.

The Prime Minister hesitated between a voluntary and a statutory incomes policy, eventually settling for a half-way house. Led by Jack Jones, the TUC agreed to a limit of £6 per week on wage rises, while in his 1976 budget Healey announced a 3 per cent maximum. This incomes policy was a success in that inflation fell from 27 to 13 per cent from 1975 to 1976. But unemployment rose to 1.2 million, and between 1975 and 1976 the purchasing power of workers on average wages dropped by 7 per cent. This naturally created friction within the Labour Party, especially as the Cabinet was abandoning the policies for economic planning and the acquisition of shares by the National Enterprise Board championed by Tony Benn. The government did, however, feel obliged to rescue British Leyland from bankruptcy, which in effect meant a state takeover; and Benn himself subsidized a number of workers' co-operatives in collapsing companies. When Wilson interrupted this by moving him from Trade and Industry to Energy, Benn failed to resign, thereby discrediting himself for the remainder of the government's life.

Following Wilson's surprise resignation in 1976, the Labour Party chose Callaghan in preference to Foot as his successor – a significant sign that the parliamentarians remained essentially a right-centre body while the party outside was moving to the left. Callaghan, though experienced and popular with the unions for his opposition to *In Place of Strife*, had been an unsuccessful minister, especially at the Treasury. He was essentially a 1950s conservative politician, highly illiberal on social issues, and rather anti-feminist in contrast to Wilson, who had promoted more women than any other Prime Minister. He seemed an inappropriately old-fashioned leader for the kind of party that Labour had become. On the other hand, his avuncular, reassuring style pleased the general public and equipped him to fend off the shrill attacks of the new Conservative leader, Margaret Thatcher.

Table 19.1 Registered unemployment in Britain, 1965–76

Year	Number registered unemployed
1965	329,000
1966	353,000
1967	556,000
1968	554,000
1969	534,000
1970	579,000
1971	724,000
1972	899,000
1973	575,000
1974	542,000
1975	866,000
1976	1,332,000

Callaghan was also a more relaxed and secure personality than Wilson; his colleagues appreciated his Cabinet style, involving more open debate and less intrigue. When the government's tiny majority disappeared in 1977 he managed to keep it going first by a pact with David Steel, the new Liberal leader, and then with the Nationalist MPs.

The 'winter of discontent'

However, by the end of 1976 the economy was very weak. The balance of payments had deteriorated, the pound's value had fallen to $1.70, and Britain's currency reserves came under severe pressure. Consequently the Chancellor, Healey, sought a loan from the International Monetary Fund. This was humiliating in itself, but it also exacerbated the friction in the party because the International Monetary Fund insisted on expenditure cuts of around $2 billion. The Conservatives condemned this as the result of a succession of economic booms generated by Keynesian finance. Healey substantially agreed with the monetarist diagnosis, and he effectively began the application of what became known as Thatcherite policies two-and-a-half years before the Conservatives returned to power. The result was a fall in living standards and an increase in unemployment to 1.5 million. Though even this was not high by the standards of the 1980s, it seemed a disaster to a generation accustomed to virtually full employment. It led many workers to believe that things could not be worse if the Conservatives ran the government, a belief neatly exploited in 1979 by the slogan 'Labour Isn't Working'.

Yet by the autumn of 1978 there were grounds for thinking that the government's tough policies were effecting some improvement. Income growth was being restrained and the balance of payments improving. By-elections showed that Labour had deprived the Scottish Nationalists of their momentum by its devolution policy. But at that point Callaghan's tactical sense failed him. A maximum wage increase of 5 per cent was announced. This was unnecessarily tight, but the unions would probably have gone along with it in the short term because they assumed it to be the prelude to an autumn general election. However, the Prime Minister was not sure that he could win an election and the moment passed. The control exercised by the unions thereupon rapidly broke down. The rising cost of living seemed to them to justify bigger wage rises, and as a result a mass of strikes occurred, especially among public sector employees. This 'winter of discontent' fatally undermined the Labour government because it destroyed their claim to be competent to handle the unions. Meanwhile the fiasco over the devolution referendum in Scotland broke up the government's pact with the Nationalists exposing Labour to defeat in Parliament on 28 March 1979 and a general election. In the end Labour had failed just as Heath had earlier in dealing with the combined effects of inflation, militant unions, poor investment in industry and a balance-of-payments deficit. The consequence was to drive much of the Labour Party further to the left while a section of the Conservatives moved sharply to the right. Both were repudiating the consensus policies that had dominated the post-1945 era.

The origins of Thatcherism

In long-term perspective, the ousting of Edward Heath from the Conservative Party leadership by Margaret Thatcher in 1975 appears as an ideological turning-point. This was not, however, at all obvious at the time. The party seemed simply to be ridding itself of an unpopular and unsuccessful leader. In fact a struggle was going on within the Conservative Party at two levels – ideology and class. Although Mrs Thatcher and her followers took socialism and the state as their ostensible targets, in a sense their real enemy lay within the Conservative Party itself. Ever since the Edwardian period there had been a powerful resentment directed towards the gilded, upper-class leadership by Conservatives of more modest social standing. This gained force from an ideological attack by the 'radical right' in the aftermath of the Boer War. Balfour became the first victim of this rank-and-file pressure, and from 1911 onwards most Conservative leaders were drawn from the middle class. However, almost all of them attempted to educate their party towards a more liberal Conservatism. Influenced by their experience of two world wars and by the enfranchisement of the working class, they shifted the political agenda in the direction of welfare and collectivism. Consequently the party's history, from one perspective, began to seem like a series of retreats dictated by the left which made the party's rank-and-file feel let down by their leaders. Heath's personal remoteness simply exacerbated the feeling; as one Conservative put it: 'Like Macmillan and R.A. Butler, you always had the impression that Heath (and some of his ministers) found some of the activists at Conference distasteful – backward-looking, complacent and reactionary.'

The reaction against Keynesianism and Socialism

In contrast Mrs Thatcher was the first leader who articulated, and apparently believed in, all the opinions of rank-and-file constituency activists, notably over taxation, welfare 'scroungers', making Britain a Great Power again, cocking a snook at foreigners, and pandering to racialism. This often involved a simple expression of views rather than a change in policy. In January 1979, for example, Thatcher made a bid for the racist vote when she argued that white Britons had legitimate fears about being 'swamped by people with a different culture'. Heath had sacked Powell for a speech only a little more inflammatory. Herein lay the strength of Thatcher's position as party leader, in spite of the parliamentarians' dislike of her views.

Thus, in spite of the apparent social similarities between them, Heath and Thatcher were very different Conservative leaders. Thatcher was a real outsider, partly because of her sex and partly because she gloried in the lower-middle-class morality and economics of the grocer's shop. The experience of the Second World War also proved to be decisive. Heath emerged from that period prepared to come to terms with the state and recognize it as a force for good. And like other soldiers, he lost his prejudices against foreigners; the key objective after 1945 was the reconstruction of Europe, hence his warmth towards the EEC. By contrast, Thatcher's experience was very narrow. She emerged unaffected by the depression of the 1930s and, having made no contribution to the war effort, lacked either a sense of collective national cause or any understanding of foreign affairs.

However, between 1970 and 1974 Thatcher kept her head down and served as a loyal Minister for Education under Heath. In this period some Tories became steadily more outraged over government policies on immigration, Rhodesia, the EEC and Northern Ireland. Yet they represented the diehard fringe which most Tory leaders had to suffer. What fatally undermined Heath was his failure to handle the trade unions, and his return to collectivist and Keynesian economic and social policies. In fact, Mrs Thatcher had been as guilty in this respect as most of her colleagues. At Education she had been a big spender, and had abolished more grammar schools than any of her predecessors. Nor did she show any interest publicly in Conservative ideology. She simply became a convert to the new Conservative economic ideas.

Among politicians the real inspiration was Enoch Powell. His belief in classical liberal economics had been carried defiantly through the 1950s and 1960s, in the face of the interventionism practised by Macmillan. By 1974 Powell had become very marginal as a result of his advice to vote Labour in protest against Heath's European policy. But his ideas were taken up by Sir Keith Joseph, one of Heath's leading ministers. Within weeks of the party's defeat in February 1974 Joseph, in a characteristic confession of past error, announced his conversion to Conservatism! What he meant by this was conversion to economic liberalism. He argued that Conservatives had been beguiled by semi-socialism and the mixed economy; in future they must allow market forces to rule and not try to cheat them by state intervention. Above all, Conservatives like Joseph felt dismayed at the effects of Barber's Keynesian policies in terms of inflation and the attempts to impose incomes policies. He was increasingly attracted by monetarism, which had long been the creed of a number of minor economists who believed that governments could limit inflation by controlling the money supply. Joseph began to promote his philosophy through the establishment of the Centre for Policy Studies under the directorship of Alfred Sherman, which effectively acted as a rival to the party's Research Department. Like a number of the men who subsequently became known as Thatcherites, Sherman's origins lay on the left; a former Communist, he brought the doctrinaire approach of the far left into the far right of Conservatism.

The Thatcherite coup

Thus, by the autumn of 1974 Sir Keith Joseph had articulated a sweeping repudiation of Heath's record over inflation, incomes policy and state subsidies. This did not make a general move to the right inevitable but as Heath had led his party to three general election defeats there was bound to be a challenge to his leadership, and that challenge was mounted by the new right. Heath had been the first Tory leader to be elected to his job, and his arrogant refusal to contemplate the need to defend his record was therefore particularly unwise. He did not face an ideological challenge – the majority of the MPs appear to have been content with traditional policies; but by his stubbornness Heath placed those policies in danger.

Joseph seemed the obvious person to challenge Heath in a ballot of MPs, but he quickly ruined his chances by some tactless remarks and withdrew in November 1974. Mrs Thatcher stepped into his place, since no one else of any stature was prepared to take the risk. She was not remotely expected to win. However, her supporters used shrewd tactics; by emphasizing that she was well behind Heath they made it easier for the large number of MPs who were exasperated with the leader to give vent, safely, to their feelings by voting for the challenger. In the event the vote on 4 February 1975 produced a major shock; Thatcher received 130 votes to only 119 for Heath. This 'peasants' revolt', as it was dubbed, destroyed Heath's leadership. Moreover, although it was not an ideological rejection of his brand of Conservatism, the ballot left the supporters of Heath too demoralized and too far behind to make an effective response. Thus on the second ballot Thatcher comfortably defeated her four opponents and seized the leadership. Her victory was an unintended revolution. She had not been elected because she offered a right-wing policy, but after its defeats the party was ready to welcome a return to basic Conservative principles. By boldly attacking socialism and championing the cause of free enterprise, she began to restore to her party the sense that it occupied the moral high ground. In a speech in 1977 she declared:

> The tide is beginning to turn against collectivism, socialism, statism, dirigisme, whatever you call it … It is becoming increasingly obvious to many people who were intellectual socialists that socialism has failed to fulfil its promises, both in the more extreme form in the Communist world, and in its compromise version.

As yet her colleagues did not realize how literally their new leader took these rhetorical flights. For some years she was obliged to surround herself with former Heath supporters, who clearly believed that they would be able to control her once in office. In any case, many felt uncertain whether they would manage to recover power under Mrs Thatcher. No one knew whether the country was yet prepared to accept a woman as Prime Minister, especially one so aggressively middle class. The avuncular and chauvinistic Callaghan continued to enjoy a big lead in terms of personal popularity. However Mrs Thatcher was lucky for a second time. Had Callaghan held an election in the autumn of 1978 he might well have won. Delay, and the industrial chaos of the winter of 1978–9, gave Thatcher her opportunity. Even so, the Conservatives won only 43 per cent of the vote, not one of their better performances, but it was enough to deliver a parliamentary majority.

Further reading

General accounts:

Brian Harrison, *Finding a Role? The United Kingdom 1970–1990* (2010)

Alwyn Turner, *Crisis? What Crisis? Britain in the 1970s* (2009)

Richard Coopey and Nicholas Woodward, *Britain in the 1970s: The Troubled Economy* (1996)

Dominic Sandbrook, *States of Emergency: The Way We Were, Britain 1970–74* (2010) – detailed narrative.

Dominic Sandbrook, *Seasons in the Sun: The Battle for Britain 1974–1979* (2012) – right-wing account.

P. Hennessey and A. Seldon eds, *Ruling Performance: British Governments from Attlee to Thatcher* (1987)

On Heath and the Conservative crisis see:

John Campbell, *Edward Heath* (1993)

A. Seldon and Stuart Balls, eds, *The Heath Government 1970–74: A Reappraisal* (1996)

R. Shepherd, *Enoch Powell* (1996)

Aspects of multi-party politics:

H. Drucker ed., *Multi-Party Britain* (1978)

B. Sarlvik and I. Crewe, *Decade of Dealignment* (1983)

David Dutton, *A History of the Liberal Party in the Twentieth Century* (2004)

T.M. Devine, *The Scottish Nation 1700–2000* (1999)

C. Harvie, *Scotland and Nationalism* (1994)

K.O. Morgan, *Rebirth of a Nation: Wales 1880–1980* (1981)

Vernon Bogdanor, *Multi-Party Politics and the Constitution* (1983)

For Labour's decline see:

M. Holmes, *The Labour Government 1974–79* (1985)

Martin Pugh, *Speak for Britain! A New History of the Labour Party* (2010)

Ben Pimlott, *Harold Wilson* (1992)

K.P. Morgan, *Callaghan: A Life* (1997)

S. Fielding, *The Labour Party: Socialism and Society since 1951* (1997)

The emergence of Thatcherism is discussed in:

C. Kavanagh, *Thatcher and British Politics: the End of Consensus* (1990)

Ben Jackson and Robert Saunders eds, *Making Thatcher's Britain* (2012)

P. Cosgrove, *Margaret Thatcher: A Tory and Her Party* (1978)

The Era of Thatcherism

'I have changed everything.' Few would disagree with Mrs Thatcher's own view that her assumption of the premiership in 1979 marked a turning-point in modern British history, comparable with 1914 or 1945. However, many of the claims made by both contemporary supporters and critics were considerable exaggerations, for after 12 years of Conservative rule many of the central objectives of Thatcherism had not been achieved. Moreover, any assessment is complicated by the fact that 'Thatcherism' developed over time; some of the original elements like monetarism were abandoned as unworkable, while others such as privatization that had hardly been mentioned at the start loomed large in the late 1980s. Admittedly, Mrs Thatcher had made it clear in 1979 that she intended to curtail the role of the state, restore market forces and create an 'enterprise culture', though as this was the kind of general rhetoric usually employed by Conservatives after a long period in opposition it was not clear what this meant.

Thatcherism as anti-Establishment Conservatism

The new Prime Minister had two reasons for being cautious during the early years of her premiership. First, her victory reflected popular dissatisfaction about the unions, taxation and inflation rather than a positive consensus about the alternatives. At 43.9 per cent the party's vote was modest, in fact the lowest polled by any party that had won a majority of seats since 1922, and it subsequently *diminished*, making it difficult to argue that the country had ever given a genuine mandate for Thatcherism. Second, the Prime Minister felt conscious of leading a minority within her own party. She was sustained by the ideas generated by several right-wing think tanks, notably the Centre for Policy Studies (1975) and the Adam Smith Institute (1977), but the official policymaking machinery remained in the hands of the 'One

Nation' Tories. Even in cabinet only three leading ministers shared her economic philosophy – Sir Keith Joseph, Sir Geoffrey Howe and John Biffen – the majority subscribing to what Mrs Thatcher derided as the 'wet' school of Conservatism. Her sense of being an outsider was heightened not just by her ideas but by her sex and her modest social origins. She and her followers were disdainful of the traditional Tory elite, which they accused of betraying the party's principles in an attempt to imitate socialism.

As a result, for much of her premiership Mrs Thatcher sounded more like a leader of the Opposition attacking conventional ideas and institutions. In the course of a decade she alienated many of the central elements in the British political system. Her unpopularity in Scotland and hostility to devolution accelerated the demise of Conservative Scottish MPs, provoked nationalism and undermined the Union. She disparaged the civil service, which she considered to be infected with Keynesianism, the House of Lords, which rejected her government's proposals on several occasions, the Church of England, which she regarded as too liberal or even Marxist, the BBC, which was seen as anti-Conservative, and the universities, which had long been centres of liberalism. This was symbolized in 1985 when Oxford University decided by 700–300 votes to refuse her an honorary degree. More surprising, in view of Mrs Thatcher's emphasis on the enterprise culture, was the alienation of many in the business community who were alarmed by her anti-Europeanism and felt that she understood only the simplicities of the 1930s grocer's shop in which she had grown up, not the complexities of modern, research-based industries that required support from government.

Monetarism and depression

The new government took office determined to reduce inflation which, partly due to wage settlements already agreed, reached 22 per cent in May 1980. However, Joseph and Howe believed that they had the answer to the problem with 'monetarism' – the idea that prices could be controlled by restricting the supply of money to the economy. Though advocated by several marginal economists, monetarism remained an unproved theory; it was not even clear what exactly constituted the money supply and for several years chancellors of the exchequer changed their definition in an effort to apply the theory to the real world.

By 1981 inflation had begun to fall, largely because the economy had once again slipped into a depression. In his budget of that year Howe astounded the political world by resorting to a severe dose of orthodox deflation, including major tax increases and a reduction in the public borrowing requirement from £13.5 billion to £10.5 billion. This decisive repudiation of Keynesianism was strongly opposed by a group of leading ministers, fearful of the unemployment that would result, but as they shrank from resignation Thatcher felt she had their measure; one by one she sacked them, replacing them with her supporters.

Meanwhile, the economic and social consequences of Howe's budget proved horrendous as the British economy suffered its worst depression since the 1930s, with unemployment eventually exceeding 3 million. During 1980–1 the gross national product contracted by 3.2 per cent and eventually around 25 per cent of British manufacturing capacity was lost during this period. The consequences of this experiment were a huge, and permanent, balance of payments deficit which, in turn, resulted in high interest rates because of the need to defend the pound, and massive unemployment which prevented the government from reducing overall government spending and involved unmeasurable long-term costs for the workers affected and their families. However, the government argued that its strategy was designed to put the economy on a stronger footing and when growth resumed between 1983 and 1988 they hailed an 'economic miracle'.

One long-term by-product of the experiment was the taming of the trade unions, whose membership fell from 13 million to 10 million in 1980–3 alone. In 1981 only 4.2 million working days were lost in strikes compared with an average of 13 million during the 1970s. The explanation was simply that continuously high unemployment had killed support for militancy. The government pursued its advantage in 1982 by removing the financial immunity from the costs of strikes that the unions had enjoyed since 1906. Unions could now be fined for unlawful strikes and pay penalties for secondary picketing, while workers who had been sacked as a result of closed shop agreements received compensation. But the government's greatest triumph came with the miners' strike, which ran from April 1984 to April 1985. This enabled them to avenge the defeat suffered by Edward Heath

Table 20.1 Registered unemployment in Britain, 1974–85

Year	Number registered unemployed
1974	542,000
1977	1,450,000
1978	1,381,000
1980	1,668,000
1982	2,809,000
1985	3,149,000

in 1974. This time the Cabinet was well prepared for the confrontation as coal stocks were high and the Cabinet insisted on maintaining full electricity supplies so that the economy could weather what was expected to be a long dispute. By January 1985 71,000 of the 187,000 miners had returned to work and their defeat decisively broke the political power of the coal industry. However, it was a pyrrhic victory for the government as the subsequent closing down of the coal industry obliged Britain to import coal from abroad at a much higher cost for the next twenty years.

Deindustrialization

Meanwhile the underlying causes of Britain's economic weakness persisted: low investment, poor productivity, inadequate management and wage inflation. Increases in wages and salaries continued to run ahead of output during the 1980s. Although the government rejected any idea of a policy for incomes, in practice it had a simple policy of restricting public-sector wages in order to mitigate the inflationary effects of increases awarded in the private sector. During 1979–85, when private-sector wages rose 11 per cent, those in the public sector fell by 1 per cent; within the public sector the government favoured its supporters by allowing above-inflation increases to the police and armed forces while holding down wages in teaching, universities, nursing and local government.

A succession of ministers at the Department of Trade and Industry insisted that there was little or nothing governments could do to promote manufacturing industry. As a result several million industrial jobs disappeared with disastrous long-term social and economic consequences for British society. Poor management was also a factor in industrial decline. Among motor manufacturers Austin, Morris and Rover all dwindled with the result that after a few years only foreign companies made cars in Britain. General Electric, Britain's largest private employer up to the 1990s suffered from the retirement of its funder, Arnold Weinstock. Thereafter the company suffered from a succession of reckless directors, dazzled by a programme of acquisitions, who effectively killed off the company by the 2000s. The period saw one major economic gain in the exploitation of North Sea oil, although the opportunity presented by the earnings and the sales of nationalized industries which might have been used to finance a state-led investment programme to improve the economic infrastructure and re-equip industry, was lost. Ministers preferred to allow the extra income to flow into short-term consumption and imports. In theory the growth of employment in the service sector was expected to compensate for manufacturing decline, but the new jobs often required different skills, they were often women's jobs and were concentrated in the south-east where expensive housing continued to be a deterrent to workers. Above all, the service sector failed to make inroads into Britain's huge balance of payments deficit, which began to lock the country into a spiral of decline. The deficit caused speculation against sterling, which in turn led the government to defend the value of the pound by maintaining high interest rates. But the higher cost of borrowing only deterred industry from making the investment required to improve productivity.

Since 1945 governments of all parties had assumed that the public would not tolerate unemployment of even 1 million, but the Conservatives managed to retain office in 1983 and 1987 despite mass unemployment. Even the official figure of 3.2 million unemployed in 1985 underestimated the total by half a million because the government repeatedly changed the methods of calculating it with a view to excluding people; eventually 1 million were transferred from unemployment benefits to disability benefits. In effect the government had succeeded in persuading the public that full employment had ceased to be feasible. Mass unemployment was not politically toxic. Between 1985 and 1988 the economy grew by 4 per cent a year and inflation

Table 20.2 Britain's visible balance of trade deficit, 1946–85 (in £ millions)

Year	Deficit in millions of pounds
1946–50	−160
1951–55	−345
1956–60	−94
1961–65	−218
1966–70	−297
1971–75	−2,263
1976–80	−1,969
1981–85	−2,397

Table 20.3 Employment by sector, 1977–85 (in millions)

Sector	1977	1981	1985
Manufacturing	7.3	6.2	5.5
Construction	1.2	1.1	0.9
Agriculture, forestry and fishing	0.4	0.3	0.3
Energy and water supply	0.7	0.7	0.6
Service	12.9	13.4	14.0

fell from 22 per cent in 1980 to 7 per cent in 1985 and 3 per cent in 1986. Consequently, although unemployment remained unprecedentedly high, as in the 1930s, it affected only a minority of people concentrated in certain regions. Mrs Thatcher relied on the support of the more buoyant areas such as the south-east of England.

The boom of the mid-1980s was largely fuelled by consumer credit and a policy of financial deregulation, the effect of which was to encourage a major increase in lending by building societies in the form of additional mortgages which amounted to loans that could be diverted into ordinary expenditure. The financial institutions got into the habit of irresponsible lending to homebuyers, many of whom were subsequently unable to maintain their payments. In addition there was a rapid increase in credit cards, bank overdrafts and hire purchase agreements, and as a result private household debt rose from £16 billion to £47 billion between 1980 and 1989 and mortgages from £43 billion to £235 billion. Whereas in 1980 debt amounted to 29 per cent of national income, by 1989 it amounted to no less than 62 per cent.

Consequently, the economic miracle hailed by the Chancellors of the Exchequer rested on inflated debt and consumer spending, not on improved productivity or export growth. It was only a matter of time before the bubble burst as the debts were called in. Unfortunately in his 1989 budget, the Chancellor, Nigel Lawson, recklessly exacerbated the danger by cutting taxes. As the economy began to take a downward turn Lawson claimed it was suffering from no more than a temporary 'blip', but it soon became clear that a second major depression had begun. By 1990 the economy was stagnant and during 1991–2 it contracted. As monetarism had long since been abandoned as unworkable, the government had few weapons at its disposal except for the use of interest rates, which at 13 per cent severely handicapped industry. Eventually this second depression discredited Mrs Thatcher's economic experiment. It emerged that the rate of growth in the British economy during 1979–91 had been, on average, only 1.75 per cent. This compared with 2.4 per cent in the previous decade and even higher rates in the 1960s – the decade so disparaged by Thatcherites. After 12 years Mrs Thatcher left the British economy demonstrably weaker than she had found it.

Delusions of grandeur

Like most twentieth-century prime ministers Mrs Thatcher felt tempted to boost her standing by capitalizing on the remnants of Britain's previous status as a Great Power. For her this was especially important, partly because her inexperience in foreign affairs and her gender meant that she was suspected of being a liability in this field. As soon as she became leader she consciously tried to compensate for this by adopting a belligerent tone towards the Soviet Union. She also cultivated a resurgence of patriotism within her party among those who regretted Britain's decline as a Great Power. Whereas previous party leaders had marginalized those Conservatives who sought to slow the retreat from empire, Mrs Thatcher attempted to articulate their feelings. She genuinely despised the diplomacy of the Foreign Office, not least because of its handling of the emotive issue of the illegal regime in Southern Rhodesia. British diplomats engineered a conference at which Britain effectively signed away power to an elected – and thus black – majority government. This resolution of a long-standing problem sat awkwardly with the views of most Thatcherites and it left the Prime Minister with the feeling that she had been bamboozled by Lord Carrington, her Foreign Secretary. Subsequently she relied more on her own instincts by adopting an uncompromising line with the Commonwealth, in particular resisting the pressure to impose sanctions against the apartheid regime in South Africa. However, Mrs Thatcher was tilting against windmills. Faced with the need to deal with the remnants of empire in the shape of Hong Kong, she simply agreed to surrender the territory to China when Britain's treaty expired in 1997.

War for the Falklands

Yet like other post-war premiers Mrs Thatcher found it possible to refurbish Britain's status as a Great Power by cultivating the special relationship with the United States. This was attractive since the US President, Ronald Reagan, shared her preference for market economics and her hostility towards the Soviet Union. They agreed a deal whereby Britain allowed the United States to keep cruise missiles on her soil and in return received the Trident nuclear missile as a substitute for the ageing Polaris submarine system. This kept alive the illusion of Britain as an independent nuclear power, but at a considerable cost. Britain's conventional weapons suffered from economies which had near-disastrous results when the Falklands War broke out – the government had been on the verge of scrapping Britain's two remaining aircraft carriers, without which the expedition could not have been carried out.

The Falklands War of March–April 1982 was a remarkable throwback to the era of minor Victorian wars in that it took place, more by accident than by design, in an area so remote that most British people had never heard of it. This small group of islands, populated by 1,200 people of British origins, had for many years been regarded by all British governments as being of no importance, in fact as rather a nuisance. Their policy was gradually to loosen the ties between Britain and the Falklands so that the islanders could be led into a closer relationship with Argentina, which claimed the islands as her territory. Mrs Thatcher's government fully accepted this policy, to which end a Foreign Office minister, Nicholas Ridley, had been dispatched to the Falklands to persuade the people to accept it. As a result of the defence economies of 1982 the one British ship in South Atlantic waters, HMS *Endurance*, was withdrawn. This error on the government's part was interpreted by Argentina as a sign that Britain was backing out. Thereupon General Galtieri tried to accelerate the process by invading the Falklands in the belief that Britain would either give them up or be unable to intervene.

This misjudgement placed Mrs Thatcher in a crisis. For political reasons she had to recover the Falklands – not to do so might well have destroyed her premiership. Accordingly, a 28,000-strong task force was mobilized and transported with some difficulty to the South Atlantic. The lack of adequate air cover made the operation extremely risky. However, by May the islands had been recovered, though with serious losses to British shipping that put Britain's capacity to meet her commitments to NATO in jeopardy. Politically the war had the effect of accelerating an improvement in the government's popularity prior to the 1983 election. In the longer term the financial consequences proved to be serious. Since the government could hardly afford to admit that it had fought a war to retain a territory formerly considered to be useless, it reversed its policy by spending large sums of money on the defence of the Falklands with a view to exploiting the material resources of the region.

Although the Prime Minister believed that she had restored Britain's standing in the world, the 1980s made little difference to Britain's position. Even the special relationship with America dwindled as President Reagan began to show more interest in cultivating relations with Germany, the real power in Europe. The Falklands was entirely peripheral in all senses. Above all, Mrs Thatcher's aspirations to restore Britain to her world role were subverted by Europe. She regarded Europe as a means of reimposing interventionism by the back door. Although the government won some domestic popularity by routinely obstructing European legislation, the public appreciated moves to bring British maternity leave up to European standards and to raise minimum wages. However, Thatcher was closer to popular attitudes in voicing her dislike of the trend towards economic union, which she expressed in a famous speech at Bruges in September 1988. Yet she was declaiming against forces beyond her control for her government committed Britain to joining the single European market from 1992 and to eventual membership of the European Exchange Rate Mechanism. This latter effectively meant that Britain surrendered her control of currency policy, so that British sovereignty, as traditionally understood, was coming to an end by 1990.

Breaking the mould of politics

Initially the Labour Party's defeat in 1979 appeared no more than the result of the immediate circumstances in which it had been fought: the industrial action during the 'winter of discontent'. However, 1979 has to be seen in the context of a protracted decline in Labour support from 48 per cent of the vote in 1966 to 28 per cent in 1983. This suggests that underlying social and structural changes were working to the party's disadvantage as opposed to simply the passing impact of issues and personalities. By the 1980s the generation that had first voted in 1945, a uniquely pro-Labour one, was disappearing from the electoral register. Meanwhile, the steady shift from industrial to white-collar occupations gradually diminished Labour's traditional sources of support; by 1988 manual workers comprised only 45 per cent of the electorate and a little more than a third of the workforce belonged to a trade union. Each new redrawing of the constituency boundaries gave the Conservatives extra seats in suburban districts while the industrial centres shrank. Labour had also lost touch with some working-class voters, notably homeowners, who comprised 62 per cent of the population by 1985. By identifying themselves strongly with home-ownership through the sale of council houses the Conservatives had driven a wedge into traditional Labour support.

However, as other left-wing parties coped with similar social changes, these trends need not have been disastrous for the Labour Party but for errors of tactics and strategy with which they coincided. Following the resignation of James Callaghan in 1980, Michael Foot was selected as leader, largely because he seemed most likely to be able to restore party unity. But although a traditional left-winger, Foot proved to be unable to contain the resurgence of the left led by Tony Benn, who almost defeated Denis Healey for the deputy leadership in 1981. The rank-and-file members were reacting against the years under Wilson and Callaghan which now appeared to have been a betrayal of the principles of the movement. At the 1981 party conference the activists succeeded in imposing a system of regular reselection upon Members of Parliament and in placing the election of the leader in the hands of an electoral college comprising MPs, trade unions and constituency parties. Subsequently Labour committed itself to an unusually left-wing programme including extensive nationalization, unilateral disarmament and withdrawal from the EEC and NATO. The resulting manifesto on which Labour fought the disastrous election of 1983 was aptly dubbed 'the longest suicide note in history'.

The Social Democrat breakaway

Yet the defeat of 1983 had already been heralded by a major split in the party in February 1981 when three former ministers, Shirley Williams, David Owen and William Rodgers, joined with Roy Jenkins to issue the 'Limehouse declaration', which paved the way for the establishment of the Social Democratic Party. Jenkins, who had taken the initiative in breaking with his old party, had felt inclined to join the Liberal Party. However, the Liberal leader, David Steel, urged, mistakenly as it turned out, that a separate organization would offer a better means of attracting support from Labour. During 1981–2 local co-operation between Liberals and Social Democrats enabled the two parties to promote an agreed candidate in every constituency. Meanwhile, they scored a series of spectacular victories in by-elections and by November 1981, according to opinion polls, their 'Alliance' enjoyed the support of 45 per cent of voters. Twenty-nine Labour MPs and one Conservative joined the Social Democrats. Amid the economic failures of doctrinaire Thatcherism and Labour extremism, it seemed for a time that a major new force was about to break the mould of British politics.

However, the new strategy suffered from several flaws. Although the Social Democrats were impressive at parliamentary level, they lacked roots in the country. Notably unsuccessful in attracting Labour voters, most of them lost their seats at the next general election. Although they performed better in Conservative territory, they did no better than the Liberals. Consequently, the rationale for launching a separate party rather than joining the Liberals was never fully justified. Nonetheless, support for the Alliance reached a peak around March 1982, though by then Conservative support had begun to revive and was strengthened by the Falklands War, which decisively interrupted the progress of the Alliance by depriving it of the initiative. At the 1983 election the new grouping performed well, winning over 25.4 per cent, only slightly behind Labour on 27.6. However, the electoral system created a complete travesty of democracy by returning 209

Labour MPs compared with 23 for the Alliance. Although the Conservatives' vote *fell* to 42.4 per cent, they won many more seats, giving them a huge overall majority. These distortions of public opinion were so great that they created widespread support for the introduction of a system of proportional representation.

After the fiasco of 1983 Foot was replaced as leader by Neil Kinnock, a pragmatic left-winger who recognized that Labour could easily be relegated to third place behind the Alliance if it persisted with existing policies. With considerable skill and courage he led the party back towards a more centrist position and dramatized his strategy by public condemnation of prominent left-wingers, including Derek Hatton of Liverpool, Ken Livingstone of the London County Council and Arthur Scargill of the National Union of Miners. However, full revival appeared for some years to be an intractable goal. Although the Labour poll increased modestly to 30.8 per cent in 1987, this only slightly reduced the government's majority. Labour, meanwhile, widened its advantage over the Alliance, whose vote fell to 22.6 per cent. Between 1983 and 1987 the Alliance had missed its opportunity, largely due to the prima donna behaviour of David Owen who had succeeded Jenkins as Social Democrat leader and stubbornly resisted the pressure to merge with the Liberals so as to offer voters a single party. However, the members of both parties backed a merger and when this was subsequently achieved Owen was quickly marginalized and withdrew from politics. He had, however, damaged the new Liberal Democrat Party, whose vote fell to 18 per cent in 1992 when the Conservatives won a fourth victory by a narrower margin. The main achievement of the Social Democrats had been to force Labour back into centrist politics and make it electable again.

The growth of poverty and inequality

The 1980s marked a watershed in British social history. Ever since the innovations of the Edwardian Liberal governments the state had effected a modest but steady redistribution of income, by means of graduated taxation and social welfare, from the richer to the poorer members of the community. This progress was upheld by all subsequent governments, but after 1979 it went into reverse. Not only did the decade witness a notable increase in poverty, it also saw a wider gulf between what Disraeli had described as the 'two nations'. Whereas in 1979 the top 20 per cent of wage earners had enjoyed 37 per cent of all income after tax, by 1988 they had 44 per cent; conversely, the poorest 20 per cent, who had received 9.5 per cent of income in 1979, earned just 6.9 per cent by 1988.

This shift in favour of the wealthy was partly achieved by adopting a regressive system of taxation. By stages the government cut the standard rate of income tax to 25 per cent and the top rate to 40 per cent. This was supposed to stimulate enterprise and wealth creation. However, there was no evidence that it worked in this way and the most successful economies, Japan and Germany, flourished despite higher rates of tax than Britain's. The tax changes had the effect of enriching a small number of high earners, but for the majority of people the tax burden *increased* because of major additions to other forms of taxation paid by the poor and by those on average incomes. For example, National Insurance payments rose so that they yielded three-quarters as much as income tax, and there were extra indirect taxes on consumption, notably value added tax which increased from 2.5 per cent to 17.5 per cent.

Although the government criticized welfare expenditure for its undesirable effects on the poor, it did not hesitate to extend the welfare state in the shape of subsidies for the middle classes. By far the most costly subsidies took the form of income tax relief on mortgage payments, which began to go out of control in this period; from £1,000 million in 1979, mortgage relief cost the Exchequer £7,000 million by 1990. The Treasury sacrificed a further £7,000 million by failing to levy capital gains tax on house sales. In addition the government paid £10 billion annually in tax subsidies to pension funds for wealthier people and introduced a new subsidy for personal pension schemes and a new tax subsidy for the purchase of shares of £100 million.

Trimming back the welfare state

All these transfers of income to relatively well-off people had to be financed by extra taxes on consumption paid by poorer people and by cuts in welfare for the working classes. One way of achieving this lay in modifying the level of unemployment benefits by linking them to prices, not to wages, which meant that the growing number of unemployed fell further behind the rest of the community. Child benefits, which had replaced family allowances, were simply frozen for several years so that their value fell sharply. After 1988 the social security system was reorganized so that those who depended on National Insurance were to receive loans from a Social Fund. However, those who were deemed unable to repay the loans were denied assistance.

Moreover, the local Department of Health and Social Security offices operated within annual expenditure limits, so that payments had to be made in the light of the resources they had available, not in accordance with the applicants' needs. At this time some 300,000 children lost their right to school meals, those aged 16–18 lost their claim to unemployment benefit, and students' housing benefit was withdrawn. The elderly suffered in two main ways: 700,000 lost their housing benefit, and the link between pensions and national earnings was abandoned.

The consequences of these changes in welfare, combined with the return of mass unemployment, proved to be dramatic. During the 1980s beggars reappeared on the streets of British cities and increasing numbers of people took to sleeping in the open – sights once associated with the Victorian era. Indeed, in 1989 200,000 people were prosecuted under the Vagrancy Act of 1824. The number of homeless families rose from 56,000 in 1979 to no fewer than 128,000 families, some 370,000 people, by 1989. The cause lay in the 1980 Housing Act which promoted the sale of council houses at high discounts, such that by 1986 643,000 had been sold, by 1996 another 1,100,000 and from 1997 to 2010 a further 900,000.

The consequences of increasing poverty and unemployment showed themselves in terms of the break-up of families, higher divorce rates, more suicides, mental illness and, above all, crime, which rose by 79 per cent under Mrs Thatcher's premiership. The emergence of a large 'underclass' alienated from the mainstream of society was marked by the outbreaks of rioting in many of the depressed urban districts. Beginning with the Bristol riots in 1980 this phenomenon spread to Brixton, Toxteth (Liverpool) and Moss Side (Manchester) in 1981, to Handsworth (Birmingham), Tottenham and Brixton in 1985 and to Newcastle in 1991. The government exacerbated the situation with its attempt to reform the local rating system by requiring even the poorest to contribute towards the new 'poll tax'. This provoked a massive non-payment campaign even in comparatively well-off areas and led around 1 million people to fail to register as parliamentary voters by 1992. In this way some poor people lost their political rights, albeit temporarily, another throwback to Victorian times. By the end of the 1980s there were ominous signs that British society had begun to break down under the social strains and economic setbacks of Thatcherism.

Rolling back the state

The attack on the state concentrated on four main areas: local government, education, health and nationalized industries. Much of this work was concentrated in Mrs Thatcher's third term because by then there seemed less reason to fear the unpopularity likely to be aroused. For some years the government gave no indication that it planned to return state-owned industry to the private sector, but it was eventually realized that the sales would provide the resources required to pay for tax cuts. The result was a succession of privatizations, including British Telecom, British Aerospace, Britoil, British Airways, the Trustee Savings Bank, British Gas, Rolls-Royce, Rover, Jaguar, and the Electricity and Water Boards. The most eccentric privatizations involved prisons which resulted in a large number of escapes, the Ministry of Defence's use of private security firms to guard barracks, and proposals by English Heritage to sell ancient monuments under its care. During his 1992–7 administration John Major also sold off the railways to a multitude of private companies; this was supposed to lead to more investment and managerial expertise but the state paid higher subsidies to the private railways, ticket prices rose and punctuality decreased.

These policies were imposed in the face of public opposition; four out of five people opposed water privatization, for example. Moreover, resistance was well founded as the government obtained very poor deals because state concerns were disposed of at well below their value for fear that private investors might not want to undertake the risks in managing them. The greatest scandal was the sale of cemeteries worth £7 million for £1 by the Conservative-controlled Westminster Council. Some Conservatives regarded the industries as assets paid for over decades by taxpayers and which, like the state's oil holdings, had earned revenue for the Exchequer. Harold Macmillan memorably denounced the policy as 'selling the family silver'. Subsequently the privatized companies, especially gas, water and electricity, attracted criticism for exploiting their monopoly status to fatten their profits by sacking staff and raising prices to consumers. Indeed in the case of electricity, ministers had insisted on raising prices before privatization to make the sale appear more attractive to investors.

Shrinking local government

Mrs Thatcher's approach to elective local government reflected the traditional Conservative mistrust. Faced with a local authority whose policies she disliked, such as the Greater London Council and even the metropolitan boroughs, she simply abolished them. The government attempted to restrict local expenditure by reducing grants and setting limits, but as this antagonized even Tory councils it was replaced by 'rate capping', which was designed to penalize authorities whose spending exceeded what Whitehall deemed appropriate. The replacement of rates by the poll tax was intended to make councils more responsive to their electorate, but it soon transpired that central government would largely continue to dictate spending. Ministers also attempted to cut local government down to size by forcing councils to sell off their houses while not allowing them to use the proceeds to build new ones. Schools were also given financial incentives to opt out of council control, though very few did so. These attacks on local government provoked thousands of resignations by Conservative councillors and permanently weakened the party's standing in local government so that it disappeared altogether in major cities such as Manchester, Liverpool, Sheffield and Newcastle, where it was replaced by the Liberal Democrats.

Meanwhile, a succession of initiatives in education succeeded in alienating almost all levels of the educational profession. The demoralization in the teaching profession led up to 20,000 teachers to leave the profession each year, making the shortages in foreign languages, mathematics and science even worse than they were already. Private business was invited to fund City Technology Colleges outside local authority control, but few materialized as companies felt reluctant to pay the government's bills. The doctrinaire nature of the thinking was underlined by the otherwise inexplicable decision to abolish the schools inspectorate and leave its functions in the hands of non-professionals. Mrs Thatcher also began to reduce funding for higher education, leading to a major decline in academic salaries and the loss of thousands of experienced lecturers who retired early or went abroad as universities struggled to keep within their resources. Many young scholars chose not to pursue careers in science because the rewards and opportunities were so poor. Students themselves suffered from the freezing of grants and the pressure to take out loans or jeopardize their academic work by taking on part-time jobs. The government would have gone further in restricting the universities but was deterred by the anger of middle-class parents. However, it found a more subtle line of attack by adopting a divide-and-rule strategy. It removed the polytechnics from local authority control, granted them university status and relied on a new breed of managers to put students through degree courses at lower costs. This led to an increase in the proportion of 18-year-olds in higher education from 14 per cent to 28 per cent, though at the cost of a reduction in the quality of the education provided.

However, Thatcher hesitated to tackle the National Health Service because of its popularity, claiming defensively that it was 'safe in our hands'. However, during the 1980s expenditure cuts resulted in the closure of thousands of hospital beds, a withdrawal by thousands of nurses because of poor pay and a major increase in waiting lists which, by 1988, had reached 700,000, with some patients waiting two years for operations. An attempt to introduce market forces into health care resulted in an increase in the number of administrators and a major rise in salaries paid to administrators. As in education, a new breed of managers tried to push more patients through the system at a lower unit cost, but this resulted in elderly patients being dispatched from hospitals too soon only to be readmitted to complete their recovery. By 1992 many hospitals were unable to admit even seriously ill patients because they had exhausted their annual resources before the end of the financial year. It was in this period that the first cautious attempts at dismantling the NHS were made. Dentists, for example, increasingly refused to accept NHS patients, and the introduction of charges for dental and eye tests in 1988 resulted in a 40 per cent fall in the number of eye tests. The underfunding of health services provoked some people into making use of private health schemes although the expansion of the private health sector introduced inefficiency into the cost-effective NHS; private health charged inflated prices and diverted scarce resources into profits for its investors.

The threat to civil liberties

Yet while restricting the social role of the state Mrs Thatcher's government took a wholly different view of its *political* activities, so much so that it extended the right of the state to interfere in the lives of its citizens and effectively curtail the civil liberties of some of them. For example, trade unionism was banned at GCHQ at Cheltenham on the grounds that it might be a threat to national security; the miners' strike saw new restrictions imposed by the police and the courts on freedom of movement and protest; and the 1986 Public Order Act extended the powers of the police to restrict public meetings. The decade also witnessed a huge increase in phone tapping, to 30,000 cases each year, by the agents of the government. Yet by far the most serious threat to civil and political liberties during the 1980s arose in connection with the secret operations of the security services. A succession of civil servants – Sarah Tisdall, Kathy Massiter, Clive Ponting – suffered prosecution for revealing abuses and errors at the heart of the official machine. Massiter helped to expose misconduct at MI5, which subjected several trade unionists and officers of the National Council for Civil Liberties to investigation for no other reason than that they held left-wing opinions. The Prime Minister was antagonized when the publication of *Spycatcher*, the memoirs of a former MI5 employee, Peter Wright, appeared to corroborate accusations of abuses committed by the security services. Wright claimed that there had been a systematic attempt to destabilize Wilson's government because of alleged contacts with the Soviet Union and that he had participated in burglaries and bugging of the Prime Minister's premises. Ignoring the possibility that there might be a threat to democratic politics, the Thatcher government concentrated on coercing public employees into silence, banned *Spycatcher* and spent huge sums of money in a futile attempt to prevent its circulation in Australia. In 1988 the Appeal Court eventually ruled that Thatcher's action in preventing quotation in the press had been illegal as well as 'futile and plain silly'. These reactionary policies had the effect of stimulating fresh concern about civil liberties in Britain in the form of a campaign for a Freedom of Information Act and reform of the illiberal Official Secrets Act, which dated from 1911. However, the government, concerned that juries were now refusing to convict civil servants such as Ponting who had revealed that ministers had lied during the Falklands War, created a more restrictive Official Secrets Act in 1988. This made it illegal for any government employee or newspaper to publish any information that the government itself defined as affecting national security; no public-interest defence was allowed, nor were illegal acts such as unauthorized telephone tapping to be revealed.

Presidential government and the limited revolution

After three successive victories in 1979, 1983 and 1987, the dominance of Thatcherism appeared to be complete the more so as she represented the presidential style of premiership rather than that of a traditional Prime Minister. One symptom of this was her reluctance to appear in the House of Commons except for brief exchanges at Question Time; in the four years up to 1990 she made only two full speeches there and overall made a fifth as many as her three predecessors. The longer she remained Prime Minister, the less she attended Parliament, retreating into the circle of her personal advisers and isolated from her critics both within and outside the Conservative Party. Her penchant for filling the role of head of *state* was underlined by her extraordinary use of the royal 'we', as on the celebrated occasion when she told an astonished press: 'We have become a grandmother.' Like other presidential prime ministers Mrs Thatcher also took care to bolster her regime by the extension of political honours. Like Lloyd George she lavishly rewarded editors and newspaper proprietors who supported her, allowing the Australian Rupert Murdoch to acquire a dominant share of national newspapers in return for his support. She granted ten times as many knighthoods to Tory backbenchers as Edward Heath had done. Those who donated large sums to party funds were recognized; for example, peerages went to seventeen industrialists whose companies had contributed £5 million to the party or one of its front organizations. Two-thirds of the newly created knights belonged to companies whose donations totalled £11 million during the Thatcher premiership. Although this practice was by no means new, the scale of it suggested a return to an earlier era. A similar mind-set allowed Mrs Thatcher's former ministers to be more than usually eager to gather lucrative company directorships. In particular there emerged a conspicuous connection with the newly privatized businesses in that several former ministers obtained well-paid positions with the very companies that took over the industries they had sold. Although transfers between official employment and private industry were neither new nor illegal, the extent to which politicians had begun to enrich themselves by this means provoked debate.

The poll tax and Scotland

Inevitably the absence of effective checks on the government began to manifest itself in the character of its decision-making. Although originally in a minority in her Cabinet, Mrs Thatcher had steadily eliminated her critics, in the process weakening Cabinet government and relying more on a small body of personal followers. The most singular result of this trend was the adoption of the community charge, better known as the 'poll tax'. By imposing the same charge upon poor householders as on wealthy ones, the scheme offended the sense of fairness that remained widespread in British society. Yet although almost all her ministers considered the poll tax to be unwise, none except Nigel Lawson was prepared to express their opposition. The tax was introduced experimentally in Scotland, where its unpopularity contributed to Conservative losses in the 1987 election. During 1988 it emerged that local councils in Scotland were actually unable to collect the tax, and by 1989 1.2 million Scots payers had received sheriffs' warrants for failure to pay. By 1990 the extension of the scheme to England had provoked similar resistance, even in middle-class and Conservative areas; for example, non-payment rates stood at 51 per cent in Liverpool but also at 39 per cent in Bath. As a result local government was in danger of breaking down as collection grew increasingly difficult. The fiasco played a major part in destroying Thatcher's hold over Conservative MPs, who began to see her as a liability.

For Scots the decision to impose the poll tax in Scotland first symbolized the distant and uncaring rule of Westminster. As Scots voted heavily against

Thatcher in four successive elections but got a Conservative government every time, they increasingly resented the 'democratic deficit'. Her aggressively English, middle-class style and values also antagonized Scots opinion. As a result the Conservatives lost their traditional working-class Protestant vote and then their middle-class voters who favoured a constructive role for the state, culminating in the 1997 election when no Conservatives were elected in Scotland. In this way Thatcher seriously damaged her party and hugely accelerated opposition to the Union with England.

The limits of Thatcherism

These developments underlined the fact that despite her power at the centre, the impact of the Prime Minister's philosophy in the country proved to be surprisingly limited. In economics there were only two enduring legacies. The dismantling of state-owned industry was extended by Major and by the post-1997 Labour governments. The destruction of trade union power reflected the contraction of union membership due to dwindling industry, legal restrictions on the right to strike, and the weakening of union influence in the Labour Party after the defeat of the coal miners.

Conversely, studies of public opinion conducted by the British Social Attitudes Survey consistently showed that faith in collectivist policies – state welfare, the NHS, public spending, state education – remained as strong as ever. In fact, growing job insecurity undermined the Thatcherite belief in the bracing effect of market forces on society. Not only were manual workers stripped of their traditional protection against unfair dismissal, but middle-class, professional employees now began to be the victims of redundancy comparatively early in life, a process that made well-paid professionals in banks, accountancy and building societies vulnerable and destroyed the traditional expectation of a secure career with rising salaries and pension rights. In the long run this began to undermine the work ethic in middle-class England, which had been far from Mrs Thatcher's intention.

Several other aims of Thatcherism also proved to be elusive. Although the government hoped to stimulate enterprise by reducing taxation, its own statistics cast doubt on its claims. In 1979 just over 35 per cent of gross domestic product was consumed by taxes of all kinds, but by 1984 this had *increased* to 38 per cent and was still at 37 per cent in 1990. Throughout the 1980s the tax burden remained higher than it had been in the 1970s, despite Conservative claims to be the low-tax party. Nor was there much evidence that an enterprise culture had been fostered in Britain. Between 1980 and 1989 the self-employed section of the labour force rose from

8 per cent to 12 per cent; however, this was largely a by-product of high unemployment as some of those who lost their jobs used redundancy money to launch small businesses, many of which went bankrupt during the depression of 1990–3. More people became owners of shares as a result of privatization during the 1980s, though by the end of the decade the number had dwindled and the proportion of shares owned by individuals fell from 28 per cent to 21 per cent. The explanation is that when buying shares the public had not seen any risk because the initial share prices of the privatized businesses had been set so low that they seemed bound to rise and yield a quick profit.

Mrs Thatcher had repeatedly insisted that Britain must pay her way in the world, but this goal also proved to be beyond reach. The modest balance of payments deficit she inherited ballooned to £13.6 billion by 1989. The collapse of manufacturing industry meant that Britain had less and less to export and meanwhile demands on public spending increased. This retreat from financial responsibility was mirrored more widely in British society by the huge increase in indebtedness during the 1980s following deregulation of banks and building societies. Whereas in 1981 16.5 per cent of national income had been saved, by 1987 this had fallen to a mere 2.4 per cent. In effect the British economy relied upon consumer indebtedness.

Women and the liberal society

Thatcherism also found itself at odds with the growing liberalism of British society. For example, the enactment of the notorious 'Section 28' which banned schools from 'promoting' homosexuality proved damaging and unpopular as it deterred teachers from discouraging homophobia; it also gave Conservatives a lasting reputation as the anti-gay party. Similarly, Thatcherism appeared hostile to feminism as Thatcher herself disparaged the movement and excluded women from her cabinets. Yet the political conformation of the 1980s was irrelevant to the process of social change in this period, notably a revolution in attitudes towards female employment. Women benefited from the expansion of employment in the service sector such that among women aged 24–44 the proportion in work rose from 52 to 68 per cent in 1971–87. The marriage rate fell by half between 1971 and 1991. By 1994 20 per cent of families with dependent children were headed by a lone mother. By 1990 41 per cent of mothers with children under five worked compared with only 23 per cent in 1983. Such evidence of gains in the status of women was bitterly attacked in the reactionary newspapers, including the *Daily Mail, Sun* and *Daily Telegraph,* but society as a whole largely accepted it. The experience of growing up under a female Prime Minister inevitably encouraged a generation of girls to pursue careers. The Scottish Nationalists led the way with prominent women MPs including Winifred Ewing, Margot MacDonald and Margaret Bain. But Thatcher also galvanized Labour women into returning to institutional politics. In 1986 the party conference responded by agreeing that among vacant, winnable seats half of candidatures should go to women. Partly as a result 60 women were elected as MPs in 1992 and a massive 119 in 1997, of whom 101 were Labour. In short the pattern of long-term social and political change suggests that the impact of Thatcherism has been greatly exaggerated.

The crisis over Europe and the downfall of Thatcher

Important as the poll tax was, the underlying reason for the Prime Minister's downfall lay in a failure of economic strategy. By 1990 financial deregulation and reckless lending by banks had got out of hand, leading to high inflation, rises in house prices and unsustainable mortgages for many people. In this situation the government recognized only one weapon – raising interest rates. This was considered necessary as a means of defending the value of the pound, which had risen in anticipation of British entry into the European Exchange Rate Mechanism. However, higher interest rates had the effect of reducing investment and profits, thereby helping to trigger another recession. Thus, by 1990 unemployment had begun to increase again and mortgage rates rose to 15.5 per cent leaving many homeowners unable to repay their mortgages. The onset of a second major depression destroyed Mrs Thatcher's credibility and made her claims to have achieved an economic miracle look thin, especially as the economy had grown more slowly than in previous decades. Things were exacerbated when, in October 1990, the new Chancellor of the Exchequer, John Major, committed an error in taking Britain into the Exchange Rate Mechanism with the pound valued at 2.95 German marks. This was far too high a level and forced British companies to try to cut costs or lose competitiveness in the midst of a serious recession.

The downfall of Thatcher

Yet it was Europe that provided the final trigger for Mrs Thatcher's overthrow. Since July 1989 when he had been sacked as Foreign Secretary for his

Image 13 Sir Geoffrey Howe and Michael Heseltine oust Mrs Thatcher from the premiership, 1990.

pro-European views, Sir Geoffrey Howe had been the target of leaks and attacks by the Thatcherites. But in November 1990 he seized the initiative by resigning and, in a devastating speech in Parliament, he argued that the Prime Minister's determination to sabotage European policy had made life intolerable. This encouraged Michael Heseltine into making a leadership challenge in which he won 152 votes from MPs while Mrs Thatcher failed to obtain enough to retain the leadership on the first ballot. Acknowledging that her support had collapsed, she withdrew from the contest and was replaced by John Major. The underlying explanation for this extraordinary outcome was that, though immensely popular among the rank-and-file members, Mrs Thatcher had never converted a majority of the MPs to her brand of Conservatism. They accepted her as long as she delivered victory, but by 1990 they judged that public disenchantment was so deep that they would lose next time. In this the party's instincts proved very sound, for her successor, who appeared a very different personality, managed to avoid bearing the responsibility for the policies of the previous decade and engineered a revival in the opinion polls.

However, as Major was an unknown quantity, many MPs had assumed that he was more of a Thatcherite than was really the case. He soon made it clear that while he accepted much of her economic thinking, he would break with her social policies and he abandoned the poll tax. Major had little use for the right-wing think tanks, the Adam Smith Institute and the No Turning Back Group, and indicated that he would not fight another election on a Thatcherite programme. On this basis Major eventually went to the polls in April 1992 against the background of a small but sustained Labour lead, retaining 42 per cent of the vote against Labour's 35 per cent. However, the Conservatives suffered a net loss of 34 seats, leaving a majority of only 21. In effect Major had escaped the blame for Mrs Thatcher's policies.

Conservative Euroscepticism

Nevertheless, this remarkable victory proved to be a poisoned chalice as Major had to handle the legacy of an economic depression and the increasingly divisive issue of Britain's role in Europe. While cultivating anti-European prejudice, Mrs Thatcher had begun to lose control over British policy in Europe. Symptomatic of her frustration was a bitter and emotional outburst by one of her ministers, Nicholas Ridley, in June 1990 when he denounced economic union as 'a German racket to take over the whole of Europe'. In this Ridley reflected the fundamentalism of many Tories who feared the loss of British sovereignty and saw economic union as a threat to their free-market philosophy.

He also spoke for a generation of older people who had fought in the Second World War and felt outraged that countries like Germany had become so successful since 1945 while victorious Britain had steadily declined. This led to the formation of the Bruges Group, a Thatcherite organization designed to force Major to veto all progress towards economic union. Although Major refused to bow to this pressure, his position was weakened by his small majority and by the fact that by 1992 the parliamentary party had become more pro-Thatcherite in composition as older MPs of the Macmillan era retired.

As Major hung on to office, the depression deepened. By 1992 unemployment was officially 2.85 million, though actually 3.5 million; 48,000 businesses went bankrupt in 1991 alone, and in that year gross domestic product diminished by 2.5 per cent. As a result of the chronic weakness of the economy the pound lost value under the European Exchange Rate Mechanism and the government repeated the tactics used in the 1920s, trying to sustain the currency by raising interest rates instead of seeking a realignment of currency levels. But by September the pound was falling inexorably, leading the Bank of England to throw away £60 billion in a vain attempt to save it, while the Chancellor pushed interest rates up to a punishing 15 per cent. The inevitable outcome was a humiliating climb down as sterling was withdrawn from the European Exchange Rate Mechanism, allowed to float, and thus was effectively devalued by around 15 per cent. This fiasco marked the end of Thatcherism as a doomed and quixotic attempt to recapture a half-remembered, half-imagined era in which the state had played a minimal role in social and economic affairs. More immediately it destroyed Conservative claims to competence in managing the economy and led to a heavy defeat in 1997.

Further reading

Accounts of the period:

M. Holmes, *The Thatcher Government* (1984)

Paul Addison, *No Turning Back: The Peacetime Revolutions of Post-War Britain* (2010)

A.W. Turner, *Rejoice! Rejoice! Britain in the 1980s* (2010)

M. Adeney and J. Lloyd, *The Miners' Strike 1984–1985* (1987)

Hugo Young, *One of Us* (1989)

Charles Moore, *Margaret Thatcher: The Authorized Biography* (2013) – a detailed, partisan account by a Thatcherite.

C.F. Collete and K. Laybourn eds, *Modern Britain since 1979* (2003)

For analyses of Thatcherism see:

D. Kavanagh, *Thatcherism and British Politics: The End of Consensus?* (1990)

Peter Riddell, *The Thatcher Era and Its Legacy* (1991)

S.R. Letwin, *The Anatomy of Thatcherism* (1992)

R. Jowell, S. Witherspoon and L. Brooks eds, *British Social Attitudes: the 1987 Report* (1987) – suggest the impact of Thatcherism on society was only superficial.

On economic aspects see:

W. Keegan, *Mrs Thatcher's Economic Experiment* (1984)

Will Hutton, *The State We're In* (1995)

Andrew Gamble, *Britain in Decline* (1986)

On external affairs see:

L. Freedman, *Britain and the Falklands War* (1988)

D.G. Boyce, *The Falklands War* (2005)

J.W. Yong, *Britain and European Unity 1945–1992* (1993)

On party political developments:

P. Dunleavy and C. Husbands, *British Democracy at the Crossroads* (1985)

D. Butler and D. Kavanagh, *The British General Election of 1983* (1984), *1987* (1988), and *1992* (1993)

K.O. Morgan, *Michael Foot: A Life* (2007)

John Campbell, *Roy Jenkins* (2014)

D.N. MacIver ed., *The Liberal Democrats* (1996)

Alan Sykes, *The Radical Right: British Social Imperialism to the B.N.P.* (2005)

21

New Labour and the Blair Era

While John Major's majority was whittled away at by-elections between 1992 and 1997, the Labour Party reinvented itself by electing a new and largely unknown leader, Tony Blair, who was thought likely to enhance the party's appeal to voters in the middle classes and south of England. Taking advantage of Labour's demoralization after four election defeats, he radically re-cast the party as 'New Labour', which involved abandoning Clause Four – the part of Labour's constitution that committed the party to nationalization – vetoing income tax increases, accepting existing levels of expenditure, giving a higher priority to crime, retaining Tory trade union legislation and tacitly abandoning the goal of full employment. The paradox was that at the 1997 election, when the electorate was anxious to repudiate Thatcherism, Labour was returned to office pledged to maintain much of its predecessor's agenda. But the details of the New Labour programme made little difference; voters had already made up their minds to change the government. Labour emerged with 419 seats and a majority of 179; the

Table 21.1 British governments, 1974–2010

1974	Labour	(Harold Wilson)
1976	Labour	(James Callaghan)
1979	Conservative	(Margaret Thatcher)
1983	Conservative	(Margaret Thatcher)
1987	Conservative	(Margaret Thatcher)
1990	Conservative	(John Major)
1992	Conservative	(John Major)
1997	Labour	(Tony Blair)
2001	Labour	(Tony Blair)
2005	Labour	(Tony Blair)
2007	Labour	(Gordon Brown)

Conservatives polled just 31 per cent and returned only 165 MPs, while the Liberal Democrats had 46 MPs, their largest total since 1929.

Continuity or change?

The new government went some way to distinguishing itself from Thatcherism. It implemented a minimum wage, initially at £3.60 an hour, rising by 2006 to £5.35, quietly redistributed income to poorer families through tax credits and reduced child poverty from 3.4 million in 1998–9 to 2.3 million by 2010–11. As a result, between 1997 and 2007 the poorest 20 per cent of people enjoyed a 12 per cent rise in incomes. However, these were exceptions to what was essentially a policy of continuity; although Labour had posed a moral challenge to Thatcherism under Neil Kinnock's leadership it had never posed an intellectual challenge.

Economic Conservatism

The survival of the government through three successive elections reflected Labour's success in managing the economy without a crisis, something that had upset all previous Labour administrations eventually. As Chancellor, Gordon Brown made control of inflation a priority, to which end he handed control of interest rates to the Bank of England; for the next ten years the economy enjoyed modest growth and a steady fall in unemployment. There was, however, a downside to all this. Initially the Bank increased interest rates, causing unemployment and hampering manufacturing industry, which continued to decline. This led to a huge balance of trade deficit of £7.2 billion on goods by 2007, though the £2.65 billion surplus in services reduced this to £4.7 billion. To a large extent the buoyancy of the economy was due simply to deregulation of banks, feverish borrowing and massive personal indebtedness which was channelled into spending on consumer goods and services. Brown effectively extended Conservative economic strategy, hoping that the service sector would replace the jobs lost in manufacturing. One result was that although unemployment fell steadily it remained high, so that even in 2004 after years of improvement there were still 1.4 million out of work, and meanwhile 1 million unemployed had been shifted onto disability benefits. In effect, since 1979 Britain had endured a quarter of a century of mass unemployment.

Continuity was also conspicuous in New Labour's close relationship with business and its determination to maintain privatization. By 1998 it had sold £12 billion of public assets, including the Tote, the Royal Mint, Ministry of Defence property, Air Traffic Control and the London Underground. However, by this time privatization was reaching its limits. Attempts to sell Brixton Prison failed, while Blakenhurst Prison was handed back to the state! New Labour also spent several years trying – and failing – to make the disastrous railway privatization work. Instead of attracting private investment, the railway companies enjoyed larger public subsidies than they had under state ownership. Instead of benefiting from the supposed management skills of the private sector, what was essentially an engineering business was now run by accountants with calamitous consequences. After a series of accidents at Hatfield, Potters Bar and Paddington caused by the inability of Railtrack to maintain safety, the government reluctantly embarked on a partial renationalization, replacing Railtrack with the non-profit-making Network Rail in 2001.

More surprisingly the government continued the Conservative policy with a step-by-step dismantling of the National Health Service. The process was especially marked in dental services but also involved buying in services, expensively, from private hospitals and employing private companies for some aspects of work such as cleaning, which resulted in lower standards and the spread of fatal infections, including MRSA, *Clostridium difficile* and Legionnaires' disease in hospitals. New hospitals were built via the private finance initiative (PFI). Although it reduced government borrowing this was far more expensive than building by state investment, and in the long term it saddled hospitals with huge repayments to the private owners of NHS hospitals. As with railways, private control and high standards proved incompatible; at one new PFI hospital in Cumbria the sewage system collapsed, ceilings fell in and window frames blew out. Hospitals increasingly resorted to exploiting patients by imposing high charges for parking, telephones and television. By 2007 many NHS hospitals were struggling under financial deficits, staff demoralization, government targets and the loss of beds.

Social and political reform

Although Tony Blair was a reluctant reformer he found himself bound by existing party commitments. For example, a Freedom of Information Act was enacted but watered down and actually repudiated by him later on. He refused to abolish the hereditary element in the House of Lords but reduced it to 92 peers. He granted devolution but distrusted Scottish Labour and tried to impose his own men on Wales and on London.

Women, sexuality and the moral crisis

Conversely his governments had a stronger record on social reform, abolishing the notorious Section 28, legalizing same-sex relationships at 16 and allowing homosexuals to engage in civil partnerships in 2005. In an increasingly tolerant society politicians increasingly came out. However such reforms helped to trigger one of Britain's periodic moral crises cultivated by the reactionary newspapers especially the *Mail, Sun, Express* and *Telegraph* whose fears peaked around the Millennium celebrations. Although British society was now overwhelmingly secular the *Mail* believed the Millennium should be a celebration of 2,000 years of Christianity and its columnists complained about the decline of marriage and family and the growing equality enjoyed by women which they blamed for the emasculation of men; each summer the press reported that girls were obtaining better examination results than boys as though it was a national disaster. The number of marriages declined from 426,000 in 1972 to 267,000 by 2002 and the fertility rate dropped from 2.95 in the 1960s to 1.77 by 2006, well below replacement level. One by-product was a rise in single-person households from 370,000 to over a million between 1979 and 1997.

Greater acceptance of feminism was but one symptom of the wider trend towards a more liberal society, especially among the younger generations. They increasingly accepted women as workers and equals, were relaxed about sexuality, lived secular lives outside the churches, were tolerant towards people of different races and favoured membership of the European Union. These long-term trends angered reactionary commentators in the press who felt impotent to influence underlying changes in society. But did their complaint amount to a moral crisis? Blair himself pandered to the newspapers by joining in their criticism of single mothers. However social change was beyond the reach of press and politicians and the public remained unmoved by criticism of single mothers for example. Manufacturing decline had destroyed men's jobs while the expansion of the service sector advantaged women, who filled 70 per cent of all the professional employment created between 1981 and 1996. The other cause of their advance was a huge increase in the number of women with university degrees, with the result that women comprised half the workforce by the end of the decade. In effect society had experienced a quiet social revolution for women since the 1980s.

Such advances engendered a 'Men's Movement' dedicated to the idea that female equality threatened to make men redundant, similar to the scares about gender confusion in the 1920s and just as ineffective. In reality younger men were adapting to women as breadwinners and to more equal relationships. However, feminists continued to point out that women earned only 80 per cent of male wages compared with 66 per cent in 1974. Thirty years after the passage of the Equal Pay Act progress remained very slow, especially in the City of London where only 11 per cent of directors were

Table 21.2 Women in the British labour force, 1911–96 (as a percentage)

1911	1921	1931	1951	1961	1971	1981	1996
29.6	29.5	29.8	30.8	32.4	36.0	38.9	50.1

female, and in private business generally. However, women became a majority among solicitors under thirty and formed 60 per cent of medical students, though only 22 per cent of GPs and 3 per cent of surgeons.

Another symptom of the moral crisis of the 1990s was the popular fear about crime and disorder fomented by the press and encouraged by politicians including Blair and successive Home Secretaries who introduced no fewer than 54 pieces of criminal justice legislation involving thousands of new crimes resulting in a prison population of 80,000 by 2007 compared with just 11,000 in 1930. During 2000–4 the government imposed ASBOS (anti-social behaviour orders) on 1,143 adults and on 1,177 children including eleven-year-olds.

Yet despite these efforts the public thought the government was soft on crime. The obsession with crime, vigorously propagated as a means of boosting newspaper circulation, flourished perversely in the face of a sustained *fall* in crime amounting to 39 per cent between 1995 and 2004. However, this success contrasted with a comprehensive failure to handle drugs going back several decades. During the 1960s and 1970s Britain had had a total of only 2,000 drug addicts who attended their local GPs for

Image 14 New Labour: Tony Blair embarks on the 1997 election campaign.

treatment and supplies and were an insignificant problem. However, successive Conservative and Labour governments competed with each other to be 'tough' and intolerant of drug use. Consequently drug users were forced to find their own supplies; inevitably criminals moved in to supply drugs thereby extending the habit enormously. As a result of the tough policy Britain had 327,000 drug addicts by 2006. Although leading policemen believed the policy could not be enforced and wanted to legalise cannabis, the politicians stubbornly refused to see that they were out of step with society. In 2005 11 million people aged 16–59 admitted to taking drugs and 70,000 were arrested annually for possession of cannabis; as some 60 per cent of cannabis was home-grown it had become an indelible part of British culture.

The declining work ethic

Like Mrs Thatcher, Tony Blair found that social change was largely beyond his control, though he devoted much attention to it. He was especially concerned by the continuing decline of the work ethic in Britain. By 2005 2.7 million people, whom the authorities thought should be employed, claimed incapacity benefits. More widely, 7.9 million Britons were economically inactive, including over a fifth of those aged 16–65. This was partly a response to the increasing stress experienced by British employees, who worked longer hours than their counterparts elsewhere in Western Europe. GPs, for example, increasingly switched to part-time employment to make life more tolerable.

Another cause of scepticism about work lay in the growing unfairness and inequality in incomes during the 1990s. Redistributive social policies checked the trend towards inequality under Thatcher but did not reverse it. Indeed this period saw the emergence of a class of 'super-rich' people. In 2001, for example, executives' pay rose by 28 per cent, six times the average; in 2005 company directors' pay again rose 28 per cent at a time when inflation was 2.5 per cent and average earnings were growing by 3.7 per cent. This became less acceptable because lavish payments in terms of salaries, pension and share deals became routine regardless of performance. After the Hatfield disaster, the Railtrack chairman, Gerald Corbett, enjoyed a £444,000 pay-off; Lord Simpson of Dunkeld received £1 million from Marconi after presiding over a 98 per cent loss of its share value; Sir Robert Horton presided over bad investment and redundancies at BP but simply moved on to run Railtrack which proved another fiasco. British business appeared to work on the basis that nothing succeeds like *failure*.

Meanwhile many employees who enjoyed company pensions aimed to retire early. However, as pensioners had become 18 per cent of the population, and rising, they were regarded as a growing problem. The low political priority enjoyed by the elderly was underlined by the demise of the post office system on which they relied; by 2007 4,000 post offices had been closed as the government withdrew business and a further 2,500 subsequently closed. Some elderly people were denied care in local authority nursing homes unless they sold their homes to pay for it, a practice that appeared to many people to contradict the spirit of the welfare state. Many also felt aggrieved by the failure of the private pension schemes that the Conservative government had encouraged them to undertake. Diminishing returns on investment funds meant that private pensions largely failed to meet expectations, for which the actuaries were seriously at fault for failing to advise pension providers of the trends. Company pensions also became problematical as many companies simply took 'holidays', that is, they stopped paying into their schemes for a time and gradually abandoned them altogether. As a result many younger people refused to invest in pensions policies. For many years the government evaded the looming crisis, merely urging people to contribute more towards their old age, but only 5 per cent of gross domestic product was spent on pensions compared with 11 per cent in other European countries. By 2006 it was decided to boost the state pension by restoring the link with earnings and to raise the pensionable age to 68.

Educational advances

A key New Labour aim was to push education higher up the agenda; indeed, it symbolized the rapprochement between New Labour and the middle classes. Although the comprehensive schools had achieved impressive results in terms of high and improving rates of examination success at GCSE and A level, New Labour pandered to middle-class fears by labelling them as a failure and pressurizing them for further improvement. This involved taking 'failing' schools out of local authority control and introducing private businesses into their running; for example, Jarvis, the company notorious for the Potters Bar train crash, was thought a suitable adviser for such schools. Eventually the government decided to launch several hundred City Technology Colleges in which private companies, including garage owners, American banks and advertising agencies, were given powers in return for small contributions to funding. Despite the extra money pumped into the new colleges, the results varied: some succeeded in raising standards, but others failed. Meanwhile, education suffered from growing perceptions that standards in terms of literacy, science and languages were steadily deteriorating, despite the evidence of improving examination results. When the government made foreign languages optional at 14, there was an immediate withdrawal, while physics experienced a 38 per cent fall between 1990 and 2005. Schools also had to cope with a growing drain on their resources to private companies, including those which charged heavily to provide supply teachers, a multitude of 'advisers' who were designed to help them meet official targets, and profit-making examination boards whose staff operated as salesmen when visiting schools. As a result, by 2007 schools spent more on examination entry fees than on buying books.

Similar problems in terms of improved statistics in the context of declining standards afflicted higher education in this period. The expansion of student numbers was vigorously continued, such that by 2002 one in three school-leavers attended university against a government target of 50 per cent. However, this expansion entailed many drawbacks. Dissatisfaction among students increased as grants were ended and replaced by tuition fees, initially £1,000 a year rising to £3,000, leaving many handicapped by debts after graduation. Moreover, as many were admitted with low academic qualifications and subsequently experienced financial difficulties, a fifth of all students failed to emerge with a degree; in some universities as many as a quarter or even a third failed.

Many of those who did graduate were obliged to take sub-graduate employment which raised questions about the purpose of university expansion. Although ministers insisted it improved economic growth no evidence was produced for this. In fact the expansion was driven by the universities' short-term financial crisis, not by the needs of the economy. Dozens of courses in engineering, technology, physics and chemistry were closed down, largely due to insufficient applications from students qualified in mathematics. But a huge expansion of law courses resulted in an over-supply of students unable to find employment in the legal profession.

However, if university expansion proved irrelevant to the economy it became an important engine of social change. Research had long demonstrated that the experience of a university education undermined received ideas and values, resulting in a more liberal outlook. The huge growth in student numbers accelerated this process, making the young notably liberal towards race, religion, gender and sexuality, and more relaxed about Britain's role in Europe than the older generations. This was to have major political implications as the older parties were trapped in the thinking of earlier generations.

The British presidency

Tony Blair proved to be an unusual premier in several respects. He had emerged as Labour leader despite having no roots in the party and, as it transpired, no respect for its traditions. His favourite tactic consisted in positioning himself against his party as a means of emphasizing the break with the past and enhancing his appeal to non-Labour voters. Initially Blair was thought to harbour Liberal sympathies, fostered by coalition talks with the Liberal Democrat leader. However, he subsequently emerged as highly *illiberal* and he and his ministers went out of their way to repudiate liberalism. In reality Blair retained the Conservative values acquired from his family, especially his father, which asserted themselves in his response to most issues of both domestic and external policy. He made no apology for his frank admiration for Mrs Thatcher. In time Blair's Conservatism became increasingly obvious as key government policies such as the Iraq War (2003), school trusts (2006) and the replacement of the Trident nuclear weapon system (2007) could be sustained only with Conservative support in the face of Labour opposition.

Blair's detachment from his party was but one symptom of what observers saw as his presidential style of government. Like Lloyd George and Mrs Thatcher, Blair largely avoided speeches in Parliament, making do with brief exchanges at Question Time. He also by-passed the Cabinet, relying on small, informal groups of personal advisers to make policy, and imported growing numbers of friends, often from outside Labour circles, to make policy. Lord Levy was his representative in the Middle East, Lord Adonis ran his educational policy, and Lord Birt was appointed to devise a transport strategy, for example. Moreover, as in the American presidency, the focus was heavily on handling the media, an approach typified by the influence enjoyed by Blair's notorious 'spin doctor', Alastair Campbell, and by the Prime Minister's dutiful relationship with Rupert Murdoch, the Australian newspaper proprietor who owned *The Sun* and *The Times*. As a result, for much of his premiership Blair seemed to be conducting an unending election campaign. Presidential government became most marked in his personal control of foreign policy, involving Britain in four wars, and controversial methods of suppressing criticism. He refused to publish the advice of the Attorney General on the legality of the Iraq War, during which it emerged that improper use had been made of intelligence to justify government policy. In effect Blair had misrepresented the Joint Intelligence Committee, pressurized its head, John Scarlett, and subsequently promoted him as head of MI6.

Governmental blunders

Presidential government also suffered from a crisis of competence. Neither Blair nor his ministers had any experience of managing institutions, apart from David Blunkett who had run Sheffield city council. Lacking either knowledge of the British system of government or British political history he developed the habit of introducing initiatives that proved impractical, created burdens for the administration and sometimes had to be abandoned. Ministers who were increasingly drawn from men whose only experience was in PR or party political research found it hard to run their departments, especially as they were moved so frequently. For example, John Reid occupied nine posts in ten years. The result was a succession of administrative failures and blunders including the fiasco of the Millennium Dome and the Olympic facilities whose cost rose from an original £3 billion to £9 billion in two years. By 2007 the government was spending £2.2 billion a year on private consultants and advisers, a practice that was not only hugely extravagant but which also generated schemes that proved to be unworkable. Most government departments experienced costly failures through the introduction of new IT and computer systems which were intended to make administration more efficient but frequently failed to work. Among the victims of computers were the Passport Office and the Child Support Agency, which was near collapse by 2004 when it owed money to half a million parents. During 2003–7 the Assets Recovery Agency spent £65 million trying to recover just £23 million from convicted criminals. Gordon Brown's Child Tax Credit system proved complicated and inefficient; the IT failed to work and government repeatedly paid out too much money which had then to be recovered. Among the many PPI scandals the worst was the attempt to upgrade the London Underground through Metronet, a private company. By 2007 when £2.5 billion had been spent Metronet was bankrupt. Expenditure on the National Health Service increased by £57 billion but only 30 per cent got through to patient care, most being diverted to debts, administration, salaries and pensions. The costs of a proposed national identity card scheme ballooned to £5.75 billion by 2007, rising at a rate of £840 million per six months, before being abandoned in 2009. The Home Office became so infamous for repeatedly introducing new bills and for its incompetence in handling prisoners, paedophiles, asylum seekers and drugs that its own head denounced it as 'unfit for purpose'; it was split into two ministries in 2007.

Political honours

As under Lloyd George and Thatcher presidential government also involved an extravagant resort to honours and rewards to prop up the regime. Increasingly honours were awarded to prominent failures such as the heads of the Child Support Agency and the Joint Intelligence Committee. So discredited was the system that in 2004 at least 300 people were known to have refused to accept honours. Blair also emulated Mrs Thatcher in expanding his personal patronage by a dubious use of titles to finance party work, by-passing the normal vetting procedures to advance personal friends and donors. By 2007 it emerged that all but one of those who had donated £1 million to the Labour Party had received peerages. In order to evade criticism, both the Conservative and Labour parties obtained huge commercial loans, rather than donations, prior to the 2005 election, hoping to turn them discreetly into donations later. However, the nomination of dubious individuals for honours led to a police enquiry, involving Blair himself being interviewed by the police, a humiliation that had never previously befallen a Prime Minister. Widespread public belief in political corruption cast a shadow over the later stages of his premiership.

Changes in the political system

Although devolution was still opposed by a third of Labour MPs and most ministers, by 1997 the party judged that it could no longer risk being undermined by the Scottish Nationalists. The result was the creation of a 129-member Parliament in Edinburgh with powers to legislate and raise up to three pence in the pound in taxation, and a 60-member assembly in Cardiff which took over the powers of the Welsh Secretary of State. The government also created an elected Mayor for London and encouraged local councils to adopt their own elected mayors. For the Prime Minister these concessions to local control went against the grain and he devoted much fruitless effort to attempting to prevent Ken Livingstone becoming GLC Mayor and Rhodri Morgan Chief Minister in Wales.

The significance of devolution

While one Labour politician asserted that devolution would kill the SNP stone dead, a Welsh first minister wisely observed that devolution was a *process* not an event. He was right. It immediately accelerated the pace of change as the nationalist parties performed better in devolved elections than in Westminster ones. In Scotland the SNP vote rose to 28 per cent in 1999 and to 44.8 per cent in 2011 while Labour's share fell to 36 per cent in 1999 and to 29 per cent in 2011. In Wales Plaid Cymru's vote rose from under 10 per cent to 28 per cent. Moreover the new institutions proved successful in that they gave Scots and Welsh voters a more effective means of realizing their priorities and views than was possible through Westminster. As a result

Labour policies in Edinburgh and Cardiff proved to be more progressive than those followed in London. The Scottish Labour–Liberal coalition introduced free care for the elderly, refused to implement tuition fees for students, empowered local communities to buy out landowners, and pioneered a Freedom of Information Act and a ban on fox hunting. In 2007 the Welsh abolished prescription charges when Westminster was increasing them. The Welsh example was especially significant as enthusiasm for devolution had been less than in Scotland. However, the Welsh gained self-confidence and developed an appetite for more powers in Cardiff. By 2001 21 per cent spoke the Welsh language and all public business was transacted in both languages. Above all devolution proved to be a success in that Scotland showed it could govern itself effectively via both a Labour–Liberal coalition and an SNP minority government while Wales had coalitions between Labour and the Liberal Democrats or Plaid Cymru. Consequently it transpired that devolution would do more to promote than to hinder independence for Scotland; it was a catalyst for national sentiment. Although the electoral system had been carefully constructed to prevent the SNP winning a majority, the party formed a minority government in 2007 and shocked Westminster by winning a majority in 2011.

Elsewhere Blair was much more conservative about constitutional reform. Although he greatly reduced the hereditary element in the House of Lords, he resolutely resisted the idea of a wholly elected second chamber. His opposition lay partly in the fear that an upper house elected by proportional methods would claim to be more representative of public opinion than the Commons; his 65 majority there in the 2005 election reflected a mere 35 per cent of the vote. In this spirit Blair abandoned his earlier sympathy for reforming the electoral system, which seemed odd as Britain now enjoyed five different electoral systems: first-past-the-post for Westminster, single transferable vote in Northern Ireland and the Scottish councils, closed regional party lists for European Union, the additional member system for Scotland, Wales and the London Assembly, and the supplementary vote for elected English mayors. In this context traditional first-past-the-post elections appeared increasingly anachronistic.

Breakthrough for women

The other political breakthrough of these years was triggered by Labour's introduction of all-female lists of candidates in many constituencies, a system which, in the landslide of 1997, resulted in the election of no fewer than 119 women MPs, most of them Labour. However, the significance remained

Table 21.3 Women MPs, 1964–97

Year	Women elected	As a percentage of all MPs
1964	28	4.4
1966	26	4.1
1970	26	4.1
1974F	25	3.9
1974O	27	4.3
1979	19	3.0
1983	23	3.6
1987	41	6.5
1992	62	9.8
1997	119	18.0

Note: F = February; O = October.

unclear. Neither Blair nor Brown were very sympathetic towards feminism, and disillusion quickly set in when the Chancellor reduced benefits paid to single mothers; a protest motion was signed by 101 members including only nine women. The new female MPs remained loyal and kept their criticism private. Meanwhile the careers of many leading Labour women petered out including Mo Mowlam, Clare Short, Estelle Morris, Margaret Beckett, Patricia Hewett, Ruth Kelly and Jackie Smith; Harriet Harman and Tessa Jowell survived but their efforts for women were thwarted. Nor did the culture and behaviour of the House of Commons change significantly as a result of the larger female element and some feminists accused the new members of being a failure. On the other hand, women improved their profile in Parliament reaching 127 in 2005 and 141 in 2010. Even this was easily exceeded by the Scottish parliament (37 per cent women) and Wales (41 per cent). The momentum was also maintained because the Conservatives felt obliged to catch up, returning 46 women in 2010.

Multi-party politics

Meanwhile, the years from 1997 to 2007 consolidated the pattern of three-party politics in Britain. After their breakthrough in 1997 the Liberal Democrats confounded the pundits by gaining a growing share of the vote, reaching almost 23 per cent and 62 MPs in 2005. In the process they became a party of government in major cities such as Liverpool, Newcastle, Sheffield and Hull, as well as in Scotland, and they partly displaced both major parties in parliamentary elections, being the main alternative to Labour in northern industrial areas and the main opponent to the Conservatives in southern, rural and suburban districts. Studies also showed that their support had ceased to be merely a temporary protest vote; Liberal Democrats enjoyed a distinctive profile for their championship of civil liberties, opposition to the Iraq War, liberal attitudes on social issues such as drugs where the main parties were increasingly out of step, support for Europe, fair taxation of wealth and support for state social welfare.

Much extra Liberal Democrat support came from Labour voters increasingly disillusioned with the right-wing trend of policy under Blair. After reaching 420,000 in 1997, Labour membership collapsed to less than 200,000 by 2007. The Prime Minister's penchant for big business and business donations and his concern to cultivate middle-class votes alienated traditional support, provoking several trade unions into cutting their financial contributions to the party and even subsidizing left-wing, anti-Labour candidates in some cases. As only 13 per cent of Labour MPs now came from a background as manual workers, it appeared that the original rationale for the party was approaching its end.

Meanwhile, the Conservatives experienced a protracted crisis arising from three successive election defeats in 1997, 2001 and 2005, leading them to appoint, and then quickly reject, no fewer than three leaders after John Major – William Hague, Iain Duncan Smith and Michael Howard. The party had become the victim not only of short-term antagonism towards Mrs Thatcher but of underlying social trends that worked against it: greater employment for women that robbed the party of its volunteer workers, wider university education that undermined Tory values, and the general tendency of society to become more liberal. This left Conservatives looking extremist, hard-faced and negative – the 'nasty party' as one leading Tory put it. In addition, the party had acquired a reputation for incompetence in economics in the declining Major years. Above all, the more Blair occupied natural Conservative territory, the less need middle-class voters saw to vote Conservative. Throughout northern England as well as in Wales and Scotland the Conservatives had become the third party, their organization and local government presence had drastically declined and, with an average age of 62, the party members were beginning to die out.

The Iraq War and the attack on civil liberties

Following the attack by Islamic terrorists in New York in September 2001 Tony Blair committed Britain to President Bush's strategy for eradicating the sources of such threats. However, the policy was misconceived from the start as it focused on the regime of Saddam Hussein in Iraq, a secular Muslim state that had no involvement with Islamic terrorism. Perversely, Bush and Blair ignored the two states that *did* harbour Islamic terrorism – Saudi Arabia and Pakistan. This led to an invasion of Iraq in 2003 designed to change the regime. In order to persuade his critics of the necessity for this Blair claimed that Saddam possessed 'weapons of mass destruction', by which he meant chemical and biological weapons, and that he could inflict them on Britain in 45 minutes. It transpired that there was no basis for these claims and that Blair had misused the intelligence reports on Iraq to bolster an unpopular policy. By 2004 even he admitted that no such weapons would ever be found.

Moreover, after a rapid invasion the American and British troops became bogged down in a costly war of attrition as Iraq descended into chaos. Meanwhile, the war began to have highly damaging effects. It turned Iraq, which had posed no threat to the West, into a focus for Islamic extremism and it multiplied the terrorist recruits from such countries as Pakistan. In this way the Bush–Blair strategy proved counter-productive. It also led them to pursue terrorism by invading Afghanistan, a less controversial move but an equally futile attempt to resolve the intractable problems of a country of which the Western leaders were ignorant; Britain concentrated troops on only one province of 34, Helmand, but after a decade had failed to defeat the enemy. The Afghan war helped to spread the terrorists to other countries and further complicated relations by offering to the Muslim world more proof of the determination of the West to wage a war on Islamic society. The Iraq War also caused new domestic disaffection by antagonizing British Muslims and by making Britain herself a target for Islamic terrorism, notably in the London bombings of July 2005. Finally, the war largely discredited the special relationship between Britain and America to which the Prime Minister was so devoted. It became clear that he had secretly committed himself to American strategy in April 2002, subordinated British national interests to his friendship with Bush, and in the process had ignored expert military, legal and political advice. By 2007 Iraq was widely recognized as the worst blunder of British foreign policy since Munich in 1938 and it went a long way to destroying the Prime Minister's reputation. But for the loyalty of Labour MPs, the acquiescence of the Conservatives and two whitewash investigations on the war by Lords Hutton and Butler, it would have ended his premiership. By this stage the wars in both Afghanistan and Iraq were being recognized as British defeats, though not officially admitted, and the government steadily withdrew troops to bases away from active combat prior to leaving altogether.

Domestic terrorism

The external conflict with Muslim countries also led politicians to exaggerate the threat of terrorism at home; it was never comparable in scale with that earlier posed by the IRA, for example. But the public, aware that it had been deceived over the war, subsequently became very sceptical about official warnings about terrorism. This led the government and MI5 into a series of attempts to manipulate opinion by launching reports about threats to national security. In 2002 they reported a plot to spread ricin, a deadly poison, from a flat in north London, in 2004 a scheme to explode Canary Wharf and another designed to blow up the Old Trafford football ground, while in 2006 they placed tanks around airports over claims that terrorists were taking bottles containing dangerous substances on board aeroplanes. Yet these scares all turned out to be baseless. Meanwhile, the Prime Minister suggested Britain had 250 terrorists while MI5 thought there were only a couple of dozen; by 2005 there were officially 800 terrorists, but by 2006 MI5 variously reported 1,200 and 1,600, as well as 30 terror plots. In effect, the more money was spent on intelligence gathering, the bigger 'terrorism' became.

However, these claims were used to justify a mass of legislation on terrorism and an attack on civil liberties by Home Secretaries David Blunkett and John Reid, classic working-class authoritarians who joined the Prime Minister in criticizing judges and disparaging liberal values. They argued that the threat posed by Al-Qa'ida justified a surrender of traditional rights. In particular they insisted on arrest and detention without trial for suspected terrorists, as a result of which some Muslims were kept indefinitely in Belmarsh Prison in south-east London with no charges being brought under the Prevention of Terrorism Act. Eventually in 2004 the Law Lords ruled that this was illegal. Blunkett claimed that despite the lack of evidence he knew that the men were guilty. Instead the government resorted to house arrest for suspects and attempted to persuade Parliament to allow the police to detain them for up to 90 days for questioning. However, the House of Commons refused to extend the existing 14-day period to more than 28 days. In fact, the police already enjoyed more extensive powers than their contemporaries abroad and resorted freely to stop-and-search methods for detaining young male Muslims. Moreover, they abused terrorist laws by applying them to non-terrorist offences, including the notorious arrest of an elderly delegate at the Labour Party conference who had shouted 'rubbish' during a speech. The 1997 Protection from Harassment Act, amended by the Serious Organised Crime and Police Act of 2005, was invoked against peaceful protesters even for sending e-mails. Under the Terrorism Act of 2000 police were able to stop and search people and vehicles engaged in environmental campaigns. In effect, the police were out of control. The most notorious example occurred in 2005 when they shot and killed an innocent Brazilian, Juan Charles de Menezes, after mistaking him for a terrorist. As was usual, no policemen were prosecuted or even disciplined for the killing. A by-product of the controversy aroused by official policy was a partial politicization of the police. In the 2005 election, for example, Sir Ian Blair, chief of the Metropolitan Police, intervened improperly in the campaign to advocate the government's new proposal for national identity cards. Originally these were supposed to help fight terrorism but as they had failed to do so in other countries the claim was soon abandoned, though not the scheme itself. As a result of these measures although Britain was not a police state, by 2007 she was halfway down the road to becoming one. Its cumulative record on civil liberties made the Blair government the most reactionary one Britain had had since Lord Liverpool (1812–27), whose policy had arisen in similar circumstances out of official panic caused by wars and domestic subversion.

The crisis of national identity

The approach of the millennium crystallized doubts and fears about Britain's role, leading to a wider debate about national identity in the new century. At the Great Exhibition in 1851, Queen Victoria's Jubilee in 1897, the Empire Exhibition in 1924 and the Festival of Britain in 1951 national celebrations had been organized with some conviction and purpose. But 2000 approached without any bold, imaginative project, and with both government and industry reluctant to subsidize the event. The Millennium Dome, which was widely disparaged at the time and subsequently failed to find a useful role, only seemed to underline the mood of uncertainty. It crystallized the frustration in newspapers such as the *Daily Mail* about the apparently inexorable growth of a liberal society. The traditional props to national pride and identity such as empire and monarchy had lost their appeal and relevance, leaving the country uncertain and resentful of the loss of Great Power status but unsure what to put in its place.

The growth of Europhobia

Although Britain's membership of the European Union suggested one alternative role, for many British people it only accentuated the problem. From an economic perspective this was perverse for by 1988 European investment in Britain had doubled to £46 billion, and Europe accounted for 58 per cent of all British exports by value and 64 per cent of manufactured exports. However, the politicians' obsession with maintaining a special relationship with America continued to distract Britain from her new European role. This was accentuated by the influence exerted by *The Sun*, *Daily Mail*, *Daily Express*, *Daily Telegraph* and *The Times* which systematically distorted popular perceptions of Europe by neglecting the beneficial effects of European legislation, by fostering xenophobia and by exploiting Europe as an all-purpose scapegoat for British failures. At their most extreme, Europhobics in the UK Independence Party propagated the idea that the European Union was essentially an extension of Nazi Germany by economic means. One symptom of this retreat into negativity and isolationism was the withdrawal from European languages in British schools, a trend inevitably damaging to the economy in the long run.

Under huge pressure from Tory anti-Europeans, John Major had negotiated an opt-out from the EU social chapter. However, in 1997 the new Foreign Secretary, Robin Cook, signed up to the social chapter, bringing a series of benefits to British parents and employees. Moreover, Tony Blair appeared to be pro-European, though he shrank from arguing the case for Europe at home. He suggested that Britain would join the single currency after a referendum. However, the referendum was never held, partly because a majority were consistently opposed to losing the pound and partly because Gordon Brown insisted that five economic conditions must first be met. In time the issue of the single currency faded but was replaced by public and press agitation about immigration from EU countries into Britain. Yet despite the concern, by 2007 people born abroad constituted only 8 per cent of Britain's population compared with 10 per cent in France, 11 per cent in Germany and 12 per cent in the United States. It was also recognized that immigrants boosted the economy because as young workers they were taxpayers, accepted low-paid jobs refused by others, and kept the NHS going.

Institutional weaknesses

To some extent prejudice about Europe was exacerbated by the loss of confidence in British institutions. Most people, especially in the south of England, had never recognized that 'Britain' was an artificial concept, a political structure presiding over four nationalities, a federal state without a federal constitution. The disappearance of several of the pillars of identity, including empire and manufacturing, that had made Britain a success in the Victorian era left the country insecure. The role of the BBC, which had promoted British national identity since the 1920s, also changed. After devolution the BBC abandoned its traditional national role, telling its programme makers: 'We broadcast to the nations of England, Scotland and Wales.'

During the 1990s there was also a significant loss of support for the monarchy, a trend that reached a peak following the death of Diana, Princess of Wales, in 1997 and revelations about the infidelity of the Prince of Wales. Following the re-emergence of a Republican movement, around a quarter of the population believed the country would be better off without the Royal Family. The main stumbling block lay in the apparent unsuitability of the heir to the throne. Prince Charles managed to defuse some criticism of his marriage to Camilla Parker-Bowles by refusing to acknowledge her legal title, Princess of Wales, acting instead as though he had a morganatic marriage by calling her Duchess of Cornwall. However, the underlying difficulty lay in his stubborn refusal to accept the restrictions of a constitutional monarchy by keeping clear of politics – the failing that had caused Edward VIII to abdicate in 1936. He organized a body of his own advisers, ran campaigns and, encouraged by Tony Blair, he badgered ministers on several subjects, especially education, farming, GM food, health, homeopathy, hunting and architecture. The cumulative effect of all this was that the monarchy was ceasing to act as the source of unity for the British people that it had been for previous generations.

The revival of Englishness

Yet the role of the Queen seemed increasingly important as the only obvious link between the four nations that made up the United Kingdom. However, the tercentenary of the Union between England and Scotland in 1707 brought into focus the question whether it would endure another 300 years. By 1997 two-thirds of Scots identified as Scottish not British and polls suggested that support for independence among Scots fluctuated between 52 per cent and 25 per cent. Some Scots saw a viable future for their country as a small but prosperous nation within the EU, like Norway. Nor did either Thatcher or Blair grasp the problem, indeed both weakened their parties by their lack of personal and political sympathy with Scotland, effectively undermining the Union thereby.

Meanwhile, Scottish devolution generated a reaction among the English on the basis that the Scots enjoyed financial subsidies, that Scots MPs voted on English matters at Westminster and that England had no Parliament of its own. By the 1990s only 44 per cent of English people identified as British and regular displays of the flag of St George on sporting occasions signified the re-emergence of English nationalism. Even though the number of Scots

MPs at Westminster had been reduced from 72 to 58, it appeared that the question of the constitutional relationship between the two countries had not been resolved or even thought about.

However, Englishness was largely a narrow and negative reaction; the English did not know what they wanted in terms of institutions and were uncertain about their role and purpose as a nation. They fell prey to claims that their traditions were under threat from subversiveal forces. Symptomatic of this mood were the bizarre claims about attempts to stop the celebration of Christmas which surfaced every December. This was especially odd since the population was overwhelmingly non-Christian. However, such fears gained credence from the publication of irresponsible books suggesting a Muslim takeover of Europe, the demonizing of Muslims by politicians and newspapers and condemnations of 'multiculturalism' which helped to make Islamophobia respectable. This was partly a panic reaction to the perceived threat of terrorism. It resulted in a huge increase in stop-and-search methods among young Muslims, amounting to harassment by the police. Between September 2002 and December 2004 701 were arrested, but only 119 were even charged and a mere 17 convicted. However, the London bombings by young Muslims in July 2005 served only to make ministers persist with what fast became a counter-productive policy. They refused to recognize what the security services told them – that some British Muslims had become antagonized by the wars against Iraq and Afghanistan and by the pro-Israeli bias of government policy. Instead they pressurized the Muslim community by criticizing the wearing of veils and asking universities to report on the activities of their Muslim students, in the process alienating the community and steadily pushing moderate and loyal Muslims into the arms of the extremists.

None of these underlying issues could be effectively tackled as long as Blair remained Prime Minister. He had largely discredited himself by his actions over Iraq, but refused to admit to error. But as a result of his unpopularity he was forced to announce in 2006 that he would not seek re-election again, thereby creating an unprecedented situation as interest inevitably centred upon the date of his retirement. He eventually announced his departure in May 2007 leaving Gordon Brown his unopposed successor.

Further reading

For accounts of the Blair government:
D. Butler and D. Kavanagh, *The British General Election of 1997* (1997)
C.F. Collette and K. Laybourn eds, *Modern Britain since 1979* (2003)

Anthony King and Ivor Crewe, *The Blunders of Our Governments* (2013)

R. Heffernan, Philip Cowley and Colin Hay eds, *Developments in British Politics* (2011)

A. Rawnsley, *Servants of the People: the Inside Story of New Labour* (2000)

John Kegan, *The Iraq War* (2004) – the author was for it in the first edition but changed his mind by the second!

For interpretations of New Labour see:

Anthony Seldon, *Blair* (2004)

J.E. Cronin, *New Labour's Pasts* (2004)

M. Foley, *The British Presidency: Tony Blair and the Politics of Public Leadership* (2000)

On national identity problems see:

Paul Ward, *Britishness since 1870* (2004)

Alvin Jackson, *The Two Unions: Ireland, Scotland and the Survival of the United Kingdom 1707–2007* (2011)

W.L. Miller ed., *Anglo-Scottish Relations from 1990 to Devolution and Beyond* (2005)

Richard Finlay, *Modern Scotland* (2004)

Tom Devine, *The Scottish Nation 1700–2000* (1999)

Martin Pugh, *Britain: Unification and Disintegration* (2012)

22

Crisis and Coalition

The emergence of Gordon Brown as Prime Minister in June 2007 had long been expected, but for some time it was uncertain whether this would result in a departure from New Labour thinking or an extension of it. Supporters of Blair argued that only the New Labour strategy enabled the party to retain support in southern and middle-class England and thus a parliamentary majority. Yet Brown, unlike Blair, was rooted in the traditional Labour Movement of urban Scotland, and the early abandonment of a controversial scheme to build huge new casinos appeared to herald a switch from the current obsession with materialism and the free market to the more puritanical tradition. In fact, however, there was to be more continuity than change. Brown, after all, had been the architect of New Labour economic policy. More intellectual than Blair, he had been convinced of the desirability of relying on market forces, expanding credit, reducing income tax and using the private finance initiative (PFI) to curtail the size of the state. He also attempted to maintain Blair's authoritarian approach in external affairs by trying to extend the period of detention without trial to 42 days, a proposal he was forced to abandon.

After a brief honeymoon period the new premier's popularity abruptly collapsed as a result of both personal and political factors. A poor communicator, Brown remained essentially a student politician, trapped in internal faction-fighting, insecure within his own government, and unable even to smile convincingly for the cameras. However, the New Labour enthusiasts were mistaken in simply blaming Brown. By 2005 Labour's vote had fallen to 35 per cent and the movement sensed that New Labour had run its course. However, no one opposed Brown for the leadership, a mistake as it exposed him to the charge of being a Prime Minister without a mandate. Though tempted to remedy this by holding an early general election, he hesitated and eventually backed away, thereby losing his best chance of victory and fatally exposing himself as an indecisive leader. In 2008 Labour was ousted from the Scottish government by the SNP and Ken Livingstone lost the election for Mayor of London; in local elections, Labour polled 24 per cent, behind both the Liberal Democrats on 25 and the Conservatives on 44 per cent. In the European elections in 2009 Labour ran third overall but actually came *fifth* in several regions. Symptomatic of the collapse of party morale was the membership, which had now dwindled from a peak of 405,000 in 1997 to 176,000 by 2007. The fall in membership combined with trade union disaffection, the demise of its municipal base and an organizational decline suggested that the pillars that had historically sustained the party were tottering.

Yet none of this would have been fatal had it not been for a sudden deterioration in economic and political conditions. The start of a dramatic collapse of British banking in 2007 forced the government onto the defensive, thereby undermining Brown's reputation for economic management. As recently as June 2007 he had used his Mansion House speech to lavish praise on the City of London, only to be faced with the results of irresponsible practice by deregulated financial institutions a few weeks later.

The expenses scandal

Finally, the eruption of a prolonged corruption scandal in 2008, involving the abuse of expenses and the misuse of influence by MPs and peers, resurrected the impression of sleaze surrounding politics that had characterized the 1990s. For four years the Speaker of the House of Commons, the hapless Michael Martin, fought to suppress evidence of wrong-doing under the Freedom of Information Act. But it eventually emerged that many MPs of all parties had paid public money to their relations, sometimes for doing minimal work, and had claimed the costs of renting houses they already owned; several Tory peers had used public funds for personal gain by investing in family businesses and trying to change the law to benefit companies that employed them. A vast dossier of embarrassing material was also published, showing that politicians had used their expenses to pay for everything from extravagant luxury furnishings to indulgences, including clearing moats, installing duck houses and pruning wisteria, as well as petty expenditure on dog food, lavatory paper and pornographic magazines. Suddenly politicians became the target of real public anger and derision. Although all parties suffered to some extent, the government was most in the firing line as the scandal triggered a long-growing crisis of confidence culminating in the resignation of seven ministers in one week. As a result, around 130 MPs withdrew at the 2010 general election, effectively marking the demise of a political generation; eventually, five MPs and two peers, including a former minister, were prosecuted and given prison sentences. These events trapped Gordon Brown in a prolonged period of crisis about his leadership that was not resolved until he quit in 2010. But although Labour politicians generally recognized that he would inevitably lead them to defeat at an election, the party, betraying a lack of focus and ruthlessness quite unlike the Conservatives, conspicuously failed to force him out.

The banking crisis and economic recession, 2007–15

After 2010 conventional wisdom had it that the economic collapse after 2008 was the result of excessive spending by the Labour governments. This was shrewd politics but a complete misconception. Britain's debt-to-gross domestic product ratio actually *fell* from 42.5 per cent in 1996–7 to 35.9 per cent in 2006–7. In reality the cause of the crisis lay in the collapse of banking and the need for the government to keep the banks open by injecting £300 billion and creating a deficit. As Sir Nicholas Macpherson, the Treasury's top civil servant, put it: 'The 2008 crisis was a banking crisis pure and simple.' The mistake made by Brown as chancellor since 1997 had been to base his management of the economy on the same principles as his Conservative predecessors: financial deregulation of the banks, the expansion of consumer credit, rising property prices and a growing service sector. This meant ignoring rising personal debt, a dwindling manufacturing sector and the decline of house-building while the financial sector enjoyed inflated profits. In 2006 the pay of top directors had risen 37 per cent, while in 2007 bonuses in the City of London increased by 30 per cent to a record £14 billion. However, in 2007 the boom collapsed when a former building society, Northern Rock, went bankrupt, the first to do so since the 1860s. Following deregulation it had aggressively tried to increase its market share by lending 125 per cent mortgages, often to people unable to afford them. In the ensuing panic, savers queued up to withdraw their funds. Yet no sooner had it been bailed out by the Bank of England than the government discovered that many other institutions had been equally irresponsible; with shares in Bradford and Bingley, HBOS and Royal Bank of Scotland collapsing, the government used taxpayers' money to write off their debts. In effect the state became the owner of several British banks.

The banking collapse triggered a major economic recession afflicting America and Europe, in the process discrediting both politicians and economists who had largely ignored warnings about the reckless reliance on credit; even the Queen was heard to enquire why no one had seen the crisis coming. But although ministers had been careless, they responded effectively to the crisis. The Chancellor, Alistair Darling, took steps to limit the recession by reducing VAT, offering £21 billion of tax cuts, and borrowing £78 billion in 2008 and £118 billion in 2009. The Bank of England, whose governor, Mervyn King, had been negligent towards the banks, eventually reduced the bank rate to 0.5 per cent and adopted 'quantitative easing' to the tune of £75 billion in 2009 in an attempt to stimulate the economy. As a result, unemployment in Britain was contained to 7.8 per cent, less than that elsewhere, and Britain was spared the worst effects of recession for a time. However, during 2009–11, a significant recovery was frustrated by the refusal of the banks to co-operate. While they remained reluctant to lend to small businesses and to home buyers, the housing sector stagnated and output was flat or declining; instead the banks exploited the resources devoted to quantitative easing to repair their own balances and to boost profits. Britain's huge financial sector was largely parasitic on the economy.

Malpractice in British business

In this situation the CBI and the Institute of Directors energetically defended the policies of financial institutions, including the payment of huge salaries, pensions and bonuses to their directors, on the grounds that this was a necessary means of retaining business talent in Britain. Such self-serving claims were, however, exploded by revelations about company boards awarding themselves ever-increasing sums regardless of the success or failure of their businesses. In fact these years were characterized by unending revelations about incompetence and malpractice in private companies. In 2008 an American company, appointed to mark SATs tests for schools, simply failed to deliver the results. In the same year Metronet, the company appointed under the costly PFI to repair London's Underground, collapsed. By 2010 the NHS had been obliged to pay £63 billion for new hospitals worth only £11 billion under PFI contracts. Hospitals paid £2.6 billion annually to recruit staff from private agencies, including £1,760 daily for a single consultant, forcing many close to bankruptcy. The privatized energy and water companies were increasingly found to be exploiting customers by inflicting higher prices in order to reward their shareholders and directors; during 2008–13 gas charges rose 52 per cent and electricity 32 per cent although wholesale costs *fell*. The protracted disaster of railway privatization continued as several railway companies simply abandoned their franchises while the surviving companies relied on raising ticket prices and on a £5 billion state subsidy to survive; a state company alone managed to run the East Coast line efficiently but on the expiry of its contract the government perversely gave it to another private company. When British Airways opened Terminal 5 at Heathrow it promptly broke down, and during the winter of 2010–11 flights were cancelled because the privately-owned airports proved unable to handle a modest snowfall. Between 1995 and 2011, 53 per cent of British dairy farmers were driven out of business because the supermarkets and big dairies forced them to sell milk below the cost of production. Tesco became notorious for failing to pay its suppliers for one or even two years, driving some into bankruptcy. In 2011 the public was shocked to learn that large parts of the public service had quietly been sold to private businesses. For example, Southern Cross, a company that had taken over care homes handling 31,000 elderly people from local authorities, collapsed through financial mismanagement, but its owner, Blackstone, had expropriated four times its original value, leaving taxpayers to pick up the bill. At a home in Bristol people with learning disabilities were discovered to be suffering physical abuse at the hands of staff at Castlebeck that charged local authorities £3,500 per person per week. Private companies including G4S and Serco were found to be both inefficient and fraudulent, claiming payments from the government for tagged offenders who were actually dead. A private hospital, Hinchingbroke, lost so much money that it abandoned its contract. Meanwhile a new scandal arose in the form of 'internships' whereby companies employed young people without payment. Many others broke the law by failing to pay the minimum wage. Poor families fell into the hands of loan sharks, notably Wonga, who charged them up to 6,000 per cent interest on loans. Consumers who tried to obtain official application forms from the DVLA or passport office via the internet were ambushed by private companies who charged them for forms that were actually available free. Several pharmaceutical companies were exposed for paying doctors to put their name on research that validated their claims about new drugs with which they had never been involved and get it published in medical journals as their own work. However, even these malpractices paled into insignificance by comparison with the major banks, which were involved in a never-ending succession of scandals including mis-selling insurance against loss of income, tax evasion, fixing libor rates and criminality including, in the case of HSBC, funding Mexican drug barons! Finally, evidence continually emerged about the extent to which big companies including Amazon, Starbucks, Facebook, Google, Boots and Shell, largely escaped paying the tax due on their huge profits. In 2016, for example, Google appeared to pay a

3 per cent tax rate. However, by reducing HMRC employees from 91,000 to 60,000 the government made tax collection even less effective; it also opposed EU efforts to target the tax havens where companies diverted their profits to escape tax. The overall effect of this catalogue of misconduct was to crystallize popular misgivings about the extension of the free market into inappropriate sectors and the exploitation of public resources by private interests.

Deficit mythology

However, these revelations made only a limited impact on official policy largely because New Labour was as committed as the Conservatives to the free market and opposed to regulation. Having adopted Conservative economic strategy since 1997, Brown and Darling found themselves unable to attack the ideas that had led to the crisis or to find a coherent alternative. As a result, Labour allowed the Conservatives, whose earlier policy of deregulation had largely caused the banking crisis, to escape blame and to change the terms of the debate. Thus, in the approach to the election of 2010 the Conservatives claimed that the crisis had been caused by excessive state expenditure rather than by private irresponsibility by banks and consumers, and focused the debate entirely on how the financial deficit should be reduced.

To this end the new chancellor, George Osborne, deliberately exaggerated Britain's deficit which had actually been a normal feature of the eighteenth, nineteenth and twentieth centuries. After 1945, for example, the deficit had been two-and-a-half times what it was in 2008, but the government had handled it successfully by expanding the economy and keeping unemployment within 2 per cent. However, policy after May 2010 was driven by political rather than economic considerations; if reducing the deficit was an overwhelming priority it enabled Osborne to shrink the state by adopting drastic reductions in spending. He imposed massive cuts that involved the loss of 600,000 public sector jobs and 700,000 private sector ones; local government suffered especially heavily from 40 per cent cuts resulting in the closures of Sure Start places for children and libraries.

Osborne argued that austerity would solve the problem by 2015, but the target was repeatedly missed and even postponed to 2019, in effect an admission that it was impossible to eliminate a deficit simply by austerity; after five years the deficit remained at £90 billion. In effect austerity checked the modest revival by reducing the demand for goods and services, and as a result the economy shrank for two-and-a-half years from 2010. Many homeowners used their spare money to reduce existing mortgage debt, which they had hitherto increased as a means of boosting their living standards, rather than to spend. By 2011 real incomes were falling and consumers, fearful of unemployment and shorter working hours, were cutting expenditure. The once-dominant service sector shrank while manufacturing, though benefiting from the falling value of the pound, was now too small to drag the rest of the economy out of recession. Osborne tacitly admitted his failure by putting extra resources into the economy and was forced to borrow an additional £40 billion so that during 2013–15 Britain enjoyed improved growth and falling unemployment. However, this was far from a real recovery as it was based largely on a resumption of consumer borrowing and on a policy of inflating house prices which had damaging consequences for young buyers. Moreover, most of the new jobs involved low-paid, part-time, unskilled employment that failed to generate the extra revenue required. The Bank of England repeatedly indicated its intention of raising interest rates which had remained at 0.5 per cent for eight years, but each time it backed away, fearful that the recovery was too fragile and consumer indebtedness too high.

The causes of economic decline

The obsession among politicians with the immediate problem of the deficit made it difficult to focus on the fundamental causes of Britain's continuing economic weakness. She was experiencing the long-term consequences of the loss of her manufacturing industry, and with it skilled, well-paid jobs, in the Thatcher-Blair era; manufacturing now constituted only 10 per cent of gross domestic product. Increasingly society was polarized between well-off professional and business employees on the one hand and a growing mass of unskilled workers in insecure, low-paid occupations on the other; Britain had steadily become a less skilled, low-wage economy. This trend was exacerbated by the weakness of trade unions whose traditional role in modifying the distribution of income between capital and employees had been undermined by legal restrictions and loss of membership. A bigger, more effective union movement had become an economic necessity. Instead Britain suffered from extreme and growing inequality of wealth and income which hampered economic growth; societies with a more equal distribution like Germany performed much better. The worst symptom of Britain's unskilled labour force was its poor and deteriorating productivity. By 2015 productivity was 28 per cent lower than in France, 29 per cent lower than in Germany and 30 per cent lower than in America. This reflected poor management and low investment. In turn this was partly a consequence of the self-serving conduct of British management and of the banks, which had become notoriously reluctant to lend to business and narrowly focused on shareholders, salaries and empire-building through takeovers. In industry as a whole 10 per cent of profits had been paid to shareholders in 1970, but by 2015 they received a staggering 70 per cent while investment and productivity slumped. Governments also remained resigned to the takeover of successful British business by foreign companies. For example, between 1990 and 2014 Britain's 207 aerospace companies had dwindled to 47, victims of foreign multinationals looking for short-term profits rather than growth. A shocking catalogue of flagship British businesses became foreign-owned, including Cadbury, Tetley, Weetabix, Jaguar, Asda, Rolls Royce, Raleigh, Branston Pickle and Newcastle Brown. The government's reluctance to intervene on behalf of British industry became apparent in 2015–16 when it was taken by surprise by cheap Chinese steel imports that undermined domestic output, leading to thousands of job losses in steel works at Redcar, Rotherham, Sheffield and Port Talbot. Meanwhile the privatized energy companies, now owned by French, German, Australian and Canadian conglomerates, simply redirected their British profits abroad. Indeed the government offered generous concessions to foreign governments; new nuclear power stations were contracted to French and Chinese state-owned companies who were to sell Britain energy at twice the current rate. British car-making became entirely foreign-owned; and although this attracted much-needed Japanese investment, two out of three car components were now made abroad. In effect the British economy was increasingly a *colonial* one reliant on foreign investment and ownership which was contingent on retaining access to the European Union market.

The coalition era

The election of 2010 should have been a clear Conservative victory. The party faced a divided and tired Labour government that had blundered into an economic crisis. It had chosen a new leader, David Cameron, who frankly aimed to shed the Thatcherite reputation by appealing to the progressive middle ground and by adopting a wider range of candidates including women and members of ethnic minorities. By 2008 the Conservatives were 20 per cent ahead of Labour in the polls. Yet in May 2010 they won only 36 per cent of the vote, historically a very low share. Why was this? Partly because they were tainted by sleaze and because their own policies had been

Table 22.1 The general election of May 2010

Conservative	Labour	Liberal Democrat	Others
306	258	57	28
36 per cent	29 per cent	23 per cent	[including 6 SNP, 3 Plaid Cymru, 1 Green, 8 DUP and 3 SDLP]

responsible for the banking collapse; during 2009 Brown had partly recovered his reputation by managing the international crisis effectively. Conservatives also made a cardinal error by agreeing to televised debates by the leaders which enabled the Liberal Democrat leader, Nick Clegg, to boost his party's support. Above all, many voters retained underlying doubts about what Cameron really intended; and despite some changes in personnel his party remained in many ways handicapped by socially reactionary attitudes that were out of touch with liberal society.

In effect the 2010 election confirmed the trends of the last twenty years – that Britain had returned to multi-party politics. As predicted, no party won a majority. In these circumstances, there were four options: a minority Conservative government, a Conservative-Liberal Democrat coalition, a Labour-Liberal Democrat coalition, and a limited confidence-and-supply agreement by the Liberal Democrats to support a government without joining it. However, the Labour ex-ministers were unprepared for coalition, several openly disparaged the Liberal Democrats, and Brown, as a rejected leader, represented a handicap. Moreover, Clegg appointed a pro-Tory negotiating team that was pleasantly surprised by the readiness of the Conservatives to offer coalition. The explanation is that the Conservatives were anxious to return to office and David Cameron's poor electoral performance had put his survival as leader in serious doubt, leaving coalition as his safest option. He calculated that a coalition would enable him to extend his strategy by using the Liberal Democrats to drag his party towards the centre ground and perhaps in the long run to absorb elements of Liberalism as had been done in the 1920s and 1930s under the leadership of Stanley Baldwin. For their part the Liberal Democrats felt that by accepting ministerial posts they would greatly raise their status and fundamentally change British politics by familiarizing the public with the idea of coalition government.

Initially these calculations appeared justified. Within a scant four days of the election an agreement had been reached and the coalition was launched amid scenes of relief and goodwill. Although coalitions had often been disparaged as a novelty or even as un-British, since 1852 no fewer than twelve coalitions governed Britain, sometimes for long periods of time and with notable success. Despite attacks by the extreme right-wing press, many voters liked the idea of parties setting aside their differences to focus on resolving national problems. The partners quickly agreed on dismantling many of Labour's authoritarian measures including identity cards and made deficit reduction the centre of their strategy.

Coalition breakdown

However, after a year the coalition had begun to break down. For the Liberal Democrats there was nothing inevitable about the effects of coalition; they had recently worked with Labour in three Scottish coalitions and successfully kept their vote together. However, in Scotland they had implemented progressive policies whereas the 2010 coalition meant abandoning their opposition to drastic expenditure cuts and accepting higher tuition fees and plans to expose the NHS to private companies, to which most of their supporters were opposed. This rightward shift was in fact consistent with Clegg's strategy since becoming leader; he had attempted to refashion the Liberal Democrats as a liberal Conservative party, repudiating the ex-Labour recruits won in 2001 and 2005. However, the link with the Tories proved to be toxic and their vote swiftly collapsed. Although Clegg attempted to distance himself from Tory policies from April 2012 onwards he had completely lost credibility in the country. The large Liberal Democrat base in local government was steadily eliminated and in 2015 the party won barely 8 per cent of the vote and returned eight MPs. Clegg's mistaken strategy had virtually undone all the progress made since the Liberal revival in the late 1950s.

For their part Tory MPs felt that the Liberal Democrats enjoyed too much influence. As a result the 2010 parliament proved very disrespectful; one Conservative, Nadine Dorries, famously derided Cameron and Osborne as 'two posh boys who don't know the price of milk'. As early as November 2010 Conservatives had rebelled in 59 of 110 parliamentary divisions. Five Cabinet ministers opposed House of Lords reform although it had been agreed beforehand. In November 2012 53 Conservatives rebelled over Europe, signalling their distrust of David Cameron. In 2013 he was effectively prevented from going to war over Syria by a vote of 285–275 when 30 Tories opposed his policy. In the process Cameron effectively abandoned his original strategy for liberalizing the Conservatives. The one progressive policy he insisted on in the teeth of internal opposition was the enactment of same-sex marriage, but beyond that he moved to the right for fear of undermining his leadership and losing votes to UKIP.

Above all Europe destroyed the Prime Minister's strategy. Polls suggested that half of Conservative voters contemplated Britain leaving the EU and several Cabinet ministers defied Cameron by supporting them. His leadership was under threat and his popular vote undermined by the rise of UKIP, which prospered on claims that Britain should repatriate powers from Strasbourg, suffered from 'benefit tourism' and had too many immigrants. This propaganda was largely a myth though it was not challenged. Whereas the NHS spent £30 million treating European visitors in 2013–14, EU countries spent £155 million on British tourists. One think tank calculated that on leaving the EU Britain's economy would shrink by £56 billion and three million jobs would be lost. However, Cameron felt obliged to pander to his right wing and to appease UKIP by promising to hold a referendum on EU membership after renegotiating the terms of membership. This was an exact repeat of Harold Wilson's attempt to contain a similar party split and protect his own leadership by holding a referendum in 1975. However, even this did not prevent two Tory MPs defecting to UKIP, whose vote share reached 25 per cent in local elections in 2013. The underlying significance of these developments was that Cameron simply abandoned his long-term strategy to recreate Conservatism as a more centrist, progressive party as he was dragged steadily to the right.

Meanwhile relations within the coalition reached their nadir in the referendum campaign to introduce the Alternative Vote (AV) system in parliamentary elections. Cameron, now under extreme pressure from his own followers, who believed that AV would make it impossible for them to win a parliamentary majority, adopted scaremongering tactics to secure its defeat, disparaging AV as 'obscure' though it was actually the system by which he had been elected Tory leader. The defeat of AV largely destroyed any remaining goodwill between the two coalition parties, especially as it was followed by Conservative refusal to enact another policy agreed with the Liberal Democrats – reform of the House of Lords. They retaliated by withdrawing support from the Tory plan to reduce the number of MPs by fifty and redraw the boundaries. For the third time – the others being 1917–18 and 1930–1 – the Labour and Liberal parties had thrown away a reform of the electoral system that they urgently needed to prevent the Conservatives winning a majority of seats for a minority of votes. In this situation the coalition would probably have collapsed, had not the government already legislated to make a five-year term almost impossible to avoid.

Corporatism and jobbery

One of the most sinister developments of the post-2010 period was the increasing penetration of the public service by private business and the influence exerted over elected politicians by corporate interests. By 2015 taxpayers gave £93 billion annually to business in grants, subsidies and tax breaks but its agents continued to seek concessions. The obvious method was via lobbyists. By 2015 one in five of the staff of MPs and peers were lobbyists who received passes (against the rules) giving them access to ministries as 'advisers'. Financial services alone spent £92 million annually lobbying ministers and won concessions including checks on banking reform, cuts to corporation tax and the abandonment of a not-for-profit pension scheme for the low-paid. In total 124 peers who received payments from financial services formed the majority on the Lords committee scrutinizing financial services. In 2015, when HSBC Bank threatened to transfer its headquarters to the Far East, the Chancellor reduced its tax bill by £1 billion within weeks. Another favoured method involved an exchange of personnel between ministries and companies, a practice extended in 2011 when the coalition paired executives from 38 companies with ministerial 'buddies'. For example, in 2012 25 Department of Health civil servants were found to be paid via their private companies to reduce their tax. In 2013 employees of gas companies worked for the government to design a subsidy scheme for gas-fired power-stations. Executives from arms companies were routinely seconded to the Ministry of Defence. Former HMRC tax inspectors went to work for accountancy firms to help them advise clients on avoiding tax, while representatives of accountancy firms worked for HMRC to influence it from inside. The pharmaceutical group AstraZeneca made £5 billion in profit in 2013–14, on which it paid no UK corporation tax due to a tax-avoidance scheme, its top accountant having spent several years advising the government on changing the tax rules.

These relationships were consolidated by extensive political connections including the distribution of an unusually large number of peerages by Cameron. But influence largely operated behind the scenes. One study in 2013 identified 38 firms, many of which donated to the Conservative Party, that had had 700 meetings with ministers. Conservative politicians enjoyed links, often via their relations and their advisers, with private healthcare companies keen to win lucrative contracts. Official committees established in response to medical pressure to reduce alcohol consumption and the salt, fat and sugar content in processed foods were staffed by representatives of the food and drink industry. In 2012 two companies that had donated £182,000 and £267,000 to the Conservative Party won employment-scheme contracts from the Department of Work and Pensions. Lord Green, who had been disgraced for malpractice at HSBC Bank, was elevated to the peerage and appointed a junior minister by Cameron. George Osborne was advised on employment policy by a party donor and hedge-funder who owned the notorious Wonga loans company. In 2016 when Google was exposed for paying little tax it emerged that it had planted many of its employees in Downing Street under Cameron's premiership while ministerial staff had gone to work for Google; regular meetings between Google and the Chancellor ensured that its interests were protected. The entrenchment of jobbery and influence on this scale in British government had not been seen since the eighteenth century. It posed a major threat to democratic government through the subversion of civil servants and politicians by private interests.

The growth of poverty and inequality

The backwash from the banking crisis accentuated wider concerns dating from the 1980s that Britain was an increasingly unequal society. Between 1979 and 1997 the redistribution of resources from rich to poor had been reversed by government policies, and, despite progressive innovations including minimum wages and tax credits between 1997 and 2007, the trend towards inequality had continued. Unpaid tax was variously estimated at £35 billion to £100 billion. By 2014 the richest five families in Britain enjoyed more wealth than the lowest 20 per cent representing 12.6 million people. By 2007 the ratio of the pay of bosses to that of their employees had risen to 98:1. The banking crisis provoked a series of revelations about the extraordinary remuneration routinely sought by management in Britain. In 2012–13 the boss of Centrica, now owners of British Gas, earned £5.7 million compared with the equivalent of £120,000 earned by the British Gas chairman in 1978. The ten most highly paid British executives received £70 million in 2006, rising to £170 million in 2008. In 2009 the chief executive of Lloyd's received £1 million pay and a £1.79 million bonus, the Royal Bank of Scotland's Sir Fred Goodwin enjoyed a pension of £693,000 annually, and the boss of G4S, forced out by his failure to provide security for the Olympic Games, left with a £1.2 million pay-off and a £16 million package – examples that underlined the entrenched habit of rewarding *failure* in British business. In the FTSE's worst year, 2008–9, the pay of directors in the 100 leading companies rose by 31 per cent. Even Northern Rock's chief executive departed, disgraced, but enjoying a £750,000 pay-off and a £2.5 million pension pot. In 2008 Network Rail was fined £14 million and missed its performance targets but was not deterred from giving a £500,000 bonus to its executive. However, exposure and criticism made little impact on the bonus culture: by 2014–15 city bonuses totalled over £100 million.

The attack on the welfare state

Meanwhile the new century saw a sharp increase in poverty, mass unemployment and a fall in living standards. Real wages fell by 9.2 per cent between 2008 and 2014, the longest decline since the 1860s. By 2011 unemployment stood at 7.8 per cent, although this understated the situation as some 4.6 million, or 15 per cent of the workforce, were ranked as 'self-employed'; this did not mean they had a job or an income, only that they had been shifted by officials off the unemployment figures. A million workers also became victims of zero-hours contracts which meant that their hours fluctuated from week to week, forcing many into lives of desperate insecurity. In effect the spread of *under-employment* meant that society was going backwards to a labour market typical of the Victorian era. By 2013 five million workers earned less than the living wage, the worst offenders being care homes, 48 per cent of which failed to pay it. Many employers failed to pay even the legal minimum wage, but few were challenged because the government required workers to pay heavily to fight illegal employer practices, thereby reducing the numbers going to employment tribunals by 79 per cent.

Meanwhile the press, television and politicians encouraged widespread prejudice against welfare as insupportably high and against those who claimed benefits as scroungers. The poorest members of society became the target of £16 billion of welfare cuts, including the 2.6 million receiving disability payments whom ministers believed to be capable of working. However, the attacks were largely misplaced. For example, the huge sums paid as housing benefits did not go to families but to their landlords so that the state subsidized inflated rents. Of the £167 billion spent on welfare no less than £93 billion actually went to pensioners and only £3.6 billion to job seekers. Moreover, the majority of claimants were actually in work but earning insufficient income to support their families. A French company, Atos, was paid by the government to assess fitness for work. However, it was so incompetent that it rejected blind people and cancer sufferers; between December 2011 and February 2014 2,380 people who had been rated fit for work by Atos, and consequently refused benefits, were so ill that they died! Meanwhile under government pressure to meet targets for cuts many Job Centres imposed sanctions on as many as 900,000 welfare claimants by 2012–13, usually for trivial reasons, forcing them off the unemployment records and onto food banks. Sanctions were a major cause of the rapid spread of food banks after 2010 which were helping to feed a million poor people by 2014–15; the number of banks run by the Tressell Trust alone increased from 56 in 2009 to 445 by 2015.

Another symptom of the welfare crisis involved expenditure on the National Health Service which was widely blamed on growing longevity. However, this was another popular myth. In fact NHS spending problems resulted from three policies: first, the adoption of a market for health in the 1980s which increased the size and cost of management from 5 to 15 per cent of expenditure; second, the building of hospitals through the private finance initiative which meant paying £60 billion for just £11 billion of new hospitals; and third, the use of private agencies to supply staff which cost £2.6 billion by 2014, a single nurse costing £1,800 per day by this method. But the underlying cause of the financial crisis was simply that, contrary to popular belief, Britain spent relatively little on healthcare: 9 per cent of gross domestic product compared with 11–12 per cent for France and Germany and 17–18 per cent for the United States. The coalition reorganized health provision by forcing care to be increasingly handed by commissioning groups to private companies who had the right to take legal action if denied contracts. In this way the gradual dismantling of the NHS continued.

The housing crisis

Inequality also acquired a generational element as the coalition safeguarded the income of pensioners but targeted the young. A fifth of all 16–24-year-olds were unemployed. Students lost the weekly educational maintenance grant that had helped the poorest to stay in education, while university students were hit by a tripling of annual fees to £9,000. In 2015 the Conservative government extended the discrimination by withdrawing housing benefit from 18–21-year-olds, excluding those under 25 from the national living wage, and replacing maintenance grants for students with loans. While the older generation enjoyed their assets in the form of rising house prices, younger people found themselves obliged to abandon the ambition to buy their own homes because of high interest rates on mortgages and demands for much higher deposits than before. As a result, by 2010 the average age of first-time buyers stood at 37 and the trend towards home-ownership, a key feature of British society since the 1920s, went into reverse. Whereas in 2003 home-ownership peaked at 72 per cent, by 2014 it had fallen to 65 per cent. The quality of housing also deteriorated in that whereas in the 1920s an average new house was 1,020 square feet, by 2010 it had shrunk to 645; show houses were often fitted with three-quarter size furniture to obscure the fact!

However, this was only one aspect of a wider housing crisis. Between 1959 and 2009 real incomes increased by 169 per cent but housing by 273 per cent. The underlying cause lay in a fall in building since the late 1990s, so that by 2010 only 100,000 homes were built annually against a need for 250,000. Any improvement in the rate was checked by shortages of bricklayers, plumbers and electricians. In London many new homes were bought by foreigners who wanted them as investments, not to live in, and often left them empty. Council houses had been sold at the rate of 212,000 in 1979–90, 193,000 in 1997–2007 and 141,000 in 2010–14, representing a social disaster for those obliged to rent. A third of ex-council homes fell into the hands of private landlords. As a result rents in private accommodation increased rapidly and tenants became vulnerable to bad landlords owing to the abolition of the rent tribunals that had given some protection since 1915. The situation was exacerbated by the diversion of funds into property by those seeking profitable investments. Buy-to-let landlords, who received state subsidies on their mortgages of £14.5 billion annually, could outbid ordinary purchasers and effectively pushed up the cost of houses. The worst effects were felt in London where a high proportion of new housing was bought by wealthy foreigners as an investment; government caps on housing benefit also meant that some London councils were forced to send tenants to other parts of the country, in effect a form of social cleansing.

Reactions

As a result of these social problems 2010–11 saw the emergence of a spontaneous protest movement known as UK Uncut, orchestrated by the online forum, Twitter. The occupation of stores notorious for evading taxes, including Topshop and Boots, combined with huge demonstrations of students against higher university fees and growing trade union militancy provoked by dwindling pensions and falling real wages, seemed to signify a shift in the moral-political climate towards egalitarianism that had not been seen for several decades. Popular disaffection reached a climax in August 2011 when rioting erupted in Tottenham before rapidly spreading to other parts of London including Wood Green, Hackney, Lewisham, Croydon,

Brixton, Peckham, Enfield and Walthamstow, as well as Birmingham, Manchester and Liverpool. Residents fled as rioters burned vehicles and shops and engaged in widespread looting. Although 1,500 arrests were eventually made, the disorder provoked severe criticism of the police for being very slow to react and for initially watching the looters rather than arresting them. Thoughtful observers discerned a pattern in these events for the Tottenham riots stood in a line of similar outbreaks in Birmingham, Brixton, Tottenham, Liverpool Toxteth and Bristol since the 1980s. The immediate cause of the Tottenham riots lay in provocation by the police – as in *all* the other cases. But the underlying factors were social and economic. The 2011 outbreaks seemed to coincide with areas of extreme unemployment and deprivation, Tottenham suffering the highest unemployment rate in London. Some observers thought that recent government economies had ignited resentment; youth services in Tottenham, for example, had been cut by 75 per cent. The riots reflected a profound alienation among many young and ill-educated men who felt they had no stake in British society. Their anger had been ignited by extensive publicity about the misdemeanours of bankers, politicians and the press; the immorality of privileged people in grabbing any advantage seemed to offer an easy excuse for those lower down the scale to do the same. The sense of alienation was further exacerbated by the bizarre severity of the sentences subsequently handed down by magistrates, some of whom succumbed to political and media pressure; one awarded a six-month prison sentence for the theft of two bottles of water.

National disunity

Protests against inequality were only one aspect of the continuing fragmentation in British society in these years. Other symptoms included English resentment towards Scottish separatism, an obsession with immigration, scaremongering against Muslims, extremist attitudes towards the European Union and the further decline of institutions such as the Church of England. In 2016 it emerged that weekly attendances at church had fallen below a million amounting to under 2 per cent of the population and under half the level of the 1960s; though retaining 26 Anglican bishops in the Lords it had effectively ceased to be a national church. In this situation Britain largely lacked the constructive political leadership needed to redefine national identity. A weak Prime Minister, David Cameron increasingly pandered to extremist right-wing emotions failing to emerge as a national leader. In particular he found it impossible to manage the Conservative Party, a majority of whose MPs and voters wanted to leave the EU. In desperation he adopted Harold Wilson's strategy of 1975 by promising a referendum on membership by 2017, thereby putting party interests before national ones.

Britain was also badly served by her press, which fostered the negative mood and had become narrow and largely right-wing. The deterioration had begun as far back as 1961 when the Victorian radical Liberal newspaper, the *News Chronicle,* folded, followed by the sale of the pro-Labour *Daily Herald* which ended as a scurrilous tabloid, the *Sun.* Meanwhile the BBC abandoned its traditional neutrality and increasingly took its agenda from tabloid newspapers dominated by right-wing proprietors and editors. By 2010 a high proportion of its staff were known Conservatives and its reporting became selective; for example it interviewed nineteen businessmen for every one trade unionist and followed the tabloid agenda with programmes designed to exploit resentment towards benefit claimants. Newspaper misconduct reached a fever pitch with revelations about illegal phone-tapping and bribes to police and civil servants. The scandal that enveloped Rupert Murdoch's newspapers culminated in the close of the venerable *News of the World*, reducing the range of the press still further. But despite some prosecutions and the appointment of the Leveson Committee which recommended independent regulation of the press nothing was done, largely because many politicians were too intimidated by the press.

Honours and the celebrity culture

On the positive side there was some revival of the popularity of the Royal Family, after years of decline arising from repeated marital breakdowns, promoted partly by the longevity of the Queen and partly by the marriage of Prince William in 2011; republicanism stood at 26 per cent to 63 per cent who favoured a monarchy. Despite this the monarchy continued to lose its relevance. Polls showed that only 37 per cent were interested in the royal wedding in 2011, against 47 per cent who were not, while over half expected that in fifty years' time Britain would not have a monarchy. While the Queen herself enjoyed wide respect, misgivings grew about the succession. In 2015 legal action finally forced the publication of some of Prince Charles's letters to ministers. The government had tried to keep them secret because it felt, correctly, that his interference in policymaking was unconstitutional and would damage his role as a national figurehead. Charles's insistence on extending his political role ominously recalled the crisis of 1936 under Edward VIII.

However, beyond the Royal Family Britain struggled even more to find heroes and role models. The problem accelerated under David Cameron's premiership with the deterioration of the Honours List. Cameron notoriously appointed 102 Tory peers from 2010 to 2015, more than anyone since 1958 when life peerages began, attracting criticism for choosing political cronies, party donors and ex-MPs discredited in the expenses scandal. The House of Lords swelled to 826 members, the world's second-largest second chamber. Moreover, Britain continued to reward her *failures*, including, in 2016, Lin Homer, who had been accused of 'a catastrophic failure of leadership' at the UK Border Agency and an inability to collect taxes when running HMRC.

Yet dubious honours were but a symptom of the wider cult of celebrity vigorously promoted by the media including the BBC which routinely used celebrities to attract viewers. Unhappily this often meant promoting those who were not genuine celebrities, in that they had little or no achievements, but were manufactured by exposure on television. The most damaging consequence of the celebrity culture was recognized in these years in the scandal over the activities of the former television presenter, Jimmy Savile, for abusing women and girls in television studios and hospitals over many years. It emerged that Savile was merely one among many prominent media personalities and politicians who were convicted for sexual misconduct. The cumulative significance of these revelations was that the British found it increasingly difficult to discern who and what was meritorious, thereby exposing another flaw in national identity.

Sport and national identity

The one aspect of national life that unquestionably boosted British identity and pride in this period was the growing success in sport. In Victorian times sport had been regarded as personifying the iconic British qualities: teamwork, fair play, discipline and respect for rules; but during the twentieth century the decline of British football and poor Olympic performances had undermined this tradition. Eventually, however, the trend was arrested as Britain won 28 medals at Sydney (2000), 30 at Athens (2004), 47 at Beijing (2008) and 65 at London (2012), reflecting major increases in state financial support. Significantly the new sporting success drew on many elements in British society, women as well as men, Scots as well as English, and the talents of a diverse multi-racial community. For example, British cricketing heroes included the Sikh, Monty Panesar, and Nasser Hussain, a Muslim whose parents hailed from Madras and Cornwall. The Beijing Games saw the remarkable triumph of the mixed-race Louis Smith, the first Briton to win an Olympic medal in gymnastics for a century. Boxing produced such iconic figures as the Muslim Olympic medallist, Amir Khan, the mixed-race James de Gale, who won gold in 2008, and the black Nicola Adams, who claimed the first ever women's boxing gold in 2012. The huge medal totals in 2012 would have been impossible without the talents of such iconic competitors as the Somali immigrant, Mo Farah, and the mixed-race athlete, Jessica Ennis. In this way sport offered irrefutable evidence that Britain had emerged as a successful multi-racial society.

The Scottish referendum and the English Question

By contrast political divisions proved more intractable. Although the Conservatives, with only one Scottish MP, commanded no legitimacy in Scotland, the coalition had the advantage of eleven Scottish Liberal Democrats including popular Scots-British figures such as Charles Kennedy and Menzies Campbell. Initially Cameron adopted a conciliatory approach towards Scottish demands, agreeing to additional powers for the Edinburgh Parliament including further scope to vary income tax. In a referendum in 2011 Welsh voters approved extra taxation powers for their Assembly. These amendments further legitimized devolution as a successful experiment, although they provoked disquiet in England as social policies increasingly diverged; for example, Edinburgh abolished prescription charges altogether in 2011 while in England they were increased to £7.40. However, events took a serious turn in 2007 when the SNP formed its first minority government and, although the electoral system had been carefully contrived to make a nationalist majority impossible, in the 2011 elections the SNP shocked metropolitan opinion when it was re-elected with 69 seats out of 129.

This was a significant development because it demonstrated that the economic recession had not made Scots feel the need for the support of London; on the contrary, they had been reassured by the experience of SNP rule. Endowed with a majority the first minister, Alex Salmond, now saw the way forward to a referendum on independence at a time of his choosing. Although Cameron did not want to be responsible for the break-up of the United Kingdom his own narrow experience and his tendency to bully left him out of his depth in dealing with Scottish opinion. With middle- and working-class Scots committed to defence of the welfare state and a positive role for the state in the economy, Scotland had effectively become a different country. However, English opinion proved slow to recognize the fact and as a result the end of the Union suddenly loomed large. This was underlined by the referendum of September 2014 which was seriously mismanaged by London. Cameron refused to allow a compromise solution known as 'devo-max' to appear on the ballot although it had majority Scots support. Although he claimed to be passionate about the Union he and his ministers largely kept away from Scotland during the campaign for fear of antagonizing voters. Meanwhile English voters took little interest in the pro-Union campaign which was entirely negative, involving scares about the consequences of independence that only betrayed the weakness of the case for the Union.

Despite this independence was rejected by 54 per cent to 46 per cent. However, Cameron promptly threw away the victory by announcing that Scots MPs would not be allowed to vote on English matters in Parliament, a move almost calculated to break up the Union by creating two classes of Westminster MPs. This immediately made Scots voters feel that they had been fooled, and support for the SNP immediately soared. Given a chance to consolidate the United Kingdom Cameron had revealed himself as a narrowly English leader. Moreover, the Labour and Liberal Democrat parties swiftly became discredited because they had campaigned with the Conservatives for the Union, thereby cutting another bond between the two countries. Meanwhile the SNP had in effect won the argument and gained thousands of new members; consequently a second referendum looked likely and the survival of the Union increasingly improbable. Indeed, the increase in *English* hostility towards Scotland, encouraged by the Prime Minister himself, made separation appear morally certain.

The referendum also exacerbated the national question by focusing attention on England, the undue concentration of resources on London and the neglect of the regions leading to a seriously unbalanced economy. During the Victorian era regions such as Lancashire had taken huge pride in being the world's greatest textile manufacturer, but the disappearance of such a role undermined faith in centralized British government. Regions such as the north-east suffered all the same problems as Scotland but so far lacked the political will to change policy. Yet the metropolitan elite had remained so complacent that England had generated little constructive debate about how to restructure her system. Belatedly the coalition proposed to re-balance the economy. However, this was largely undermined by austerity policies for the cuts fell heavily on local government whose central income fell by 40 per cent after 2010; but whereas the south-east lost £305 per head the north-east lost £665. Coalition plans to build the HS2 railway and a third runway at Heathrow Airport were calculated to accelerate the flow of people and trade into London from the provinces. Eventually proposals were made to improve railway connections in the north of

England, but following the 2015 election they were abandoned, proof that the metropolitan mentality retained its grip.

Immigration: myth and reality

Another symptom of the negative mood of this period was a growing obsession with immigration. High unemployment, low wages and rising housing costs made immigrants easy targets for attack though they caused none of these problems. But the issue was exploited by a succession of extremist groups. Although the British National Party dwindled in elections in 2001–11, some alienated youths defected to the English Defence League which provoked violent confrontations at marches and demonstrations in Muslim areas. However, anti-immigrant prejudice gained respectability from regular exploitation in the tabloid press, on television and by UKIP, which topped the poll in the 2014 European elections on an anti-EU, anti-immigrant programme. Many mainstream politicians pandered to extremist propaganda that blamed immigrants as a financial burden, as 'benefit tourists' and for undermining wages. With net immigration at 256,000 in 2010 David Cameron promised to reduce it below 100,000; however, he completely failed, for by 2014 it had risen to 298,000 and by 2015 to 330,000. Although it could not afford to admit it the government privately welcomed high immigration because immigrant labour was largely responsible for economic growth; moreover, by raising minimum wages the government effectively made Britain more attractive for immigrants.

Table 22.2 The changing composition of Britain's population (England and Wales)

	2001		2009		
Non-white population	6,600,000		9,100,000 (one in six)		
Mixed-race population	672,000		986,000		
Other white (non-British origin)*	1,400,000		1,900,000		
Irish	646,000		574,000		
Local variations: white population as percentage, 2010					
Blaenau Gwent (South Wales)	96	Birmingham	63	Harrow	48
Copeland (Cumbria)	96	Leicester	60	Tower Hamlets	47
North Tyneside	92	Slough	57	Brent	38

* Includes Poles: 75,000 (2003) – 545,000 (2011).

In fact the attacks on immigrants by newspapers and politicians were baseless propaganda. Because most immigrants were young they took less out of the NHS and other services than the rest of the population, and because a higher proportion were employed they contributed more; in fact they subsidized British finances to the tune of £20 billion between 2000 and 2011. At a time when birth rates were dangerously low the influx of young workers enabled Britain to fund the pensions of the older generation and thus avoid the crisis facing Italy and Germany. Immigrants filled unskilled jobs picking strawberries and Brussels sprouts which British workers refused to do; care homes, the NHS and the construction industry could not have functioned without them. Employers were especially appreciative of Polish workers as reliable, industrious and adaptable. Immigration also supplied skilled workers, notably in engineering and medicine, and businesses insisted that they needed more of them. Universities relied heavily on the large fees paid by foreign students, most of whom were not strictly immigrants and returned home after qualifying.

Yet despite the controversy society evolved and adapted to immigration; in these years Britain emerged as a successful, multicultural society with 9.1 million, or one in six of her population, being non-white by 2009. As a result of the high level of inter-racial marriages and partnerships she had almost a million children of mixed race. By 2014 children from non-white communities were outperforming their indigenous counterparts. Indeed some communities became crucial elements in the British success story, notably those whose families had originated in India and trained in medicine and dentistry in large numbers; young Asians were actually ten times more likely to study medicine than young white people. Paradoxically these communities also strengthened the concept of Britishness in that black and Asian people were more likely to embrace the self-description 'British' than 'English'; conversely, according to the 2011 census, growing numbers of indigenous people dropped the designation 'British' in favour of 'English' when completing their forms.

Islamophobia

Immigration also contributed to an increase in the proportion of people admitting to racial prejudice which had fallen from a high of 38 per cent in 1987 to 25 per cent by 2001. This largely took the form of hostility towards Muslims, encouraged by the politicians' 'war on terror' and the demonization of Islam in the press. British policy towards Muslims continued to be fraught with contradictions at home and abroad. For example, after proposing that

Britain should go to war to depose President Assad of Syria, Cameron was surprised when several hundred British Muslims did so voluntarily. He plunged into a new war with Libya which overthrew the regime but left a chaotic, unstable society behind it. This in turn resulted in refugees from Libya and other African countries joining those from Iraq and Afghanistan trying to enter Europe. Each Western intervention in the Islamic world had destabilized Muslim regimes, thus promoting mass emigration; in this way Western policy continued to be counter-productive. However, public opinion had now begun to recognize this and reacted against further intervention in the Middle East. When David Cameron committed himself almost casually to joining President Obama in a new war in Syria he was shocked to be defeated in Parliament by a combination of Labour, Conservative and Liberal Democrat members.

Meanwhile at home Cameron initially adopted a conciliatory approach by appointing a Muslim, Lady Warsi, as a minister and deputy-party chairman. But he also followed the practice of the tabloid press by implying that loyal, law-abiding British Muslims were responsible for acts of terrorism by Islamists abroad or should at least apologize for them. He also condemned multiculturalism and blamed Muslims for separatism, a criticism that seemed inconsistent with his government's policy of promoting schools based on religion which was almost calculated to promote separatism. In 2016 the Prime Minister criticized Muslim women for not speaking English, citing this as a cause of Islamism. Yet the government had reduced by £205 million the funding to teach English to immigrants; and in any case Islamist extremists were recruited from English-speaking men not women. Such interventions thus caused resentment and signified the confusion in official policy. A prominent Conservative Muslim, Lady Warsi, was alienated by the Prime Minister's public criticisms of Muslims, so much so that she resigned from the government. She reflected the Muslim community's resentment towards official discrimination. For example, in 2011 Muslims were reportedly 42 times more likely to be the objects of stop-and-search than white people. In this way government strategy gradually unravelled.

The end of the coalition

To general surprise the election of 2015 made a new coalition unnecessary for although the Conservatives won only 36.9 per cent, compared with 36.1 per cent in 2010, they achieved a majority of twelve. For this outcome there were five main explanations. First, the Conservatives benefited from the Liberal Democrat collapse, gaining 26 of their seats which gave them a majority. Second, the Chancellor had carefully cultivated the older voters who backed his party with higher pensions, allowing them to cash in private pensions and offering investment bonds at much higher rates than commercially available. Third, the Labour Party suffered from the fact that the election turned largely on the deficit, for which it was blamed, as well as for its supposed sympathy for benefits and immigrants. Fourth, Labour was hopelessly undermined in Scotland where the SNP gained 40 of its 41 seats after taking over Labour's traditional role as the left-wing party and as the opponent of austerity north of the border. Finally, in the election the Conservatives had shored up their vote by cultivating anti-Scottish opinion in England, an interesting revival of tactics employed against the Irish Nationalists to undermine English Liberals in the Victorian-Edwardian period. However, their propaganda exacerbated the threat to the Union with Scotland by making English hostility to the Scots more respectable. Surprisingly Cameron's victory failed to consolidate his leadership or to revive his original plan to refashion Conservatism along progressive lines because it immediately accentuated Conservative demands for a referendum on EU membership. No sooner had the Prime Minister announced that ministers would be obliged to follow the government line in the referendum campaign than he abandoned this in the face of Conservative criticism.

In the weeks leading to the referendum on 23 June 2016, the Prime Minister was dismayed to find that several leading ministers rejected his renegotiation of the terms of British membership, and the campaign rapidly deteriorated into a bitter row among Conservatives. The country was shocked by the eventual 52–48 per cent vote for leaving the EU. Cameron immediately paid the price for his miscalculation by promising to resign. But why, after over forty years, did the British decide to leave? The vote was partly the outcome of long-term factors. Over several decades the public had enjoyed sustained anti-EU propaganda in the press and found it difficult to recognize the positive aspects of membership. Many people simply blamed Europe for anything they disliked. Moreover, Cameron and the other Conservative leaders paid the price for having attacked the EU over a long period, so that when they eventually argued that it was essential to remain they lacked credibility. The same was true of the Labour leader, Jeremy Corbyn, a long-term opponent of the EU whose belated support failed to carry Labour voters.

There were also several short-term explanations. The government unwisely changed the system for registering voters from household to individual registration, which effectively excluded many young voters who were the most pro-EU. The Remain campaign relied heavily on the authority of professional economists and financial institutions, who supported membership. However, they had become so thoroughly discredited by the banking collapse, the failure of pension schemes and the inability to foresee the 2007 economic crisis that they commanded almost no influence among voters. In effect the Remain campaign relied too heavily on a negative approach warning of the dangers of leaving Europe but failing to develop a positive case. Also, the case for membership was inherently complicated. By contrast the case for Brexit could be expressed in simple terms: Britain should take control, recover her sovereignty, save the money paid to Europe, stop immigration and prevent 77 million Turks coming to Europe. Though largely untrue, this was comprehensible to voters.

But above all, the referendum reflected fundamental social divisions in British society, in particular the dangerous alienation in many working-class communities which felt marginalized and neglected by the London elite and were angered by years of austerity for which they carried the burden. Hence large votes to leave in such areas as County Durham and South Wales. Perversely they benefited hugely from EU funding and relied on foreign investment attracted by the ability to sell manufactured goods within the large European market. The real problem for them and other neglected regions like Cornwall was the dominance of London that starved them of British resources, not Europe, but it was easier to fix on a simple scapegoat such as immigration from Europe.

* * * *

By comparison with 1870 British society between 1970 and 2015 was transformed in several ways. Life expectancy rates for men rose from 48 in 1901 to 84 by 2005. Women enjoyed far more independence, were better educated than men and comprised half the labour force. Society as a whole was far better educated and trained in that whereas young people had mostly abandoned education at 12–13 it became common to extend it well into their twenties. Britain had developed into a consumerist society in which shopping had become the major preoccupation in many people's lives. The dominance of heavy industries notably coal, steel and shipbuilding, typical of the late-Victorian economy, had given way to employment concentrated in the service sector; hitherto major employers including textiles, railways and engineering had greatly diminished. As a result industry accounted for a mere 10 per cent of British gross domestic product. Admittedly some things had not changed. Britain still suffered from poor productivity and relatively low investment and was let down by banks that concentrated on their own profits rather than on supporting the wider economy.

However, it comes as a shock to recognize the extent to which Britain had actually gone *backwards* between 1870 and 2015, returning in some respects to the earlier era.

- Large numbers of Victorian workers had experienced lives of extreme insecurity as a result of casual employment, low pay and irregular work, but this insecurity had returned for millions engaged in zero-hours contracts, part-time jobs and unpaid internships. The Victorian docker who turned up on Mondays seeking a day's work was not far removed from modern retail employees who did not know how much work they would have from week to week.
- From 1979 onwards society suffered from a huge rise in inequality of wealth and income with dysfunctional effects on the economy, whereas late-Victorian and Edwardian Britain had begun to find ways of taxing great wealth and redistributing it.
- Many of those dependent on state benefits shrank from their hostile treatment at modern Job Centres just as their poor predecessors had from the Victorian poor-law system.
- In schools modern Britain had returned to the Victorian pattern in which it was not compulsory for teachers to be trained.
- Whereas the Victorians and Edwardians had increasingly recognized that a railway system fragmented among many companies was not efficient, Britain had reverted to the old pattern.
- The long-term trend to home-ownership, pioneered by the Victorian building societies, was thrown into sharp reverse.
- The Post Office, a triumph of Victorian public enterprise, had been steadily undermined by successive governments and thousands of the branches that had been a comfort to elderly citizens had been closed.
- Whereas late-Victorian Britain had embarked on a major expansion of elective local government, modern Britain withdrew functions such as housing, education and utilities to central and to private control.
- The local and regional press, such a strength of Victorian cultural and political life, had suffered from extensive closures resulting in a narrow focus on a London press owned by a handful of wealthy men.

Such trends underline the extent to which the era from the 1970s to the 2000s was an age of reaction. Moreover, widespread social problems only exacerbated political divisions. Those suffering falling real incomes, unemployment and expensive housing commonly found scapegoats in benefit recipients and immigrants. Consumerism and the internet had largely replaced the influence of politics, religion, empire and monarchy in the lives of British citizens. In some ways the British had still not quite adjusted to the loss of empire; their desire to retain symbols of super-power status such as the Trident nuclear weapon and their reluctance to accept their role in Europe were obvious symptoms of the maladjustment. Yet several experienced diplomats including Sir Jeremy Greenstock, formerly ambassador at the United Nations, argued that since 2010 Britain had lost influence in world affairs. Although the special relationship with the United States, which some saw as an alternative to Europe, remained intact, it was increasingly nominal; President Obama had clearly downgraded the relationship in favour of more important powers such as Germany and China. But the most acute dilemma was the prospect of British departure from the EU which threatened not only to undermine her economy through the loss of foreign investment and jobs, but to accelerate her decline as a world power. Moreover, it was not clear whether the referendum on EU membership would actually resolve the issue even if Britain voted to remain a member. In addition, the referendum exacerbated the whole question of the future of the United Kingdom because the SNP demanded separate votes for the constituent parts of the country, and argued that if England voted to leave Europe Scotland would try to rejoin following a vote for independence. It would be difficult to find a period since 1870 when the future of Britain was so clouded by division and uncertainty.

Further reading

On the origins and implications of the coalition see:

Tim Bale, *The Conservative Party from Thatcher to Cameron* (2010) – focuses on high politics, tactics and personalities.

T. Heppell and D. Seawright, *Cameron and the Conservatives* (2012) – emphasizes Cameron as the Tory Blair.

G. Baldini and J. Hopkin eds, *Coalition Britain* (2012)

David Laws, *22 Days in May: The Birth of the Lib Dem-Conservative Coalition* (2010) – Lib Dem account.

Rob Wilson, *Five Days to Power: the Journey to Coalition Britain* (2010) – Conservative account.

Vernon Bogdanor, *The Coalition and the Constitution* (2011) – negative view of coalition generally as anti-democratic.

For analyses of the economic crisis see:

Charles Ferguson, *Inside Job: The Financiers Who Pulled Off the Heist of the Century* (2012) – exposes the dysfunctionality and criminality of Anglo-American banking.

L. Elliott and D. Atkinson, *The Gods That Failed: How Blind Faith in Markets Has Cost Us Our Future* (2008)

Vince Cable, *The Storm: The World Economic Crisis and What It Means* (2009)

Several analyses of British society as dysfunctional:

R. Wilkinson and K. Pickett, *The Spirit Level: Why Equality is Better for Everyone* (2009)

Owen Jones, *The Establishment and How They Get Away With It* (2014)

D. Hancox, *Fight Back! A Reader on the Winter of Protest* (2011)

Various aspects of the national identity problem:

J.L. Esposito, *The Islamic Threat: Myth or Reality?* (1999) – valuable corrective to Islamophobic books.

Z. Sardar, *Balti Britain* (2008)

Christopher Walker, *Islam and the West* (2005) – classic scare-mongering book on how Muslims are taking over Europe.

Christopher Harvie, *Scotland: A Short History* (2014)

Kevin Jeffreys, *Sport and Politics in Modern Britain: The Road to 2012* (2013)

Helen Brocklehurst and Robert Phillips eds, *History, Nationhood and the Question of Britain* (2004)

Danny Dorling, *So You Think You Know About Britain?* (2011) – a geographer explodes the myth that Britain is overpopulated.

D. Morley and K. Robins eds, *British Cultural Studies* (2001) – useful essays on the diversity of society.

Martin Pugh, *Britain: Unification and Disintegration* (2012) – puts current problems into historical context.

Index